W9-BBM-636
ST. MARY'S CITY, MARYLAND 20686

This book offers a unique and fascinating investigation into the lives and careers of the British in eighteenth-century Russia and, more specifically, into the development of a vibrant British community in St Petersburg during the city's first century of existence as the new capital of an ever-expanding Russian empire.

Based on an extremely wide use of primary sources, particularly archival, from Britain and Russia, the book concentrates in a series of chapters on the activities of the British within various fields such as commerce, the navy, the medical profession, science and technology, and the arts, and ends with a broad survey of travellers and travel accounts, many of them completely unknown. Also included are many attractive and unusual illustrations which help to demonstrate the variety and character of Russia's British community.

BY THE BANKS OF THE NEVA

BY THE BANKS OF
THE NEVA

CHAPTERS FROM THE LIVES
AND CAREERS OF THE BRITISH
IN EIGHTEENTH-CENTURY
RUSSIA

ANTHONY CROSS

CAMBRIDGE
UNIVERSITY PRESS

Published by the Press Syndicate of the University of Cambridge
The Pitt Building, Trumpington Street, Cambridge CB2 1RP
40 West 20th Street, New York, NY 10011-4211, USA
10 Stamford Road, Oakleigh, Melbourne 3166, Australia

© Cambridge University Press 1997

First published 1997

Printed in Great Britain by Bell and Bain Ltd, Glasgow

A catalogue record for this book is available from the British Library

Library of Congress cataloguing in publication data

Cross, Anthony Glenn.
"By the banks of the Neva": chapters from the lives and careers
of the British in eighteenth-century Russia/Anthony Cross.
p.   cm.
Includes bibliographical references.
ISBN 0-521-55293-1
1. British–Russia. 2. Russia–History–1689–1801. I. Title.
DK34.B7C76 1997
947'.00421–dc20
96-3825
CIP

ISBN 0 521 55293 1 hardback

FOR JANE AND TOM

CONTENTS

ILLUSTRATIONS

PREFACE

This has been a difficult book to write and an even more difficult one to finish. It is with some embarrassment that I recall it was as long ago as 1973 that I published an article entitled 'The British in Catherine's Russia: a preliminary survey' with every expectation of finishing a book within two years, rather than two decades. The survey was basically sound, although the use of the word 'preliminary' was well-advised. What I was then surveying was indeed the tip of an iceberg and with every year that passed, the imposing size of that iceberg slowly revealed itself. More and more fascinating individuals were discovered, more and more archives, family and public, were found, more and more areas of British activity were recognised. I have frequently sought refuge from the colossus by writing other books, other articles, some, but not all, connected with Anglo-Russian relations, and including a book whose title, '*By the Banks of the Thames*', echoes that of the present volume but which was considerably easier to write, not least because the materials were more circumscribed, the number of individuals involved infinitely smaller.

My fascination with the general theme of Anglo-Russian relations in the eighteenth century dates back to my postgraduate study of the career of Nikolai Karamzin, the Russian man-of-letters who visited, and wrote about, England just after the French Revolution; but if I were to single out two works which influenced the direction and range of my research specifically into the activities of the British in eighteenth-century Russia at an earlier stage, I would name Matthew Anderson's *Britain's Discovery of Russia, 1553–1815* (London, 1958) and James Cracraft's article, 'James Brogden in Russia, 1787–1788' (1969).

The second of these publications introduced me to the records of the Russia Company and the register of the English Church in St Petersburg, which I have subsequently used frequently and profitably. The Guildhall Library, where they are held, stands at the head of a long list of archives and libraries in Britain, Ireland and Russia in which I have had the good fortune to work and/or from which I have received microfilms and photocopies and innumerable kindnesses from their staffs. They include: the Public

Record Office, Chancery Lane and Kew; the Scottish Record Office, Edin-
burgh; the Public Record Office of Northern Ireland, Belfast; the British
Library, London; the National Library of Ireland, Dublin; the National
Library of Wales, Aberystwyth; the Royal Irish Academy, Dublin; the
National Maritime Museum, Greenwich; the Royal Society, London; the Uni-
versity Libraries and Archives of Aberdeen, Edinburgh, Glasgow, Cambridge,
Hull, Leeds, Nottingham and the School of Slavonic Studies, London;
Birmingham Reference Libraries; the County Record Offices of Bedfordshire
at Bedford, Cornwall at Truro, Derbyshire at Matlock, Hampshire at Winch-
ester, Kent at Maidstone, Lincolnshire at Lincoln, Wiltshire at Trowbridge
and the Greater London Record Office; Dr Williams' Library, London; the
United Society for the Propagation of the Gospel, London; the Library of
the Grand Lodge of England, London; the private archives of Earl Cathcart,
Mr Robert Dimsdale, Mrs Eleanor Rosser and Mrs Joyce Sanderson. In
Moscow I was given access to important sources in the the National Library,
the Archive of Foreign Affairs and the Russian State Archive of Ancient Acts,
and in St Petersburg to sources in the Russian National Library, the Archives
of the Institute of History and the Institute of Russian Literature (Pushkin
House) of the Russian Academy of Sciences, the Archive of the Russian Academy of Sciences, the Naval Archive, and the Central State Historical Archive.
I apologise for any omissions in this list.

Over the years my research has been facilitated by the granting of sabbati-
cal leave from the universities of East Anglia, Leeds and Cambridge and I
have received generous grants to aid my work from those universities and
also from the British Council and the British Academy.

Some of the material in my book has been reworked from articles I have
published in scholarly journals and appears with permission of the editors
of *Canadian Slavic Studies, European Studies Review, Journal of European
Studies, Mariner's Mirror, Oxford Slavonic Papers, Scottish Slavonic Studies,
Slavonic and East European Review* and *Study Group on Eighteenth-
Century Russia Newsletter.*

My book is about people and there are many people I wish to thank who
have made, often unknowingly, a contribution – be it in the form of snippets
of information or bibliographical leads, words of understanding or a sympathetic ear. My colleagues in the Study Group on Eighteenth-Century
Russia have been particularly supportive and long-suffering and I value
highly their expertise and their friendship. I wish from their distinguished
ranks to single out Roger Bartlett, who, particularly in the early years, supplied me with all manner of helpful morsels from archives and recondite
publications and whose knowledge in certain areas of my investigation is
without equal.

Teresa Jones has survived ten years as my secretary at Cambridge and my

indebtedness to her skills and her patience in seeing this book through to
the end is beyond measure.

Finally, my book is dedicated to my elder daughter Jane and her husband
Tom, to whom I made the promise that I would finish the typescript by their
wedding day – which I did, but only after calling for the adjudication of the
third umpire.

NOTE ON RUSSIAN DATES

Dates of events in Russia are shown in both Old and New Style variants (a
difference of eleven days in the eighteenth century and twelve in the nineteenth century), even though the New Style was adopted in Great Britain
only in 1752.

INTRODUCTION

Of the five centuries during which the British and Russians have been in more or less constant contact, the eighteenth century is the most interesting, the most attractive and the most varied in the forms that contact assumed, or so it appears to my undoubtedly prejudiced eye. The sixteenth century had the excitement of 'first-footing', the fascination of a rapprochement between a Russia ruled by Ivan the Terrible and an England under Elizabeth, and came to a close with a masque of the Muscovites in a Shakespearean comedy; the seventeenth century had its periods of warming relations under the enlightened Boris Godunov and of considerable cooling under Aleksei Mikhailovich; the nineteenth century, on the other hand, throws us deep into 'Great Power' struggles and love–hate relationships, Russophilia and Russophobia, Anglomania but never quite Anglophobia, the first really bloody conflict between the two nations notwithstanding; and the twentieth century, tsarist and soviet, offers infinite variety in cultural, ideological and political counterpoint and confrontation, with the pendulum swinging violently from Russian Fever to Red Menace, from ally to foe.[1] The eighteenth century had something of all these features and much that was distinctly its own.

In Peter I and Catherine II, it had pre-eminently two rulers on the Russian side whose personalities and activities made them the stuff of legend and whose generally positive attitudes towards Britain and the British brought to relations between the two countries the colour and drama which were conspicuously missing on the British side in the first Georges. These attitudes were, nonetheless, part of a wider preoccupation with Europe, with Russia's place within it and with Russia's demands upon it. Peter and Catherine consciously embarked on the 'Great Experiment' of trying to bring Russia into Europe and of using Europe, for a limited period, as mentor and training ground to achieve that goal. This is the significance of Peter's oft-quoted assertion that 'Europe is necessary to us for a few decades and then we shall turn our back on it', which is not a Slavophile rejection of Europe but an aspiration to equal status within it. Europe for its part viewed Russia with varying degrees of condescension, superiority, amusement and growing fear.

In the age of the Enlightenment it was prepared in principle to assist the sun's rays in illuminating and warming the frozen north, believing unshakeably in its own cultural superiority and the need for Muscovy to emerge from a state of ignorance. At the same time Europe viewed Russia as a vast and highly desirable export/import market which it was cynically prepared to exploit to its advantage. The fear element in European perceptions of Russia inevitably derived from its growing military might, its territorial expansion, its increasing ability to disrupt the long-accepted balance of power.

The relationship between Britain and Russia, while obviously being part of this greater scheme of things, was, nevertheless, distinctive and 'special', or at least many on both sides wished to see it so. In his *View of the Importance of the Trade between Great Britain and Russia*, written in 1789 at a time of great tension in the relations between the two countries, Anthony Brough donned the enlightener's mantle in his influential defence of much less dignified commercial interests: 'There is no nation on the records of history that has so rapidly risen from a state of darkness and barbarism, to a great height of splendour and civilization, as the Russians have done during this century. The causes of this rapid and wonderful change have been many; but I would venture to affirm, that her intercourse with Great-Britain has been the greatest.'[2] He went on to affirm that Peter 'knew that the interest of Russia depended on her connexion with England: he came in person to our Court, to cement the friendship that already existed between the two nations' and he further suggested that 'the great plans he formed, she [Catherine] has executed'. This led him to the formula that 'there is no Russian, who is a friend to his own country, but what must be at the same time a friend to Great-Britain', which was near to the favourite maxim of the then Russian ambassador in London, Semen Vorontsov, that 'tout bon Anglais doit être bon Russe et tout bon Russe doit être un bon Anglais', but without its generous reciprocity.[3] For all the impetus that Peter and Catherine gave to Anglo-Russian relations it is nonetheless noteworthy that it was precisely in the intervening decades between their reigns that the two lynchpins of Anglo-Russian entente arose: the concepts of 'the most favoured nation', enshrined in the first commercial treaty of 1734, and of 'faithful allies', emerging from diplomatic negotiations in the 1740s and 1750s. Of course, such concepts inevitably blur the realities of the ceaseless blips in the relationships, but perception is more powerful than truth; as the success of the campaign to dissuade Pitt from action against Russia in the 'Ochakov Crisis' of 1791 demonstrated, Russia enjoyed a generally favourable image, influenced by many different factors, including the fame of the Northern Semiramis, anti-war sentiment, commercial self-interest and threats to employment for the British both at home and in Russia.

Politics and all its trappings of ambassadors, negotiations, secret agendas, alliances and treaties loomed large, but they were the constant rumble in the background to what really characterised Anglo–Russian relations in the eighteenth century. It was the transmission of ideas, technological know-how and information, and the interflow of people embodying those ideas, teaching or acquiring skills, working, learning and observing, that occupied the foreground.

In an earlier book, 'By the Banks of the Thames': Russians in Eighteenth-Century Britain (1980), I sought to describe one side of the exchange, to look at the activities of Russians in Britain subsequent to the epoch-making visit of Peter I himself. Peter initiated the tradition of Russians coming to Britain to study; indeed, of the approximately 400 Russians identified as residing here, the overwhelming majority were students. Some were attending the universities of Oxford and Cambridge, Glasgow and Edinburgh, but others were apprenticed to British specialists in such areas as instrument-making, weapon production, shipbuilding, and agriculture, or were learning seamanship in the British navy, or visiting factories, mines, canals and industrial centres. Even the Russian Grand Tourists of the last decades of the century came to admire and marvel at 'le pays de la richesse, de la sécurité et de la raison',[4] and to study how the landed gentry managed their estates and created their landscape gardens (although many, it must be admitted, partook in equal, if not in greater measure, of the more social and leisured aspects of their tour). The Russian embassy and church in London acted as the focal point and organisational centre for the activities of Russians in Britain, but from ambassador and chaplain to humble embassy clerks and church choristers, these official representatives were also often keen students themselves of British achievements, particularly in agriculture.

The largely positive reaction to Britain experienced by Russians of all classes and backgrounds, punctuated rather than punctured by individual disappointments and disillusionments, may be seen as part of the growing European cult of all things British, the French-fostered Anglomania which spread to Germany and eventually to Russia. Among the beneficiaries of such a cult were the British themselves. 'De tous les peuples qui habitent sur notre globe, les Anglais sont à ce que je crois les plus heureux et les plus à envier', wrote a Russian visitor in 1772.[5] With the heroes and heroines of French and German novels (many of which were translated into Russian) increasingly being cast as English, the British visitor to Europe, and particularly to Russia, often received a warm welcome on the basis of these literary portrayals.

In transferring attention from the Russians in Britain to the British in Russia, we are not dealing with a mirror-image, with a simple reflection of the reverse flow from Britain. The picture is of course complementary, but there is much that is different, both in the numbers of people and the nature of the activities involved and in the wider implications of the British presence in Russia. There is thus no overall correspondence between chapters, which are, nevertheless, organised along thematic lines in both studies, and it is instructive to highlight the continuities as well as the divergences.

The title of the book was chosen with some care. 'By the Banks of the Neva' obviously echoes the first part of the title of the previous work; both are quotations and emphasise the dominant role of the capital cities. Russians, however, travelled and worked in other parts of Britain, as did the British in Russia, but to a much greater extent and over a vaster area. These wider geographical boundaries are implied in the second part of the titles, but in the present work the comprehensiveness to which I aspired in 'By the Banks of the Thames', either in the body of the work or in the checklist of Russians visiting Britain, was never considered feasible or desirable. The chapters in 'By the Banks of the Neva', which themselves include chapters from the lives and careers of numerous British subjects, are offered as parts of a much larger picture of the British presence in eighteenth-century Russia.

It is not possible to speak of a Russian community in eighteenth-century London. There was an embassy, or rather a townhouse, in which the ambassador and his staff lived and worked, and there was a Russian Orthodox church, known as the embassy church but not physically attached, where Russian visitors worshipped and to which Russian students were called periodically. The ambassador and the chaplain were the influential people among a group of some dozen or so assistants and helpers. How different this was to the situation in St Petersburg: here there was an ever-increasing and vibrant community, in which the key figures were the merchants of the British Factory (the name given to members of the Russia Company), and in which the church also played a central role, but the building belonged to the Company and the chaplain was its appointee. The British ambassador was essentially on the periphery of the community, a guest invited to its balls and other social functions but whose ambience was essentially the court. He had a house but not an embassy and no other staff but a secretary and the occasional assistant. The government appointee of more significance for the community was in reality the consul-general, who, more often than not, was also the agent of the Russia Company and a former merchant himself.

It is for such reasons that this book omits a chapter on the British ambassadors and the course of Anglo-Russian diplomatic relations and opens instead with a detailed study of the composition and increasingly rich and varied life of the British community, its clubs, institutions and entertainments. Although the Anglo-Russian commercial agreements guaranteed equal rights for British and Russian merchants in the receiving county, the Russian merchant in eighteenth-century Britain was a rare phenomenon, whereas his British counterpart with his often large family and conspicuous lifestyle was a dominant figure in the St Petersburg community. Merchants inevitably appear in the opening chapter, but it is in the second that more detailed attention is given to the careers of certain prominent individuals and of the consuls-general within the wider context of 'Factory matters'. There is no intention to investigate the vicissitudes and argue the statistics of Anglo-Russian trade: this is the territory of economic historians who seldom, however, see the people behind the trade figures and the names of commodities and firms. In contrast to what can only be a sampling of case histories and categories of activity, given the overwhelming number of merchants trading in Russia down the century, the third chapter attempts to trace the history of the English church in St Petersburg, physically and spiritually at the centre of the community, and to offer a detailed study of its chaplains, whose interests frequently went far beyond the theological.

The British went to Russia to find employment, to make their fortunes, and to practise and/or teach a whole range of skills (which many Russians also acquired during their periods of study in Britain) that were considered vital for Russia's modernisation. The men whose careers are described in chapters 4, 5 and 6 were all 'necessary foreigners' in the sense that their expertise, be it as doctors, naval officers, shipbuilders, instrument-makers, watchmakers, engineers or mechanics, was in demand – even if it was always hoped by the Russian authorities (and by Russians whose own prospects the foreigners' presence seemed to damage) that the demand would be short-lived. Each of the areas covered in these chapters could well merit monographic treatment, given its importance and the wealth of material, but it should be emphasised that the context for these studies is essentially that of an on-going British presence and they do not pretend to be, for instance, histories of Russian medicine or technology, within which the extent of a specifically British contribution might be confidently fixed. The chapters dealing with doctors and with specialists and craftsmen nevertheless attempt to be as inclusive as possible within their own parameters and to supply information that was hitherto unknown or overlooked. The challenge offered by naval officers and shipbuilders is of a different order. Hundreds of men were involved at some period from the beginning of Peter's reign to beyond that of Paul in the development of the Russian navy and were active in every campaign in the Baltic and in the south. This chapter seeks to demonstrate the extent of the British presence and the significance of the very real contribution that was made.

The British in the Russian navy is a self-recommending subject, the British in the Russian army during the same period, much less so. British mercenaries were very conspicuous in the armies of seventeenth-century Muscovy,[6] but the situation changed in the eighteenth. British officers, notably Scots and Irish, figured prominently, however, in many battles during the first half of the century. Beginning with Peter's mentor General Patrick Gordon (d. 1699), the list would include other Gordons, Lacy, Ogilvie, Fullerton, Campbell, the venerable General George Brown, and, pre-eminently, Field-marshal James Keith (d. 1758), of whom much has been written but who still awaits a biographer. British officers gave their services as 'volunteers' in the wars against the Turks during the reigns of both Anna and Catherine; among them we find the Earl of Crawford in the 1730s and the noted Welsh-man Henry Lloyd, the diplomat William Fawkener, Hugh Elliot and many others in the 1770s. There is material enough for a chapter, but it remains one still to be written.[7] It is the navy that provides the great military theme for the British in eighteenth-century Russia and a constant refrain in Anglo-Russian relations. Count Semen Vorontsov, the Russian ambassador in London, underlined their relative importance when he wrote in 1787 that 'I would very much like us to take as many Prussian officers as wished to enter our army and as many British officers as wished to serve in our navy'.[8]

The men who are the subject of chapter 7 are distinct from those discussed in the preceding three chapters – distinct not in their going to Russia to seek their fortunes but in the nature of what they offered. These were the archi-tects, painters, engravers and landscape gardeners who catered for the court and the aristocracy. Foreign architects in particular had long practised in Russia, but the creation of St Petersburg led to a spectacular increase in the number of architects and other artists seeking employment in Russia. The British, however, were notable only by their absence before the reign of the great Catherine. France and Italy were and remained the dominant cultural influences, but a consequence of the Anglomania reaching Russia in the last decades of the century was the readiness to recognise and employ British artists. Painters contributed very little, but the skill of mezzotint engravers such as Walker and Saunders was highly valued. Cameron's contribution as an architect was distinctive, but it is in landscape gardening that the British left their indelible mark. The 'English gardens' that soon became a feature of many imperial and aristocratic estates were created in some cases by Russians sent to Britain to study the art but overwhelmingly by a phalanx of talented British gardeners in Russia, whose activities are little recognised there and scarcely suspected back in the land of their birth.

Some of the most valuable comments about the gardeners and their work are found in the diaries and accounts of contemporary British travellers to Russia. Visiting Russia 'out of curiosity' had its origins in the 1730s, but during Catherine's reign Russia formed part of the 'northern tour', offering new and exciting variations on the traditional Grand Tour. Books published by travellers (and by armchair travellers, taking advantage of the vogue) helped to form British opinion about the new Russia, emphasising its pro-gress towards civilisation or exploiting old prejudices. Many more British travellers visited Russia than is usually conceded and they have left a wealth of unpublished letters and journals. The travellers' itineraries, reactions and impressions provide the substance for the closing chapter.

The ranks of these visitors contained many people, men and women, for whom Russia was but a brief interlude in their lives and who usually came from, and returned to, careers and lives of eminence and record in Britain. At random one might cite, to indicate the range and type of visitors from the 1770s to the 1790s, Sir Nathaniel Wraxall, the Rev. William Coxe (accompanying, firstly, Lord Herbert, and later, Samuel Whitbread II), Sir John Sinclair, Sir Richard Worsley, Jeremy Bentham, John Howard, Patrick Brydone, the Duchess of Kingston, Lady Elizabeth Craven. These are names which appear in the *Dictionary of National Biography*, a distinction enjoyed by few of the hundreds of people who appear in the earlier chapters of this study. To be sure, all the ambassadors receive their accolade, as do men who, like the travellers, were known before they went into Russia or who returned to enjoy some reputation for their subsequent writings or activities in Britain. Such were John Perry, Sir Charles Knowles, John Elphinstone, Samuel Bentham, and the former chaplains John Glen King and William Tooke. But invariably, the Russian episodes in their lives, which lasted from perhaps just a few years to many, are treated superficially and inaccurately through ignorance of the essential source material.

Neglected in British biographical sources, a number of the British claimed their place in the great but unfinished *Russkii biograficheskii slovar'* (25 vols, St Petersburg, Moscow, 1896–1916) and in other more specialised dictionaries of Russian military leaders, artists or clockmakers. Without any attempt at an exhaustive listing, the following are to be found either in the completed volumes of the dictionary or in the listing for projected volumes: Belli (Bailey), Berd (Baird), Bottom, Farvarson (Farquharson), Gainam (Hynam), Gaskoin (Gascoigne), Golidei (Halliday), Greig, Gutri (Guthrie), Keit (Keith), Kroun/Krovn/Kron (Crown) and Villie (Wylie). In some cases the original names are obvious, in others, they are obscured by the eccentricities of transliteration. We have a situation where British origins are lost for Russian readers amidst a plethora of foreign names (mainly German) absorbed into Russian, but equally so for British (and American) scholars using Russian sources (and some of the original documents offer the most bizarre of variants), who write of Belli and Kuzens or Cuzins (Cozens) and Menas (Manners), or who, knowing what sometimes happens in transliteration, render back Gutri correctly as Guthrie and Gop as Hope but can be sometimes undone, as in a notable instance, when the entrepreneur Gomm reappeared as Home.

It is not extravagant to suggest that we are dealing with a legion of forgotten men and with a community whose size and way of life and importance both for Britain and Russia have been but dimly perceived. The impulse to reconstruct that community is archaeological rather than antiquarian; and the move towards a sort of supplementary volume for the *DNB* – a *DEBR*, a dictionary of expatriate Britons in Russia, albeit only for the eighteenth century – is prompted not solely by the wish to rescue worthy men from unjust oblivion but by the need to show at an individual level the nature and variety of their activities in St Petersburg and in other parts of Russia and their interaction both with their fellow-countrymen at home and in Russia and with Russians. In sum, this is a case study of a significant and powerful expatriate community which may serve as a basis of comparison with other outposts of empire in other countries and in the same or other centuries.

1

THE COLONY BY THE BANKS
OF THE NEVA

I

The views upon the banks of the Neva exhibit the most grand and lively scenes I ever beheld. The river is in many places as broad as the Thames at London: it is also deep, rapid, and as transparent as chrystal; and its banks are lined on each side with a continued range of handsome buildings. On the north side the fortress, the Academy of Sciences, and the Academy of Arts, are the most striking objects; on the opposite side are the Imperial palace, the Admiralty, the mansions of many Russian nobles, and the English line, so called because the whole row is principally occupied by the English merchants. In the front of these buildings, on the south side, is the Quay, which stretches for three miles, except where it is interrupted by the Admiralty; and the Neva, during the whole of that space, has been lately embanked by a wall, parapet, and pavement of hewn granite; a magnificent and durable monument of imperial munificence.[1]

Such were the impressions of the Rev. William Coxe on his first visit to St Petersburg in 1779. A visitor to the city some 200 years later would immediately recognise the scene and locate the buildings described; but if he was unfamiliar with the city's history, he would undoubtedly be puzzled by the reference to the 'English line'. However, for a century and a half up to the October Revolution, the English Line or Embankment was almost as famous as the Nevskii Prospekt and seemingly a permanent reminder of the link between the British and Peter's city. The link has now been re-established with the renaming of the embankment in 1994 to mark the visit of Queen Elizabeth II.

In the first years of its existence from 1703 the city would have seen few Britons and few indeed would have wished to be there, as hordes of peasants, soldiers and prisoners drove the piles and attempted to drain the marshy islands of the Neva delta. It was a place where there was 'on one side the sea, on the other sorrow, on the third moss, on the fourth a sigh'.[2] The city nevertheless grew rapidly, initially on the Petersburg (now Petrograd) side, to the east of the Peter and Paul Fortress, where the fifteen major wooden houses in 1704 had increased to 150 by 1709. The victory over Charles XII at Poltava in 1709 brought security to the new city, which became Russia's capital officially in 1712. The sense of permanence was increased by the construction of more stone buildings and in 1714 building in stone outside the capital was forbidden by imperial decree. The great series of buildings by the Italian architect Domenico Trezzini, including the Peter and Paul Cathedral, the Summer Palace, the Twelve Colleges and the Exchange and Warehouses, was built from 1710 onwards. The last of these, the Exchange and Warehouses (1723–35), was to be the heart of Petersburg's commerce and house the headquarters of the association of Russia-based members of the Russia Company, known as the British Factory, which was obliged to move from Moscow in 1723. It is from 1723 that a real British community in the capital may be said to date, although a number of Britons, particularly those in Russian service but also some merchants, had been there during the previous decade. There is little information, however, about precisely where in these early years the British lived.

In 1704 the Admiralty, which was then merely a shipyard, was begun on the mainland, or Admiralty Island, on the left bank of the Neva. In its immediate vicinity there grew up a Foreigners' Quarter, a far more temporary and haphazard area than its Moscow counterpart. Among the mass of wooden huts Prince Menshikov was said to have built a large lodging-house where foreign workmen could hire a room; nearby stood a tavern where they passed their dreary nights. Beyond this settlement others grew up on this side of the river, where small craftsmen and tradesmen settled. But fire, which along with flooding was a constant danger, devastated large areas of the city on the Admiralty Side in 1736 and 1737; this led to decrees forbidding the construction of wooden buildings without stone foundations and to the removal of wooden structures standing next to stone buildings. It also saw the setting up of the Commission for the Orderly Development of St Petersburg. Even more significant was to be the creation in 1762 of the Commission for the Stone Construction of St Petersburg and Moscow. Already in the first third of the century, along the waterfront to the west of the Admiralty, houses had been built both in wood and stone for members of the Russian aristocracy and for important foreigners: the British shipbuilders Joseph Nye and Richard Cozens had houses there in the 1720s, for example. Several of these houses survived into Catherine's reign, but were subject to considerable alteration and rebuilding, dictated not only by necessity but by changing tastes and styles. One building to keep its original baroque façade from Petrine times until after the end of the eighteenth century was the mansion of Count Boris Sheremetev. In 1753 this was bought by the British Factory and converted for use as the English Church; it was to become the centre of the British community's life in more senses than one. One of the important provisions of the Anglo-Russian Commercial Treaty of 1734 was that British merchants were spared the imposition of having soldiers billeted in the homes they rented; noble Russian house-owners were therefore more than pleased to have them as tenants. A decree of 1759 allowed merchants to buy houses in their own name, and British merchants were among those who acquired plots on Vasilii Island and built there stone and wooden houses; more importantly, the richest among them were able to buy some of the elegant three-storey stone houses erected in the 1760s and 1770s to the west of the church. In the 1770s, 1780s and 1790s many of the most prominent British merchant families lived there for varying periods of time, including the Cayleys, Sutherlands, Glens, Bonars, Porters and Warres; noted doctors such as Rogerson and Halliday also had houses there, as did the widow of Admiral Greig; British ambassadors frequently rented houses in the same row. Their presence and that of the church gave rise to the name 'English Quay' or Line for that part of the Neva embankment towards the end of Catherine's reign.[3]

The embankment itself, known during the Soviet period as the Embankment of the Red Fleet, stretches for a little over 1.25 kilometres; its extension, the Admiralty Embankment, joining it to the Palace Embankment, was only completed in the mid-nineteenth century. It ended at what was originally called St Isaac Square, where a wooden church had stood. This church had been demolished to make way for Falconet's famous Bronze Horseman statue (officially unveiled only in 1782), and a new church, designed by Rinaldi, was begun in 1768, further back in the square. The front of the square, renamed Peter's Square, faced the river, which at this point was crossed by a pontoon bridge to Vasilii Island. Halfway along the English Embankment, which was faced in granite between 1767 and 1788, stood another bridge, built originally of wood in 1788 but replaced by an elegant stone structure, designed by Starov; this raisable bridge spanned not the river but the Kriukov canal, flowing into the Neva and connecting with the Moika and the Admiralty Canal. To cross the bridge westwards was to enter the heart of the British community. The houses on this half of the embankment overlooked the river with 'balconies large enough to drink Tea in', according to the description of one captivated English visitor,[4] but access to them and to the church was from the rear, through courtyards lined with buildings and outhouses. This back street, running parallel to the English Embankment and known successively as Galley, Old Isaac, Red, and now once again Galley Street, had more modest houses on its other side, where tradesmen and craftsmen of all descriptions (mainly British or German) lived and had their shops. It was to Old Isaac Street that the British would come during Catherine's reign to visit the English Inn, the coffee house, the subscription library, and on Sundays, the church. To these and other institutions we shall return, but first it would seem appropriate to hazard some estimate of the size and growth of the British community and the role it played in the life of the city.

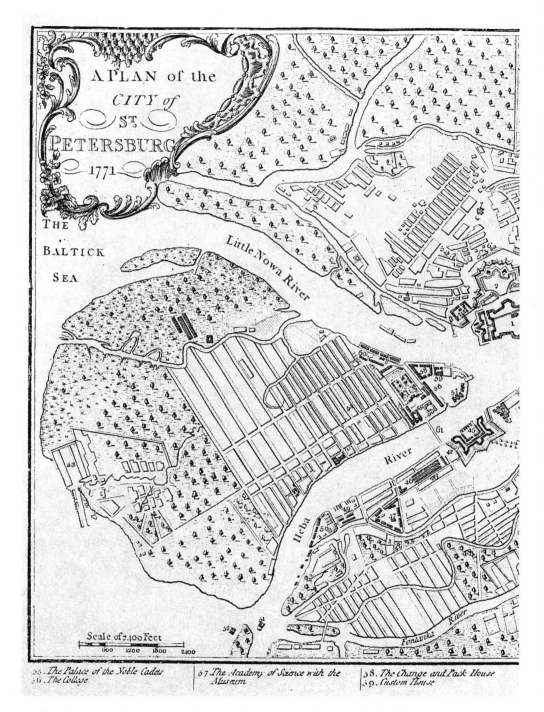

1 Plan of St Petersburg, 1771. (Plate 29 from John Andrews, *Plans of the Principal Cities in the World*, London, 1771.)

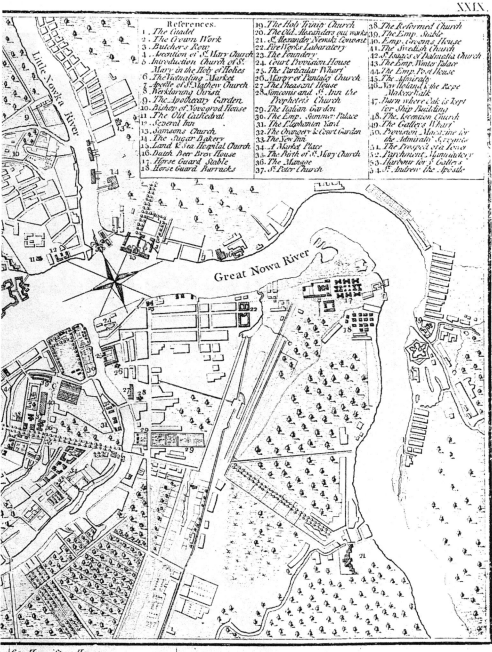

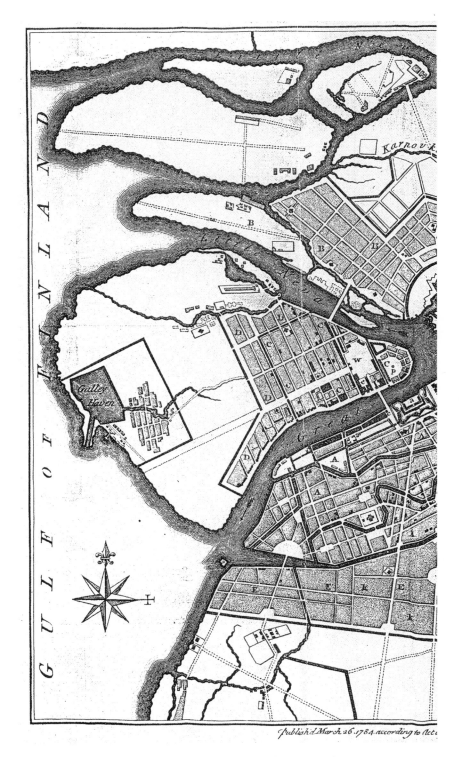

2 Plan of St Petersburg, 1784. (Engraved by Thomas Kitchin, sr., for William Coxe, *Travels into Poland, Scandinavia, and Russia,* London, 1784.)

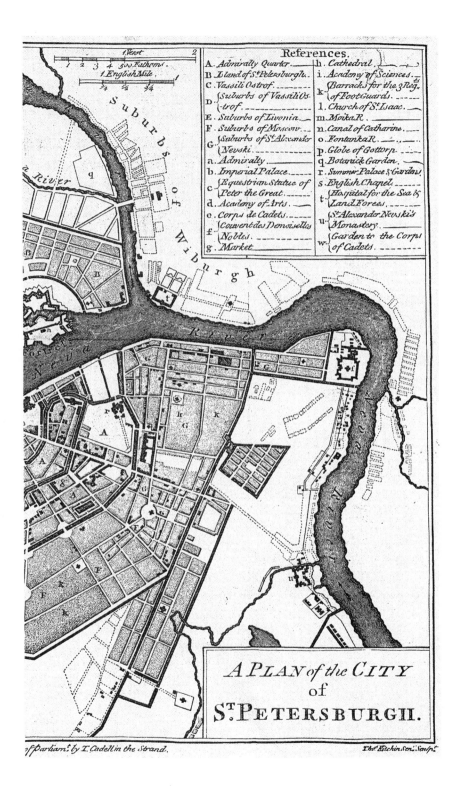

II

It is probable that there were not more than 200 British subjects resident in
St Petersburg towards the end of Peter's reign after the arrival of the British
Factory, although this figure would not include men serving in the Russian
navy. The Anglo-Russian commercial treaties of 1734 and 1766, particularly
the latter, brought a great increase in trade and in the number of people
involved directly or indirectly with that trade. There was a notable upsurge
of confidence, a more 'civilised' way of living in what was changing from a
'frontier town' to a great capital. There was a marked increase in the number
of women and families and a greater sense of permanence and security in the
community. Catherine's reign was not only 'a time when almost everyman of
Genius in Europe is offering at the Shrine of this most Illustrious of Sovereigns',[5] but also one when men of lesser pretensions and calibre, anxious to
find employment, flooded into Russia. The British population more than
doubled in the 1760s; by the beginning of the 1780s the congregation of the
English Church was said to number 482, but this gives but a partial picture.[6]
Further figures for a little later in the century are 930 in 1789 given in Heinrich Storch's account of the city and 1,500 by an English tourist in 1792.[7]
These totals may be judged within the context of the city's overall population
growth – from some 70,000 in 1725 to 95,000 in 1750, 192,000 in 1784,
and 220,000 in 1800.[8] At no time, however, were the British among the
best-represented foreign groups. According to Storch, of the 32,000 foreigners resident in St Petersburg (who made up almost one-seventh of that city's
population in 1789) 17,660 were German, 3,700 were Finnish, 2,290 were
French, 1,860 were Swedish, 930 were British and 50 were Dutch. It will be
readily appreciated that such figures are very imprecise – Storch arrives at his
totals on the basis of very dubious calculations – and the status of 'resident' is
never defined. Nonetheless, although the figure of 1,500 may be taken to
represent the upper limit of the British community in Russia in the last years
of Catherine's reign, the composition of the population was constantly
changing. Great family dynasties were begun in the eighteenth century and
continued for generations: there were many families who were to remain in
St Petersburg until the final dispersal of the community after the October
Revolution of 1917 (for example, the Cattleys, the Cazalets, the Hills and
the Whishaws). There was also a constant flow of men and women, staying
for periods of a few months or a few years, an increasing number of tourists
(particularly in the last decades of the century), large numbers of naval officers, craftsmen, and workmen of all kinds, to say nothing of the crews of
the hundreds of British ships. Over the century there were literally thousands
of Britons who gained some experience of Russia, mainly of the capital and/
or Kronshtadt; there were also pockets of British merchants in Riga, Narva

and Archangel, officers with the Black Sea fleet in Nikolaev, and a small community in Moscow, estimated at 126 in 1805.[9]

Under Catherine the British enjoyed the halcyon days of their influence, partaking of the benefits and security that an enthusiasm for their country, its way of life, institutions, history and literature was to bring – an enthusiasm which was widespread among, if limited to, the upper classes and emerging intelligentsia. The St Petersburg British not only embodied, or appeared to embody, solid British virtues and British ways, but they were also on the spot to cater for the material needs that accompanied Russian Anglophilia, to provide those luxury goods that became indispensable to the Russian elite. Edward Daniel Clarke, a Cambridge don travelling through Russia in 1800, argued that 'whatever they [the Russians] possess useful or estimable comes to them from England. Books, maps, prints, furniture, clothing, hard-ware of all kinds, horses, carriages, hats, leather, medicine, almost every article of convenience, comfort, or luxury, must be derived from England, or it is of no estimation.'[10] Twenty years earlier, a Scots gardener, recently arrived in the capital, noted that 'the Russ are so excessive fond of everything which comes from England that the Rascals of Traders in the Market will swear that many things manufactured in Russia is Angloiskey (that is English) purposely to advance the price'.[11] Foreign merchandise was traditionally sold at the Gostinyi dvor, the capital's official trading centre, next to the Exchange and near the Customs House, on the spit of Vasilii Island; ships came up to the adjacent wharfs or anchored in a channel of the Little Neva.

In the beginning of summer, when the ships arrive at St. Petersburg, the wharfs, at the custom house where they deliver their cargoes, become the morning and evening lounge for all the beauty and fashion of that splendid city. It really is an amusing and pleasant sight. The English bring horses, carriages, dogs, cattle, curious plants, and animals: and the Germans, singing-birds, fruits, flowers, and other curiosities and nicknacks; which, all being set out and arranged for sale, produce a very lively and entertaining scene.[12]

It was a scene dominated by the British skippers and crews and the merchants: Aleksandr Radishchev, the future author of *A Journey from Petersburg to Moscow* (*Puteshestvie iz Peterburga v Moskvu*, 1790) which brought him the wrath of Catherine, was appointed to the Petersburg Customs House in 1780, and soon found that, although he knew French and German perfectly, it was necessary for him to learn English in order to carry out his work satisfactorily.[13]

In 1782 a relaxing of the trading regulations saw a mushrooming of shops throughout the city, frequently in parts of houses belonging to the Russian nobility. By 1791 there seem to have been no fewer than four establishments known as 'The English Shop' in various parts of St Petersburg: owned by Messrs Hoy and Bellis at 74, Malaia Millionnaia, Samuel Hawkesford on the corner of Nevskii Prospekt near the Admiralty, Benjamin Hudson in the house of Countess Matiushkina and William Hubbard on Pervaia Liniia on Vasilii Island.[14] There was indeed some competition to be known as *the* English shop, for a little earlier Hoy and Bellis announced that the English shop had moved, whereupon Hudson immediately advertised that the English shop (i.e. his) was where it had always been.[15] Hubbard's shop on Vasilii Island was soon to be taken over by Mrs Sarah Snow, who began to advertise in detail the wares she had for sale:

At the English Shop, which is situated on Vasilii Island at no 249 Cadet Line and was owned formerly by Mr Hubbard and now by Sarah Snow the following goods are on sale at most reasonable prices: the latest editions of English books, hats, stockings, English cloth, wide and narrow cotton fabric, Irish linen, muslin, charlatan, blankets, velveteen, nankeen, corduroy, ladies' hats, flannelette, flannel, various sets of buttons, watch chains and keys, gloves, trays, tea and coffee machines, pocket books, buckles, sealing wax and seals, magnesia, quills, ribbons, fans, needles, camisoles, table linen, children's toys, sporting weapons and many other items of gold, silver and haberdashery; ladies' dresses and hats are also made to order.[16]

This announcement appeared in the pages of the twice-weekly *St Petersburg News (Sanktpeterburgskie vedomosti)*, which provides ample evidence of the growing dominance of the consumer market by British goods. A sample of items from the newspaper over the years 1790–2 shows the sale of English razors and strops; the auction at the Exchange of English scissors and candle-holders, and, later, of English cloth, chandeliers and plated tea-urns (*nakladnye samovary* – the Russian samovar was after all a variant on the English urn); the arrival of English books, prints and statues; the import of English watches, and of eight-day wall clocks, 'playing various attractive arias'.[17] The emphasis is always on 'English' origin. The trend was bolstered by Catherine's decree of May 1793, which, following the rupture in Franco-Russian relations, prohibited the import of French goods; long lists were published of items, 'the greater part of which merely encourage excess and ruinous luxury and the others can be replaced by Russian products and articles or be obtained from places with which our subjects may carry on permitted and profitable trade'.[18] Although towards the end of Paul's reign it was the turn of all goods of English origin to be forbidden by a decree of 22 November/4 December 1800, the effect was to be minimal, for the Emperor was assassinated a few months later; by the beginning of May 1801, an English visitor was writing: '. . . went into the Shop of Mrs Hoy, a great English house that sells *everything*'.[19]

The historian of St Petersburg in Catherine's reign, Academician J. G. Georgi listed beer, cloth, horses, coal and pottery as particularly prominent imports from Britain.[20] Coal and beer came from Britain as useful ballast for

British ships; coal was used almost exclusively by the British, but beer had a much wider appeal. Prince M. M. Shcherbatov, author of a trenchant critique of the 'new' Russian aristocracy, held Countess Anna Vorontsova, wife of the grand chancellor, responsible for introducing the vogue for English beer at the end of Elizabeth's reign; it was drunk 'not only daily at aristocratic tables but also by common people, who scorning Russian beer, drank it to excess'.[21] The Earl of Buckinghamshire, British ambassador at the beginning of Catherine's reign, wrote of the popularity of Burton ale, and some years later, the Rev. William Coxe, another Cambridge traveller, opined that he had 'never tasted English beer and porter in greater perfection and abundance'.[22] Interesting information about Russian preferences for ale rather than porter and on shipping practices is found in a memorandum drawn up by the steward of a later British ambassador, Lord Cathcart, on the basis of discussions with a British merchant:

3 hogsheads of Porter – Mr Thomson thinks proper to observe the Rushians don't Drink it and tho' it comes Cheap from London, it pays the same Duty here as Burton Ale, that they are fond off – 5 Great Casks of Burton Ale – There is nothing to be saved by ordering it from Burton as it is always Ship'd very New and the Casks often come two thirds or half full, besides it is seldom sold to the Advantage of those who order it, and can only answer the end of the Brewers, who Ship it almost all for their own accounts. – It is of more advantage to the Consumers to pick and chuse the best here on the Key, and then the Casks are fill'd up and gag'd, and they are sure of having what they pay for, and four years in five as cheap as it would come to cost any body that would order five or ten Casks, even if they came all good and full, which never hapens but Mr Thomson has been long of opinion that Ale does not answer the great expense of it, and tho' it is generally agreeable to the Russians, it is not consid'd according to it's cost – Five casks of Ale on account of the very high Duty will amount to as much as the ten Hogsheads of Common Claret.[23]

Shcherbatov, taking Countess Vorontsova to task for her addiction to English beer, also attacked Count Petr Shuvalov for being the first to buy expensive English horses to pull his carriage.[24] The Russian aristocracy's wish to imitate the life and habits of the English gentry was particularly noticeable in its cult of English horses, carriages and dogs. As early as 1740 the Empress Elizabeth purchased sixty-three pairs of dogs of different breeds from the British prime minister, Robert Walpole, and put aside a large house which had formerly belonged to Artemii Volynskii for her hunting hounds and their handlers, who included two highly paid Englishmen.[25] The British Factory, for its part, kept its own pack in the 1780s and 1790s, 'though the frost sets in generally & puts an end to the hunting about the beginning of November'.[26] Catherine on her walks around the grounds of Tsarskoe Selo was inevitably accompanied by her greyhounds, a gift of Baron Thomas Dimsdale. It became as fashionable for a lady to own an English dog as it

was for a gentleman to own an English horse. Georgi estimates that between
200 and 300 English horses were imported annually in the period 1780–
90.[27] Horses arrived in specially adapted ships, and many were on sale in
the capital from British agents. A typical advertisement in 1790 offered a
stallion and seventeen mares for sale and the services of a stallion for breeding at 25 rubles a time.[28] British grooms, ostlers, blacksmiths and dealers
flourished: grooms offered to teach the English style of riding; saddlers provided and repaired the saddles and bridles; blacksmiths shoed the horses and
repaired the imported carriages. In 1783 an English newspaper reported that
'a very commodious travelling-coach, of an uncommon size, and containing
a variety of conveniences, is just finished by Hatchett of Long Acre for the
Empress of Russia'.[29] Hatchett was appointed imperial coachmaker and supplied coaches not only for Catherine but also for Potemkin and other members of the Russian aristocracy; in 1790 he found it necessary to send his
son Charles to St Petersburg to try and collect payment from Potemkin and
obtain new orders.[30] With all the enthusiasm for things equine and equestrian
it is not surprising that the British also took a leading role in promoting
horse-racing. In July 1792 a race was organised on Vasilii Island with a silver
cup worth 150 rubles as the prize.[31] Its organiser was the riding-master
Charles Hughes, who had recently arrived with blood stallions and breeding
mares for the famous stud of Count Aleksei Orlov near Moscow. Orlov more
than anyone helped to make English thoroughbreds popular in Russia.
Among the numerous English horses he bought were former winners of the
Derby and St Leger, and early in the 1770s he had twenty English stallions
and thirty English mares out of a total stud of 100 horses.[32]

British grooms and coachmen frequently entered the service of the Russian
aristocracy (the Grand Duke Paul, for example, had a coachman named
Clark, who 'had driven three Kings');[33] so too did British valets, tutors and
governesses who occupied positions more commonly associated with the
French. 'Mrs Lake seeks a position with a young noble lady to teach history
in English'; 'a recently arrived Englishwoman, who was a nanny in several
genteel families in her homeland, seeks a similar post'; 'an Englishwoman
seeks a position as a housekeeper or children's nurse with a noble family.[34]
Some of the men advertised their ability 'to dress hair and shave beards', as
well as a knowledge of languages other than English, although many offered
instruction in the English language.[35] Some, it may be suspected, were of the
quality of the man who told a British visitor that 'in summer I be clerk to a
butcher at Cronstadt, and in winter I teaches English to the Russian nobility's
children'.[36] Perhaps persuaded by the growing Russian interest in English as
well as the number of British children in the capital, a certain John Elmore
set up a school in 1792 on Vasilii Island on the Seventh Line, 'at which

children of both sexes will be taught in English reading, writing and arithmetic'.[37]

III

The British community in St Petersburg has been called 'a sort of transplanted City of London in miniature'.[38] Although it has been possible to give some idea of the types of employment pursued by people at the lower end of the social spectrum, there is little documentary evidence about their day-to-day existence. What little there is originates from the more privileged members of that society and is designed to entertain, amuse or shock. Such were the letters sent by Dr Matthew Guthrie, physician to the Noble Cadet Corps, to a Scottish journal in 1792–3, purporting to be the compositions of English sailors on a jaunt in St Petersburg,[39] or some of the anecdotes included by James Walker, Catherine's engraver, in a work he published some years after his return to England. Walker, tells, for instance, a story about a Mrs Muslin, an English cook who married an ostler known as 'Brandy Bob',

having first consulted the British chaplain on the subject, freely owning she had kept him company for several years before. The clergyman questioned her in what way, and hoped that nothing improper had passed between them. She hesitated; and, wishing to wrap up the thing as well as she could, and in the most learned and polite words her vocabulary furnished, stammered out, that she had been his – 'Not concubine, I hope,' said the divine. 'Oh, Lord, no, your reverence, not that! only a little prostitution now and then, as I believe you call it.'

But the further point of the anecdote is to demonstrate the 'unconquerable prejudices to which the lower class of the English adhere in foreign countries', for Mrs Muslin, 'being a British-born subject, thought the Russians mere scum'.[40] But James Meader, one of the empress's gardeners, has little to say in favour of English girls coming out to St Petersburg as servants:

The two Girls you sent to me & Bush [another gardener] are Dam'd bad ones. Bush's is a Thief & Whore & ours is the same besides a most abominable Liar. [. . .] they are worse than any Russ Girls I have had before tho I must keep ours till her Year is up or I may be put to the Expence of freighting her back tho I believe her Inclinations are for Petersburg to cohabit with some fellows who came in the same Ship with her.[41]

There is, as might be expected, considerably more material about the life-style of the wealthy stratum of the community – the prosperous merchants, the diplomats and those high in Russian service, doctors, artists, naval officers. One of the English chaplains during Catherine's reign wrote:

The English stationary at St. Petersburg are mostly merchants, acquire and expend a great

3 The New Isaac Bridge and the English Embankment. (Lithograph, 1820s, by unknown Russian artist.)

4 Exchange and Warehouses, Vasilii Island, St Petersburg. (London, 1755, after original engraving by M. Makhaev.)

deal of money, live like their countrymen at home . . . In the houses of the Britons settled here a competent idea may be formed of the english manner of living. Furniture, meals, establishments; everything is english – even to the chimney fire. Here where wood is in such plenty, the Englishman fetches his coals from home.[42]

A similar picture was painted by Lady Elizabeth Craven, visiting the capital in 1786:

I find English grates, English coats, English coal, and English hospitality, to make me welcome, and the fire-side chearful – I have never yet been fortunate enough to make any acquaintance in the world of commerce; but if all English merchants and their families are as well informed and civil as those I find here – I should be very glad to be admitted into the city of London as a visitor, to enjoy a little rational conversation, which at the court-end is seldom to be found.[43]

According to James Brodgen, the son of a prominent member of the Russia Company in London visiting Petersburg a year or so later (and also noting, incidentally, 'the English fire Place where they burn new Castle and Scotch coal'): 'the houses of the English and the other civilised Europeans are fitted up with every convenience, even at the expence of appearance, by which as in all other things we are so peculiarly distinguished from the Russians, whose prevailing passion seems to be the desire of shew'.[44] Not all observers were so impressed: Lionel Colmore in 1790 found the English 'very cold and stiff, I mean where there are women. The bachelors live very comfortably; but you know how the English women are in that circle of life; they are all so very *proper*, that it becomes tiresome to find conversation.'[45] In contrast the British diplomats and their families found much to commend. Lewis de Visme, Secretary to the Embassy in 1768, reported that 'the British Factory here are the greatest resource for excursions; I never yet saw so many worthy, reasonable and sober People get together, their whole way of life is open and generous, with more cordiality than can possibly be conceived among Rival Merchants', and Lady Cathcart enthused in similar terms.[46] Much inevitably depended on the eye of the beholder and a negative interpretation may be easily given to qualities which were advanced as positive. It was, for instance, noted with approval that 'the English merchants live with that cautious reserve which every where distinguishes them' and were 'usually divided into sets, and a line is drawn around each circle of acquaintances'.[47] Some sense of the different circles existing within the community during Catherine's reign may be gained from the unpublished diaries of British visitors, whose own acceptance and entrée depended on their social status and/or the letters of recommendation they brought with them from home.

The British community, or at least its most prominent representatives, enjoyed a generally distinctive and cordial relationship with the Russian nobility. Patrick Brydone, visiting the Russian capital in 1776, some three years after the publication of his very popular *Tour through Sicily and Malta*, noted that the British were 'on a better footing wᵗ the Court and Nobles than any set of Merchᵗˢ I have ever seen out of England', adding that 'the Present Empress has distinguish'd them very much'. Baroness Dimsdale also recorded in 1781 that 'the Empress is very partial to the English', while Robert Hynam, the imperial watchmaker, suggested that Catherine was 'acquainted with the conduct and character of every Englishman in Petersburg' (or, at least, of those that 'mattered').[48] Many members of her court were frequently in the company of the British and attended some of their institutions and major events.

The subscription balls, organised during the winter season by the British merchants, were important occasions for such social intercourse. It seems likely that they were instituted early in Catherine's reign – Lady Cathcart mentions them in 1769: 'our Family are invited & our going is thought vastly obliging & to ourselves very Pleasant'.[49] In the 1787–8 season there were seven balls, and Brogden has left a delightful description of the first of the series, which was attended by Prince Potemkin, Count Bezborodko, the foreign ambassadors, many Russian nobles, and most of the British merchants:

Country Boamkin, as they call Country Bumkin, is a very favourite dance, tho' they make it quite different from the dance so called in England. The supper is very elegant, but so much in fashion is everything English that Beefstakes, Welsh Rabits & Porter is the most fashionable meal. I myself saw the Duke of Capriola, the Neapolitan Embassador, in his red heeled shoes, very busy at a great Beef Stake, a dish I dare say he had never tasted in Italy. Those dishes are as fashionable among the ladies as the Gentlemen; the former, tho' they do not eat many sweetmeats at Supper, pocket them & apples without Scruple.[50]

(Walker also provides an amusing anecdote about the Russians' addiction to roast beef: his family, unexpectedly visited by the three Countesses Protasov, was obliged to seek help from a neighbour who supplied 'a most famous cold round of beef with, however, strong injunctions that it should be immediately returned after dinner', which it was, only for the princesses to decide to stay on 'for another slice of that most excellent beef at supper'.)[51]

The balls were held at the English Inn, which was run in the late 1780s and 1790s by a Scotsman, Joseph Fawell; and both the balls and Fawell were celebrated in a poem written in 1791 by the Russian poet Ivan Dmitriev: '. . . at that hour, when Terpsichore / Summons through Fawell everyone to her temple of amusements and delights'.[52] In the 1787–8 season Fawell had specifically changed from masquerades to balls in accordance with the wishes of the subscribers.[53] Three years earlier, he had offered 'two masquerades at six rubles for both occasions, admitting one male and one female. Tea, coffee, lemonade etc. are served free of charge. The large room is reserved for contre-danses, the small for minuets, and the other rooms are for cards.' In the same year, 1784, Fawell was advertising concerts by visiting artists.[54] It is difficult to establish when and precisely where the first English inn was to be found. Stolpianskii discovered a reference as early as 1747 to one run by Antony Walter in the home of Vice-Admiral Golovin by the Kriukov Canal and in the 1770s there was another run by a certain Fraser 'near the Galley Yard'. All the innkeepers, Fawell included, held lotteries and sold various goods from apples (Golden Pippins) to oysters ('twelve days from England').[55] Fawell's inn was a large house, owned by a Russian nobleman on the English Embankment but entered from Isaac Street. Apart from its assembly rooms, it offered lodgings mainly for visiting British tourists and enjoyed a high reputation. Although in 1776 Brydone was complaining that there were 'no coffee houses at Petersburg',[56] by 1790 Fawell was operating within his hotel a 'subscription Coffee Room' and Charles Hatchett was enrolled as a 'Visitor'.[57] Hatchett took rooms above another 'English Coffee House', run by a Frenchwoman and her daughter and located, according to the newspaper, nearby at 117 Isaac Street.[58] A walk across the road would take the more serious-minded members of the community to another typically British institution, the subscription library, which was housed in one of the rooms or courtyard wings of the English Church.

The library seems to have been established in the 1760s and the first mention of its existence is found in a letter by Lady Cathcart of September 1770; thanking her correspondent for sending her books, she writes:

Mrs Montagues remarks upon Shakespear we had admired last year with' knowing the Author; they were lent to us by a Gentleman who Commended them very much at the same time. I believe his Copy & mine are the only ones that have reached Petersb^g. when any thing of the kind appears, it is handed about among the Merch^{rs} who are universally very clever & sensible Men, & what they approve they send for, & place in their Public Library.[59]

Its first known librarian was Peter Holsten, a naturalised Englishman and member of the Russia Company. This information appeared on the title page of a poem published in St Petersburg in 1776 by Holsten, who two years later began to publish *Das Englische Wochenblatt in deutsche Sprache*, a weekly news-sheet based on English materials he himself translated and arranged.[60] In 1781–3 Holsten edited a further journal entitled *Englisches Magazin* and once again put to good use the opportunities that the post of librarian afforded him. It is only in 1787 that further references to the library are encountered, when Holsten had retired or been replaced as librarian. The Venezuelan Count Francisco de Miranda, who was taken on a tour of inspection by the British chaplain, suggested that the initiative for the library had come from the ladies in the community; he found the collection a good one, approaching 2,000 volumes, and met the librarian whom he called

Howel (possibly Fawell and a relation of the innkeeper).[61] He also mentioned a catalogue, but this was certainly manuscript and has not survived. It was only in 1821 that the first printed catalogue appeared, listing over 1,200 titles in thirteen categories. The Rules state that the library was open six days a week, between ten and three during the day and seven and nine in the evening, and that subscribers could introduce visiting British citizens as temporary members.[62] There was another collection of English books and newspapers available nearby at perhaps the most famous establishment created by the British community in St Petersburg – the English Club, which was to prove so popular with the Russians that by the middle of the nineteenth century it remained English in name only.

The origins of the English Club, as opposed to those of other institutions so far described, are well documented.[63] It appears that a number of foreign merchants were in the habit of gathering at a small inn run by a Dutchman called Cornelius Gardiner in the late 1760s; when he ran into financial difficulties it was suggested by one of the merchants, an Englishman by the name of Francis Gardner (1745–1813), that they should establish a club, of which the Dutchman would become the manager. The club was officially established on 1/12 March 1770, when fifty founder members signed its constitution, the twelve articles of which included an annual subscription of six rubles, the election of a six-man committee every half year, methods of electing new members, provision for billiards and cards (no gambling), and a separate reading room. The first committee consisted of two Britons (Robert Hay and Henry Fock) and four Germans, in the house of one of whom (Conrad Kuzel) the first meetings were held on New Isaac Street, which ran from the back of St Isaac's Square parallel to Old Isaac Street and near the Moika River. Gardner seems never to have served on the committee, but remained a member for forty-three years and was esteemed as the founder of the club: his portrait hung in one of the main rooms.[64] By the end of 1771 membership had grown to 250; by 1780 this number had increased to 300, which thereafter remained the maximum. Members were drawn from all nationalities, and the British were well represented but never in the majority. The club's minutes, incidentally, were recorded in German rather than in English. It was originally intended that no one above the rank of brigadier (the fifth position in the Table of Ranks) should be admitted, but this was soon relaxed and the provision finally removed in 1801. By 1774 it was necessary to move to new rooms, in Count Buturlin's house on the Moika near the Blue Bridge; in 1778 a further move was made to the house of Countess Skavronskaia, by the Red Bridge, and there the club remained for the last decades of the eighteenth century. Most of the most prominent British merchants served at some time or another on the committee (which was increased to seven members by the end of 1770); James Walker, the engraver, seems to have been one of the few non-merchant Britons to be elected. Walker retained fond memories of the club long after he had returned to England; he notes the mixture of nationalities and social status, 'yet such is the excellency of its regulations, assisted by the urbanity and politeness of the nobles, that they set down pellmell to dinner at the same table, upon perfect equality ... In twenty years that I had the pleasure of being a member, and three times a director, I never saw but one serious quarrel ...'[65] The club was open daily, from morning to midnight, and members could dine there twice a week (or four times, according to another account).[66] Georgi called the English Club not only the oldest but also 'the most exclusive and most respectable' of the capital's clubs;[67] it seems to have provided the stimulus for the formation of several other clubs and societies, such as the Bürger Club (or Schuster Club, after its founder), the Club of the Nobility, the Musical Club (later the Musical Society) and the Dance Club. Dr Matthew Guthrie was a prominent member of the Musical Club, and Charles Hatchett records visits to it and to the Dance Club, which consisted of '300 members of all Ranks & Nations, not frequented much by genteel Women'.[68] But it was societies of a somewhat different sort that proliferated in St Petersburg in the 1770s and 1780s – the lodges of Freemasonry. And it was in the English Masonic Lodge of 'Perfect Union' that the English Club, whose motto was 'Concordia et Laetitia', found in some respects its closest parallel and complement.

IV

The links between early Russian and British Freemasonry are of a somewhat obscure, even legendary character. Peter the Great was reputed to have acquired a knowledge of Freemasonry from Sir Christopher Wren during his visit to London in 1698 and to have founded a lodge in Moscow on his return in which he served, characteristically, not as Master but as Junior Warden. A few years later, he performed once again the functions of Warden in a select and secret club, known as the 'Neptune Society', which met at the Moscow School of Mathematics and Navigation. Among the members were two Scots – General James Bruce and Henry Farquharson, the latter being the mathematician from Marischal College, Aberdeen, recruited by Peter for his new school.[69] However it is another Scotsman, General James Keith, who is generally recognised as the founding father of Freemasonry in Russia. Keith, who entered Russian service in 1728, was appointed Provincial Grand Master of Russia in 1740 by the Grand Master of England, who was in fact his cousin, John Keith, Earl of Kintore. Keith's role in Russian Freemasonry was celebrated in a masonic hymn which was sung during the reign of Elizabeth, but of his activities before he finally left Russia virtually nothing is known.[70] He is said to have attended a lodge in St Petersburg in 1732, during the term of office of the far more obscure first Provincial Grand Master of Russia and Germany, a Captain John Phillips (appointed in 1731).[71] But it was only in 1771, forty years after Phillips's appointment and thirty years after Keith's, that the Grand Lodge of England entered into its Engraved Lists its first lodge in Russia, 'Perfect Unity'. 'Perfect Unity' would, however, have remained but a name, without any insight into its working and membership, were it not for the fact that a copy of its minute book, covering a single year of its short existence, is still preserved in the archives of its parent body.

It seems likely that 'Perfect Union' was founded in the summer of 1770, a few months in fact after the establishment of the English Club. Its first Master, while it was still unconstituted, was Giuseppe Brigonzi (d. 1789), the famous Italian 'machinist', creator of elaborate scenaries and stage machinery, first for Locatelli's company, with which he had come to Russia in 1757, and then for the imperial theatres. It was during Brigonzi's terms of office that the approach was made to the Grand Lodge of England for a constitution, which was granted on 1 June 1771; and it is with the election of Brigonzi's successor, the British merchant William Gomm, jr., on 13/24 June, St John the Baptist's Day, that the copy of the minutes begins. Brigonzi became Master of Ceremonies and the other officers of the Lodge in 1771–2 were Ivan Golovkin, Senior Steward; Dirk Jäger, Junior Steward; John Cayley, Senior Warden; Samuel Swallow, Junior Warden; François van Zanten, Secretary; Timothy Raikes, Treasurer; Sebastian de Villiers, Orator. The officers, who incidentally were re-elected en bloc in the following year (1772–3), represent a spread of nationalities – four Britons, one Russian, one German, one Dutchman, one Frenchman and one Italian – that was characteristic of the Lodge's membership as a whole. There seem to have been about fifteen founder members, who had increased to twenty-three when the decision was taken on 6/17 February 1772 to limit membership to twenty-four and to invite no more than six visitors at any one time, in addition to the four masons (all Russians) who enjoyed the status of 'perpetual visitors'. This decision was taken on account of the small size of the rooms in which the Lodge met (unfortunately, there is no indication of precisely where the Lodge did meet, but it is likely that it was in the 'English Line'), although the membership was soon to be increased to thirty 'with the Reservation of admitting supernumeraries of the British Nation, our Lodge being always considered as British in its Foundation'.[72] During the period covered by the extant minute book (from 13/24 June 1771 to 23 July/3 August 1772) there were no less than seventy-five men connected with the Lodge either as members, perpetual visitors or visitors; of these, thirty were British, nineteen Russian, sixteen German, five Italian, four French and one

Dutch. While half the actual members were British, the cosmopolitan mix of the Lodge is very evident and parallels that of the English Club. Indeed, over one-third of the members and visitors were either at that time or soon to become members of the English Club: and the Club's founder, Francis Gardner, received the degrees of Apprentice and Fellow Craftsman as a visitor in 1772.

The British members included some of the most influential merchants: Samuel Swallow was currently British consul-general and agent of the Russian Company, a position which Cayley, a partner in the firm of Thornton, Cayley & Co., was also to hold from 1787 until his death in 1795; but Gomm, Raikes, John Farquharson, John Sutherland (Baron Sutherland's brother), John Thomson, Charles Innes and others were all prominent figures. Only one of the British members was not a merchant: John Robison (1739–1805) had arrived in Russia in 1770 as private secretary to Admiral Sir Charles Knowles, whom Catherine had invited to revitalise the Russian navy; he was to become professor of mathematics at the Naval Cadet Corps in Kronshtadt in 1772, before returning to Scotland in 1773 to become professor of natural philosophy at Edinburgh University.[73] Among the British visitors to the Lodge were many other merchants as well as William Tooke, the English chaplain from Kronshtadt, William Richardson, tutor to the children of Lord Cathcart (the British ambassador) and a future professor of humanity at Edinburgh, and Captain, later Sir George Collier, captain of HMS *Flora*, which was to convey the ambassador, his family and Richardson back to England in August 1772. It was to Collier that the copy of the minute book was entrusted for delivery to the Grand Lodge in London.

The decision to send the copy arose from the Lodge's wish to remain 'a *British* Lodge whose Foundation & Existence is national, immediately and directly depending on Your Grace alone [the Duke of Beaufort, the then Grand Master of England], and consequently not subject to the control of anyone else'.[74] It was a desperate and ultimately unavailing attempt to avoid submitting to the authority of the third Provincial Grand Master appointed by the Grand Lodge of England but the first Russian to hold the post. It is possible that 'Perfect Union' knew of the approach made to the Grand Lodge by the government official and dramatist Ivan Perfil'evich Elagin (1725–93) when it sought its own constitution and hoped thereby to pre-empt any question of allegiance, but the Grand Lodge unfortunately did not see it that way. Although it granted 'Perfect Union' its constitution, in February 1772 it made Elagin its Provincial Grand Master and sent the Master of 'Perfect Union' a letter calling for the Lodge's submission to Elagin's authority and describing 'the Year 1772 as the Era of Masonic Splendour and Dignity in Russia'.[75] 'Perfect Union' reacted negatively to the demand and informed Elagin that with Respect to the fundamental question, suggested by the Letter from the Grand Lodge, it has been unanimously resolved, that this Lodge shall exert its utmost Efforts, in order to preserve the privilege, which it derives from the Constitution, of having no dependance, nor official Correspondance to that Effect with any other than the Grand Lodge in London.[76]

Congratulating Elagin on his new eminence and wishing him success in the erection of new and prosperous lodges in Russia, 'Perfect Union' was willing to regard him and his followers as their true brothers, but never as their masters. The ill-feeling continued throughout the summer of 1772, but on 28 October the Committee of Charity of the Grand Lodge of England again resolved that 'Perfect Union' must submit. And submit it eventually did, but evidence suggests that it was only towards the end of 1774. Certainly by 1776 it was under Elagin's authority and the name of its Master at that time, John Cayley, appears on a list of masons designated by Elagin for higher degrees.[77] English masons were soon visiting other Lodges in the capital, particularly 'Urania' with its high percentage of German merchants in its membership. Francis Gardner is particularly mentioned in this respect, and visitors after 1775 included the British merchants James Whittaker and Caleb Wilkins, who were by then possibly members of 'Perfect Union'.[78] No information is available about the Lodge's membership and activities in the second half of the 1770s or about how long it continued to exist, although this would not have been later than 1784, when Elagin decided to close all the lodges under his control.

V

The eighteenth-century Briton proved an eminently clubbable person. Large numbers of men joined clubs and societies in Britain which frequently met in taverns and coffee-houses, where they indulged their mutual interests in lively conversation, sympathetic company and good food and drink. Many societies indeed did much to help the advancement of learning, offering a forum for scholarly papers and informed debate, but many more were content to promote simply good fellowship and conviviality. Good fellowship was one of the ideals of Freemasonry, but the secrecy which surrounded its rites and activities inevitably gave rise to rumours of conspiracy and political intrigue. But there were other societies which attempted to conceal their very existence, for their activities were of a kind that scandalised respectable society and threatened public morals. The Hellfire clubs, of which the Brotherhood of the Friars of St Francis, formed by Sir Francis Dashwood in England, and Robert Burns' Court of Equity in Scotland are prominent examples, enjoyed a notoriety for blasphemy, satanism and sexual orgies but seemed to have little difficulty in recruiting followers even among the most exalted members of society. The British in Russia, as we have seen, were eager to imitate many institutions that flourished in their homeland, but were they prepared to risk imitating societies that could only bring disrepute and scandal to their community? The answer seems to be 'yes', even though the existence of such societies remained unsuspected for over 200 years. The activities of 'Perfect Union' were a closely guarded secret, but at least there were contemporary or near-contemporary references to the lodge's existence; in the case of the British Monastery and the Order of the Beggar's Benison there were no such references, although the activities of the former, if not of the latter, could hardly have escaped comment.

One of the most notorious of Petrine institutions was the Most Drunken Synod (*Vsep'ianeishii sobor*) and numerous accounts exist of its elaborate ceremonies and processions, designed as obscene parodies of church rituals and institutions, and of the prolonged drinking orgies, ending with the participants blind drunk, retching or unconscious. Seen as a calculated attack on Muscovite conservatism and the authority of the church or a creation of the dark sides of Peter's nature, the Synod was no passing fancy, but something which, coming into existence as early as 1692 and operating according to statutes drawn up by the Tsar himself, retained his interest and support virtually until his death. It seems probable that the idea of the Synod arose from Peter's meetings with foreigners in Moscow's Foreign Quarter, known to seventeenth-century Muscovites as the 'Drunken Quarter' (*P'ianaia sloboda*), but while it is impossible to say whether Britons were involved in the Synod's foundation, they were certainly involved in its subsequent activities. What was never realised until the discovery of documents in a Leningrad archive in the early 1920s was that members of the British community in Moscow were soon to form an association in imitation of the Most Drunken Synod.[79]

In a letter of 1708 Peter mentions 'the British *arkhierei*' (a bishop or above in the church hierarchy) as one of the members of the Most Drunken Synod,[80] but it is the copy of a warrant (*patent*) issued to William Lloyd, a British merchant, on 10/21 August 1709, instructing the British 'Metropolitan' in Moscow to promote him from 'deacon' to 'archdeacon' and to allow him to take part in the tributes to Bacchus, that seems to provide evidence of the existence of the British Monastery in Moscow. The warrant is included with the other documents which are concerned with the Monastery's activities in 1720, by which date it had transferred to St Petersburg, and include the code or statutes of the Monastery and, most importantly, a list of the members and the offices they held. The original membership of the Monastery will probably never be established, but may well have included many of the people listed in 1720 who were known to have been in Moscow in the early years of the century. The list gives fifty-five positions in the Monastery, but not all have accompanying names. The first fifteen offices all bear ecclesiastical titles, ranging from Metropolitan down to Assistant Cellarer; then follow titles drawn from a whole range of professions and occupations, including orator, solicitor-general, various professors, keeper of the seraglio, ranger, bagpiper, wine-waiters and cooks. Of the forty-six people named in the list at least twenty-eight are British (the documents are in Russian and the transcription of names makes identification in some cases difficult).[81] It is clear that the Monastery brought into its orbit some of the most influential and notable members of the British community – leading merchants of the British Factory and respected scholars and professional men. Merchants such as Samuel Gartside, Henry Hodgkin, William Lloyd, William Waite, Robert Nettleton, James Spilman, Samuel Meux and William Elmsal were all partners in large trading firms, bankers, commission agents, or factory owners; Nettleton after long years in Russia returned to London to become an outstanding Governor of the Russia Company; Spilman traded in Russia for over thirty years and is known for the little book he published in 1742, *Journey through Russia into Persia*, describing new British trading ventures. With all these men Peter was on the friendliest of terms, dining in their houses and addressing many of them by their Christian names. The same was true of Henry Farquharson, already mentioned as a member of the 'Neptune Society', and Stephen Gwyn, one of two scholars recruited from Christ's Hospital in London to work with Farquharson in the Moscow School of Navigation; both Farquharson and Gwyn transferred to St Petersburg in 1715 to become professors at the Naval Academy. Other Britons included surgeons, instrument makers, John Wells the 'master painter', and Sir Henry Sinclair, a cousin of Peter's physician Dr Robert Erskine who had come to Russia in 1716. But the Monastery, despite its majority of British members, enjoyed the same range of nationalities that was to be apparent in other British-dominated societies later in the century: there were Germans, including notably Baron Heinrich von Huyssen, the tutor of the tsarevich and one of Peter's most enthusiastic propagandists, and Johann Paus, chief translator at the Academy of Sciences and man of letters (among whose papers, incidentally, the documents about the Monastery were discovered); some Dutchmen, including two members of the famous Kellerman family of merchants; and a few Russians, mainly among the ancillary staff but also Osip Bazhenin, a prominent shipbuilder and entrepreneur.

If the appelation 'Monastery' corresponds to 'Synod', its alternative title 'the Bung College' echoes 'the most drunken', for among the several meanings of 'bung' in the seventeenth and eighteenth centuries were those of 'drunk' and 'tavern keeper'. The Monastery undoubtedly followed the Synod in its addiction to drink; it also shared its delight in childish obscenity and pranks: the statutes include a list of punishments for recalcitrant members, ranging from slaps on bare buttocks, tossing in a blanket, pouring cold water down coat sleeves, to the rather more sadistic one of setting two hungry ducks to do their worst on an offender whose penis had been smeared with egg yolk and oats. The preoccupation with the private parts is also found in the curious designation of one office-holder as 'staff-surgeon and pinkle smith or prick farrier' (*khuev kuznets*) and of another as 'cunt-peeper'. The members of the Monastery also took part in the 'revels' of the Most Drunken Synod and one of the documents states that they should sport leeks in their hats on such occasions. This Welsh element, possibly out of deference to Lloyd, was also continued in the Monastery's banner, which carried a representation of St David with a border of leeks. It appears that the Monastery met in St Petersburg in a house on Dvorianskaia Street (now Kuibyshev Street), opposite the home of Petr Ivanovich Buturlin, who had been elected Prince-Pope of the Synod in 1717.

It seems certain that the Monastery was dissolved with the death of Peter, and the British community returned to less spectacular pursuits. It was possibly the Monastery that Jonas Hanway had in mind when he wrote in 1753 that 'the British factors in St Petersburg, as may be observed in all small societies, contribute much to each other's amusement, and are now become sober and virtuous, as well as more elegant in manners than in times past, when they were debauched and low in their pleasures'.[82] It was only during the reign of Catherine II that the British again organised themselves into societies and clubs; but if these were in the most part impeccably respectable, one at least would seem to have revived, if unknowingly, some of the more dubious activities of its Petrine predecessor.

One of the strangest and longest lasting of the Scottish convivial and Hell-fire clubs was the Most Ancient and Puissant Order of the Beggar's Benison and Merryland, which was founded at Anstruther in Fife in 1732 and existed until 1836. In organisation and nomenclature the Order was pseudo-chivalric (cf. the Knights Templar of the masonic tradition particularly associated with Scotland): presided over by a Sovereign, the Knights, as the members were called, met together in the Temple, which was suitably 'tyled' (i.e. guarded against intruders, as with the masons) before the ceremonies began. And what ceremonies! The god that ruled the temple was the phallus, and the main activity was its display and measuring. Novices were tested by 'frigging' (masturbation), a practice indulged in by all the Knights. After the exhibitionism there usually followed a session of voyeurism – local lasses were hired to pose nude before the assembly. Another practice was the reading of suitable literature (e.g. Cleland's *Fanny Hill*) to excite the Knights. The Order convened twice a year, at Candlemas (2 February) and on St Andrew's Day (30 November), and the ceremonies would be followed by a banquet accompanied by bawdy toasts, singing and speechifying, before the proceedings ended with 'secresy enjoined upon faith'.[83]

The Order's Code of Institutes and its Diploma, abounding in sexual *double entendre*, were drawn up in 1739 by one John McNaughton, Collector of Customs at Anstruther, a founder member and a key figure in its early history. Six years later McNaughton became Sovereign of the Order, a position he held until his death in 1773. When he moved to Edinburgh in 1766 as Inspector General of Customs, he set up a branch of the Order there, but this significant expansion of its activities was soon to pale before the 'agreeable prospect of extending the interests of our Empire, & ye beneficient purpose of our Guardianship over ye province of Russia'. This astonishing piece of information is found with other documents about the Order among the papers of Alleyne Fitzherbert, British envoy extraordinary at the Court of Catherine II between 1783 and 1787.[84]

The man responsible for opening up the 'agreeable prospect' of an outpost for the Order in the Northern Palmyra was William Porter, a St Petersburg merchant, who had been admitted to the Russia Company in 1770 and who possibly had been a member of the order before coming to Russia.[85] He seems to have written to McNaughton proposing the establishment of a 'Consistory' in St Petersburg and giving the name (unfortunately unknown to posterity) of the man willing to act as 'Prince' or 'Viceroy', and receiving in return a letter for the new 'Prince' and descriptions of the ceremonies connected with the initiation of Knights, the arrangements for dinners, including seating plans and order of toasts. These descriptions significantly amplify what has hitherto been known about the actual ceremonies of the Order and also introduced the titles of office-bearers such as Chancellor (the office held by Porter), Cup-Bearer, Usher of the Pink Rod and Benison King-at-Arms. Apart from the customary 'blessing' ('May your Prick & purse never fail you' – even then discreetly reduced to 'P – & p –') at the end of the Sovereign's letter to his new Viceroy, and the unexpected addressal of Venus during the initiation of the Knights, there is little in the wording of the new documents to suggest immediately the true nature of the Order. It is only in the context of what has been related earlier about its activities in Scotland and the wording of its diploma that the unending string of *double entendre* is to be recognised. Thus the Prince is inevitably termed 'most potent'; his sceptre 'can never in the nature of things be weak'; uprightness – *rectus* – erection is the quality of his rule; the usher is predictably 'Pink Rod'; the novitiate Knight pledges to serve the Order 'employing at its call those Arms which Nature has given me for its use, and to spend my last drop before I retire or quit my post'.

The intriguing questions raised by the documents are ones for which there are no definitive answers. Did the St Petersburg Consistory meet and how long did it exist? Did it perform the same ceremonies as its parent body in Anstruther? Who were the Knights? It seems that the Consistory was indeed established and existed for a number of years, the evidence for which is the copy of the 'speech composed & spoken by W.P. as Chancellor of the Order of the Beggars Bennison in Russia 1773' among the Fitzherbert Papers and a letter from Samuel Bentham to his brother Jeremy in October 1780, where there is a glowing appreciation of Porter's talents and the information that 'He is master of a great flow of language, so as at a kind of private spouting club there is here to be able to attract the attention and astonishment of the company for 2 or 3 hours together on any subject'.[86] If the Order indulged in other than debates and speech-making there is no allusion to the fact and no evidence of any scandal, but it is possible that the Knights, whoever they were (for again we have no list), were successful in preserving the 'secresy enjoined upon faith'. Nevertheless, Porter, whom Bentham describes as an intimate of Sir James Harris, the British ambassador between 1777 and 1783, seems to have informed Harris's successor, Fitzherbert, about the Beggar's Benison and supplied him with the documents that were copied into a note-book around 1785. At all events, the establishing of the Order in St Peters-burg in 1773 was a remarkable event, coming two years after the erection of the Lodge of 'Perfect Union'. Opposed to Freemasonry in all its ideals and consciously parodying its rituals, the Order in St Petersburg drew its Knights from the same small community, including, almost certainly, mem-bers of the respectable English Club, to which Porter was later to belong. But it was also to find parallel organisations among the so-called 'erotic' clubs frequented by members of the Russian nobility in the late 1780s and 1790s – St Petersburg was said to have had a 'Philadelphian Society' and Moscow both an 'Adam' and an 'Eve' Club, although this would seem to be the same gathering.[87] (The medal worn by a Knight of the Beggar's Benison, incidentally, depicted Adam leading away Eve on one side, beneath the legend 'Be fruitful and multiply', and on the other, Adonis surprising a sleep-ing Venus and ready to enact the legend 'Lose no opportunity'.)[88]

VI

It is remarkable how many of the various institutions described in the preced-ing pages flourished or originated during the late 1760s and particularly the early 1770s. The phenomenon seems largely attributable to the sense of opti-mism and security that the successful re-negotiation of the Commercial Agreement in 1766 brought to the British community, the ensuing increase in its size, and the evident goodwill of the empress. Rumours about the siz-able British community were possibly among the factors that persuaded a company of professional English actors to try its luck in the Russian capital towards the end of 1770. Amateur theatricals had inevitably found a place in the life of the British community just as they did in that of numerous Russian aristocratic circles and in such institutions as the Smol'nyi Institute for Young Gentlewomen, but the series of plays performed by a small group of British residents at the home of the merchant Timothy Raikes on the English Embankment in 1767–8 was particularly noted. The German academician Jakob von Stählin, who was apparently present on several occasions, mentions only one play by name, *The Jealous Husband* (possibly Cibber's *The Careless Husband* or Hoadly's *The Suspicious Husband*?) and gives as performers Raikes, a Miss Cook (possibly Sarah Cook, who was to marry Admiral Greig in September 1768, or her sister Elizabeth), and a Mr and Miss Brooks.[89] But the arrival of a professional company inevitably had a much wider impact, and not only on the British community. Shortly after their first performances in October 1770, Lord Cathcart saw fit to include in one of his dispatches 'a little anecdote which shows the regard of the Empress, and her court for British subjects':

Some English players arrived here from Copenhagen and fitted up a house to act in. They were chiefly encouraged to stay by the Russians, who regularly frequent and applaud them, and indeed seem much entertained though they do not understand the language. A box had been prepared for her Imperial Majesty, to which she had easy access, and on Saturday she came unexpectedly, seemed to be pleased, and sent Mr Fawkener who was the only gentleman known to her present, a message by her chamberlain that she thought herself at home when she was among English people. Next morning the manager was sent for by one of her secretaries who showed him 1000 Roubles and bid him take them from a lady who thanked him for having admitted her and her company the night before without tickets.[90]

An advertisement announcing the opening of the theatre on 2/13 October identified the house as belonging to the merchant F. G. Wulf (a founder member of the English Club) on the Moika near the Summer Garden, but it is a description of the early months of the theatre's existence by William Richardson in his *Anecdotes of the Russian Empire* (1784) that adds information of considerable interest.[91] Richardson suggests that the theatre was not in Wulf's house, but in a barn in the grounds – 'with great diligence, and much tinsel, they furbished up an old barn into the likeness of a theatre' – and that the quality of the performance was such as to win over an audience that came to laugh but stayed to cry. Moreover he identifies the opening play as the popular tragedy *Douglas* by John Home, and that the part of Douglas himself 'was performed by a female player with inimitable pathos'. He then mentions the visit of Catherine, who 'ordered a better theatre to be prepared'. In fact on 10/21 November 1770 Catherine issued a decree, granting the company 'the wooden stable standing on the meadow [Tsaritsyn lug] opposite the [Summer] Garden, as well as whatever they may require from

the old theatre in the same meadow, in order they may have their own theatre'.[92] Work on creating what became known as 'the new English theatre'
was completed early in 1771 and the first performance in the new building
was given on 9/20 February. Richardson gives the text of the 'Prologue' delivered on the occasion by the actress who had performed the role of Douglas.
Her identity as well as the title of the first play of the new season are found
together with a fuller version of the prologue in an item published in *Scots
Magazine*: the actress was Mrs Fisher, wife of the director of the company,
and the play, Nicholas Rowe's *Jane Shore* (1714); the prologue itself was an
elaborate paean to Catherine, ending with the lines (among several omitted
by Richardson in 1784 in the wake of Catherine's declaration of the Armed
Neutrality): 'BRITANNIA's friend! long may she live! renown'd/ For arts
and arms, with endless glory crown'd.'[93]

    The company gave regular performances throughout 1771 and early
1772 – in its extensive repertoire there were, in addition to *Douglas* and
Jane Shore, Bickerstaffe's *The Padlock, Love in a Village* and *The Maid of
the Mill*, Murphy's *Old Maid* and *The Apprentice*, Farquhar's *The Incon-
stant*, Centlivre's *The Busy Body* and *The Wife Well Managed*, Garrick's
The Fatal Marriage, O'Hara's *Midas*, and, most notably, Shakespeare's
Othello (which was performed on 7/18 January 1772).[94] The success of Fisher's company was obviously great among the Russians as well as the British
and Germans, so much so that Nikolai Novikov in his satirical journal *Zhiv-
opisets (The Painter)* rebuked his fellow-countrymen for being 'astonished
by a troupe of strolling English provincial players, for we too have our actors,
who can match the finest English actors and actresses'.[95] But the success of
the company was short-lived, and a contemporary source suggests that, 'qua-
relling among themselves; they [the actors] separated and went home: except
a few who remained and got employment as teachers of the English language'.[96] Several left in June including Robert Bowles (1748–1806), who was
to enjoy a long career in the theatre in Norwich and London, but Mrs Fisher
and another of the leading ladies, Margaret Andrews, returned in September
after an unsuccessful attempt to recruit replacement players.[97] In January
1773 Mr Fisher, calling himself the 'ex-proprietor of the English theatre' was
indeed advertising English lessons[98], but he may well have returned to England in April that same year. If the Alexander Fisher advertising his departure
was Mr Fisher the actor, he was also the Freemason of that name who visited
'Perfect Union' in April 1772; and almost the last we hear of the English
theatre itself dates from the summer of 1772, when the Masons of 'Perfect
Union' used the building to celebrate their great Feast of St John on 13/24
June with a 'Concert Supper and Ball', attended by some eighty guests.[99]
Memories of the company's visit, however, lived on: Patrick Brydone later
records that the Empress 'honour'd with her presence an English play they

had some years ago, altho' she did not understand a word of the language'.[100]

The visit of Mr Fisher's company of English actors was an unrepeated event in the cultural life of the Russian capital, but other British entertainers, relying on their acrobatic, conjuring and equestrian talents rather than on their voices and thereby attracting a much wider public, were fairly regular visitors. By mid-century foreign troupes and individual artists were coming to Russia in ever-increasing numbers, bringing new acts and spectacles to add to the traditional attractions of the Russian fairgrounds and carnivals. Acrobats and equilibrists figured prominently among the early British performers, but the particular British contribution during Catherine's reign was, not surprisingly, equestrian: a stream of skilled trick-riders and their troupes did much to bring the excitement of the circus ring to Russia.[101]

During the 1750s, the second decade of Elizabeth's reign, three visits by British performers are recorded, beginning with an unnamed family (husband, wife, son and five-year-old daughter) arriving in the capital in 1750 and performing on the tight-rope, followed by the equilibrist Michael Stewart, exhibiting his skills on the slack wire in both St Petersburg and Moscow in 1756–7, and ending with the act of a man named Berger and his French wife in 1757–8. Berger was an acrobat and jumper, capable of somersaulting across twelve men or jumping across ten with raised and bared swords; his wife performed spectacular balancing acts. In 1767 'the famous English equilibrist' Michael Maddox was performing in St Petersburg, marking the beginning of a long and extraordinary career in Russia; he was followed in 1772 by a Mr Sanders, who proclaimed that he had performed his act, which included the use of birds and mechanical contraptions in addition to high-wire balancing, before many crowned heads of Europe before deigning to come to Russia. But Russia obviously had its attractions for Sanders, who was active in Moscow and St Petersburg and other provincial towns before last being seen in Moscow in 1790, offering English lessons (like Mr Fisher before him).[102]

It is generally little known, certainly in England, to what extent the careers of the most renowned of the early English riding-masters turned showmen were connected with Catherine's Russia, but almost all the men mentioned in the history of the early English circus (with the conspicuous exception of Philip Astley) visited Russia on short or, in some cases, prolonged tours between 1764 and the early 1790s.[103] The first to come to Russia was Jacob Bates in 1764, who is credited with introducing the delights of trick-riding to Russia; his repertoire included balancing tricks on two or three horses at full gallop. He soon returned to France where he set up its first circus in 1767. In contrast, James Price already enjoyed a great reputation for his performances in London from the mid-1760s before bringing his troupe to Russia in 1779. The programme that Price offered in St Petersburg, Moscow and other towns between 1779 and 1792 was very varied: he danced on the top of a ladder, shot bullets through previously selected cards from a pack thrown in the air by his wife; his obviously light-footed wife, known as La Spaniola, danced on hen's eggs; the troupe formed a fifteen-man pyramid, erected for some unknown reason 'in honour of Julius Caesar'; and as the *pièce de résistance* a compressed air balloon was released. Between the visits of Bates and eventual departure of Price the Russian public saw performances in 1776 by the former dragoon Sampson and his wife, who had been billed in England as 'the first Equestrienne', in 1775 by Wilton and his wife, also in 1776 by Fletcher, and in 1780 by Miss Lamayne Mason. In 1792 there arrived Charles Hughes (d. 1797) who was responsible for arranging the horse-races mentioned earlier. Hughes was a bitter rival of Philip Astley, for whom he had formerly ridden, and his Royal Circus, set up in 1783 in partnership with Charles Dibdin, vied in popularity with Astley's Amphitheatre.[104] Hughes's visit to Russia was, however, his swan-song, and despite proclaiming on his return that he had been favoured by the attentions of Catherine and her court and had indeed set up an imperial circus, he lost his former popularity. For his performances in St Petersburg, which were held in the theatre of a house on Old Isaac Street, he relied much on the acrobatic skills of his young boy riders, who, according to the newspaper advertisement, performed numerous if not by that time particularly original tricks.[105]

VII

As a coda to the portrayal of the life of the British community in St Petersburg a few pages might be devoted to the British presence in the old capital Moscow during the later decades of the century. I use the word 'presence' because it is really only meaningful to speak of a British community there in the first two decades of the eighteenth century before St Petersburg became first the home of the diplomatic corps and then, more significantly, the centre of foreign commercial activity. Only at the beginning of the nineteenth century is there any sense of a revival of a community with the appointment of an English chaplain to the United English and Reform Church. This is not to say that Moscow was devoid of prominent British citizens during Catherine's reign in particular and many aspects of Anglomania were not slow to emerge during the same period.

Moscow was to have, for instance, its own English Club, founded in 1782 some twelve years after its St Petersburg counterpart.[106] It seems to have adopted the same rules and offered the same amenities. The *Moskovskii kur'er* (*Moscow Courier*) reported in 1805 that 'the occupation of members is the playing of cards, billiards and the reading of all foreign and Russian journals – for a special payment'.[107] This was undoubtedly 'the great Club' that Charles Hatchett visited in April 1791:

it consists of 300 Members of English, Russian & Germans & it is exactly on the same Plan as the great Club at Petersburg, the annual subscription is R 25. dinner 1/2 Ruble per head paid separate as well as Wines, Porter, Cards – there are besides two Billiard Tables.[108]

Hatchett, however, uses the appellation 'English Club' in connection with another gathering:

Mr Jackson & I dined with a club held at Godaines and established by Mr Rowand & Mr Bourgarel the members consist chiefly of the few English who reside in Moscow except Mr Dickinson and a few foreigners who understand the language in all about 30. they meet every Friday fortnight from October to April.[109]

In the size of its membership and the months when it met, this club recalls the English masonic lodge in St Petersburg, although it was probably simply a British merchants' dining club.

Hatchett had letters of introduction to all the leading British merchants in Moscow. The name of James Rowand, who together with the Swiss merchant Bourgarel is credited with founding this second club, is frequently encountered in travellers' accounts. He was a Scottish merchant banker in partnership with John Thomson in St Petersburg and lived in considerable style in the house by the Iauza River where in 1799 Alexander Pushkin was apparently born.[110] It was, however, Robert Dickinson (b. 1744?), an habitué of the real English Club rather than of Rowand's, who lived with a splendour, Hatchett suggests, that would be the envy of an English nobleman. Dickinson was the head of the great silk and linen mills that were still called by the name of their founder, John Tames, who had been a close friend and associate of Peter the Great. According to the Oxford don John Parkinson, it was Tames, a Dutchman, who had brought Dickinson from Riga to be his associate in Moscow. Parkinson took a particular interest in Dickinson on discovering that he also hailed from Lincolnshire, and described his house as 'situated on an Eminence out of the Town, of which it commands a charming view'.[111] A similar description with the added detail that 'the principal apartments are fitted up with silks made at his own manufactory' is found in the manuscript diary of Sir Richard Worsley, the noted antiquarian, who was invited to dine with Dickinson in September 1786.[112]

Hatchett, Parkinson and other British visitors to Moscow in the 1780s and 1790s were frequently in the company of Michael Maddox, already mentioned as performing on the tight-rope in St Petersburg in 1767. It was in Moscow that he settled and embarked upon the career that ensured him a place in Russian theatrical history.[113]

In 1776, a year or two after moving to Moscow, Maddox (1742–1822) became the partner of Prince P. V. Urusov, who had just received a ten-year lease of the Znamenskii Theatre (the former Vorontsov mansion on the Znamenka) and authority for all theatrical productions in the city. Urusov was a mere figurehead and it was Maddox who became, in the words of an Englishwoman who met him that year, 'manager of the Diversions at Moskow'.[114] These diversions included not only the production of plays for which the innovative stage machinery owed much to Maddox's skills as horologist and contriver of wondrous mechanical effects, but also the introduction of masquerades in a special hall attached to the theatre. At about the same time Maddox began to develop in imitation of London's Vauxhall Gardens and Ranelagh his own Vauxhall on the southern edge of the city. The Rev. William Coxe, visiting it in 1778, records how 'we entered by a covered way into the gardens, which were splendidly illuminated. There was an elegant rotunda for a promenade, either in cold or rainy weather, and several apartments for tea or supper. The entrance money was four shillings.'[115] In 1780 the Znamenskii Theatre burnt down but within a few months a new theatre, the Petrovskii, was built nearby on part of the site occupied today by the Bol'shoi. Maddox was the sole proprietor and was granted control of public theatrical activities in Moscow for a period of twenty years. He possessed 'a structure which for elegance of architecture, as well as for dimensions and solidity, may vie with any in Mosco';[116] it was indeed one of the largest theatres to be found in Europe, with four tiers of boxes and two large galleries. Hatchett noted that 'the Theatre is capable of holding 5000 people by M's account and is tolerably neat. The boxes have Veils of light Silk to draw before the Front that those in them may be seen or not at their pleasure.'[117] In 1797 there was published a large album of plans of the theatre, which provides a permanent record of the Petrovskii, which was itself to be destroyed by fire in 1805 and bring Maddox's career as a theatrical impresario to an end.[118]

It was inevitable that Moscow should follow St Petersburg's predilection for all things English. A traveller at the end of the century noted that:

the number of English horse-dealers, and English grooms, in Moscow, is very great. They are in high favour among the nobles. . . . It was usual to hear the nobles recounting the pedigree of their favourites, as if on an English race-course: 'this', say they, 'was the son of Eclipse; dam by such a one; grand-dam by another'; and so on, through a list of names which their grooms have taught them, but which have no more real reference to their cattle than to the moon. English saddles and bridles also sell at very advanced prices.[119]

The pages of *Moscow News* (*Moskovskie vedomosti*) provide ample evidence to support this assertion. In 1795 alone there were many advertisements from a whole range of British breeders, traders and grooms, offering inter alia 'to anglicise tails' (*anglizirovat' khvosty*).[120] In their number were several who gained mighty reputations in Moscow. Such were John Smith and John Jackson, but it is very appropriate that it was John Banks who, in that paper's very first issue of 1795, was offering his stallion Woodpecker of impeccable pedigree for mating with a very limited number of mares at 600 roubles a session.[121] Banks (1758–1831) spent the last fifty years of his life in Moscow achieving fame not only for his knowledge of horses but also for his marriage to a young Russian ballerina when he was, according to the memoirist Zhikharev, already 'an old man' (in fact, in his mid-forties).[122]

The 1795 issues of *Moscow News* also supply information about Englishwomen seeking positions as companions and housekeepers, an Englishman prepared to teach English 'in the most modern style', and the offer of English goods from best mahogany furniture to the latest hernia trusses.[123] Inevitably, Moscow also had its 'English shop'; indeed, as in St Petersburg, it had several competing for the title. It was, however, the shop owned by Richard Davies (d. 1814) at no. 140 Moroseika that was the best known and longest lasting.[124] Mention might also be made of a Richard Morphew, goldsmith, giving notice of his intention to return to England. This was the jeweller from Deptford in Kent who arrived in St Petersburg in October 1781 and whose amusing first letter back to his family, published as a curiosity in *The Times* some sixty years ago, speaks of his intention to buy as soon as possible a Russian wife for fifteen to twenty rubles.[125] He was returning home alone.

In one area Moscow did provide a precedent: Moscow University had an English-born teacher of English language and literature. In St Petersburg the teaching of English in official institutions such as the Naval Cadet Corps had been in the hands of Russians who had trained in England and the same was initially true of Moscow University.[126] However, from 1784 until his death in 1809 John Bailey taught two courses, one for beginners in the English language, the other for more advanced students in translation in which he used works by Milton, Shakespeare and Pope. Described as a 'tall, red-cheeked, brown-haired, imposing man', Bailey apparently earned the respect of his pupils. There is a letter from him to the British ambassador in September 1801, enclosing a poem he had written on the occasion of Alexander I's accession. He described it as 'lame, as being composed during a severe fit of the gout'; it fortunately has not survived.[127]

2

FACTORY MATTERS AND 'THE HONOURABLE OF THE EARTH'

Of the three ships – the *Bona Speranza*, *Bona Confidentia* and *Edward Bonaventure* – which set out from England in 1553 to seek a northern sea route to the East, only the last succeeded; the first two singularly failed to live up to their names. Edward VI had supplied the captains with a letter to be presented to rulers of the lands they were to encounter; it alluded to the function of merchants 'to carry such good and profitable things, as are found in their countries, to remote regions and kingdomes and againe to bring from the same, such things at they find there commodious for their owne countries'. Although Edward was dead by the time a reply was received, it came from a totally unexpected quarter. Ivan IV, to whom Richard Chancellor, captain of the *Edward Bonaventure*, had delivered the letter, replied promising 'free marte with all free liberties'.[1] For the sober John Milton, writing over a century later, 'the excessive love of Gain and Traffick [which] had animated the design' detracted from what otherwise might have seemed 'an enterprise almost heroick'.[2]

I

The company which was formed to exploit that trade and which received its royal charter in 1555 was the Company of Merchant Adventurers, better known as the Muscovy Company. It operated as a joint-stock company, enjoying a monopoly of trade with Russia and acting as a body; the British merchants in Russia were not independent traders, but servants or employees of the Company, headed by its factors or agents (hence the name Factory). In 1613 the Company became 'regulated', a development which allowed its members to engage in trade in their own name and using their own capital, but still subject to its general rules and restrictions. However, throughout the remaining years of the seventeenth century the 'regulated' company's monopoly of trade was made even more exclusive by admitting only those merchants who had served an apprenticeship within the Russia trade and by raising the admission fees to £50. Thus membership of the company, which stood at 201 merchants in 1555, dwindled to fifty a century later and to no more than fourteen in 1694, when a parliamentary enquiry was ordered after complaints about the company's administration. Finally, on 25 March 1699 an Act of Parliament 'to enlarge the Trade to Russia' became law, enabling any British subject to become a freeman of the company on payment of a fine of £5. A new era in the history of what now became known as the Russia Company had begun; to the two established methods of obtaining the company's freedom – by patrimony and by servitude – was added 'by act of Parliament', which brought a sharp increase in membership through-out the eighteenth century. In the preceding 150 years British trade with Russia had been fitful, interrupted on occasion by political events, and in general had yielded supremacy to the Dutch. The eighteenth century was to see the emergence of Britain as 'most favoured nation' and a rapid develop-ment in trade between the two countries. The authority and influence of the Russia Company grew at home, as did that of the British Factory in Russia, particularly after the transfer of its activities to St Petersburg towards the end of Peter's reign.

In London the 'new' Russia Company's affairs down the century were administered by a governor, four consuls, and a court of twenty-four assist-ants, who were all elected annually on 1 March at the General Court, which was the assembly open to all freemen of the Company.[3] The Court of Assist-ants, presided over by the governor, met at least once a month to transact the business of the Company; it is the minute books of its proceedings, aug-mented by the account books and other miscellaneous documents, that form a rich and indispensable source for tracing the often complex relationships between Company and Government and Company and Factory.[4] The Court had much real business to conduct and, in addition, its elected officers were often involved in one or other of its several permanent and *ad hoc* com-mittees, vastly consuming of time but of time freely given. The Company's paid staff was in fact minimal: a secretary and a sergeant. The Court was particularly intent on safeguarding its privileges and collecting the monies necessary for the proper functioning of the Company. The Company's funds came essentially from the tariff of duties imposed, at different rates, on all goods that freemen of the company imported into Britain, but also from mulcts exacted from all apprehended 'interlopers' or non-freemen attempting to break the Company's monopoly. As trade expanded, the Company was obliged to maintain a network of agents at many English ports and trading centres; in 1787, for example, eighteen places had agents: Bristol, Falmouth, Hull, King's Lynn, Lancaster, Liverpool, Lyme Regis, Newcastle, Plymouth, Poole, Rochester, Southampton, Stockton, Sunderland, Truro, Whitehaven, Whitby and Yarmouth. These agents, whose job it was to collect the dues, were local merchants, free of the Company, who received honoraria. The Company also appointed a 'Collector' for Scotland, where the collection was not always without incident, given a fairly widespread belief among Scottish traders, at least in the early decades of the century, that the Company's authority, agreed before the Act of Union, did not thereby stretch north of the border.[5]

The money collected by the Company was put to a number of purposes. It was used, for example, to maintain the Company's London headquarters, which had originally been at Waldo and Batson's Coffee House but which transferred in 1748 to the Royal Exchange, where the Seamen's Office also became home to the meetings of the Court (previously held in the Ironmongers' Hall, then the Slaters' Hall); it paid for the services of the secretary and sergeant, and was used to support specific charities; and it provided for navigational lights in The Sound, and for an agent at Elsinore at the entrance to the Baltic. Of particular importance for present concerns, however, was its use in maintaining an agent at St Petersburg and, later, at Kronshtadt, and in paying for the chaplains at St Petersburg and Kronshtadt. Extra levies were, however, raised also from imports to provide protection for the increasingly large convoys that left twice a year during the shipping season from London for the Baltic.

The Company was fortunate down the century in the quality of the relatively small number of men to hold the office of governor. They were all experienced and energetic, committed to the Company's cause, skilful in cajoling the Admiralty to provide convoy support, prepared to advise and inform government ministers, and to defend the trade from the bar of the House. And should commercial self-interest alone be seen to motivate their actions, they, and Edward Forster in particular, were indefatigable in their 'good works', in extending the Company's charitable concerns. Samuel Holden, Sir John Thompson, Robert Nettleton, Edmund Boehm and Forster served a total of eighty-five years between them, taking the Company from before the first Commercial Agreement of 1734 to the fourth such agreement of 1813, so embracing the golden age of its power and influence.

Behind the three treaties which lay at the heart of Anglo-Russian commercial relations through the eighteenth century were literally years of complex negotiations, sometimes aborted by wars and by changes of monarchs and policies, but providing a continuum of endeavour and concern. One treaty did not simply lead to renewal nor always to immediate renegotiation. When the momentous first commercial treaty was signed in 1734, the British minister resident could not achieve the king's wish that it should 'be perpetual, as our treaties of commerce generally are with other countries' and settled for fifteen years, 'for this being the first treaty of commerce this court ever made, they were resolved not to bind themselves for ever'.[6] Nevertheless, 'our english merchants here are very much rejoiced that the treaty is signed, which certainly will put their trade on a much better footing than it ever was in this country'; and the British goverment also rejoiced in the astuteness of its diplomacy, particularly when assured by the Russians that 'all the articles were in favour of the english'.[7]

Article XXVIII, which begins 'il est convenu et conclu entre les Hautes Parties contractantes que les sujets de l'une et de l'autre seront toujours considerés et traités comme la nation la plus favorisée dans leurs Etats respectives', highlighted above all others that favour, enshrining at the same time a reciprocity that was no reciprocity at all in terms of each side's capability at the time to utilise its advantages.[8] However, neither an interpretation of the treaty as the Russians hoodwinked or deceived by perfidious Albion nor one, indeed, as the British deluding themselves, given the huge specie deficit in favour of Russia that always characterised the trading, is satisfactory. Douglas Reading, author of the classic account of the 1734 treaty, concludes his book with the reflection that 'the treaty itself was a masterful British commercial triumph. Russia, on the other hand, might read her own peculiar success between the lines in the £25,000,000 sterling which she collected from British merchants and the British Admiralty long before the close of the eighteenth century.'[9] The stakes were in reality even greater and the context wider. N. C. Hunt, in a study which is both an extension and critique of Reading's work, suggests that there was a 'coincidence between what the Russia Company wanted and the national interest in the widest concept. The Commercial Treaty of 1734 was an integral part of British foreign policy at a particularly difficult juncture; it also made its contribution to national security by facilitating the supply of naval stores.'[10] The astuteness of Russian diplomacy, both at that time and later, is, however, emphasised by Herbert Kaplan, for it 'played a key role in the development of Russia's international market, for without it the country could not have concluded satisfactory commercial treaties, issued advantageous tariffs, or arranged to sell its important products on the market profitably. That success reflected Russia's knowledge of its material resources and the demand other countries placed upon them.'[11] There was, in short, a harmony of interests in a relationship which Arcadius Kahan has described 'as primarily a businesslike one in spite of fluctuations in the degree to which their political interests converged. Both partners valued the economic benefits that accrued from their trade relationship, and each tried to use it to achieve their particular ends, to satisfy their own objectives and short-term needs.'[12]

Although Elizabeth, who was well aware of the advantages of Britain as a dependable trading partner, was prepared to extend on a temporary basis the 1734 treaty when it expired in 1759, the political and economic situations of the two countries had changed markedly over the preceding decades. There were to be two changes of ruler and six years of hard bargaining before the second treaty was signed in St Petersburg in July 1766. Russia was not interested in repeating the concessions it had previously made; it was under pressure from its own merchants to adopt a much more stringent and protectionist line, it wished to encourage its own industrial development, and it fully understood how Britain had become even more dependent on what Russia supplied. The resulting treaty was one that brought none of the 'improvements' the Russia Company had requested (more in hope than conviction) and certain privileges were lost. Not least of these was the concession to trade with Persia overland through Russia, which had been hard won in 1734 and removed under Elizabeth through British abuses and mismanagement.[13] There was, however, considerable elation once again among members of the Factory, some twenty-four of whom sent a letter to George Macartney, the British ambassador responsible for the final negotiations, giving 'a public acknowledgement of the entire and unreserved approbation of every article in this Treaty from us who are so immediately and so nearly concerned in its Consequences'.[14]

Its 'Consequences' were enormous. Modern economic historians have weighed and measured, counted and tabulated the imports and exports between Russia and Britain and in so doing have followed the grand tradition of the eighteenth century itself, when the Russia Company in particular sought to justify the trade by a wealth of statistics, culminating in J. Jepson Oddy's colossal *European Commerce* (London, 1805). However, the degree to which Britain's Industrial Revolution was indebted to, and dependent on, continuing imports from Russia of vital raw materials, including, from a much longer list, bar iron, timber, hemp and flax, has been made with notable vigour and superabundance of tables by Kaplan, who also emphasises, as have countless others, that the imports and exports at St Petersburg travelled predominantly in English bottoms and that their outward destinations were not only British but other European ports.[15] Furthermore, the British were ideally placed to supply luxury goods not only of British manufacture but commodities from the colonies and from wherever the British traded, those extras which became the essentials of the elite, as was seen in the preceding chapter.

Guaranteed for twenty years, the 1766 treaty expired at a time when Britain's premier role was threatened by Russia's negotiations for treaties with other countries, notably France. Tension during the Russo-Turkish war, culminating in the Ochakov crisis, made the possibilities of another treaty remote. The apprehension of the Company and the Factory are caught in a memorandum submitted to the Government in April 1791, where it is said that 'there are at this time resident in several parts of the Russian Dominions many of his Majesty's Subjects who having been settled there with their Families under the Protection of a Treaty of Commerce & easy under the Expectation of its renewal now find themselves in a situation of very uncertain security'.[16] Catherine's increasingly hostile reaction to the French Revolution, particularly the Terror, however, brought about a political rapprochement with Britain and cleared the way for the renewal of the commercial treaty, negotiated this time in London, in August 1793, but for a period of only six years.[17] This restored old privileges and added new concessions with regard to the new Black Sea ports and ushered in a further period of British trade dominance that was to last until Paul introduced a series of punitive measures against the British in 1800. Under Alexander, relations underwent another period of decline at the time of Tilsit. Although a fourth and final treaty was signed in 1813, the days of British commercial hegemony in Russia had passed.[18]

It is against this background of commercial treaties and a parent body, functioning in London and close to Government, that the merchants of the Factory in St Petersburg plied their trade, enjoyed privileges that incensed Russian and other foreign merchants, made their fortunes and, not infrequently, lost them in bankruptcy, and increasingly spent much, most, or all of their lives there. Kahan to a certain extent and Jennifer Newman notably, in a recent and highly illuminating study, have shown how the British firms conducted their business within Russia and the 'very delicate Experiment' that was the nature of their financial affairs.[19] Considerable financial resources were needed for the purchase of goods for import or export and for the expenses of transportation and taxes. But they were needed even more to survive the potential hazards that threatened to arise, on the one hand, from the requirement to offer extended credit (for up to a year) to Russian merchants and intermediaries and, indeed, to Russian purchasers of luxury items and, on the other, by disasters, such as harvest failures, wars, falls in exchange rates and international financial crises, such as hit Amsterdam, the heart of European banking, in 1763 and again in 1774. These last two events caused disarray in the ranks of the Factory but also allowed the Russian government to display its magnanimity towards the British traders. On the first occasion, the Russian vice-chancellor gave the assurance that 'not a single House sho^d be distressed; though their Bills of Exchange sho^d go back for non payment'; on the second, 'Her Imperial Majesty, on receiving information of the many failures in Amsterdam and London, has given orders to the court-banker, to assist any of the British Factory at this place with a loan of money, if necessary, on the present emergency' and both George III and the Russia Company were quick to applaud this 'example to all Sovereigns of the protection which is due to the interests of commerce'.[20]

Financial problems on a major scale loom large in the case studies of two of the most prominent and publicity-attracting members of the British business community during Catherine's reign that provide part of the present chapter. They are but pieces in what might be called the mosaic which is

formed from the varied activities and no less varied personalities of the Factory. The actual phenomenon of factory-owning by the British is the subject
of a further section, but this is preceded by an examination of the way
Government and Company sought to safeguard and promote their interests
in Russia through their appointed commercial representatives in St
Petersburg.

II

It is difficult to establish how many of the governors of the Russia Company,
despite their prominence as principals of firms engaged in the Russia trade,
had had actual experience of Russia. One certainly had – Robert Nettleton,
who was governor from 1753 until his death in 1774. Nettleton, who was
involved initially at Riga exporting pitch, later moved to St Petersburg, where
he is known to have become a partner in a sugar refinery. He was also a
member of the British Monastery with the rank of 'archimandrite' in 1720
and was noted as taking part in the great masquerade of 1723. It was, nonetheless, in that very same year that his name was prominent in a list of
merchants petitioning George I for assistance in building an English church
and it had been in his house that divine services had been held since 1720.
Three decades were to pass before the Factory achieved its church and among
the people most prominent in securing the building and raising the funds
were Nettleton, who was then governor of the Russia Company, and Jacob
Wolff, the British minister resident in St Petersburg, who had been Nettleton's companion in the British Monastery, where he had held the office of
'notary'.

Prior to 1750 Wolff had occupied the post of consul-general and although
he was not the first, he was, in terms of effective service, the last to make
the transition from British commercial representative to accredited diplomatic agent in eighteenth-century Russia. The relationship of consulships to
diplomatic posts within the British foreign service was generally recognised
as ill-defined and actual practice frequently gave the lie to theoretical differences.[21] In the case of Russia, where commercial matters were almost always
at the forefront of diplomatic negotiations, the role of the consul was further
complicated by his relationship to the British Factory and its parent body.
It was only in Catherine's reign that the tradition was firmly established of
offering the position of agent of the Russia Company in St Petersburg to
the person receiving the king's patent as consul-general, when promotion to
minister was seemingly no longer an option. The overlap of various functions
was also accentuated in Russia by the fact that the consul-general and the
diplomatic representative were always in the same city – initially Moscow,
then St Petersburg (with a short return to Moscow in the reign of Peter II),

whereas in many countries the consul or consuls were appointed to the major trading ports, while the ambassador or minister resided in the capital or followed the court. Although the Russia Company was later to appoint agents to Kronshtadt, Archangel and Riga, these were not consuls with royal patents, and its main agent was of course in the capital.

In *Lex Mercatoria Rediviva: or the Merchant's Directory*, published in London in 1752, Wyndham Beawes, himself a merchant, but not of the Russia Company, made a rare attempt in English published sources to define the duties and character of the 'Consul'. Ideally, a consul should be fluent in the language of the country in which he resided, conversant with its mores and its commercial practices, able to settle differences between merchants of his own nation; loyal to his own country but enjoy 'the esteem of the governing people where he lives, if possible, as by this means he may often influence and obtain favours for his fellow-subjects in their commercial concerns'.[22] Somewhat earlier, in 1711, the Board of Trade had proposed that consuls (or ministers resident, if there were no consuls) should call together every six months the British merchants trading at their place of residence, 'consult with them upon the present state of British trade to that place, and to propose what they think proper for the improvement or advancement thereof', and transmit such proposals, duly signed by the merchants, to London. In the 1760s, consuls were required to send in regular commercial reports and statistics.[23] The Russia Company had always expected such reports from its agent in Russia, if it did not always receive them. In a letter to its last agent to hold the office in Russia in the eighteenth century, the governor requested accounts of the general state of the trade of Russia, imports into St Petersburg, exports from St Petersburg, both in general and on British ships, and exports from Archangel and other ports.[24] By that time the Company's agent had long since been also the king's consul-general and there was no duplication of effort. It is, however, instructive to identify down the century the men who were responsible for British commercial interests as agents and/or consuls-general (occasionally, also ministers resident) and to describe, where appropriate and possible, their careers. They are to a large degree forgotten figures, but within the context of the life of the British community and of the Factory, they were more significant than the ambassadors and envoys whose names are infinitely better known to posterity.

The first person to be appointed consul-general was Charles Goodfellow (d. 1728), but his appointment was unique, not to say eccentric, in almost every aspect. Behind it lay a crisis in the character of the Russia Company, hastened by the actions of a group of merchants, securing a monopoly on the export of tobacco to Russia.[25] In April 1698, towards the end of his stay in London, Peter granted for a period from two to seven years 'the Whole and Sole Importation with Exclusion of all others of Tobacco into Muscovy' to Peregrine, Marquis of Carmarthen, and 'his assigns'. In so doing, Peter clearly snubbed the Russia Company and disappointed a consortium of Virginia merchants, seeking free trade within Russia, and seemingly rewarded excessively Carmarthen, who had been his boon companion in London. The tsar was delighted with the immediate advance of £12,000 he received to bolster his depleted resources, Carmarthen was equally delighted with the promise of five shillings per hogshead of exported tobacco, and the group of assignees – rich merchants, bankers and projectors, some of whom were prominent Eastland (Baltic) traders – were left to organise their trade and to carry on the war of attrition against the old-style Muscovy Company. A Commons committee had concluded as early as 27 January 1697 that it would be 'advantageous to the Trade of this Kingdom, That all Merchants be admitted into the Russia Company, upon reasonable Terms', but the Company fought a rearguard action until March 1699, when entry 'by act of Parliament' on payment of £5 was made available to all. On 14 April seventy-three persons, of whom forty-eight were connected with the tobacco contract, availed themselves of the new dispensation; a fortnight later, the remaining contractors were admitted.

It is at this juncture that Goodfellow makes his appearance. He had first gone to Moscow in 1695 as agent for the Hudson's Bay Company and apparently never relinquished the post, despite his other future commitments. It seems that he was never the agent of the Russia Company, nor, indeed, even a member during his sojourn in Russia. One of the last measures the old-style Company had taken was to forbid from 1 May 1699 the employment of anyone who was not free of the Company as a factor in Russia. The Tobacco Company had in fact already secured Goodfellow's services in this capacity, but he could not return to England to take the oath; the enlarged membership of the Russia Company, however, resolved on 26 April that 'the tobacco contractors may employ Mr. Goodfellow for their factor this year in Russia, notwithstanding their former order'. Moreover, Goodfellow was later allowed to trade on his own account and he subsequently exported large quantities of flax, hemp and potash. He continued to do this throughout his time in Russia, despite the fact that in September 1699 he was appointed not only consul-general but also minister. He was appointed in direct response to the tobacco contractors' wish for a consul to protect the tobacco trade and British commerce as a whole.[26] At no point were there raised those questions of conflict of interests or of the differing functions and status of consul and minister that became so important later in the century. In fact, Goodfellow seems to have proved a very loyal servant both of his country and of the Tobacco Company, which soon ran into great difficulties, lost its monopoly after two years, but continued to exist and operate in Russia until 1714, the year in which he finally returned to England. He must then at long last have become free of the Russia Company. Over the next decade or so he traded as Goodfellow, Ransom & Parsons, Russia merchants and he rose to positions of influence within the Company itself, firstly as a member of the Court of Assistants from 1719 and then as a consul from 1725 until his death.[27]

Goodfellow died on 25 October 1728 and was buried at Bath Abbey. He was much admired by the first British permanent envoy to Russia, Charles Whitworth (later Baron Whitworth), who arrived early in 1705. When in 1707 Goodfellow requested permission to return to England after a particularly trying year, Whitworth wrote of him that 'he has had very flourishing business, is very easy in his fortune and has stay'd here these two years only in consideration of the Tobacco Company, not to leave their business in disorder'.[28] Although he received permission of the king, the Russia Company (on the condition that Whitworth stayed), and the Tobacco Company to return, it appears that he did not, and he outstayed the ambassador.

Although commercial matters remained prominent throughout Peter's reign and efforts to conclude a commercial treaty were made on more than one occasion, the functions of the consul-general were subsumed in the successive appointments of ministers resident, but resident very briefly up to the rupture in diplomatic relations in 1719. (George Mackenzie, for example, held office only from September 1714 to May 1715; James Haldane never got to Russia at all; and James Jefferyes arrived but was not received in 1719.) In the year of Peter's death, John Deane, who had earlier served in the tsar's navy, arrived unannounced at Kronshtadt as consul-general, but was promptly expelled as a spy. The merchants of the British Factory assured the College of Foreign Affairs that they had not requested his presence in St Petersburg and before his departure from London the Russia Company had warned against his suitability.[29] Not until 1728, following the deaths of Catherine I and George I, did the change in the political climate permit restoration of the office of consul-general as a preliminary step towards full diplomatic links.

The new consul-general was Thomas Ward, a son of the former chief baron of the exchequer, Sir Edward Ward (1638–1714), but whose background and qualifications for the post remain obscure. It would appear that Ward was also the first person to be appointed as the Company's agent. A special committee, informed of his appointment as consul, recommended to the Court of Assistants that 'the Company should grant a Power to the said Mr Ward to be their Agent in Russia to take care of their Trade and to endeavour to have such Greviances [sic] as the Company lyes under redressed'. His document of appointment was agreed and signed on 10 May 1728.[30] He was requested to administer the oath to all freemen of the Company in St Petersburg, to guard against infringements of the Company's rights, and to ensure that only freemen were involved in importing and exporting between Russia and Britain; as to his emoluments, he was granted port charges according to a scale of size of ship.[31]

Ward arrived in St Petersburg in August 1728 only to find that Peter II had removed the court from a place 'where there is nothing to be seen but marshes and water' to Moscow and, furthermore, that his commission as consul-general was not acceptable to the Russians. It was one of those disputes over protocol that had punctuated Anglo-Russian relations since the time of Ivan IV and revolved around the absence of an accompanying letter from the king requesting the tsar to receive and protect his consul. The Russians referred to the precedent of Goodfellow; the British denied it; and more than a year passed before Ward was officially recognised.[32]

In his dispatch of 27 October/7 November 1729, informing London of his recognition, he raised the question of a commercial treaty and aired his view on the apparent paradox of Anglo-Russian trade:

The advantage arising to any nation by commerce consists in selling as much of the produce and manufactures of that nation, and taking in return as few commodities for its own consumption, as it possibly can; the remaining must be paid in money. I own, at first view the trade to this place seems quite the reverse, for I have said before that we buy for double what we sell for; but then, my lord, it must be considered that naval stores are not consumed in England only, but are made use of to carry on our trade to all the different parts of the world and to bring back from hence the balance which we gain upon them, so that all nations with whom we have traffic, are concerned in paying us again for our naval stores.[33]

Ward was to become so involved in commercial matters that, following the accession of Anna Ivanovna a few months later and after subsequent moves to accredit him as minister resident, he was to request that he should remain consul-general and that his secretary Claudius Rondeau, who had carried on in his own name most of the official correspondence with London, should become minister.[34] In the event, Ward died suddenly on 4/15 February 1731 with his credentials as minister unpresented. Rondeau was to acquire both the post destined for Ward and, within a matter of months, Ward's widow, for widows were a commodity much sought after in the British community.[35]

Although George, Lord Forbes was sent out in 1733 as minister plenipotentiary to conclude the negotiations and sign the first commercial treaty on 2/13 December 1734, it was essentially Rondeau who prepared the often difficult ground. Rondeau, son of a French Protestant who had settled in England and with some experience in trade, proved persistent and resourceful in his interpretation of British interests, both governmental and factorial, and in his patient dealings with the Russians. Representing the British government but as yet not agent of the Company, he had few illusions about the conduct of certain members of the Factory. 'I am very sorry to inform your lordship,' he wrote to Harrington in January 1732, 'that, I believe, there never was an english factory so disunited as this; but I shall do all it is possible to be done to persuade them to live in friendship, and as countryman ought to do; but all I can hear since my arrival at this place they do their utmost to ruin one another.'[36] This was precisely at the time when half of the Factory was denouncing the late consul Ward's involvement in commercial activities allegedly contrary to Company rules, while the other half wrote letters, dissociating themselves from the action.[37] Nevertheless, Rondeau proved tireless in cajoling the Factory into a sense of corporate responsibility, calling meetings to discuss their complaints as well as their aspirations for the proposed agreement. Forbes was subsequently appointed 'in compliance with the Czarinna's repeated desire of having a person of quality there',[38] but Rondeau's very real qualities are eloquently exhibited in the three volumes of dispatches that he has left, spanning virtually the whole of Anna's reign. Interestingly, it was only subsequent to the signing of the treaty that the Russia Company, making an award of £150 to Rondeau in recognition of his great services, decided also to appoint him officially as their agent from 17 April 1735 on the same terms and with the same obligations as Ward.[39]

Between the death of Rondeau in October 1739 and the appointment of Jacob Wolff in 1744 the post of consul-general was not filled. The British envoy and plenipotentiary Edward Finch was instructed during his brief stay of some twenty months between June 1740 and February 1742 to 'protect and countenance Our trading subjects to any of the Czarinna's dominions in the full and quiet enjoyment of all the privileges and advantages in trade, which they are, ought to be, or have been in any time possession of',[40] and although these were a routine inclusion in instructions, he was zealous enough in carrying them out. The affairs of the Russia Company were, however, in the able hands of the agent it appointed on 14 February 1740, Onslow Burrish, who also acted as secretary to Finch for a few months after his arrival, helping him, for instance, to encode confidential dispatches.[41] Burrish was the only person acting as the Company's agent in the eighteenth century who did not also have a governmental appointment. Moreover, it was spelt out that he should not himself be involved in trading and should sever ties with any British commercial house in Russia. He has been characterised as 'an efficient agent, who knew how to find his way through the intricate maze of Russian officialdom', but he remains a man without a past and without a face and his activities are barely reflected in the Company's minutes.[42] One can only assume that he died in office sometime in 1744, when the proposal to appoint Wolff was first made.

Jacob Wolff (1698–1759) is today one of the least known representatives of the British government in eighteenth-century Russia, but he was its devoted servant over a period of some fifteen years and a prominent and respected member of the business community in St Petersburg for much longer. The first reference to him in a Russian context is in the list of members of the British Monastery, which indicates, if nothing else, that by 1720, when still only twenty-two, he was on familiar terms with most of the leading British merchants in the new capital. Indeed, he, Nettleton and sixteen other members of the British Factory petitioned the new empress, Catherine I, on 25 February/8 March 1726 for a lowering of tariffs and for protection from various trading abuses by Russian merchants.[43] Apart from this, it is only in the 1730s that his name begins to appear with increasing frequency as a partner in the firm of Shiffner & Wolff. It is this partnership which possibly provides a clue to the otherwise obscure origins of Wolff. His partner was Matthew Shiffner (d. 1756), said to be the son of an archbishop of Riga. Shiffner became a naturalised Englishman in 1711, joined the Russia Company, and settled eventually in London, conducting the English end of the business from his office in Broad Street. His sons Henry (1721–95) and John obtained their freedoms by patrimony in 1743 and 1750 respectively and joined the firm.[44] Wolff, described by a British ambassador as 'a subject of this country [i.e. Russia], and only naturalised an englishman',[45] was probably also from a Baltic German family and took similar advantage of the Naturalisation Act (Act 7 Anne, c. 5 (1708)). Finally, it is not without significance that Shiffner & Wolff, irrespective of their own merits, became the most successful firm (among the British) precisely in the reign of Anna: Matthew Shiffner's wife had been governess to the Duchess of Kurland, the future empress, who was godmother to the Shiffners' daughter Benigna.[46]

In the run-up to the commercial treaty of 1734, Shiffner & Wolff was granted, and not without considerable controversy in at least two cases, a series of contracts for crown products – goods such as hemp, potash, tallow and pitch which were, at different times, a monopoly of the state. In 1730 the firm, working through consul Ward, contracted for some 1,500 barrels of potash and considerable amounts of hemp, glue, codfish and rhubarb.[47] After Ward's death the firm took a further 360 tons of potash on 8 per cent commission and then agreed to ship out 3,600 tons of Siberian iron over a five-year period, given the Russian government's guarantee to prohibit their sale by others outside Russia.[48] Shiffner & Wolff had handled rhubarb since 1730, but in 1735 they became the principal conduit for the export of rhubarb, that most prized commodity and 'wondrous drug', throughout Europe.[49] As importers into Russia, the firm secured a contract with the Admiralty College in 1732 to supply between 80,000 and 100,000 yards of British woollen cloth annually for a period of three years. This was the first step, but an important one, in wresting from the Prussians the valuable woollen contracts. 'I am in great hopes,' wrote Rondeau, 'as m-rs Sheffner [sic] and Wolff are honest men, they will furnish good cloath and by that means put that branch of our manufactory again in good repute, which has suffered very much of late years by some of the british factory delivering bad cloath.'[50]

It was thus with considerable business success and a well-earned reputation for honourable trading that Wolff was to become British consul-general in 1744, a post which had lapsed in name since 1731. Lord Tyrawley, the British ambassador, professing his ignorance of the 'Bracking of Potashes, a technical term' and other mercantile matters, suggested to the secretary of state that someone be appointed who 'is Master of the Trade here, and that Possesseth the Russ & German Languages, both which are necessary for this Business' and recommended Wolff as 'very Current in all these Matters, [and] Capable of being of great Use from his personal Friendships with the people in power in this Country'.[51] The matter was referred to the Company, which in December 1744 approved of the proposal but only after a long discussion and the defeat of a second candidate for the consulship, Hugh Norris. Only subsequently, on 22 February 1745, did the Company appoint Wolff its agent.[52]

Wolff was also in good standing as a banker and there was hardly a British envoy who was not in debt to him or a high Russian official (with Ostermann and, later, Bestuzhev at the top of the list) to whom he had not passed on financial 'presents' from the British government. That he was a man to cultivate was obvious to all. In 1748 the Austrians made him a baron and 'imagined they had entirely gained him to their interests'. However, as Lord Hyndford, who had warmed considerably to Wolff over the two years he had been ambassador, informed London in a dispatch, not only had he disappointed the Austrians in their hopes of gaining a hold on the supply of cloth to the Russians, but he had secured the British contract on a much more solid basis. 'I could not help doing this piece of justice to baron Wolff, whom I shall always esteem for his attachment to the interest of the british nation.'[53] The king was pleased to allow Wolff to accept the Austrian honour, and, two years later, when the Russian chancellor Bestuzhev suggested that the consul's promotion to minister resident would not be unacceptable to the Russian court, the king readily agreed, although stipulating that 'you should not interfere in any business without his express order and that you are not to expect or have any salary or pay in consequence of His Majesty's credential letter'.[54] Apart from stressing Wolff's qualities, including the supremely rare one in a British diplomat in eighteenth-century Russia – the ability to speak Russian – Bestuzhev hinted that the post would give Wolff diplomatic immunity and save him from (unspecified) enemies who were seeking to destroy the consul's credit and, with it, that of the whole British Factory.[55]

Wolff as minister was instructed to concern himself only with things commercial and protect the interests of the Russia Company, which he did as best he could virtually to the end of Elizabeth's reign. The Company repeatedly congratulated him on his efforts to sort out the numerous blatant violations of British merchants' privileges and rights, the commercial treaty notwithstanding. A classic case was the non-delivery of consignments of iron promised by Kurt von Schönberg, Director of Mines, who received some £18,000 in advance. The story began in 1742, before Wolff became consul, and took some six years of unrelenting effort on his part before the matter was resolved.[56] When, in 1751, a letter from an anonymous British merchant denounced Wolff for showing preference to 'Russ Creditors in prejudice of the English', the Company recorded that it had been treated 'as such Clandestine Aspersions deserve, with Disregard & Contempt'.[57] That Wolff was envied and mistrusted by some members of the Factory was to be expected. One possible reason was hardly reputable. If, and there seems only the assertion of an envoy as evidence, Wolff was originally 'made King's consul chiefly to support the persian trade' (the long desired concession achieved in the 1734 treaty), it is somewhat surprising that he is nowhere mentioned in the *Historical Account of the British Trade over the Caspian Sea*, published in 1753 by Jonas Hanway, who had been a member of the British Factory for the last seven years of Wolff's consulship. It was in that work that Hanway had described merchants as 'the Honourable of the Earth', but had also included a chapter, referring specifically in its title to 'The complaints of the merchants of Great Britain, particularly the Russia traders, with respect to foreigners, obtaining acts of naturalisation, without any intention of continuing in this kingdom', which possibly explains, while in no way excusing, his silence about Wolff.[58]

Wolff died on 5/16 October 1759. His successor to the post of consul-general was Thomas Wroughton, a 'natural-born subject' who nonetheless received a lukewarm reception from his fellow merchants. Wroughton had received his freedom of the Russia Company on 29 June 1753 by servitude, having been apprenticed to Robert Dingley, a member of the Court of Assistants, since March 1745, and had gone out to St Petersburg about 1755.[59] His appointment as consul-general was not made in consultation with the Russia Company and when he wrote early in 1761, seemingly expressing his willingness to act for them, the Court of Assistants resolved 'after great Debate' not to appoint an agent.[60] Wroughton, however, seemed destined to follow Wolff in his promotion to minister resident: recalled to London at the end of 1761, he did in fact receive his credentials, but on his return to St Petersburg in March 1762, he was not received at court.[61] He left St Petersburg for the last time in May to pursue a successful diplomatic career that was to bring him a knighthood in 1780, and he left believing, not without reason, that his position as minister had been undermined by Robert Keith, the British envoy extraordinary in St Petersburg.

Soon after Wroughton was appointed consul-general, Walter Shairp, a

Scottish merchant in whose house he had lodged during his first years in the Russian capital and who was himself many years later to hold the same office, wrote revealingly in a private letter that:

He's a Gay and Lively young Fellow fitter for a Court Life than Business & it is by that Means he got himself appointed Consull by People in Power here but much against the Consent of the Russia Company & every Body in that Trade, so he'll be opposed by them as one [who] don't deserve any such Office, far less so to a Man in the Trade, so he'll encounter many Difficulties & I am certain never make the fortune by it that Bⁿ Wolff left which was about £120,000 & He got made Consul when many wished [?] more to protect his Capital than to increase it; I join in the opposition to Wroughton tho' we are personally Good Friends as I think it my Interest & [?]. And I know he is no Favourite of Our Friend Mr Keith's.[62]

A companion or framing piece is provided by the pages that Sir Nathaniel Wraxall was to devote to his meeting with Wroughton in Warsaw in the summer of 1778 in his controversial *Historical Memoirs of My Own Time* (1815):

He had been very handsome in his youth; and though grown somewhat corpulent, still preserved many of the graces, and much of the activity of that period of his life. His education, if it had not given him a very cultivated mind, had completely fitted him for the world; and a residence of more than twenty years at the two Courts of Poland and Russia, in a public character, rendered his conversation, upon all points connected with the History of the North of Europe, no less entertaining than informing.[63]

Indeed, Wroughton told Wraxall some anecdotes about Elizabeth and Catherine that could not 'without violating decorum, be commemorated in the present Age', but, nevertheless, 'always spoke with admiration and respect, though with freedom' about Catherine. It was Catherine who was instrumental in obtaining for him the post of consul and it was her obvious predilection towards him that brought the wrath of Peter III, who refused to receive him as resident minister. The essential truth of what Wraxall reported is clear from the correspondence between Wroughton, Keith and members of the British government in 1761–2. For a consul-general, Wroughton was too patently involved in things political, but the new government of Lord Bute was initially influenced by what he wrote to believe that Catherine was 'the Ruling Genius', not her husband, the new tsar. Keith stoutly resisted Wroughton's interpretation of events and policies, but the coup that deposed Peter III was also effectively to depose Keith as ambassador but was too late to save Wroughton, who had left St Petersburg in May for Dresden.[64]

Shairp, who was then in London, received details of the 'revolution' of June 1762 in a letter from his partner Samuel Swallow (1724–76) and suggested that the change would be for the better and bring no disadvantages to trade. Two years later, Shairp was mentioning that Swallow had been elected agent of the Russia Company in St Petersburg and that the appointment would not be without benefit to his firm.[65] There seems to have been no pressure on Swallow to give up his partnership then or even earlier, for on 23 March 1762 the royal patent for Swallow as consul-general had been dispatched from London.[66] Shairp made no mention of this appointment, although he did describe Swallow (and Keith) as enjoying Peter III's favour. Swallow in fact had managed skilfully to walk the tightrope between Peter and Catherine from the time they were grand duke and duchess, working in 1755–7 as a go-between for the British ambassador, Sir Charles Hanbury-Williams, in his correspondence with Catherine, privy to her affair with Hanbury-William's protégé Stanislav Poniatowski, but still trusted by Peter, for whom he acted in financial matters. It was to Peter that Hanbury-Williams wrote on 13/24 August 1756 as follows:

As I know your Imperial Highness honours Svalov [sic] with your patronage, I can assure your Imperial Highness that he is a young man of good sense, and devoted to your service. This last merit is a great recommendation to me, and I have thought of a means which may some day make his fortune. Baron Wolff is the King's consul at this court. He is old, and if he were to die, I shall have enough influence at my court to arrange that Swallow should succeed him, especially if the King knew that this would be agreable to your Imperial Highness. The appointment would be worth from three to four thousand roubles a year to him.[67]

Within days Peter duly obliged with a letter to King George II.[68] Consul-general for only a few months under Peter III, Swallow retained his post for the first fourteen years of Catherine's reign, dying on 5/16 January 1776 at the age of fifty-two. Less than two years earlier, the very same Nathaniel Wraxall who had reported at length on his conversations with Wroughton, visited St Petersburg on an earlier tour and 'received the greatest marks of hospitality and politeness' from Swallow. Endeavouring 'faithfully to preserve the substance of the information; which, as memory is treacherous, I instantly committed to paper, on quitting Mr. Swallow', Wraxall gave in six pages of quoted speech the consul's views on Catherine's character and rule. Although Swallow exonerated the empress of all blame for Peter's death and generally considered her 'a great princess', Wraxall deemed it politic to omit all mention of the conversation from the first three editions of his travels published in 1775–6; it was unobtrusively inserted only in the fourth edition of 1807.[69]

Swallow, free of the Company on 28 November 1752 (a few months before Wroughton), came to his consulship in a way similar to Wroughton's. The Russia Company for its part reacted to Swallow as it had to his predecessor: as governor, Nettleton, having received a letter from Lord Bute informing him of Swallow's appointment and then a letter from Swallow recognising Peter III's help, but asking for the Company's 'Worthy Commands and Advice', simply acknowledged their receipt. Only in March 1764, after the receipt of another letter from Swallow and a petition signed by seventeen of the trading houses of the Factory in his favour did the Company elect him its agent – at a most crucial time in the negotiations for a renewal of the lapsed trade agreement.[70]

Swallow's experience and good standing among his fellow merchants made him an excellent informant and supporter of, first, the Earl of Buckinghamshire and, second, Macartney during the treaty negotiations. He was one of the first British consuls to respond to the Board of Trade directive of 1765 to submit annual trade figures and was thanked for the 'accuracy of the accounts transmitted'. He was as assiduous as preceding and succeeding agents in tackling the perennial problem of the 'brak' (brakovka) – the quality/quantity control over packaged goods (particularly hemp, flax and hides) which, despite being legislated for in the commercial treaties, was simply ignored and abused – and in 1774 he was especially congratulated by the Company for his representations on the matter. The minutes of the Company reflect his care in sending translations of edicts and compiling reports about the plague in Moscow in 1771, his informing them of an outbreak of cattle disease near the capital in 1774, and generally indicating his attentiveness to anything affecting the conditions and prospects of trade.[71]

Swallow's long years of service to both the British government and the Russia Company brought him no fortune. He had a sixth share only in the firm of Shairp, Maister and Swallow (later Shairp and Swallow) and the reckoning after his death brought his widow and three surviving children virtually nothing. She was obliged to turn to the Company, which in March 1777 awarded her an annual pension of £100 for her 'peculiar distress'.[72]

For Walter Shairp (1721–87), friend of Wroughton and partner of Swallow, the triangle was completed by his own appointment as consul-general in the spring of 1776. It was an auspicious appointment in that the Russia Company, responding to an invitation from the government to provide a name, recommended Shairp at the meeting of its General Court on 1 March and, when this was accepted, proceeded soon afterwards to appoint him its agent and rule that 'it is the Opinion of this Court [of Assistants], that no Person can be properly qualified to be Agent for this Company unless he hath been bred to, and experienced in Mercantile affairs, particularly in the Trade carried on to and from Russia'.[73] The piquancy of the situation was that Shairp had been an 'assistant' since 1768, and having absented himself from the Court on this occasion, returned graciously to accept his appointment.

Shairp's experience of the trade stretched back to 1747, when he received his freedom by Act of Parliament, and something of his early career (and that of Wroughton and Swallow) is known from the letters he wrote to his father between 1744 and 1770. He was soon to form a partnership with a merchant called Thomas Allen (free on 23 December 1746) that survived until 1753, when Allen withdrew and was replaced by William Maister. Maister, born in Hull and son of a member of parliament, who had left him a considerable fortune, had just become free in June 1753 after having served his apprenticeship with Messrs Amyand & Co. in London.[74] Shairp wrote of his feelings of confidence in his business prospects at this period and of his pleasure in his recent marriage to Eleonora Lindeman (born in Russia of Danish parents), although he was less pleased by the size of her dowry.[75] He was now to spend most of his time in London and it was there in November 1758 that he heard of 'one of the most Shocking & Dismall Disasters'. William Maister, fearing that he had brought financial ruin to the firm, shot himself in St Petersburg. Subsequently, Maister's brother Arthur (free on September 1761) joined the firm, taking a one-sixth share like the third partner, Swallow.[76] After what was to be his permanent return to Russia with his large family in 1776, Shairp seems not to have relinquished all his business interests. The firm which traded as Shairp, Swallow and Maister, becoming Shairp and Swallow in 1772, continued after Swallow's death as Shairp & Co., bringing in almost immediately his eldest sons Thomas Charles (b. 1756) and Stephen (b. 1757), both free by patrimony on 28 November 1778, and eventually, his other two sons, Walter (b. 1761) (at the London end), and Alexander (b. 1769).[77] Shairp, while consul, also seems in the 1780s to have leased from Potemkin an iron foundry at Osinovaia roshcha on the Chernaia rechka on the Vyborg side.[78]

Shairp's eleven years as consul and agent included the difficult period of the Armed Neutrality, yet by November 1781 he was expressing his opinion that prospects for trade were very good, indeed 'without Precedent', and the following year he was detailing welcome information about the lifting of restrictions on timber exports.[79] His involvement in preparations for the renewal of the trade treaty was cut short by a deterioration in his health and he was to die soon after the Company had granted him a year's leave of absence.

The office of consul-general, coupled with that of agent of the Company, had undoubtedly become an enviable one during Catherine's reign. Although such a position no longer held the possibility of further career moves into the diplomatic service as minister resident, the position was clearly prestigious and powerful in a city where the British community and, within it, the British Factory had a significant presence. Certainly, following Shairp's death on 28 July/8 August 1787 there was no shortage of candidates for the consulship. Although the Russia Company minutes reflect only the division of opinion over two contenders, there was a third candidate whose aspirations were disappointed. William Statter, a merchant who had been in St Petersburg at least since the late 1760s, had hoped to use his good standing with high Russian officials to secure the post: even before Shairp's demise, he had requested Count P. V. Zavadovskii to intercede on his behalf 'when a vacancy occurs'. Both Zavadovskii and Count A. A. Bezborodko, the state secretary, duly recommended Statter warmly to Count Semen Vorontsov, the Russian ambassador in London, and urged him to use 'every effort to secure the consulship'.[80] In the event, the Russia Company, invited by Lord Carmarthen, the secretary of state for foreign affairs, to recommend once again 'a successor, provided that person was not in trade', sent forward the name of John Cayley ahead of that of Walter Shairp's son, Stephen, but only after two votes on counter-proposals. Cayley, recommended for 'his well known Character, the long Residence in Russia and great experience in Trade', received his royal commission as consul-general on 21 September 1787 and was elected agent on 2 October, receiving an annual allowance of £300, postage and other dues.[81]

The son of Matthew Cayley, merchant of Kingston upon Hull, John Cayley became free of the Company on 26 February 1754 after apprenticeship to Messrs Napier and Hassenfeller.[82] He became a partner in the firm of Ritter, Thornton and Cayley, which became in turn Thornton, Cayley & Co., then Thornton, Cayley and Son – introducing Cayley's son John (b. 1761), when the consulship required Cayley senior to relinquish trading. Cayley, who married Mary Cozens, daughter of one of Peter the Great's famous English shipbuilders, in 1756, soon established himself as a leading figure in the British community. He was a founder member and senior warden of the Lodge of 'Perfect Union' in 1771 and rose to be its master in 1777; he was elected to the English Club in 1774 and to its committee in the following year.[83] A less flattering glimpse of Cayley, when consul, is provided by James Walker in an anecdote recounted by one of Cayley's daughters. The consul was in a line of foreign diplomats and consuls in the Winter Palace waiting to be presented to the Empress. When his turn came, he 'bowed, but unfortunately standing under a glass-cut chandelier, and being somewhat fidgetty, as most of my countrymen are upon great occasions, had got somehow or other the toupee of his bag-wig entangled in the wire of the drops; so that, when he bowed, (and that he did very low,) there was at least two feet between his bald pate and the suspended perriwig, and he could not on rising get his head into dock again'.[84]

Cayley's eight years as agent and consul were often fraught in various ways. He took up his post at a time when merchants of the Factory were worried by the commercial treaty signed with the French in 1786 and by the continuing failure of negotiations for the renewal of the British treaty, all of which threatened to undermine the position of the most-favoured nation. A symptom of this malaise was the action of at least six merchants who, faced with new charges following the lapsing of the provisions of the old treaty, 'had entered themselves in the first Class of Petersburgh Burghers in Order by the Payment of an Annual Tax upon their Capitals to enjoy the Privileges of Native Burghers'; other merchants, concerned with the legality, if not the ethics, had asked, via Shairp, for a ruling from the Company. Cayley inherited the problem, which was solved when the offending merchants withdrew.[85] In Britain, following the outbreak of the Russo-Turkish war, the Russia Company was about to be engaged in a vigorous defence of Anglo-Russian relations, and Anglo-Russian trade in particular, before the growing clamour of the 'war party' in the government, but Cayley's letters to the Company convey little anxiety, other than on the more mundane level of collecting church dues from recalcitrant Factory members, and sending out the encouraging import/export figures, and tackling, as ever, the abuses of brack.[86] The improvement of relations led to the renewal of the 1766 agreement, and Catherine, in response to an approach from the Company, presented it with her portrait. One of Cayley's last duties was to make sure that the empress' ministers were made fully aware of the Company's gratitude.[87] Cayley's health was deteriorating and granted a leave of absence like his predecessor, he at least, succeeded in returning to England. 'Universally regretted for his amiable manner and excellent qualifications', he died at his daughter's home in Richmond on 28 July 1795.[88]

To all intents and purposes, Cayley was the last of just three consuls-general and Russia Company agents who covered the long reign of Catherine. In fact, his disappointed rival of 1787, Stephen Shairp (1757–1826) was elected to replace him at the end of 1795 and served during the last few months of Catherine's life. No less than seventeen of the British commercial houses in St Petersburg decided to show their support for Shairp before the Company itself had met to consider the question of Cayley's successor; they believed that there would be many candidates for 'a Situation in itself so respectable & in point of emoluments not unworthy of attention', but none so qualified as Shairp. Interestingly, they took issue with the government's stance that a 'person not in trade or prepared to quit it' be appointed, arguing that someone 'in Trade and personally interested in obtaining for it every possible facility & encouragement appears to us rather an object of desire than a ground of disqualification'. Shairp was subsequently elected consul and agent, but was obliged to quit the trade.[89]

Stephen Shairp was to have an eventful time as consul, spanning critical moments in Anglo-Russian relations under both Paul I and Alexander I, but emerging with great credit and involuntarily and increasingly involved in political matters. He had had some preparation, serving briefly as secretary to the British ambassador Sir James Harris and acting as chargé-d'affaires in the short period between Harris's departure and Alleyne Fitzherbert's arrival in October 1783,[90] but the challenge of coping with the vagaries of Paul was of a different order. In July 1796 Shairp reported that the Russians seemed disinclined to re-open negotiations on a new commercial agreement and by the time the current treaty had lapsed in 1799 there was a worsening situation in Anglo–Russian relations that soon led to stringent measures against the Factory. A number of protectionist measures were apparent earlier in the reign and in April 1799 Shairp informed the Company that the emperor had vetoed the free export of timber which his father when consul had welcomed.[91] By the beginning of 1800 Shairp was back in London and reporting in person before a committee of the Company about the situation in Russia.[92] When, in June 1800, the British ambassador Charles Whitworth and Justinian Casamajor, whom he had hoped to leave as chargé-d'affaires, were ordered to leave the country, Britain was without any official representatives. In August Shairp was instructed by the government to return to St Petersburg, consulting first with Whitworth who was then in Copenhagen, and to encourage all British ships to leave Kronshtadt as soon as possible, and to obtain 'any information on the present temper of that court, on the actual condition and readiness for sea of the Russian Navy' – and everything to be carried out with 'the utmost caution and secrecy'.[93] It is all very reminiscent of the mission of John Deane seventy-five years previously – and the outcome was the same: Shairp's application at Kronshtadt for a passport to proceed to the capital was turned down, but at least he was able to communicate with the vice-consul, his brother Alexander. It was to be Alexander Shairp, who, among many other tasks in 1800–1, organised the collection of some 40,000 rubles from the Factory to distribute to British crews ordered to leave their ships and march off to detention camps in the interior.[94] One blow came after another in 1800. The sequestration of British ships was followed by the confiscation of all goods and possessions belonging to British merchants, including their residences, and by a prohibition both of imports of British goods and the sale of those already in Russia. Finally, on 22 November/4 December 1800, Paul decreed that the debts of Russians to British traders should be liquidated and a special Commission on Commerce be set up to investigate.[95] Back in London, Shairp was publishing a letter in *The Observer* on the plight of the merchants, reporting on the activities of Father Smirnov, the Russian priest acting as Russian chargé-d'affaires in London, and attempting to convey to his brother the government's order to destroy 'all papers or Archives belonging to his Majesty's late Mission at Petersburgh'.[96] There was no need: Paul was himself destroyed.

Shairp returned to Russia with the resumption of relations and was soon involved in securing compensation for merchants and shipowners for the losses incurred by the embargo of 1800. The Russian government went a long way to meet the various claims, but not as far as many British claimants wished. There is a long screed from Shairp, dated 7/19 November 1802, to the agent of the organisation of British shipowners which gives a full account of the difficult negotiations.[97] British confidence never fully recovered despite the fact that trade flourished for the few years up to Tilsit and that at the opening of the new Stock Exchange in 1806 the emperor was symbolically to distinguish trade with Britain by presenting gold medals to members of the Factory. It was in 1806 that Shairp, back in London on leave of absence, was knighted by the king for his services. He was to stay as agent and consul for another six years, resigning in 1812 when he was presented with plate to the value of a hundred guineas, an honour the Company usually reserved for its governor.[98] It was the following year, after the defeat of Napoleon, that the fourth and final commercial agreement was signed in St Petersburg.

III

As the century wore on, more and more members of the British Factory, writ large, also became owners of factories.[99] Foreigners – Dutch rather than British – had been responsible for the few manufacturing enterprises established in seventeenth-century Muscovy, but it was Peter who was inevitably to give new impetus and direction to industry and manufacturing. He was determined to involve the Russian merchant class – and, to some extent, the gentry – in developing industry with the ultimate goal of lessening Russian dependence on European expertise, capital and exploitation. Stating the aim was easier than attaining it, and Peter and his successors recognised the need to grant concessions – loans, labour and land allocations, and tax exemptions – not only to Russian merchants but also to foreigners in order to encourage them to set up manufactories. In return, foreign entrepreneurs were expected to meet, both qualitatively and quantitatively, the Russian demand for the articles and goods they produced, but also and far more importantly, to reveal their 'secrets', to train apprentices, and to prepare the skilled Russian workforce that would eventually, in theory at least, make the foreign presence superfluous. In April 1720 the Russian resident in London was instructed to advertise the privileges and concessions that the tsar had made available to foreigners willing 'to seek ores and set up factories'.[100] Three years later, in December 1723, the College of Manufactures (*Manufaktur-Kollegiia*) was established to control all developments in the Russian manufacturing industry, which previously had been the responsibility, along with mining and heavy industry, of the College of Mines (*Berg-Kollegiia*). Over subsequent decades, until its abolition in 1779 in the wake of Catherine II's relaxing of manufacturing restrictions, the new college licensed enterprises, Russian and foreign, and decided on the concessions to be extended.[101] The British in no way dominated the Russian manufacturing scene but were responsible, particularly in the 1750s, for introducing factories which made significant contributions to Russian industrial development in terms of organisation, technology and product. In so doing they were sometimes perceived as working in the interests of the Russian state rather than of the Russia Company (and hence Britain), when in fact they were consistent as ever in serving their own financial interests.

The first British subject to own a manufactory in eighteenth-century Russia was probably William Lloyd, the Welshman mentioned in the preceding chapter as a prominent member of Peter's Most Drunken Synod in Moscow and, later, of the British Monastery in St Petersburg. On 16/27 August 1709, a week after he had issued the patent promoting Lloyd within the hierarchy of the Synod, Peter signed an order giving him a ten-year lease on the glass manufactory that had been opened four years earlier outside Moscow on the Sparrow Hills. Lloyd was given a monopoly over the sale of glassware and window glass throughout Russia and for export to Persia and Turkey, while undertaking to teach the skills of glass production to twelve Russian apprentices.[102] However, the business did not prosper and in 1713 a great fire destroyed the works and machinery. In 1715 five of the British specialists whom Lloyd employed in his factory – William Mills, Richard Wilcox, Israel Rogers, Thomas Bell and Edward Quin – sought Peter's permission to transfer to the new glassworks at Iamburg, where, evidently, other British workers were already employed.[103] A report submitted to Lord Townshend, the secretary of state, in August of the same year praises the quality of the new factory's products and adds: 'There was heretofore another Glass-Work set up by British artists at Muscow, but as their sudden gains made it's undertakers too remiss, sloath & their own private differences soon put out that fire: Prince Mentizicoff having had the gift of that at Jamburg brought down from Muscow the ablest of these artists, to which the Czar the rather consented, because that this Glass-Work would be more to his purpose, as being only about 2 days Journey from Petersburg.'[104]

Although Samuel Gartside petitioned to set up a rope-yard and develop whaling and fishing at Archangel in 1720,[105] it was in the new capital that enterprises in which British merchants were involved were certainly established during this time. Paul Westhof (d. 1726), son of a Dutch merchant, and a partner, apparently also of Dutch descent, were responsible for setting up the first sugar refinery on the Vyborg Side on the banks of the Big Nevka. Production began in 1720, but the following year the factory was virtually destroyed by a high flood. It was necessary to rebuild and this could be done only with the injection of capital from two British merchants, Henry Hodgkin and Robert Nettleton (fellow members, with Westhof, of the British

Monastery). The Mining College under whose authority the factory remained until 1723 issued an agreement, which incorporated in essence the typical concessions and obligations with regard to the foreign factory owner. Westhoff & Co. could enlist specialists from abroad and also hire 'free' Russian labour. The Russians were to be bound to the factory for seven years, during which Westhof was obligated to teach them all the secrets of preparing sugar. For three years the factory would not pay taxes either on imported sugar cane or on the sale of the end product. The government furthermore forbade the import of sugar products by others until Westhof's factory was fully operational and producing sugar equal in quality to imported sugar and costing the same or even less for the Russian consumer.[106] Westhof also set up a rope-yard adjacent to the sugar refinery, but it is not known whether his British partners were also involved. Another British merchant, Hill Evans, also established a rope-yard in 1722. Five years later, it was said to be producing various types of hemp cordage, up to 6,000 poods a year at a cost of 7,000 rubles, for export and internal use, and employing seven apprentices.[107]

Rope-yards and sugar refineries figure prominently among the manufactories established by the British later in the century. In the 1750s there were ten rope-yards active in St Petersburg alone, two of which had British owners in Robert Cramp and James Gardner. After Gardner's death in 1756, his widow took over the business during the minority of her son Francis (1745?–1813). Francis, regarded as the founder of the English Club and an active freemason, was to be in charge for more than forty years and was eventually succeeded by his son James (b. 1787). The rope-yard was still active in the 1820s.[108] The Gardner yard on the Vyborg Side appears in a 'List of Factories, Manufactories and Works Operative in St Petersburg in September 1794', along with three other British-owned rope-yards – one, belonging to David Gilmore, was located on the Petersburg Side, while those of John Claxton and of Thomas Vernon, continued after his death by his widow Elizabeth, were on Vasilii Island.[109] At Kronshtadt, Alexander Cook, a Scottish merchant, was given permission by the Admiralty College (rather than the College of Manufactures) to establish a rope-yard in 1774. It was argued that since Kronshtadt was a town in its own right the regulation forbidding the erection of new factories within forty miles of the two capitals did not apply.[110] The fact that Admiral Samuel Greig, the hero of the battle of Chesme, was Cook's son-in-law may also have helped.

It was inevitable, given the enthusiasm for British beer among both British and Russian residents, that British brewers would also attempt to establish themselves in the capital. In 1783 the Hammersmith brewer George Blake, future author of *Strictures on a New Mode of Brewing* (1791), sought the advice of the learned Dr Joseph Black about the prospects of setting up a brewery to produce 'Beers of any Quality or Kind in nearly as great Perfection as in London', but was ultimately dissuaded by the Russians' alleged 'envy and jealousy of Foreighners [sic]'.[111] By the early 1790s, however, three (unnamed) British brewers were active in the capital, according to Georgi, and indeed one was advertising in 1790 'for sale at the new English brewery in Nevskaia Sloboda near the small Okhta ferry locally brewed English-type strong beer without added colouring, at 60 copecks a gallon'.[112] The 1794 list of factories gives thirteen breweries, but only one of them is designated as British (belonging to Dorothy Ronald, widow of a merchant). By the end of the century it was also reported that 'we have very good beer made at Petersburg by an English brewer, Smith'.[113]

At least five more British-owned enterprises appear among the 162 listed in 1794 (of which some 20 per cent were owned by foreigners) and include playing-card, braid and starch manufactories, sugar refineries, and the recently formed ironworks of Francis Morgan and the Baird brothers, James and Charles, which is discussed in a later chapter.[114] The starch factory and sugar refineries are also mentioned in Georgi. The starch and indigo works of Gressen and Parland in the heart of the city near the Moika began operations in 1790 and launched an impressive advertising campaign which emphasised that their indigo was superior to the imported variety in the quality of Russian materials and possessed the two-fold advantage of being twice as effective and twice as cheap.[115] The sugar refineries were, however, of much older vintage and take us back to the 1750s.

The Westhof refinery, which later passed into British ownership (Meux and Stephens), was still in existence in May 1752 when Nicholas Cavanaugh (1725–83) obtained a thirty-year lease on two brick houses belonging to members of the Golytsin family. These houses were situated on the Neva embankment between the 11th and 12th Lines of Vasilii Island, and Cavanaugh was subsequently permitted by the College of Manufactures to convert them into a refinery. The original capital was provided by a consortium of Russia Company merchants, including Charles and Robert Dingley, Jonas Hanway and various members of the Gomm family, but it was eventually to be Charles Dingley and William Gomm, jr., in conjunction with Cavanaugh and a further partner, William Warre, who emerged as joint proprietors by an agreement of 1768. Dingley was, however, to die the following year and, as will be shown, Gomm was already beset by financial problems in other areas of his commercial empire; but Cavanaugh, who also acquired the former Westhof refinery on Vyborg Side in February 1767, prospered, producing and storing large amounts of expensive sugar to meet what was to prove a steadily increasing consumer demand.[116] Nicholas Cavanaugh was succeeded by his son John (b. 1764), about whom an Irish compatriot Catherine Wilmot wrote in 1805: 'He is by way of a *Lothario*, but a Merchant to his fingers ends, & besides remarkably accomplish'd in sundry lan-

guages & general information with a capital *head piece*!'[117] Under John the
business continued to flourish. The Vyborg factory burnt down in 1788 but
was replaced by a new well-equipped refinery, which impressed a French
visitor who found it operating under a German director and with a workforce
of twenty Russians. The same traveller also mentions a further sugar refinery
owned by the Cazalet family at Ekaterinoff.[118]

In the last year of Charles Dingley's life, when he sought to contest for a
parliamentary seat none other than that of John Wilkes, *The Political Register* attempted to portray his business ventures in Russia as deeply unpatriotic.
It produced a set of four queries which read as follows:

i. Who was the first person that introduced the art of printing linnens at Russia, to the
manifest prejudice of the artificers in that branch in this country? ii. Who introduced the
art of refining sugar in Russia, and erected a sugar-house there, to the detriment of exportation of refined sugars from hence? iii. Who was privy to, and active in measures productive of the emigration of the manufacturers of this country to that empire, to the great
prejudice of the manufactories of this kingdom? iv. Lastly, can you tell who counterfeited
the Russian stamp, with a view of defrauding the empire of its dues, to the private emolu-
ment of an individual?[119]

The last accusation seems to refer to the avoidance of the so-called 'stamp
tax', which accrued to the government from the sale of paper stamped with
the government seal and required for all contracts and petitions, but no evidence has been found of Dingley's involvement in any fraudulent activity.
However, the first three queries are interrelated and all seem to refer to the
early 1750s when not only was the Cavanaugh refinery established but also
two other prominent British-owned manufactories, in which Dingley and
William Gomm were involved.

The setting up of a 'manufacture of paper-hangings' in Moscow beyond
the Tverskie Gates in 1751 provoked an anguished reaction from British
manufacturers who appealed to the lords commissioners for trade, who in
turn made representations to the king. The matter was referred to the British
envoy extraordinary in Russia, Guy Dickens, who produced a detailed report
in January 1753. His conclusion was one that the British manufacturers,
anxious to continue their profitable export trade, could well have expected
but would not have welcomed, namely that 'there is no direct prohibition
to be laid on the paper-hangings imported here from abroad, but only dutys
more or less in proportion, as the manufacture introduced here shall prosper;
which is indeed the same thing, but how to prevent it, is hard to tell, when
our own people will act a part so contrary to the interest of England and if
I am rightly informed to the oath they had taken to the Russia company'.
The offending Britons were principally George Thomson, who is described
as 'formerly book and warehouse keeper to the charitable corporation' and

'the person who introduced this manufacture', and his associate Martin Butler, in whose name the business was registered and who had been a wall-paper manufacturer in England and possessed the technical know-how. There had been an attempt by a Petersburg-based merchant, Thomas Nesbit (d. 1757), to set up a rival manufacture, and although he had received permission from the Office of Manufactures (which was responsible for St Petersburg and district), this was overturned by the Senate, on appeal by Butler. The Butler–Thomson enterprise had been authorised by the senior body, the College of Manufactures, and guaranteed a ten-year monopoly on the usual conditions. Dickens further reported that two British commercial houses in St Petersburg were strongly supportive of the Moscow manufactory – Peters and Thomson (not surprisingly, for John Thomson was George's brother), and Gomm & Co.[120]

Information is not available on the production achieved by the manufactory or its commercial success, although the demand for the product generally grew steadily over the next decades. William Tooke in 1799 noted that 'as these hangings are greatly used in Russia, they are therefore made in large quantities' and cited five manufactories in Moscow.[121] But the Butler–Thomson enterprise had long since ceased to be one of them. Although in 1760 there was a further ten-year extension of their monopoly, when a petition from a Russian to establish a similar manufactory was rejected, by 1770 John Thomson was writing enigmatically that 'it's a poor business now to what it was and growing very profitable when they violently demolish'd us from a mistaken Policy'.[122] He was describing to his correspondent, Dr James Mounsey, the situation of the Butler family and of Martin Butler in particular, who had 'recover'd his judgement but not his health', despite spending a year of intended recuperation in London. Mounsey, who had practised in Moscow, had in fact treated Butler in 1756, when he fell seriously ill after inhaling toxic fumes while carrying out colour-mixing experiments.[123]

Longer lasting than the paper-hanging manufactory was the noted textile enterprise associated with the names of Richard Cozens and William Chamberline. Established in 1753 at Krasnoe Selo, some twenty miles from the capital on the old Narva road, it was given a ten-year monopoly on the production of printed cotton, which began in 1755.[124] Although no evidence of Dingley's direct involvement has been discovered, William Gomm was a partner and there would seem little doubt that the manufactory was the one alluded to in the first of *The Political Register*'s queries. It is also significant that when Cozens and Chamberline sought an interest-free loan of 30,000 rubles from the government in 1756, one of their guarantors was Nicholas Cavanaugh, who in 1753 had married Mary Cozens, one of Richard's sisters, and who was himself to be very involved with the purchase and export of Russian linens.[125]

Almost nothing is known about William Chamberline, who died in 1759 leaving a widow (who married another British merchant) and a daughter Margaret, who in the 1790s was wealthy enough to purchase a house on the English Embankment.[126] In contrast, the origins of Richard Cozens are clear: he was the son (b. 1726) of Peter the Great's famous shipbuilder Richard Cozens (1674–1735) and brother of Alexander Cozens, who returned to England and became a well-known painter.[127] He benefitted from the hereditary nobility bestowed on his father which allowed him to purchase 300 serfs for his factory in 1757. Neither Cozens nor Chamberline, as far as is known, had any previous experience or skill in cotton-printing; they enlisted Swiss specialists to train their workforce and, more significantly, in 1757 they acquired the services of the Dane Christian Lieman. During the years of its monopoly, the factory flourished, raising its production from 120,000 arshins of cloth in 1756 to 1,360,000 arshins in 1762. When the Cozens monopoly ended in 1763, Lieman left to set up his own and increasingly successful rival manufactory at Schüsselburg. The Cozens mill was, however, to continue for another fifteen years. It was in 1767 that Count J. J. Sievers visited Krasnoe Selo and was greeted not by Cozens, who was ill, but by Gomm, 'aussi interessé dans la fabrique', who conducted him on a tour of inspection that left Sievers 'surpris et enchanté; surtout de l'employ donné aux enfans de 8. à 12 ans; capables de gagner 12. 15 à 18 R° par an; jusques là des bouches inutiles a chargé à la famille'.[128] Sievers was also 'surpris de la finesse des Toiles que l'on fait déjà de Coton et de Lin' and even more surprised when he heard Gomm elaborate plans for the factory to produce vast quantities of linen for the Spanish market. These came to nothing, not least as a result of Gomm's impending financial disaster. Cozens' own affairs, it seems, worsened rapidly in the 1770s; eventually in 1779, he leased his factory to a Moscow merchant and was soon afterwards declared bankrupt. His name appears in a list of British residents in 1782–3, together with five children, the youngest of whom, Henrietta, was to marry the Rev. Thomas Percival of the English Church in St Petersburg in 1795. Henrietta was born in March 1767 at Krasnoe Selo, where her mother was to die a few months later. Cozens' grief was such (this was the time of Sievers' visit, incidentally) that it became a matter of local legend and was purveyed to posterity with the stylistic embroidery of a sentimental traveller, who chanced to stay in Cozens' house near the former factory nearly thirty years after the event:

This Englishman passionately loved his wife. He lost her and buried her in the garden. Every day he visited the stone shrine he had built there specifically to preserve her coffin. His dog, which also loved his wife, was there all the time, and when it also died, it was buried alongside. I could discover no signs of the shrine and it is not known what became of that rare and faithful husband. This example of tender and passionate love is preserved in the accounts of local people. I am living but a few paces away from the remains of that beloved wife; my eyes do not find a monument, but my heart tells me that they are near.[129]

'The rare and faithful husband' was still alive in the 1790s and by that time was the owner of sawmills in Kronshtadt, although he was still heavily in debt for them to the firm of Thornton & Cayley, jr.[130]

It was during the first decade of Catherine's reign, when the Cozens mill was still flourishing, that the Gardner porcelain factory was founded in 1766 in the village of Verbilki on the Dubna River some fifteen miles from Dmitrov in Moscow Province. This was the most famous and longest surviving of all the manufactories and works with which the British as private enterpreneurs were connected in the eighteenth century, with the possible exception of the much later Baird works in St Petersburg. Certainly, its products remain as a very visible reminder of its existence and its excellence to this very day.

The Gardner porcelain factory is the one concern that Tooke, in his comprehensive survey of manufactories, firmly connects with a named British entrepreneur, while commenting with some condescension that 'the produce of Mr. Gardner's manufactory comes at present tolerably well into commerce, and he has even made a complete service for the court: his porcelain is cheap, has a pretty white glazing, but is not particularly substantial, and the painting will admit of improvement'.[131] But even Tooke, generally well informed, calls the proprietor 'our countryman Mr. Henry Gardner'. The origins of Gardner are obscure and have given rise to much confusion, but the founder of the porcelain factory was a Francis and his father, a James. However, as we have seen, there was in St Petersburg at the same period Francis Gardner of English Club Fame, whose father was also a James (d. 1756), a treasurer of the British Factory since the early 1730s and owner of the rope-yard, who, to complicate matters even further, also had a brother named Francis (d. 1755).[132]

The Moscow Gardner arrived in Russia in 1746, described in an official document as a 'timber merchant' (lesopromyshlennik), but soon opening a banking office on Nemetskaia Street.[133] Otherwise almost nothing is known about his activities until c. 1760, when, according to a family memoir, he conceived of the idea of establishing a porcelain factory and set off on protracted and extensive travels that took him to Siberia, the Ukraine and the White Sea, prospecting for the clay, quartz and other materials necessary for his hard-paste porcelain. On 1/12 December 1765 he submitted his proposals to the College of Manufactures and on 24 February/7 March of the following year he received permission but with two important reservations: his factory would have to be established outside Moscow and he was refused serf labour, in keeping with Catherine's new legislation. Resorting to a far from unknown strategem to circumvent the law, Gardner bought serfs in the name of a Russian intermediary of gentry status and then acquired in his own name the village of Verbilki, in which some of them lived. He acquired a serf workforce of over 100, augmented by a number of hired hands, and he brought in skilled craftsmen and artists from Saxony to train them. Gardner's venture succeeded brilliantly, despite difficult years. A Russian visitor could write as early as 1770 of the fame of the factory, whose 'products were on sale throughout Russia'.[134] By the 1770s the factory was producing not only tableware for both general and elite markets, but also the figurines or 'dolls', as they were then termed, for which it became and has remained famous, initially imitating Meissen designs but increasingly adding types of purely Russian inspiration.[135] However, 1777 was to prove the real turning point in the factory's fortunes. In that year production reached a new high of 17,670 rubles after a succession of years at 6,000 rubles and below. Disaster threatened, however, when Gardner's deceit over the purchase of serfs was discovered, although ultimately no action was taken. Instead, Gardner received a commission from the empress that was to guarantee the factory's future success. Three years after the great 'Green Frog' service she had ordered from Wedgwood arrived from England for her palace of La Grenouillère on the Tsarskoe Selo road, she commissioned Gardner to prepare three services which were to be decorated with the insignia of the imperial orders of St George, St Alexander Nevskii and St Andrew and to be used at the annual dinners in the Winter Palace at which knights of the orders met on their respective saint's day. The services were for sixty, thirty and thirty place settings respectively and were completed by 1780. The empress was so delighted that she commissioned a further service for the 140 knights of the order of St Vladimir, which was completed in 1785. The translucency of the porcelain in this service revealed the growing mastery of the factory. The resourceful Gardner, who was well paid from the imperial purse for his efforts, nevertheless reused the moulds for the services to produce tableware with other designs for wider sale and set up retail shops in Moscow and in Tver. Gardner lived on to the end of Catherine's reign (the date of his death has not been established) and was eventually succeeded by his son Francis, who died in 1799. The business, however, remained in family hands until 1892. Many Gardner pieces are to be found in museums and private collections in Britain, but particularly noteworthy are the forty-one pieces from the services of the imperial orders which were acquired by Mr Gwenoch Talbot in the 1920s and formed part of his great collection, which is now in the Ashmolean.[136]

IV

The name of William Gomm, jr. has loomed large in the preceding section on account of his involvement in so many enterprises in the 1750s. He is, nevertheless, a man who merits further close attention. As was evident from his conversation with Count Sievers in 1767, Gomm was a dreamer, a schemer, or, in eighteenth-century terms, a 'projector'. The Russian ambassador in London, Semen Vorontsov, understood the type very well, writing some years after Gomm's death about someone else's plans: 'Je ne crois pas que le projecteur est allé exprès en Russie pour l'abîmer, mais je crois que c'est un homme d'une imagination ardente, remplie de théories hardies, neuves et gigantesques, comme l'a été le défunt Gomm et comme l'a été Law.'[137] Gomm, as an outstanding example of the foreign entrepreneur in eighteenth-century Russia, has attracted special attention in recent times, but the full range of his activities has scarcely been recognised.[138]

Gomm (b. 1728), the son of William Gomm, a landed gentleman of Lewkner in Oxfordshire, was indentured for two and a half years from 31 July 1746 to Andrew Thomson of London and George Thomson of St Petersburg and received his freedom of the Company on 1 March 1749.[139] He was soon to go to Russia, where his connections with the Thomsons and his partnership with Dingley put him, in the 1750s, at the heart of several of the manufacturing concerns already described. Gomm during this period also paid 16,000 rubles for the export monopoly on Ukrainian tobacco, but soon found it would not sell abroad with any degree of profit and he was forced to surrender the concession.[140] It was, however, the description of Gomm as 'the great Russian timber merchant' by none other than the musicologist Dr Charles Burney that highlights the particular sphere of business which made and eventually destroyed his reputation.[141]

It was in 1752 that Count Petr Ivanovich Shuvalov, who managed to promote important economic reforms as a senator and to profit by them as a private individual, received a monopoly on vast and rich timber lands in the north of Russia around Archangel (to add to his considerable concessions by the Caspian and in Siberia) and the right to export annually up to 652,000 pieces of timber, including 1,000 masts, as well as a large amount of birchwood. Two years later, finding himself unable to exploit the concession, he turned to Gomm and signed a contract, allowing Dingley, Gomm and Co. to fell, retrieve and export the timber over a period of twenty years, but under his overall supervision.[142] In 1760, however, Shuvalov not only conceded (for an agreed sum) the whole undertaking to Gomm, who received a new contract, confirmed by the Senate, for a thirty-year monopoly, but he also arranged for him to receive a state loan to the tune of 300,000 rubles (on the surety of Cozens, Cavenaugh and Poggenpohl, a merchant originally from Westphalia to whom Gomm was related by his recent marriage).[143] Despite conflicting accounts, it seems clear that Shuvalov was glad to get out of the business, for Gomm had already significantly overreached himself. The conditions for timber extraction on the Kola peninsula had proved insuperably difficult and less than 50,000 trees of all sizes were collected in 1755. Gomm, working through his associate William Ramsbottom, transferred his operations to adjacent areas bordering the rivers Onega and Mezen'.[144]

Mezen' was ultimately as great a failure as Kola, for, despite developing a wharf with warehouses, smithies and sawmills and gathering a considerable quantity of timber, it proved impossible to bring the rafts of timber down the river to the White Sea and the stocks were left to rot. Onega was, however, to be a much greater success. Within a decade, wharves, large sawmills and much else had been constructed. Timber was being shipped abroad in great quantities both on British and Dutch ships and on Russian ships constructed at the Onega and Archangel yards, although the total amount up to 1764 of 308,941 pieces of timber fell vastly short of the quantities originally planned for export.[145] Jacob Sievers' travels as governor of Novgorod province took him to Onega and Archangel in 1766 and he enthused at what he saw, while the British ambassador, Sir George Macartney wrote in his *Account of Russia in the Year MDCCLXVII* that 'the creation of a new port at Onega, in the White Sea, utterly unknown a few years ago, but now annually frequented by near 30,000 tons of shipping, is entirely owing to the genius and industry of Mr. Gomm, an English merchant at St Petersburgh.' Macartney's high assessment was shared by the British chaplain in St Petersburg, the Rev. John Glen King, who confidently advised a friend, Mrs Elizabeth Allen, who was to become the second Mrs Burney, to invest £5,000 in Gomm's enterprises. Sadly, by the time Macartney's book appeared in 1768, Gomm's prospects, to say nothing of his fortune or, indeed, of Mrs Allen's investment, had plunged.[146]

Although the end was much protracted, its beginning coincided with the accession of Catherine. In 1762, Shuvalov died, leaving enormous debts. In the investigation into his affairs that followed early in the new reign, attention was inevitably turned to the timber concessions and the various payments and loans involved, particularly from the State Copper Bank. In addition to Catherine's antipathy to monopolies and mercantilist thought in general, there were anxieties, voiced by the Admiralty College in 1760, that timber supplies for the Russian fleet might be affected, and pressures from other groups and individuals wanting to be involved in the timber trade. By her *ukaz* of 8/19 May 1763, the empress set up a commission headed by General P. I. Panin to investigate the whole question of the timber concessions and the ways in which the treasury could recover outstanding loans. Its detailed report, benefitting from an on-the-spot inspection by General Weimarn, revealed the complexities and shortcomings of Gomm's operations and estimated his debts at 737,000 rubles, comprising the 300,000 borrowed from the Copper Bank, 200,000 still owed to Shuvalov's heirs for the purchase of the concession (but now to revert to the state) and 237,000 rubles of accumulated interest. The commission came up with the eminently pragmatic recommendation that, if the state were to recover any of its money and Gomm's firm to be saved from bankruptcy, Gomm should not only be allowed to continue in accordance with the 1760 contract, but be required also to build more ships in Archangel (three a year) and in Onega (as many as possible) and to increase the export effort, while operating under official supervision and meeting a strict timetable of repayments. Gomm emerged apparently stronger from the investigation and his appointment as a Court Banker in the summer of 1765 only consolidated his standing, while exciting the resentment of the French in particular at further signs of British commercial dominance.[147] It is nonetheless indicative of continuing Russian anxieties about the soundness of Gomm's business concerns that the Russian ambassador in London was asked at the end of 1766 to make enquiries about Gomm's relatives and associates. In a letter of 1/12 December, he reported on one of Gomm's brothers, almost certainly John (d. 1772), that 'he had acquired his capital through marriage rather than through trade' and that 'his credit on the exchange was steady but modest'. An indication, however, of the success of the Onega timber exports was the information that so much mast timber had been received in 1765 that the market price in England had fallen.[148]

The storm clouds were, in fact, soon to regather. By March 1767 Gomm had presented himself to the empress as 'me voilà arrivé à cet Epoque de malheur que j'ai toujours craint et que j'ai predit' and rumours were soon spreading that his firm faced bankruptcy following the refusal of banking houses in Amsterdam to honour his bills of exchange.[149] This news reached Catherine in May during her voyage down the Volga and she ordered a full investigation into Gomm's affairs over the preceding two years, but this time not simply the timber concessions but 'all his other enterprises, such as his various manufactories, mills and his trade in iron, for one might conclude that all these are sustained out of state money'. The information she received was hardly reassuring and she remarked that 'the cotton-printing factory is worth at most 100,000 and he [Gomm] is not alone; as for his other factories they are not worth mentioning and all are worse than it'. So much for the Cozens manufactory and the Cavanaugh refineries. Catherine ultimately decided that it was necessary 'either to lose a great deal or to help him further', but the latter had to be done 'secretly'.[150] A loan of 200,000 rubles from the governor of Moscow only temporarily lifted his credit on the Amsterdam exchange, where the ruble consequently fell against the Dutch stuiver.[151]

Gomm in fact was not to recover, although it seems he was allowed to carry on his timber operations for a few more years, receiving a monthly allowance (as did Ramsbottom). He continued to be seen as a person of some importance in the business community, being elected, for instance, master of the British masonic lodge 'Perfect Union' in 1771–2. However, a graphic illustration of the downturn of his business at the Petersburg end can be seen by comparing the export/import figures for 1764 and 1765 with those for 1772 and 1773. In 1764, imports stood at 531,893 rubles (by far the biggest of any British firm), and exports at 107,040 rubles; in 1765, the figures were 373,703 rubles (still easily the largest) and 82,913 respectively. In 1772, in stark contrast, the firm is not even listed; and in 1773, imports worth a mere 67 rubles were recorded and no exports at all.[152] It was in 1774 that the timber concession was totally removed from Gomm and bids from foreign and Russian merchants were sought by the College of Commerce.[153] In August of that year John Jervis, the future Earl St Vincent, visited the Gomm 'villa' on a hill overlooking the manufactory at Krasnoe Selo, enjoyed his day with the family, and characterised Gomm as 'formerly an eminent merchant, afterwards the Court Banker and now [page torn! 'dabbling in'?] Politicks in Retirement'.[154]

Ahead lay several increasingly difficult years (according to a subsequent petition he addressed to Catherine in 1780 and a copy of which he sent to his former patron, Sir George Macartney).[155] He refers to his thirteen years of misfortune and to the seven of those that had passed since a further enquiry had apparently exonerated him but had done nothing to improve his parlous situation. His goods had been seized for his creditors and he had been compelled to live off the generosity of friends and relations until even that source had dried up. He saw himself very much as a hapless victim and still believed that he had been unjustly deprived of his Onega timber monopoly. Given Russia's 'failure to convert its own resources into a major merchant marine and navy and thus transform the country into a significant sea power',[156] the passage in which Gomm alludes to the start he had made on providing 'une flotte de plus de cent gros navires marchands' demands attention. If he had been allowed to continue – and there is here as near an admonition to Catherine as he could legitimately express in a petition for help! – Russian merchant ships manned by Russian crews would be carrying Russian goods 'sur toutes les mers de l'Europe sous le Pavillon Russe'. His plea for imperial clemency for himself and his associate Ramsbottom did not fall this time on deaf ears. By an ukaz of 7/18 August 1782 Gomm was finally freed from his debts to the Russian treasury.[157]

The last years of his life saw a change of direction: admired by Macartney in the 1760s, Gomm was employed in the 1780s by a later ambassador, Sir James Harris, as a member of the embassy. When Harris left Russia in 1783 for The Hague, Gomm followed him and became Secretary of Embassy there in 1788–9 and chargé-d'affaires for a brief period when Harris eventually moved to another post. On hearing in 1788 of his new ambassadorship, Harris wrote that 'while good things are showering down on my head, will more fall on that of my friend Gomm? who wants them much more than I do, and for whom I wish them much more than for myself. I do not mean by this, that I am not fully sensible of their value, but to convey my feelings on the situation of a man who has taken such a fatiguing share in my labours, and who is twenty years nearer the grave than I am.'[158] Gomm was in fact just five years away. He retired to Bath, where he died on 9 April 1792 at the age of sixty-five, having outlived his two brothers, his wife and two of his three sons.[159] The plaque in the abbey commemorates his years as a member of the British Factory in St Petersburg and his service for his king. It says nothing of his life's vicissitudes. In a family memoir drawn up in the 1830s by his grandson, Field Marshal Sir William Gomm, William Gomm was remembered as opening 'an extensive commerce and navigation in a previously obscure and unproductive corner of the Russian empire' and described, with that relaxed sense of chronology so often encountered in family memoirs, as having 'the contracts made by the Czar Peter . . . perfidiously broken by his successor'.[160]

V

The November 1791 issue of *Gentleman's Magazine* recorded on the same page the deaths in distant Russia of Prince Potemkin and Baron Sutherland. Potemkin was accorded a brief biography, although 'his death, at this period, will be of no importance out of Russia', while Sutherland was simply described as 'banker to the Empress of Russia'. Other than the implication that both men would have enjoyed Catherine's favour and trust, there was nothing to suggest any connection between them, not even the fact that they were coevals, born in 1739 and dying within a few hours of each other.[161] Yet in Court circles in St Petersburg their names were very much linked in what became known as 'the Sutherland affair'.

Richard Sutherland was the eldest son of the Scottish shipbuilder Alexander Sutherland, who was recruited into Russian service in 1736 and had a distinguished career at Archangel and St Petersburg, where he died in 1760. Following an earlier shipbuilder's son, Richard Cozens, jr., Richard Sutherland sought a career in business. He was apprenticed to Robert Dingley and became free of the Russia Company by servitude on 14 June 1763.[162] He soon entered into partnership with John Watson (d. 1782) as Watson, Sutherland & Co. He was to be joined over the next few years by his younger brothers, John (1742–73), George (1745–93) and Alexander Hendras (1753–1820). John was a member of the influential British masonic lodge from 1771 until his premature death at the age of thirty-one, while the youngest brother, Alexander Hendras, was to leave for England to control the London end of the business. Richard, the head of the family and the firm, married Sarah (d. 1787) in about 1765 and had a daughter Sarah (b. 1766) and a son Richard (b. 1772), who became a partner not later than 1790.

Sutherland was a pillar of the British community and enjoyed the good life; he was famed for his wealth and for the lavishness of his table. A visitor to his home in the English Line in the autumn of 1787 described how he 'dined the day before yesterday at Mr R. Sutherlands, who is a *very* great man here & lives in a very expensive manner'. Catherine remarked on his death that 'on dit que c'était un grand gourmand', a comment, suitably expanded, that found its way two years later into the diary of an Oxford don in the Russian capital: 'Old Sutherland was very much attached to the Empress who when he died observed to Whitworth [the British ambassador] unfeelingly at Court that Oisters would now be cheaper; alluding to his great fondness for them.'[163]

Sutherland established a reputation for business acumen and financial expertise that led to his appointment as court banker, a position held a few years earlier by the ill-fated William Gomm. On 26 November/7 December 1788 he was created Baron of the Russian Empire, a title the empress had bestowed previously on Dr Thomas Dimsdale, who had inoculated her against smallpox in 1768, and on Robert Rutherford, the British merchant and consul at Livorno, who arranged the provisioning of the Russian fleet during the war against the Turks in the Mediterranean in 1769–74, but which Sutherland was uniquely among the British to bear in Russia.[164] His elevation had come at the end of a year when the rate of exchange for promissory notes on foreign exchanges fell dramatically and his advice and mediation with the College of Commerce were sought and appreciated by a large group of foreign and Russian merchants: 'votre situation vous fournit les moïens de former et de proposer, ou il appartient, un plan convenable pour retablir et rassurer le credit du public, en tachant de rapprocher les cours du change de leur équilibre'.[165] Sutherland as court banker was responsible for administering financial transactions abroad, in particular for attending to the expenses involved in the running of Russian embassies in European capitals. His integrity does not seem to have been questioned until the late spring of 1791, when complaints about his administration of finances began to reach the Empress.

Irregularities were reported from Aix la Chapelle and from London, but it was when the Russian minster in Florence, Count Demetrio Mocenigo, turned to the Empress in connection with the loss of 120,000 rubles in a business transaction through Sutherland's negligence that matters were brought to a head. On 18/29 August Catherine instructed her state secretary, the poet Gavriil Derzhavin, 'to inspect the documents presented by him [Mocenigo] and seek the necessary explanation from Our banker Sutherland, and when the business was completely clarified, to report to Us'.[166] Derzhavin spent much of the summer of 1791 making his investigations, reporting directly to the empress, but 'since the whole ministry was on Sutherland's side, for everyone was in debt to him ... the empress, undecided, sent him [Derzhavin] away on about six occasions, saying he was still new to such affairs'.[167] Derzhavin, incidentally, was himself still in debt to the banker and had received two demands in 1788–9 for repayment of a loan.[168] It was only in the spring of 1792 that the Mocenigo part of what had become the much more serious 'Sutherland affair' was settled, but in the interim there had occurred Sutherland's demise on 4/15 October, which Derzhavin in his memoirs erroneously suggests resulted from Sutherland taking poison when the empress ordered a full investigation.[169] The three-man committee, of which Derzhavin became a member, began its wider enquiries, however, only in April 1792. It was quickly established that sums in the region of 2 million rubles had been misappropriated by Sutherland; he had lent large amounts to many of the magnates close to Catherine and 'in addition had himself used significant sums for his own needs'.[170] Potemkin (to the tune of 800,000 rubles), Prince A. A. Viazemskii, Count I. A. Osterman and Grand Duke Paul were all deeply in debt to Sutherland. Catherine was incensed by Paul's debts but ordered the treasury to bear the cost of most of the large debts while requiring some smaller debtors to repay. The scandal seemed to be about to be laid to rest, but Catherine, anxious to avoid similar incidents in the future, decided to establish another committee early in 1794 to make further enquiries.[171]

The 'Sutherland affair' illustrates the spectacular rise and no less spectacular fall of a particularly prominent member of the British Factory, albeit in the context of Russian court politics and finances; it could not but have repercussions within the British community itself and especially among members of the Sutherland family and their associates. That this more intimate, 'British' side of the story can be told at all, however, is due to the preservation of a number of letters among the family papers of an outsider, who made the acquaintance of the Sutherlands and others in happier times and was later involuntarily involved in their wrangling and misfortunes.[172] Samuel Whitbread II (1764–1815), later famed as a Whig politician, had gone to Russia in 1785–6, soon after graduating from Cambridge, as part of a European tour under the tutorship of the Rev. William Coxe, who had earlier accompanied Lord Herbert, the future Earl of Pembroke. The visit was not, of course, without its mercantile dimension. Whitbread was the heir to the famous brewery firm started by his father Samuel Whitbread I (1720–96), free of the Russia Company in 1784 and importer of large quantities of isinglass. The young Whitbread was to write that 'My stay at Petersburg, however, will be remembered by me with delight, from the pleasure I had in the company of a select half dozen, who I am proud of calling my friends',[173] although in 1800, when he received most of the letters in question, he might well have wished to reconsider. The letters were in the main written by Richard Sutherland, jr., whom Whitbread had met as a fourteen-year-old and for whom he arranged to send out as a tutor a young man named John Browne. Richard, jr. and Browne were to become central figures in what might be termed the aftermath of the Sutherland affair. Things had, however, begun to go wrong even before the scandal broke.

Browne soon neglected his tutoring to pay court to Richard's sister Sarah, whom he married on 12/23 December 1788, despite the baron's strong opposition and refusal to give a dowry. Richard, jr., however, persuaded the baron to 'concede to me the permission of my sharing with him my own peculiar Capital, and his become an associate in my Commercial Establishment; this being agreed to he was accordingly nominated a partner bearing the half share of my capital'.[174] The firm was about to embark on a series of bewildering name changes, to some extent characteristic of many commercial houses in St Petersburg but occasioned in the case of the Sutherlands by acrimony and dispute. The Russia Company's minute book might still describe the firm in early 1792 as 'Alexander Hendras Sutherland, Richard Sutherland, George Sutherland and Peter Bock Merchants and Copartners', but this was incorrect even in 1788, omitting the name of Richard Rigail.[175] Early in 1789 Alexander Hendras Sutherland withdrew in protest at Browne's partnership, 'alleging he would not be a partner with one, he so much detested and a man of such low extraction' and within months the baron himself, 'without rhyme or reason', engineered the exclusion of Bock, substituting a William Whishaw, 'merely as a working tool, he not having any Capital of his own'. The firm now became known as Sutherlands & Co., comprising the baron and his son, George Sutherland, Rigail, Browne and Whishaw. 1791 brought the death of the baron, followed within weeks by that of his daughter Sarah, probably in childbirth. There exists a letter from April 1792, written by Browne, her husband, to Whitbread, in which he speaks of the investigation into the baron's affairs and concedes that 'undoubtedly there is ground for enquiry on the present occasion'. More interestingly in the present context, he anticipates that 'the sensation (which this enquiry must naturally cause) will affect the credit of the house of trade with the profits of which I should be much at ease'.[176] That his apprehension was well-founded is evident from the letters Richard Sutherland was also to address to Whitbread, beginning in June 1800. Sutherland, dreaming, not unnaturally, of 'the fruition of a propitious fate', instead found that:

I being, at that time, a minor, there was not anyone to ward off the blow; everyone endeavouring to lucre himself, no one thought of me besides which, by the ubiquitary rumour of my father's downfall being, solely from the unity of our surnames, misapplied to me, my Commercial Establishment tho' fully unconnected with the Bankership, received a severe shock: notwithstanding which it upheld itself above two years longer, & was again in a flourishing situation, when by the Circumvention of an insidious partner, it received it's last irreparable Blow.[177]

The villain of the piece was Whishaw, who apparently had persuaded Hope & Co, the famous merchant bankers of Amsterdam, that without further reorganisation the St Petersburg house could not continue. This led to the expulsion of George Sutherland, who 'was so aggravated by this severe shock that, in less than three months he resigned his breath', and of Sutherland's cousin Richard Rigail, and to the creation of the new house of Sutherland, Browne and Whishaw from the spring of 1793. By the beginning of 1794, however, Whishaw had convinced Browne and Sutherland that their establishment was no longer viable and that they should declare their bankruptcy. This they did and the prominent British merchants Timothy Raikes, Stephen Shairp and Laurence Brown were appointed assignees to the estate.

Thus began the long winter of young Sutherland's discontent and the ultimate fall of the house of Sutherland. The year 1800 marked the nadir of his fortunes and he turned to Whitbread, with whom he had not been in contact for over a decade, with an initial plea to intercede for him with his uncle, Alexander Hendras Sutherland, who had prospered as a Russia merchant in London.[178] He sent Whitbread no less than five letters in as many months, including one so long he himself called it a 'Pamphlet', detailing his story from the mid-1780s. Browne and Whishaw received 'handsome allowances' from the assignees and were absolved of their debts. Whishaw went on eventually to form a new partnership with John Henley, to prosper and found one of the great merchant family dynasties,[179] while Browne left for England sometime in 1794 after a violent argument with Richard Sutherland, who 'was surprised to find ... that he had out of madness locked all the doors, even the privy; and had thrown the Keys God knows whither – some say, into the River'. Worse was to follow, for the 'Government enforcing it's prerogative, confiscated and seized, not only my father's but even my own peculiar property, my Cloaths, my bed, were taken, my dinner thrown out of the saucepans and the Kitchen fire extinguished'. Debts piled upon debts and one business venture after another turned into farcical misadventure. Inheriting his father's title, Richard was able to acquire estates and serfs legally, which he did, projecting a vast farm in the English style, and showing himself utterly incapable of managing his affairs. He lashed out at all and sundry, pillorying the 'purse proud' 'factorial gentlemen', while wallowing in self-pity – and was rebuked in like measure for his fecklessness and 'a complexion bordering on insanity' by his uncle and by Browne. He disappears from our view with his last letter to Whitbread of 19/31 October 1800, in which he characterised himself as 'like a man in a labarinth, who walks, unguided, up & down, to seek his weariness; & no sooner has he measured, with much toil, one Crooked path, in hopes of getting his freedom; but it betrays him into a new affliction'.[180]

VI

Two years before his death, the British consul-general and agent of the Russia Company, John Cayley of the 'suspended perriwig', drew up his last will and testament, dated 16/27 June 1794 in St Petersburg.[181] It is in most respects an unremarkable document, in which the testator with characteristic thoroughness sought to provide for his wife and family, issuing no threats or exclusions and making no surprising bequests. It is the will of a solicitous paterfamilias, but it is also a good merchant's will, systematic and precise, with its revealing codicil, listing down to the last copeck what each of his sons and daughters had already received as wedding settlement or loan and was to be deducted from the final portion. Cayley made careful provision for his 'dearly & justly beloved wife', ensured that the one or two family heirlooms, be it his gold watch or his father's portrait on a snuffbox and silver platter presented to him by the Corporation of Kingston upon Hull, were routed through his eldest son, and was compassionate in the financial arrangements for a recently bereaved daughter and her young children. If not quite a conversation piece in the late eighteenth-century fashion, more a faded family photograph *avant la lettre*, John Cayley's will, chanced upon in a catalogue of ephemera, appropriately has found its niche in a university archive largely devoted to the fates and fortunes of British families and individuals in Tsarist Russia. It is, of course, only one of a countless number of similar wills drawn up by merchants of the British Factory and preserved to this day in family and public archives, but therein lies its interest as a characteristic document, revealing relationships within the St Petersburg British community. The Cayley will provides a further insight into the networks and lifestyles of this community which, as we have already seen, was essentially held together by family and business ties.

In a long and gossipy letter of March 1764 John Thomson brought Dr James Mounsey, his old friend in retirement in Scotland, up to date about mutual friends and the sizes of their families: 'Mr Caley has got eight Children alive, Mr Regail seven Mr Cavenaugh six and all the Women breed fast.'[182] The successful renegotiation of the Commercial Treaty in 1766 was to herald both an unprecedented increase in the volume of trade and in the number of merchants seeking admission to the Russia Company, including many who were to settle in the Russian capital. But the fast-breeding wives of already established Petersburg merchants made their own significant contribution to the rapid growth in the size of the British community. Infant mortality was high, but the almost yearly production of a new child meant the survival of large families. The register of the English Church provides in its entries of births, marriages and deaths an eloquent, if partial commentary. The children born in the 1760s and 1770s grew to adulthood, married and had children of their own, all within the span of Catherine's reign; and it was this generation which enjoyed the prosperity of successful fathers and partook of the delights of a more sophisticated and cosmopolitan capital.

In his will John Cayley names some twenty beneficiaries in the following order: his surviving sister Elizabeth at Hull and brother Edward at Whitby; his nieces Jane and Harriet Cozens (b. 1759 and 1767); his sister-in-law Mary Cavanaugh (1722?–1806), her son John (b. 1764) and daughter Sally (b. 1759); his brother-in-law Richard Cozens; his niece Mary Raikes (b. 1756); his wife Sarah Cayley (d. 1803); his son John (b. 1761); his daughter Elizabeth Poggenpohl (b. 1757) and her three children; his daughter Sally Moberly (1764–1837); his other sons Cornelius (b. 1762), George (b. 1763), William (1766–1803) and Henry (1768–1850). Of known direct relations, only Arthur Cayley, jr. (son and heir of John's late brother Arthur of Archangel, with whom William Cayley had served his apprenticeship) is omitted. There were two distinct circles of his family within the St Petersburg context – first, John Cayley's in-laws, the relations of his wife, and secondly, the in-laws acquired by the marriages of the Cayley children.

John Cayley had married Sarah Cozens on 19/30 December 1756 and became part of that circle, mentioned in an earlier section, of the Cozenses, Cavanaughs, Poggenpohls and Gomms, united in some cases by marriage and in all cases by business. It was with the younger and infinitely more populous generation that the net spread inevitably wider, but not so wide as to destroy what remained a very close family circle, comprising in the late 1780s and the 1790s essentially the Cayleys, Cavanaughs, Raikes and Moberlys. The Cayleys were very fortunate in losing comparatively so few of their children in infancy: two daughters died within months, but five sons and two other daughters survived and married. The Cavanaughs on the other hand lost three of four sons and one of four daughters, while only one of four Raikes' sons survived, but all three daughters (according to the church register).[183]

Timothy Raikes (1730–1810), a prominent merchant of whom more later, had married Mary Cavanaugh (b. 1756) in 1776 and was thus related also to the Cozens and, distantly, to the Cayleys, but the latter link became closer, when John Cayley, jr. married his second wife Harriet Raikes (b. 1779) in 1799. His first wife had been Anne Halliday, which linked the Cayleys with the large family of a near neighbour, Dr Matthew Halliday. This wedding had taken place on 8/19 February 1792 as a joint event with the wedding of his younger brother William, who married Elizabeth Cavanaugh (b. 1762). Sally Moberly's husband, Edward, whom Cayley had made an executor, represented new blood in the community. He hailed from Knutsford in Cheshire, but came to St Petersburg probably at the beginning of the 1780s. He gained his freedom of the Russia Company by Act of Parliament on 17 August 1788, the same day as Matthew Anderson, and became a partner in the firm of Anderson, Brown & Moberly.[184] In July 1785 he married Sally and by the early years of the next century they had no less than eight surviving sons and three daughters. Sally's sister Elizabeth had married Wilhelm Poggenpohl in December 1782. He was the son of the German merchant who was linked with Cavanaugh and Cozens (and with Gomm) in the 1750s and the brother of Johann, also in commerce and a member of the English freemasonic lodge in the 1770s. Wilhelm in contrast had entered the Russian foreign service in 1771, spent many years at the London embassy, latterly under Count Semen Vorontsov, where his wife helped to care for Vorontsov's young daughter, the future Lady Pembroke. They had returned in about 1788 to St Petersburg, where her husband died the year before Cayley drew up his will. The Poggenpohl conection extended the net to include the Nicolays – Heinrich von Nicolay, who was to become President of the Academy of Sciences in 1798, was Elizabeth's brother-in-law – and other influential members of the Russian bureaucracy and aristrocracy.[185]

A revealing and lively picture of the lifestyle of this extended family group is provided by the letters which James Brogden sent from the Russian capital to his father and sister in London in 1787–8. Brogden's father John was a Russia merchant of the same vintage as John Cayley, his friend since the 1750s, and he had long been prominent in the running of the Company's affairs. James Brogden, born in 1765, was paying his first visit to Russia, beginning 'now to think of myself as something of a Merchant', and indeed, obtaining his freedom of the Company by patrimony in February 1789, three months after his return, and on the same day and by the same means of admission as Stephen Thornton, who was to meet him on his very first day in St Petersburg and became his close companion throughout his stay in Russia. Stephen was in fact the son of Godfrey Thornton, Cayley's partner, first in St Petersburg and then in London, where he also became a leading figure in the Russia Company.[186]

Brogden was immediately drawn into the Cayley circle and toasted as 'the *New Member* of the society' at a dinner at the Raikes's. He was soon writing that 'I am indeed very pleasantly situated, being *domesticated* in the most agreeable circle in this town – the Raikeses, Cavanaughs, Cayleys, with Mr & Mrs Mauberly, who is Mr Cayley's Daughter, & several others who are related to the different branches of this society & live together upon the most intimate footing, tho' they still associate with the rest of the Factory.' The three families met 'very frequently' and they lived 'in a very grand manner – five servants at table'. Brogden was persuaded by Cayley 'to take up my lodging in his house, or rather a small house separate from his, where S. Thornton now lives', explaining in a further letter that Cayley's house was 'situated in the English Line, which is joined to a Lane they called the *back line* by a long yard, at the bottom of which is a small house over the gate-way'.[187] The Cayleys lived at no. 247 Galernyi dvor (no. 70, according to present numbering) and the Raikeses at no. 245 (no. 68, the so-called Stiglits Palace), both houses being to the west of the English Church. Their immediate intervening neighbours were the Sutherlands and the Hallidays. Cayley had bought the house with Godfrey Thornton in the 1770s and was to buy it outright in 1789: it remained the Cayley home until at least 1870. Three of the Cayley sons were then living at home, apparently Cornelius, William and Henry, all destined for a career in trade, like their eldest brother John, who was also frequently mentioned, but he was already in business with Cavanaugh and about to take a partnership in the family firm, following his father's appointment as consul. Only George was away, breaking the mould and studying medicine at Edinburgh.[188] None of the Cayley sons was married at the time of Brogden's visit (but at least two were by the time of the will) and, together with Cavanaugh and Thornton, they led a very active social life in which Brogden participated to the full, although, as he would have his father believe, with reluctance: 'Petersburg is a very agreeable residence for a few months, but is much too gay for me. Balls, Plays, dancing, Eating & drinking seem to be the most important concerns of life to the majority of its enhabitants.'[189]

Brogden was much taken with Timothy Raikes, one of the more interesting and 'original' characters in the British Factory. Of Yorkshire stock, Raikes was apprenticed at the age of fifteen to Robert Nettleton (after whom he was to name his first-born son in 1776) and received his freedom of the Russia Company by servitude on 29 May 1753.[190] He soon moved to St Petersburg where, early in Catherine's reign, the firm of Reinholt and Raikes was established. After a few years and not later than 1771, he formed a partnership with James Saffree (1722–81), a fellow freemason (Raikes was the lodge's treasurer), but in the 1780s his firm became simply Timothy Raikes and so continued until his death.[191] Customs figures for various years show the firm's exports at four to six times greater than imports, but without any indication of the goods involved. Brogden mentions that Raikes took him to see 'his linen Warehouses' as well as the hemp wharf and the tallow warehouses. Raikes was undoubtedly very versatile in his commercial dealings. At the end of the 1760s, for instance, he supplied a large amount of silver to the Petersburg mint, but as late as 1773 Lord Cathcart, who found him 'a very worthy and obliging man', was still interceding on his behalf for payment.[192] In the 1780s Raikes set up a factory to produce nails and tin on the Uslanka river, a tributary of the Svir' in the province of Olonets.[193]

'A blind cleaver little witch of a Man' was Catherine Wilmot's description of Raikes in 1805, some five years before his death at the age of eighty, but she delighted in his company, as did her sister.[194] His hospitality was legendary and several British travellers have left accounts of their visits to his home. And not only the British – the Venezuelan Franciso de Miranda visited the Raikeses in the same year as Brogden, finding there 'very good company' and much talk about literary matters. It was at Raikes' house in the 1760s (long before his marriage) that some of the English indulged in amateur theatricals, and the remark of a young Englishman to his stepmother that 'the English here are only those of the factory: a money getting unletterd race, not excepting your old flame Mr R-' would seem less than just.[195]

Raikes was a cousin of Robert Raikes (1736–1811), the founder of Sunday Schools, and of his brothers, Thomas and William, who were prominent Russia merchants and Russia Company consuls in the 1780s and 1790s. It was Thomas's son, also Thomas (1778–1848), who visited St Petersburg, met Pushkin, and published *A Visit to St. Petersburg in the Winter of 1829–30* (London, 1838).[196] If in the case of Timothy Raikes, it was collateral branches of the family that achieved fame in the nineteenth century, it was the direct line for the Cayleys and Moberlys. Almost all of John Cayley's family remained in Russia for many decades and multiplied greatly. His youngest son, Henry, married Mary Doughty in 1814 and produced perhaps the two most noted Cayleys in that century: his second son was the outstanding mathematician Arthur Cayley (1821–95), Sadlerian Professor of Mathematics at Cambridge and corresponding member of the Russian Academy of Sciences; his third son was the poet Charles Bagot Cayley (1823–83), who produced verse translations of Dante's *Divine Comedy* and Homer's *Iliad*.[197] The progeny of Edward and Sarah Moberly is celebrated by a granddaughter in *Dolce Domum* (1911), a biography of her father George Moberly 1803–85), headmaster of Winchester and Bishop of Salisbury: 'they had a large family of eight sons and three daughters. These eleven persons have had between them the unusual number of 93 children and 256 grandchildren.'[198]

The foregoing has been an excursus into the lattice of strong and complex family networks that grew up within the British community, particularly in the last decades of the century, and may also be seen as yet one more variation in what has been essentially a set of variations on a theme of considerable richness. Numerically, the British traders, merchants and manufacturers, together with their families, represented by far the largest and most important group within the British community in St Petersburg and it has been possible only to hint at a few of its personalities and problems. Inevitably both British and Russian reactions to 'the British merchant' and his way of life and of conducting business were mixed, as was apparent from some of the evidence introduced in the opening chapter.

The general Russian image of the British during Catherine's reign was a very positive one, fed, it is true, on the reading of the so-called English novel and influenced by an incipient European Anglomania, in which, nevertheless, there was even room for admiration of mercantile virtues in the projection of the Briton 'as loyal and steadfast'.[199] The Russian poet who wrote that line had worked on Catherine's Legislative Commission and in her Instruction (*Nakaz*) to that body the empress had clearly stated her belief that

it is better to do Business with a People who demand little of us and whose Commercial Wants render them in some measure dependent upon us; with a People who, from the Extent of their Views on Business, know where to bestow the Superabundant Merchandise; who are rich, and can take off many Commodities; who will pay for them in ready Money; who (to use the Expression) are obliged to be faithful; who are peaceable from fixed Principle; whose Account is in Gain, and not in Conquest.[200]

The British view of the Factory, when negative, was invariably harsh in its expression. To George Norman's already quoted 'a money getting unletterd race' could be added Richard Sutherland's obviously far from unprejudiced verdict that, when 'money is the *passe partout*, 'tis that which makes the pot boil tho' (as the proverb says) the devil pisses in the fire'. Even Walter Shairp had a sober view of his own kind, commenting on one occasion that wars were particularly good for trade and on another, in connection with the bankruptcy of a friend, that 'at this same Time others are making Great Fortunes as you know Men in Trade are like Beasts of Prey that feed upon the Distruction of their Fellows'.[201] On the other hand, there were inevitably those who were inclined to romanticise and idealise both their calling and its practitioners. Hanway is the supreme example, managing to combine mercantile interests, patriotism and Christianity into a powerful credo. For him, 'the merchant whose mind is strong enough to pursue gain without indulging any anxious fears, and without forgetting the more essential duties of life, is in a happy employment, was it only for this reason, that there are few callings so free and independent'.[202] Finally, there are the later views of William Porter, he of Beggar's Benison notoriety or English Club respectability, who wrote:

Liberal sentiments, enlarged views & a considerable portion of general information, together with strict integrity and a high sense of character are leading features in the portrait of a British Merchant. They are more peculiarly so among persons of this class who reside abroad ... The members of the Russia Company, at that time residing in St Petersburg were certainly not exceptions to this general observation.[203]

3

'IN ANGLORUM TEMPLO':
THE ENGLISH CHURCH AND ITS CHAPLAINS

The western half of the newly renamed English Embankment today looks
distinctly shabby, but a number of buildings still impress by their elegant
proportions. No. 56 is an excellent example of the work of the Italian architect Giacomo Quarenghi, whose restrained Palladianism is evident in a whole
series of buildings in different parts of central St Petersburg. The building,
or rather the rebuilding of the original structure, was begun in 1814, three
years before Quarenghi's death. Although it underwent some reconstruction
in the 1870s, it retains its characteristic features: a row of half columns and
corner pilasters of the Corinthian order at first-floor level, supporting a pedi-
ment, topped by three statues. It now houses the St Petersburg City Excursion
Bureau and the lofty central hall is used as open-plan office space. Long
curtains cover most of the walls, and it is only when these are drawn back
to reveal brass commemorative plaques, an organ and religious inscriptions
that the building's original function becomes clear. This was the English
Church, the focal point of the British community's life in pre-Revolutionary
St Petersburg. A British visitor describes the impression it made on him in
1827, a few years after it was opened:

On the Sunday immediately after our arrival, I attended service in the English church, a
very handsome and substantial edifice, situated about the centre of the English Quay,
where it presents a noble front to the river, being decorated by a colonnade, placed on
a massive and well-distributed basement story, in which are the apartments of the Rev.
E. Law, nephew of the late Lord Ellenborough, and Chaplain to the Factory. The church
was first built in 1754, and reconstructed in its present form in 1815. The entrance,
properly speaking, is from a street at the back of the Quay, through a handsome gateway.
The interior is neat and simple, and has the great advantage of being well warmed and
comfortably fitted up. There is a state pew for the British Ambassador on the right of
the altar and opposite to the pulpit; it is surmounted by the Royal Arms of England. The
altar-piece is a Deposition from the Cross, a very creditable painting, on the sides of which
are two handsome Corinthian pillars of marble. The female part of the congregation, as
in the Lutheran churches, sat apart from the rest, and occupied the left side of the church.
. . . The church has no gallery, and, although capacious is insufficient to accommodate
more than a part of the English residents.[1]

5 The English Factory House, better known as the English Church, St Petersburg. Engraving from *Gentleman's Magazine* (1796).

Quarenghi's church in St Petersburg, like St Andrew's Church in Moscow (built in Victorian Gothic and consecrated in 1885), is a reminder of the importance of spiritual matters for the expatriate British, but the history of the English Church in Russia goes back to at least the seventeenth century. It is to a study of this early history and of the personalities and activities of the chaplains appointed to minister to the spiritual needs of the British congregation that this chapter is devoted.

I

It was William Tooke (1744–1820), one of the most notable of the church's chaplains, who was responsible for what seems to be a unique account of the British congregation in Russia. A prolific author and translator, he completed a translation of Heinrich Storch's *Gemälde von St Petersburg* (1792–3) – a very informative guide to the history of the city – some years after his retirement in 1792 from the St Petersburg chaplaincy. The third chapter of Storch's original work describes the various religious congregations but makes no mention of the English Church, an omission which Tooke saw fit to remedy by inserting a brief history up to 1800 in his translation.[2] Tooke begins his history with the appointment of the Rev. Thomas Consett, who was in fact to be the first chaplain to the British Factory when it moved to St Petersburg in 1723 but who had previously served in Moscow and Archangel from 1717. His words suggest that prior to Consett's arrival there had been no independent British congregation in the old capital, an impression

6 The English Church in present-day St Petersburg.

seemingly confirmed in the monumental history of Moscow published in London in 1823 by Robert Lyall, a Scots doctor formerly in Russian service. Questioning the testimony of Adam Olearius, the famed German scholar and diplomat who had written that in the 1650s there had existed in Moscow separate churches for both the British and the Dutch, Lyall suggests instead that there had always been a combined congregation, generally called the Dutch, or sometimes the Reformed, Church. The ministers of this church, he states, had been Dutch or Swiss until the year 1808, when the Rev. Benjamin Beresford became 'the first Briton who ever held this office',[3] although this ignores Olearius's specific naming of a Scot, Andreas Gordius (Andrew Gordon?) as pastor in the 1650s.[4]

There is, however, evidence that there were English chaplains at various periods in seventeenth-century Moscow. In 1625 a pass was issued to the Rev. Thomas Rhodes (d. 1636?) 'to travaille into Muscovia for three yeares (provided he repayre not to the cittie of Rome)'.[5] Rhodes, a graduate of King's College, Cambridge and ordained as priest at Peterborough in 1621, became acquainted with Arthur Dee, Tsar Mikhail's body-physician, but little else is known of his activities in Moscow. Nor indeed of those of his successor, Ambrose Frere, who left England in 1627 'to goe to reside in the dominions of the Emperour of Russia to preach to the English nation there'.[6] No other names of chaplains are known and it is interesting that both Rhodes and Frere were in Moscow before the creation of the *Nemetskaia sloboda* ('New Foreign Quarter') on the right bank of the River Iauza in 1652. Indeed in 1648 the British merchants had been expelled from Moscow to Archangel and the few British Protestants remaining in Moscow would have attended either the Lutheran or the Reformed (Calvinist) churches. Where the British congregation originally gathered cannot be established, but at some period in the century they would seem to have used a separate building, possibly part of the so-called Old English House (*Staryi angliiskii dvor*), now to be seen near the Rossiia Hotel, off Red Square, or part of a second house acquired in 1628 by the Muscovy Company's agent Simon Digby in Belyi gorod and known as the New House (*Novyi dvor*). A letter of March 1703 from two prominent British merchants in Moscow to a friend in London refers to 'a great deale of Church Furniture wch formerly belong^d to the old Muscovie Companie here' and also to the church plate and pulpit cloth and cushion which had been taken back to London.[7]

The same letter is, however, even more important for what it reveals about the situation in Peter's Russia. Already in 1696, the Roman Catholics in the Foreign Quarter had at long last been allowed to build their own church, possibly as a result of General Patrick Gordon's position of favour with the tsar. At about the same period Peter had allowed foreigners to settle virtually where they wished within the Russian empire, and the British merchants moved freely between Archangel and Moscow. The appointment of Charles Goodfellow as British consul-general in Moscow from 1699, the eventual arrival of Whitworth as envoy extraordinary in 1705 and the general influx of British specialists following Peter's visit to England in 1698 all contributed to make Moscow the centre for the growing British community. Not unexpectedly, moves were made to provide a church for the British congregation there, and in 1703 Peter granted 'as much ground as we desire to build a Church in &c. wth which we very shortly intend to accquaint the Company and of our Godly Designes, hoping that they will out of the Abundance of their Charity contribute largely towards building of a convenient Church & other conveniences for the parson'. The letter also contained requests for a large church bible and prayer books with 'the English Company in Moscow' stamped on the back covers in gold, as well for other books, including fifty copies of the new versions of the psalms by Brady and Tate. Finally, the letter names the chaplain already *in situ* as the Rev. John Urmston.

Precisely when Urmston arrived in Russia cannot be established, but there are reasons for suggesting that it was in 1702. Urmston himself sent a long letter to an Oxford friend in September 1703, some six months after the merchants' letter, from which it is apparent that he had not been long in Russia.[8] At the same time he speaks of the activities of the Society for the Propagation of the Gospel in Foreign Parts, which received its charter on 16 June 1701 and of which Urmston's correspondent, the Rev. Philip Stubbs of Wadham College, was a founder member. Urmston had received a consignment of books from the Society to distribute to the crews of British ships arriving at Archangel (from where the letter was in fact written), but he also intended to give them to 'Sailors & others. Artificers and Soldiers in the Emperor's Service here, at Veronits Azof, in the Army and upon the Baltick, who live like Heathens and are utterly destitute of such helps'. He is scathing about the Russians, their religion and lack of learning: 'The Russians stile themselves Christians, but indeed are too worthy of the Character some of our Country-men have given them, viz. ye Scum & dregs of Xtianity; they pretend to be of the Greek Church, but strangely ignorant, yet great Bigots' and goes on to describe the opposition to Peter and his reforms and the people's hatred of foreigners: 'if his Ma^{ty} should die in the Minority of his Son who is but 14 years old we must expect all to be murder'd'. But his description of his treatment by his own congregation is no less revealing. He regrets not having with him the Bishop of London's 'Licence or Approbation for this Place the want there of hath already gain'd some disesteem', although he has produced other recommendations, from which it appears that Urmston possibly served previously as a chaplain in the British navy:

I must keep up a good Esteem, for should our Merch^{rs} once suspect I were inferior in Learning & Repute in England to Dr Stillingfleet, Tillotson, Burnet or any other of our Learned Worthies they would not think me worthy of their Service; when in company I've had such Questions proposed to me as were never answer'd or scarce made to man before, insomuch that one would think they made it their Business to pick out dark Sayings and the difficult passages in and concerning the Holy Word of God and the Misteries therein contain'd, they are curious enquirers into Hidden Secrets especially in the Old Testament and pass regardless by what imports them more to know & practice; they are hard to please & would scarce be satisfied wth the most pious & Learned: St Paul himself had not such to deal wth.

Obviously poor Urmston failed to please. A note in the Whitworth papers reads:

Mr John Armstone (sic) was Minister to the Factory, but upon several disputes he had with most of the Merchants he was dismissed the year 1705 & Mr Thirlby, who had been at Narva while the English resided there, was called to supply his place.[9]

Urmston returned to England to become curate at Eastham in Essex until early in 1710, when he went to South Carolina with his wife, 'a poor timorous creature', and three children.[10] He worked at a mission of the Society for the Propagation of the Gospel until 1720. The Society's records thereafter note that he worked in Maryland, where he fell into disrepute, and was 'burned to death' in 1732 in North Carolina.[11]

His successor in Moscow was Charles Thirlby (1651–1715), son of a priest at Clifton near Nottingham and a graduate of St John's College, Cambridge, who was ordained priest at Ely in 1676.[12] When and for how long he was in Narva is not known, but he was to serve in Moscow until his death in 1715, two years after the death of his wife Martha. It is Thirlby who began the register of the English Church in Moscow, listing in 1706 a congregation of fifty-three men and women, headed by Whitworth, Goodfellow and Dr Robert Erskine, the imperial physician.[13] With Thirlby's death the Factory undertook to find a replacement; the Factory's treasurer was instructed 'to provide a proper person for the administration of the church offices. The Rev. Thomas Consett was accordingly invited over, and his salary fixed by a regulation made the 12th of November, 1717 (OS) at Archangel, whither the Factory had lately removed.'[14] By coincidence, Consett (1678?–1730) was also educated at St John's, Cambridge, before being ordained deacon in 1699 and priest in 1702 at York, his home town.[15] Consett was to spend nearly ten years in Russia, acquiring a wife and two daughters (and losing a son) and, unlike Thirlby, making wide contacts with Russian and foreign clerics and scholars and accumulating the materials for an important book, published after his return to England. His first years were spent at Archangel, although entries in the church register and other evidence suggest he was frequently in Moscow. However, in 1723 he moved with the Factory to St Petersburg, which was henceforth to be the trading centre of the Empire:

1723. N.B. Trade by order of his Imperial Majesty of Russia being removed from Archangel and Mosco to St. Petersburg, and the Factory obliged to repair thither, I also left Mosco the 8th of June and arrived with my wife at St. Petersburg the 23ᵈ of the said month; where, by favour of the British Factory, I am again settled as their Minister.[16]

Consett thus became the first of a long line of English chaplains in St Petersburg, ministering to a congregation that was once again united in one place, thereby removing the need for a separate minister, if not for a church, as had been requested by Whitworth in 1712, the year the city became the imperial capital.[17]

Consett soon established his reputation as an erudite scholar, 'known for his philosophical, theological and philological works, which will bring immortal glory to his name', according to a contemporary assessment.[18] In May 1724 he was elected a corresponding member of the Brandenburg Society of Sciences (as the Berlin Academy of Sciences was then known) through the good offices of Baron Heinrich von Huyssen, one of Peter's closest associates and apologists, recommending him as 'assidu à traduire plusieurs ouvrages Russes en Latin ou Anglois et à recueillir les curiosités de ce pais'.[19] Consett was thereafter to engage in a fairly regular correspondence with the vice-president of the society, D. E. Jablonski, sending him various translations and hoping to enlist his help in gaining some preferment in the Anglican Church on his eventual return to England. In St Petersburg Consett moved in circles close to Peter, which included the Bishop of Pskov, Feofan Prokopovich, and other influential members of the Holy Synod such as Gavriil Buzhinskii, head of the Troitse-Sergeevskii Monastery near Moscow, and Archimandrite Afanasii Condoidi, as well as the young Prince Antiokh Kantemir, who within a few years was to be Russia's minister in London. Consett's residence in the Russian capital, spanning the last years of Peter's life and much of the reign of Catherine I, and his access to information about not only ecclesiastical but also political matters made him a valued correspondent for the British government: two letters which he sent in 1725 to the secretary of state, Lord Townshend, cover such topics as Jacobite activities in St Petersburg and the legitimacy of the imperial succession which were of great interest at a time when Britain had no officially accredited representatives in Russia.[20]

There is no mistaking Consett's own sympathies for Peter and his consort, which he conveyed forcefully in two sermons delivered to his congregation on 30 July/10 August 1724 in celebration of the recent coronation of Catherine and on 7/18 February 1725 in Peter's memory;[21] they are no less apparent in the opening lines of his 'Preface' to *The Present State and Regulations of the Church in Russia*, published in London in 1729. But apart from the extensive introduction, in which he incorporated an account of the life of Prince Menshikov, Consett preferred to use translations of contemporary Russian documents and tracts (some of which he had sent to Jablonski in Berlin) to present an objective portrait of the enlightened acts of the Russian tsar. The fundamental text is his translation of Prokopovich's *Dukhovnyi reglament* ('Spiritual Regulation') of 1721, which sets out Peter's major church reforms, but also includes four other works by the bishop, the best known and most impressive of which is the oration on Peter's death, as well as an oration by Buzhinskii and a lamentation by Huyssen, both dedicated to Peter, and miscellaneous other tracts. Consett, in reaction to what he considered were hastily compiled general histories of Peter's reign, wished to produce something of lasting value for future scholarly studies:

as ... it is very difficult at present to distinguish the true and the genuine, and in the Process of Time this Difficulty will grow yet greater, I have thought it for the purpose to lay a sure Foundation of future History, by drawing out of the Language of the Country some authentick Records which will, and must be allow'd to be proper Materials for Historians to work with hereafter, and which yet might have been lost or neglected, as many Originals in Languages are, for want of this Care to bring them to Light, and to preserve them for general Use.[22]

He was undoubtedly right, and the recent facsimile edition is evidence that his book has retained its importance up to the present time.[23]

Pursuing happily his scholarly interests was one thing; being pastor to a contented flock was obviously something quite different. Like Urmston before him, Consett seems not to have seen eye to eye with many of the merchants of the British Factory who paid his salary. Tooke notes succinctly: 'Some differences arising between the Factory and their chaplain, he was dismissed from their service by a resolution of the 10th of July (OS) 1727.'[24] The precise reasons for this action are difficult to establish. Consett in his letter to Townshend in June 1725 refers to his refusal to administer an oath of allegiance to Catherine I to the British congregation, despite the insistence of one of the merchants, but in March of the following year Huyssen was suggesting that 'Mr. Conzet s'est reconcilié avec la Factorie Angloise.'[25] At all events Consett left Russia at the end of July 1727 for England, where he busied himself with the preparation of his book and the search for a new appointment. In February 1729 he was appointed by the East India Company to the chaplaincy at Fort St George near Madras, where he was to die on 21 July 1730, only months after his arrival.

II

The dismissal of Consett left a vacancy which the Factory obviously found very difficult to fill. The church register gives no indication of any person subsequently responsible for looking after the congregation, and it was only at the end of 1736 that the Factory approached Claudius Rondeau, the British minister resident, with its *first* request that the Russia Company find a suitable chaplain. At the same time it asked the Company 'to contribute somewhat towards the support of a Minister'.[26] If at a later date when a dispute arose, the Factory was to consider its request for a chaplain as a specific initiative from its side, which it was free to repeat or withhold whenever subsequent vacancies in the chaplaincy occurred, the Company for its part was to see the request for financial assistance as conclusive evidence of its authority to determine who the chaplain was to be whenever there were competing candidates. The chaplain was henceforth regarded in the same light as the Company's agent at St Petersburg, supported by contributions from both the Factory and the Company and by special levies on all goods exported from and imported into Russia in British ships. A special committee of the Company drew up a letter to Rondeau which stated that:

the company have laid a Foundation for supporting the Honour of the Nation, the Ease and Reputation of the Factory, and the which they hope will redound to the Advantage of their Trade in General. The Company design to allow out of the Money ariseing (sic) from the above Regulations 200 Roubles per Annum towards the support of a Minister which with the 600 Roubles the Factory propose to allow him, will be, not only an easy but an honorable support for him . . .[27]

The Company's search for 'a person of Piety and Prudence, who by his Life and Conversation, may recommend Virtue and Religion, and thereby do Honour to God and his Country and be of use to the Factory' led to the election on 27 July 1737 of the Rev. Phillip Lernoult in preference to the Rev. John Kippax.[28]

Lernoult, who was, it appears, Rondeau's nephew, had graduated from Corpus Christi College, Cambridge in 1724. He had been ordained deacon at Peterborough in the same year and then priest at Norwich in May 1727, before returning to his native Canterbury to become Chaplain at St Peter's.[29] Although Lernoult served in Russia from 1737 to the beginning of 1742 nothing is known of his activities or of his impressions of the country, which is particularly regrettable since his chaplaincy spanned the end of Anna's reign, the short reign of Ivan VI under the successive regencies of Ernst Biron and Anna Leopol'dovna, and the coup that brought Elizabeth to the throne. There is one amusing glimpse of 'the learned and reverend Mr Lerna (sic)' in the memoirs of the Scots doctor John Cook, when the elephants, brought to St Petersburg as a present for the empress by the Persian ambassador, threatened to trample them underfoot as they stood watching near the Admiralty.[30] Lernoult, nevertheless, seems to have pleased the members of the Factory. When he presented himself at a Court of Assistants on 15 October 1742 on his return to London, testimonials from the Factory were read, stating that 'during Four Years and Ten Months Residence amongst us (he) has behaved very soberly, diligently, and in an Exemplary Manner as becomes his Function'.[31]

Although Tooke in his published account writes that Lernoult was followed as chaplain by the Rev. John Forster (1697?–1781) between 1742 and 1747, a note he himself made in the church register indicates that Forster served only from 1745.[32] The Factory in fact had been again without a chaplain until Forster's arrival in St Petersburg at the very end of 1744 in his capacity as personal chaplain to John Carmichael, Earl of Hyndford, the British ambassador. Forster was an interesting character, who had earlier been tutor to Edward Wortley Montagu and indeed was later to claim authorship of Montagu's *Reflections on the Rise and Fall of the Antient Republics* (1759). Unkind Fate was to bring Forster back to Russia some thirty years later, when crippled with gout and in his dotage he attended to the spiritual needs of the notorious Elizabeth Chudleigh, Duchess of Kingston. He refused to return to Europe with the duchess because of the arduous travelling and remained in St Petersburg, where he died in June 1781 at the age of eighty-four.[33] But his time as chaplain to the Factory was without incident, although it would seem he made known his wish not to continue longer than necessary. This led to the Factory's second approach to the Russia Company for a permanent chaplain. The Company took appropriate action only after the Factory had agreed to certain stipulations, chiefly that the chaplain be provided with 'a Yearly Salary of 1000 R° with Free House & Wood' and that 'the Factory should enter into Agreement to raise upon them-selves a sufficient Fund for this Purpose by laying a Tax upon the Amount of each Factors Buyings and Sellings'.[34] On 24 July 1747 the Rev. Daniel Dumaresq (1713–1805) was elected chaplain.

Dumaresq was the first chaplain after Consett whose scholarly interests brought him significant recognition in Russia. From an Anglo-French family in Jersey, he was also the first Oxford man among the chaplains: he had studied at Pembroke College, where he received his BA in 1733 and his MA three years later; he took his BD from Exeter College in 1745.[35] In 1752, during his residence in Russia, he applied for the degree of DD, which 'the University of Oxford was pleas'd to grant me, not only without the least Scruple, but even with Readiness and Cheerfulness'.[36] He had then served five years as chaplain, and the Factory was so content with him that they offered him a further five-year period, but he preferred to continue for an unspecified time, subject to three-months notice from either side. He never-theless served five years more before leaving Russia in what proved to be an unsuccessful attempt to obtain 'some decent Establishment, to spend the rest of my days in England'.[37] Obliged to return to St Petersburg, where his duties had been carried out during his absence by a Rev. John Hooke, he carried on for another five more years, which took him into the reign of Catherine II.

Dumaresq's scholarly pursuits brought him into close contact with mem-bers of the Russian Academy of Sciences, particularly with the historian G.-F. Müller. Some fifty letters from Dumaresq to Müller survive over the period 1758–79 and provide invaluable information about Dumaresq's interests and movements. The correspondence is in French, although Dumaresq was a con-siderable linguist, having added German and then Russian to his repertoire in the early 1750s.[38] It is known that he compiled a 'Comparative Vocabulary of the Eastern Languages' (the manuscript of which has been lost) at a time when oriental studies were but weakly developed at the Academy, although Lomonosov, with whom Dumaresq was undoubtedly acquainted, was a strong advocate of their importance. It is likely that Dumaresq's work was subsequently used in the preparation of a universal comparative dictionary, two volumes of which appeared in 1787–9 under the editorship of Professor Peter Pallas and with the active encouragement of the empress.[39]

From his earliest days in St Petersburg Dumaresq had been concerned to promote Anglo-Russian scholarly interchange. When in Russia, he was constantly sending Russian publications to potentially interested parties in Britain: thus, in 1749, he sent the Duke of Richmond the *Flora Sibirica*; two years later, Lord Granville was the recipient '(merely on account of the Singularity and Novelty of the thing) [of] two copies of a Tragedy lately translated out of the Russ into French', Sumarokov's *Sinav i Truvor*; and in 1753 the same correspondent was fortunate indeed to receive the *Plan de la ville de St. Petersbourg avec ses principales vues*, a magnificent album produced to mark the fiftieth anniversary of the founding of the city.[40] During his first return to England in 1757–8 Dumaresq attended meetings of the Royal Society (to which he was to be elected in 1761) and spoke about the recently founded University of Moscow; he sent back lists of members of the Society to Counts Shuvalov and Stroganov and copies of its transactions to one of the Academicians.[41] Prior to his second, and what he (and the Academy of Sciences) thought was his final, homecoming, he was elected an Honorary Foreign Member on 24 May/4 June 1762.[42] In 1762–3 he was sending back to Petersburg such items as recent English translations of works of Russian exploration as well as the classic early English accounts of Giles Fletcher and Samuel Collins.[43]

Early in 1764 Catherine invited Dumaresq to return to Russia as a member of her newly created commission on educational reform. The commission was chaired by G. N. Teplov and its other members were P. H. Dilthey, T. von Klingstedt and his old friend Müller, who had but recently moved to Moscow to become director of, first, the Foundling Home, then, a year later, the archives of the College of Foreign Affairs. Dumaresq was to remain a further eighteen months in Russia, taking a very active part in the commission's work, which led to the submission to Catherine in 1766 of 'A General Plan for Gymnasia or State Schools'. It proposed the setting up of a network of secondary schools throughout the provincial towns of Russia that would offer identical curricula during the first two four-year stages of an overall period of twelve years. For the final four-year period there would, however, be four syllabuses to cater for the academic, military, civil and commercial professions. Entry to the gymnasia would be 'classless', which meant, of course, for all classes except the peasantry and the urban poor: elementary schools for the 'common people' were nonetheless proposed in a special appendix.[44] In the months preceding the commission's final proposals (none of which, incidentally, was adopted by Catherine) Dumaresq's letters to Müller reflect many aspects of their work, including the provision of textbooks and the training of teachers. Dumaresq seems to have had a special responsibility for recommending and acquiring books in foreign languages to be translated into Russian. In response to Müller's idea of establishing two teacher-training seminaries he cautioned that any students sent abroad for study should be well prepared, a belief repeated a month later, in June 1765, when Catherine made known her wish to send a group of seminarists to Oxford and Cambridge.[45] It was at this juncture that Dumaresq entered into correspondence with Dr John Brown, a vicar in Newcastle and energetic preacher and publicist, who had gained a reputation in England for his *Estimate of the Manners and Principles of the Times* (1757) and subsequent works on morality and education. Brown responded to a request to present his views to the empress with a long letter of 'reflections' on the great projects on which Catherine has embarked. Brown's ideas, in Dumaresq's French version, appealed to the empress, who invited him to Russia and charged Dumaresq, about to return to England, 'to concert Matters with you there, in Relation to your Voyage'.[46] Brown never went to Russia: Dumaresq, beginning a letter to Müller from London on 22 September 1766, wrote that Brown was suffering from gout and had postponed his departure: a postscript the following day conveyed the news that Brown had committed suicide.[47]

Dumaresq himself was never to return to Russia. In November 1765 the Bishop of Salisbury had offered him a good living if he could take it up within six months; in January Dumaresq took his leave of the empress and of the grand duke, for whose education his advice had been earlier enlisted, and on 1 March 1766 he arrived back in England, having stayed briefly in Warsaw at the invitation of the King of Poland.[48] Sadly, the living at Salisbury was worth only half of what he had expected. He approached the Russia Company for help in seeking advancement and the letter that was addressed to the lord chancellor on his behalf is eloquent testimony to the respect in which he was held:

The Revd Daniel Dumaresq Doctor in Divinity has served the Russia Company fifteen years as their Chaplain in Russia & hath acquitted himself with the utmost dignity and reputation, so as to reflect a lustre on our Church and Nation. He is distinguished not only for great learning but such universal benevolence as to have attracted the attention of the first people of that Country both in Church and state and especially persons of Science. He is particularly known to the Empress herself who hath upon several occasions given him very high marks of her esteem whereof her Imperial Majesties Ministers here have for a course of years given the fullest testimony.[49]

He was, however, never to receive the preferment in England that his talents seemed to merit. He resolved to retire to the country and he returned in fact to the parish of Yeovilton, near Ilchester in Somerset, where he had been previously in 1762–4 and where he was to remain virtually for the rest of his long life. His few letters to Müller after his return describe his straitened circumstances and his sense of physical and intellectual remoteness from the scholarly and cultured life of London. A letter of September 1778, after a twelve-year break in their correspondence, expresses his nostalgia about their past conversations and activities and mentions as a highlight in his life at Yeovilton his financing the inoculation against smallpox of all his parishioners.[50] In 1798 Dumaresq retired to Bath, although he continued to be nominally the rector of Yeovilton. There he met the empress' body-physician John Rogerson but missed his old acquaintance, the Russian ambassador Semen Vorontsov, to whom he wrote subsequently to tell him and to send him an engraving from a portrait miniature.[51] It was to Vorontsov that Dumaresq, then in his ninety-third year and near to death, wrote again in January 1805, mentioning the visit the ambassador had paid to him the previous May.[52]

III

Dumaresq's period as chaplain coincided with an important event in the life of the British congregation – the acquisition of a suitable place for worship. It will be remembered that a church was not built in Moscow despite Peter's grant of land in 1703 and that Whitworth's initiative in 1712 in St Petersburg was not pursued. However, soon after the removal of the British Factory to St Petersburg in 1723 a number of prominent merchants sent a petition to George I:

We your Majestie's most dutifull & faithful subjects the Merchants of the British Factory at St Petersburg do at our own Charge maintain a Minister to perform Divine Service according to the Rites of the Church of England; but being without a Church, the Rest of our Countrymen who are very numerous in & about the Place cannot conveniently enjoy their Part of this Blessing, & we being too few in number and our Trade small, find ourselves utterly unable, without some powerfull assistance, to build a Church.[53]

The 'powerful assistance' was not, however, forthcoming and another quarter of a century was to pass before the matter was raised again. In the interim the English chaplains conducted their services in a chapel fitted out in 1720 in the house in Galley Quay owned by Robert Nettleton (a signatory to the 1723 petition); this would appear to be the place described in the title of one of Consett's Sermons, dated July 1724 as 'in Anglorum Templo . . ., ex mandato Imperialii stituto'.[54] It was only shortly after Dumaresq's appointment that the Factory again communicated through Baron Jacob Wolff, the British minister resident, its wish that a church and house for the chaplain be built. At a meeting of the General Court of the Russia Company on 1 March 1748 it was resolved that 'one Quarter per cent for the Value of one hundred pounds worth of Goods according to the Company's Rates & so in proportion for every Greater or Lesser Quantity be raised now for one year of the Trade of the Company towards building these Church & House for the Chaplain', and a special committee was set up to receive voluntary subscriptions towards the building and the project was advertised in the *London Gazette*.[55] Dumaresq noted that the Factory was very pleased with the 'very happy Turn' the proposal had taken and named Cramond, Nettleton, Thornton, Dingley and, later, Hanway as merchants who had 'done much Service in this affair'.[56] The following March the Court was informed that the Factory had subscribed a total of 4,700 rubles and a year later it was announced that the sum of £1,000 had been raised from dues at the Port of London.[57] Baron Wolff meanwhile had petitioned the Empress Elizabeth for 'the Grant of a Proper Piece of Ground', but it seems not to have brought any response.[58] The Russia Company for its part forwarded to the Factory 'a Plan of a Chapel and Dwelling-house, which I believe, will be well lik'd'.[59] That was in 1751, but it was only in 1753 that Wolff found a building which he considered might be altered for the required purposes. He then informed the Company that he had 'Purchased Count Sheremitoff's House for a Place for Divine Worship on Condition that the Owners procure a grant from her Imperial Majesty for the Sale & Conveyance of said House'.[60] Because of certain regulations then obtaining in Russia, the purchase of Count B. P. Sheremetev's house was completed in the name of Baron Wolff 'as temporary Expedient till a more convenient Method could be fixed on to Register the said Building & Appurtenances in some manner more suitable to its Determination'.[61] Upon Wolff's death in 1759, the Factory proposed that the property be registered in the name of the King of England and 'provide a Sanction that might prove of the greatest Use under many Circumstances and particularly it would be a Means of freeing it from some Regulations which have at times occasion'd Trouble & Perplexity'; the Company, however, decided that the property should be transferred to the governor, consuls and Court of Assistants and gave power of attorney to George Napier & Co. of St Petersburg to effect the transaction.[62] Built towards the end of Peter I's reign and uninhabited for many years, Sheremetev's house was obviously not in the best of condition, but Dumaresq was enthusiastic about the prospect:

. . . we intend, please God, to fit up a large and lofty Room or *Salle*, in the middle Story, for a Place of Divine Worship. The Summer being the only Season proper to build or repair Houses here, we are making the best use of it we can, and hope we shall be able, towards the end of next Autumn, to remove our old Pulpit and Pews, from a ruinous *Salle* into one half-finished. But as to the full Completion of the Work, our funds are not yet sufficient for it.[63]

The new chapel, described as 'a regular structure of Italian architecture' in a note accompanying an engraving which appeared over forty years later in the *Gentleman's Magazine*, was eventually opened in March 1754; on 6/17 March the first service was performed and on 30 March/10 April, the first baptism.[64] The possession of a church at a prime location in the middle of Galley Quay, later to be known as the English Embankment, was a significant milestone in the history of the British community in Russia's capital.

IV

After Dumaresq's resignation the Factory again found a suitable but temporary replacement on the spot in the person of the Rev. Erskine, the chaplain to the ambassador extraordinary, John Hobart, Earl of Buckinghamshire, who had arrived in St Petersburg in September 1762. Erskine, like Forster before him, found the double duties too onerous and declined the offer of a permanent appointment from the Factory.[65] The Company's help was enlisted for a third time and in June of the following year it appointed the Rev. John Glen King (1732–87).

King and his eventual successor Tooke were to occupy the chaplaincy at St Petersburg for a greater part of Catherine's long reign (King for eleven years until early 1774, Tooke, the longest serving of all the chaplains, for eighteen, until 1792). Like Consett and Dumaresq, they were to enjoy the esteem of Russian clerics and scholars, but they also achieved considerable reputations in England through their published work. Very able scholars, they differed in their interests and the range of their studies, but each in his way contributed greatly to British awareness of Russia in spheres other than political.

King, born at Stowmarket in Suffolk and educated at Caius College, Cambridge, where he graduated as Bachelor of Arts in 1752, was ordained priest in 1756 at Ely and became vicar of Little Barwick in Norfolk in 1760.[66] He went to St Petersburg with his wife Anna Magdalen, who was to die at the young age of twenty-three in April 1767, leaving him with an infant daughter. It was, King suggests, to seek distraction from the grievous loss of his wife that he turned to the study of the Orthodox Church at the suggestion of Sir George Macartney, the British envoy extraordinary, who had arrived in Russia at the beginning of 1765. Shortly after his return to London, Macartney produced for private circulation his *Account of Russia, MDCCLXVII* (1768), which ends with an appendix entitled 'The Present State of the Church of Russia, 1767'. Although it is clearly indicated that the author was 'the Rev. Mr. K-', it was attributed to Macartney by John Barrow, who published large extracts from it in 1807.[67] King provides a well-informed, descriptive account of the Russian Church, its ceremonies, festivals, organisation and dignitaries. Only in the section entitled 'General Reflections on the Religious Principles of the Russians' does he abandon his restrained exposition for acid criticisms of the Russian clergy and a dismissal of icons as 'generally most miserable daubings, some of which, notwithstandingly, are said to be the work of angels'.[68]

A longer residence in Russia brought greater understanding, evident in King's *Rites and Ceremonies of the Greek Church, in Russia* (1772), a massive quarto volume of some 500 pages with numerous plates, which established his scholarly reputation in England and was to remain for many decades the standard English work on its subject. His purpose in writing a detailed account of the dogma and ceremonies of the Orthodox Church was to shed light 'on a subject which perhaps has hitherto, in general, been but little understood'. He based his researches, now that he had acquired a knowledge of both Church Slavonic and Russian, mainly on native sources, particularly the works of Prokopovich (acknowledging his predecessor Consett's translations) and of Archimandrite Platon, at that time the tutor to the Grand Duke Paul and the outstanding contemporary Russian churchman. It is noticeable that King had modified his earlier critical opinion of the Russian clergy, taking the 'opportunity of doing justice to characters, which are too often misrepresented', the higher clerics, 'whose candour, modesty, and truly primitive simplicity of manners would have illustrated the first ages of christianity'.[69]

At the end of 1769 King had requested permission of the Company to 'come to England on his private affairs', but he left only in June 1770, when he had managed to secure a temporary replacement at his own expense.[70] Unfortunately, the Rev. John Thackeray (who would have been William Makepeace Thackeray's great-uncle!)[71] died within months, and King, now in London, found a second replacement in the Rev. John Dixon, who officiated until his return in June 1772. An interesting glimpse of King in St Petersburg on the eve of his departure is provided in a letter from the sculptor Etienne Falconet to the empress: Platon, the Archbishop of St Petersburg and the Bishop of Tver wished to see the model of the Bronze Horseman prior to its casting and Falconet called in his friend King to act as interpreter in French, Latin and Russian. A pair of ear-rings made from a piece of the great granite pedestal was a gift King took with him to England for Lady Macartney.[72] The two years in London were in many ways the highpoint in King's social and scholarly life and certainly the best documented. Even before his book saw the light of day, he was elected to the Society of Antiquaries of London in January 1771 and, the following month, to the Royal Society. He was also anxious to secure a doctorate and after vacillating between a degree in divinity or law, took his DD at Oxford in March, 'as the University of Cambridge made difficulties I thought ridiculous'.[73] His main concerns were, however, the arrangements for the publication of his book, a list of eminent subscribers and a suitable dedicatee.

T H E

RITES and CEREMONIES

O F   T H E

GREEK CHURCH, in RUSSIA;

CONTAINING AN ACCOUNT OF ITS

DOCTRINE, WORSHIP, AND DISCIPLINE.

BY JOHN GLEN KING, D.D.

Fellow of the ROYAL and ANTIQUARIAN SOCIETIES, and Chaplain to the
BRITISH FACTORY at St. Peterſbourg.

L O N D O N:

Printed for W. OWEN, in Fleet-Street; J. DODSLEY, in Pall-Mall; J. RIVINGTON, in
St. Paul's Church-Yard; and T. BECKET and P. A. DE HONDT, in the Strand.
MDCCLXXII.

7 *The Rites and Ceremonies of the Greek Church, in Russia* by Rev. John Glen King
(London, 1772), title page.

Wanting Macartney to see 'the book you made me write'; King was disappointed to discover he was in Ireland (and reluctant, it seems, to let King come to visit him), but it was Macartney who used his influence to secure the necessary permission for the book to be dedicated to George III. King certainly capitalised on his acquaintance with Macartney and his successor in Russia, Lord Cathcart, to gain entrée to certain fashionable houses in London and to meet prominent politicians such as Edmund Burke. In January 1772 King was received by George III and, subsequently, by the queen, to both of whom he presented copies of his book.[74] A month later, the diarist and novelist Fanny Burney commented:

It is amazing to me how such a man as Dr. King can have ingratiated himself into the good graces and acquaintances of the first men of the nation, which he really has done. It would be curious to discover by what methods he has so raised himself above his possible expectations; at least, above what his friends could conceive he formed! When he left Lynn, about nine years since, he knew – nobody, I was going to say; and now he is acquainted with all the men of letters in England![75]

King had known the Burney family well in King's Lynn during his earlier years and apparently had kept up contacts: in a footnote to his book he expresses, for instance, his gratitude for advice on the tonal system of Russian hymns to his 'ingenious friend' Dr Charles Burney, Fanny's father and a noted musicologist.[76] It is Fanny, however, who is in constant attendance to see 'the ridiculous side of this man's character' and provide a whole series of amusing cameos of King in 1771–2, 'spouting Shakespeare, Pope, and others', imitating Garrick in *Macbeth*, and 'talking three hours upon any given subject, without saying anything'.[77] Fanny could also never forgive King for an earlier incident, noted in chapter 2, which connected them all with Russia: a few years before, King had advised Mrs Elizabeth Allen, who was to become the second Mrs Charles Burney, to invest £5,000 in the White Sea ventures of the prominent British merchant, William Gomm (whose activities were examined in the previous chapter); Gomm went bankrupt and Dr Burney was left to regret 'the loss of my 2nd wife's Dower'.[78]

Highly content with the contacts he had made and the honours he had received (if disappointed in his wish for a church preferment), King left England – doubtless expecting that his success would accompany him to St Petersburg. In London he had let it be known that Catherine had read parts of his *magnum opus*; this was more than unlikely since when a few years later he sent the Empress a copy of another work, she said she was unable to read it, 'faute d'être suffisamment familiarisée avec la langue anglaise'.[79] A more revealing reaction to King's work from both Catherine and Platon is found in the letter by the then Metropolitan's conversation in 1805 with Reginald Heber, the future Bishop of Calcutta; he suggested that King's work was 'not to be depended on; he had excellent opportunities for information, but was obstinate and attached to his own system' and added that King 'had hoped to gain the Empress Catherine's favour by his work, and affected to go often to court. She at last sent him word that "the Greek Church needed not the apology of a stranger".'[80]

King informed the Company that he was 'obliged' to resign the chaplaincy in June 1774, but it is not clear whether or not he had secured a living. If he had, it was at or near Blackheath, where he settled, married for a second time in 1776, and produced in 1778 his twenty-three-page *Letter to the Right Reverend the Lord Bishop of Durham, Containing Some Observations on the Climate of Russia, and the Northern Countries.* The essay reflected the general interest manifested by many visitors in the effects of extreme cold, the way people dressed and warmed their homes, kept their food, travelled and amused themselves. Inevitably King's attention focussed on the so-called 'flying mountains', and perhaps the most arresting feature of his publication is the yard-long engraving of the great ice mountain built for the Empress Elizabeth at Tsarskoe Selo. Other interests and activities of King in the years following his return are reflected in his correspondence with a member of the Russian Academy of Sciences, Professor Jakob von Stählin.[81] King had assembled a collection of Russian medals in bronze and he was anxious to enlist Stählin's help in completing the set; in exchange, King sent prints and engravings (some after paintings by Reynolds) and held out the carrot of possible election to the Royal Society. King also informed Stählin of progress on a major project – engravings of Roman coins with representations of emperors and noble families; some ninety engravings had already been prepared – he estimated an overall total of 1700 – and he had written to Catherine and Betskoi to inform them of his work.[82] Stählin also sent King a collection of Russian medals to sell in London; and it was in connection with the sale of a collection of coins that King decided to make a final visit to Russia in June 1781. The widow of a close friend wished to dispose of a large collection of Saxon and English coins, which King took to Russia and succeeded in selling to Aleksandr Lanskoi, Catherine's current favourite.[83]

In July 1783 King was presented to the living of Wormley in Hertfordshire. Somewhat later, he was also to purchase chapels in Somerset and London. It was in London that he died on 3 November 1787 and was buried at Wormley.

V

Finding a successor for King in 1774 presented no difficulty. The Factory recommended, and the Company accepted, William Tooke, who had been chaplain at nearby Kronstadt since 22 March 1771.[84] Unlike his predecessors, Tooke was not a graduate of either Oxford or Cambridge, although much later in life (in 1784) he was admitted sizar of Jesus College, Cambridge. Soon after finishing his schooling in London, he decided to devote himself to literary pursuits, producing in 1767 an edition of John Weever's *Funeral Monuments* and in 1769 *The Loves of Othniel and Achsah*, said to be a translation from 'the Chaldee', but in reality a work of his own devising on philosophy and religion. Thus began a career of literary endeavour that was to continue over fifty years up to his death in 1820. In 1771 he was ordained priest and preferred for no obviously good reason the chaplaincy in Kronshtadt to a safe living in Essex. During his Kronshtadt years Tooke began to cultivate the acquaintance of members of the Academy of Sciences and other scholars and to earn the esteem of the British Factory. He was also a visitor to the British Masonic Lodge 'Perfect Union' in the capital and was admitted to the degree of Master Mason on 8/19 March 1772.[85] An excellent linguist, he soon added a knowledge of Russian to his Greek, Latin, Hebrew, German and fluent French; a notebook has survived in which he has recorded an English–Russian vocabulary arranged according to such topics as 'Merchants goods', 'Weights and Measures' and 'Animals', and an extensive 'Alphabet of English and Russ Words'.[86]

Once established in St Petersburg, Tooke was soon pursuing his scholarly activities and ministering to a rapidly growing congregation at a time when the English star was very much in the ascendant. The first work he was to publish was *Pieces Written by Mons. Falconet, and Mons. Diderot on Sculpture* (1777), a translation of various letters and articles concerned principally with the equestrian statue of Peter I, 'the Bronze Horseman', on which Falconet was then engaged. The volume included the first plate to be published of the statue, drawn by Falconet himself and engraved by Bajin. Falconet was a close friend of Tooke (as he had been of King); an even closer friend was the Academician Johann Gottlieb Georgi, who had arrived in Russia in 1770 and took part for the next four years in one of the Academy's expeditions to Siberia. Georgi was widely informed on numerous subjects of interest to Tooke and it was with particular enthusiasm that Tooke began to translate his *Beschreibung aller Nationen des Russischen Reiches* (1776), which was to present the English public with its first comprehensive and scholarly account of the nations within the Russian empire.[87] The first volume of Tooke's translation appeared in London in 1780 and the fourth and last in 1783, when Tooke was himself in England. Travelling overland from Russia, Tooke visited Emmanuel Kant at Königsberg and in Berlin he met members of the Berlin Academy of Sciences and his old friend Abel Burja, formerly pastor to the French Reformed Church in St Petersburg (where Tooke himself had often preached) and the author of *Observations d'un voyageur sur la Russie...* (1785).[88] In London Tooke, who had been elected to the Royal Society on 5 June 1783, was admitted as a Fellow on

8 Rev. William Tooke (1744–1820). Engraving by Joseph Collyer from an original painting by Sir Martin Archer Shee. (National Portrait Gallery, London.)

26 February 1784.[89] Like King a decade earlier, Tooke moved in literary and social circles, but without making himself a figure of fun. Often in the company of his old schoolfriend, the publisher and antiquarian John Nichols (to whom we owe, incidentally, so many details of Tooke's career and life), he was introduced by him to Samuel Johnson, whom he delighted with the news that the Russians intended to translate *The Rambler*.[90] He also seems to have met Jeremy Bentham and agreed to take letters back with him for Samuel

Bentham, then in Russian service. Samuel was not amused, writing in turn to his brother that 'It is unlucky that the packets were entrusted to this Parson's Care. He is the most tittle-tattle man imaginable . . .'[91]

Shortly after his return to St Petersburg, Tooke set off on extensive travels down the length of the Don to Azov before returning to St Petersburg at the beginning of January 1786. As he travelled, he sent to London descriptions of his journey, full of archaeological, ethnographical and botanical information, which were published in the Gentleman's Magazine under the initials 'M.M.M.' (the Tooke family motto: 'Militia mea multiplex').[92] Some of what he wrote was mere pedantry or just irrelevant; much was of undoubted interest: he provided information about 'the manners and customs of the Kosacs' and included in the last three of his four letters from Azov 'the only account of the Krimea ever given to the publick' (although he himself never travelled there and simply translated from notes supplied to him). In the first of two final letters from St Petersburg he described earlier journeys he had made to Central Asia in 1771 and 1773, and in the second, he gave a potted history of Russia up to the end of the seventeenth century. The thirteen letters are the only evidence at this period of Tooke's scholarly activities, apart from the letters that he sent regularly to Nichols. Tooke was acquainted with many of the leading figures at Catherine's court, and he was certainly known to the Empress herself, not least by his regular attendance at her annual *diners de tolérance*, when representatives of all the religious denominations in St Petersburg gathered under the presidency of Gabriel, Metropolitan of Novgorod and St Petersburg.[93] It was, however, the friendship of scholars and men of letters that Tooke sought and prized: he numbered among his close colleagues Bachmeister, Euler, Georgi, Pallas, Storch and other academicians, principally of German extraction, and it was under their guidance and from their work that he gained his sound economic, geographical and historical knowledge of Russia. During his last years in Russia he was elected to membership of the Imperial Free Economic Society of St Petersburg, and just prior to his departure, Princess Dashkova arranged his election to the Academy of Sciences as a Corresponding Member.[94]

Inheriting a fortune from a relative in England, Tooke resigned his chaplaincy and left Russia in September 1792 with his wife, daughter and two sons, Thomas and William, who were both to enjoy illustrious careers. There ensued a decade of intensive work that was to make Tooke the foremost interpreter of Russian history and culture for the British public at the turn of the century. The path he chose was that of translator and compiler rather than of original author. In a remarkable and extensive defence of his position, he argued that too many trifling works were being published and that writers 'should rather chuse to simplify and to compress in compilations, than furnish more receptacles for dust and cobwebs to Book-collectors, and increase the oppression of their already groaning shelves'. The translator's task was difficult but honourable:

Indeed if he have executed his task with fidelity and elegance, he may in some degree appropriate it; he becomes part-owner of it; he is unquestionably author of the translated book; and that book is as much an original in England, for instance, as that from which it is taken is in Germany. Add to this, the labour and pains, the toilsome drudgery it costs, to become thoroughly master of a foreign tongue, its various idioms and phraseology; not to mention that he must also have those of his own, with a great choice of words at command, a matter of no vulgar attainment; and the liberal mind will hardly begrudge him the portion of praise which legitimately accrues to him from his performance.[95]

Tooke's earlier translations from Falconet had a coda to the title, 'with several additions'; this was characteristic of Tooke's method. He preferred to insert his own original observations and material into the text he was translating or in footnotes. The history of the English congregation which he was to insert into his translation of Storch's *Gemälde von St Petersburg* is another example. But perhaps the most interesting illustration is found in what became his most noted and frequently republished compilation – *The Life of Catharine II. Empress of Russia*, which first appeared in 1798.

Shortly after the death of Catherine, a French writer by the name of Jean-Henri Castéra quickly cobbled together a *Vie de Cathérine II* (1797), which despite all its deficiencies proved remarkably successful. It was translated into several foreign languages, including three separate English versions. Tooke's version, called 'an Enlarged Translation from the French', was in fact twice as long as the original and included an extensive introduction and various other amplications and corrections, for which Tooke drew on the writings of numerous German and Russian authors. Second and third editions appeared in 1798 and 1799, both 'with considerable improvements' and omitting reference to the original French source. Castéra at this point brought out another edition of his own work, incorporating most of Tooke's additions but also with new material from his own researches. Tooke thereupon replied with a fourth edition in 1800, using Castéra's material. Finally, a fifth edition, with Tooke's name for the first time as author on the title page, was published in Dublin later the same year.[96] By this time, another mammoth compilation by Tooke and bearing his name had appeared in its second edition. His *View of the Russian Empire, during the Reign of Catharine the Second, and to the Close of the Present Century* (3 vols., 1799), relying on the work of numerous authorities, all carefully cited in his introduction, provided the detailed and systematic information on Russia that was conspicuously lacking in the works of other English travellers and writers. But Tooke was by no means finished with Russia. His interest in the early history of Russia, evident in the last of his letters to *Gentleman's Magazine*, gave rise to a *History of Russia from the Foundation of the Monarchy by Rurik to the Accession of Catharine the Second* in 1800. Tooke himself was at pains to 'intitle it not a history, much less the history, but simply History of Russia, diligently collected from native chronologists and other primitive sources'.[97] An interesting addition to the second volume was a 'Sketch of Mosco', taken from Johann Richter's *Moskwa: Eine Skizze*, published only months previously in Leipzig. This survey of the history of the old capital was to find a companion piece in the translation of Storch's work on St Petersburg, appearing the following year. Both works had chapters on theatre and literature, which were virtually uncharted territory for the English public; incidentally, in translating Storch, Tooke achieved the particular distinction of providing the first metric versions of Russian poems, albeit via German, to appear in English.[98]

Although one translation and one essay had appeared in 1795,[99] Tooke's major publications on Russia were packed into the space of four incredible years from 1798 to 1801: three multi-volume works, one going into five editions, another into two, and the translation of Storch; a version of A. L. Schlözer's *Probe russischer Annalen* (1768) in 1798;[100] and finally, in the 'overseeing', if not the translation, of F. C. P. Masson's notorious *Mémoires secrètes*.[101] It was the spectacular climax of thirty years' study of Russia. Tooke was to live twenty more years, translate and work unceasingly until his death, but as far as is known, published nothing further about the country whose history, geography and culture he had done so much to promote among his fellow-countrymen.

VI

During the last years of Catherine's reign the chaplaincy in St Petersburg was held by the Rev. Thomas Basnett Percival (1766–98), a graduate of St John's College, Cambridge, and formerly domestic chaplain to the marquis of Waterford[102]; but in 1796 his ill-health led the Factory to ask Tooke, then in London, to find a temporary replacement. When Percival died two years later at the early age of thirty-two 'the factory so highly approved of his substitute, that they appointed him to the office, which he continues to fill'.[103] With these words Tooke closed his account of the chaplains in St Petersburg, leaving the reader with an impression of Factory and Company working in harmony and carefully suppressing from public view a controversy that was to rage for many years. Tooke himself was in a somewhat difficult position, for he, like Percival after him, had been appointed to the chaplaincy by the ruling body of the Russia Company in London, its Court of Assistants, but at the same time it was he who had found the Rev. London King Pitt (1773–

1813), whom the Factory appointed to succeed Percival; he also knew that the book to which he had added his account of the British congregation would certainly be read with particular interest by many members of the Russia Company in London. What Tooke decided to do throughout his account was to distinguish carefully and accurately between the decisions and actions of the Factory on the one hand and those of the Company on the other.

Before examining in detail the reasons for the controversy, it is appropriate to devote a few lines to the Rev. Pitt, the last of the chaplains in eighteenth-century St Petersburg. He was enlisted by Tooke a year or so after his graduation from St John's College, Oxford, and in St Petersburg his qualities as a person and scholar quickly endeared him to all members of the British community, particularly to the British ambassador, Sir Charles Whitworth. Whitworth was one of the witnesses at his marriage to Frances Brompton (the daughter of the former Court painter) in 1798 and Pitt's only son was christened Charles Whitworth in October 1802.[104] After the rupture in Anglo-Russian relations during Paul's reign, Pitt accompanied Whitworth back to England in June 1800 and during the year he spent there, he entered into correspondence with the Rev. William Coxe about the situation in Russia, supplying him with an extensive account of Paul's reign and assassination.[105] In 1801 he received his MA from Oxford and then returned to Russia. His only published work, a sermon to his congregation on the great British naval victory at Trafalgar, dates from 1805.[106] Pitt soon afterwards again left for England on extended leave until July 1807. During this period he received his BCL and DCL from Oxford, and became rector of the parish of Hinton in Gloucestershire.[107] On his departure for England, another leading member of the British community, the imperial physician John Rogerson, commended him warmly to the Russian ambassador in London, Count Semen Vorontsov, as 'un jeune homme de mérite qui remplit les devoirs de sa vocation dans toute leur étendue' and suggested that he would seek a post for him on his return as teacher of classics and English to the Emperor's children.[108] In 1807 Pitt did in fact become tutor in English to the Empress Elizaveta Alekseevna. In 1812, shortly before his death, he also became a director of the recently formed Russian Bible Society.[109] Although Mrs Pitt returned to England after her husband's death, she was prevailed upon to return to Russia to act as companion to the empress.[110]

Although, as Tooke writes, Pitt was chaplain in St Petersburg in 1801 and continued to hold the office until his death, he was in the eyes of the Company a usurper, unlawfully preventing its appointee from taking up his post in St Petersburg. The Factory had considered that Pitt's application for the chaplaincy in 1798 was a mere formality, to be rubber-stamped by the Company. The Company, on the contrary, regarded Pitt as one applicant among several and made the election on merit. In addition to Pitt, who was warmly supported by the British ambassador, the treasurer and church wardens of the British church, the Rev. Thomas Reed (the Kronshtadt Chaplain), the Rev. John Egerton, and the Rev. George Porter also applied, and Porter, who had powerful references including one from the Bishop of London, was elected on 17 August 1798.[111] When this decision was communicated to the Factory it created an unprecedented furore. Faced with protests from the Factory, the Company defended itself against charges of favouritism in the election of Porter and declared that since the year 1737, with a single exception (that of the Rev. Forster), 'the Court have elected the Chaplains & which they think it is evident they have a right to do under the words in the Charter & the power thereby given viz. "full power & authority from time to time to make order ordain establish & erect all such statutes & ordinances for the Government good condition & laudable Rule of the said Fellowship" '.[112] A special committee was nevertheless established to investigate the grounds for the Factory's objections; it searched the Company's records and came to the conclusion that the Company and not the Factory was the decision-making body and 'that even had the practise been different the Court at any time might assume and exercise the powers given them under their Charter'.[113] A letter was drafted to the agent in which it was pointed out that 'the resolutions which have occasionally been made at the meetings of the Factory respecting the appointments have in so many instances been the consequence of the resolutions of the Court of Assistants communicated by their agent that it may be presumed that they have been so generally' and it was piously hoped that 'what has happened may cause no breach in the unvaried friendly intercourse which has subsisted between the Gentlemen with you and their friends here'.[114] A meeting of the Factory in St Petersburg on 14/25 February 1799 rejected the Company's decisions and the Company in its turn instructed their agent to withhold use of the church and chaplain's house from anyone other than their official appointee and not to pay any money levied on the authority of the Court towards the maintenance of a chaplain.[115] The Company's next move was to seek the opinion of the Solicitor General on their rights, presenting in their petition a potted history of the Russia Company since its establishment in 1555; on the basis of legal advice upholding their authority, they made a number of resolutions which were to be transmitted to their agent. The first six resolutions merely repeated what the Company had already said concerning its authority; the last two were in the nature of contingency arrangements should members of the Factory refuse to pay the official levies.[116] The Company at a later meeting also resolved to request the assistance of the foreign secretary, Lord Grenville,

who wrote to Sir Charles Whitworth on their behalf.[117] The Factory was
unmoved and an entry in the church register states that the members
'resolved to act on the original and long established system & the Rev^d
London King Pitt was appointed their Chaplain on the 10th day of September
1799 (OS)'.[118] In April 1800 the Company was obliged to raise the necessary
sums for supporting its appointed Chaplain 'by way of Company's Duty on
the several Importations into England & not heretofore under the Sanction
of this Court by a tonnage duty on Shipping in the Ports of Russia' and this
decision was communicated to the foreign secretary and published in the
London papers.[119] In 1802 there seemed at last a possibility of healing the
break between the Company and the Factory; a committee of the Court recommended 'that as it appears by the representations of the Factory that Mr
Pitt has by his conduct and abilities given so much satisfaction to the Congregation at Saint Petersburg there is no reason to doubt but that upon the
application of the Factory to the Court they would appoint him their Chaplain' and this was accepted by a Court of Assistants.[120] In January 1803 the
committee went as far as recommending that Pitt be now officially appointed
and that Porter, who had been receiving his salary in the interim, be discharged with a gift of £500; but by this time opinion in the Court itself had
changed and it found that 'it is not expedient to discharge the Rev^d Mr.
Porter as their Chaplain but that the accustomed Salary of £100 per annum
be continued to him'.[121] Ten years were to pass before the matter was finally
resolved. On 29 January 1813, the Governor of the Russia Company
informed a Committee that he had received a letter in which the Factory
'expressed their earnest wish to terminate the misunderstanding that had so
long existed between the Company & the Factory' and that the Company's
Agent had recommended the election of Pitt as 'the best means of producing
a reconciliation'.[122] On 5 February, the Governor informed the Court that
Porter had offered his resignation, although obviously with reluctance and
stressing that he had no family to support him and no church preferment.[123]
Pitt was then formally recognised as the chaplain at St Petersburg after thirteen years in the post, but by a cruel twist of fate, he died just two months
later.

   The Factory decided once more to ask the Company to seek a replacement,
but it was essentially a gesture of reconciliation and not of capitulation to
the Company's authority, dictated primarily by the fact that no suitable candidate for the chaplaincy was to be found in Russia. The Factory pointedly
stressed that the new chaplain's chief recommendation should be 'his own
individual merit – without interest or connection'. The Company was sensitive enough not to propose the still available Porter and in the election of a
successor for Pitt introduced the new procedure of requiring the candidates
to preach before the Court.[124] Thus the Company and the Factory settled

their differences, but the wounds were slow to heal. As late as 1824 a member of the Factory composed a memorandum which rehearsed the Factory's interpretation of the history of the St Petersburg chaplaincy and reiterated the view that the initiative in appointments rested with the Factory and not with the Company.[125] Although the Factory's claim as to its degree of independence, in law if not always in practice, was exaggerated, it is nonetheless symptomatic of the changed relationship between the parent body in London and the merchants in Russia which became increasingly apparent in the eighteenth century and which had its roots in the momentous Act of Parliament of 1698 which relaxed the restrictions on membership of the Company. The controversy over the chaplains was one of the most striking manifestations of this independence.

It remains necessary only to follow the fortunes of the Church building itself after its formal opening in 1754. By 1783 the Factory was obliged to draw attention to 'the great Increase in the Number of British Subjects within these few years past' and, considering the extension of the building a mere stop-gap measure, suggested that 'it would be much more eligible as well as creditable to our Country to have a regular new Church built either upon the present premises or upon any other Spot of Ground that may be found more convenient'. The Factory estimated that the cost of a new church would be in the region of 40,000 rubles 'according to a plan of Her Imperial Majesty's Architect', but foresaw that some years would pass before the necessary sum could be raised 'by a small Tax upon the Trade'.[126] The Petition was given favourable consideration at subsequent meetings of the Court of Assistants and it was resolved that the Company should contribute a maximum of £2,000.[127] The sum was duly raised but it was not until 1792 that the Factory requested the money and was refused 'until a proper place was found & the Building undertaken'.[128] Not until twenty years later, when the protracted controversy over the appointment of Pitt was finally settled, was the Company's agent in St Petersburg allowed to draw on the money collected for the new church in 1784. There was now, however, no mention of a new church, simply of effecting repairs and enlarging the existing chapel. The sum put at the disposal of the Factory was raised to £4,000 and in July 1814 Parliament made a special additional grant of £5,000.[129] 'With that munificent assistance', writes the author of the pamphlet of 1824, 'the Factory have enlarged the Church, Chaplain's residence, Library & other Offices and furnished them in a manner which reflects honour on the British nation.'

VII

Although Archangel and Moscow lost most of their British residents with the transfer of the British Factory in 1723, St Petersburg was not the sole beneficiary. Kronshtadt on the island of Kotlin in the Finnish Gulf developed into a large fortified town, the base of the Baltic Fleet and the destination of the hundreds of commercial vessels plying the Baltic during the ice-free months. The Russia Company had an agent at Kronshtadt, many British merchants maintained offices there and the sizable British community was swelled by hundreds of visiting British sailors and travellers. Early in the nineteenth century a visitor described the scene in detail:

Never, even in the Thames, did I observe a more extensive or denser forest of masts. It was gratifying to find that they were nearly all belonging to our country, and of course so many practical testimonies to our wealth, reputation and enterprise. Besides the crews of these vessels, every second person we saw was English; the beach, quays, streets, and taverns (their keepers and servants also of the same nation) were crowded with them, bustling to and fro with the characteristic hurry of commercial business, and occasionally, it must be confessed, dealing out to each other, or strangers unluckily in their way, some of the choicest flowers of nautical eloquence. This is not an occasional, but on the contrary, a constant scene all the months in which, from the absence of the ice, the Gulph of Finland is open to traders; so that the place might be taken for an English colony.[130]

He also notes that 'besides two or three Russian churches, is an English one with a resident Clergyman, supported by contributions from the merchants'.[131]

The origins of the Kronshtadt chaplaincy are unclear. Sadly, the register of births, marriages and deaths (with deaths predominating) is extant only from 1807 and the records of the Russia Company also lack vital information. The first references in the latter source date from the beginnings of Catherine's reign, but a reliable eighteenth-century account written by J. C. Grot, pastor to the Lutheran Church in St Petersburg, indicates that the first English chaplain at Kronshtadt was Robert Thomson, who served from 1728 until his death in 1745.[132] Thomson was thus appointed some months after Consett left St Petersburg and it must be surmised that he was able to attend to the spiritual needs of the British in both Kronshtadt and St Petersburg until Lernoult was appointed to St Petersburg in 1737. Grot also supplies the names of all the Kronshtadt chaplains down the century, but it is only Thomson's successor, Thomas Northcote, who is unknown from other sources. Northcote served from 1746 until 1748, when the chaplaincy fell vacant until the appointment of the Rev. Lewis Lewis (d. 1768) in 1761.

On 27 August 1760 the Court of Assistants of the Russia Company decided that the five-ruble levy on British ships for church dues should be split equally between St Petersburg and Kronshtadt.[133] On 16 March 1764 the Company ordered the Factory to pay Lewis 250 rubles as his entitlement from the ships' levy collected since 1760 and that the remaining money 'be appropriated for the Repairs Support & Maintenance of the British Chapel at Cronstadt'. At the same time the Company agreed to pay £100 towards the purchase of a piece of land on which to build a house for the chaplain.[134] It would thus appear that there was in existence a separate British chapel, but when and where it was built is unknown. A recent architectural history of Kronshtadt makes no mention of a British church at any period, but notes that from 1719 religious services were frequently held in private houses for 'foreigners of the Evangelical faith' and that in 1752 the wooden church of St Elizabeth was built to cater for their needs.[135] Two contemporary sources speak, however, of a separate British church in the 1780s, 'en faveur des gens de mer',[136] and this would seem to be the original dating from earlier in the century and not a recent structure. It is true that the Russia Company was moved to appoint Tooke to the Kronshtadt chaplaincy in 1771 (following a three-year gap) when it was informed that the Factory had at last acquired the necessary land for a new building. The Company requested 'an Estimate & Plan & Elevation of the intended New Church and Parsonage House designed to be built thereon' and an indication of how much the Factory was prepared to contribute.[137] But there the matter was to rest until 1802, when once again the Company was obliged to consider the position. In the interim Tooke and his successors had to make do as best they could.

Of the eight men who served as chaplains at Kronshtadt at various times during the eighteenth century little is known, with the exception of Tooke. Tooke was followed in 1774 by Henry Dixon, who was elected in preference to the Rev. William Gordon,[138] but on Dixon's retirement in 1777, Gordon tried again, this time successfully. Gordon was the son of a schoolmaster from Monymusk in Scotland; after his resigning the Kronshtadt post in 1783 on account of ill-health, Gordon was presented to livings at Darlington and then at Speldhurst in Kent, where he remained until his death in 1830 at the age of 84.[139] Gordon's replacement, the Rev. Samuel Furly (b. 1759) had graduated from Magdalene College, Cambridge, in 1781. He was briefly curate at Lanlivery in Cornwall before being ordained priest in April 1783 and leaving to take up the Kronshtadt chaplaincy. He served until 1792 and is last seen as vicar of Lostwithiel in Cornwall between 1804 and 1807.[140] He was succeeded at Kronshtadt by the Rev. Thomas Reed (1763–1805). More is known about Reed's death and the fate of his family than about the thirteen years he was at Kronshtadt. Frequently ill, Reed finally resigned at the end of 1804.[141] He was apparently offered a teaching position in Moscow, but died during the journey from St Petersburg, leaving his wife and two daughters destitute.[142]

During the nineteenth century, chaplaincies were established in other cities such as Moscow, Archangel, Riga and finally Odessa, when the British communities grew to sufficient size. The chaplaincy at Archangel seems to date from 1835, but there was an earlier attempt to persuade the Russia Company to appoint a chaplain. In a letter dated 12 December 1788, Edward

Blechynden informed the Company that the British subjects at Archangel were willing 'to grant a Sum of Money towards building a small place of Worship & the maintaining a British clergyman there'. The Company expressed caution and a decision was postponed 'until further Information is obtained'.[143] Whether or not such information came we do not know, but no action was taken for nearly half a century.

4

'DOCTORS ARE SCARCE AND GENERALLY SCOTCH'

The observation that doctors in Russia were 'scarce and generally Scotch' appeared in a book of travels published by one John Richard in London in 1778.[1] The fact that the book was apparently the production of an armchair traveller whose knowledge of Russia would seem to have been limited to the superficial perusal of other people's accounts and conversations with visiting Russians increases rather than minimises the interest of the remark. If Richard were reflecting British opinion about the state and composition of the Russian medical services, then that opinion reveals its usual compound of half-truth and fiction. Doctors, virtually all foreigners before the reign of Catherine II, were indeed scarce in Russia; the majority of them were German, however, and only a small minority British, of whom the most prominent and visible were indeed Scots. But it was not so in pre-Petrine Russia.

I

Within four years of Richard Chancellor's unsought visit to Moscow in 1553 there arrived the first English physician to practise at the Russian court. What precisely prompted Richard Standish to accompany the returning Russian ambassador, Osip Nepeia, is unknown, although several other Englishmen, including an apothecary Richard Elmes, were also attracted by the inducements offered. Certainly, they were royally treated by Ivan IV and it is recorded that 'there were given unto master Standish doctor in Phisick, and the rest of our men of our occupations, certaine furred gownes of branched velvet and gold, and some of red damaske, of which master Doctors gowne was furred with Sables'.[2] Standish had little time to enjoy his good fortune or to incur imperial wrath, for he died in 1559, less than two years after his arrival in Russia. Standish, nonetheless, has the honour of beginning what was to become a firm tradition of British doctors in Russian service, a tradition which throughout the rest of the sixteenth century and for much of the seventeenth was decidedly English and Cambridge.[3]

Standish, who had been a Fellow of Trinity College, Cambridge from

1548, was followed to Russia in 1567 by a former colleague Richard Reynolds (d. 1606), who despite being 'jolyvated with 200 roubles',[4] was to return to England within a year and enter the Church. Reynolds, incidentally, had also been accompanied by an apothecary, Thomas Carver, who stayed on in Moscow only to perish in the Muscovy Company's house which was gutted in the great fire of 1571. A decade later, it was another English apothecary, James Frencham, who was responsible for establishing the court pharmacy (*apteka*).[5] Frencham had travelled to Russia in 1581 with a third Fellow of Trinity and one who made a mark by his diplomatic as well as medical abilities. Robert Jacob (d. 1588) was Queen Elizabeth's own physician and sent by her in 1581 to attend Ivan IV. It was Jacob who was to suggest Lady Mary Hastings to the tsar as his next bride, but Ivan's death in 1584 brought an end to the project and the doctor's return to London. Two years later Elizabeth dispatched him again, this time with a midwife, to advise Tsar Fedor's consort Irina on matters gynaecological, recommending him as 'a man previously known to you, full of faith in the medical art in which he excels'.[6] Mark Ridley (d. 1624), another Cambridge man who also attended Queen Elizabeth, followed Jacob to Russia in 1594 and served for four years as physician both to the merchants of the Muscovy Company and to Tsar Fedor.

In the seventeenth century British doctors were much in evidence at the courts of the Romanovs.[7] Two are particularly noteworthy. Arthur Dee (1579–1651) spent some twelve years in Moscow as personal physician to Mikhail Fedorovich, before returning to England with his twelve children on the death of his wife in 1634. Dee was the son of the eminent astrologer and mathematician John Dee, whom the Russians at an earlier date had tried unsuccessfully to recruit. Arthur shared his father's alchemical interests and during his time in Moscow completed his *Fasciculus chemicus* (published in Basle in 1629). He enjoyed the favour of both tsar and patriarch and was richly rewarded for his skills.[8] Mikhail's son, Aleksei, also received the services of an English doctor over a period of nine years from 1660 and was equally generous in his appreciation. Samuel Collins (1619–70), who began his studies at Cambridge before completing them at Padua, is perhaps the best known of all the early British doctors in Russia, for he alone has left as a memorial of his visit a published account, which is much quoted by scholars and much prized by collectors of Russica. *The Present State of Russia, in a Letter to a Friend at London* was not, however, intended for publication and appeared posthumously and anonymously in 1671 in London. The 'friend' was the Hon. Robert Boyle, philosopher, scientist and leading member of the recently founded Royal Society, with whom Collins had been in correspondence over a number of years and had talked during a brief return to England in 1662–3. Some of the Russian material Collins communicated to Boyle was included in the latter's treatises on cold and air. Although Boyle seems not to have been immediately responsible for the publication of Collins's *Present State*, it was obviously not prepared without his participation. Internal evidence clearly shows that the work is a concoction from several letters, written over an extended period of time, rather than a single missive. Ranging widely beyond scientific subjects, Collins's little book offered English audiences salacious anecdotes and superior dismissals of Russian customs and mores.[9]

II

The tradition of the Romanov tsar and his British body-physician continued with Peter, although the person in question was soon to assume wider powers as a result of a reorganisation of the Russian medical services.[10] Already under the first Romanov, the old court pharmacy, founded on the initiative or, at least, with the participation of Frencham, was transformed into the Apothecaries' Department (*Aptekarskii prikaz*), which had high among its duties the verifying of the qualifications of the increasing number of foreign physicians and surgeons seeking positions in Russia. Its function as the central administrative body for medical affairs was strengthened under Peter. It was renamed the Apothecaries' Chancery and then the Medical Chancery (in 1721). At its head was the Archiater or chief physician, who invariably combined this position with that of principal body-physician to the tsar. It was a position of considerable responsibility, potential influence and consequent danger, as the careers of its relatively few holders exemplify. Several of the archiaters did much to promote the status of doctors in Russia, attempt a reorganisation of hospitals and services, and institute training for native Russians. By happy coincidence the first and last archiaters were Scots and the only British doctors to hold the post, which was abolished by Catherine II in 1762, some fifty-six years after Peter I had created it.

Robert Erskine (1677–1718) was a scion of a noble Scots family, son of Sir John Erskine of Alva and close relative of the Earl of Mar.[11] Apprenticed to a surgeon-apothecary in Edinburgh at the age of fifteen, he left for Paris in 1697 to continue his studies, passing through Holland at precisely the time Peter the Great was working in the Zaandam shipyards, but certainly not thinking of a future career in Russia. He returned to Holland to take his MD at Utrecht in 1700. Why Erskine decided to sail for Russia some four years later is unclear, when he not only had to his credit degrees and recent election to the Royal Society (30 November 1703) but also influential friends in the medical and scientific world, a growing reputation in London, and the offer of a good position. Perhaps the last came too late, for as he wrote to his mother on 14 June 1704, hours before his departure: 'If I dont like the Countrey I shall return to London very quickly, where a Gentleman has promis'd me two Hundred Pounds a year, since Munday last.'[12] It has been suggested that Erskine was invited to Moscow to become personal physician to Prince Menshikov; at all events, he appears already as 'Phisician to the Czar' in a list compiled by the British ambassador in 1705.[13] A year later, he was appointed to the newly created post of archiater and was well launched on an auspicious career. In February 1710 he was to write to his brother that 'I'm well and kindly entertean'd here and if 'twas not that I am so far from my Relations and good friends, I could leave my Bones in this cold climate.'[14] And he did.

Erskine spent the last fourteen years of his life in Russia, divided more or less equally between Moscow and St Petersburg, where he moved with the Russian court in 1712. A fellow countryman in Russian service wrote that 'amongst other obligations Russia owes this physician, it was he that put the great Imperial Dispensary in the excellent order it is in at present: it furnishes the armies and fleets, and the whole empire with drugs, and makes a great addition to the Czar's revenues'.[15] Work began in 1706 on providing the Apothecaries' Chancery with enlarged premises and facilities near the Kremlin to include a pharmacy, laboratory, library and adjoining herb gardens. Erskine was responsible for keeping the collections of natural history acquired by Peter during his first visit abroad and for increasing and cataloguing the Chancery's holdings of medicinal herbs, composing his own herbal (which has survived). After the move to the new capital, the collections were temporarily stored in both the Summer Palace and Erskine's own house, before the Kikin Palace was acquired in 1718 as the home of the new Kunstkammer. It was here that major new foreign collections, such as the exotic specimen and anatomical 'cabinets' of the Dutchmen Albert Seba and Frederik Ruysch, acquired in 1716 and 1717 respectively with Erskine's active participation, were brought. These were to become star attractions in the specially designed Kunstkammer on Vasilii Island, which was begun in the lifetimes of both Erskine and Peter but only opened in 1728. Erskine was also the driving force behind the creation of the St Petersburg botanical garden, laid out in 1714, appropriately enough, on Apothecaries' Island, and was its first superintendent.[16]

As body-physician Erskine travelled everywhere with Peter, most notably on the tsar's second foreign journey which took him to Denmark, Germany, Holland and France between February 1716 and October 1717. This was in many respects the climax of Erskine's career, although it threatened also to mark its nadir. At Gdansk/Danzig on 30 April/11 May 1716 the tsar, in an act of imperial munificence following the recent nuptials of his niece and the Duke of Mecklenburg-Schwerin, bestowed on Erskine the rank of actual state counsellor and with it, hereditary nobility.[17] At the same time he reconfirmed the titles of archiater and president of the medical chancery. The events that threatened to undermine Erskine's reputation were connected with the aftermath of the Jacobite rising of 1715, in which his elder brother, Sir John Erskine of Alva and other friends and relations were conspicuously involved. During the embassy's residence in Copenhagen, Erskine's help was solicited on behalf of his brother; more damagingly, he was specifically named as a reliable contact in correspondence between Swedish ministers in Paris, London and the Hague, who were conspiring to bring a reconciliation between the tsar and Charles XII and the overthrow of George I in favour of the Pretender. The intercepted correspondence was published by authority in London in 1717. Peter the Great, at that time in The Hague, denied all knowledge of the plot and declared his physician totally innocent of the charges. Both tsar and physician would seem to protest too much, although George I had the good grace to accept the explanation.[18] Erskine did not abandon his Jacobite friends and at the end of 1717 was certainly in correspondence with the Duke of Ormonde, travelling to Russia in the hope of arranging a marriage between the Pretender and a daughter or niece of the tsar.[19]

Erskine's last will and testament, drawn up on 29 November/10 December 1718, less than a month before he died, reveals his considerable wealth and possessions, including a house in Petersburg and two country estates.[20] There is also a reference to his library, money from the sale of which was to go to his heirs. Peter bought it for 3,000 rubles and it eventually became part of the library of the new Academy of Sciences. From 1714 until his death Erskine had added to his other responsibilities that of chief librarian of the collection of the Apothecaries' Chancery, which was also housed in the Summer Palace. Erskine's own books complement those of the basic collection, which was also to become part of the Academy library, and contributed some 2,300 titles. While about a fifth of Erskine's books are on natural history and the vast majority are on medical and scientific matters, others show his wide-ranging interests over many fields.[21]

An early writer on Russian medical matters, himself an English doctor in Russia, suggests, after discussing Erskine, that 'there is little mention made of British physicians, from the time of Peter the Great's death, to the accession of Catherine the Second'.[22] Since even James Mounsey, the last archiater, was omitted from his survey, it occasions no surprise that other British medical practitioners in Russia during that particular period – and there were quite a number – were omitted. There are omissions too in the list of 511 doctors practising in Russia throughout the eighteenth century which was compiled by a leading Russian authority.[23] In this very small total a mere nineteen are British (including one from Ireland) and of these, six (including Erskine and Mounsey) are indicated as practising in the first half of the century. The list is, however, of 'doctors', i.e. men who had studied at foreign universities and received their MD (Moscow University awarded its first medical degree only in 1794) and were then given their right to practise in Russia after examination by the Medical Chancery. Surgeons (*lekar'*), both Russian graduates of the surgical schools and foreigners without degrees, are excluded. There were, however, other British doctors – not only surgeons – who served in Russia during the reigns of Peter and his immediate successors, and the majority of these were Scots.

When Erskine arrived in Moscow there was already an English doctor there by the name of Richard Lee. It is possible that he was assigned to the British Factory but nothing is known of his activities. A copy of R. Platt's *The Natural History of Oxfordshire* (1677) – now in the Bodleian Library – bearing his signature on the title page and dated 'Moscow, 1715', merely corroborates the entry in the church register for 1706.[24] Erskine's own good offices were inevitably requested for fellow countrymen seeking their fortunes in Russia. Two instances of a specifically 'medical' nature are known, in which Erskine's assistance took a very similar form.

In 1713 Thomas Garvine, who a few years earlier had been apprenticed to a Glasgow surgeon, was himself already attached as a surgeon to 'the hospital at Petersbourg'.[25] Erskine's involvement led to Garvine's appointment as physician on an embassy which was to go to Peking in response to a request from the Chinese emperor for an able doctor and efficacious drugs (of an aphrodisiacal kind). The embassy, led by Lorenz Lange, a Swede in Russian service, set out from St Petersburg in August 1715 and arrived in the Chinese capital in November the following year. Lange's account of the embassy soon appeared in English as an appendix to F. C. Weber's well-known work on Peter's Russia, but nothing is said about Garvine's medical performance.[26] It was presumably successful and Garvine arrived back in St Petersburg at the beginning of April 1718. Within weeks he departed for Scotland and was last noted in 1738, when he was admitted as a surgeon-freeman by the Royal College of Physicians and Surgeons of Glasgow. He is caught, however, for posterity in a recently discovered painting, completed after his return to Scotland and depicting him proudly wearing the blue, fur-lined coat presented to him by the Chinese emperor.[27]

The other physician to be helped by Erskine left his portrait in words rather than in paint, for in 1763 John Bell of Antermony (1691–1780) published his *Travels from St. Petersburg in Russia, to Diverse Parts of Asia*, an account which even the demanding Dr Johnson found satisfying. It exemplifies those sturdy values that earned its author the name of 'honest John Bell', whose aim was to give 'the observations, which then appeared to me worth remarking, without attempting to embellish them, by taking any of the liberties of exaggeration, or invention, frequently imputed to travellers'.[28]

Bell had arrived in St Petersburg in 1714, anxious to see 'foreign parts' and armed with letters of introduction to Erskine. Erskine was soon able to recommend him to A. P. Volynskii (1689–1740), appointed by Peter to lead an embassy to Persia and seeking a 'a person who had some knowledge in physic and surgery'.[29] Bell concedes that he 'had employed some part of my time in those studies', but the extent of his medical training is not known. It is thought that he turned to medicine for some two years after completing his first degree course at Glasgow University in 1711.[30] At all events, Bell set out with his embassy on 15/26 June 1715 and in August met his 'friends, Messieurs Lange and Girvan' in Moscow on their way to China.[31] The account of the embassy to Persia, which lasted until the end of 1718, a few weeks after the death of his benefactor Erskine, is the first of four accounts that make up his book. Within months of his return to St Petersburg Bell was successful (through the good offices of Volynskii) in becoming a member of a new embassy to China under Lev Izmailov. In January 1722 the embassy returned to Moscow, where it found Peter and his court preparing to celebrate the end of the Great Northern War. Bell's third narrative covers the Derbent expedition, commenced in May 1722 and commanded by Peter himself. It was Erskine's successor as archiater and body-physician to the tsar, Johann Blumentrost, who invited Bell to take part. The expedition, lasting less than a year, provided Bell above all with an opportunity to praise Peter unstintingly, whose 'prudence, justice, and humanity, very much overbalanced his failings; which principally, if not solely, arose from his inclination to the fair sex'.[32] Sometime in 1723–4 Bell returned to Scotland, although this is nowhere mentioned in his book, and remained there for some ten years.

His Russian adventures were not yet, however, at an end. He returned in 1734 to act as personal secretary to Claudius Rondeau, the British minister at St Petersburg. And it is with the account of a fourth journey that he undertook in 1737–8 to Constantinople (on clandestine diplomatic business for the Russians who were then at war with the Turks, while openly acting for the British) that his book concludes. Bell's diplomatic career had a further high point when, following the death of Rondeau in 1739, he acted briefly as unofficial British chargé-d'affaires.[33] This diplomatic episode was followed by a commercial one, when Bell set himself up as a merchant in Constantinople, before finally returning to Scotland in 1746. The previous year at the age of fifty-five he had married Mary Peters, daughter of a prominent Scottish merchant in St Petersburg. Bell's last known visit to Russia was to visit his in-laws in 1751–3.[34] The remaining years of a long life were passed in quiet seclusion and good works at Antermony, near Glasgow. He tells his readers that he had no intention of publishing anything about Russia until prevailed upon by a friend around 1760, but what he produced was a great success with the public and eagerly subscribed to by many of his friends among the British in Russia. In 1779, a year before his death, he was still interested enough in things Russian and above all in the personality of Peter to gather together 'sundry Anecdotes' of his hero.[35]

Garvine and Bell represent two of the British surgeons active in Peter's reign, but there were others. The register of the English Church, which occasionally and succinctly indicates a man's profession at the time of his marriage or death, supplies the names of two more – John Goodson, who died in 1725 (and who indeed may have been the John Goodman noted in Moscow in 1705!) and James Selkirk, who in November 1726 captured as a bride one of the few available widows in the British community.[36] Selkirk was still active in the mid-1730s, when he is described as surgeon to the guards regiments in St Petersburg.[37] The ever-growing needs of the ever-growing army and navy demanded more and more medical personnel and many of the British surgeons inevitably were attached to either the navy and army hospitals, distinct from but sharing the same site in the capital, or to the fleet or regiments. Lewis Calderwood began his career in Russia in 1728 also as surgeon to a guards regiment in the capital, but within two years was appointed first surgeon to the court, which at that period was established at Moscow rather than St Petersburg. When Anna moved the court back to St Petersburg, Calderwood went too and remained there for a number of years. There is a glimpse of him in 1736 at Peterhof, where he had gone temporarily as duty court surgeon.[38] It is, however, for his outstanding contribution to teaching and medical administration that he (exceptionally as a practitioner without a MD) is accorded a place in Chistovich's list.[39] He moved to Moscow where he worked until his death in 1755 at the *Gofshpital'*, the great hospital and surgical school, founded in 1706 by Peter I's personal physician, the Dutchman Nicholaas Bidloo (d. 1735).

The rupture in Anglo-Russian diplomatic relations between 1720 and 1731 did not obviously dissuade Scots of Jacobite sympathies from seeking employment in Russia, but the 1730s and 1740s nevertheless brought an influx of British surgeons and physicians – Scots with a sprinkling of Irish. One of the reasons was clearly put in a letter that the Countess Erroll sent to Admiral Gordon on 23 June 1737, recommending Dr Francis Hay, a son of the Laird of Pitfour: 'he has been bred Chirugeon and Phisician and as our country is overstock'd with them of that Profession, he goes to try his fortune abroad and would willingly put himself under your protection'.[40] There is no further sighting of Hay; glimpses of other practitioners are sometimes just as fleeting. Mere names from the 1740s are the surgeons William Freer of Leith and William Mitchell, whose wife died in St Petersburg in 1749.[41] Of the two Irish doctors, Francis Dease was with the army during the Russo-Turkish war from 1738 until his death in 1741, while Dr Henry Smith was 'physician to the Guards' at the same period.[42] More is known about Smith's career, at least its beginning and end. He left London for St Petersburg in the summer of 1731 to be 'one of the Czarinna's physicians at Moscow' on the recommendation of the eminent Professor Hermann Boerhaave of Leyden and characterised by Lord Harrington in a letter to Rondeau as 'a person of whom I have heard a very good character, and therefore desire you to do him all the service you can at that court'.[43] Smith seems, indeed, to have flourished. He was to serve virtually twenty years before obtaining his discharge in March 1751 and returned to London, recommended by the British chaplain in St Petersburg as 'one of the very first Phisicians in this Country: Nor have his Skill and Pains been unrewarded, for it is well known that he has made his Fortune by his Profession'.[44] If he had, he was an exception and he must have had a lucrative private practice to supplement his official modest salary. 'Sollicitous to be rich' but without conspicuous success was Silvester Malloch, who in the late 1730s was principal surgeon at the port of Astrakhan and previously seems to have been in the employ of the Persians. In 1740 Malloch was replaced as principal surgeon at the Admiralty hospital with authority over all the naval, army and civil surgeons, but allowed to stay on in a subordinate position as chief surgeon to the army hospital.[45]

The purveyor of this information and more about Malloch was his successor as principal surgeon, his fellow countryman John Cook, who was the author of a book about his experiences in Russia. Almost a century after Cook arrived in Russia, another Scotsman who had flourished in Russian service and achieved the rank of general, Alexander Wilson, sent a copy to none other than Alexander Pushkin, commenting that Cook 'lived in Russia from 1736 to 1750 and according to his lights described all that he saw and all that happened to him. There is much that is trivial and a fair amount of gossip but his service under Prince Golitsyn, his journey with an embassy to Persia, his anecdotes about the learned, intelligent but amoral Tatishchev are worthy of some attention, as are many other details about a period about which little has been written.'[46] Perhaps inspired by Bell's success and to some extent imitating in his own preface Bell's protestations of truth and simplicity, Cook had printed at his own expense the two-volumed *Voyages and Travels through the Russian Empire, Tartary, and Part of the Kingdom of Persia* (Edinburgh, 1770). Cook was at that time a doctor in practice in Hamilton, but virtually all we know about him is contained in his book. Although written in a graceless style, the work is underestimated and unjustly ignored. It is a mine of information about many things, not least about the activities of the Scots and English in various parts of the Russian empire

during the reigns of Anna and Elizabeth; it is also a unique contemporary
source for the workings of the Medical Chancery and the trials and tribulations of medical practitioners in Russian service.

Cook's motives for going to Russia, where he arrived in July 1736, were
original, to say the least; having been very ill for a long period, 'I resolved
to go for Russia, hoping that the voyage, and change of air, would do me
some service, or at least that I could but die.'[47] He duly survived to tend the
sick instead for some fifteen years in Russia and even longer afterwards in
his native Scotland. It is not known where Cook received his initial medical
training, but he had no MD and therefore was appointed as a surgeon to
the naval hospital in St Petersburg. Cook provides an account of the history
of the Medical Chancery, paying fulsome tribute to Erskine; he explains the
various duties of physicians, surgeons, surgeons' mates and apothecaries (in
a passage subsequently quoted with admiration for Peter the Great's wisdom
by the *Critical Review*); and even more interestingly, he describes in detail
the army and navy hospitals in St Petersburg and their regimen.[48] He gives
amusing accounts of his meetings with the then archiater, the Livonian Dr
Johann Fischer, and of his examination by the Medical Chancery board:

I was brought to my examination before nine gentlemen, but only two of them could
speak Latin; however one of them interpreted to the rest, and from them to me. Having
finished it, they told me that they had little to say against my qualifications but that as
I seemed very young they could not think my experience could be great. They examined
me on anatomy, surgery, medicine and pharmacy. They proposed sundry diseases and
caused me write such medicines, &c. as I thought fit for such complaints, and very politely
dismissed me after they had kept me about three hours: however they gave me a few
glasses of wine, and allowed, nay entreated me to sit down.[49]

Despite differences of opinion about where and for how long he should serve,
Cook began work in the naval hospital. He was there, however, only for
some five months before being suddenly transferred in mid-March 1737 to
the 'galley-haven' at the western end of Vasilii Island, where there was a
small hospital for non-serious cases. In August of the same year he was commanded to join the Russian forces in the south and become physician to
Prince Mikhail Golitsyn and the regiment he commanded. Cook remained
near Voronezh with Golitsyn throughout the war against the Turks and,
although anxious to return to St Petersburg, then agreed to accompany the
prince and his family to Astrakhan, where they arrived on 5/16 March 1740.
The prince, who had been appointed governor of the city and wished to
retain Cook, persuaded the Medical Chancery to appoint him to the post of
the unfortunate Malloch. Cook was, nonetheless, allowed back to the capital,
where he had 'contracted a great kindness for Miss Hadderling', the daughter
of an English shipbuilder with the rank of captain in the Russian navy, and

on 6/17 August 1741 they were married in the English church.[50] He soon
thereafter returned to Astrakhan, where he supervised the building of the
naval hospital. In 1745 he resigned his post in order to join Golitsyn's
embassy to Persia. His last appointment was as surgeon-general to the army
commanded by Field Marshal Peter Lacy and stationed at Riga. Cook, whose
son was born in August 1748, was soon keen to return home with his family
but encountered great difficulty in obtaining his discharge. John Bell, who
had come to his rescue at the very beginning of his stay in Russia, re-appeared
again like a guardian angel to secure his release.[51] Cook arrived back in
Scotland in August 1751. The previous year he had been awarded his MD
(by testimonials) from the University of St Andrews and he settled down to
private practice (and a little authorship) until his death in 1790.[52]

Given that Cook mentions so many Scots, it is perhaps surprising that the
name of James Grieve is not among them, for although their paths did not
cross during their early years in Russia, they almost certainly did in the late
1740s. Grieve is worthy of note in several respects, not least because he was
the first in a long line of graduates from Edinburgh's famous medical school
to serve in Russia – his dissertation 'De morbis oculi' was accepted and his
diploma awarded on 5 June 1733.[53] A year later, on 19/30 May 1734 he
was given the right to practise in Russia. It was to the edge of Asia that he
was sent as physician to the Kazan' and Siberian Factories' Office. After some
years at Kazan', he moved to Orenburg, where he served from June 1742 to
1744, before receiving an appointment at the St Petersburg army hospital
and responsibility for the medical care of the guards regiments quartered in
the capital. On 12/23 October 1747 he was made the capital's City Physician
(shtadt-fizik). He attended the Empress Elizabeth and also briefly served as
deputy to the incumbent archiater. However, in 1751 he transferred to
Moscow as its City Physician. Chistovich, from whom these career details
are taken, then states that after nearly twenty-three years' service Grieve was
allowed to retire for reasons of 'old age and family circumstances' and left
for Scotland on 17/28 April 1757 with his wife and son James.[54] Grieve
seems, however, to have been back in Britain by the beginning of 1753. On
6 February of that year he was given licence to practise and admitted as a
Fellow of the Royal College of Physicians of Edinburgh.[55] About the same
time James Grieve became a Licentiate (only graduates of Oxford and Cambridge were made Fellows) of the Royal College of Physicians of London.[56]
And it would seem to be in London, or possibly Bath, that he practised. In
Bath Abbey there is a memorial plaque to his wife Elizabeth (heiress to the
famous Anglo-Dutch linen factory of Tames), who died on 22 March 1757,
aged thirty-three.[57]

It was during his time in London that Grieve began to translate S. P. Krasheninnikov's *Opisanie zemli Kamchatki* (Spb., 1754), a classic of Russian

exploration. It may well have appealed to Grieve by being connected with an expedition which set out during his own early years in Russia but, more likely, he saw the translation as his contribution to British knowledge of Russian natural history and geography. As such it continued that significant Scottish tradition, exemplified in Erskine, Bell and Cook and stretching on down the century. *The History of Kamtschatka* eventually appeared in London in 1763 and a second edition was published in Gloucester in 1764. It was favourably reviewed in the *Critical Review* but was heavily criticised by Professor August Schlözer, who reported to the Petersburg Academy of Sciences that the translation was bad and the translator 'had omitted whole sections, whole chapters even, because he didn't understand them'.[58] The book was prefaced by an 'Advertisement', in which occurs the statement that 'the gentleman, who undertook this Translation only for his amusement, was frequently interrupted in the course of the work by the necessary duty of his profession, and prevented from revising it before it went to the press by his sudden departure for Petersbourg'.[59] One can only speculate when or why Grieve suddenly went to Russia – it might well have been notification of the Empress Elizabeth's last illness or, less likely, simply a wish to see Joanna, his daughter by a first marriage (?), who in 1754 had married another Scots doctor, James Mounsey (1710–73), the last archiater. However, he was soon to return again: on 10/21 May 1762 Mounsey petitioned the Russian College of Foreign Affairs (or possibly the Russian ambassador in London) to seek suitable employment in Britain for Grieve on his leaving Russian service.[60]

If Grieve in fact returned soon afterwards, he would have been followed within weeks by his daughter and son-in-law, for on 17/28 July 1762 Peter III, Mounsey's patron, who had made him archiater soon after his accession, was murdered and within a week Catherine II had announced the archiater's retirement for reasons of ill-health. It is true that in June he was telling a friend in Scotland that 'my health is but invalitudinary and my offices will be too heavy for me long to bear, and I have long ago been much troubled with *hamewae* [homesickness]';[61] but it was not ill-health that made him scamper to depart and leave a friend to arrange the sale of his house;[62] or to build his mansion at Rammerscales near Lochmaben with an underground passage and provide each room with two doors.[63] Ten years after Mounsey's departure, another Scots doctor wrote to him from St Petersburg that 'if you had remained in the country for a few months longer that [sic] everything would have been cleared up, the false impressions been removed, and like gold tried in the fire, you would have shone brighter after the false smoke had dissipated. Do not imagine, however, my dear friend, that there was ever the smallest tache attempted to be thrown upon your integrity or your ability in your profession which was always incontroverted. The whole was nothing more than a court intrigue . . .'[64] Mounsey lived until 1773, unmolested and

9 Dr James Mounsey (1700?–73). Engraving by George Schmidt, 1762.

in regular receipt of his pension from Russia. He even went to Courland in
1771 for ten months at the request of the the duke, Peter Bühren, but did
not proceed to St Petersburg. It is interesting that Mounsey was seemingly
not content with the honours he had won in Russia and the fortune he had
undoubtedly amassed: in 1772 the Duke of Queensberry with the support
of Robert Keith, formerly British ambassador in Russia, petitioned for a
baronetcy for Mounsey for conduct 'singularly meritorious with regard to
this country'.[65] Mounsey died before the matter was settled.

John Cook recalls how he and Mounsey, when both were young surgeons
at the naval hospital in St Petersburg, correctly diagnosed a skull fracture

only to have their diagnosis dismissed by the chief surgeon – with fatal results.[66] Although also without a medical degree but with some general schooling at Edinburgh University, Mounsey arrived in Russia by a more conventional way than Cook: he was recruited by the Russian ambassador Prince Kantemir in July 1736 on a three-year contract.[67] They soon parted company, for although both joined the Russian forces fighting against the Turks, Cook was with Lacy's army, while Mounsey was with Munnich's by the Dnieper. A decisive moment in Mounsey's career was his meeting in 1737 with General James Keith, who received a serious knee wound shortly after-wards. Mounsey counselled against amputation and was allowed to accompany Keith to Paris, where the general recovered after a successful operation. For some reason Mounsey was not permitted to re-enter Russia and was dismissed. Returning to France he took his MD at Rheims and was eventually re-admitted to Russian service in 1741 and allowed to practise as a doctor. Over the next fifteen years Mounsey travelled widely with Russian armies, serving for instance with Keith in Finland in 1742–3 during the war against Sweden, until in 1756 he resigned his post and 'settled in Moscow where I had great reputation and no ungratefull Practice'.[68] He was then suddenly summoned to St Petersburg and 'without my desire or inclination' was appointed on 29 September/10 October 1760 body-physician to the empress with the rank of state counsellor. He attended her for a little over a year and was one of the three physicians to sign her death certificate. Peter III, by a decree of 20/31 January 1762, only increased Mounsey's glory by raising him to the rank of privy counsellor and giving him the offices of archiater and body-physician – offices which, as Mounsey assures his corre-spondent, were not always automatically granted to the same person. Indeed, 'First Physicians of other Monarchs may be great as to themselves by per-sonal merits but the greatness of their office and power bears no manner of comparison with mine.'[69] But it is not all vainglory; indeed, the suggestion that 'I can do more good to those under me than any of my Predecessors ever could' is more the measure of the man. During his short term as archiater he compiled important legislation affecting the status and duties of medical personnel, which Peter III signed and the Senate ratified. Doctors were given the ninth class in the Table of Ranks which conferred hereditary nobility and other medical practitioners were incorporated into the service hierarchy for the first time; salaries were increased and pensions provided. With the end of the Seven Years' War Mounsey was anxious to increase the number of practitioners in civil posts in the districts and *gubernii*. At the same time he was concerned that practitioners should be conscious of their responsibilities, including the need to research, record and publish their observations, and to this end he composed a special 'Memorandum' ('Nastavlenie vsem vracham ob ispolnenii lezhashchikh na nikh obiazannostei').[70]

Mounsey's recommendations derived from his own experience and aspirations. In addition to his career as practising surgeon, doctor and administrator, Mounsey pursued, whenever his duties allowed, scholarly and scientific interests which won him a considerable reputation in Britain. On 8 March 1750 he was elected a Fellow of the Royal Society; the recommendation spoke of his 'extensive Learning, Curiosity and knowledge in Natural History', which had already been demonstrated in a number of past communications.[71] Since 1747 Mounsey had been in regular correspondence with the polymath and scientist Henry Baker FRS, who published some of the letters in the Society's *Philosophical Transactions* and engineered Mounsey's election.[72] Their correspondence, which continued until 1771, covered many areas of botany, zoology and mineralogy, and Mounsey frequently sent him specimens of rocks and minerals and consignments of seeds.[73] Among the latter were seeds of the 'true' rhubarb, *Rheum palmatum*, dispatched to Baker in 1761. A year later, Mounsey brought seeds for Sir Alexander Dick, President of the Royal College of Physicians of Edinburgh, of which he was made an honorary fellow on 2 November 1762.[74] Seeds were given also to Professor John Hope, who successfully planted them in the Royal Botanical Gardens in Edinburgh; Hope subsequently sent an engraving of the plant and a report, acknowledging Mounsey's involvement, to the Royal Society, which was published in 1765 in its *Philosophical Transactions*.[75] The history of British interest in acquiring medicinal rhubarb from Tibet, Mongolia and China via Russia (which had a virtual monopoly in the rhubarb trade until 1782) and in cultivating it here is fascinating and complex. It involved not only Mounsey, to be sure, but other Britons in Russia, such as John Bell, as well as leading British botanists and gardeners. Nonetheless, the award of a gold medal by the Royal Society for the Encouragment of Arts on 17 January 1770 consolidated for his own time and for posterity the role and reputation of 'Rhubarb' Mounsey.[76]

The careers of Mounsey and Grieve take us briefly into the momentous reign of Catherine II. The careers of two other Scots do the same, but for longer periods. It is appropriate to delay discussion of Matthew Halliday, the longest serving of British doctors in eighteenth-century Russia, but mention might be made of North Vigor (d. 1769), who received his MD from Edinburgh with a thesis entitled 'De Diabete' in 1747. He was given a six-year contract from 26 June/7 July 1749 as a junior physician in the army hospital in St Petersburg. Returning to Britain in June 1755, he became a Fellow of the Royal College of Physicians of Edinburgh with right to practise from 7 November 1758.[77] At some stage he became a general practitioner at Bodmin in Cornwall, where Daniel Dumaresq, the former English chaplain and now near-neighbour, met him in 1763 and wrote that Vigor had no wish to return to Russia.[78] But return he did, probably attracted by news of the better conditions in Catherine's Russia: in 1766 he was re-admitted to Russian service with a salary of 1,600 rubles and the position of physician to the Empress's maids of honour.[79]

III

Although Mounsey was hurried on his way by Catherine, she could not fail to appreciate the sound sense that informed much that he had proposed as archiater. The post of archiater itself was abolished but its last holder's aim to enhance the standing of his profession was consolidated. On 12/23 November 1763 Catherine issued a decree establishing a Medical College to replace the old Medical Chancery. At its head was to be a president, an informed layman, who would be in charge of the administrative and business office and also preside over the medical department of seven voting medical practitioners, representing the various grades from doctor to apothecary. The duties of the college were principally to expand medical care for the population at large, to increase the number of native medical personnel and to supervise the working of apothecary shops. Further decrees followed in 1764 and subsequent years as Catherine attempted to improve medical facilities beyond the capital cities and to do battle with some of the great ills of the age – infant mortality, syphilis, smallpox and the plague.

The first president of the Medical College was Baron Aleksandr Cherkasov (1728–88), who consistently earned Catherine's benevolence, if not that of his medical associates. Cherkasov, however, has particular claims for attention in the present context because of the many years he spent studying at Cambridge and (probably) Edinburgh,[80] and also because he was involved in negotiations which led to one of the most publicised medical events of Catherine's reign – the inoculation against smallpox of the empress herself by an English physician.

Catherine had a great fear of smallpox and the ravages it caused, striking at all levels of society: she had seen its disfiguring effect on her late husband and she was moved by the recent death of the young fiancée of her minister Count Nikita Panin. Anxious for her own safety and for that of her son during an outbreak of smallpox in the capital in the early summer of 1768, 'I considered myself obliged to get away and travel with the Grand Duke from one place to another. This prompted me to put an end to such fears and by being inoculated against smallpox to relieve both myself and the whole country from worrying uncertainty.'[81] It was to England that she turned as the home of the most experienced and celebrated practitioners of variolation. This was a relatively time-hallowed technique of administering to a healthy person matter from the pustules of a smallpox patient in order to induce a mild form of the disease and was popularised in Europe earlier

10 Dr Thomas Dimsdale (1712–1800). Engraving by Ridley for the *European Magazine* (1802).

in the eighteenth century largely through the efforts of Lady Mary Wortley Montagu and was not unknown in Russia.[82] Although initially it appears that Daniel Sutton, the most famous inoculator of the day, was to be invited, the choice fell on the Quaker physician Thomas Dimsdale (1712–1800), who was then in practice in Hertford.[83]

Dimsdale came from a family of doctors and had himself worked for a while as a surgeon in Hertford between 1734 and 1745, before offering his services to the Duke of Cumberland's army fighting against the Jacobites. Subsequently, he took the degree of MD at Aberdeen in 1761 and became a fellow of the Royal College of Physicians of London. Dimsdale had long been particularly interested in smallpox inoculation, but it was an interest that was undoubtedly quickened and given direction by the work of Sutton and his sons from the late 1750s. His great debt to the Suttons was acknowledged in a work published in 1767, *The Present Method of Inoculating for the Small-Pox*, which presented his own variations on what was essentially the Suttonian method and reported in detail a number of experiments he had carried out. The book, which ran into four editions in the year of publication, brought him instant fame, and could hardly have come at a better time as far as his own future was concerned. Cherkasov learnt of Dimsdale's work and suggested to the Russian ambassador in London that Dimsdale be approached. Dimsdale showed some initial reluctance, and not without reason: he was well established, with family, reputation and fortune, and he was already fifty-six. But he was flattered and persuaded, and on 18 July 1768 he set out with his second son Nathaniel, aged twenty and a medical student at Edinburgh (where he returned to finish his degree in 1771).

Despite his understandable apprehension, shared to the full by George III who feared a major diplomatic crisis if things were to go wrong, Dimsdale found Catherine welcoming and confident. Quaker physician and Russian empress seemed to have got on like a house on fire, as John Thomson, a Scottish merchant in St Petersburg and apparently privy to their meetings, confided in a letter:

[H]e is an ingenious, plain, free man whose open manner I was sure would obtain a freedom with the great Lady. He spoke so bad French as not to be able to explain himself intelligibly and what she comprehended whet'd her desire to know all and comprehend what he said to reconsile her to the arduous undertaking she meant him to undertake unknowen yet to everybody. He had free access every morning to her bedchamber. They conversed for an hour or two together according to the time she could spare and he was not alter'd by sitting tete a tete on the canopy with her, nobody disturbed them [except] Count Orloff who often made the third on the canopy. She made the doctor speak to her in English what she could not comprehend in French and she comprehended it justly. She accustom'd herself to treat him like an old man and an intimate friend and bid him go away when her time came to prepare to see others. I was a faithfull secretary tho' the only person acquainted with their daily entretien. She was charmed with the simplicity of her doctor and she determined to be inoculated.[84]

Catherine herself suggested that 'by many successful experiments since his arrival he fully demonstrated his faultless skill in this art as a result of which I became even firmer in my intention'.[85] The operation took place in secrecy in St Petersburg on 12/23 October; the following day Catherine went to Tsarskoe Selo to follow Dimsdale's prescription of fresh air and exercise. Within ten days she released the news of her full recovery and returned to the capital to be present at a Te Deum on 2/13 November. It was in the evening of that day that the Grand Duke Paul was inoculated. On 22 November/3 December a great service of thanksgiving for the recovery of both empress and heir was held, at which the famed preacher Bishop Platon spoke of the 'assistance from Britain, that island of wisdom, courage, and virtue'[86] and on the same day the rewards bestowed on Dimsdale were also announced. The British ambassador swiftly sent off a dispatch to London, describing how Dimsdale had been made a baron, body-physician to the empress and a state counsellor with the rank of major-general and given a life pension of £500 per annum;[87] and the ambassador's wife, Lady Jane Cathcart, noted in her diary that 'Le qui fait encore beaucoup de plaisir à nous même avec toute la ville de Pétersbourg c'est que le Baron Dimsdale est un homme d'une purité des plus distingués en tout sens et qui portera tout ces torrents d'honr, de richesse, & de prosperité, avec une approbation universelle n'en étant lui même changé en rien.'[88] Dimsdale's success was extraordinary and he became part of Catherine's publicity drive (which also included popular prints) to spread the message of inoculation throughout her country.[89] The aristocracy and nobility, led by Grigorii Orlov and including whole families such as the Shcherbatovs, queued up to follow the empress' example and it is estimated that the Barons Dimsdale (for Nathaniel was created a Baron in his own right) inoculated some 140 persons over the next two months.[90] They also supervised the setting up of inoculation clinics in both the capitals.

The Dimsdales left for home in January 1769, loaded with sumptuous presents, including the portraits of Catherine, Paul, Panin and others that still adorn the family collection.[91] Before they left, Dimsdale had written a number of papers for Catherine, describing the treatment of both her and her son and and others matters connected with smallpox. These were subsequently published in Russian in 1770, together with a translation of Dimsdale's *Present Method* (1767). On his receipt of the Russian edition, Dimsdale wrote to the empress that he had been asked to publish an English edition of his writings and add a memoir of his visit to Russia; this he would not do without the empress' approval of the manuscript and he hoped equally for permission to dedicate the work to her.[92] The empress readily agreed and went on to review the progress of inoculation in Russia: 'et je crois assurer sans me tromper que l'inoculation n'a fait dans aucun pays des gagnes plus rapides qu'en Russie où elle date au juste que depuis votre voyage'.[93] In 1776 Dimsdale published two of the five papers or treatises as part of a volume entitled *Thoughts on General and Partial Inoculations*; only in 1781 did all the five treatises, prefaced by Dimsdale's detailed account of his 1768 visit, appear as *Tracts on Inoculation*. By this time Dimsdale was preparing for a second important if less momentous visit to Russia. In the interim his reputation in England had gone from strength to strength. He was elected to the Royal Society in March 1769, and in 1774, at the express command of the king, he had inoculated Chief Omiah, brought from the South Seas by a Captain Furneaux who had been on Captain Cook's great second circumnavigation. Dimsdale divided his time between Hertford, where he established a very successful Inoculation House, and London, where he became a partner in a banking firm, and entered Parliament as MP for Hertford in 1780. He maintained close links wiith the Russian embassy in London and was ever willing to offer assistance or carry out commissions for his Russian friends.

In 1781 the empress requested his return to Russia to inoculate Paul's sons, the Grand Dukes Alexander and Constantine, aged three and two respectively. It was to be a visit graphically chronicled in the recently published journal of his third wife, Elizabeth. Travelling out with the former chaplain to the British Factory, Dr John Glen King, the Dimsdales arrived in St Petersburg on 28 July/8 August and remained there until they moved three weeks later to Tsarskoe Selo. On 27 August/7 September Dimsdale inoculated Alexander and Constantine – 'Alexander had the Disorder very full for inoculation, tho' not one alarming Symptom ever appeared, the Baron was naturally anxious until it was over.'[94] They eventually left St Petersburg in mid-October and arrived at Dover on 30 November, a little over five months from the beginning of their outward journey.

Dimsdale was then in his seventieth year. His energies seemed nonetheless unabated, although in 1784 he underwent a successful operation for cataracts which had rendered him almost totally blind. His continuing devotion to Catherine, the true architect of his fame, is touchingly shown in a letter to her of 19 June 1783, in which he prescribes for her 'une Medecine plaisante agréable et sur pour les maux d'estomac causés par une indigestion qui peuvent revenir et qui demandent une purgation légère' as well as sending a pony for one of the Grand Dukes and 'deux petites jeunes Chiens de la Race de Canada qui sont fort à la Mode ici'.[95] In 1785 he made known to Catherine his willingness to travel to Russia for a third time to inoculate two of the Grand Duchesses, but perhaps fortunately for all parties, the offer was not taken up.[96] Dimsdale at last retired from medical practice, although he enjoyed a second term in Parliament until 1790, when he resigned his seat in favour of his son Nathaniel. It was in Hertford on 30 December 1800 that he died at the ripe old age of eighty-eight.

Dimsdale's work of inoculation in Russia was continued by a Scottish doctor, whose fate it has been to be largely forgotten both in his homeland and in his adopted country. Omitted from Chistovich's list and where mentioned in other sources, then invariably with inaccuracies and confusion,[97] Matthew Halliday (1732–1809) lays claim nonetheless to be among the longest serving British doctors in Russia. He hailed from the Scottish Borders, that fertile breeding ground of so many of his fellow practitioners in Russia, and seems to have gone to Russia in 1756 or thereabouts. He may have received some medical training at Edinburgh but no degree and therefore would have been engaged as a surgeon, probably at the army hospital in the capital. The first mention of him is in the English church register, when he married Mrs Anna Regina Kellerman on 18/29 December 1758.[98] Thereafter the entries of the births (and deaths) of their children, including triplet daughters only one of whom survived, are frequent and over a long period (1759–81). Sadly, there is no information about his work or position during the last years of Elizabeth's reign and the brief reign of Peter III. It is already two years into the reign of Catherine before a letter from Halliday to Mounsey reveals something of his activities and interests. He writes on 5/16 September 1764 from Brussels, the latest port-of-call in a European tour that had already taken him to Vienna and Paris. In the absence of other evidence, one can only speculate that Halliday had been sent, possibly by the recently established Medical College or by Catherine, to investigate latest developments in medicine. He refers to treatment for cancer in both Vienna and Paris, where he met Elizabeth's former body-physician, Antonio Ribeiro Sanchez. More significantly, for it provides both a pre-history and a context for the Dimsdale visit, he is much concerned with the controversy over the effectiveness of variolation: the Medical College, he suggests, was inclined in its favour, but Dr Gerard von Swieten, for instance, believed that more died than the inoculators admitted.

It is essentially as an inoculator and faithful exponent of the Dimsdale method that Halliday swims regularly into view during the remainder of Catherine's reign and, indeed, throughout that of Paul, whose confidence he demonstrably enjoyed. In 1768 Halliday was put in charge of the inoculation house or hospital established by Dimsdale on the Sanktpeterburgskaia (now Petrogradskaia) Side of the city and he remained there, both living and working, well into the 1790s. As smallpox struck both high and lowly, Halliday inoculated grand dukes and serfs. A notice in the *St Petersburg News* in 1791 announced, for example, that Dr Halliday would be in attendance daily from 6 p.m. to 11 p.m. from 15 March and would treat patients without fee.[100] It was Halliday who took on responsibility for inoculating the seemingly endless stream of children of Paul and Maria Fedorovna: thus, he, Dimsdale's offer notwithstanding, inoculated in 1786 the Grand Duchesses Aleksandra and Elena, preferring not to treat Maria until she was more than two years old; in 1799 he was richly rewarded by the Tsar Paul with 20,000 rubles and the rank of state counsellor for the inoculation of Grand Duke Nicholas and the Grand Duchess Anna; finally, on 29 March/9 April 1800 'Adidé' inoculated the infant Grand Duke Michael.[101] Maria Fedorovna was always particularly alive to the dangers of smallpox: in early 1789 she was worried about the outbreak among the peasants at Pavlovsk and sent Halliday to inspect the children: 'And if it is necessary to inoculate them,' she instructed her bailiff, 'follow his instructions and persuade their parents to agree, making them understand that We have two children who have not yet been inoculated and who will truly be in danger, if the epidemic persists at Pavlovsk.'[102]

In 1798 Edward Jenner after many years of experiment and investigation published his discovery of cowpox vaccination. Halliday was not long in getting news of this revolutionary development and managed to obtain vaccine in the autumn of 1800. Halliday thus became one of the first physicians in Russia to carry out vaccinations, even if initially unsuccessful:

Je ne sçais pas, si Votre Excellence, avoit entendu parler de la Vaccine ou Petite-Vérole des Vaches, tant vanté en Angleterre. Par hazard, j'en ai recu de la matière cette automne, dont j'ai fait part à S.M. l'Impératrice, désirant qu'Elle ordonnerait d'en faire l'éprouve dans une des Instituts sous ses ordres. S.M.I. a eu la bonté de m'écrire de Gatchina qu'Elle en avoit informé S. M. l'Empéreur qui a bien voulu ordonner, que je fasse l'essai sur des Enfans trouvés, tirés des Villages. C'est ce que j'ai fait, sans succès pourtant, la matière étant trop vieille et trop sèche. S. M. l'Impératrice ayant au Coeur le bien de ces pauvres Orphelins, aussi bien que du Publique en général, a donné ses ordres aux Chirugiens de la Campagne dont Elle en a plusieurs, d'examiner les Vaches à présent et à l'avenir, pour sçavoir si on pourroit en trouver quelques propres pour communiquer la Virus Vaccine; en telle Cas je dois en faire la besogne, ce que je ferai avec le plus grand plaisir, à obeir les ordres de S.M.I.[103]

There is one other moment in Halliday's career that demands attention. At the end of 1771 the *Scots Magazine* informed its readers that 'Dr James's powder had been administered in the pestilential fever at Moscow, with the greatest success; and that Mr Haliday, an English physician, has been sent thither from Petersburg, with a large quantity for the relief of those who are afflicted.'[104] The dreaded bubonic plague had spread from the Danubian principalities where the Russian and Turkish armies had been locked in war since 1768 and arrived in Moscow with devastating effect at the end of 1770. In September of the following year there occurred the riots that led to the death of Archbishop Amvrosii and the dispatch from the capital of Prince Grigorii Orlov to restore order. About a month later Halliday arrived in the capital, sent obviously not merely as a courier with supplies of the antimonial nostrum known as Dr James's Powders in which the Medical College had unfounded confidence, but also possibly because many believed that smallpox and bubonic plague were closely related and might therefore be similarly treated. At all events, soon after Halliday arrived in Moscow, Orlov judged that his services were more urgently needed in Iaroslavl', where plague deaths were rising sharply, and sent him there on 8/19 November 1771. Halliday encountered confusion and bureaucratic hindrance and denounced the local authorities to the Plague Commission. However, the onset of winter curtailed the spread of the epidemic and Halliday was able to confirm the end of the plague in Iaroslavl' and the surrounding districts on 19/30 January 1772. He returned to Moscow a few weeks later, but in March he was again dispatched to Nizhnii Novgorod to report on the situation: the epidemic was already at an end, but he remained there until the autumn.[105]

Assessments of Halliday as a person, insofar as they are available, seem to swing from the somewhat negative to the warm and appreciative. Two of his countrymen, in letters to Mounsey at the time Halliday was in Iaroslavl', comment on his quick temper, 'his narrow way of thinking' and his 'more prudence than judgement'.[106] On the other hand, he had a staunch supporter in Count Semen Vorontsov, whom he had met during his early years in Russia. Vorontsov was godfather of Halliday's third son Michael (b. 1765) and Halliday had inoculated Vorontsov's son Mikhail. For Vorontsov, Halliday was 'mon ancien ami', 'ce digne vieillard'; indeed, 'toute cette famille Haliday est bonne et honnête: c'est une excellente race, et on peut se fier à elle'.[107] Halliday's sons all prospered, particularly Michael, who rose to be a vice-admiral in the Royal Navy, and the eldest, William (b. 1759), who became a doctor. William studied at Edinburgh (1780) and London, before taking his MD at Tubingen in 1785. Given the right to practise by the Medical College later that year, he served as a provincial doctor in the town of Ryl'sk, near Kursk, until 1792 when he moved to Moscow. He practised there privately and under contract for many years and is mentioned in the accounts and letters of a number of British travellers as a pillar of the small British community – and as a strong advocate of James's Powders.[108] The head of the family died in St Petersburg on 24 February/7 March 1809, aged seventy-seven. Despite all his rewards, he characterised himself as 'un pauvre vieillard, qui a une nombreuse Famille' in 1803, when threatened apparently with eviction from the house officially provided for him and in which he had lived for many years.[109] Nevertheless, he also seems to have owned some land and possibly a house on the island to the west of Vasilii Island towards the Gulf of Finland, now known as the Island of the Decembrists. It is this island which, it is commonly asserted, under a corrupted form of his name, Golodai, perpetuated his link with the city until 1926.

If Halliday is among the least sung of British doctors in Catherine's Russia, John Rogerson (1741–1823) is undoubtedly the most celebrated.[110] Halliday's and Rogerson's fathers farmed side by side at Lochbrow, not far from Lochmaben and indeed not far from Skipmyre, where Mounsey was born. Mounsey was related to Rogerson through the latter's mother and it was with letters of recommendation from Mounsey that Rogerson left for Russia in 1766. The previous year he had completed his MD at Edinburgh with a thesis entitled 'De morbis infantum'. It would also seem that he had married and possibly lost a wife in childbirth, for he left behind a son John, who also received his MD at Edinburgh in 1786, for which event his father made his first return visit from Russia.[111]

Although granted leave to practise on 5/16 September 1766, Rogerson seems initially to have had no specific post. He is known, however, to have been instructed in the art of inoculation by Dimsdale and carried out several operations on his behalf. According to the British ambassador, it was on Dimsdale's recommendation following North Vigor's death that Rogerson was appointed a court physician in February 1769.[112] Rogerson, however, seemed discontented with his lot, writing to Mounsey some three years later that 'tho' I have more than my brethren may think my just share of, it is no object for a man to promise his fortune upon', although a member of the British community believed him 'farther advanced than I ever knew any at his age and short practise'.[113] The same writer revealed a sure understanding of the extraordinarily relaxed relationship that already existed between the Russian empress and the young Rogerson: 'she consults him occasionally about her health and follows his advice and takes what he prescribes, but she much oftner, most graciously entertains him with other discourse, and all about her pay him the respect of a body phisician, and tho' he wisely courts none of them, the courtiers do the same and his practise increases'. The official appointment of Rogerson as body-physician duly came on 18/29 January 1776 and with it the rank of actual state counsellor and a salary of 4,000 rubles. Rogerson would complain no more. Shortly before her death, Catherine rewarded him for his long years of devoted service with an estate near Minsk, which had over 1,500 serfs and brought in an annual income of 6,000 rubles to add to his salary and the gifts he received from grateful patients. If the Cambridge don Edward Daniel Clarke is to be believed, these gifts were usually one and the same gold snuff-box, which Rogerson would sell to a prominent jeweller, who in turn would suggest it as an eminently suitable gift for anyone wishing to reward the doctor for his services.[114] On the day of Paul's coronation Rogerson was raised to the rank of privy counsellor, but increasingly his thoughts turned to retirement. He was nonetheless treated graciously by both Paul and Alexander and he continued to live and practise in Russia until 1816. He had always maintained close links with his homeland and had returned to Scotland on at least three occasions, buying in 1804 the mansion of Dumcrieff, where he spent the seven years of his retirement and where he died.

During his long career Rogerson treated many of the leading figures in St Petersburg society and in the British community, and the references to him as a doctor are overwhelmingly positive. Princess Dashkova, for example, relates in her memoirs how 'Mr Rogerson's great skill and care gave me back my son' after a dangerous fever in 1772, and ten years later again credited him with saving both herself and her son during serious illnesses.[115] The improvement in Nikita Panin's health in 1781 was attributed to Rogerson's 'skill and resourcefulness', and even the British and French diplomatic representatives could agree that he was 'un fort bon medecin'.[116] On the other hand, Rogerson appears as a prominent but powerless figure at many death scenes: of Natal'ia Alekseevna, Paul's first wife, in 1776; of A. D. Lanskoi, Catherine's favourite, in 1784; of Admiral Greig at Revel in 1788; of Baron Sutherland, the court banker, in 1791; and of Catherine herself in 1796.[117] His two panaceas seem to have been blood-letting and laxatives with the occasional judicious prescription of James's Powders. Of all his patients, Catherine remained the most sceptical and for the most part she succeeded in keeping him at arm's length during the many years he attended her, although he managed the odd blood-letting. Her secretary A. V. Khrapovit-skii records one typical exchange in 1788: '[The empress] unwell. Rogerson mixed a laxative in her drink. She complained . . .', but at least the next morning, 'on awakening She said that "on n'a plus de barre sur la poi-trine!" '[118] Catherine was fond of remarking that she had read her Molière and one of her letters to Baron Grimm reveals the sort of attack she launched against the unfortunate Scot: 'Je lui ai dit qu'aucun médécin ne pouvait ni savait guérir même la piqure d'une punaise . . . Je ne me suis apaisée que lorsqu'il eut convenu que lui et tous ces confrères étaient des ignorants qui ne savaient guérir personne.'[119]

Possibly as a result of Catherine's continual taunts, Rogerson seems to have held no great brief for himself as a physician. Unlike many of his colleagues he also did not seek a reputation as a scholar and wrote no learned papers on either medical or scientific matters. Nevertheless, tributes to him even in these areas are not difficult to find: Colonel Francisco de Miranda, who met him in Kiev at the time of the empress' visit to the Crimea, considered him 'a learned man'; a Russian contemporary affirmed that 'he has much experience and, in addition to his knowledge of medicine, enjoys the reputation of a scholar'.[120] He was, of course, more than prepared to send seeds and plants and minerals, and to promote Anglo-Russian scholarly interchange. A notable instance of the latter is revealed in his letters of 1773 and 1776 to the historian and Principal of Edinburgh University, William Robertson, in which he speaks of his efforts to bring Robertson's works to the attention of the empress and to gain her permission for the use of documents relating to Russian discoveries in America.[121] His influential position at the Russian court brought in its wake election to leading learned societies both in Russia and in Britain. In December 1776 he became the first Briton to be elected to the Russian Academy of Sciences. Already a member of the Edinburgh Philosophical Society (later the Royal Society of Edinburgh), he was elected in 1779 to the Royal Society after being recommended by Dimsdale and others as 'a Gentleman distinguished for his proficiency in several branches of natural knowledge' and, more revealingly, as 'likely both from his talents & situation to become an usefull & valuable Member'.

Finally, in December 1782, he became an Honorary Fellow of the Royal College of Physicians of Edinburgh.[122]

Catherine, seeing Rogerson in the Hermitage one day, said to her secretary that 'he was gathering information'.[123] He was, indeed, well-informed. Without irony, a friend wrote that 'Rogerson, qui connait mieux que personne tout ce qui se fait à notre cour, dans notre capitale, dans nos provinces, dans nos maisons, dans nos familles, a du vous donner les meilleurs renseignements possibles sur notre pays.'[124] Rogerson had entrée to almost all the fashionable homes in the capital, both as doctor and as friend. He was a good friend and certainly did not betray the confidences of his imperial mistress or lose the respect of those who trusted him, such as the Vorontsov clan. Nevertheless, his position and activities and indeed some of his 'weaknesses' inevitably made him the target of anecdotes and malicious gossip. Some of the stories, touching on his pronunciation of Russian, his somewhat ungainly and comic appearance, his spontaneous gestures that led him, on one occasion, to slap Catherine on the back for taking the medicine he had prescribed, are affectionate and amusing. Most notoriously and groundlessly, he was said to examine Catherine's potential favourites to see they were free from disease. Enemies liked to dwell on his political intriguing: the Comte de Ségur said on one occasion that 'As he dabbles in politics as much as in medicine, and it is through his hands that bribes are supposed to pass, I cannot but be pleased at his absence', while Fedor Golovkin sourly recorded that 'his position, which demanded knowledge, and his gambling for high stakes opened all doors. He was even employed for secret negotiations with Vienna and other courts, and politics in general was after gambling his dominant passion.'[125] His love of gambling is well attested and perhaps the most famous incident occurred during a game at Count Bezborodko's during which the doctor continually revoked but always blamed his partners. Bezborodko thereupon sought the empress' permission to fire off a cannon in the grounds whenever Rogerson subsequently revoked, an action which almost led to an unseemly brawl.[126]

A series of sixty-four letters which Rogerson sent to Semen Vorontsov in London over the period 1791–1819 survives as the most substantial legacy he left for posterity, but survives only because Vorontsov ignored his plea that 'Je compte que mes lettres lues, vous les jetez dans le feu.'[127] The letters, at times guarded when transmitted openly, but usually unconstrained, reveal him as no idle intriguer, but a man of considerable integrity, intellect and knowledge; they demonstrate his attachment to friends, his support for just causes, his considered opinions on a wide range of topics, from monetary reform to problems of education, from international negotiations to aspects of relations between Russia and Great Britain. Like his correspondent, Rogerson was a committed 'Anglo-Russian'. One aspect of the letters which does him no little credit is his lasting devotion to Catherine. In the first letter he wrote after her death, he believed that 'les grandes, rares et admirables qualites de Catherine paraissent a present dans tout leur eclat. Je n'ai rien à regretter qu'elle. Je regarde ma carrière comme finie; je mourrais si je reprendrais un nouveau service. Le sien c'était la liberté la plus parfaite.' Her death remained a deep, haunting tragedy: 'Je suis encore trop frappé de la mort de l'Impératrice: tout me rappelle encore cette fatale journée.'[128]

In June 1769, nearly three years after his arrival in St Petersburg, Rogerson was joined by a former fellow-student from Edinburgh, Matthew Guthrie (1743–1807). Guthrie likewise came with letters of recommendation from Mounsey to members of the British Factory, as well as a letter from a James Wright of Stirling to the British ambassador, Lord Cathcart, which provides some new biographical detail.

The bearer Mr Guthrie was bred a Surgeon at Edinburgh and has been practising in that way for some time in London and is reckond to know his business well he is nephew to Mr Guthrie the Historian at London his friends have advisd him to goe to St Petersburgh where they hear there is great demand for people of his profession . . . he is a pretty sort of man and good of his business & have taken out his degrees both at Edinb and entred a regular Surgeon in London.[129]

Guthrie had not in fact completed his studies at Edinburgh and wisely decided to return soon afterwards to Scotland, where he received his doctor's diploma from the University of St Andrews in April 1770. Possibly arriving back in Russia with Admiral Knowles and his family early in 1771, Guthrie was certainly with Knowles the following year and seems to have been the unnamed surgeon appointed to accompany the admiral and his staff on their 'secret' expedition to Moldavia in February.[130] Guthrie remained with Rumiantsev's army in the south until the cessation of hostilities; his involvement with questions of quarantine and plague prevention became the subject of a subsequent scholarly paper, in which he also mentions another British surgeon, George Smyth, who had apparently survived two attacks of the plague.[131] Back in St Petersburg, Guthrie only received the right to practise in 1778 and was appointed chief physician to the Noble Land Cadet Corps in March, a post which he kept until his death and which allowed him ample time to devote to his scholarly pursuits.[132]

In 1781 Guthrie married Marie Dunant (d. 1800), a Frenchwoman (née Romaud-Survesnes) who had been acting Directress of the Smol'nyi Institute for Young Noblewomen and was recently widowed.[133] Two of the three daughters of the marriage survived childhood and made excellent matches. The elder of the two, Anastasia Jessy (1782–1855), married the fifty-eight-year-old Charles Gascoigne in 1797 (whose brilliant career in Russia is charted in a later chapter); Anastasia won a reputation for her beauty and

11 Dr Matthew Guthrie (1743–1807). Silhouette by unknown artist.

for being mistress of the father of Paul's favourite, Anna Lopukhina. She was one of three women described by the malicious pen of Count Golovkin as being particularly influential at court in Paul's reign.[134] Perhaps a consequence of that influence was Paul's special decree of 31 December OS 1797, which gave Guthrie an extra 500 rubles a year and the rank of state counsellor.[135] It was an elevation that obviously delighted him and when Sir John Carr, Byron's 'Green Erin's knight and Europe's wandering star', visited him in 1804, he was quick to inform him of his own 'hat and feathers, and the rank of a general'. Carr rhapsodised about this 'gentleman of the most aimiable manners, a philosopher, and well known to the world for his various scientific and literary productions', but inevitably others were not so impressed. A decade earlier, a young Tory buck, Lionel Colmore (1765–1807), thought him 'the most pompous man I have ever met with; in person and manners the very counterpart of Lishmahago in *Humphry Clinker*, and a perfect Quixote in physick and mineralogy'.[136] Colmore, nevertheless, was quite happy to exploit Guthrie to obtain books for a friend. Guthrie, indeed, was ever ready to offer his services. His name appears in the letters, diaries, journals, published and unpublished, of numerous visitors, mainly but not exclusively British and many of whom arrived with letters of introduction to him. Sir John Sinclair (MP and Scottish improver), Baroness Dimsdale (third wife of the Baron), John Howard (prison reformer), James Trevenen and Samuel Bentham (naval officers), John Parkinson and William Coxe (Oxbridge dons and travelling tutors) are names to provide a mere sample. One person who responded wholeheartedly to the Guthries' hospitality was the Venezuelan Francisco de Miranda. His diary in the summer of 1787 lists endless teas, dinners, 'long literary conversations', arranging of loans, introductions, all steming from 'mi unico confidencial amigo el Dr Guthrie'.[137]

Earlier in this chapter it was suggested that Rogerson received his scholarly accolades less for his scholarly activities than for his position of influence. In contrast, Guthrie achieved his by dint of unrelenting correspondence, productivity and lobbying. He loved 'communicating' and there were few British societies of note to escape his approaches. In St Petersburg he was a founder member of the New Music Society from 1778. In the previous year he had become the first Briton to be elected to the Imperial Free Economic Society (followed two years later by Arthur Young), but the Academy of Sciences eluded him.[138] Not so the Royal Society, to which he was elected on 11 April 1782 during a last visit to Britain. He was made a corresponding member of the Society of Antiquaries of Scotland on 25 June of the same year. In 1783 he became a founder ordinary foreign member of the Royal Society of Scotland – like Rogerson, he had belonged to the earlier Philosophical Society. He soon became a member of the Philosophical Society of Manchester; and finally, 1792 brought him corresponding membership of the Society of Arts, the Society of Antiquaries of London and the Society for Promoting Natural History.[139] Behind these elections and beyond is a long list of publications, stretching from 1776 (when a letter from Guthrie to Dr John Hope about a variety of botanical, zoological and mineralogical matters was printed by Andrew Duncan in *Medical and Philosophical Commentaries*) to 1802, when his wife's *Tour Performed in the Years 1795–6, through the Taurida, or Crimea* appeared in London under his 'editorship'. Within the confines of the eighteenth century Guthrie's work represents the culmination of that transference of scientific, geological, geographical, botanical and zoological knowledge from Russia to Great Britain, initiated by Erskine and continued by a whole line of Scottish doctors – and English clerics. The bibliography of Guthrie's printed works and manuscripts, which Dr Jessie Sweet appended to her specific study of Guthrie as a gemmologist, provides a clear statement of the range of Guthrie's interests and his importance as a scientific

opulariser and communicator – as emphasised in the specific area of medicinal plants in yet another article by Appleby.[140] There are, however, areas
other than the strictly scientific into which Guthrie ventured and which
deserve particular attention.

At the end of December 1790 there appeared in Edinburgh a new journal
entitled *The Bee, or Literary Weekly Intelligencer*; its editor, James Anderson, laid out an ambitious diet of pleasantly useful compositions and
expressed the wish to establish 'a friendly literary intercourse among all
nations' with the cooperation of talented correspondents at home and
abroad.[141] The prospectus was tailor-made for Guthrie, who made his debut
under the pseudonym 'Arcticus' in April 1792 and appeared in all subsequent
volumes but one until *The Bee* closed at the beginning of 1794. From volume
XII to the final volume XVIII Arcticus established himself as the journal's
major contributor as well as acting as intermediary for other correspondents
from Russia, pre-eminent among whom was Professor P. S. Pallas. Guthrie
was responsible for no less than fifty contributions, made up of his own
original compositions but mostly of other people's that he had translated
and edited. Some of his original pieces had nothing to do with Russia and
reveal their author as a contented, prosy paterfamilias, waxing lyrical about
the splendid British constitution and cautioning against 'the florid display of
new lights', emanating from across the Channel; many of the pieces are in
the popular science mould, usefully explaining experiments and discoveries
by men such as Lowitz and Pallas and providing descriptive tables of Russian
birds (in collaboration with Pallas) and of gemstones (from his own
collection). It is, however, the items of a historico-biographical, literary and
ethnographic-folkloric nature that have particular significance, partly as
an indication of the development of Guthrie's interests and partly for their
novelty in a British context.

Guthrie supplied a number of historical anecdotes and pieces about Peter
the Great, including an accomplished translation of Mikhail Lomonosov's
oration on Peter (1755). Guthrie was not only contributing to the British
cult of Peter but also providing the British public with a rare translation of
a Russian literary work. He went on to translate as 'Ivan Czarowitz, Or the
Rose Without Prickles That Stings Not' a little allegorical tale by Catherine
the Great herself, which was to reach a wider audience by also being published as a separate book in 1793. Guthrie was later to translate Catherine's
opera *Nachal'noe upravlenie Olega* (1787), which he was anxious to publish
in Britain but which remained in manuscript. His translation of Archbishop
Platon's oration on the coronation of Alexander I did, however, appear in
a London newspaper in 1802.[142] The descriptions of village crafts, such as
the preparation of vegetable dyes, and of popular superstitions, represented
in three items in *The Bee*, were to lead Guthrie into more searching investi-

THE BEE,

OR

LITERARY WEEKLY INTELLIGENCER,

CONSISTING OF

ORIGINAL PIECES AND SELECTIONS FROM PERFORMANCES
OF MERIT, FOREIGN AND DOMESTIC :

A WORK CALCULATED TO DISSEMINATE USEFUL KNOWLEDGE
AMONG ALL RANKS OF PEOPLE AT A SMALL EXPENCE,

BY

JAMES ANDERSON, LL.D.
F.R.S. F.A.S. S.

Honorary Member of the Society of Arts, Agriculture, &c. at BATH ;
of the Philosophical, and of the Agricultural Societies in MAN-
CHESTER ; *of the Society for promoting Natural History,* LONDON ;
of the Literary and Philosophical Society, NEWCASTLE ; *of
the academy of arts, sciences, and belles lettres,* DIJON ; *of the
Royal Society of Agriculture and Rural Economy,* ST PETERSBURGH ;
correspondent member of the Royal Society of Agriculture,
PARIS ; *and author of several performances.*

VOLUME SEVENTEENTH

APIS MATINÆ MORE MODOQUE.   HORACE

EDINBURGH :
PRINTED FOR THE EDITOR
M,DCC,XCIII—VOL. V.
FINE PAPER.

12 *The Bee*, edited by James Anderson, vol. XVII (Edinburgh, 1793), title page.
Contains contributions by 'Arcticus' (Matthew Guthrie).

gations into the life and customs of the Russian village. The fruit of his research was 'Noctes Rossicae, or Russian Evening Recreations', a huge work divided into ten 'dissertations', covering dance, song, musical instruments, games, rites, and early Russian history, and remaining in manuscript.[143] Fortunately, the first five, and most interesting, chapters were published in St Petersburg in 1795 as *Dissertations sur les antiquités de Russie*, with a long subtitle spelling out the subject matter as well as the author's intention to establish links between the beliefs and traditions of the Russians and the Ancient Greeks. Its appearance in French and in St Petersburg gave it a wider impact and influence than would have been the case with an English version. Although the British public's knowledge of what Guthrie was propounding was thereby limited to reviews, the work found a sympathetic response in Russia itself among historians, writers and poets, Derzhavin and Pushkin included.[144]

Among the items Guthrie sent to *The Bee* was an obituary of Admiral Greig, who had died during the recent Russo-Swedish war. Although Rogerson was in attendance when he died, his physician on board ship was Dr Robert Simpson. It was Simpson who penned a series of moving letters to Sarah Greig, reporting on the admiral's fight against the fever that had struck him on 23 September/4 October and to which he succumbed on 15/26 October 1788.[145] Simpson had been recruited into Russian service by Greig as a surgeon for the frigate *Natal'ia* in 1774 in the latter stages of the Mediterranean campaign. In February 1777 he received the right to practise and was officially assigned to the Baltic fleet as a surgeon. He then apparently resigned, but was re-engaged at the outbreak of hostilities against the Swedes and assigned to the *Rostislav*. His subsequent naval career was as senior physician at the Kronshtadt naval hospital, broken only by his attending Count Ivan Chernyshev on a visit to Vienna, until his retirement in May 1794.[146] He had recently married and he settled with his wife Francis (d. 1811) in St Petersburg, where they produced over the next thirteen years eleven children, of whom the eldest (Charles) also became a doctor. Simpson died in 1822 at the age of 73 and an imposing monument to him can still be seen in the Smolenskii Lutheran cemetery.[147]

A further British doctor active during the Mediterranean campaign was Jonathan Rogers (1739–1811), who was appointed body-physician to the admiral in charge of the Russian expeditionary force, Count Aleksei Orlov. It may indeed have been Rogers who was the mysterious author of 'A Character of Count Orloff, by Dr Blay, his body-physician, an Englishman' that appeared in the *Scots Magazine* in December 1770.[148] Although the tone of this little piece was eulogistic, Rogers seems to have spent much of his time ashore at Livorno, complaining about his pay and conditions.[149] After the return of the fleet to Kronshtadt Rogers was appointed physician to

Count N. V. Repnin's embassy to Constantinople in 1775–6. He subsequently was given the right to practise as a doctor and was appointed to the Izmailovskii guards in St Petersburg. In 1785 he returned to England for reasons unknown, possibly ill-health. He was nevertheless back in the Russian capital a few years later: the Oxford don John Parkinson records a conversation with him in 1792 about the Repnin embassy.[150] In 1799 he departed Russia for a second time, reportedly for reasons of ill-health but, more likely, because of antipathy to the political climate under Paul. In 1803 he was invited back into Russian service and on 12/24 August was named chief physician to the navy. Two years later, he became the first physician-general (*general-shtab-doktor*) to the new Naval Ministry, retiring on 13/25 July 1809 with further rewards and the rank of actual state counsellor.[151] It was while holding this last post that Rogers compiled an important *Pharmacopaea navalis Rossica* (Spb, 1806). On 26 April/8 May 1811 the seventy-one-year-old Rogers married at Kronshtadt a Miss Bridget Fraser, 'having first taken the Oath of Celibacy'. A month later, he died.[152]

The early years of Alexander I's reign saw the deaths of a number of distinguished British doctors – Guthrie, then Halliday and Rogers – but the first to go was by far the youngest: John Grieve, who died from a stroke on 21 December 1805/2 January 1806, aged fifty-two.[153] He was born in Edinburgh in 1753, the year his relative Dr James Grieve arrived back from Russia. John studied at the university for some four years, during which he became one of the presidents of the Edinburgh Physical Society in 1776–7, but for some reason he decided to take both his MA and MD at Glasgow in 1777.[154] The following May he left for Russia with a letter of recommendation to Admiral Greig from Sir Alexander Dick, the President of the Royal College of Physicians of Edinburgh, in which it was said that 'he has had a very regular complete Education and has made the greatest Proficiency in his Profession of any of his fellow Students at the University of which he can produce many Attestations. And as I know him to be a Sensible Steady Young Man I have every reason to think he will do Credit to my Recommendation.'[155] Grieve's first spell was limited by ill-health to some five years spent as physician to the army division stationed at Voronezh (where four decades earlier, his countryman John Cook had been attached to Lacy's army). Grieve returned to Britain with the inevitable letter from Guthrie (as did Rogers two years later), and he was to spend the next fifteen years in Britain, the last eleven in private practice in London.

It was during these years that Grieve achieved significant scholarly and public acclaim for his medical researches and practice, first in Scotland and then in London. The number of British societies to which he was elected (at least twelve) make even Guthrie's achievements in this area seem puny. His election to the Royal Society of Edinburgh on 26 January 1784 was neatly balanced a decade later by election to the Royal Society of London on 22 May 1794 (the fifth Scoto-Russian doctor to be so honoured during the century).[156] In the interim other Scottish and English agricultural, antiquarian, medical and scientific societies queued to honour him. His list of publications was, however, small. A communication on a case of dropsy he had observed in Russia appeared in *Medical Commentaries* in 1784, the year in which his important paper on the medical applications of fermented mare's milk, *kumys*, was read to the Royal Society of Edinburgh by his friend and mentor, Professor Joseph Black.[157]

Although Grieve had contemplated returning to Russia while Catherine was still on the throne, it was only to be towards the end of Paul's reign that he did, and it seems likely that his decision was encouraged by Rogerson. Rogerson was anxious to retire, or as he put it, 'il faut que je change du climat', but was advised by friends to avoid giving offence to Paul and to seek instead leave for a year.[158] Grieve seems to have arrived early in 1798 and Rogerson set out for England that summer, returning to the capital in late October 1799. Commenting on Rogerson's return, a friend noted that 'son ami Grieves, qui soigne actuellement la santé de Sa Majesté l'Empéreur, et dont l'Empéreur parait fort content, lui facilitera probablement son projet de retraite'.[159] Rogerson did not retire, but Grieve's career flourished. He was soon made body-physician and by a decree of December given a large mansion not far from the Winter Palace as 'an eternal and hereditary possession'; in March 1800 he was created an honorary member of the Medical College.[160] He found similar favour with Alexander I, but this was cut short by his premature death. He left a young widow Frances (d. 1811) and two daughters, but was predeceased by two other children, named after the emperor and his consort.[161]

The two sojourns of Grieve in Edinburgh as student and as returning scholar more or less encompassed a new and important period in relations between Edinburgh and, more specifically, its university, and Russia. The links that had hitherto existed through correspondence or had been one-way (with Scots leaving to work in Russia), now assumed a new dimension: between 1774 and 1787 no fewer than sixteen students from Russia spent some time at the university, and in their number were several who studied medicine.[162] Grieve was a young student at the university when John Robison returned from Russia in 1774 to be professor of natural philosophy, bringing with him the first three students, and he was still there when Princess Dashkova arrived with her son Pavel, who in April 1779 was to become the first Russian to receive an Edinburgh degree. When Grieve came back to Edinburgh at the end of 1783 he found among the medical students Daniil Pishchekov, whom he may have known in Voronezh. It is possible that it was Grieve who, in a letter to *Gentleman's Magazine* under the pseudonym 'Medicus' in 1786, was to make more widely known ways of treating 'the itch' and other skin diseases from Pishchekov's thesis.[163] Overlapping for a time with Pishchekov and another Russian student, Iurii Bakhmetev, were not only John Rogerson, jr., whom his father came to see in 1786, but also two other Scottish students who, soon after receiving their degrees, went out to Russia to practise.

Charles Stewart and George Cayley were taken into Russian service within a week of each other in August/September 1789. Stewart was appointed as doctor to Olonets Province, north of Petersburg, where Charles Gascoigne had his home and foundry at Petrozavodsk; but in March 1794 he was transferred as army divisional doctor to the newly acquired Polish provinces. He retired because of illness in April 1794 after a final year as doctor at Dubno in Volynsk Province.[164] Cayley (b. 1763), who was the son of John Cayley, the prominent merchant and British consul-general, was in fact returning home. At Edinburgh he had become an ordinary member of the Natural History Society on the same day in April 1786 as another Russian student, Pavel Bakunin (who was to succeed Dashkova as Director of the Academy of Sciences in 1794), and later that year he joined the Medical Society.[165] Cayley's first appointment in Russia was to the Vyborg field hospital where he remained at least until the war with Sweden ended (1791); it seems likely that he then resigned and set up in private practice in Moscow, where he was certainly working in 1792–4.[166]

As war followed war and epidemic followed epidemic, the demand for surgeons and doctors, native or foreign, was equally unending. The *London Chronicle* had reported in 1783 that 'The Empress of Russia has, we are assured, sent to this kingdom for fifty surgeons who will be liberally encouraged to serve in the Russian army.'[167] As the war against the Turks reached its climax towards the end of the decade, a British participant commented that 'notwithstanding the great want of them several regiments are without surgeons. Medical assistance of all kinds is as bad as conceivable. Scarcely any man recovers from the dysentery ... If 2 or 3 young men of abilities were to come here they could not fail of doing well.'[168] In the intervening years there had never been more than a trickle of surgeons and physicians prepared to try their fortunes in Russia.

In October 1783 a William Miller left for Russia, recommended as 'a Gentleman of Experience, long Practice & eminence in the art of Surgery and Physic'.[169] In November of the following year Charles Brown from Carmarthen, who had received his doctor's diploma from Aberdeen on 26 March 1771 after studying in Newcastle, London and Paris, was given the right to practise.[170] He apparently had some difficulty in finding a suitable appointment, for early in 1785 Samuel Bentham, who had just taken over the management of Prince Potemkin's estates at Krichev in White Russia, persuaded

him to spend a few weeks there. He decided to return to London the following year and subsequently he accepted a position as a physician at the Prussian court.[171] Staying somewhat longer in Russia was another Brown, William Brown, a Scot, who became a surgeon with the fleet in June 1784. Three
years later, given the right to practise as a physician, he travelled out to
Barnaul in Siberia with the American explorer John Ledyard. He served as
a local doctor in Kolyvan *guberniia* until his retirement in 1793, when he
returned to Edinburgh to join the Incorporation of Surgeons and to write a
number of treatises on the treatment of fever as well as 'Hints on the Establishment of a Universal Written Character'.[172]

It was directly to the provinces that Samuel Hunt (b. 1751) was sent on
receiving the right to practise on 12/23 November 1786. The first Cam-
bridge-educated doctor to work in Russia in the eighteenth century, Hunt
had spent some eleven years at Caius College, where he received his BD in
1773 and his MD in 1778 for dissertations on 'De febre intermittente' and
'De medicamentorum facultatibus'.[173] In Novgorod Severskii, where he
worked until 1796, he was made responsible in April 1787 for carrying out
the smallpox inoculation of the local population. Early in the reign of Paul,
he was dismissed for refusing an appointment as Inspector of the Novgorod
Medical Commission. Soon afterwards he became personal physician to
Count Kirill Razumovskii, the last Hetman, at his estate of Baturin, and he
subsequently served one of the count's sons, Lev Kirillovich. A Scots doctor
of a later reign, Robert Lyall, met him some time before his death and records
that the old man (he was then nearly eighty) had been shabbily treated by
the widow of Razumovskii's son, left without a pension and forced to return
to Moscow.[174] Sharing a Cambridge connection with Hunt was John Debraw
(d. 1788), who had been apothecary to Addenbrooke's Hospital. Apparently
learning of Potemkin's Krichev enterprise from Jeremy Bentham and the
returned Dr Charles Brown, he decided to make his way to Russia without
any previously agreed contract. He was a man of considerable ability as a
doctor but proved to be erratic and disruptive in his dealing with Samuel
Bentham and his British workmen. He spent the summer and autumn of
1786 in Krichev without seemingly doing anything of note in the medical
field or in any other other area. His skill as a doctor won him, however, the
attention of Potemkin and the offer of the position of first physician to the
army in the south, where he was to die the following year. Samuel Bentham,
who was himself engaged in the war, wrote in a letter to his brother: 'Debraw
you know I suppose is dead. He had just been made 1st Physician to the
Army, the Patent for which did not come from Petersburg till after his death,
had it come before it would no doubt have saved his life for he died more
of disappointment than of anything else.'[175] Debraw's widow, petitioning in
1792 for money promised to her but not received because of Potemkin's

death, gave a rather different version: her husband had died in an accident at Kremenchug following 'some chymical, but dangerous Experiments'.[176]

It is fitting that the last Briton to enter the Russian medical services during Catherine's reign should not only be a Scot and one who had studied at Edinburgh but also the longest-serving of any British doctor and the most celebrated. The career of James Wylie (1768–1854) stretched over sixty years and four reigns, but only eleven of those sixty years came within the reigns of Catherine and Paul. To follow Wylie in any detail through the years of his greatest triumphs would therefore be to distort excessively the chronological limits and context of this study, but by the end of the reign of Paul he was already well and truly launched.[177]

Although he had studied a number of years at Edinburgh, Wylie received his MD only much later in 1794, and then from the University of Aberdeen. In the interim he had been assigned on 9/20 December 1790 as surgeon to the Eletskii infantry regiment, which had recently transferred from the south to the Baltic and was commanded by Samuel Bentham's close friend, Colonel Henry Fanshawe. Wylie soon earned a considerable reputation, firstly by successfully treating an outbreak of intermittent fever by a 'solutio mineralis' of his devising, and, more enduringly, by his skill as a surgeon. In 1794 he was promoted to staff-surgeon, but in the following year, when the commander-in-chief of the army, Count Repnin, requested his transfer to army headquarters as chief surgeon only to have his request refused, Wylie decided to retire. He became the personal physician to Count Boris Stroganov and practised in the capital. The great breakthrough in his career came in Paul's reign when his skills as a surgeon were enlisted to perform the lithotomy that saved the life of the Danish ambassador, following which he was appointed court 'operator' on 25 February/8 March 1798. The next year, when Rogerson was in England, Wylie successfully lanced a tumour on the throat of Paul's favourite, Count A. P. Kutaisov. This brought his elevation to the rank of the emperor's personal surgeon (23 July/3 August 1799) and spawned the bon mot that 'Dr Wylie had made his fortune by cutting Count Kutaisof's throat'.[178] It was to Wylie (rather than to Grieve) that Rogerson on his return would seem to be referring in the following passage: 'je ne vais pas chez le Maître, qui est maintenant beaucoup prevenu en faveur de mon compatriote, qui a été placé là par le favori dans le tems qu'on était faché contre m-r Beck'.[179] A further honour for Wylie at this period was the bestowal of the degree of doctor of medicine and surgery by the Medical College on 15/27 March 1800 and his election as an honorary member (at the same time as John Grieve).

Under Alexander, Wylie became effectively head of all Russian medical services. As Chief Medical Inspector of the army from 1806 until his death in 1854, Wylie became president of the Medico-Surgical Academy in 1808, and in 1811, became director of the Medical Department of the War Ministry (when the military medical administration was separated from the civil). A gifted and committed administrator, Wylie still found the time and opportunities for authorship (for example, a dissertation on yellow fever in 1805 and an important general pharmacopeia in 1808, the year he founded a medical journal) and for operating, particularly during the Napoleonic Wars. In May 1814 he was made body-physician to the tsar and in this capacity attended Alexander on his visit to London. It was during that visit that the Prince Regent knighted Wylie at Ascot with the sabre of the Cossack ataman Platov. Under Nicholas, Wylie continued as actively as ever for more than two decades, taking part in the war against Turkey in 1828 and playing a leading role in the fight to control the great cholera epidemic of 1830. On 9/21 December 1840 Wylie's fifty years of service in Russia was marked with special celebrations and the award of a gold medal. He bequeathed his fortune to the building of the Mikhailovskii hospital in St Petersburg, in front of which a monument to him was unveiled in 1859.

This monument, which is still standing in St Petersburg, if in a less prominent place, may be said to celebrate the considerable contribution made not only by Wylie but also, symbolically, by all the British doctors, particularly the Scots, since the reign of Peter the Great. It is a contribution made by a number of men who were very visible, occupying positions of distinction in the Russian medical service and/or at court, and by others who fulfilled very necessary but unsung tasks as obscure provincial or military doctors and surgeons in a country where their expertise was sorely needed. Men such as Erskine, Mounsey, Rogerson and Wylie by their eminence and influence would figure in any account of Russian medicine in the eighteenth century: others such as Guthrie, Bell and Cook have left published works by which they are remembered, if not primarily as doctors; while yet others such as Halliday, certainly, and the Grieves are less known than they deserve to be. It might be argued, nonetheless, that it was an Englishman, Thomas Dimsdale, who was not really in Russian service, who made the most significant, and obviously the most publicised, impact by his successful inoculation of the Russian empress. During the reign of Alexander, Scottish doctors reached a pinnacle of influence when the heads of the military, naval and civil medical departments were Wylie, Sir James Leighton, and Sir Alexander Crichton respectively. Leighton and Crichton are outstanding examples of still more British physicians active in Russia in the first half of the nineteenth century (e.g. Archibald Crichton, Galloway, Hutchinson, Keir, Lefevre, Lyall, Morton), but the eighteenth century essentially came to an end with another trinity of Scots doctors, Guthrie, Grieve and Wylie, who had the melancholy task of conducting the autopsy and the embalming of the murdered Paul I and of announcing (through Wylie) the cause of death as apoplexy!

5

'SUR LE PIED ANGLAIS': SHIPBUILDERS AND OFFICERS IN THE RUSSIAN NAVY

Although believing strongly that the experience and expertise gained by young Russian officers serving with the British navy was ultimately of greater value than the presence of British officers serving in the Russian navy, Count Semen Vorontsov (the Russian ambassador in London during the last years of Catherine's reign) was more than ready to acknowledge the considerable contribution made by British officers. His statement that 'notre service, depuis le chevalier Knowles et surtout par les soins de l'amiral Greigh, etait sur le pied anglais', made in the wake of the Russian naval victories in 1788–91 over Swede and Turk, recognised, moreover, the crucial organisational and inspirational role that Knowles and Greig in particular had fulfilled.[1] In less than 100 years a Russian navy had been created out of nothing and at virtually every stage in its evolution and in almost every aspect of its activities a British contribution was apparent.

I

One hundred years (plus a few months) separated the death of Admiral Samuel Greig in October 1788 from the discovery by the young Peter I in June 1688 of a dilapidated little boat on the Romanov estate of Izmailovo. This was the boat that was to be immortalised as 'the grandfather of the Russian fleet'. Moreover, it was, according to the introduction that Peter himself wrote for the *Naval Regulation* (*Morskoi ustav*) of 1720, 'an English boat', possessing the wondrous advantages of sailing against the wind.[2] Whether the boat was indeed English – and legend subsequently embroidered the account to suggest that it had been a gift from Elizabeth I to Ivan IV – or of English design cannot be established, but Peter's informant was Franz Timmermann, a Dutchman. And it was another Dutchman, Karsten Brand, who was to repair the little boat. He had originally been brought to Russia by Peter's father to build ships on the Caspian. Dutch expertise and a strong Dutch presence was to dominate early Russian maritime interests (particularly Peter's), and Dutch masters were recruited to build ships for the Azov campaign of 1696. Holland was undoubtedly the most powerful

magnet drawing the tsar to the West, but as he himself writes, although he
learnt much in the shipyards of Amsterdam, the Dutch masters were unable
to instruct him 'in the Mathematical Way' he required. His dissatisfaction
was, however, resolved by the intervention of an Englishman who 'told him,
that with us in England, this Kind of Structure was in the same Perfection
as other Arts and Sciences, and might be learn'd in a short Time. His Majesty
was glad to hear this, and hereupon went in all haste to England, and there,
in four Months Time, finish'd his Learning; and at his Return brought over
with him two Master Ship-builders, John Deane and Joseph Noy [Nye].'[3]

Peter's visit to England during the first months of 1698 confirmed his high
opinion of Britain's pre-eminence in both the building and the commanding
of ships. He himself was constantly on the water, sailing with spirit, if not
always with success, the small yacht *Dove* that had been made available for
his personal use. He visited Portsmouth to watch a mock sea battle and
Deptford for a demonstration of firing by a new bomb vessel, and he was
often to be found in the Royal Yard at Deptford. And of course, he drank
deeply with numerous sea captains and particularly with his boon companion, Admiral the Marquis of Carmarthen, before reluctantly sailing away
on the *Royal Transport*, King William's gift of a state-of-the-art yacht.[4] A
contemporary English source suggests that thereafter Peter 'often declared to
his Lords, when he has been a little merry, that he thinks it a much happier
Life to be an Admiral in England, than Czar in Russia', a version patriotically
adjusted in a Russian collection of anecdotes to read that if he were not tsar,
he would wish to be an English admiral.[5]

Unable, however, to fulfil the dream, Peter attempted to recruit skilled
representatives in all those areas vital for the success of his navy and in this
endeavour he was aided and abetted in no small measure by Carmarthen.
Carmarthen had drawn up a memorandum for the tsar 'of what may be
proper for him to doe whilst in England, and to carry from thence in order
to the erecting and well establishing after the English Manner such a Navy in
Muscovy as his Majesty shall think most fitt for his Service'.[6] He highlighted
essentially four groups of specialists: first, master shipbuilders, riggers and
smiths, together with their assistants; second, 'Ingenious English Sea Officers', but not too many of them; third, ordinary seamen, who would instil
in the Russians with whom they served typical English skills and discipline;
and fourth, instructors to teach 'the Art of Navigation'.

Tracing the careers and fates of the many British subjects recruited by Peter
during his sojourn in England (and in subsequent years) is made easier by the
existence of four contemporary accounts written by Britons with first-hand
knowledge of Russia. These accounts, differing considerably in range and
intention, are all frankly partisan in their interpretation of events but provide
a counterbalance to other writings where the role of the British for a number

of reasons is minimised or overlooked. Three of the authors exemplify categories of expertise sought by Peter – shipbuilder, hydraulic engineer and naval officer, whilst the fourth was the informed and involved British ambassador, Charles Whitworth (1675–1725), whose *Account of Russia as it was in the Year 1710*, which was produced as an information document for government circles but published only long after his death, devotes by far its largest section to naval matters. The most comprehensive of the accounts, entitled *The Russian Fleet under Peter the Great*, is essentially a log-book of the movements of the Baltic fleet until 1724. This was not published until 1899 when it was attributed to an anonymous 'contemporary Englishman'. However, the subsequent discovery of the autograph copy in which the account is continued into 1725 and in which the author's name is revealed as John Deane significantly enhances the work's value.[7] He is indeed the very same Captain John Deane (1680?–1761) whose career is spoken of in such sympathetic but selective detail in the narrative. Deane entered Russian service in 1712 but in August 1720 he was disciplined for disobeying orders, reduced to the rank of ensign (*poruchik*), and sent off to Kazan; the following November with the end of the Great Northern War he was released from Russian service, with the instruction from the tsar 'never to return to Russia'.[8] He did, however, attempt to return in June 1725 in his new capacity as British consul-general, but he was apprehended at Kronshtadt and dispatched home at the beginning of July.[9] He is not, however, the John Deane who was responsible for the *Letter from Moscow to the Marquess of Carmarthen, Relating to the Czar of Muscovy's Forwardness in his Great Navy &c. since His Return Home*, bearing the dateline 8 March 1698/9 and subsequently published by its recipient in London in April 1699. This is the John Deane who, together with Joseph Nye, became the first British shipbuilders to enter Russian service, personally recommended to Peter by Carmarthen, as was John Perry (1670–1732). A disgraced naval officer, court martialled for negligence, but a knowledgeable engineer, Perry was to be entrusted by Peter with major canal and hydraulic works. Although he was eventually to return to England to earn fame but certainly no fortune for his success in damming a breach in the Thames embankment, his reputation is based on what was to be perhaps the most influential contemporary foreign account of Peter's Russia, *The State of Russia under the Present Czar* (1716), a record of fourteen years of mainly personal trials and tribulations intertwined with negative comments on the Russians and a contrasting eulogy of the reformer-tsar.

It is difficult to establish with any certainty how many people Peter took into his service as a result of his visit to England. Estimates vary widely, from a few dozen to Sir John Barrow's 'not much less than five hundred persons' in a detailed list that inspires little confidence with its 'two hundred gunners'.[10] Whatever the number, nearly all of these first recruits were inevitably destined not to command ships but to build and caulk and rig them. These were early days in the history of the Russian navy, when eyes were directed exclusively towards the Turks in the south; the Baltic meant as yet virtually uncontested Swedish waters, and Archangel in the north was the port of call for the merchant ships of Holland and Britain and not the scene of military activity.

It was to Archangel that the *Royal Transport* came on 9 June 1698, carrying many of the specialists who were to make their way to Moscow and Voronezh. It was in Moscow, however, that the *Royal Transport*'s ill-fated captain, William Ripley, another of Carmarthen's recommendations, was murdered in June the following year, at about the same time as John Deane died there.[11] The son of Sir Anthony Deane, Charles II's eminent shipbuilder, Deane was Peter's prize capture, but he suffered continually from ill-health during his few months in imperial service. He did, however, produce a model of a machine to move the *Royal Transport* from Archangel to the Volga, which the tsar liked, 'but gave no Orders for putting it in Execution, so I believe she will lie where she is now, and perish'.[12] Deane also managed to accompany the tsar to Voronezh at the end of 1698 and on the basis of this visit to write 'a true Account (from my own Knowledge) of the Czar (our Master's) Navy'. He describes the extent of the fleet 'chiefly built by the Dutch and the Danes', with the exception of the galleys designed by Italian masters, before mentioning that both he and the tsar had been able to set up 60-gun ships. The implications of this are spelt out with typical trenchancy by Perry: Peter 'made those English that he had brought over now his chief Master Builders, and he discharg'd all the Dutch Builders, except what were to finish the Ships which they had begun, and those that were left under the Command of the English; and that there should be none but English fashion ships to be built for the future'. Whitworth provides a similar version and adds that 'the last ships built by the Dutch were eleven frigates at Stupena [Stupino on the River Voronezh] in 1703'.[13]

Deane's mantle now fell on Joseph Nye, who himself was already at work on a 60-gun ship in 1698. After Deane's death, Nye was joined by Richard Cozens (1674–1735) and together they dominated Russian shipbuilding in the south over the next decade.[14] Shipbuilding was conducted with varying degrees of success at Stupino, some twenty miles north of Voronezh, and at Voronezh itself, where ships were constructed on dry land and floated off on the spring floods or by use of sluices, usually mismanaged with the result that the channels were severely silted. Whitworth gives a total of thirteen ships that were completed at the yards of Voronezh by 1710, of which two of 70-guns are attributed to Cozens and six ships to Nye, including, interestingly but unidentified, a yacht he had designed 'in imitation of the transport'.[15] In 1705 a site six miles to the south at Tavrov was selected for a new yard. The site was again badly chosen and the foundations of the docks were swept away in 1707 and again in 1708. Nevertheless, in the summer of 1707 four 80-gun ships were laid down by Nye and Cozens, followed by four smaller ones (48-gun and 24-gun) in 1709. It was early in 1709, prior to Poltava, that Peter visited Voronezh and, dismayed by the state of the installations and condition of the ships, he decided on a fourth site for a yard. It was to be 100 miles to the south, near the mouth of the Osereda, a tributary of the Don. Cozens was sent to inspect the site, where it was first necessary to build a fortress for protection against attack by Cossacks and Tartars, and although he and Nye are said to have worked there up to 1712, nothing is known about their activities.

Whitworth lists the names of many British specialists who were key figures in the construction of what was meant to be the Azov fleet. In Voronezh, Cozens' under-master was Robert Hadley, his assistant was Robert Davenport, and his two apprentices were Francis Kitchen and William Snelgrove; Nye's under-master was Henry Johnson and his assistant was William Gardner. Both yards had a nominal workforce of some 500 men, but were always considerably below strength. Cozens and Nye were also charged with the maintenance of existing Dutch-built craft, most of which were, however, 'most decayed'; they were assisted by Henry Bird and an apprentice Leonard Chapman. Almost all these men were to serve many years, transferring in due course to the Baltic. In addition to the shipbuilders there were masters of other necessary skills, such as Henry Wright the mast-maker, Nicholas Baggs the block-maker, William Mansfeldt the carver, Henry Atherley the caulker, and Samuel Hopkins the painter, the majority of them recruited by Peter in 1698. A hundred miles north of Voronezh at Dobrov Richard Halley and his assistants Robert Davies and Thomas Daniel were producing the anchors and other ironwork for Peter's fleet.[16] Another list among Whitworth's unpublished papers and dated 1705 includes, in addition to most of the men mentioned above, many others in similar and allied trades and indicates that recruitment was a continuing process.[17]

Two men who appeared on both lists were John Beckham and John Perry. Both entered Russian service in 1698 with the rank of captain and were naval officers as opposed to master craftsmen. Beckham, one of two known British officers with the Azov fleet, was essentially in overall command until his death in unknown circumstances in 1711.[18] Perry on the other hand was recommended to Peter as an engineer. All but the last of his fourteen years in Russian service were to be spent in the south, devoted to ambitious maritime projects (such as the Volga–Don waterway) that were never quite brought to fruition or were frustrated for reasons largely beyond his control; to a certain extent his career mirrored the overall frustrations and half-successes of Peter's southern naval adventure. John Deane, with whom Perry travelled out to Russia, relates in his letter of March 1699 that 'Capt. Perry, who was sent to make a Communication between the Rivers Wolga and Done, near Astracan, is returned from Surveying the same; he makes it appear Feasible enough to be done; accordingly his Majesty has ordered 40,000 Men to be rais'd, and Materials provided for doing the same; which he has promis'd to Finish in Five years, tho' I believe it may be done in less. When that is perform'd, then the Czar may carry his Ships from the Black Sea into the Caspian Sea, and extend his Conquest that way.'[19] It was an optimism that foundered within three years on the hostility of the governor of Astrakhan, the lack of manpower, the immensity of the undertaking, and financial retrenchment after the defeat at Narva. After 1701 Perry's talents were switched to solving some of the problems connected with the various ship-yards on the Voronezh and Don rivers. For example, given the task of over-seeing the repairs of numerous rotting ships at Voronezh, Perry managed to create a huge dry dock by first floating no less than fifteen vessels over cradles positioned on the river bank and then gently lowering them and the water level by the skilful manipulation of sluices he had constructed. These and other considerable feats he details in the first part of his book which was essentially written as a petition to the British authorities to intercede on his behalf for the salary which he had never received. Perry was finally obliged to escape from Russia in 1712 under the protection of Whitworth 'without their giving me any Money, Pass, or Discharge'.[20]

Whitworth had paid an earlier visit to London in 1710, when he finished his *Account*, which reflected much that Perry and other informants had told him. By 1712, however, what he had written about the situation of the fleet in the south had lost its value for any prognosis of future development. In November 1710 hostilities had broken out between Russia and Turkey, bringing the following year the disaster on the Pruth, when with his army surrounded, Peter was obliged to agree to give up Azov, Taganrog and his forts on the Dnieper. As a direct consequence he lost a beloved fleet that had been slowly developed and augmented under the guidance of British special-ists but had never had the opportunity to be tested in battle; in truth, only three of the ships at Voronezh were fit to be sent down river and few of the battleships already at Azov or Taganrog were ready for combat in the spring of 1711. Peter was forced to hand over four ships (under the command of Captain Andrew Simpson) to the Turks and destroy many others on the Sea of Azov; many ships were broken up at the yards on the inland rivers, but among those that remained at Tavrov to the end of Peter's reign were Cozens's 70-gun *Staryi Dub* and *Spiashchii Lev* and several ships built by Nye, including the 60-gun *Sulitsa* and *Tsvet Voiny*.[21]

Cozens and Nye by that time had long been transferred to the north-west, where a British contribution to the emerging Baltic fleet was even more in evidence. From 1700 Russia was involved in the Great Northern War and, recovering from the defeat at Narva, began to harry the Swedes by land and water. Prior to the establishing of the Admiralty yard in St Petersburg in November 1704, two shipyards had been created on the south-eastern shore of Lake Ladoga at Olonets and it was there that the first British shipwrights were to be employed. William Snelgrove was transferred from Voronezh, where he had been an apprentice in Cozens' yard, to Olonets in 1703 and he built a number of small ships there over the next few years, before working with Richard Bent on a 50-gun man-of-war in 1708–11. Bent had arrived in Russia in 1705 with his fellow master-builder Richard Brown and both had gone first to Voronezh. By 1708 they were at Olonets and appear in Whitworth's lists as heading the Olonets and Novoladozhskaia yards respectively.[22] Bent died in 1710, but Brown, who had learnt his trade in the yards at Chatham, 'has since given the world a demonstration of his great genius that way by building the Tsar several ships, from 90 to 16 guns, that may vie with the best in Europe for the part that concerns the builder'.[23]

Nye, Cozens and Brown were the 'big three' of Russian shipbuilding in the last decades of Peter's reign, but the corps of master-builders was increased by the arrival in 1715 of Richard Ramsey and by the promotions in 1718 of Davenport and Hadley, who had worked originally in Voronezh.[24] The first three dominated the building at the Admiralty yards in St Petersburg, where they were joined by Ramsey. Davenport was assigned to Reval to oversee the repairs to the Baltic squadron, while Hadley worked at Kazan, from where supplies of oak timbers were sent to St Petersburg. Some twenty of the fifty-four ships-of-the-line built for the Baltic fleet between 1708 and 1725 came from British shipbuilders as did at least three of the thirty-one frigates, as well as numerous other smaller craft.[25] The standing of the British builders was acknowledged in July 1723 when five of them received significant promotions: Nye, Cozens and Brown were made captains-commodore and Davenport and Hadley, captains of the first rank. (Ramsey had joined with the rank of captain and was made captain-commodore in 1732.) John Deane, writing in 1724, suggests that Peter had 'always showed great respect to his shipbuilders; frequently on public occasions sitting amongst them and calling himself one of their fraternity. But of late he seldom does them that honour, and this summer has given them much distaste by introducing a custom, that every master shall watch his work night and day in the yard at St Petersburg.'[26] However, in the summer of the same year another observer, present at the launch of the 66-gun Derbent that Cozens ('much loved by the emperor') had built, commented that 'his majesty was in an extremely good mood and therefore there was an awful lot of drinking on the new ship'.[27]

Of all the early British shipbuilders Cozens is perhaps the best known, but not simply for the quantity and quality of the ships he built. Rumour had it, the *Dictionary of National Biography* records it, and the tradition lives on among descendants of Cozens, that his son Alexander (d. 1786), often termed the father of British landscape painting, was in fact sired by Peter the Great at Deptford. Another version suggests that somehow or other the shipbuilder himself was Peter's son. Chronology and reason point to the fact that Richard Cozens and his wife Mary (née Davenport and possibly a sister of the shipbuilder of that name) produced Alexander while they were at Voronezh and several later children at St Petersburg, where their births are recorded in the records of the St Petersburg English church. The Cozens' children intermarried with some of the leading merchant families in the Russian capital (as noted in chapter 2). Richard Cozens himself took Russian citizenship and spent the last two years of his life at the yards in Archangel, where he died in 1735.[28]

All six shipbuilders in fact continued in Russian service into the reign of Anna Ivanovna. Even allowing for a number of 'lost years' in the careers of such as Ramsey, the six men served a total of some 200 years – an average of thirty-three years. Davenport died in 1735, the same year as Cozens; Nye, old and infirm, retired to England in 1737 after thirty-nine years in Russia; and Brown died in 1740. The relatively unsung Brown was in many respects the most influential British master-builder. He, rather than Nye and Cozens, was responsible for producing the first effective men-of-war for the Baltic fleet and it is to his, rather than to others' achievements that Deane returns again and again in his account.[29] He also became the most highly paid, combining his work in Petersburg with the supervision of fleet repairs at Kronshtadt in the last years of Peter's reign. Under Anna he was made chief superintendent of shipbuilding (*ober-intendant*), given a stone house on Vasilii Island and finished his career with two great ships of the line, the mighty 114-gun *Imperatritsa Anna* and the aptly named 66-gun *Osnovanie blagopoluchiia* ('Foundation of Prosperity').[30]

Carmarthen had recommended that Peter recruit British naval officers – but not too many. There were indeed very few in the original party, but with Russia's involvement in the Great Northern War and the consequent development of a Baltic fleet the demand for experienced officers inevitably grew. Attempts have been made, notably by F. T. Jane and R. C. Anderson, to list British officers in Russian service down the century, but Peter's reign presents particular difficulties.[31] While making use of Deane's generally reliable account in their search for names, Jane and Anderson neglected the primary source of information, the 'general naval list', which virtually doubles their totals to over sixty officers.[32] It is clear that prior to the end of the War of Spanish Succession in 1713, Peter was unable, or did not seek, to enlist many officers. Over a fifteen-year period from 1698 to 1712 nineteen officers can be identified as joining the Russian navy with a maximum of three in any one year (1703 and 1704). In truth, there was little to attract a British officer, given the picture painted by Deane of tensions between foreigners and Russians, bad conditions and pay perpetually in arrears – not that the pay, if and when paid, compared favourably with similar rates in the British navy.[33] A career in the Russian navy on a short-term contract and bringing instant promotion could, however, appear attractive to an officer on half-pay and with few prospects of advancement. The twenty-six officers who went to Russia in the years 1713 and 1714 obviously thought so. Following the Northern Crisis of 1716 and the subsequent cessation of diplomatic links between Britain and Russia the recruitment of British officers slowed to its earlier trickle. Between 1719 and 1725 a mere eight officers joined. The year 1717, however, proved to be a very special one in many respects. At the beginning of the year George Paddon, who had been dismissed from the Royal Navy in 1714, became the first Briton to join the Russian navy with the rank of (rear-)admiral and at the end of the same year there arrived a group of six officers, recruited by Peter during his recent visit in Holland. All were Jacobite sympathisers, who had resigned or been dismissed from the British navy following the uprising of 1715. They included Captains-Commodore Thomas Gordon and Thomas Saunders, both of whom were to become admirals. Although they were not the only Jacobites to be recruited, there is no foundation for Jane's statement that 'in Peter the Great's reign, in nearly every case the British officers were attainted persons – Jacobites and the like', nor for his accompanying verdict that 'there were not more than half a dozen who would have been suffered to remain had they been in the British Navy at that time'.[34]

When the Great Northern War came to an end with the Treaty of Nystadt in November 1721 the map of the Baltic was considerably redrawn. Russia now possessed Ingria, Livonia, Estonia and parts of Kurland and Finland; it had ports at Reval and Kronshtadt from which it controlled the sea with a fleet that had not existed two decades earlier. Russia's emergence as a naval power in the Baltic followed the victory at Poltava and the defeat on the Pruth. However, in 1710 it was Sweden and Denmark who contested the sea: Sweden had forty-three battleships and Denmark forty-one, while Russia had none. By 1721 the Swedish navy was reduced to twenty-four battleships and the Danes to twenty-five, while the Russians had moved to a position of supremacy. Russia had twenty-nine seaworthy battleships of thirty-six to ninety guns, having acquired (by building, purchase or capture) no less than fifty-three ships and lost (by ways other than in action) nineteen over a twelve-year period.[35] Although Deane only gives five Britons among the commanders of the twenty-nine ships in 1721, plus two admirals,[36] many British officers had been in command of Russian ships of the line since 1710, but not to the exclusion of Danes, Dutch and Russians. However, no Briton built or commanded a galley and it was the galley fleet that brought the Russian navy its first great triumph at Hangö-udd in August 1714. Four British officers were nevertheless commanding battleships present at the action; and one more, the Irishman John Delap, was in Siniavin's squadron that captured three Swedish ships on 24 May/4 June 1719 in a battle hailed by the most eminent of Russian naval historians as 'our first real sea victory, sending the tsar into rapture'.[37]

The war at sea was not one of great set battles but rather of skirmishes and raids and pursuits; it was frequently more of a struggle with the elements and an effort, all too often unsuccessful, to avoid sandbanks and rocks; above all, it provided a harsh training school for Russian officers and seamen. Foreign officers were there to instruct and discipline and set an example – and the tsar was constantly on hand to ensure they did. In the year following the Treaty of Nystadt, Peter, 'desirous to cultivate discipline in his seamen on the Baltic, gave orders for a squadron to go out under the command of Vice-Admiral Gordon, of whose capacity that way he conceived a good opinion from his long serving in the British, just esteemed by the Tsar the best regulated navy in the world'. Gordon duly took out fourteen ships and 'departing five or six leagues from Kronslot, continued out near three months; sometimes under sail disciplining the people in forming lines of battle, other whiles at anchor, exercising their guns, and practising all the different parts of the duty of a seaman'.[38] Peter's admiration for the British navy needs no underlining and it is obvious that throughout his reign he sought to bring in sound practices affecting every aspect of a ship's preparation, victualling, manning, and command, frequently following British example. Deane may well have emphasised how much there was still to do, but his report nevertheless highlights how much in fact was achieved. The British government had long since manifested its anxieties at the growth of Peter's navy and the arrival of Admiral Sir John Norris's combined Anglo-Swedish fleet in the Baltic in 1719 was a misplaced show of strength. The title of a pamphlet published in London that same year under the initials N. N. (hiding George Mackenzie, who had been British minister-resident in Russia in 1714–15) eloquently testifies to British alarm: *Truth is but Truth, as it is Timed! Or, Our Ministry's Present Measures against the Muscovite Vindicated by Plain and Obvious Reasons: Tending to Prove, that it is no less the Interests of Our British Trade, than that of Our State, that the Czar be not suffer'd to retain a Fleet, if needs must that he should a Sea Port, in the Baltick*. Mackenzie mentions the training of Russians aboard British ships and the British shipbuilders in St Petersburg but not the officers in the Russian navy.[39] While their presence is easy to attest, their contribution is more difficult to assess.

Although a basic career outline is available for the majority of British sailors serving with the Russian fleet, biographical details are missing for all but a few of the most conspicuous (i.e. high-ranking) officers. Nonetheless, a few general observations might be made. Earlier, an indication was given of the years in which British officers were recruited into Russian service. The lengths of time they served inevitably varied greatly. Despite the often adverse conditions encountered, not all of them were anxious to leave or indeed allowed to leave. Perry and Deane both describe the stratagems used to keep valued individuals in Russian service ('the Tsar himself in his cups frequently toasting: "A Health to all brave officers, that never design to leave me; especially during the war!"'). By contrast, the British minister Claudius Rondeau wrote in a dispatch of May 1729 that 'several good foreign officers who are in this service daily ask their discharge to return home, and it is granted them without any difficulty, which shows the politics of this country are strangely changed since the death of the late Czar'.[40] However, all the nineteen officers still in service at Peter's death continued to serve under his successors, in almost every case until their own deaths. They included men who had joined relatively late in Peter's reign but also others from the beginning of the century; they included men who achieved eminence as well as those of more modest attainments. Among the latter was certainly the worthy John Nicholas, who joined as a boatswain in 1702 and slowly climbed the ranks until he became a captain with the rank of brigadier in 1733. When he retired in 1752, he had completed fifty years' devoted if unspectacular service in the Russian navy.[41] In contrast to Nicholas was Paul Dukes, who arrived as a captain-lieutenant in May 1721 but was released in December the same year following the peace agreement.[42] This was the time of the exodus of another eight officers, mainly from the large group which had arrived in 1713–14, and who were not looking for another period on the reduced pay that Peter had been quick to introduce.

Some twelve officers had died before 1721 while still on active service. The circumstances of their deaths are not always known, although it is certain that none was actually killed in battle against the Swedes. Captain Edward Vaughan, who arrived in 1714, was killed the following year on his ship, the *Narva*, which blew up at anchor off Kotlin Island when its powder was struck by lightning; Captain Hutchisson was given command of the refitted *Royal Transport*, which left Archangel in September 1715 with other ships for the Baltic, but, as Deane describes, 'was cast away upon the coasts of Sweden: Captain Hutchisson saved and made prisoner of war, with about 20 more, but is since dead in Marstrand Castle'; Adam Urquhart, who arrived in 1717 with Gordon, was in command of the *Portsmouth* when it ran aground on a sandbank off Kronshlot and he was killed by a falling mast in the subsequent operation to free it.[43] Although there is only one instance

of an officer absconding, cases of courts-martial, punishments and dismissals
are not infrequent. Thomas Edwards, for instance, who enlisted in 1714, was
dismissed in 1717 as 'unsuitable'.[44] Deane, who omits to record his own exile
to Kazan in 1720 and subsequent pardon with the signing of the Treaty of
Nystadt, describes the court martial following the incident in which Urquhart
lost his life in 1719. Deane had captained the *Devonshire*, which was some
way behind the *London* and the *Portsmouth* when they went aground.
Robert Little, a captain of the first rank who was commanding the *London*,
was demoted to most junior lieutenant and sentenced to six months' confinement. He was pardoned in 1721 and, unlike Deane, was restored to his
former rank and continued to serve until his death in 1735.[45]

Of particular interest in Deane's account of Little's actions is the ill-
concealed animosity that existed not only among foreign officers in general
but among the British in particular, touching on questions of seniority – and
of politics. Earlier, reporting disparaging remarks made to the tsar by
Gordon about his fellow admiral (the Dane Sievers), Deane has the Russian
admiral Apraksin declaring that 'he looked upon Gordon and his associates
as men of turbulent dispositions and malevolent principles; that having set
their native country in a flame without finding their account in it some of
them were forced to fly from justice, and were now caballing to foment divisions in Russia'.[46] Apart from being a newcomer, Little was also a Jacobite.
Several of the nineteen officers continuing to serve after Peter were also, not
unexpectedly, Jacobites; there were also at least three longer-serving Welsh-
men and one, possibly two Irishmen, who may not all have been of similar
persuasion but had little reason to return to Britain. Three Jacobites were flag
officers under Peter, but the first to hoist his flag had been George Paddon.

Given the very advantageous contract he had negotiated and the fact that
he had lost his commission in the British navy, Paddon would undoubtedly
have served many years in Russia, but eighteen months after his arrival in
May 1717 he was dead. He was nonetheless able to make his mark both as
commander and, more significantly, as reformer. Within days of arriving he
sailed with the fleet under Apraksin, who in June left 'the charge of the fleet
to Rear-Admiral Paddon, with directions to go out and exercise them in
forming lines of battle'.[47] His main contribution was, however, to advise and
further the work of the recently established Admiralty College. He worked
with Vice-Admiral Cruys, who was also vice-president of the college, on Russian versions of the British and Dutch regulations for the fleet and Admiralty
and also made a whole series of proposals, many of which were subsequently
adopted. He suggested, for instance, how fully rigged masts could be erected
outside winter barracks so that crews could hone their skills. He recommended the keeping of ship's logs and that examinations should precede
promotion.[48]

Paddon's role was largely taken over by Gordon, who was a particular favourite of the tsar. They had met in Amsterdam early in 1717 when Peter asked Gordon to recruit other disaffected British officers, who included Thomas Saunders (d. 1733). Both arrived with the rank of captain-commodore and their careers thereafter were closely linked – but it was always Gordon who was ahead.[49] Gordon already had a long career in the Scottish and English navies behind him; however, when he refused to take the oath of allegiance to George I, he resigned his commission in 1716 and went abroad. He was already fifty-six or fifty-seven years old when he joined the Russian navy, which he served for nearly another quarter of a century: he died in 1741 during the short reign of Ivan VI, his fifth Russian monarch. Promoted at the beginning of January 1719 to rear-admiral, he became vice-admiral following the Treaty of Nystadt (when Saunders became a rear-admiral) and a full admiral (Saunders, a vice-admiral) on 6 January 1727, two days before the death of Catherine I. Increasingly, Gordon's experience and presence were required in the Admiralty College. Of his duties there he wrote to a friend in March 1722, 'I have no idle time on my hand, for I am appoynted one of the Commissioners of the Admiralty where I am oblig'd to be every day to regulate the affaires of the Navy' and adds amus-ingly, 'I ranke with a Lt generall and none but 2 mareshalls, 4 generalls, 3 admiralls, the Chancellor, & so many Lt generalls as are older in Commission than I, so that in this great Empire there is 20 can sitt above me. I doe not inform you of this out of vanity, but only to tell you that my expence is much more than I care for'.[50] Gordon's earlier duties had been primarily to lead the fleet in its yearly cruises and manoeuvres. In August 1721 he also staged a mock sea battle, in which Peter took great delight, remembering, no doubt, a similar battle he had witnessed at Portsmouth many years before. Gordon's final years from 1724 until his death were largely spent at Kronsht-adt, where his periods as commander-in-chief alternated with short spells in the office by, first, Saunders, then, Lord Duffus, the third Jacobite admiral, who had arrived in 1722 to be 'intendant of Maritime Affairs ashore, accord-ing to the method of France'.[51] Duffus fell ill within months of his Kronshtadt appointment and died in April 1732,[52] whereupon Gordon resumed the com-mand. The admiral was, however, to be involved in one last naval action during the War of Polish Succession. In June 1734 the Russian fleet under his command appeared off Danzig/Gdansk to assist Field Marshal Münnich's army in the siege of the fortress. It was another Russian field marshal, his compatriot James Keith, who wrote to him subsequently that 'all the Poles that I have seen assure me that the so sudden surrender of the town was entirely owing to the appearance of the fleet which cut off all hopes of suc-cours, and therefore they look on you as the main instrument of the loss of their liberty'.[53] It was freedom of another sort that Gordon received rather than lost in June 1736, when his native Aberdeen made him an honorary burgess.[54]

Perhaps the most valuable contribution to the development of Peter's Baltic fleet came not from a sea-going officer but one who was to assume the mantle of John Perry. Unlike Perry, however, the Welshman Edward Lane left no book to bring him fame; largely ignored by posterity, he was, unlike Perry, able to accomplish much he was asked to undertake and to receive the rank and, apparently, the financial rewards that were his due. Of his background or early experience in Britain, little is known, other than that, according to Whitworth, he had 'taught navigation on board the "Woolwich", but he enlisted in the Russian navy as early as 1702 with the rank of ensign. He first went to Voronezh, but within a year was transferred to Olonets. His promotions to captain-ensign and junior captain in 1706 and 1711 are recorded but nothing more. Perry, who left in 1712, makes no mention of Lane, either in relation to his own work in the south (when his assistant was a Luke Kennedy) or to his later surveying for a Volga–Ladoga link. It was in 1712 that Lane's name is first mentioned in connection with the great harbour constructions that dominated the last fifteen years of his life. On 1 January 1715 he was promoted to first rank captain 'for his particular services in harbour works'; in 1721 he became a captain-commodore with the pay, nevertheless, of a rear-admiral; and the following year he was created officer commanding the Kronshtadt ports.[55]

The date 7/18 May 1704, the day when the Russian flag was raised over the fort of Kronshlot, is considered to mark the founding of what was eventually to become known as Kronshtadt. Kronshlot was built on a sandbank to the south of the island of Retusari, which under Russian control was called Kotlin Island. The fort with its fourteen cannon, together with two batteries on Kotlin Island itself, defended the young St Petersburg from attacks by the Swedes from the Gulf of Finland. However, Kronshlot soon became the name used for some two decades to describe both the fort and the island until on 7/18 October 1723 Peter cut the first turves for what was to be the fortress (and town) of Kronshtadt. Peter 'having laid the Foundation of a New City, on the Island Retusari, commonly call'd Crownslots, order'd the City, as also the Port, to go, for the Future, by the name of Crownstadt; and a Penalty to be inflicted on Any that shou'd transgress this Direction'.[56] Lane's great contribution was to help effect this rapid transition in the period following Poltava.

Lane was involved simultaneously in the creation of the first harbours on Kotlin Island from early 1712 and the transforming of the original Kronshlot fort into New Kronshlot. It was soon realised that the design of the compact pentagonal tower fort allowed only one-fifth of its fire-power to be effective against enemy ships attacking from the main channel. Lane was given the task of producing a new design which was essentially an elongated pentagon with cannon on at least three bastions able to provide protection and with gates constructed to give access to an inner harbour on the side facing Oranienbaum. Work began at the very end of 1715 but ten years were to elapse before New Kronshlot was completely finished. During the same period Lane was responsible for the harbours, docks and canals being constructed on Kotlin Island. He had at his disposal an enormous workforce comprising convicts, prisoners and serfs drawn from all parts of Russia, who toiled in inhuman conditions, starved, fell ill and died like flies. Like St Petersburg, Kronshlot/Kronshtadt was built on bones. But piles were driven, channels were dug, moles, piers, breakwaters were erected, firstly for the naval harbour (*voennaia*) and then, from 1718, for the commercial harbour (*kupecheskaia*). Lane surveyed the route for the main canal that would allow ships to pass from the sea into a series of dry-docks for repairs. It would appear that he also constructed another heavily armed fort, similar to the New Kronshlot, which came to be called the Citadel, to guard approaches to the new harbours. Among his many other responsibilities and achievements during these years was the weighing up of the *Lesnoi*, a 90-gun ship built by Peter, which had sunk as it left harbour after hitting an anchor. He also built a lighthouse on a sandbank off the west coast of Kotlin, called 'the London' after the ship commanded by Captain Little that had foundered there in 1719. Finally, Lane was put in charge of the construction of the main fortress of Kronshtadt from 1723.[57]

Although Kronshtadt was the scene of Lane's major and lasting activity, he was involved in many other projects, including construction of the harbours at Reval and Råger Wik and the surveying of a better route for the Volkhov–Neva canal link. A start on the harbour at Reval seems to have been made in 1713 under the supervision of the hydraulic engineer I. L. Luberass, but Lane was called in 1722 when Peter came to rely increasingly on his expertise.[58] It was, however, to Råger Wik (present-day Paldiski in Estonia) that Lane was duly sent in December 1721 to carry out a survey. Here, according to Deane, the tsar had decided in the summer of 1718 that a harbour should be built but 'deferred the execution of his design till peace'. The tsar approved Lane's plans and in the summer of 1723, when sailing with his fleet off Råger Wik, he came ashore to lay the foundation stone of the harbour. Work was to begin during the winter under the supervision of Lane and Luberass and considerable progress was made, despite adverse conditions.[59] The British could not but view with great suspicion a new Russian harbour to the south of Reval. Already in August 1723 an English diplomat was writing that 'if he [the tsar] compasses that, and lives he will still grow a more troublesome neighbour, being able to go sooner from that port, and come later home, than at Reval'.[60] Deane was at pains to establish the state of the harbour in 1725 and in the postscript he added to the copy he presented to George III gave a detailed description, received, however, at second hand, for 'no foreigners were permitted to approach the Works'.[61]

It was a sign of Lane's standing that in February 1725 he was specifically called from Kronshtadt to St Petersburg to be present at the lying-in-state of the late emperor and to offer his allegiance to Catherine I. He was to survive Peter by four years, remaining to the end responsible for the docks and har-bours of Kronshtadt. Deane's assessment of him in 1722 as 'a sober ingenious man [who] has done great things for the tsar' was echoed by Rondeau, who wrote in 1729 that 'he was reckoned one of the greatest men in his way in Europe; his death is a great loss to this country, for they have not another person capable to keep up the works he has built'.[62]

For all his eagerness to bring British shipbuilders, artificers and officers into Russian service Peter clearly understood that they should be obliged to train cadres of Russian specialists. While the tsar was in London, the first request was made for young Russians to serve on ships of the Royal Navy, initiating a tradition that continued down to the times of Nelson.[63] In April 1697, even prior to the tsar's visit, Mr Brook of the Royal Society had been instructed by the government to meet his request for 'some mathematicians to instruct his people in the art of navigation, fortification etc';[64] the last of Carmarthen's 'proposals' was precisely in the same spirit and moreover specific in suggesting young graduates from Christ's Hospital. In the event two young men from the Royal Mathematical School of Christ's Hospital, Richard Grice and Stephen Gwyn, seventeen and fifteen years of age respect-ively, agreed to go to Russia with Henry Farquharson (Liddell Mathematical tutor at Marischall College, Aberdeen) whom Peter had appointed to head a proposed school of navigation and mathematics in Moscow.[65]

Although given generous contracts in London, they nevertheless found themselves forgotten in Moscow for a whole year, left without any means of subsistence and living in cramped conditions in a single room in the home of Henry Crevett, the Englishman who worked as interpreter for the *Posol'skii prikaz*. Even when Peter at last instituted the school in 1701, they saw no improvement in their salaries. Years later, John Perry wrote of Farquharson that 'I cannot forbear to mention the hard Usage he, who is my Fellow-Sufferer, hath met with in the Czar's Service, by his being long and unjustly kept out of his Pay, as we have often lamented our hard Fortunes together.'[66] Nevertheless, all three men were to spend the rest of their lives in Russia, although in the case of Richard Grice, this was a matter of a decade until his murder by a gang of Moscow thieves early in 1709.

As Nicholas Hans has shown, Peter's new school was to be closely mod-elled after Christ's Hospital with 'the same division into preparatory schools, the same curriculum and the same organisation'.[67] The best pupils from the lower schools entered the upper school, which was dedicated to the training of future naval officers and teachers of mathematics and navigation. Farquharson was officially appointed teacher of mathematics, while Grice and Gwyn were described as teachers of navigation, but all three taught a range of subjects which included algebra, astronomy, geography, geometry, navigation, trigonometry, surveying – and English. They taught in English originally, but were soon to acquire a good command of Russian. Within a few years, the Anglo-Russian axis was given a particular emphasis when groups of Farquharson-trained 'navigators' were sent to England to gain practical experience on ships of the British navy.

The Moscow school was housed in the Sukharev Tower (a landmark only dismantled in Soviet times), where Farquharson was able to practise his skills as an astronomer. Perry relates how the tsar would order from England all the telescopes and other instruments that the Scot recommended and would ask to be informed whenever an eclipse was to take place.[68] Astronomy was undoubtedly one of the activities of the Neptune Society, variously described as masonic and alchemical, whose members were Peter and his close associates, including Farquharson and his fellow Scot James Bruce, whom rumour held to be a necromancer.[69]

In 1716 Farquharson and Gwyn, who a few years earlier had completed a survey for the straight road the tsar wished to see between Moscow and St Petersburg,[70] found themselves taking the somewhat longer road to the new capital to become professors in the Naval Academy, created the previous year by Peter to replace the Moscow navigational school. Gwyn died in 1720, but Farquharson was active for another twenty years, producing a stream of textbooks and manuals for his students. His prowess as a linguist was such that he not only wrote in Russian many of his later works, devising equivalents for the many necessary technical terms, but he was also responsible for monitoring the quality of works translated by others into Russian.[71]

In March 1737 the Admiralty College successfully petitioned the Empress Anna to bestow on Farquharson the rank of brigadier, for 'although Farquharson himself did not himself seek promotion to this rank, he fully merits it for his outstanding services to the state, having introduced the study of mathematics into Russia and having instructed in the art of navigation almost all the Russians in Her Majesty's fleet, from the highest to the lowest'.[72] It is precisely to 1737, two years before the venerable mathematician's death, that the following little cameo refers, penned by a compatriot in Russian service, Dr John Cook:

One day Mr Farcharson Professor of Astronomy came from the Academy to drink tea with me, but, although all the younger officers had studied under him, and particularly the gentlemen at that time on guard, whom he well knew, he could not gain admittance till the commander gave orders. Indeed the Captain ran to the gate, and conducted his old regent with great deference to my house. When seated, the good old professor told him, that he was glad to have lived so long as to see many gentlemen in the fleet, formerly his pupils, of distinguished learning, who could prescribe laws to him. Compliments on both sides were not wanting.[73]

For once, a great experiment had not failed. Farquharson was arguably the most able and influential person Peter had brought into his service, a man who dedicated over forty years of his life to the training of young Russians in the skills of mathematics and navigation and who helped maintain respect for British expertise during the long period when Russians were no longer welcome on British ships.

II

There is little disagreement among either contemporary observers or latter-day historians, both Russian and foreign, that the Russian navy following the death of Peter went into a steep decline that was only truly arrested with the accession of Catherine II. The differences are essentially in emphasis, in the order of importance of various factors and in the apportioning of the blame. Undoubtedly, the single most important factor was the removal of Peter himself, a man passionately dedicated to his navy and prepared to sacrifice virtually anything and anyone for its well-being. Experienced observers such as Deane well realised, however, that 'the vast charge he is yearly at to discipline his men and keep up his fleet to its present height, whilst little or no service is done in return of such expense, must inevitably exhaust his treasures and render him less formidable'.[74] Peter's successors understandably lacked his commitment and his willingness to allocate the necessary resources. For all her desire to continue her husband's policies Catherine I failed to provide the money for equipment and repairs and for the building of new ships – only two battleships were completed during her reign. Under Peter II, the situation was infinitely worse. The new tsar hated the sea and took the first opportunity to move the capital back to Moscow – and most of his nobles followed him gladly. Two key admirals, Apraksin and Cruys, died within months of each other; crews were well below strength; training was neglected; and the fleet became less and less seaworthy. Rondeau, visiting Kronstadt with the shipbuilder Nye in August 1728, saw 'about twenty six men-of-war of the line, that are all unrigged; they appear very handsome, but they are not all fit for service, some being laid aside as entirely useless and others to be repaired'.[75]

Nearly five years later, in February 1733, he was again describing 'the Russian fleet, that has been so very much neglected since the death of Peter the first' and adding that, although Cozens was being sent to Archangel to build two new men-of-war, they 'I believe will be of little service, for, though there was a great many tolerable good seamen in this country in the time of

Peter the first, they are almost all dead or dispersed, so that I have been assured there is not enough good seamen left to man above five or six ships'.[76] However, the dispatch containing these remarks also included full details of the reforms recommended by the commission set up at the beginning of the reign of Anna Ivanovna. The reforms were essentially bureaucratic but not thereby unnecessary, for administrative chaos could not but encourage fundamental disorder aboard ship. Veselago, discussing the improvements of an organisational and material kind, stressed the failure to imbue the fleet with the high morale and commitment that he discerned under Peter.[77] It is, nonetheless, a considerable leap from such a view to a British scholar's that 'in this atmosphere of dislike and indifference [under Anna and Elizabeth] Russian sea-power might have ceased to exist on any significant scale but for the leadership and exertions of British officers'.[78]

With the deaths of Apraksin and Cruys and the disgrace of his arch rival and superior, Piter Sievers (d. 1740), Admiral Gordon, now in his seventies, emerged as the most influential admiral of Anna's reign, temporarily heading the Admiralty College and commander-in-chief at Kronstadt until his death. His friend Thomas Saunders, who had been a member of Anna's naval commission and been promoted to Vice-Admiral of the White for his services, died in 1733, a few months after Lord Duffus. Of the other survivors from Peter's reign whose careers have not been specifically detailed, three deserve particular mention: two, the Irishman James Kennedy and the Welshman William Lewis achieved eminence in the Russian navy by comparatively conventional means, whereas the third, William Walton, occupies a rather special niche within the context of Russian voyages of exploration and discovery.

Walton entered Russian service in October 1723 as a mate or steersman (*shturman*) and achieved officer status in 1730.[79] In 1733 he was assigned to accompany Captain Vitus Bering on his great second expedition across Siberia to Kamchatka and the Pacific. Bering's first expedition had been launched in the last months of Peter's reign to establish whether land masses of Asia and America were connected. The success of that first expedition from which Bering returned in 1730 was limited and the questions asked far from satisfactorily answered. The Admiralty College, with the participation of the Academy of Sciences, moved to mount a new expedition with far-ranging scientific, astronomical and geographical tasks and numbering over 500 men. Walton was assigned as assistant to Captain Martin Spangberg, a Dane like Bering, whom he had accompanied on the first expedition. Spangberg's group was given the specific task of sailing to Japan; its three ships, under the command of Spangberg, Walton and the Dutchman Alexis Schelting, finally set out in June 1738, sailing from Okhotsk for Bolsheretsk on Kamchatka and thence south towards the Kurile Islands and Japan. The ships

separated and independently made their way back to Bol'sheretsk, Walton
having reached the island of Hokkaido. The following year the three ships
set out again for Japan and on this occasion, Walton, who was very much
at odds with Spangberg, deliberately slipped away and made his own way
to the main Japanese island of Honshu. The reports submitted by Spangberg
and Walton were distrusted in St Petersburg, because of the intriguing of the
commandant of Okhotsk, who alleged that they had reached the coast of
Korea and not of Japan. Only in 1746 was the issue resolved in their favour
and the importance of their discoveries recognised: they had mapped the
Kurile islands and part of Japan, demonstrated the non-existence of the 'Land
of Gama' and had been the first to find the route to Japan from the north.[80]
By then Walton was dead. He had died on the return journey from Siberia
on 4/15 December 1743, leaving a wife and a son, born three years earlier
in Iakutsk.[81]

Kennedy and Lewis had both arrived in 1714 as 'under-lieutenants'
(*podporuchik*) and despite a certain amount of leap-frogging in their promotions, both became on the same day in January 1733 'captains of the rank
of colonel' (following the naval reforms, this rank replaced the earlier one
of captain-commodore). It was, however, during the reign of Elizabeth that
they both achieved the rank of admiral but not without certain colourful
episodes in their service records.

Kennedy, who had taken part in the siege of Danzig under Gordon, was
in action again when Russia became involved in the War of the Austrian
Succession against France and Sweden. He was frequently in command of
the ships flying the flag of Vice-Admiral Mishukov. In 1743 he was detailed
to bring the newly-built *Sviatoi Pavel* from Kronshtadt to join the fleet. The
ship was caught in a storm that threatened to sink it and Kennedy subsequently submitted a report to the effect that those responsible for installing
the guns and the rigging deserved to be hanged. The Admiralty College, however, held him responsible, censured him for the language used in his report
and docked him half a year's salary. Two years later his promotion to the
newly restored rank of captain-commodore was blocked on account of his
'unreliability' and frequent drunkenness; in a reign in which the dignity of
Russians was high on the political agenda, he was given a sum of money
for his long service, since 'this would be more tolerable than promoting to
flag-officers such people under whom Russian subjects would be forced to
endure hardship'! Nevertheless, he was not to be denied. He was promoted
to captain-commodore in 1747, rear-admiral in 1752 and retired on 5/16
May 1757 as a vice-admiral on half salary.[82]

Lewis was promoted to vice-admiral on the same day as Kennedy, but
their careers had diverged over the previous twenty-five years since their last
mutual promotions and Lewis's was not yet over, although political events

had threatened to end it in that same year of 1757. A change in the alignment of allies in the Seven Years' War brought Russia to the side of Austria and France against Prussia and England. Lewis commanded the Reval squadron that joined the Kronshtadt fleet in the capture of Memel in July 1757, but with the arrival of the British fleet in the Baltic, requested and was granted permission to reside in Memel until the conflict between Russia and England was resolved. However, on the accession of Catherine II, Lewis was made a full admiral and received the order of Alexander Nevskii. At the beginning of 1764 he retired on full pension after fifty years in Russian service and continued to live in St Petersburg until his death in March 1769. In the 1740s Lewis had been successively commander at Archangel, Kronshtadt and Reval. In 1743 he had been in command of the White Sea squadron which left Archangel in an attempt to join the Russian fleet moving against the Swedes, but the ships were dispersed in a storm: Lewis was court-martialled but acquitted. Earlier, under Anna Ivanovna, he had been dismissed from the service and exiled from Russia 'for not more than two days' for daring to petition personally the empress for the restitution of pay, but was soon pardoned and restored to his former post. He was in fact generally regarded with favour and given special responsibilities, be it the safe conduct back to Kiel in 1727 of the newly-wed Duke and Duchess of Holstein (she was Peter's daughter Anna), or, of more significance in the present context, the task of recruiting master shipbuilders and assistants in Holland and England in 1733.[83]

Anna's reign saw not only the official restoration of diplomatic links between Britain and Russia but also, following on the work of the naval commission, new initiatives to attract British expertise and experience into the Russian navy. The Russian resident in London, Prince Antiokh Kantemir, informing the Admiralty College of Lewis's arrival in May 1733, said that the pay offered was not attractive but that Lewis had nevertheless managed to find three men willing to enlist as shipbuilders.[84] They are not identified but were probably the three who eventually arrived in 1736–7. Alexander Sutherland was the first to arrive and was joined by his brother John and by John Lambe Yeames the following year. Most of the six British shipbuilders who had worked for Peter and continued under Anna had died or retired, but the newcomers ensured that British dominance in building ships for the Baltic fleet continued through the remaining years of Anna's reign and that of Elizabeth. In the second quarter of the century, following Peter's death, British builders were responsible for twenty-one out of forty-one ships-of-the-line and seven out of eleven frigates. In the following quarter, the figures were twenty-seven out of sixty-one battleships and ten out of twenty-two frigates.[85] Only in the last two decades of Catherine II's reign did the reliance on British and foreign masters wane and Lambe Yeames remained as virtually the only reminder of a great tradition. The activity of the Sutherlands fell wholly within the boundaries of Anna's and Elizabeth's reigns, John dying in 1757 and Alexander in 1760.

John, who was initially recruited only as a shipbuilder's assistant (*podmaster'e*), remained a comparatively minor figure, working in St Petersburg and Kronshtadt on a small number of mainly small craft, including two prams and a fireship, although just before his death he finished the 80-gun *Sv. Pavel* at Kronshtadt.[86] Alexander Sutherland went initially to head the shipbuilding yard at Archangel, where the building of battleships for the Baltic Fleet had been resumed in 1733 when it was decided to make greater use of larch as opposed to expensive oak. Over a ten-year period he was responsible for some ten ships-of-the-line and frigates at Archangel. The last ten years of his life were spent at St Petersburg, culminating in the building of two great battleships, the 80-gun *Sv. Andrei Pervozvannyi* and the 100-gun *Dmitrii Rostovskii*. He enjoyed regular promotions, finishing with the rank of colonel.[87] A rank higher, that of brigadier, was achieved by Lambe Yeames towards the end of a long and distinguished career. He was yet another of the band of Britons to serve fifty years in the Russian navy. He worked with Alexander Sutherland at Archangel, making the yards there the most productive in Russia. He remained by the White Sea until 1765 by which time he had built no less than twenty-six ships ranging in size from the 66-gun battleships to pinks. In 1763, early in the reign of Catherine II, he was made surveyor-general (*ober-sarvaer*) with the rank of colonel. Transferring to St Petersburg, he built another thirteen ships, including the 100-gun *Trekh Ierarkhov* by 1783.[88] He was a legendary figure, delighting in taking British and other visitors around the Admiralty yard in St Petersburg, while proclaiming to the end that things were done better in England.[89] 'The great Ship builder at Petersburgh an englishman but a thick skull', in the opinion of Samuel Bentham, died in December 1787 at the age of eighty.[90]

Two years after Lewis's visit to London, the Admiralty College instructed Prince Kantemir to recruit twelve British naval officers: six lieutenants to be appointed as captains of the first rank and six midshipmen as lieutenants. This he did without difficulty and the first officers began arriving in Russia in the summer of 1735.[91] A more senior British officer, Captain Thomas Mathews (1676–1751), also offered his services and arrived in St Petersburg in July of the same year to negotiate terms with the Russian authorities. He was soon on his way back to England, for reasons Rondeau makes clear in his dispatch of 6/17 September: 'the Czarinna would very willingly have employed him in her service, if he would have accepted of the rank of her first vice-admiral; but m-r Mathews not being willing to engage without he was made an admiral, has taken leave of the Czarinna'.[92] Two years later, in a dispatch of 18/29 June 1737, Rondeau was writing that 'Last Saturday arrived here Captain Obrion who is entered into the Czarinna's service as a rear-admiral. As I find he is come with leave of the King I shall do all I can to serve him.'[93] Although he let it be known that Admiral Wager, his English commanding officer, had thought him worthy to be a full admiral in Russia, Captain Christopher O'Brien was obviously prudent enough to bide his time. He was assigned to Kronshtadt to inspect the harbour and fortifications and in November was provided with a stone house there. His promotion to vice-admiral came in the last months of Anna's reign and he became commander-in-chief of Kronshtadt during the short reign of Ivan VI. He retired in 1742.[94]

The British officers and masters, of whom at least six were also recruited at this time, arrived in Russia just as a new conflict with Turkey began; inevitably, many, if not all, were to be sent to the south to join the Don or Dnieper Flotillas. In January 1737 Rondeau was reporting that 'about four thousand seamen with a rear-admiral, nine captains, a great number of lieutenants and masters, having been sent from hence with anchors, cables and all sorts of materials for shipping to Tabaroff on the river Don and to Branska on the Dnieper. Among the officers there is five english captains and a great many english lieutenants.'[95] One of the captains, William Griffiths, was to die a few days into the march; a year later, two more English captains, Somerset Master and William Talbot, were dispatched to the Dnieper.[96] No British shipbuilders were involved either at Tavrov on the Don or at Briansk on the River Desna, which flows into the Dnieper, but British officers were to command Russian ships on the Sea of Azov for the first time since 1711.

The war, which included decisive victories by the Russian armies and the capture of the fortresses of Azov and Ochakov, finished as disastrously as Peter's campaign at the Pruth. Russia, left high and dry by Austria's withdrawal from the war, was forced to sign the Treaty of Constantinople in October 1739, ceding virtually all its gains with the exception of Azov and losing its right to have its battleships sail the Azov or Black Seas. It was not first and foremost a naval war: at sea it was a war of skirmishes and stand-offs, for the Russians had few ships of the line and the Turks had many. The navy was there to supply support for the land operations, notably in the Crimea. Vast numbers of small boats and some prams and galleys were built on the upper reaches of the rivers; many were lost as a result of poor construction and bad weather rather than enemy fire; and those that remained in 1739 had lost their raison d'être.[97]

Some six British officers were initially assigned to the Don flotilla and at least ten to the Dnieper flotilla, but very little is known of their activities at sea. Indeed, from a British point of view the campaign was memorable for a prolonged and acrimonious dispute or disputes between Rear-Admiral Bredal, the experienced Norwegian sailor who had been in the Russian navy since Petrine days and was now commanding the Don flotilla, and a number of British officers under his command. Although the dispute is reflected in official Russian naval records, there is a substantial and inevitably biased contemporary British account by John Cook, the Scottish doctor who was sent to Tavrov and who, early in 1738, met there a number of the British officers involved. The previous year the Russian attempt to open the naval campaign on the Sea of Azov with the battleships up the river at Tavrov was thwarted by the impossibility of floating large vessels over the river's bar to the sea; on Bredal's advice it was decided to build a large number of small boats armed with two-pound guns and able to transport some forty men. However, the British officers, 'Capt. Kenzie, Lieutenants Leslie, Every, and Smallman, were of another opinion, protested against the admiral's plan, and sent a report of the soundings [of the bar at Azov], subscribed by them all, which they had carefully taken. They alledged that it was possible to build vessels fit to carry twenty or even thirty guns: that if they were provided with a sufficient number of such vessels, they would not only be in a condition to protect their transports, but did not doubt to give a very good account of the Turkish fleet, notwithstanding the largeness of their ships, or the number of their cannon.'[98] In the event no such ships were built. The friction between Bredal and Every in particular came to a head during the summer campaign of 1738, when the admiral ignored Every's sighting of the Turkish fleet during reconnaissance and set sail with ultimately disastrous results. The Russian flotilla was to be hemmed in by the Turkish fleet by the Spit of Fedotov (Fedotova kosa) near the top of the Crimean peninsula; Bredal ordered his ships to be burnt and crews, guns and equipment to retreat to Azov by land. Cook's colourful account depicts a craven Bredal pleading illness and driving off first in a cart, while Captain Kensey 'resolved to remain, live, or bravely die with those under his command'. When all arrived back eventually at Azov, the British officers 'spoke their minds too freely to the admiral's face', with the result that they were court-martialled, Kensey and Leslie were sentenced to be dishonourably discharged and Every and Smallman to be executed.[99] Cook leaves the story at the point when the officers were summoned back to St Petersburg. All were reprimanded, but Leslie at least continued to serve into the 1740s, while Kensey was dismissed in July 1741 for his refusal to answer questions and was accompanied back to England by Denis Every. Every, however, was to rejoin the Russian navy for a further three years from 1754 with no loss of seniority and promotion to captain of the third rank.[100]

With the end of the war against Turkey, the remaining British officers were transferred back to the Baltic fleet. Many were coming to the end of their contracts and left Russian service over the next few years. The Admiralty's recruitment through Kantemir of the officers and masters in the mid-1730s was the last Russian initiative of its kind for nearly thirty years. The number of British officers in the Russian navy during the reign of Elizabeth was noticeably diminishing, but it was during this period that Lewis and Kennedy became admirals. Almost duplicating their careers and providing a strong sense of continuing British presence among the upper echelons of the Russian fleet were Peter Anderson and Thomas Mackenzie. Anderson arrived in 1735 as a lieutenant and Mackenzie a year later, as a master, but with a contract providing for promotion to lieutenant after two years, if merited. Throughout their long years of service Anderson always retained his seniority. Although both were captains of the first rank at the end of Elizabeth's reign, Anderson became rear-admiral in 1764 and vice-admiral in 1769, before retiring in 1770, while Mackenzie was promoted to rear-admiral in 1765, the year of his retirement and the year before his death. Both took part in the war against Sweden at the beginning of Elizabeth's reign and in the Seven Years' War at its end, although it is interesting to note that Mackenzie joined Lewis in Memel when Russia was ranged against England in 1757.[101]

Elizabeth's reign was one in which, it is usually emphasised, the pendulum swung back in favour of all things Russian. While that may be so in certain respects, the empress was Peter the Great's daughter and well able to combine patriotism with an appreciation of what foreigners could do for Russia. British officers undoubtedly continued to make a significant contribution during her reign – and British shipbuilders in the shape of Sutherland and Yeames even more so. She looked to Britain for a replacement for Farquharson, but in vain – the British who were approached, such as Thomas Wright of Durham, required salaries that the Russians would not meet – and the experiment of sending Russians trained by Farquharson from the Naval Academy to England was tried instead, and with some success.[102] In 1752, when the new Noble Naval Cadet Corps was opened, an English professor of mathematics and navigation by the name of Newberry was apparently brought from London, but of him and his subsequent career nothing is known.[103]

III

Commitment to the well-being of the Russian fleet was one of the areas in which Catherine the Great most conspicuously followed the example of Peter I and by the end of her reign she possessed a navy that had struck far more effectively than his against both Turk and Swede. She had few illusions about the state of the navy she inherited and her review of the fleet off Kronshtadt in June 1765 only confirmed her worst fears: 'Nous avons des vaisseaux et du monde dessus à foison, mais nous n'avons ni flotte, ni mariniers ... Il faut avouer qu'ils ont l'air de la flotte pour la pêche des harengs, qui part

d'Hollande tous les ans, et non en vérité d'une flotte de guerre, pas un vais-
seau ne tient son rang.'[104] She had already taken steps to ameliorate a dismal
situation by persuading the British government to accept a number of young
Russians for training in the British navy. Between January 1763 and early
1766 some thirty Russians came to Britain in an experiment which was to
prove highly successful in terms of the contribution that most of these men
made subsequently to the Russian navy but which was only to be repeated
in the last years of Catherine's reign.[105] The policy of recruiting foreign, predominantly British officers was, however, pursued with somewhat more consistency and brought many men of experience and calibre into Russian service. Between 1764 and 1772 perhaps fifty British officers joined the Russian
navy. The second great influx came in the 1780s, when Anglo-British
relations improved after the temporary cooling occasioned by the Armed
Neutrality of 1780: no less than thirty-eight officers arrived in a body in
1783 and many more were recruited in subsequent years. The two periods
of the most intensive and successful recruitment coincided not unexpectedly
with the availability of numerous officers on half pay after the peace treaties
concluding the Seven Years' War and the war against the American colonies
and France and Spain. They also occurred, by coincidence rather than design,
a few years before the Russian navy's involvement in its most important
actions of the century, during the war against Turkey in 1768–74 and against
Sweden in 1788–90 and the Turks again in 1787–91. These wars brought
the spectacular naval victory against the Turks in the Mediterranean at
Chesme Bay in June 1770 and a significant action against the Swedes at
Hogland in July 1788. In both battles a good percentage of the Russian ships
were commanded by British officers. Indeed, British officers were prominent
throughout both campaigns and made a notable contribution to the marked
advance of the Russian navy in the last decades of the century.

A number of British officers recruited in the reigns of Anna and Elizabeth
continued to serve under Catherine, notably Vice-Admiral William Lewis and
Captains of the first rank Peter Anderson and Thomas Mackenzie. As we
have seen, Catherine immediately promoted Lewis to full admiral and Anderson and Mackenzie to rear-admiral. Within a few years all had retired or
died, but from the outset the lack of experienced commanders among the
upper echelons of her navy was keenly felt by the empress. In Charles
Douglas (d. 1789), who resigned his commission in the Royal Navy on 20/
31 March 1764 to become a rear-admiral in Catherine's navy, she undoubtedly saw an important capture, but he was soon to disappoint her: within a
month of his arrival, he returned to England to fetch his family, but he
decided to rejoin the Royal Navy, was rewarded in due course with a baronetcy and in 1787 became a rear-admiral.[106] However, undaunted, Catherine
recruited another Scot, Captain John Elphinstone (1722–85) in June 1769,

who was within a month promoted to rear-admiral. More significantly, at the end of the following year she secured the services of Admiral Sir Charles Knowles, the most senior British officer ever attracted into the Russian navy. They were both to make their mark, but the greatest value accrued from those officers who were initially appointed lower down the scale and whose subsequent rise to the top was attributable to what they accomplished in the Russian, rather than British, navy. There are many examples from preceding reigns as well as from Catherine's, but pre-eminent among such men was Samuel Greig (1735–88), who was accorded his 'indubitable right to stand alongside the most distinguished Russians of the age of Catherine II' by the compiler of the *Dictionary of Notable People of the Russian Land* (1836).[107] In the following detailed account of Greig's career spanning nearly twenty-five years in the Russian navy, the attempt will be made to interweave something of the careers of just a few of the many other British officers who also sacrificed years of their lives, and, indeed, not infrequently, their very lives, to the service of Russia.

Greig was born in Inverkeithing in Fife, where the museum has a number of exhibits commemorating the town's most illustrious son and which is dominated by a copy of the famous portrait of the admiral by Ivan Argunov. He learnt his craft as a seaman on his father's merchant ships before joining the Royal Navy as a master's mate sometime before 1758. Over the next six years Greig served with distinction but with modest reward: he was involved in the reduction of Goree in 1758, at the blockade of Brest and the action at Quiberon Bay in 1759 and at the reduction of Havana in 1762. Since 1761 he had been acting lieutenant, but this rank was not confirmed for a number of years, by which time the prospects of advancement and fortune in the service of Russia seemed all too attractive to forgo. Greig was one of the group of five Scottish officers who arrived in St Petersburg in the early summer of 1764 and as a captain of the first rank, was second in seniority after Rear-Admiral Douglas. The other members of the party were captain of the second rank William Roxburgh, Greig's kinsman, who was to distinguish himself in the forthcoming Mediterranean campaign and achieve the rank of rear-admiral before his eventual retirement in 1776, and two lieutenants, Cleland, who returned to Britain within months, possibly with Douglas, and William Gordon, who died in 1768.[108]

Greig soon managed to make his mark in Russia. At the beginning of 1765 he submitted to the Admiralty College a new method for the armament of warships and was allowed to try it out on the frigate *Sv. Sergei*. The college also approved of his subsequent suggestion that in the construction of new ships, the underwater section should be covered not with tar alone but with a mixture of tar and sulphur. In 1768 he was allowed to supervise the armament of the 66-gun *Trekh Ierarkhov*, the ship he was to command at Chesme,

13 Admiral Samuel Greig (1736–88). Painting by D. G. Levitskii, 1780s.

and the innovations which he introduced were recommended for other ships of the line. Nevertheless, in a letter of 10/21 May 1768 Greig complained of his frustration and of his lack of a promotion he felt he merited:

The humble efforts that I have made, to introduce Naval order and Energy into the fleet, and the late Improvements that have been made in the British Navy, has met with such opposition from the different Departments of the College of Admiralty, and has been so little Countenanced by any at the Board there, that I have not the least Incouragement to make any further Attempt. Their steady adherence, & vehement attachment to old Rules & Customs, overballances every Reason that can be advanced on that Subject; and perhaps in a Country where Subordination is so great, my want of equall Rank, lessens & abates the force of my arguments with my Superiors, in matters of themselves so plain & evident. I cannot in the Compass of a Letter pretend to enter into any Particulars of the present Situation of the Fleet; I shall only observe to your Excellency, that if her Imperial Majesty, is really in earnest to have her fleet put upon a creditable footing, or even upon an equall footing with the fleets of our Neighbours in the Baltick, a very different Plan must be followed from that pursued at present.[109]

That the empress was indeed anxious for her fleet to compete with the best was not in doubt and the war with Turkey that began that very year provided a great opportunity to test the mettle of her navy. 'Nothing on earth will do so much good for our fleet as this campaign. All that is stagnant and rotten will come out, and it [the fleet] will be soundly refurbished,' she wrote at the beginning of 1770 to Count Aleksei Orlov, the commander-in-chief of the new Russian Mediterranean fleet, who throughout that year flew his flag on board Greig's ship, the *Trekh Ierarkhov*.[110]

Possessing a fleet only in the Baltic, the Russians decided to split it, forming two squadrons under Admiral Grigorii Spiridov and Rear-Admiral Elphinstone that would constitute the Mediterranean fleet; the remaining ships were placed under the command of Rear-Admiral Anderson at Reval and Kronshtadt. In the passage of the two squadrons to the Mediterranean British assistance in terms of victualling, medical help, docks and repairs, even refits, proved to be not only generous but critical to the success of the expedition.[111] Greig, now a brigadier, was in command of the second division of Spiridov's squadron and arrived at Port Mahon, Minorca on 2/13 December 1769, but was soon detailed to Leghorn to fetch Orlov. Between March and June 1770 the Russian forces were involved in a number of essentially piecemeal, badly coordinated and inconclusive actions on land and sea, including the sieges of Koron and Modon, the landing at Rupino and the engagement at Nauplia. Greig's role in those few actions at which he was present with Orlov during this period was a relatively minor one; the centre of the stage was occupied by Spiridov and by Elphinstone, who had arrived with the second squadron in May, and they were soon engaged in acrimonious mutual recriminations and squabbles about their respective seniorities and responsibilities. The gathering of the fleet under the not-to-be-disputed command of Orlov in the middle of June brought at least a semblance of unity.

On 24/25 June (5/6 July) 1770 two actions were fought which subsequently came to be called the Battle of Chesme, although Greig, in his own account of the events, calls the engagement during the morning and early

afternoon of the first day the Battle of Chios.[112] This first battle was comparatively brief but bloody, resulting in heavy losses on both sides and the
destruction of Spiridov's flagship, the *Sv. Evstafii*, as well as that of his
opposite number, Hassan Pasha's *Real Mustafa*. The Turks retired to the
mouth of the harbour of Chesme, where the second and decisive action was
to be fought during the coming night, directed, on the specific nomination
of Orlov, by Greig, who had transferred to the *Rostislav*. Greig's command
consisted of four battleships, two frigates and the bomb-ship *Grom*, supported by four fireships. By the time the fireships entered the fray around
2 a.m. on 25 June/6 July, their objective had already been in part fulfilled
by a projectile from the *Grom* that had set fire to one of the Turkish battleships. The fireships were commanded by four volunteers: two Russians,
Lieutenant Dmitrii Il'in and Midshipman Prince Vasilii Gagarin, and two
Britons, Lieutenant Thomas Mackenzie and Captain-Lieutenant Robert
Dugdale. Dugdale's fireship was intercepted by the Turks, but Mackenzie
managed to reach his target – a ship that was, however, already in flames.
It was Il'in who administered the coup de grâce by reaching the end of the
Turkish line and setting it alight, leaving Gagarin with nothing to do.

Mackenzie was to describe the battle and his own success in two letters
which were soon published in both English and Scottish newspapers and
journals.[113] It was a stunning victory that devastated the Turkish fleet,
brought death to some 10,000 Turks and gave the Russians control of the
Mediterranean with minimal loss of life and ships. There was no gainsaying
the extent of the Russian victory, although inevitably rivalry for the victor's
laurels was fierce. The official national hero was Orlov, whose alleged contribution was to be immortalised by the addition of a second barrel to his
surname – Chesmenskii, but it is to Orlov's credit that he never attempted
to minimise Greig's role. Lord Cathcart, the British ambassador in St Petersburg, wrote later in 1770 that Greig had 'received every encomium courage
and conduct could deserve', while Sir Horace Mann, writing to Greig from
Florence in 1776, congratulated him on 'the signal services you have rendered
Her [the empress] and the whole Russian Nation by raising it to a pitch of
Glory that astonished all Europe and that might be envied by the greatest
Maritime Powers, Envy itself cannot rob you of the least share of it, whilst
your respectable friend Count Alexis [Orlov] has the noble generosity to
declare that the greatest success of that ever memorable day was totally
owing to you'.[114]

At the very beginning of 1772 there appeared in London *An Authentic
Narrative of the Russian Expedition against the Turks by Land and Sea*,
'compiled from several authentic journals, by an officer on board the Russian
fleet'. The identity of the officer has never been established but, on the basis
of internal evidence which suggests that he was a junior officer aboard the

Ne tron' menia, Thomas Newberry, a midshipman, would seem a likely candidate.[115] Praised in a review as 'animated with that ingenuous warmth that accompanies the faithful relation of public and important actions' and possessing 'even a respectable talent as a writer',[116] the author provides what might be called 'the Elphinstone version', the account of the Scottish rear-admiral's contribution to the Mediterranean campaign up to and including his leaving Russian service early in 1771. It was widely reviewed and was to influence and colour both contemporary and subsequent British attitudes towards the events and the *dramatis personae*. In short, it is responsible for the comparative lack of recognition in Britain of Greig's role and for the aureole surrounding the hero Elphinstone, undone by the machinations of the envious Russians. Greig in fact is mentioned simply by name on three or four occasions and even his contribution at Chesme is seen as the result of a chance decision, although he is commended for leading the attack 'with great spirit'.[117] Elphinstone in contrast always takes centre stage. Describing the action at Nauplia in May 1770, the author proclaims that 'this was certainly a bold action; it shews what invincible courage can do, when animated with the love of glory, and a passionate desire to promote the service we are engaged in. The hazard, and the danger, to be sure were very great; but it is in opposing and rising above these considerations that we discern the hero.'[118]

There can be no question that Elphinstone was a courageous and enterprising leader; he was also impetuous, obstinate and vainglorious. On his voyage from Russia to the Mediterranean he had clashed with Admiral Geary at Portsmouth over port procedures, and in the Mediterranean he and Spiridov were frequently at odds, Elphinstone considering that the empress had placed him under no one's ultimate command but Orlov's.[119] His plans for the attack at Chesme having been rejected and his proposals for swift action after the battle to pass the Dardanelles and fall on Constantinople similarly ignored, Elphinstone soon found himself a source of irritation to Orlov, who wrote to Catherine at the end of June that he 'would be obliged to remove Elphinstone's command, if he did not change his behaviour'.[120] The loss of his flagship, the *Sviatoslav*, on a sandbank during the siege of the fortress of Pelari proved to be the final straw and Elphinstone was sent back to Kronshtadt to face charges of negligence. On reading his defence, Catherine said she thought that 'Elphinstone belonged to the ranks of the mad who are carried away by their first impulse and pay no regard to logic', but that a further matter of his possible embezzlement of funds should be hushed up so as not to offend the British court which had been so helpful to Russia in the war against the Turks.[121] No formal verdict was ever delivered, but Elphinstone sealed his fate by appearing in his Royal Navy uniform at his audience with the empress. The *Scots Magazine* which recorded every stage

14 Captain John Elphinstone (1722–85). Mezzotint by unknown English artist, 1780s. (National Maritime Museum, London.)

of the affair, said that Catherine had observed that 'it was high time that a man should quit her service, who had thrown off her livery'.[122] Elphinstone left Russian service on 19/30 July 1771; three days later, his sons, John and Samuel, who had been with their father throughout the campaign, also resigned their commissions.[123]

It was suggested at the time, and repeated in more recent accounts, that 'a great number of English, who were in the Russian service, and who are unwilling to serve under Count Orlow' followed the Elphinstones back to England.[124] This might be considered, however, in the light of a report written soon after Chesme, in which the Turks were described as 'much exasperated against the English, believing them not only to be the cause of the Russians coming into their seas, but that most of the officers and men on board the Russian ships were English, notions which I am told have been industriously propagated among them by the French'.[125] Whilst the exaggeration is obvious, the British presence was, nevertheless, much in evidence, to a degree perhaps not widely appreciated. It is of course very difficult to give a reliable estimate of the numbers of British officers, to say nothing of the mates, masters and able seamen serving with the Russians in the Mediterranean. In 1769 the *Scots Magazine* made frequent reference to the recruitment of both officers and men and in November reported that Elphinstone's squadron was 'chiefly manned, both men and officers, with English and Scots. The flag-ship carries 80 guns, and, of 800 hands, has but 150 Russians on board'.[126] The author of *An Authentic Narrative* names a Mr Boyd, the pilot of the *Saratov*, 'a man of great humanity, and a brave and judicious seaman', who died in action, and a Mr Glasgow, second mate of the pink *Sv. Pavel*, and also refers to seamen in connection with the siege of Pelari:

At the beginning of September, forty or fifty English and Swedish seamen who were just arrived in a vessel which was purchased at Leghorn [a frigate, also confusingly called *Sv. Pavel*], sent a letter to the English in the fleet, who had before voluntarily offered to mount the breach under the command of Lord Effingham, that they were desirous of sharing the honour with them. The next day thirty more Englishmen, from various vessels, sent to desire that they might be permitted to join their countrymen in the same hazardous undertaking.[127]

It was, incidentally, to Thomas, Earl of Effingham (1747–91), one of the 'gentlemen volunteers' on Elphinstone's flagship, that *An Authentic Narrative* was dedicated. Effingham and his brother Richard, who were both officers in the British army, were among those who left with Elphinstone, but this was not generally the case with the naval officers named in *An Authentic Narrative*.

Three ships in Elphinstone's original squadron were chartered British merchantmen, armed and used principally as transports and storeships. All were commanded by British officers, two of whom, James Body (d. 1780) and George Arnold, continued in Russian service after their ships were reclaimed by the British authorities.[128] A fourth ship, the already mentioned six-gun pink *Sv. Pavel*, was commanded by James Preston (1738?–1813), who was dismissed on Admiral Spiridov's orders in 1771, but contrived to be readmitted in 1788, becoming a rear-admiral during the reign of Paul.[129] Roxburgh, Greig's relation, who was Elphinstone's flag-captain on the *Saratov* when it foundered, also became a rear-admiral. It is a matter worthy of record that in addition to Preston and Roxburgh, no less than seven other officers eventually achieved the rank of admiral in the Russian navy, beginning with Greig and including the fire-ship commanders Dugdale and Mackenzie, Samuel Gibbs (1743–95), Robert Hall (1761–1844), George Tate (1745–1821) and Robert Wilson. This is out of an estimated minimum total of thirty-eight British naval officers serving throughout, or during some stage of, the war against the Turks. This war also involved a Russian squadron operating on the Black Sea and on the Sea of Azov; and it was to that theatre that Admiral Sir Charles Knowles came in 1772.

When Knowles left England at the end of December 1770 he was approaching seventy years of age and had already served over fifty years in the Royal Navy, the last five of them with the title of Rear-Admiral of Great Britain.[130] His career, full of incident, achievement and disappointment, included a controversial spell as Governor of Jamaica, two celebrated court cases from which he emerged the loser against the Spanish government and the winner against Tobias Smollett, and a great reputation as an engineer and inventor. Far from seeking a quiet retirement Knowles remained ambitious and in search of financial security. Responding to an initial indication from Count Chernyshev in 1769 that 'a proper plan was much wanted for the better Construction, Equipment, Discipline and future preservation of the Russian navy', he 'made a tender of his Services', managing to retain half of his British salary, while receiving benefits from Russia way above the norm for an admiral.[131] Despite the *Scots Magazine*'s assurances to its readers that Knowles had been appointed 'Chief President of the Admiralty', the title Catherine was to give him after his arrival in February 1771 was 'General-Intendant' with responsibility for shipbuilding and shipyards, administration and supplies (a somewhat wider brief than that enjoyed by Lord Duffus in Petrine times). He was reputedly 'in such high favour at that court, that he frequently dines in public with the Empress, and the Grand Duke, her son. Several new regulations are daily making in the marine affairs by his express directions.'[132] A memorial he prepared for the empress at this time details changes necessary for the good running of the dockyards, but he was equally active throughout the summer of 1771 designing new schooners and battle-ships, with the assistance of the shipbuilder Lambe Yeames, for use not only in the Baltic but also in the south. It appears that the 80-gun *Sv. Prorok Iezekiil'*, launched in 1773, was designed by him, and that following the great fire that destroyed numerous galleys and other small ships in June 1771, he built 'a schooner frigate' with shallow draught that 'proved a remarkable fast sailer', applying principles he had read and verified in a work by La Croix which he afterwards translated as *Abstract on the Mechanism of the Motions of Floating Bodies* (1775).[133]

In July 1771 Catherine wrote to Count P. A. Rumiantsev, commander-in-chief of the Russian first army that had swept the Turks from Moldavia and controlled the area around the Danube delta, describing Knowles as 'a skilled and enterprising old man' and passing on his designs for 'the best method of building fire-ships'.[134] Earlier that year she had urged Rumiantsev to be ready for the campaign of 1772, which promised 'an end to the woes of humankind by a daring enterprise', namely an attack by 40,000 Russian

15 Admiral Sir Charles Knowles (1704–77). Mezzotint by John Faber (1750s) from an original painting by Thomas Hudson. (National Maritime Museum, London.)

troops on Constantinople itself. She specifically required the prospecting for
suitable timber, the sounding of the rivers and the preparation of enough
boats, both newly built and captured from the enemy. In his reply Rumiantsev had tactfully tried to suggest that the scheme was impracticable and
that he was a soldier, not a sailor, but this was to provide a reason for
dispatching Knowles to oversee the creation of a suitable Danube flotilla.[135]
At the beginning of the following February Knowles left St Petersburg on
his 'secret expedition', accompanied by the Dutchman Captain Kingsbergen,
three British lieutenants, John Wilkinson, Thomas Lawrence and George
Arnold, a British shipbuilder William Oxenham, and his interpreter and adjutant Grigorii Mulovskii, Count Ivan Chernyshev's illegitimate son, whom he
had met originally in England.[136] However, 'upon Sir Charles's arrival at
Ismael instead of finding there, as the Empress assured him he would, above
four score vessels fit for transport, or other service, there was not one in a
condition to go as far as the mouth of the Danube, which at once prevented
the attempting to carry into execution this wild and romantic scheme'.[137]
Knowles did what he could, inspecting installations and shipbuilding at
Izmail, Kilia, Galatz and Iassy. Two frigates were completed according to
his design and two more were laid down before they left: these were the
frigates which Catherine ordered Vice-Admiral Siniavin, who was in command of the Azov flotilla, to repair and make seaworthy for operations in
1775. Knowles detailed Kingsbergen to join Siniavin, but he himself seems
to have decided to return to St Petersburg via Kiev rather than visit Azov
and the yards on the Don.[138]

Back in the Russian capital by late July, Knowles was to make tours of
inspection at the ports of Kronshtadt, Riga and Reval and it was the state of
Kronshtadt, 'Ville Frontière de la premier [sic] consequence', that particularly
appalled him: 'J'étois touché d'y voir l'ouvrage le plus stupendueux dans
l'univers tomber en déperissement et en danger d'être totalement ruiné.'[139]
He proceeded to write a number of reports for the empress, urging a fundamental reform of the Russian naval administration. Catherine, sympathetic
in principle to his recommendations, although twice characterising them as
too sweeping and too vague, was concerned that were she to initiate the
reforms and Knowles then to depart for England, as he was regularly suggesting he might, everything would stall and revert to its former condition. In
the event, Knowles remained until the end of June 1774 but, receiving none
of the recognition he expected in his homeland, he was said to have regretted
he had not stayed in Russia. In Russia, although he had ruffled many feathers,
he had proved a catalyst for change. He had proposed much, achieved a
great deal, particularly at Kronshtadt, and had essentially fulfilled what he
had promised Catherine at the outset: 'framing a Plan for the better Regulation of Her Imperial Majestys Marine and leaving the execution of it to

Younger Men and Posterity, to carry into Execution'.[140] In the words of the *Scots Magazine*, which had assiduously reported his activities during his three and a half years in Russia, he had taken 'uncommon pains to establish the English exercise throughout the navy';[141] this, in the Russian ambassador's variant, was 'le pied anglais', for which he gave recognition to Knowles but, pre-eminently, to Greig.

In stark contrast to the temperamental and troublesome Elphinstone and Knowles, Greig proved himself not only courageous and highly capable, but loyal, discreet and diplomatic, and his career prospered accordingly. He was immediately promoted to rear-admiral after Chesme and, flying his flag, he was to take part in several of the many subsequent engagements in the Mediterranean. In October 1772, for instance, he was in command of a detachment (flagship the *Pobeda*) which made a successful raid on the town of Chesme, but by the late spring of 1773 he had seen his last action of the campaign. He returned to Russia with his squadron for a few months before setting out from Kronshtadt again on 21 October/1 November 1773 and reaching Leghorn in February the following year. He was still at Leghorn when the Peace of Kuchuk Kainardji was signed in July 1774. In February 1775 he left the Mediterranean for the last time. On his voyage back to Russia Greig put in at Dover for water and provisions and the British papers noted with admiration that 'the cleanliness on board will be a clear proof of how it preserves the lives of the sailors, as the Admiral declared, that during the eight months not a single man died out of 3,000, the complement of the squadron'.[142] They had evidently no suspicions that an even more newsworthy item was connected with Greig's homeward voyage, one of the incidents which might be seen as casting a shadow on an otherwise unblemished career. On the day the admiral sailed from Leghorn, 12/23 February, Count Orlov brought to his flagship, the *Isidor*, the mysterious and unfortunate adventuress know as the Princess Tarakanova, where they were entertained by Greig and his wife Sarah and by the British Consul Sir John Dick and his wife. Tarakanova, allegedly the daughter of the Empress Elizabeth by Count Razumovskii, was then detained on board ship and taken to St Petersburg, where she was soon to die in prison, if not in the dramatic fashion portrayed in the famous painting by the nineteenth-century Russian artist Flavitskii. Captain James Trevenen, an English officer who came to know Greig a few years later and to venerate him as 'my third tutelar genius, my household god, my successor to [Captain James] Cook and [Captain James] King', noted that 'Greig has been censured by many for the part he took in that affair, but as far as it relates to the ship it is without cause. If Count Orlov, having decoyed the woman on board, put her in his charge as his prisoner, he could not do otherwise than carry her to Petersburg.' However, if Greig had brought his wife from Russia 'for the express purpose of serving as the decoy duck; and if he entered as a principal into that matter, it becomes an affair of treachery in which I should have been very much ashamed to have borne a part'.[143] On 16/27 May 1775 Catherine sent Greig a note in which she said that 'the travellers would soon be taken off your hands' and that 'I shall always remember your services and shall not fail to give you marks of my benevolence towards you'.[144] The question mark remains and Grieg's complete loyalty to the empress was only really put to the test when direct confrontation with Britain was involved.

Already a knight of the orders of St George (2nd class) and of St Anna on the completion of the Mediterranean campaign, Greig was soon the recipient of new honours: on 10/21 July 1775 he was promoted to vice-admiral and appointed commandant of Kronshtadt; a year later, on 8/19 July 1776, on the occasion of Catherine's inspection of the Russian fleet, the last squadrons of which had finally returned from the Mediterranean, he received from her the ribbon of the Order of St Alexander Nevskii. The next year saw his triumphant return to Scotland and visit to London:

> Adm. Greig went from Edinburgh to London, was introduced to the King on the 10th and had a conference with Lord George Germaine on the 12th of September – on Thursday, Oct. 2 the Empress of Russia's birthday, the Russian frigate at Leith gave a round of twenty-one guns, which was answered by the same number from the castle of Edinburgh; and on that occasion the Admiral gave a grand entertainment, in Fortune's tavern, Edinburgh, to the Prince d'Aschkow [Pavel Dashkov, the son of Princess Ekaterina Dashkova], the Lord Provost and Magistrates, and many of the nobility and gentry in the city and neighbourhood. Next day his Excellency was presented with the freedom of the city, on which occasion the Lord Provost gave an elegant entertainment in his own house. – on the 9th of October his Excellency set sail from Leith Road on his return to Russia.[145]

A further mark of esteem from Britain followed on 14 March 1782, when Greig was elected a Fellow of the Royal Society 'for many eminent services in his Profession as well as for a very extensive knowledge in the various branches of Physics'. Also in 1782, he was made a full admiral and on 7/18 August of the following year he was elected an Honorary Member of the Russian Academy of Sciences.[146] Finally, mention might be made of his previously unnoticed contribution to the *Regulations on Merchant Shipping (Ustav kupecheskogo morekhodstva)*, promulgated in 1781: for drafting the first eight articles he received from the empress a snuffbox with her portrait.[147]

Among all these honours and distinctions, his appointment as commander of Kronshtadt was of particular significance. Greig was both to continue and complete much that Knowles had begun and to initiate much more of his own. Knowles had been gone almost a year by the time Greig returned for the last time from the Mediterranean, but their paths had crossed for a few months in the summer of 1773, when both were back at Kronshtadt and, according to one source, Knowles' help was enlisted in the fitting out of Greig's new squadron.[148] Knowles had found much amiss at Kronshtadt and work was under way to rid the harbour of the accumulated rubbish of decades and to repair rotten timber and decayed brickwork. He had been particularly concerned with the state and inadequacy of the Peter Canal and recommended the building of three new dry docks, two of which were in fact completed by the end of 1774.[149] Knowles' major contribution, however, was his insistence on the need to replace the antique windmills that had been used to empty the dry docks by fire-machines imported from Britain. An order was eventually placed with the Carron Iron Works near Falkirk, where Charles Gascoigne, the director, had produced with the help of the noted engineer John Smeaton a 'Grand Plan for converting the Mill N into a Fire Engine for draining docks of Cronstadt', but by the time the group of fourteen workmen had arrived from Scotland to construct the engine late in 1774, Knowles had already left.[150] Greig assumed responsibility for the installation and the first tests were run in June 1777, shortly before Greig's visit to Scotland. He was so impressed with its performance that he was allowed to order another some years later, but it never became operational. The original engine became one of the sights of the capital and Catherine writes of her visit to see 'la machine à feu qui vide le canal' in 1782, the year in which Greig was raised to full admiral.[151]

Greig was as concerned as Knowles with problems of fitting and arming the Russian fleet and following Knowles, he turned to Carron, but not only for guns: in 1786 he entered into negotiations with Gascoigne himself, the inventor of the gasconade or carronade, to 'établir une fonderie d'artillerie ici en Russie'.[152] After fierce opposition from his associates and initial opposition from the British government, Gascoigne, whose activities will be examined in some detail in the following chapter, was eventually allowed to leave for Russia. He was to reorganise after the Carron system the Aleksandrovskii cannon works at Petrozavodsk on Lake Onega and the nearby Konchezerskii foundry and later to set up a branch of the Petrazavodsk works near Kronshtadt on Kotlin Island, which was designed to make use of the old cannon there and to supply the immediate needs of the fleet.

Under Greig's surveillance the port of Kronshtadt was subjected to a new face-lift in the 1780s. William Tooke, the British chaplain in St Petersburg during this period, commenting that 'the harbour for the ships of war is extremely remarkable and frequently visited by foreigners to their great satisfaction', drew attention to 'the large mole surrounded by a pier of granite, constructed under the supervision of admiral Greig'.[153] This was but one of the projects initiated by Greig with the empress' active encouragement. Describing her visit to the fire engine in 1782, she also noted the progress that was being made with replacing the wooden linings of the docks with granite; Kronshtadt was taking on that appearance of solid impregnability, considerably increased in the nineteenth century, which led a writer at the time of the Crimean War to remark that 'a Scotsman built those walls which years afterwards checked the career of his fellow-countryman Sir Charles Napier'.[154] Catherine had issued the ukaz for the stone reconstruction of the harbours at the end of 1781 and Greig took over responsibility on 21 February/4 March 1783, following the death of Engineer-General Bauer. But the overall replanning of Kronshtadt was hastened by one of those all-too-frequent occurrences in the Russian capital – a vast fire, devastating the Admiralty on 13/24 May 1783. Within two weeks it was decreed that the Admiralty was to be transferred to Kronshtadt. By March the following year Greig had submitted proposals to the Admiralty College for the siting of the buildings with particular attention paid to problems of fire prevention, but it was only on 28 January/8 February 1785 that the 'General Plan for the Building of the Admiralty at Kronshtadt, Composed by Admiral Greig' was confirmed.[155] The plan covered not only the disposition of the new Admiralty buildings but also the construction of barracks, hospitals (including a quarantine hospital on the island of Seskar), a prison, the naval cadet college, and the dredging of the Military, Middle and Commercial harbours.[156] The hospital and prison proved an inevitable magnet for the English philanthropist and reformer John Howard, who visited Greig in 1781 and was greatly impressed both with the admiral and his plans; a second visit in September 1789, after the admiral's death, dismayed him however, for he found that the standards in the hospital had worsened and that the new prison which had been marked out in 1781 was still not built.[157] The most detailed and enthusiastic description of what was happening at Kronshtadt under Greig is found in the diaries of General Francisco de Miranda, who spent three days with the admiral in July 1787. Miranda comments with approval on the system of 'summer' and 'winter' hospitals whereby the sick were transferred to light and spacious summer quarters, whilst the main building 'is whitewashed, ventilated and cleaned to receive them back in winter'; he is also impressed by the 'new barracks, constructed under the direction of the admiral, which are certainly very good and can hold 10,000 men, and when completed, up to 30,000'.[158]

Although Greig's success in persuading Gascoigne to enter Russian service in 1786 apparently led him to be ostracised for a time by the British community in St Petersburg,[159] an earlier incident demonstrates his unwillingness to act when he considered British interests were truly at stake. The Armed Neutrality of 1780 created a difficult situation for the British officers in Russian service, but Greig was not slow to make his position clear, as a dispatch from the then British ambassador, Sir James Harris, reveals. On reading the terms of the Declaration, Greig had composed a memorandum for the empress, pointing out that 'if she carried her present measures into execution, she would act in direct contradiction to herself'. Greig furthermore assured Harris that 'and he spoke in the name of all his countrymen, that if ever the Empress should require of them to serve in a manner hostile to us, they would, to a man, quit her service. Notwithstanding his high rank and lucrative post, I am sure he is sincere, as far as regards himself, and am happy to give this strong and undoubted testimonial of his character and principles.'[160] Further evidence of his stand is contained in a letter he wrote at about the same time, suggesting that 'the Empress probably judges (and not without Reason) that I'm too partial in my Principles, to make a good Neutral Commander. And we have seen that little good is to be expected from those who are employ'd to act inconsistently to their Principles.'[161] Later in 1780 there was an incident revealing Catherine's continued respect for her admiral. There was an 'attempt to burn the Russian fleet' and Harris reported that 'everyone imputed it to the nation and people against whom they were the most indisposed. Count Panin fixed it upon the English sailors, and impressed the Grand Duke with this idea.' The empress, however, 'treated the whole as an idle tale'.[162] Harris gave a more detailed account of the incident to Samuel Bentham, recently arrived in St Petersburg, who passed it on to his brother Jeremy:

On Monday evening, the fleet being all out in the road at Cronstadt, about 7 o'clock, a smoke was seen to issue from the middlemost ship. Admiral Greig saw it from his window, ran instantly to the water side, and went off on board. With some difficulty he made his way through the smoke towards the magazine or powder room, in the passage of which he found a large bundle of oakum just lighted and the match which was still burning. He got it out before it burst into flames, and by that means saved the ship, if not the greatest part of the fleet ... The Admiral examined every body on board immediately, and has found one man who is much suspected.[163]

It would seem to be this incident which Trevenen had in mind when he wrote of Greig that 'he never lost the Empress's good will and she supported him through everything, even once when the Grand Duke seemed to become his enemy', although there is no evidence at all for his suggestion that 'Greig's conduct in that affair wanted manliness'.[164]

Certainly, there is no lack of courage or decisiveness in another affair at Kronshtadt which happened during Greig's command, although once again rumours were rife in St Petersburg that he was to some degree to blame. On the first day of Easter 1785 a group of sailors went on the rampage after they had been given watered vodka as well as short measures by the local *otkupshchik* (the Kronshtadt merchant exercising the state vodka monopoly). Greig, accompanied only by his adjutant and an orderly, immediately went among the rioters, most of whom fled when they saw him. Other officers, including four British (Captain John Biggs, Captain-Lieutenant John Green, and Lieutenants Nicholas Brown and Stephen Scott), came to his assistance with guards, who proceeded to round up the sailors. Greig in his letter to Count Bezborodko, Catherine's secretary, categorically denied that complaints about the *otkupshchik* had been addressed to him prior to the disorders, although characteristically he added that in principle he had much sympathy with the words allegedly uttered by him: 'if the vodka's bad, they should not drink it; at least it would cut down the number of drunks', for drunkeness was always harmful, 'for good order and military discipline, as well as for health'. The letter is also remarkable for Greig's protestations of loyalty to Catherine, of his clear conscience before God, of personal honour and courage, and for his appeal to all 'who have a profound knowledge of the human heart'. 'Although it would be extremely vain of me to praise my personal courage (insomuch that it would be shameful for anyone in my position to be without it), I am nevertheless sure that all will agree that the feeling of guilt brings fear to the bravest of men when he finds himself among those whom he knows in his conscience he has wronged and who are in a position to take their revenge.'[165] Both the sentiment and its expression point directly to Greig's connections with one of the great social and moral movements of the age – freemasonry – an aspect of his career and character which is seldom, if ever, given the prominence it deserves.

In November 1779 the Lodge 'Neptune' at Kronshtadt received its warrant from Prince G. P. Gagarin, grand master of the newly formed Chapter of the Swedish order in Russia. Greig, who was a senior warden at its foundation, became master in 1781, a position he retained until his death. Unlike 'Perfect Union', the St Petersburg lodge founded in 1771 (described in chapter 1), 'Neptune' had no pretensions to be a British lodge and worked the currently dominant Swedish rite with its ten degrees and a pageantry which was an undoubted attraction for a predominantly military lodge. Three lists of members of 'Neptune' for the years 1780–1 only have been preserved and show over 88 per cent of the masons to be naval officers or connected with the Naval Academy, but at no time did British masons represent more than 10 per cent of the total membership, which grew from fifty-two in 1780 to sixty-two at the end of 1781. In addition to Greig, the other full British members were all naval officers: Captains-Lieutenant Francis Dennison and Robert Wilson, who had been in the Mediterranean campaign, Captain James Nasse, who had been British consul at Trieste before coming to Russia and joining the navy in 1777, and Lieutenant Charles Newman, but it is probable that others were to become members, particularly following the new influx of British officers into Russian service after 1783. The lodge helped to create a bond, if only a fragile one, between the British and the Russians and cement their allegiance to Greig, and many of them were to distinguish themselves in the forthcoming Swedish campaign by their courage and absence of fear in the face of death.[166]

Greig had one more crisis to weather on the eve of the Swedish war which was to cost him his life. On 23 April/4 May 1788 there arrived in St Petersburg John Paul Jones (1747–92), Scottish born but an officer in the Continental Navy since 1775. In April 1778 he masterminded what has been called 'one of the most curious incidents in our island's history: the American invasion of England', a somewhat excessive description of his raid on Whitehaven.[167] It and similar exploits nevertheless brought him fame in America and in France and a notoriety in Britain which was to be remembered keenly by the British officers at Kronshtadt. Jones received from the empress the rank of rear-admiral, giving him seniority over all the British officers with the exception of Greig. They immediately drew up a memorial for the empress in which they argued that Jones, 'who has violated every principle of honour and honesty and the laws of God and men, not only cannot be worthy of trust, but must bring disgrace and contempt upon any Corps of Officers or service into which he may be admitted'.[168] Greig, who a few years earlier had written to his friend, Charles, now Sir Charles, Douglas that 'the dastardly conduct of the Rebels hitherto, shews them to be very unworthy of that Liberty & Independence which they urge as the specious Pretence of their Rebellion',[169] agreed to sign the petition, but with some reluctance. When it became clear that the empress could hardly concede on a matter involving her judgement and authority, Greig dissuaded his brother officers from presenting the document. The immediate crisis was also defused with the removal of Jones to the Black Sea to command the sailing fleet.

Since August 1787 Russia had been at war again with Turkey and Greig himself had been preparing to accompany most of his Baltic fleet to the Mediterranean to reinforce the existing squadron of six battleships. An advance detachment of three battleships under Admiral von Dessen had already left for Copenhagen when the Swedes decided to move against Russia in the hope of a quick and decisive victory. Their action was altogether too precipitate and when the Swedish fleet put to sea on 29 May/9 June 1788, Greig was able to marshal most of his Baltic fleet and set out on 22 June/3 July. The war at sea, which was to prove costly for both sides in terms of ships and men, dragged on for over two years until the peace of 3/14 August 1790, but for Greig the war was to be a very short one, a matter of little more than three months. During that period he fought an essentially indecisive action at Hogland on 6/17 July and was then successful in blockading the Swedes at Sveaborg, but died on board his flagship, the *Rostislav*, at Reval on 15/26 October, before he was able to effect his plans for attacking the Swedish frigates gathered at Porkala. Greig had, nevertheless, wrested the initiative from the Swedes, frustrated their plans to attack St Petersburg, captured at Hogland the flagship of Count Wachtmeister, the *Prins Gustaf*, and a few days later outside Sveaborg fired the Swedish battleship *Prins Gustaf Adolf*, which had run aground whilst taking evasive action. Catherine's delight in her admiral's victories knew no bounds and Greig was made a knight of the Order of St Vladimir (1st class) and of St Andrew.

Greig in his own sober account of the battle for the empress paid tribute to the bravery of the greater part of the officers and men under him, but declared himself 'very much dissatisfied with the conduct of some of the captains, who I shall be under the necessity of suspending'.[170] These officers, who had kept their ships at long range during the battle and allowed the *Vladislav* to fall into Swedish hands, were sent back to Kronshtadt, where they 'were put in chains, with an iron collar round their necks, in which condition they are doomed to perpetual slavery', according to the *Scots Magazine*'s lurid account.[171]

The Battle of Hogland proved controversial in another respect. Greig was accused by the Duke of Sudermania of using 'fire-shells' and rebuked that 'projectiles of such a kind are not used by civilised nations'. In his reply, Greig suggested that the Swedes had been the first to use them both against his own ship and against that of Admiral von Dessen, although he admitted that von Dessen had himself fired up to fifteen of the same projectiles. He added an interesting passage:

Your Royal Highness will graciously consider that the fleet under my command was fitted out against the Turks, and that this war service being of a desperate nature, there must be some excuse for carrying out desperate arms never intended to be used against a civilised nation. If, then, Y. R. H. should be disposed to promise me that such destructive arms will not hereafter be used by the Swedish fleet, I in my turn hereby plight my honour that neither shall the Russian fleet make use of them, it being my earnest desire to reduce the cruelties of war to such an extent as the nature of the service will allow.[172]

Greig's 'earnest desire to reduce the cruelties of war' was everywhere apparent, particularly in his directives to Russian landing parties not to cause hardship to the Swedish villagers. Greig's role was a difficult one, but as a foreigner in command of the Russian navy, a mason believing in international brotherhood and master of a lodge practising the Swedish rite, he nevertheless gave Catherine no reason to doubt his selfless dedication to her service.

A number of legends grew up around Greig's death: one version had it that 'Greig died of a broken heart for not having succeeded better'; another, that he had succumbed to 'chagrin over the jealousy to which both he and the other British officers were exposed from the Russians', yet another, that he was poisoned. There was also a confused story that the masons were preparing to kill him for not surrendering the Russian fleet to his Swedish brothers.[173] His death, however, resulted from a fever after an illness of some three weeks. Catherine sent her physician, Rogerson, a fellow Scot, to attend

Greig, but to no avail. His death occasioned national mourning on an unprecedented scale, certainly for a foreigner. The French ambassador, the Comte de Ségur, wrote that 'l'impératrice fit une perte qui lui coûta de justes larmes; l'amiral Greig mourut. Chef actif, administrateur éclairé, habile amiral, guerrier intrépide et modeste, il emporta au tombeau l'estime de ses ennemis, et les regrets de tous ceux qui l'avaient connu.'[174] Catherine had a gold medal struck in his memory and ordered her architect Giacomo Quarenghi to prepare a design for his mausoleum. In addition to the state funeral held at the Lutheran cathedral in Reval where he was to be buried,[175] at least two special memorial Lodges were held in the capital. Funeral orations were delivered in which Greig was praised for his public and private life, for his services to Russia on the one hand and to masonry on the other, for those 'great and attractive qualities which adorned our lamented and esteemed Brother, which did credit to mankind and him a god-fearing, wise, generous man, in a word a true Freemason'. The German orator of the Lodge 'Urania' did not restrict himself to mere panegyric; his portrayal of Greig contains reference to his idealism and simplicity of manner but also to human weaknesses which prevented him from achieving 'that perfection for which he strove'.[176]

Captain Trevenen's memoirs, which have supplied interesting insights into Greig's career and character, also provide a final remarkable pen portrait of the admiral in his last years which is an essential accompaniment to the formal portraits painted by Levitskii and Argunov:

His person was rather large and excessively awkward. His legs very large; his belly and breast rather sunken; his shoulders round and his head stooping forward. In his winter dress at Kronstadt nothing could look more like an old Scotch wife well wrapped up in cold weather. His dress, when not in uniform, was plain, almost to an affectation of plainness, only that I believe (though it was not always my opinion) that he had not a spark of affectation of any sort in him. The features of his face were large and marked, but as for character there was nothing observable but much seriousness and reflection and perhaps somewhat of profundity. When he was not speaking there was a heaviness, almost dullness, marked in it, but his countenance brightened much in conversation. He was in general very silent, but sometimes, in particular companies, he knew how to make himself entertaining by producing with much good nature and pleasantness some of that inexhaustible fund of knowledge and information that he had acquired by constant application in the latter years of his life; for in his early stages his education had been evidently much neglected. His remarks were always judicious, for he was capable of observing and reflecting as well as of application to gain the ideas of others. With all this he was certainly slow and heavy from nature. In affairs of writing, however, method supplied all quickness of parts and in the active business of a fleet he threw off that part of his character and was busy, energetic and decided.[177]

Greig left a widow Sarah (1752–93), a daughter of Alexander Cook, owner of a rope-walk in Kronshtadt with a contract to supply the Russian fleet.

They had married in the English chapel in St Petersburg on 21 August/1 September 1768. The Greigs had four sons, Alexis (1775–1845), John (1776?–92), Samuel (1778?–1807) and Charles (1785–1817), and a daughter, Jean (1783–1820). Alexis, the first-born who was made a midshipman at birth, became the most famous and was the only one of the family to take Russian citizenship. He rose to the rank of admiral and like his father before him and his own son Samuel after him, he was made an honorary member of the Russian Academy of Sciences for his wide-ranging services, which included presidency of the design commission for the noted Pulkovo observatory.[178] Although his sister was to remain in St Petersburg and eventually marry the Reverend John Paterson, a prominent figure in the Russian Bible Society, in 1817, Alexis's three brothers all left Russia. John, a midshipman in the Russian Navy, joined the Royal Navy, Samuel became commissioner to the Russian Navy in London, and Charles, after an apprenticeship in a British commercial house in St Petersburg, eventually joined the Royal Navy pay office.[179]

IV

The Russian navy without Greig was hard to conceive. Count Zavadovskii called Greig 'the first admiral the Russian navy ever had' and looked with an apprehension which was shared by Bezborodko at the people who were to succeed him.[180] Catherine, realising her 'très grand besoin de quelques bons et entendus marins', turned to Vorontsov in London in March of the following year with a list of fifteen rear-admirals, including Sir Charles Douglas, and seven senior captains in the Royal Navy whom she would like to see in Russian service, but none was available.[181] While there might seem a hint of panic in her appeal in 1789, she had pursued her policy of recruitment at all levels at intervals throughout her reign. Following her captures of Douglas in 1764, Elphinstone in 1769 and Knowles in the following year, she had early in 1783 ordered Simolin, Vorontsov's predecessor, 'to sound Admiral Rodney, and to try every possible means to induce him to enter into the Russian service, and in case he should decline, to use his utmost endeavours to engage Admiral Hood or Commodore Elliot [both reappearing on her 1789 list], or some other officer of high rank and high reputation'.[182] Simolin was successful only in meeting her second request for promising 'officers of an inferior rank' – and overwhelmingly successful, if the *London Chronicle* was to be believed: 'Upwards of three hundred British Naval Lieutenants, Midshipmen and Surgeons, embarked in the course of last week for Petersburgh, in order to serve on board the Russian ships of war', it announced at the beginning of September 1783, but it scaled down its assessment in the following issue to 'a certain number of marine officers', of whom a dozen were soon to leave London.[183] Nonetheless, over forty officers made their way to Russia at this time. Some four years later, in March 1787, Vorontsov informed Bezborodko that many British officers, worried by the prospect of a long peace, were approaching him with a view to entering Russian service, but since he had no instructions, he could do nothing. Although he could not promise admirals, he said that he knew personally Admirals Howe and Rodney who would undoubtedly help him to select suitable candidates.[184] Catherine responded immediately, authorising her ambassador to recruit between twenty and thirty of the best officers available for service on the Baltic, the White Sea and Black Sea, which he did, if not without some difficulty.[185] Looking back in 1802 to his own initiative in 1787 and the empress' request to him in 1789, Vorontsov, writing to his old friend Admiral Nikolai Mordvinov, who had spent some years with the Royal Navy in the 1770s, recalled how none of the British admirals had wished to enter Russian service and the British government, 'still indignant for the imposition of the Armed Neutrality', had opposed the recruitment of other officers. 'However, I succeeded in persuading a number of them, who resigned from service to their country, and they included Trevenen, Marshall, Thesiger and Crown, of whom the last is still serving with distinction as a rear-admiral and the merits of the others are well known in the Russian fleet'.[186] Some thirty officers seem to have been recruited in the years 1787–9; and for the whole period from the Peace of Kuchuk Kainardji in 1772 to the Peace of Jassy in 1792 upwards of 100 British (and a few American) officers joined the Russian navy. Overall, a figure well in excess of 150 British officers would seem a fair estimate for the reign of Catherine. If in the 1760s there were probably as many Danish officers recruited as British, the British increasingly dominated thereafter, although the names of Italian, Greek and a very few Dutch officers also appear. By 1783 only some fifteen British officers who had joined the Russian navy during the early years of Catherine's reign were still serving; at least eleven others had died, and many more had left for Britain. Of the native Russian officer corps, only a quarter of those who had taken part in the 1769–72 campaign remained in active service, according to Vorontsov's estimate, and the rest had retired or dispersed to their distant estates.[187] The influx of British officers in 1783 was therefore timely, not least because Russia's annexation of the Crimea in that year increased the ever-present tension in the region and there was urgent need to develop the Russian naval presence.

A number of the newly arrived British officers were soon dispatched to the south, three or four to Astrakhan to join the Caspian flotilla, but the majority to the Black Sea and Sea of Azov. In the Black Sea, Russian naval strength was divided between recently founded Kherson on the Dnieper and the newly acquired port of Sevastopol in the Crimea itself. It was Thomas

Mackenzie of Chesme fire-ship fame, now with the rank of rear-admiral, who was responsible for initiating the construction of the harbour at Sevastopol and who died there in 1786.[188] Coincidentally, Robert Dugdale, the other British fire-ship commander, who was promoted to rear-admiral on the same day in January 1783 as Mackenzie, was transferred to Kherson from the Baltic, but remained for just two years before returning to a shore post at Kronshtadt.[189] Both were thus removed from the scene when, in August 1787, the Turks, incensed by Catherine's triumphant and self-advertising progress to see her 'New Russia', declared war. Undoubtedly, many of the officers recruited by Vorontsov in 1787–8 would have been sent to the Black Sea but for the attack in the Baltic by the Swedes in May 1788, and in the event none went. Once the war against Sweden had come to an end, however, several British officers immediately and successfully petitioned the Admiralty College to be transferred to the Black Sea, where action and promotion beckoned.[190] British officers were nevertheless engaged in various early battles against the Turks, with varying fortunes.

Benjamin Teesdale (d. 1799), who had been in the Russian navy since 1771, was transferred to Kherson in 1783. In September 1787 he was captain of the 66-gun *Maria Magdalina* that left Sevastopol with the fleet under the command of Rear-Admiral Count Voinovich and was soon caught in a violent storm. The 44-gun *Krym* foundered with all hands, including Lieutenant John Mettam (who had joined as a midshipman in 1783), while the *Maria Magdalina* lost its masts and rudder and, after floating helplessly for several days towards the Bosphorus, was captured by the Turks and Teesdale and his crew imprisoned. On the conclusion of the war Teesdale was released but was immediately arrested by the Russians. When the empress was asked whether he could be included in the general amnesty following the peace, she ruled that Teesdale had ceased to be in Russian service the moment his ship was captured, and therefore he could be given the requisite passport to leave Russia as soon as possible.[191]

The misfortunes of Teesdale and Mettam coincided with the beginning of the protracted struggle for control of the Liman and for the fortress of Ochakov, which eventually fell to the Russians in December 1788. The Liman was the great bay or lagoon formed by the estuaries of the Dnieper and Bug rivers and stretched for some thirty miles westwards before joining the Black Sea at a point less than two miles wide and guarded on opposite sides by the Turkish fortress of Ochakov and the Russian fort of Kinburn. In the wresting of the Liman from the Turks one Englishman and one American were destined to play conspicuous roles. The American was of course Rear-Admiral John Paul Jones, commander of the sailing fleet who had raised his flag on the 66-gun *Vladimir* only in the summer of 1788. Jones, who has left his own detailed account of the battles for the Liman, was, however, recalled to St Petersburg at the end of the year, after clashing with Prince Charles of Nassau-Siegen, the commander of the rowing fleet, and with Potemkin; the following summer, he was dismissed from Russian service on trumped-up charges of rape.[192] It was, however, the multi-talented Samuel Bentham (1757–1831), brother of the more famous Jeremy, who, despite the fact that he held a commission in the Russian army, was to render the navy invaluable service. Soon after his arrival in Russia in 1779 he was recommended to Admiral Greig as possessing 'a good deal of universal knowledge, but his particular turn & almost innate taste is for every thing that regards the mechanism of a ship';[193] and it was his creation of the so-called Liman flotilla and his courageous participation in its actions against the Turkish fleet that earned him an inscribed sword from the empress and a place in Russian naval history. At Kherson Bentham was given the task of turning a miscellaneous collection of small craft, including the barges on which Catherine had made her recent trip down the Dnieper, into fighting ships, which he armed with 'great guns of 36 and even 48 pounders'.[194] Unexpected fire-power and great manoeuvrability gave the flotilla of some forty ships a distinct advantage over the ponderous men-of-war of the numerically superior Turkish fleet in the treacherous waters of the Liman. Bentham provided his brother with a long and graphic account of the various actions of the flotilla, in which his fellow army officer Henry Fanshawe (1756–1828) also served with distinction. It also contains interesting references to Paul Jones, not least that Bentham and Fanshawe had declared that 'nothing but the presence of the enemy could induce us to serve *with* him, and no consideration whatever could bring us to serve *under* him'. The success and subsequent rewards enjoyed by Bentham and Fanshawe aroused among the naval officers, Jones included, 'a most terrible envy, so much so that we are actually both of us kicked out of the flotilla for peace and quietness sake'.[195] Bentham and Jones had both left the Liman when the Russians stormed Ochakov on 6/17 December 1788. A volunteer in that action and 'marching at the head of a column of 200 Russian grenadiers' was a Lieutenant Fox, who had arrived in the area only weeks before and who was apparently assigned to Paul Jones's flagship. Two years later, Fox was shot dead during the storming of Izmail and 'and is remembered in the Russian army to this day as a great hero'.[196]

British officers distinguished themselves in several of the many engagements between the Russian and Turkish fleets over the three years the war had still to run. Three in particular might be mentioned, but not solely on account of their services during this war, for they virtually spent the whole of their long careers in southern seas. Although the name of John Priestman does not appear in either the listings of Jane or Anderson, it was frequently found in the letters and accounts of travellers who met him either at Kherson

16 Samuel Bentham (1757–1831). Oil painting (1784) by unknown Russian artist.
(National Maritime Museum, London.)

or at Nikolaev. Priestman had entered Russian service in September 1786
and joined the Black Sea fleet at Kherson. It was in Kherson in 1789 that
John Howard, who had come to see the state of medical care for the Russian
forces, died from fever and it was Priestman who read the funeral service.
Many travellers subsequently heard from him details of Howard's melancholy fate. Priestman finished the war as a captain of the first rank and soon
transferred to Nikolaev, the new city and naval centre built at the confluence
of the Bug and Ingul rivers. Promoted to rear-admiral under Paul I, he
became a vice-admiral on the accession of Alexander I and commander of
the Black Sea rowing fleet. In 1804 he was made commandant of Nikolaev,
where he died in 1811. Edward Daniel Clarke, meeting him in 1800 when
Anglo-Russian relations were at a new low, praised 'the blunt sincerity of

his character, his openness and benevolence of heart'. 'That so distinguished a naval officer should be in the service of our enemies, merely from want of employment at home, cannot be too much regretted. Great Britain has not, perhaps a better or braver seaman.'[197]

This was a typically extravagant Clarke judgement, which could be over-turned a dozen times solely with examples from many officers in the Black Sea fleet. Let two suffice. Thomas Messer and Henry Bailey (or Bailly), joining as midshipmen in 1783, were sent to Kherson and the Don flotilla respectively, but were both fighting with the Black Sea fleet in 1788 and both essentially stayed with it until their deaths in 1829 and 1826. Both Messer and Bailey appear in Anderson's list, but poor Bailey is described as 'not mentioned after 1783'. In Anderson's later fundamental work on naval battles in the Levant there are several references to a 'Belli's' conspicuous role in several engagements against France in the 1790s and in one instance a footnote suggests that Belli was 'apparently an Irishman, Baillie, by birth', but no further connection is made.[198] Although Bailey's and Messer's careers kept more or less in step, with seniority to Messer by a matter of months, Bailey's was more newsworthy. For his outstanding service during the battle with the Turkish fleet at Cape Kaliakra on 1/11 August 1791, one of the last actions of the war, he was awarded the Order of St Vladimir, 4th class. In the wars against Revolutionary France, when Russia found itself an ally of Turkey, Bailey was in the Mediterranean as part of Admiral Ushakov's fleet as captain of the *Schastlivyi*. He took part in the siege of Corfu at the end of 1798, receiving the Order of St Anne (2nd class), which the following year became 1st class, when he led a land assault party of 500 men that took Naples. Paul I, making the award, allegedly said 'Bailey wished to surprise me, and I'll surprise him'. Bailly added further battle honours during the same campaign, including the two foreign orders of St John of Jerusalem and of St Ferdinand (from the King of the Two Sicilies). He was particularly prominent in actions in the same waters in 1806–7 and for eighteen naval campaigns received the customary award of the Order of St George (4th class). Messer had received the same award in 1799 and, weeks before Bailey received the same promotion, he became a rear-admiral on 20 January/1 February 1806 on his appointment as commandant of the port of Sevastopol. In 1826, the year of Bailey's death, Messer became a vice-admiral and in 1828, forty-five years after he first entered Russian service, he was commanding a squadron, beseiging Varna in 1828.[199]

Although the main actions of the war against the Turks in 1787–91 were fought on the Black Sea, it was to the Mediterranean that Rear-Admiral Samuel Gibbs was sent in 1789. Gibbs, who had joined the Russian service in the same year as Greig and had been with him at Chesme, was to organise a squadron of privateers to harass Turkish shipping. He succeeded in collecting a small number of vessels that were to fly the Russian flag and to be led by a Maltese corsair, Guliemo Lorenzo. There were two other squadrons already active, one of which, consisting of six ships, had Russian officers on board to oversee operations: one of these officers was in fact a British lieutenant named George Smith. The squadrons proved an irritant to the Turks, but Gibbs found that his authority was disregarded at will by commanders and crews who were pirates in all but name, and he was called the following year to Kronshtadt.[200] There exists, and in several copies, a journal allegedly kept by William Davidson, an English seaman who served for nine months in 1789 as a member of the crew of one of the Russian privateers. Known as 'the Bloody Journal', it is a stark day-by-day account of ruthless acts and massacres on such a scale that, not surprisingly, its authenticity has been questioned.[201]

Although the British public's awareness of the Russo-Turkish conflict was dramatically increased by the 'Ochakov crisis' of 1791,[202] the public was undoubtedly as unconcerned as it was uninformed about specific naval engagements in the Black Sea and about the exploits of British officers serving with the Russian fleet. The Baltic was nearer to home, the geography more understandable, the flow of visitors to St Petersburg immeasurably greater, and the news of victories and deaths more immediate. British participation in the war was considerable, the heroism displayed by British officers conspicuous, the loss of life and limb far from negligible. The timing of the Swedish attack meant that the majority of the officers recruited in 1787–8 stayed to fight in the Baltic, where they joined others who had come in 1783 or even earlier, like Greig himself, so emphasising the unbroken British presence at Kronshtadt in Catherine's reign, indeed, down the century.

The complex and numerous engagements in the Baltic during the three years of the war have been traced by R. C. Anderson with the same clarity he brought to the Black Sea conflict. The Swedes lost twelve battleships and gained one from the Russians during the war, while the Russians lost four and gained six, not counting the addition of newly built ships. In 1790 the Swedes had a mere sixteen battleships, whilst the Russian Baltic and White Sea fleets had forty-six. Russian superiority over both Sweden and Denmark 'had been more or less assured ever since the days of Peter the Great, but after this war with Sweden it became far more marked than before'.[203] Such statistics, however, take little account of the great loss of smaller craft, such as galleys and cutters, which operated in large numbers in the Baltic, and of the accompanying loss of life on both sides.

Vorontsov in his letter to Mordvinov had mentioned with pride four men he had recruited for the Russian navy in 1787–8: James Trevenen (1760–90), Robin Crown (1754–1841), Samuel Marshall (1766?–90) and Frederick Thesiger (d. 1805). Two of these, Trevenen and Marshall, were killed in action and were, together with Admiral Greig and Captain Samuel Elphinstone (1758–89), the subjects of the 'Anecdotes of Distinguished British Officers who Fell in the Russian Naval Service during the Last War with Sweden', which Dr Matthew Guthrie sent to an Edinburgh periodical in 1793, suggesting that 'possibly many of these brave men may never have any other monument erected to their memory than the volume of the *Bee* where these short notices may be inserted'.[204] He was essentially correct about Marshall and Elphinstone, but not, of course, about Greig, whose obituary had appeared in the *London Chronicle* at the beginning of 1789, or, indeed, about Trevenen, accorded a long obituary in *Gentleman's Magazine* in August 1790. What Guthrie did not and could not know was that Trevenen was the assiduous writer of long and detailed letters and diaries, most of which were preserved within the family and provided the material for a biography compiled in 1805. This ultimately became the basis of the memoir published in 1959, which gives us a contemporary British 'insider' view of the naval war against Sweden and forms a unique trilogy with John Deane's account of the Petrine navy and Thomas Newberry's(?) *An Authentic Narrative* of the Mediterranean campaign. The year before Guthrie's notices appeared, a fellow Scot and a kinsman of Greig, Andrew Swinton, had published an account of his travels in Russia in 1788–90 and there is much in the book about the admiral and about British participation in the Russo-Swedish war. Swinton named not only Trevenen and Elphinstone but also Lieutenants Helenus Hay and John Green, who both died in the Battle of Rochensalm, otherwise known as the first Battle of Svenskund, on 13/24 August 1789.[205] This was a battle, fought between the Swedish rowing fleet and two Russian squadrons of miscellaneous craft such as galleys, gunboats, shebeks and cutters, several of which were commanded by British officers, that went largely unnoticed in contemporary accounts, despite its significance not least in loss of ships and men. The Battle of Vyborg Bay in June of the following year, on the other hand, attracted much attention, not least in Britain. William Tooke, writing in 1798, described the action as 'particularly fatal to the British officers':

Captain Denison, a gallant and skilful commander, had his head shot off by a cannon-ball; captain Marshall, in attempting to board one of the enemy's ships, fell into the sea and was drowned; captain Miller, equally bold and enterprising, was severly wounded in his leg; captain Aikin, likewise a spirited and brave commander, had his thigh-bone shattered so as to render amputation necessary, and about four years afterwards died of an epidemic fever at Cronstadt. Several others were severely wounded; and captain James Trevenen, after having gallantly distinguished himself in the action, was mortally wounded by the last shot fired by the enemy, and died on the fifth day after.[206]

Marshall had been in Russian service barely more than a year. Son of a

Commissioner of the Royal Navy, he had arrived with a high recommendation from Admiral Rodney and a considerable reputation made during the War of American Independence, when he set fire to sixty American craft in Chesapeake Bay. The manner of his death became legendary and is described in several travellers' accounts, if always with differing details.[207] Two weeks before Marshall's death, Trevenen spoke of him as 'a young man of genius, but excentric'.[208] In the same letter Trevenen mentioned Dennison – not surprising since they shared the same father-in-law in John Farquharson, a leading Petersburg merchant.[209] Dennison was among the most experienced of British officers in the Swedish war, having begun his career in 1771 as a midshipman in the Mediterranean campaign. A captain of the first rank at the outset of the war, he took part in all the major battles and received virtually the same promotions and awards as the younger and seemingly more dynamic Trevenen.[210] Although it is not apparent from Tooke's account, the shot that proved fatal to Trevenen also maimed his friend James Aiken, who despite becoming a captain of the first rank himself after one display of bravery in action after another, preferred to stay with Trevenen as his second-in-command. Aiken was sent to England to recover from his wounds, as, indeed, was John Miller, a captain-lieutenant, but both returned in 1792.[211]

Trevenen was by all accounts, including his own, a remarkable young man. It was Trevenen alone for whom Tooke provided a long biographical footnote, largely based on the published obituary, where it was said that he had been 'honoured with repeated marks of the Empress's favour; and doubtless had he lived would soon have arrived at the first rank in her service. He was a man of strong natural abilities, greatly improved by cultivation, and possessed a high sense of honour and a liberal enlightened mind.'[212] Such a view was shared by Vorontsov, recommending him unhesitatingly to Bezborodko and Greig. Bezborodko was soon describing him as 'an excellent man, who promises to become a distinguished admiral'.[213] This was written soon after the Battle of Hogland, where Trevenen had been one of five British commanders of ships in the Russian line, the others being Dennison, Elphinstone, Scott and Tate. Elphinstone, who as a very young midshipman had been with his father Rear-Admiral Elphinstone at Chesme and who had rejoined the Russian navy in 1783 as a captain, was the real hero, whose actions led to the capture of the Swedish vice-admiral.[214] Elphinstone duly received his Order of St George (3rd class); Trevenen and Dennison also received theirs, but only after making known their sense of grievance at being initially overlooked. Trevenen, whose courage was matched only by his ambition and self-esteem, was to make a similar complaint two years later, although his career prospered at a rate to cause resentment among the Russian officers. After Hogland, he was given a squadron to block Swedish fleet movements

17 Captain James Trevenen (1760–90). Oil painting (c. 1788) by Charles Allingham.

off Hangö-udd, which he did so successfully that he was promoted to captain of colonel's rank. The following year brought its share of triumph and disaster. In September Trevenen at the head of a large squadron successfully attacked the port of Barö-sund, for which he received a gold sword. Many British officers were involved in the operation and in his report he commended Lieutenants Joseph Lally, Alexander Ogilvy and Vincent Barrer as well as Aiken, together with several Russian officers.[215] During the action the 64-gun *Severnyi Orel* ran aground and was wrecked; on the 15/26 October, on the voyage to Reval, Trevenen lost in a similar way his own

64-gun *Rodislav*. By an unhappy coincidence, four days later, Thesiger lost his 66-gun ship, the *Vysheslav*, which was wrecked on its voyage from Reval to Kronshtadt. The empress received the news of the loss of the three ships at the same time and exclaimed, according to her secretary, 'So even the English lose ships! If Russians had been the captains, it would have been said: from incompetence.'[216] Trevenen and Aiken were to be court-martialled and it was only in April 1790 that the trial was resolved in their favour and the blame laid on the pilot. Trevenen had already been assigned the command of the *Ne tron' menia*, on board which he was to meet his death.[217]

While it is obviously not possible to give a roll-call of the names – let alone provide details – of all the officers who served with great distinction against the Swedes, a final exception might be made for Robin Crown, not simply because he was cited by Vorontsov or even because his actions throughout the campaign were truly heroic, but because of his wife! Crown left the Royal Navy in February 1788 and joined von Dessen's squadron destined for the Mediterranean. He was at Copenhagen when the Swedes attacked Russia, and took command of a cutter purchased in England. Over the next few months he plied the Baltic, raiding Swedish commercial shipping, capturing a 12-gun cutter and then, in May 1789, the 40-gun frigate *Venus*, for which he was promoted to captain of the second rank and given the Order of St George (4th class) and the command of the captured ship. He commanded the *Venus* throughout the rest of the campaign, rewarded with a gold sword and promotion to captain of the first rank for a series of notable exploits, culminating in the capture of the 64-gun *Retvizan* at Sveaborg on 23 June/4 July 1790.[218] It was, however, to Crown's period of command of the *Merkurii* that one must return to find his wife, the indomitable Martha, who wrote to Trevenen about 'their' activities:

We were sent from the fleet on the 28th of April [all the dates are New Style] to reconnoitre Karlskrona. With much difficulty in getting through the ice we arrived on our station the 8th instant and observed in Karlskrona 15 sail of pennants. The 14th we were chased by two frigates and a cutter, and indeed so we have been ever since, but from foggy weather have lost sight of them for a day or two. Yesterday in endeavouring to regain our station we met them again and were obliged to put in her [the island of Bornholm]. On the 11th we captured a cutter mounting 12 guns and were so fortunate as to receive no damage but having some of our rigging shot away. I am of the opinion that some very heavy blows will be struck this campaign.[219]

Martha in fact performed very much like a proto-Florence Nightingale in caring for the wounded and she was subsequently awarded the Order of St Catherine.

Not all wives of British officers found themselves in similar situations. Martha Crown had believed herself on the way to the Mediterranean, but was eventually returned safely to Kronshtadt, where she was to bestow on her children such names as Platon Valerian and Anna Catharina and enjoy the fruits that her husband's successful career was to bring. Many of the wives, particularly those who suddenly found themselves widows, were not so fortunate. The archives contain letters from, and on behalf of, such widows, petitioning for pensions and assistance. Greig, for instance, wrote for Admiral Mackenzie's widow, who was living in poverty in Kronshtadt in 1786. Lieutenant Mettam's wife 'became poor & unfortunate tho' married to a russian Adml after the death of her Capt' and found employment as a nanny in a noble house.[220] Others soon remarried: Ruth Dennison married William Rogers, a member of the British Factory, and Trevenen's widow Elizabeth contracted an unfortunate union with Thomas Bowdler, editor of *The Family Shakespeare*.[221]

Much has seemed to revolve around Trevenen and there remains one aspect of his early career which has particular resonance in the Russian context. Trevenen, who as a sixteen-year-old midshipman had accompanied Captain Cook on his last voyage to the South Seas, came initially to Russia not with the intention of fighting but of exploring. He had already been on Kamchatka, at the harbour of St Peter and St Paul (Petropavlovsk), where Captain Clerke, who had succeeded the murdered Cook, was himself to die in August 1779. It was therefore not surprising that, having failed to interest the British government in his project for exploration and trade along the coasts of China and Japan, Trevenen should petition Catherine through Vorontsov in February 1787. What he proposed was new perhaps only in its emphasis on the advantages to Russia of trade with China and Japan from Kamchatka, for exploration of the region had been growing apace over many decades. Indeed, Trevenen in referring to the specific question of trade with Japan, showed his acquaintance with his British predecessor, Lieutenant Walton's voyage of 1738.[222] Catherine's reply had been swift and positive and she obviously realised how Trevenen and his interests could fuse with the objectives of an expedition already planned by the Russians, but about which Trevenen as yet knew nothing. In December 1786, a matter of months before Trevenen had presented his plan to Vorontsov, Captain Mulovskii, who had been Knowles's adjutant, was appointed to command a squadron of three ships to explore the coast of Kamchatka. The ships were already equipped and waiting at Kronshtadt, when Trevenen, delayed by a serious injury en route, eventually arrived in October 1787. It was apparently envisaged that Mulovskii's squadron would have sailed via the Cape of Good Hope, while Trevenen would have been given another to sail via Cape Horn. However, the war with Turkey had begun in the interim and Trevenen was informed 'that the voyage being laid aside for which I was more particularly destined, the Empress and Count [Bezborodko] expected that I should enter into the marine service to serve in the present war'.[223] In the event, it was in the war with Sweden that he, and Mulovskii, were to serve and die. There was by that time, however, another Russian expedition already on the eastern seaboard under the command of Englishman Joseph Billings (1761–1806), who had been assistant to the astronomer on Cook's last voyage.

According to Samuel Bentham, who was in the Russian capital when he arrived early in 1784, Billings had failed to gain support in London and therefore 'entered into the Russian service with a view of being sent on such an Expedition under the Russian flag. His proposals were attended to but nothing will be fixed for him for this year or two and probably as matters stand at present not at all.'[224] The catalyst seems to have been the Rev. William Coxe, whose *Account of the Russian Discoveries between Asia and America* (1780) had apparently been translated immediately into French for the empress' perusal and who was paying a second visit to St Petersburg precisely in 1784. According to Martin Sauer, who was appointed secretary to the expedition, it was as a result of the combined persuasions of Coxe and the naturalist Professor Peter Pallas that Catherine authorised an expedition 'to complete the geographical knowledge of the most distant possessions of that Empire, and of such northern parts of the opposite continent as Captain Cook could not possibly ascertain'.[225] It was not, however, until the late summer of 1785 that all the arrangements were made and the expedition could depart. Apart from Sauer, two other Englishmen were recruited, Lieutenant Robert Hall (1761–1844) and a 'mechanic' Joseph Edwards.[226] The expedition finally assembled in Irkutsk in February 1786 and then started on its main task of charting the Aleutians and other islands in the Bering Sea as far as Alaska. At Okhotsk ships were specially constructed in accordance with a design by Lambe Yeames and the expedition carried out its work with varying degrees of success until 1794. It was the last great Russian expedition of the eighteenth century and its progress was reported with keen interest, particularly in Britain. Coxe brought out a third edition of his *Russian Discoveries* in 1787 with a special supplement giving information on the expedition; Sir John Sinclair in a report he distributed after a visit to Russia in the same year, gave it a comparatively high profile and offered a characterisation of Billings as 'a young, active, and enterprising officer, but so deficient in judgement, that it is not supposed he will be able to prosecute so extensive and so tedious a plan with sufficient steadiness and ability'; while Dr Guthrie, apart from supplying the Royal Society with the full text of Billings' Instructions, wrote two items for *The Bee* about the expedition in 1792–3.[227] In 1802 Sauer's substantial *Account of a Geographical and Astronomical Expedition to the Northern Parts of Russia*, dedicated to Sir Joseph Banks, eventually appeared in London and was followed in 1806 by *An Account of a Voyage to the North-East of Siberia, the Frozen*

AN

ACCOUNT

OF A

GEOGRAPHICAL AND ASTRONOMICAL EXPEDITION

TO THE

NORTHERN PARTS OF RUSSIA,

FOR ASCERTAINING THE DEGREES OF LATITUDE AND LONGITUDE OF
THE MOUTH OF THE RIVER KOVIMA;
OF THE WHOLE COAST OF THE TSHUTSKI, TO EAST CAPE;
AND OF THE ISLANDS IN THE EASTERN OCEAN, STRETCHING TO
THE AMERICAN COAST.

PERFORMED,

By Command of Her Imperial Majesty *CATHERINE THE SECOND,*
EMPRESS OF ALL THE RUSSIAS,

BY COMMODORE JOSEPH BILLINGS,

In the Years 1785, *&c. to* 1794.

THE WHOLE NARRATED FROM THE ORIGINAL PAPERS,

BY MARTIN SAUER,

SECRETARY TO THE EXPEDITION.

LONDON:

Printed by A. Strahan, Printers Street;
FOR T. CADELL, JUN, AND W. DAVIES, IN THE STRAND.
1802.

18 *An Account of a Geographical and Astronomical Expedition to the Northern Parts of Russia* by Martin Sauer (London, 1802), title page.

Sea, and the North-East Sea, an English version of Gavriil Sarychev's report (Sarychev being Billings' Russian aide).

Among the incentives offered to Billings and other members of the expedition were promotions and financial rewards when certain objectives and tasks were achieved. Thus, in Billings' case, he began the expedition as a captain-lieutenant but became a captain of the second rank from June 1787 and, on reaching the coast of America, a captain of the first rank from July 1790. It is interesting that Trevenen's promotion to captain of the second rank in October 1787, was, in his own words, 'to be dated backwards [to December 1786], so as to make it superior to that of Billings', who had been an able seaman on Cook's *Resolution* when Trevenen had been a midshipman.[228] It seems likely that Trevenen was expected to take over from Billings, if and when his squadron sailed to the Pacific. Billings eventually returned to St Petersburg in 1795 and was awarded the Order of St Vladimir (3rd class); the following year he was transferred at his own request to the Black Sea fleet. Until his retirement on grounds of ill-health in November 1799 with the rank of captain-commodore, he worked mainly on surveys of the Black Sea, producing highly accurate maps for an atlas published in 1799.[229] He presumably remained in the Crimea until his death in 1805 and the last glimpse we have of him is of 'an illiterate man, whose vanity we found would be piqued if we did not take up our abode with him', penned in 1800 by the acerbic E. D. Clarke. Billings, it transpires, was opposed to 'the removal of any antiquity we had purchased, although they were all condemned to serve as building materials'![230]

A word might be said of Billings' other aide, Robert Hall, although in truth he deserves his own biography. Entering Russian service as a fourteen-year-old marine with Greig's squadron in the Mediterranean in 1774, Hall finished Billings' expedition in 1794 as a captain of the second rank. Ahead of him stretched exactly fifty years until the day he would drop dead during a service in the English church in St Petersburg on 23 January/4 February 1844. During that time he had served with the Black Sea, Baltic and White Sea fleets, had become commandant of Riga and governor of Archangel, received countless decorations and honours, including a diamond pendant to his Order of St Andrew, and had risen to full admiral and gained membership of the Admiralty Council.[231]

V

Tracing the careers of Billings and Hall has taken us into the reign of Paul and, in the case of Hall, well into the reign of Paul's third son, Nicholas I, and to the threshold of the Crimean War. Although the Crimean War is the most celebrated of all Anglo-Russian conflicts, it came at the end of a long period of confrontation and cooperation, of musical-chairs alliances, most marked during the years of the French Revolutionary and Napoleonic Wars from 1792 to 1815.

The end of the Russo-Turkish conflict with the Peace of Jassy and the defusing of the Ochakov crisis with the abandonment of Pitt's Russian armament heralded a period of Anglo-Russian rapprochement in the face of French aggression. The British ambassador Charles Whitworth was to negotiate not only a new commercial treaty but also a defensive alliance in February 1795 that was soon to have Russia committing both troops and men-of-war for joint operations against the Dutch. In June of that year a Russian force of twelve battleships and eight frigates, under the overall command of Vice-Admiral Petr Khanykov, assisted by Rear-Admirals Mikhail Makarov and George Tate, an American of Scots descent, left Kronstadt to join Vice-Admiral Duncan's North Sea fleet. With the Russian fleet were many British officers, as well as Russian officers who had been trained in the British navy, beginning with Khanykov himself, but the story of cooperation over the next few years is punctuated by all the old elements of mutual recriminations and mistrust, squabbles over precedence and botched initiatives.[232] Nevertheless, it represents a unique attempt at combined operations in the history of the two navies in the eighteenth century, threatened and ultimately scuttled by the Emperor Paul, who came to the throne on the death of Catherine II in December 1796.

Paul was not too averse to continuing the provisions of the alliance: he did in fact order Khanykov to withdraw early in the summer of 1797, but allowed the Russian fleet to reappear the following year. The attack on Holland in August 1799, however, went seriously wrong and the emperor was appalled by the Russian casualties. It was events in the Mediterranean, where the Russians had been in unholy alliance with the Turks, that led Paul to the embraces of Napoleon and to a renewal of the Armed Neutrality in December 1800. The catalyst was Malta, home of the Knights of Malta of whom Paul was the Grand Master. Furious when the French seized the island, mollified when Napoleon offered to transfer it to him, and indignant when Nelson captured it and kept it, Paul moved against the British in Russia. All British ships in Russian ports were impounded and their crews sent to detention camps in the interior: it has been estimated that 'some 2,000 seamen from some 200 ships were sent off to 102 different destinations in Russia, to be followed after a few weeks by the 400 mates and boys who had been left behind'.[233] With confrontation between the British and Russian fleets imminent, British officers on Russian ships at Kronstadt and Reval were sent to Moscow for the duration of the war, which in the event was but a few weeks. It was, however, a foretaste of what was to happen a few years later and for a much longer period. After the golden years of renewed cooperation that followed the accession of Alexander there came the treaty with Napoleon at Tilsit and, from 1807 to 1812, British naval officers were in internal exile, mainly in Moscow.

In Paul's reign and in the first years of Alexander's further groups of young Russian officers had been sent to England to gain experience with the Royal Navy, but recruitment of British officers for the Russian navy had virtually ceased. As the century ended, so did a great experiment. Although the Russians might well have wished to continue to use the Royal Navy for the training of their men, the stemming of the flow of foreign officers into Russia had been anticipated and welcomed. But British presence in the upper echelons of the Russian navy was far from being eradicated. Down the century from earliest Petrine times each influx of British (and other foreign) officers had created its own series of waves spilling into succeeding decades and had been renewed: junior officers had gone on to be captains of the first rank, rear-admirals, vice-admirals and occasionally full admirals. The intakes of 1783 and 1788 had many, many years of service still ahead, taking them into the reign of Paul and beyond, before they finally and literally died away. There were even survivors from the early 1770s.

Following Greig's death, one Scot, Samuel Gibbs (d. 1795) and one American, Tate, became rear-admirals in 1789 and 1793 respectively, during the remaining years of Catherine's reign. Under Paul, James Preston and Robert Wilson, who had both served under Elphinstone in the Mediterranean, were made rear-admirals in 1797, Priestman followed in 1798 and Crown, in 1799. During Alexander's reign a similar rank was achieved in 1803 by Hall, in 1807 by Alexis Greig (eldest son of Catherine's 'Strike Sure' admiral who was enrolled as a midshipman at his birth in 1775), in 1812 by Andrew Elliot, in 1814 by Alexander Ogilvy, in 1816 by Bailey and Messer and Brining Boyle (d. 1825), and in 1824 by James Hamilton, while promotions to vice-admiral had come to Wilson and Priestman, and then to Greig and Ogilvy, and to full admiral for Crown and Tate. Finally, the last British officer to achieve the rank of rear-admiral seems to have been Thomas Chandler in 1827, after thirty-nine years' service. Nicholas I, in fact, was also to create more full admirals of British descent than any preceding monarch: Greig, Hall and Ogilvy, in 1828, 1830 and 1841 respectively, while Messer, Hamilton and Chandler progressed to vice-admiral.

In the first decades of the nineteenth century the Russian navy thus had some fourteen admirals of British descent. British descent is not used, however, merely to permit the inclusion of Tate under the British umbrella; on the contrary, it is used to indicate that most of these officers at some stage took Russian citizenship, several during the difficult years of internal exile when Russia and Britain were at war after Tilsit, some later (Greig, for instance, only in 1830). Thus Nicholas might, with some justice, say that all his admirals were Russian citizens and that his navy had freed itself from foreign domination. His reign was the end of an era in another sense, for the 1840s brought one after another the deaths of his admirals: Crown and Hamilton in 1841, Greig in 1845, and Ogilvy in 1846.[234]

Ogilvy was one of those who took Russian citizenship in 1811. The following year he was captain of the 88-gun *Smelyi*, which was part of the fleet sent to England under Admiral Tate. The fleet returned to Russia in 1814 with the Imperial Guard Regiments from France and several of the ships were given British doctors from the Royal Navy to supervise health and hygiene during the voyage.[235] Ogilvy's ship had one such surgeon (sadly unidentified), whose journal was published in 1822 as *A Voyage to St Petersburg in 1814*. It offers a fascinating insight into life on board a Russian ship and has much of particular interest about the relations between the British and Russian officers. The author speaks briefly of the career of the rear-admiral (identified only as 'O—'), of his years of exile in Moscow, of his marriage (presumably to a Russian), before offering the following judgement:

I know not whether professional views and long estrangement from his native land may not, in some degree, have blunted the more delicate feelings of national glory: for, on mentioning accidentally in conversation, the attack and capture of some Russian gunboats in the gulph of Finland, a few years ago, by Captain (now Admiral) Sir Byam Martin, he did not seem to recollect the circumstance; he expressed doubt whether English seamen could ever, on equal terms, conquer those of Russia. This, however, is an excusable feeling, naturally arising from regard to the honour of the service to which he belongs. Let me add also, that he is a very correct officer and a worthy man.[236]

What he did not add, and possibly did not know nor could imagine, was that Ogilvy was a Russian citizen, espousing and defending as his own the Russian cause. The surgeon then turns to Ogilvy's second-in-command, a Russian identified only as Captain R– (very probably, the future admiral Petr Ivanovich Rikord (1776–1855)) and described as 'one of the strangest characters I ever met with, being a compound of extremes'. R–, who had been trained in the Royal Navy and spoke excellent English, alternated between praise and censure of Britain, British institutions and British men; it was a relationship of love and hate, of need and rejection which he embodied perhaps in an extreme form but which was not at all untypical. It lies at the heart of a debate and a dilemma that existed from the moment Peter recruited his first British sailor.

The surgeon pronounces on the overall superiority of Britain in naval matters, including administration, procedures, training and shipbuilding, and particularly in the quality of its officer corps. He seemed surprised that 'the jealousy entertained of the British officers is extremely great; so that though they have mainly contributed to, if not entirely gained, nearly all the sea

victories of the country, they do not find much favour in the eyes of their
Russian brethren'. He then gives the Russians' scathing characterisations of
Tate, Elliot and Crown. The author wonders why British officers ever both-
ered to enter Russian service, for 'Russia is poor for an Englishman. A moderate exercise of talents and industry in his own country, will always gain him
as much as perhaps great labour and anxiety there; a remark which holds
good with respect to adventurers of every class to "All the Russias".'[237] It is
not difficult to find numerous examples of such complacency, arrogance and
incomprehension in the letters and reports of British naval officers, travellers,
diplomats and others in almost any period in the preceding century – or to
find corresponding expressions of Russian resentment and xenophobia. The
great Russian nineteenth-century naval historian F. F. Veselago felt the need,
in concluding his magisterial short history of the Russian fleet with a review
of Alexander I's reign, to devote a section to 'the preference for the British
over Russians'. He gives examples of official neglect of such heroes as Admirals Ushakov and Seniavin and counterbalances them by citing instances when
British officers, virtually in their dotage (and he names Crown and Captains
John Monk (d. 1824) and Robert Borthwick (d. 1827)), were given commands for which there were outstanding home-grown candidates.[238]

   Ill-concealed British contempt for the state of the Russian navy, of its complete unfittedness for battle – attributed to every aspect of building and maintaining and manning – blinded the British government to the emergence of
Russia as a great naval power. Reporting on the 'state of their marine' had
been the concern of British observers from the two John Deanes onwards.
A century after the shipbuilder Deane sent his letter to Carmarthen, a
Lieutenant Norris of the Royal Navy, who had arrived at Kronshtadt with
one of the transport ships repatriating Russian soldiers after Paul's withdrawal from the Coalition against France, reported on 19/31 October 1800
that the Russian Baltic Fleet was 'as truly as Crazy a Rotten Fleet as ever
put to sea ... The day prior to their being to sail, the Captains of Seven
Line of Battle ships made Reports, that the Ships were not fit to go out of
the Mole, as they were then making six feet of water a day.'[239] The authority
of Admiral Knowles, a quarter of a century earlier, was particularly influential in moulding British opinion. 'The account Sir Charles Knowles gives me
of the state of their marine, would from any body else be incredible: he
assures me, such a thing as a barrel of turpentine is only to be procured from
an apothecary's shop,' wrote the British ambassador in 1772[240]. A few years
later, two officers in the Royal Navy, who had known Knowles in Russia
and apparently had access to his papers, both submitted official reports,
purporting to be their own work but coinciding in many instances in their
wording, and offering the view that Russia 'never can become a great Maritime Power'.[241]

The paradox remained: Russia's navy was despised and underestimated, despite the victories and remarkable exploits that it achieved during its first century of existence; it was judged ill-prepared and tactically naive, despite the expertise, the examples of leadership and the long years of service given by dozens of British officers, and the training received by many Russian officers in the Royal Navy. It is to the development of the Russian navy that the British made their most consistent and conspicuous contribution – as officers on active service, as administrators and as shipbuilders. Vorontsov was not far from the truth in acknowledging that the Russian navy was at least 'sur le pied anglais'.

6

'NECESSARY FOREIGNERS': SPECIALISTS AND CRAFTSMEN IN RUSSIAN SERVICE

I

In the report of the embassy, sent by the first of the Romanovs (Tsar Mikhail Fedorovich) to England in 1613–14, it is said that the ambassadors told Sir John Merrick, the experienced merchant-diplomat, that 'you know how in the past under our Great Sovereigns the Tsars of Russia many willing people from other states and from England, doctors and smiths and many learned necessary artisans, knowing about the Moscow state, that it is abundant in everything and hearing of the Tsar's grace, came by themselves and were in honour and sufficiency and earned a great deal'. They continued, in accordance with their instructions, that the tsar 'wants also to see in his country necessary foreigners, and wants to show his Tsar's grace to them more than before'.[1] The Time of Troubles had severely disrupted commercial, cultural and diplomatic ties between Russia and the West in general and Britain in particular. During the second half of the sixteenth century Russia had seen the arrival from Britain of merchants and diplomats, physicians and soldiers, and a few specialists in other areas. In 1567, for instance, Queen Elizabeth had sent as a result of a request from Ivan IV a goldsmith by the name of Thomas Green and a building and fortifications expert, Humphrey Locke. Ironically, it was silversmiths – a group of whom Boris Godunov had sent back to England in 1602 because he had, he said, a superfluity of them – that Tsar Mikhail specifically requested.

Merrick had been unable at the time to persuade any masters to travel to Russia, but by the end of the year he was offering the tsar miners and smiths willing to prospect for tin and silver near the River Shukhona, a tributary of the Northern Dvina. Over the remaining thirty years of Mikhail Fedorovich's reign British experts were prominent in the prospecting for precious metals and stones in many parts of Russia, particularly in the Urals and in the south. The tsar also welcomed British goldsmiths and silversmiths who worked for many years in the Kremlin: Martin Erdinter was entrusted in 1616 with producing a warder (*zhezl*) for the tsar, decorated with precious stones and an elegant crown; Samuel Plument in the 1730s was employed in making silver and gold thread for the vestments of the tsar's family; and Thomas Atwood produced buttons decorated with enamel and precious stones over two decades for Tsar Mikhail and his son, Tsar Aleksei Mikhailovich.[2]

British masters in seventeenth-century Moscow were working not only in the Kremlin but also on the fabric of the Kremlin itself. John Thaler and Christopher Halloway probably arrived together in 1621 and worked together for a decade or more on the restoration of various palaces and cathedrals. Thaler's initial task was to restore the women's quarters of the Great Kremlin Palace, followed by work on the sixteenth-century Golden Tsaritsa's Palace. His skill in the construction of vaulting was employed in the strengthening of the Uspenskii Cathedral, before he was entrusted with the design and building in stone of the Cathedral of St Catherine, to replace the wooden church which had been used by female members of the royal family but had burnt down in 1626. Halloway, designated as 'a master of horological and hydraulic matters', is a much more celebrated figure than Thaler, principally for the clock he constructed in 1623–4 as part of the new superstructure for the important Spasskii Tower in the Kremlin wall. Although the tsar and patriarch were both delighted by Halloway's clock, the nude figures with which he adorned some of the upper niches of the tower were decorously draped in coloured kaftans. Sadly, the great fire of 1626 damaged the tower, but Halloway restored it and the chiming clock continued to function until 1707. The young Peter the Great was able to enjoy the fruits of another of Halloway's achievements: water for a pond on the roof of the Reserve Palace (on which Peter was to sail his toy flotilla) was raised from the Moscow River by means of a machine Halloway had originally constructed for the so-called Water Tower (*Vodovzvodnaia bashnia*) in the Kremlin wall.[3]

Under Peter's father Aleksei foreigners' skills were still in great demand, particularly in the military sphere: the British, predominantly Scots, figured prominently among the thousands of mercenaries attracted into the Russian armies. Nevertheless, the British presence in the ranks of technical experts and craftsmen was not as notable as in the previous reign, the fortunes of the merchants fluctuated and fell, and it was the Dutch, the Italians and men from the German lands who were more generally in evidence and who prospered.[4] Peter's early preferences among the inhabitants of Moscow's Foreign Quarter were divided among the Dutch, the Germans and the British, but his foray to the West in 1697–8 marked in many respects a decisive turning towards Britain, exemplified most immediately and dramatically in the procession of many British into Russian service. While the recruitment of shipbuilders, riggers, smiths and seamen reflected Peter's primary concern for his nascent fleet, the engineering skills of Perry and the academic instruction offered by Farquharson and his young assistants were an indication of the tsar's wider interests and his country's needs.

Farquharson became the third of a triumvirate of Scots who nurtured and sustained the tsar's interests in science and technology, particularly in instruments and machines. Peter was, however, soon to lose the most senior of them, General Patrick Gordon (1635–99), who had joined the Russian army in 1661 and been a particularly influential supporter of the young tsar in the 1690s.[5] The second, the Moscow-born James Daniel Bruce (1669–1735), the future field marshal and count but as yet a colonel, had accompanied Peter to England with the Great Embassy and remained there for a few further months, studying, meeting Newton, Halley and other scholars, and collecting books and scientific instruments.[6] In the bill presented by the British merchant Henry Styles for expenses incurred by the tsar and his retinue during their stay in London many entries refer to such items as quadrants, clocks, hour-glasses, magnets, telescopes, mathematical and scientific instruments.[7] Bruce returned to Moscow to set up an observatory in the Sukharev Tower, where the School of Navigation and Mathematics was also to be housed, and the tradition was firmly established of acquiring scientific instruments from the leading British makers. Bruce's own collection of astronomical instruments passed after his death to the Academy of Sciences' Kunstkamera, joining similar collections belonging to Peter and others. The work of such British masters as Culpeper, Carver, Marshall and Rowley was well represented. No less than eight works by John Rowley (1674–1728) are recorded, of which two sundials and a circumferentor are extant. One of the sundials was specifically prepared as a gift from George I to Peter in 1715 and bears the tsar's monogram as well as indicating the latitude of an uncommon number of Russian towns. However, the jewel in the Kunstkamera's crown is one of the lost items: a wonderful orrery or planetarium, which merchants of the British Factory presented to the tsar in 1714 and which survived until its destruction in 1941.[8] Two years after its arrival, a British instrument maker came to work in the Russian capital.

John Bradlee (d. 1743) had arrived in Moscow in the summer of 1710 to work at the Artillery Office, at the specific invitation of James Bruce who had been in charge of the Russian artillery at Poltava and was soon to become General-Master of the Ordnance. A few years later, Bradlee was to be involved in gunpowder tests, but his primary task was to prepare instruments and 'to instruct in all kinds of instruments two young men from among the cleverest school pupils who have passed their examination in geometry'. Little is known of Bradlee's Moscow period, although it was of almost six years' duration. One analemmatic sundial, bearing the inscription 'J: Bradlee Mosco Fecit', has survived and seems to be one of those about which Bruce complained in 1715, for it does not give the precise latitude of St Petersburg (60° instead of 59° 48'). Only three pieces, however, are extant from his much longer Petersburg period – in the Hermitage collection there is another sundial (of the popular Butterfield-type dial), a ring dial, and a gunner's caliper, the last of which testifies to his position in the Artillery and Fortifications Office in the Russian capital, where he served for more than two decades.[9]

Even less is known about George Sanepens, an English mechanic and lathe-maker, whose skills were much prized by Peter, himself a very accomplished turner. There had been a turnery attached to the Mathematical School in Moscow, headed by Johann Blübero (d. 1709), where the young Andrei Nartov acquired his skills. In 1712 Nartov transferred to St Petersburg, where Peter's Turnery (*Tokarnia*) had been established in the grounds of the Summer Garden under the supervision of the recently arrived Sanepens and the German master mechanic Franz Zinger. Sanepens, who was known in Russia as Iurii Kurnosyi ('George the Snub-nosed') was responsible for the design of at least three lathes in the years before his death in 1720. One is still preserved in the Hermitage and bears the inscription in English 'St Peter-burg' [*sic*]; it was begun in 1713 by Sanepens, but completed by Nartov, who had already emerged as a craftsman of considerable ability and who was soon to be sent to England to hone his skills.[10]

It is suggested in one Russian source that, after his arrival in St Petersburg, Bradlee probably used the facilities of the turnery and would have known Sanepens as a neighbour in the new capital's 'Foreign Quarter', which grew up by the Admiralty.[11] Another member of the British 'scientific community' was John Pateling, an intriguing and largely unknown figure, who arrived in St Petersburg in 1718. He came originally for just one year, but he was to remain until his death over thirty years later, in July 1750.[12] Described as 'a master of machines', he was responsible for bringing to Russia a Desaguliers/Savery steam pump which was to raise water for fountains in the Summer Garden (from the river which was thereafter known as the Fontanka).[13] In a letter from Reval at the end of July 1718, Peter ordered that the machine should be set up as quickly as possible so that 'on my return I can see it in action'.[14] Equally remarkable, if less dramatic, was Pateling's next contribution to the cityscape of St Petersburg. The 'lanterns on posts, after the English manner', which in 1726 the French traveller A. de LaMotraye found some fifty paces apart on both sides of the first section of the Great Perspective Road (as the Nevskii Prospekt was then called) had in fact been erected some three years earlier to Pateling's design. They can be seen on the engraving after Makhaev's 'Vue de l'Amirauté et de ses Environs' which appeared in the album issued in 1753 to mark the first fifty years of the city's existence.[15]

The album was distributed to many European courts, including St James's, with a view to impress foreigners with the beauty of Russia's capital; it was accompanied by a huge city plan, which had been prepared over a number of years by the Academy of Sciences' Geographical Department under the supervision of Ivan Fomich Truskott.[16] Ivan Fomich, born in St Petersburg on 1/12 December 1721, was the son of Thomas Truscott (d. 1741), a British merchant who seems to have settled in Russia during Peter's reign and had a house on Vasilii Island.[17] John finished the Academy gymnasium in 1735 and his skill as a draughtsman, together with his fluency in at least three languages, persuaded the Academy's professor of astronomy, Louis Delisle de la Croyère, to invite him to join the Geographical Department. The department was formed only in 1739 and brought belated recognition to cartography, an area of ever increasing importance as a result of ceaseless Russian exploration, particularly to Siberia and the eastern seaboard. Truscott became an 'ad"iunkt' in 1742, a status below that of 'professor', but which made him a full (as opposed to 'corresponding', 'honorary', or 'foreign') member of the Academy of Sciences, the only Briton to achieve this distinction in the eighteenth century. He was to serve nearly fifty years, retiring only one year before his death on 18/20 May 1786. The historian of the Geographical Department, V. F. Gnucheva, wrote of him: 'his name is known to anyone with the slightest knowledge of the maps which the Academy of Sciences published in the eighteenth century. He was responsible for almost half of these maps.'[18] Truscott took a leading part in the production of the first Russian atlas (1745) and of numerous other maps and plans in the 1740s, but the first printed map to bear his name dates from 1754 and shows Russian acquisitions in the north of America, although there is a manuscript map of Georgia which is much earlier and signed 'l'étud. Trescott'.[19] (There are, incidentally, several variant spellings of Truscott's name both in Latin and Cyrillic.) A major contribution that Truscott made to the good order of his department was his compiling of a 'Register of All the Maps, Drawings and Plans of the Russian Empire' (1773), which listed 1,085 items.[20] From 1757 Truscott was joined by Jacob Schmidt (d. 1786), also with the status of 'ad"iunkt', and they worked in seeming harmony for the next thirty years. Their work brought them into close contact with the polymath M. V. Lomonosov, who had been made an 'ad"iunkt' (in physics) in the same year as Truscott and professor of chemistry in 1745, but who was very involved with the Geographical Department. A month after Lomonosov's death in April 1765, Truscott and Schmidt produced a joint memorandum on desired improvements in the department, placing the emphasis on the need to train young Russian cartographers in order to undertake the preparation of a new atlas of Russia. For all the soundness of the proposals, there was a lack of vision and initiative that has been judged as condemning the department to be a cartographic 'workshop' (*masterskaia*) rather than the true 'laboratory' it might have become.[21]

The training of Russian pupils 'with unstinting zeal' was acknowledged as a contractual obligation by the British instrument maker Benjamin Scott, but one, he argued, he could hardly fulfil given his ignorance of Russian and his pupils' lack of English. A solution was, however, at hand. 'Here in St Petersburg there is an Englishman, named Thomas Truscott, who not only understands Russian and German but also English and, moreover, is quite skilled in instrument making, for previously he spent five years studying with me.'[22] The Thomas Truscott in question was John's younger brother (b. 1726) and the Academy of Sciences agreed in July 1748 to his becoming Scott's apprentice at a salary of 100 rubles a year.[23] Scott himself had moved to the Academy at the end of 1747, having signed a four-year contract at an annual salary of 600 rubles. He had previously worked at the Admiralty as a compass- and instrument-maker for a similar salary and had obviously been in Russia for at least five years. For some twenty years from 1714 he had had a shop in the Strand in London, where he made and sold 'all Sorts of Mathematical Instruments in Silver, Brass, Ivory, and Wood . . . all Sorts of Sliding Rules, Parallel-Rules, best Black-lead Pencils', and in 1733 had published *The Description and Use of an Universal and Perpetual Mathematical Instrument*, an eighteen-inch circular slide rule, consisting of twenty circles.[24] Given that his first contract was with the Admiralty, it is possible that Scott was among the men recruited by Kantemir over the period 1734–8, who included master carpenters and engineers at a similar salary.[25]

His eventual move to become head of the Academy's 'Instrument Workshop' (*Intrumental'naia palata*) came as a direct result of the disastrous fire of 5/12 December 1747, which seriously damaged the Academy's library, kunstkamera and observatory, including 'the great globe and several quadrants and other astronomical and mathematical instruments which must be repaired and put in good order as soon as possible'.[26] Repairing the great globe of Gottorp, which Peter had acquired in 1713, was to be Scott's first major task and one which lasted until June 1750. Nartov was annoyed that he had not been given the work and characteristically wrote that it should have been done 'by Russian hands and not the hand of the master Scott'.[27] Several of the instruments which had been acquired from Rowley were destroyed and when Scott reported that Rowley's mural quadrant was irreparably damaged, the Academy resolved to order a replacement from another famous English master-craftsman John Bird. The decision was taken on 23 March/3 April 1751, the day after Scott had died after a long illness.[28] In all, Scott worked for the Academy for over three years and was frequently consulted by Lomonosov for whom he prepared a complex telescope with ten lenses, a wooden vice, and other tools and instruments.[29]

Scott was always referred to as Benjamin Scott senior, to distinguish him from his son, who also signed a four-year contract at a salary of 600 rubles but did so a year later (on 23 December 1748/8 January 1749) with the St Petersburg Mint. Benjamin Scott junior, was a medallist, but where he learnt his trade and with whom has not been established. It is possible that he and his wife Anna Elizabeth arrived in Russia only in 1747; it was towards the end of that year that he was asked to produce the first of two examples of his art, the die for a medal of the Empress Elizabeth.[30] Scott was to remain at the Petersburg mint until the very end of Elizabeth's reign – his last known work was a medal on the empress's death in 1761, extant in both bronze and gold variants. It was probably this last medal that the noted authority Leonard Forrer mistook for a portrait medal of Catherine II, for there is no evidence that Scott ever worked for her.[31] The last entry in the register of the English Church dates from 29 August/9 September 1760 (the death of the last of eight children born to the Scotts in St Petersburg) and the family probably returned to England soon afterwards.[32] Scott was responsible for a large number of dies of rubles of different values which were minted in both St Petersburg and Moscow in the 1750s and for at least six medals, including copies of medals issued to mark Peter's victories and both coronation and death medals of Elizabeth (the former, his first test piece). His work usually carries his initials or his name in full ('B. Scott fecit'). Scott was a meticulous and skilled craftsman with a talent for accurate copying rather than originality, and his contemporary, Professor Jakob von Stählin, suggested that he did not enjoy particular success as a medallist because of his weakness in drawing.[33] It was, however, as a teacher that he has rightly been accorded high praise: two of his three known apprentices, Samoila Iudin and Timofei Ivanov, developed into the outstanding Russian medallists of the century and several of Scott's medals were joint productions, bearing the initials of his pupils on the obverse sides. The standards of medal production at both the Moscow and St Petersburg mints had been in decline for many years prior to Scott's appointment and 'he was virtually the only foreigner to take seriously the obligatory clause in the contract concerning the instruction of Russian engravers and in that respect Scott's sojourn in Russia was the one to produce the best results'.[34]

The tale of the two Scotts is matched from virtually the same period by that of the two Bottoms, father and son and both named Joseph. The elder Bottom was recruited into the Russian navy in 1703, although no details of his career are recorded; his name also appears in the list of the British congregation in Moscow after 1705.[35] By 1723 he and his wife Catherine were certainly established in St Petersburg, when the first of a succession of entries in the church register records the baptism of a daughter and the last, the burial of Joseph himself in October 1753.[36] Bottom junior, who was born in 1720, has his acknowledged place in eighteenth-century Russian history as 'Lapidary to the Empress', the master craftsman (*granil'nyi master*) who was head of the Lapidary Works at Peterhof for thirty years until his death in February 1778.[37] It was Peter I who, in 1725, had established a watermill for the cutting, preparation and polishing of marble and semi-precious stones (*Shlifoval'naia mel'nitsa*) near his Marly Palace in the Lower Park at Peterhof, but he did not live to see the use of such stones in the decoration of his palace rooms. The original mill burnt down in 1731 (when it had been hired by the British merchant William Elmsall) and was replaced with a temporary building until 1734, when a new mill was built. In 1748 the Swiss lapidary Bruckner was replaced by Bottom, who had previously worked as an instrument-maker at the Academy of Sciences. Receiving a salary of 1,200 rubles, Bottom undertook 'to polish diamonds (*almazy brillantirovat'*) and cut every kind of coloured stones'; he also redesigned the lapidary works and introduced new machines for polishing and faceting as well as establishing a stone-sawing workshop. The mill's activities greatly expanded during Catherine's reign and Bottom was responsible for preparing quantities of stone brought from various parts of Russia, but from the Urals in particular, where the empress had sent an expedition early in her reign to search for 'agate and other sorts of coloured stones'. In 1774 Bottom and the director of Peterhof Skripitsyn were ordered to prepare a plan and estimates for a new stone mill. Work began in 1777 to a design by Iurii Fel'ten and was completed just before Bottom's death. It was at the new mill, a few years later, that the jasper was cut for two rooms in the Cold Bath suite that Charles Cameron was preparing for Catherine at Tsarskoe Selo.[38]

Joseph Bottom's eldest son, Alexander, served initially in the College of Foreign Affairs, but petitioned successfully in 1794 for the post formerly held by his father, citing his 'sufficient knowledge both in the cutting and preparation of gemstones and in mechanics'; he was to occupy the post until 1815.[39] Another son, John, became a clockmaker and had a shop from the early 1770s at No. 48 Bol'shaia Millionaia.[40] He was one of several British clockmakers active in Catherine's Petersburg, where the skills of British horologists were highly valued. An episode from the previous reign provides, however, an idiosyncratic introduction to the subject.

II

The register of the English church in St Petersburg records the death on 17 March/7 April 1759 of one William Winrowe.[41] The story of his tragi-comic years in Russia is preserved in the writings of that same Professor Stählin who was disparaging about the younger Scott but who found it 'essential' to interrupt his account of music and ballet in eighteenth-century Russia with a description of 'a musical instrument, the equal of which it would be difficult to find for its inventiveness and artistic finish'.[42] He was referring to an organ-clock which Winrowe, a blacksmith turned clockmaker, had designed and built in London and decided to take to Russia to sell to the empress for a goodly sum. It was an imposing piece of furniture in mahogany with bronze ornamentation and carving, ten feet tall and eight feet wide (narrowing to six). The top half held an intricate and large clock, surmounted by a gilded sphere, representing the phases of the moon. The front opened up to reveal the two keyboards of the organ, which could be played together or separately, like a harpsichord, as well as containing two barrels which could be wound up to produce 'twelve of the most beautiful and complex concertos' by such as Handel, Corelli or Albinoni. If this was not enough, there was apparently also a little figure, reminiscent of Handel, which silently conducted each piece! Winrowe, having somehow contrived to get the organ to St Petersburg in the year 1743, was allowed to instal it in a building near the empress' Summer Palace, but he was foolish enough to demonstrate its potential to 'the public', before Elizabeth had inspected it. No sale resulted, but Winrowe stayed on in St Petersburg, setting up as a clockmaker and hoping in vain that someone would buy his wonderful organ-clock. He died before a new empress came to the throne, but his heirs were allowed to re-export the organ to England, where it was to achieve considerable fame. It was bought by Messrs Moores, watchmakers and jewellers of Ipswich, who put it on display for many years. It was seen, for instance, on 9 December 1768 by Sylas Neville, who recorded in his diary quite a different account of how Winrowe refused to sell his organ to Elizabeth because she ate an apple while he was playing.[43] Ultimately, the organ came into the possession of a Mr Tucker, who placed it in the castle of Trematon in Cornwall, where it remained from early in the nineteenth century until it was again sold in 1886 for a mere £24 and lost from view.[44]

However curious and bizarre this episode might appear, it was but one in a century that took great delight in curiosities and novelties. Peter the Great might well have responded very positively to Winrowe's construction – and to another horological marvel that was sent to St Petersburg during Catherine II's reign. In the late 1760s Matthew Boulton and John Fothergill, owners of the famous foundry at Soho, near Birmingham, were anxious to increase their overseas business and saw Russia as a very promising market. Fothergill was in St Petersburg for some four months in 1767 as part of a business tour of northern European countries and established useful contacts. They also worked through the British ambassador in St Petersburg, Lord Cathcart, to promote their ormolu-ware and break what was virtually a French monopoly. It was the application of ormolu to the decoration of ornate and intricate clocks that is of particular interest and in 1771 Boulton and Fothergill sent the ambassador details of 'Minerva', 'geographical', and 'sidereal' clocks they were making. In the event, only a sidereal clock, showing the movement of the sun against a celestial globe, was eventually dispatched in the summer of 1776, after its failure to sell at Christie's in 1772.[45] It met a similar fate in the Russian capital, from where William Porter, the merchant acting for Boulton, wrote in 1779 that 'Your clock has been shewn at Court first to the Empress, afterwards to Prince Potempkin [sic] and accepted by neither though I asked only Rs 2500 ... They all praised it – it was very fine, an elegant piece of workmanship – but it did not strike the hours, nor play any tunes – how could a clock without such necessary requisites cost Rs 2500?'[46] Only in 1787, after eleven years in Russia (compared with sixteen years for Winrowe's clocks), the sidereal clock returned to Soho, minus its smashed glass case. It was not put on display and was presumed lost until it was discovered in 1987 in the former Boulton family home at Great Tew, Oxfordshire. Two hundred years after its return from Russia, it was at last destined to be sold in a sale conducted by Christie's (who had failed to sell it in 1772), but a discerning government decided to accept it in lieu of death duties.[47]

British achievements in horology were, nevertheless, much appreciated in Catherine's Russia, particularly when they were combined with automata and the added musical attractions that were found to be lacking in Boulton's sidereal clock (but not, it has to be admitted, in Winrowe's). James Cox, a London clockmaker active in the last decades of the century, is best represented in the present-day collections of the Hermitage. Pride of place is given to the exotic 'Peacock' clock, which was originally bought by Prince Potemkin from the Duchess of Kingston and placed in his Taurida Palace. It was, however, only in 1792 that the clock's complex mechanism that moved the peacock and other birds was repaired by the Russian mechanic Ivan Kulibin. The prince later acquired another piece by Cox in the form of an elephant with rider. Although the latter piece is lost, other pieces in the Hermitage, including a table clock with lion and rhinoceros in ormolu, agate and coloured glass, and a dressing-table clock mounted on rhinoceroses, similarly decorated, testify to Cox's popularity.[48] Clocks as objects of conspicuous consumption or as the necessities for the proper functioning of such institutions as the Academy of Sciences or the Admiralty were equally in demand and were expensive, if not equally so. A member of the Russian academy sent to England in 1781 reported, for example, that 'j'ai vu ici de ces montres marines de Mr. Arnold, qu'il appelle Time Keepers ou Chronometers ... On m'a dit que le prix d'une telle montre est 100 Guinees.' He felt it too dear to acquire for the Academy, but he had ordered from Dollond 'une Lunette Achromatique à triple objectif' for forty-six pounds.[49]

In the ever-increasing scientific and scholarly contacts that had followed the establishment of the Academy in 1725 the acquisition of instruments for all branches of science had remained a constant subject of Russian concern. To the instrument-makers from whom Peter and his associates purchased instruments were to be added over the following decades the names of such as Arnold, Bird, Cuff, Adams, McCulloch, Short and Herschel.[50] A few young Russians came to Britain to train with British masters: the Academy of Sciences sent Nikolai Chizhov in 1759 and Vasilii Vorob'ev in 1780, while the first pupils to arrive from the Academy of Arts (Russia's second academy founded in 1758) were Osip Shishorin and Vasilii Sveshnikov, who stayed for some five years from 1780.[51] Despite the progress made by such students, the Russian aim to 'se passer des secours étrangers dans la fabrication des instrumens' was to prove elusive.[52] Shishorin and Sveshnikov were in fact accompanied to London by their British instructor from the Academy of Arts, Francis Morgan (1742?–1802).

It was with considerable pessimism that Lord Cathcart informed London at the end of 1771 of Morgan's arrival with his family and two 'very good workmen': 'Morgan was an Optical and Mathematical Instrument maker of Reputation, and some Stock, and had the great shop in Fleet Street. His migration hither has cost the Empress 5,500 Rubles, and I am afraid will cost him his whole fortune without any advantage on either side.' Lord Cathcart enclosed a copy of the agreement Morgan had signed before he left England, 'which is a paper layable to any Interpretation may be put upon it here'. Cathcart was rightly sceptical about the 'paper', which included commitments to teaching five or six apprentices and to selling instruments at current London rates, as well as pledges about remuneration and rent for a house from which he might also ply his private trade, before finishing with the assurance that 'after all these Conditions very encouraging and advantigious for him, it is with reason expected, Mr Morgan will not have pain or trouble to prove his abilitys, as well as his Diligence in forwarding and finishing with as much expedition as accuracy, whatever her Imperial Majesty, or her admiralty may order him, in preference to any other Engagements of his'.[53]

Although this agreement made him 'Her Majesty's, and her Fleets and Admiralty Mathematical and Optical Instrument Maker', a position he seems to have retained virtually until his death, Morgan within a matter of months entered into a second agreement with the Academy of Arts to last for four years from 25 July/5 August 1772. The Academy of Arts a few years earlier had resolved to widen its curriculum to allow for the development of technical skills in its pupils and the mathematical instrument-making class was a result of that decision. On 28 May/8 June 1776 Morgan was called before the Academy's academic council (*sobranie*) to discuss a new three-year contract. From the extensive minutes of that meeting it emerges that Morgan was asked to account for the progress of the pupils under his supervision: he named six, who were variously able to prepare astrolabes, electric machines, telescopes, microscopes and sundials, polish metals and lenses, and engrave on brass, but two others 'gave little hope in anything'. He agreed to take on further pupils up to a maximum of six and he was to receive 300 rubles a year as his salary. During the period of his first contract, he had occupied a ten-room flat and workshop in Academy buildings overlooking the Neva, but he was now obliged reluctantly to move to a house less convenient for his trade on the 4th Line.[54] While continuing to live in an Academy house, he decided also to open a shop in 1779 on Nevskii Prospekt to carry on his flourishing private business. After fourteen years' teaching at the Academy of Arts, he was, however, to be dismissed on 1 June 1785 on account of the poor showing of his pupils in recent examinations. He was also reminded that he had failed to present the Academy with the second of two objects 'either rare or of new design', as agreed in his original contract of 1772. He was, furthermore, evicted from his house.[55]

Morgan seems to have given no cause for complaint in the fulfilment of his contractual obligations to the Admiralty, although information about his activities is not easily accessible, even in the voluminous *Materials for the History of the Russian Fleet*. Morgan was sent to England on at least three occasions on official business. The first was, as we have already noted, in 1780 when he accompanied apprentices from the Academy of Arts, but he equally carried out commissions for the Admiralty College. He brought back an upsetting machine to roll copper and iron sheets which he was responsible for installing at the Admiralty's Izhora works at Kolpino and for maintaining with eight apprentices assigned to his charge.[56] At the end of 1790 he was back in London, seeking to recruit shipbuilders and was commended to the Russian ambassador by Chernyshev, the head of the Admiralty College, as having given Russia some twenty years of loyal service.[57] In the 1790s the Izhora works were extended and reorganised and Morgan was responsible for constructing a furnace for the smelting of iron waste near the rolling mill. When a rifle manufactory was established there during Paul's reign, it was Morgan who was given the task of overseeing the production of cleaning rods by workmen transferred from the Kremenchug and Sestroretsk factories.[58] The training of apprentices was recognised as one of Morgan's most important and lasting contributions. It was precisely this area that the new emperor was quick to emphasise and seek to expand within months of his accession. 'His Imperial Majesty, seeing the success of the master Morgan in the training of apprentices to produce mathematical, optical and other instruments, many of whom are now themselves masters and include Anisin Vorotnikov, currently and usefully employed at the Admiralty', increased the number to twelve, allowing Morgan to take on twenty initially and reject those who proved incompetent.[59]

In addition to his work for the Admiralty, Morgan was called upon on several occasions to work for the Academy of Sciences or to supply them with necessary instruments, a tribute to Morgan's reputation as well as perhaps an indication of the Academy's reluctance fully to recognise the skill of Kulibin, who was in charge of its instrument workshop. At a meeting in October 1774 Professor Wolfgang Krafft proposed to 'retablir la Chambre de physique expérimentale auprès de l'Académie' and to make a start by buying an available pneumatic pump from Morgan. Euler and Krafft inspected the pump and found it 'très bien executée' and 'l'appareil des plus complets'.[60] This led the following year to the Academy's agreeing to pay Morgan 250 rubles for a fundamental repair of the great Rowley orrery that stood in the hall of the Library. It seems, however, that it was ultimately Kulibin and not Morgan who carried out the repairs.[61] In 1783 the Academy recorded that all its thermometers were obtained from Morgan and a year later Krafft reported that he had used a Reamur thermometer made by the British master for the meteorological observations he had recently made in America.[62] Kulibin, in devising a electrophore, was guided by the appliance that Morgan himself had already produced.[63] Morgan was a prolific and inventive instrument-maker, whose place among the capital's notable craftsmen (in Professor Georgi's contemporary guide to St Petersburg) was fully merited.[64] Like most instrument-makers he was also very interested in horology. Indeed, the lasting testimony to his skill is the turret clock beneath the spire on the Admiralty which he completed a year before his death.[65]

'Watchmaker to the Empress' was the title enjoyed, however, by another Briton, Robert Hynam (1737–1818), who arrived in the Russian capital some five years after Morgan. How or when Hynam achieved that distinction is difficult to establish. He had served his apprenticeship in London as a joiner, although when he was admitted to the livery of the Joiners' Company in 1764, he was already described as a watchmaker. He was subsequently appraised by a contemporary watchmaker as 'much-improving' in 1773, but this would seem hardly enough to secure an imperial appointment.[66] Most probably, Hynam went to Russia without a contract, keen to exploit what he considered a gap in the market – the import of English watches, clocks and objets d'art. In the Boulton and Fothergill letter-books there is a copy of a letter sent on 20 July 1776 to Hynam, still apparently in London, about his order for tea urns and a tea set and of another, the following April, to his father about the unpaid bill for 'sundry goods . . . chiefly silverware'.[67] The first extant letters from Hynam himself date from 1778: the first to his brother is concerned with the paying of bills, but it is the second, to the London watchmakers Lamb and Webb, from whom he has just received eighteen watches, that is uniquely informative about his trade and his status. He explains that he is 'in exceeding want of Horizonal Watches, and indeed of all other sorts, particularly very large Silver Horizontal Sec^{ds} Watches, and plain D° I mean without Seconds'. Wishing to reassure them that he is a man with whom it is safe to do business, he trots out details of his lofty position and income:

I think it incumbent upon me to give you every satisfaction in my power, and therefor I advice you, that the place I enjoy under H.I.M. is the same as a Patent place in England, it is for Life, my Salary is 1200 R^s or 240£ Sterling, and from different Russian Gentlemen for the care of their Clocks 65£ in the whole 305£ per annum. And I assure you what Money I earn (independant of the above) is nearly equal to the whole of my Expenses. The profits of my trade will be very considerable, if I am well served with Clocks, and Watches from England.[68]

Of Hynam's own activities as a watchmaker there is surprisingly little information. Chenakal records, however, that he 'made many table clocks and pocket watches of high quality and superb finish'; a small fob watch on a six-strand chatelaine, all encrusted with diamonds, which he made for the Empress and which is now in the Hermitage, has been elsewhere described and illustrated.[69] Hynam was, however, a man of infinite resource and invention and he was soon branching out into other areas which brought him scholarly recognition both in Russia and his homeland.

In August 1781 the Academy of Sciences was instructed by the empress to carry out tests on a machine which Hynam had presented to her to 'indiquer la vitesse du son et la distance à laquelle il se trouve' and Hynam himself asked for and was granted permission to address a public assembly on his invention.[70] That the impression was positive was recalled many years later in September 1800, when Hynam was elected a Corresponding Member of the Academy. However, although he was elected 'unanimously and without balloting', he had in fact himself sought the honour, supplying the President of the Academy Baron von Nicolay with a copy of the diploma he had recently received as Corresponding Member of the Society for the Encouragement of Arts, Manufactures and Commerce (later known as the Royal Society of Arts) in London.[71] Hynam had been awarded a Gold Medal by the Society in 1796 for an instrument he had made for gauging the cutters for wheels in clocks and watches, but on condition that he send the Society the complete instrument together with the calculations he had made for it. Hynam eventually complied and received his medal; his letters, tables and plates were printed in the *Transactions* of the Society in 1799, the year of his election as Corresponding Member.[72] Towards the end of his life he was also elected a Member of the University of Moscow and was not slow to inform his brother that he was 'the first Englishman that has had the Honor of being made a Member of the Imperial Academy of St. Petersburg, and the University of Mosco'.[73]

Hynam once confessed to his brother that 'there is no resisting, my mind must be constantly employed' and he was then, in 1800, at work 'on a small tretise [sic] upon the Balance, or scale beam'; twelve years later he was to produce three specimen standard pairs of balances.[74] Standardisation was his passion, but not to the exclusion of all else – in Catherine's reign he had invented two machines, one 'for boiling oak planks for shipbuilding, the other for weighing ponderous loads', and, much later, he was conducting experiments on magnetic fields.[75] It was, however, his creation of a standard linear measure for the Russian Empire that was to be his most conspicuous achievement.

In 1797, early in the reign of Paul I, a statute on weights and measures was introduced at the direct instigation of Charles Gascoigne in his capacity as director of the government's iron foundries at Petrozavodsk. The English inch was its basic unit of measurement. It was envisaged that Gascoigne should make the measures at his works, but he found 'difficulty in fixing their exactness with certainty' and therefore encouraged Hynam to petition the tsar for the right to produce them. After corresponding on the matter with British scholars, Hynam devised the instruments necessary to give accurate measurements and decided on 'a block of Siberian Jasper, laid in a block of Ebony' as the most suitable material, resistant to both extreme heat and cold, from which to 'to make an Arschine or Standard Measure for the Russian Empire'. This was in the summer of 1800, but Paul never quite got round to issuing the required statute and so in August of the following year Hynam petitioned the new tsar, and this time successfully. He wrote:

I am capable of dividing a measure of length to the most minute exactness, and also to make all Standards for the regulation of the Commerce of this vast Empire. I am willing to show what can be done by making at first a Standard measure of length by taking the Unite from the English Yard of three feet, and from thence to make a minutely correct divided Archine of two feet four inches, and upon the exactitude of this measure of length I am willing to rest my abilities, and to offer in future my services to Government.[76]

In 1803 the Ministry of Internal Affairs, which had assumed responsibility for such matters from the earlier First Department of the Senate, instructed Hynam to proceed, envisaging three stages of work: first, the creation of standards of weights and measures which would be retained in St Petersburg; second, the creation of measures to be sent to all provincial centres, to be used as controls; and third, the production of 'ordinary arshins', to be used by the population at large.[77] It was only in November 1807 that the emperor approved of the standard arshin which had been presented to him. Hynam in fact prepared three standard arshins – of glass (rather than jasper), steel and brass; soon afterwards he produced a brass arshin for each of the fifty-two *gubernii*. The first estimate of the quantities of the arshin that would be required for everyday use was 500,000 and, not unreasonably, Hynam was anxious to be given the contract to produce them. In 1810 he and his two sons signed a contract that seemed to guarantee the family fortune: they were to be responsible for all stages of the production of the arshins. They were given a large house on the First Line of Vasilii Island to serve as factory and family home; all the necessary instruments and machines (after Hynam's designs) were to be paid for out of government money, and the supply of iron was to be paid for through a loan. Hynam agreed to train twelve young apprentices and to supply 50,000 arshins per month at a unit cost of 40 copecks. However, costs soon exceeded estimates and Hynam also experienced great difficulties in getting arshins of good quality iron from the foundries. When at last this latter problem seemed solved with the contracting of the nearby Sestroretsk munitions factory, the war against Napoleon brought production to an abrupt close.[78] Robert Hynam's son Benjamin wrote at this time that 'Had not this present blow arrived, we should have been enabled in the course of five years to have returned him [his father], not indeed in affluence, but with a sufficiency to satisfy moderate ideas.'[79] The supply of over a million arshin measures was, however, eventually completed, but only in 1821, three years after the death of Robert Hynam, who had been succeeded as director of the factory by his second son William, who was to buy from the government the house and factory.

The Hynams constituted a whole dynasty of imperial watchmakers. Robert's first son, Benjamin (1769–1850), was sent to England for ten years to learn his trade with financial support from the imperial purse – he 'is very industrious, he learns natural philosophy, besides the watch-making', it was reported in 1785[80] – before returning with his bride to St Petersburg in 1791 and to his own appointment as watchmaker to the empress in 1793. Benjamin's elder son Robert (1793–1864) enjoyed a similar title from 1861, as well as siring ten daughters, one of whom, incidentally, married a Swan and had a family that descended to the Swann of 'Flanders and Swann' fame.[81] It is William, the younger son of Robert Hynam senior, who remains perhaps the most intriguing and least known of the Hynams. Trained as a watchmaker, he became director of the standards factory, before being expelled from Russia in 1826 for his involvement in the Decembrist uprising.[82] The collection of Hynam letters in the Greater London Record Office sheds no light on the circumstances: its last letter, dated 1/13 October 1818, is, however, from William and contains the line 'my late Father, who has bequeathed me his good name, which I hope in God never to disgrace'.[83] William in fact was arrested on Senate Square on 12/24 December 1825 and taken to the Peter and Paul Fortress. During his interrogation he pleaded that he had been there 'out of curiosity' and had been obliged to shout the same as the crowd around him 'in order to save his life'. He was, however, expelled, but pardoned in April 1832 and allowed to return to Russia, after his brother Benjamin had petitioned Count Benkendorf, the head of the Third Department. William was to be expelled once again on 5/17 May 1837 'for reprehensible conduct', but in connection with what remains a mystery.[84]

III

The 1770s, when Morgan and Hynam came to St Petersburg, and the following decade were a period of intense Anglo-Russian interchange which saw the unceasing passage of British subjects to Russia. If in 1773 it was suggested that it was 'a time when almost everyman of Genius in Europe is offering at the shrine of this most Illustrious of Sovereigns', *The Public Advertiser* exactly a decade later informed its readers that 'The Empress of Russia, who has a Sensibility to discern real Genius, and a Generosity to reward it, draws the aspiring Artist to her Dominions.' A few days later, it published a letter from a British craftsman recently arrived in the Russian capital, who wrote that 'there are several London Masons, Carpenters, Locksmiths, &c. here, and they have been well encouraged; for the Spirit of Invention in Mechanics seems as uncommon as Genius in other Respects in this Part of the World'.[85] 'Genius' was obviously not the distinguishing mark, nor British the nationality, of most who made their way to Russia, but Catherine's encouragement for foreigners was indeed positive and constant.

By her manifestos of 1762 and 1763 Catherine gave notice at the very beginning of her reign of her wish to attract large numbers of colonists to Russia and of the benefits that awaited them. Some fifteen years later there had arrived over 30,000 colonists from all parts of Europe, but overwhelmingly from the German lands. An English translation of the second manifesto was distributed in Britain, but the response was minimal.[86] There was, however, an abortive attempt in 1763 by A. R. Vorontsov, the Russian ambassador in London, to send off a group of some 200 emigrants from Britain, but none arrived, which was probably no great loss to Russia were the following characterisation of them to any degree accurate:

the people are of too volatile a disposition and of too bad characters in general to be worth receiving in any country, having neither trade nor art to set up, and being mostly common adventurers, without even an industrious inclination, whom the late circumstances of Europe had sent a-travelling, and who, not finding nor deserving employment in England, embraced any scheme or proposal which could give them an immediate and momentary subsistence.[87]

Two decades later, Vorontsov's brother Semen blocked Potemkin's plan to form a British penal colony in the Crimea, 'the English Siberia', 'acquiring every year 90 or 100 malefactors, monsters, one could say, of humankind, incapable of agriculture or handicraft and suitable only for thieving and murder, and so riddled with the diseases that their way of life brings that they are unfitted to procreate'.[88] Following Russia's annexation of the Crimea in 1783, the delights of New Russia were promoted in another manifesto, aimed specifically at attracting craftsmen, specialists and entrepreneurs to the new or planned towns.[89] In June of that same year, 1784, Samuel Bentham was writing to his brother that he had 'just received news from Petersburg of the arrival of men, women and children to the amount of 139 from Scotland. The Prince was pleased to hear it and will take good care of them in the Crim which it seems is the place of their destiny'.[90] It was not, for these were the workmen recruited by Charles Cameron, but Bentham, using his brother Jeremy virtually as his London agent, took on the task of recruiting for Potemkin British specialists in a whole range of areas – distilling, brewing, tanning, dairy farming, shipbuilding, botany, medicine and architecture. Potemkin, indeed, wished 'to have a whole colony of English ... On every occasion there appears a partiality in favour of our country that is very flattering.' In short, 'any clever people capable of introducing improvements in the Prince's Government [i.e. New Russia] might meet with good encouragement, but I should be very sorry to recommend any one who in the end should fail in their proposals'.[91] Failures there inevitably were, but during the three years of Samuel Bentham's stewardship of Potemkin's estate at Krichev in the *guberniia* of Mogilev (from July 1784 until the summer of 1787) there were also successes, as described in great detail in the recent monograph by Ian Christie.[92]

Rumours were rife in Britain that valuable British subjects were being seduced to Russia, and contrary to the prevailing British laws. In 1764, in the wake of news about the putative emigrants, a correspondent to the *North Briton*, suggesting that 'others are daily making the same agreement', asked 'are there no laws in England that prohibit Manufacturers from going abroad, and forbid our private men to enlist in foreign service? I have somewhere read, that it is highly penal to decoy a Manufacturer over sea. If there are such laws, why are they not put into execution?'[93] There were indeed such laws, frequently invoked on the British side and well known to the Russians. In 1784, during a period when British anxieties were at their height, the government saw fit to publish the appropriate extracts from Statute 5 George I, chapter 27 and Statute 23 George II, chapter 13 'for the Information of all Persons who may be ignorant of the Penalties they may incur by Disobedience to them. – And it will be observed, that they extend to those who are in any ways concerned or instrumental in the Sending or Enticing Artificers or Manufacturers out of these Kingdoms, and in the Exportation of the Tools and Instruments made by them, as well as to the Artificers or Manufacturers themselves.' The clipping from the newspaper was sent to St Petersburg by the Russian minister in London, Ivan Simolin, who continued to negotiate vigorously for specialists both for the Crimea and elsewhere.[94] In St Petersburg, Simolin's British counterpart, Alleyne Fitzherbert, greeted the arrival of Cameron's workmen with dismay and commented that 'it seems somewhat extraordinary that the magistracy of

Edinburgh should not have exerted themselves so as to prevent the artificers I have just been speaking of from leaving the Kingdom as people of that class are evidently included, not only within the meaning, but within the exact letters of the various acts of Parliament which have passed of late years in order to prevent the emigration of our manufacturers and as their embarkation was carried on, not by stealth, but in the most public manner'; two years later, he was outraged when Gascoigne arrived from the same port of origin with workmen and machinery.[95] Back in Britain, Gascoigne's former father-in-law and partner at the Carron Company, Samuel Garbett, was particularly, not to say hysterically, sensitive to Russian malpractices with regard to both British artificers and machinery.[96]

Other Britons, however, found themselves for various reasons – and not always those of personal gain – in the role of 'enticers'. An interesting and little known example concerns the young Benjamin Hynam who was sent by his father to England in 1781 at the raw age of twelve, and found himself a few years later in serious trouble for infringing the notorious statutes. Seemingly on the orders of the empress, Baron Dimsdale (into whose care Hynam had been entrusted) set out the details of Hynam's arrest in a long letter to her of 17 October 1787 'for having seduced an Artist in the Watch-making business to go into foreign service' and his subsequent release on bail. It transpired that other watchmakers had also been informed that Hynam 'would certainly be convicted and that the Sollicitor for the Treasury had orders to prosecute him with the utmost severity'. Count Vorontsov, the ambassador, thought the affair 'so unpleasant' that he could not 'possibly interfere into it as a Minister. His private view is, however, that Mr H. should be sent out of this country, & the sooner the better'. The outcome of the affair is not known, although Hynam returned home only in 1791.[97]

What Eric Robinson has called 'the transference of British technology to Russia' nevertheless continued with few serious interruptions. Many of the most significant moments or episodes were connected in some way with either the employees or the products of the enterprises of Birmingham and of the Carron Company at Falkirk. The Carron Company, founded in 1759, began producing cannon two years later and during the Russo-Turkish war achieved its first contract to supply guns to the Admiralty College. During the same period, coinciding with the first decade of Catherine's reign, the Russian government had sought to improve and modernise its armaments in both army and navy and looked with mixed success to its existing foundries and specialists to remedy the situation. There was a particular deficiency in the production of iron cannon, as opposed to brass, and Catherine herself put the position very clearly to Sir Charles Knowles:

Nous possédions cy devant l'art de fondre des Canons de Fer, pour nos Vaisseaux et Forteresses. A notre honte il faut avouer que nous avions oublié cet art utile, et qu'à présent quelque fois de Cent Canons de Fer, à l'épreuve il n'en reste souvent que dix en entier. On se donne depuis deux Ans toutes les peines possibles pour avoir un habile Fondeur de Canons de Fer, mais inutilement.[98]

Although the empress was drawing attention to the high failure rate in the testing of Russian-produced cannon – for example, only 123 out of 613 guns cast at the state Kamenskii works in the Urals between 1763 and 1768 were accepted as sound – many of the forty-five 32-pounder guns delivered by Carron in its first consignment to Kronshtadt in June 1772 failed the strict Russian proofing. The confidence of Gascoigne, then the managing director of Carron, which was expressed in his accompanying letter to Knowles, was more than a little misplaced: 'The Glory of Her Imperial Majesty's arms may be proclaimed from the mouths of our Artillery at the Gates of Constantinople.'[99] The initial order for 1,000 tons of cannon was fulfilled only in the summer of 1773 after many more guns had failed their test and no further orders for ordnance were forthcoming until the mid-1780s. The links with Carron were, however, in no way broken. Catherine had drawn attention also to the search for specialist cannon-founders and Knowles had himself commented that 'je crains qu'un bon forgeron manque plutôt que le bon fer',[100] and it was from Carron, if not directly, that they came.

As in many such areas, there was a precedent from Peter's reign. Among the specialists he personally recruited in London were Endris(?) Kreiter and Thomas Snelling (or Snolling), both cannon-founders of whose existence but not subsequent fortunes we know only from an archival document detailing their arrival, first in Novgorod, and then in Vladimir in July 1698, and of their need for money in accordance with their contracts.[101] The names of two other gun-founders, Robert Gerrard and William Pankhurst, are found in the British ambassador's list of British craftsmen at Voronezh in 1705.[102] In Catherine's reign, it was not until May 1771, after abortive searches in Sweden and elsewhere by the Admiralty College, that the Russian ambassador in London signed up two founders, Adam Ramage and Joseph Powell, whose contract and early misfortunes are detailed in the same letter in which Cathcart informed London about Morgan.[103]

Despite the efforts made to get them to St Petersburg, Ramage and Powell were neglected and forgotten until they sought Cathcart's intervention and were eventually dispatched to the Lipetsk foundries near Voronezh in October 1771. Their contract was for six years, but Ramage died in October 1775. In 1777, Powell, by then himself a very sick man, completed his contract to the satisfaction of the College of Mines to the degree that it declined to re-employ him since he had trained adequate Russian replacements.

However, a year later, after petitioning the college to be allowed to demonstrate a revolutionary new method of casting cannon, he was sent to the Aleksandrovskii foundry at Petrozavodsk for a trial period of three months. The experiment proved unsuccessful: the cannon he produced were unfit for use, and the management was unconvinced that he had anything new to offer. The College of Mines, nevertheless, saw fit to give him a further contract at Lipetsk, where he was to stay for three years. Thereafter, he transferred to the Admiralty College and headed the foundry at the Izhora ironworks until his death in 1789. He had been recommended to the Admiralty in 1782 as 'sufficiently proven in his art and having shown no little usefulness in the introduction into Russia of a new and completely unknown method for the founding of cannon',[104] but despite references to the 'English manner', it is not clear what this entailed other than the use of high-grade ore and would anyway seem to contradict the evidence of his work at Petrazavodsk. He remains a controversial figure, but, as Roger Bartlett has shown in his detailed study, not uniquely so: Powell is an example of the foreign technical expert, working in a particularly sensitive and important area, whose successes arouse envy and suspicion and whose incompetence and failures invite scorn and indignation.

Powell was dubbed a 'scoundrel' in an article written during the Cold War;[105] a similar verdict in pre-Soviet days was delivered on Thomas Inglis, who arrived in St Petersburg in 1793 to undertake a radical overhaul of the foundries of the St Petersburg Arsenal, founded by Peter I in 1712.[106] Despite Russian victories in the second war against the Turks, Platon Zubov, Catherine's young favourite and member of the war council, had decided that Russian cannon production still left much to be desired and it was at his request that the Russian ambassador in London, Semen Vorontsov, found Inglis, 'a highly skilled master'. His four-year contract obliged him, in addition to training young Russian apprentices, to design and produce new machinery, to reorganise the foundry at Briansk, as well as the St Petersburg Arsenal, and to make the Russian artillery comparable to the best in Western Europe. In addition to his son John, he was to have a team of some twelve British craftsmen, including turners, smiths and mechanics. A British master mason, Isaac Little, was soon engaged on a six-year contract to enlarge and reconstruct the Arsenal after plans drawn up by Inglis, and in February 1796 twelve young boys from the Moscow Foundling Home were sent to him as apprentices. Inglis's contract was not renewed in 1798, although it is not clear whether this was in accord with his wish to return home or, as the Arsenal's historian suggests, an indication of dissatisfaction with his work. The latter seems less plausible, given that his son John remained for a further four years, working as part of a team of eleven specialists headed by James Wilson, a master smith.[107] In the absence of a list of Inglis's workforce, it cannot be established how many of them simply continued, like John Inglis, under Wilson. They were part of a considerable body of British, predominantly Scottish, skilled workers and craftsmen that changed and grew during the last decades of the century and was to be involved in many different government undertakings and enterprises. In this connection, it is instructive to go back to the 1770s and the arrival, some three years after that of Powell and Ramage, of a group of workmen from Carron.

As was seen in the preceding chapter, it was with the prompting of Admiral Knowles and after the intervention of the empress herself that the Admiralty College placed an order with Carron in 1773 for a fire engine, 'une machine à feu', to replace the existing windmill for the pumping of water from the Kronshtadt dry dock. The engine, designed with the help of John Smeaton, could be delivered without any contravention of the existing regulations, but it was again virtually a case of smuggling out the workmen necessary for installing it at Kronshtadt. Because of this, the four smiths, four stonemasons and two carpenters under the chief engineer Adam Smith seem to have arrived in two groups and work was not begun until early in 1775. The installation took over two years and the first successful tests were held in June 1777. Some of the workmen had returned earlier to Scotland, either dismissed for unsatisfactory work or with their particular contribution completed. Only Smith and the blacksmith William Bruce remained after 1777, agreeing to remain in Russia permanently to maintain the engine in working order. For Bruce, this was to mean another six years until his death in 1783. In that year, Adam Smith's son, Alexander, came to Russia as his father's assistant. It was he who was entrusted in 1791 with trying to put together another engine ordered from Carron by Admiral Greig shortly before his death. Smith found, however, that pieces were missing and could not be obtained because the political situation created by the 'Ochakov crisis' had led to a British government ban. Undaunted, Smith proceeded to build his own small pumping engine near the Kronshtadt canal, using components prepared at Gascoigne's Aleksandrovskii works. Despite this, the Admiralty decided to terminate his contract in 1793 when he asked for his salary to be doubled.[108]

The second and largest ever group of British workmen to arrive in Catherine's Russia came at the behest of the architect Charles Cameron in 1784.[109] Cameron had been working for the empress at her summer residence of Tsarskoe Selo since his arrival in 1779, initially on the redesign and construction of suites of apartments within Rastrelli's great Catherine Palace, and subsequently, on the addition of a new wing overlooking the Great Pond, his famous Agate Pavilion and Colonnade. He had been hampered from the outset by a lack of skilled workers able to carry out his requirements accurately and responsibly and with whom he could communicate directly in his own language. Given permission to recruit suitable craftsmen from Scotland, Cameron advertised on 21 January 1784 in the *Edinburgh Evening Courant* and received an overwhelming response. On 3 May a party of 140 workmen, wives and children set sail from Leith and by mid-June were settled in Sofiia, the 'model town' on the edge of the Grand Park. They occupied small wooden houses on stone foundations built by Cameron in the south-west corner of the town in a street which became known as the 'English Line', somewhat more modest, to be sure, than its namesake in the Russian capital. No less than seventy-three workmen signed three-year contracts: they included four master masons, two of whom had particular skills in vault construction, three master plasterers, two master bricklayers, fifteen plasterers and five smiths. Thirty-nine of the men were bachelors, and of the married men, twenty-four came with their wives and families, who numbered sixty-seven. The age range of the workers is also of interest: all but four were aged forty or below, with some forty of them in their twenties. Easily the eldest was fifty-two-year-old William Lyon, arriving with his two sons George, twenty, and James, nineteen. It was, incidentally, a letter from William and George Lyon, written a month after their arrival in Russia to their family back in Scotland, that provides a unique and vivid record of their first impressions of Kronshtadt and St Petersburg, where they stayed for a fortnight in the English Inn and 'we was ordred to want for nothing but call for what ever we wanted', and their journey to nearby Tsarskoe Selo.[110] In Sofiia the Scots lived as a tightly knit community. Before they left Scotland most of the men, headed appropriately enough by David Grubb, a stonemason, had petitioned the Grand Lodge of Scotland to erect their own masonic lodge and were entered on the roll as No. 207 'Imperial Scottish Lodge of St Petersburg'.[111] The lodge was unique in Russia by virtue of that fact that it comprised operative, as opposed to speculative, masons. Sadly, there is no information about the lodge's activities or even a hint that the master architect, Cameron himself, was in any way involved.

Archival documents suggest, however, that relations between the architect and his craftsmen were at times strained; they also offer fascinating glimpses of demarcation disputes, differences in British and Russian work practices and expectations. The Lyons had written that they expected to 'do very well here and in a short time relive [*sic*] you and ourselvs', but as always money problems loomed large for the workmen. The workmen obviously signed their contracts in ignorance of what to expect in Russia and it was inevitable that, once installed at Sofiia, they would soon, individually and collectively, begin to voice certain grievances and attempt to get an improved deal. Disputes in 1785 over numbers of bricks laid, days lost for non-availability of materials, payment for the long non-working winter months, brought a long decree from the empress in August, in which the attempt was made to regularise working practices. One particularly revealing clause reads:

Insofar that it has been noted that the English workmen arrive late for work and depart early and moreover celebrate not only their own but also our festivals, which causes great delays in the work, it is required that they arrive at work at 6am during spring and summer and finish at 9pm on the longest days and at 7pm on the shortest, with two hours allowed for meals, and moreover, they are to celebrate only the festivals of their own faith and Sundays.[112]

The workmens' disputes were not, however, only with the Palace Office for Building but also with Cameron. Their growing dissatisfaction is reflected in a letter they addressed to Bezborodko, the state secretary, in September 1785:

We left our own Country on faith of the publick Advertisment for workmen in her Imperial Majestys name but soon after we Arrived those who Engaged us by the threat of denying us Subsistance we were Nessiated to accept of a Salary much below our British Agreement and sit us under the direction of the Cantor [the Palace Office] or who you think proper for under M[r] Cameron we will not be unless in the Character of Architect – If Your Excellency will be pleased to remove these our Grievances or please allow us the liberty to return to our Native County.[113]

Relations did not improve and in the next year, for instance, Cameron recommended that three masons who wished to return to Scotland be allowed to do so at their own expense and that five others be dismissed as 'lazy and incompetent'. In the event, three at least of these were allowed to stay, and the remaining workmen (one had died and another absconded) signed new and somewhat improved three-year contracts, effective from 1/12 May 1787.

With work on the Cold Baths/Agate Pavilion complex completed in 1787 and on the Colonnade (Cameron Gallery) soon afterwards, the main tasks for which the Scots had been recruited had come to an end. They had also worked on the Chinese Village and on the Grand Orangery and at Sofiia; some had been sent further afield for particular projects – to St Petersburg, to Peterhof and to Mogilev. It seems likely that the majority of workers were simply not offered a further extension of their contracts in 1790 and this led to a general exodus. During the months of April to July 1790 the lists of intending departees in the *St Petersburg News* were full of the names of Scots workmen and their families from Sofiia. For most of them the weird and wonderful Russian episode in their lives was at an end and they were to return to Scotland, undoubtedly glad to see their homeland again but without any hopes of a bright future. Not all the workmen announced their departures and not all those who did departed. It is clear that some were on the lookout for further work, convinced for a variety of reasons that their lives

and, possibly, their fortunes were now forever linked with Russia. It is difficult to say with any certainty how many in fact remained – perhaps twenty
workmen at most. There were fifteen smiths, plasterers and bricklayers still
contracted to the Palace Office in 1793 and they included several men who
were to achieve quite remarkable success and eminence.

The career of the architect Cameron will be discussed in detail in the following chapter which is devoted to 'masters of the arts' – and it is there also
that two of his workmen, the master mason Adam Menelaws and the mason
William Hastie, will equally find their appropriate place as notable architects
in their own right (in Hastie's case, as architect/town planner). The further
careers of other craftsmen, may, however, be properly pursued here. The
Lyons were among those who remained and soon called out the rest of their
family to join them in the Russian capital. There is no information about
where the two Lyon brothers worked in the 1790s and they are mentioned
again essentially to introduce their youngest sister Jane, or Jenny (b. 1771),
who claims our attention, not, to be sure, for any unexpected technological
expertise but for the fact that in 1796 she was appointed nurse to the infant
Grand Duke Nikolai Petrovich, the future Tsar Nicholas I. She was the
renowned 'nanny-lioness' (*niania-l'vitsa*), Evgeniia Vasil'evna Laion, who
stayed with the imperial family for over forty years, earning its love and
admiration.[114] Isaac Little, one of the masons, signed, as we have already
noted, a six-year contract in 1794 to work at the Arsenal with Inglis, but
the only indication of his continued presence into the nineteenth century in
St Petersburg is the registering of frequent new additions to his family.[115] By
contrast, the fortunes of James Wilson and his son Alexander can be charted
much more clearly.

The Wilsons arrived as the largest family group: James (1749–1821) and
his wife Helen brought their three sons (Alexander, aged nine; Luke, aged
five; and John, aged one) and three daughters (the twins Mary and Helen,
aged five; and Christine, aged three). During the Cameron years the only
direct reference to James Wilson relates to his preparing the iron rail for the
staircase in the Grand Duke Paul's apartments in the Grand Palace,[116] but
as the only master in a team of seven smiths, he would have been responsible
for, and much involved in, the complex ironwork throughout the new buildings. By 1793 his son Alexander, now aged eighteen, had made sufficient
progress in his father's trade to be offered a contract in his own right by the
Palace Office. It was to be a team of specialists, headed by James Wilson
and including Alexander Wilson, which followed Inglis at the Arsenal in
1799, but the new century saw the father working under his son. It was
at this time that Alexander Wilson began his important but comparatively
short-term association with Gascoigne, becoming his assistant, firstly at the
Admiralty's Izhora works at Kolpino, where Gascoigne was appointed in

1803 to supervise its reconstruction after plans drawn up by another of Cameron's former workmen, William Hastie, and then, and simultaneously, at the Aleksandrovskaia manufaktura, where Gascoigne became technical director in 1805. Following Gascoigne's death in July 1806, Wilson himself was appointed head of both enterprises, but it was his directorship of the Aleksandrovskaia manufaktura, continuing almost until its closure in 1862, that brought him particular renown.

The great textile mill and industrial complex had been founded in 1799 on the Neva some miles beyond the Aleksandr Nevskii Monastery. It enjoyed the patronage of Maria Fedorovna, the empress, soon dowager empress; it served as a source of employment for children of both sexes from the St Petersburg Foundling Home, while providing funds towards the Home's and similar institutions' maintenance; it became inevitably a 'sight' for visitors, a sort of showpiece of technological progress and of would-be enlightened exploitation of child labour. Two long and instructive descriptions of all aspects of the enterprise from the early years of Wilson's directorship are found in the memoirs of John Quincy Adams, the United States' first recognised minister in Russia, who went there in 1810, and the memoirs of Dr A. B. Granville, dating from 1827.[117] While the visitors differed in their assessment of the lot of the children from the Foundling Home, both were impressed by Wilson and the manufactory's machinery, most of which he was responsible for introducing. Adams, however, remarked that 'Mr Wilson has no pay – nothing but occasional presents; leaving him in a state of anxiety and suspense with regard to his future prospects', but by the time Granville met him, Wilson had become a major-general of engineers. He was promoted to lieutenant-general in 1829 and received countless other honours, before dying in February 1866 at the ripe old age of ninety.[118] A little-known detail of his biography is his acquaintance with Alexander Pushkin. In 1835, when Pushkin was gathering materials for a history of Peter the Great, Wilson sent him copies of the *Memoirs of Peter Henry Bruce* and John Cook's *Voyages and Travels*, works by Scotsmen who had also sought, if with considerably less success, their fortune in Russia.[119]

The Wilsons have consistently and erroneously been numbered among the workmen arriving with Gascoigne in 1786, whereas their paths have been shown to have crossed only at the turn of the century. It is, however, upon Gascoigne and the group of skilled Carron workers he in fact brought with him that attention must now be focussed. Their identities, activities and developing careers add futher strands to the complicated skein of social and working relationships in the British community and between the British and Russians during the last two decades of the eighteenth century and, in many cases, beyond.

The published correspondence between Admiral Greig and the Russian ambassador in London, Semen Vorontsov, begins with three letters from Greig in 1786, which convey some of the drama and intrigue surrounding the departure of Gascoigne, 'que j'ai engagé par ordre de Sa Majesté Impériale pour établir une fonderie d'artillerie ici en Russie', and indicate its apparent happy outcome with his arrival at St Petersburg.[120] It is an episode which a Russian scholar has recently written up as an absorbing historical narrative, involving undercover agents, diplomatic deception, clandestine payments designed 'to achieve the desired aim and advance the strategic interests of the Russian empire'.[121] Many Britons at the time and since viewed the matter somewhat differently. Pitt, apparently after an interview with Gascoigne, cleared him to go to Russia but was only told at best half the truth; Garbett, Gascoigne's former partner, and Matthew Boulton were vociferous in their denunciations of what was really involved – of patent infringements of existing legislation regarding the export of specialists and machinery. In St Petersburg the British ambassador's indignation on Gascoigne's arrival communicated itself to the British community which for a time ostracised both Gascoigne and his sponsor Greig, whose letters and actions reveal how far he was prepared to go in the service of his country of adoption. Memories of the affair were slow to fade, and Clarke, the Cambridge don, refers to Gascoigne, whom he met during his travels through Russia in 1800, as 'a British outlaw, formerly superintendant of the Carron Works in Scotland, whose improvements he betrayed to the Russian Government, and was accordingly rewarded'.[122]

Gascoigne arrived in St Petersburg on 26 May/6 June 1786, but it was only in late August that he finally left for Petrozavodsk where he was to be the director both of the Aleksandrovskii cannon works, completed in 1774 on a site near to Peter the Great's original factory, and of the Konchezerskii iron foundry, built for Peter in 1707 some twenty-five miles from Petrozavodsk. His task was to undertake a fundamental reconstruction and reorganisation of the two works in order to produce 'according to the Carron system' a steady supply of reliable cannon for the Russian army and navy, soon to be locked in war with both the Turks and the Swedes. It was an enormous task which Gascoigne approached with matching confidence, quickly but far from totally eroded by his experiences on site. Although Gascoigne was to be involved with almost every technological enterprise of note in Russia during his twenty-year career, it was Petrozavodsk which was his first, his most important and best known achievement. Nevertheless, a fascinating insight into the initial problems he encountered is provided in a series of letters which Gascoigne wrote to Greig over the two years from the autumn of 1786 to the admiral's death in October 1788 and which have only recently been made available.[123]

Gascoigne was accompanied, it appears, by eleven associates and specialists:

19 Charles Gascoigne (1738–1806). Oil painting (*c.* 1800) by unknown Russian artist.

James Baird, Gascoigne's second-in-command; Adam Armstrong, his assistant and translator (who had been tutor to the Greig children in Scotland and
heavily involved in the secret negotiations); Josiah Roebuck, the chemical
expert for testing metal; Charles Baird, cannon-turning master; George
Clark, Daniel McSween, John Glen and James Walker, masters of various
(unspecified) processes; William Brown and James Russell, cannon-boring
masters; and Timothy Roper, model master.[124] Bowie, a British specialist who
had been sent by the College of Mines to Petrozavodsk as early as 1774,
was still there, or perhaps had returned there, when Gascoigne arrived: he is
mentioned in December as sent with McSween to search for special timber
for use in the construction of the new blast furnace.[125] Over the succeeding
months Gascoigne was constantly on the lookout for further workmen. He
encouraged Greig to send him a carpenter, adding that

> we want a few good hands much, for tho the Russians are infinitely the best Hatchet Men
> I ever saw, yet they work with no other Tool & a Hatchet dont make a good joint fit to
> bear strain from *going machinery*, there is a solidity in all our Work here that they have
> had no Idea of till they saw it.[126]

He became increasingly scathing about the unreliability and incompetency of
the Russian workmen and wrote of the need for real craftsmen. 'At Carron
in every new thing my method was to engage the best workmen that could
be procured for money to make a beginning & I never once failed by taking
that method.'[127] He was soon welcoming Barlow, who had slipped away secretly from Carron to become his 'Principal Furnace Man' and was 'intimately
acquainted with every thing appertaining to Blast Air and Cupola Furnaces'.[128] Gascoigne was, however, playing a very delicate game. In the early
years he was still dependent on Carron for shipments of machinery and furnace parts, fire bricks, axles for water wheels, cranes, firebricks, fire-clay.[129]
If he could hardly expect goodwill from his former partners, he was anxious
that he should not be regarded as continuing to entice away Carron employees
nor seen as bringing an end to the export of cannon which had been resumed
in the 1780s under his directorship. He asked Greig to ask the empress for
'an order for some Guns or Carronades to Carron C°', explaining

> besides other substantial Reasons you might give as an essential and true one, that the
> Country in Scotland are outrageous gainst the Company & me, under the notion that we
> are doing a national prejudice to Scotland & they universally say the C° may expect no more
> Encouragement from this Empire, consequently so strict is every Eye upon us in Scotland,
> that I cannot get some very necessary Hands, & Instruments, which otherwise the Company
> could not object to (& that is truly the case) & the Country would not observe us were the
> Company doing Business in the Gun way for HIM, & if HIM pleases to order a few hundred,
> say 100 pieces or what she thinks right, only money as the former letters shall be paid, &
> I will undertake here to make Bar Iron, to pay the other 2/3ds of the price.[130]

The orders continued[131] – and so did the influx of men. In August 1787 when John Taylor, a blacksmith, arrived, Gascoigne hastened to inform Greig that he was 'a Man I did not want but will not be the less usefull only I fear my Friends at home may suppose he came out at my instigation; tho he never wrought with Carron Company, at least for years past he wrought several years with me as Master Ship-Blacksmith at Carron Wharf and is a masterly & industrious workman'.[132]

At the end of 1786 another blacksmith, John Routh, was sent from Kronshtadt, although Gascoigne was soon to wish 'I had asked for the one that is married – with a Scots woman – She would have perhaps kept house for the whole who are at present most egregiously cheated by their Russian servants & yet dont know how to help themselves.'[133] With their first winter behind them, the Scots were soon building their own houses and creating their own community within the larger community. Petrozavodsk was indeed to have its own 'English Street' (shown on a map of 1801). Unlike many of Cameron's workmen, Gascoigne's had gone to Russia without their families. In April Alexander Ingram returned to Scotland to bring back his own and George Clark's families and Gascoigne's youngest daughter Mary; Barlow's family came out the following spring.[134] It has not been established if, like Cameron's workmen, they asked at this time for a priest and a teacher, but in the late 1790s there was certainly a teacher at the factory school, who may have been a Scot. It seems, however, that the workmen did form their own masonic lodge.[135] The composition of the community inevitably changed over the years: Gascoigne, Armstrong, Roebuck and George Clark (and his son Matthew) were still on the official payroll by the end of the century, but others of the original team had either returned to Scotland or moved on to other ventures. It has been calculated that some twenty-eight British specialists were involved at one or other of the Olonets works in the 1790s, and if the associated Kronshtadt works, established in 1789, is included, there would seem to have been even more at the time of the government inspection in August 1800.[136] Among those listed were some of Cameron's former workmen, notably the smiths Alexander Davie and James Niven, but the works' mechanic was none other than Alexander Smith, who had built the 'fire-engine' at Kronshtadt and in 1800 had been temporarily seconded to Moscow to build another.

At the end of February 1787 Greig wrote to Bezborodko in his inimitable French to explain that he had recently been to Petrozavodsk to see for himself the general situation at the works, but at the invitation of a Gascoigne who was anxious to gain support for his proposals for radical and costly reconstruction.

Apres avoir bien considéré de toutes les Circonstances, nous sommes convenu avec Monsʳ Gascoigne qu'il sera bien inutile, de faire des petites Reparations temporaire, pour continuer le font des Cannons, qui causera un depence continuelle sans pouvoir faire assé des Cannons pour y repondre – ainsi nous nous sommes desidé, qu'il sera bien plus avantagieuse pour la Courrone, de Construire tout de nouveau.[137]

Both before and following his visit Gascoigne had bombarded Greig with letters and reports in which he rehearsed the deficiencies of existing furnaces, found wanting the iron ore from local mines ('exceedingly coldshort'), deplored the lack of coal (the advantages of which over charcoal were immense) and, while rejoicing in the force of the water power, found that the dam leaked and the water wheels were badly constructed. He complained about the climate and about the difficulties of transportation and would have preferred another foundry built nearer the sea. Nevertheless, as the months went by, Gascoigne reported his progress and successes. Two blast furnaces were working when he arrived, casting 12-pounder guns and less, and furnace no. 3, which is first mentioned in October 1786 as under fundamental repair, was to provide a virtual leitmotif to his letters until on 5/16 August 1787 it was finally 'brought into blast' and it 'continued to work to my entire satisfaction, making a perfect & compleat seperation in the Cynder which runs off freely by itself, & yeilding abundance of Iron from the materials with which she is working'.[138] Later that month the blowing machine for furnaces 3 and 4 was finished by McSween and others and was 'a compleat piece of workmanship in all its parts'.[139] Furnace no. 4 began operations in mid-September and at the end of the month the governor-general of Olonets T. I. Tutolmin came to inspect the completed Aleksandrovskii works. The red-letter day was, however, 11/22 April 1788 when Gascoigne could write: 'We have about 30 Guns bored, about 20 of these turned & the arms cut, & have this day had the first Gun proved and received by the major of Artillery on Government Account.'[140] He was confident of producing 100 cannon for the fleet by the middle of May, if they stood proof. There was the rub, for many of the cannon produced over the few years failed the stringent Russian tests. Nevertheless, the Aleksandrovskii cannon foundry emerged as one of the major suppliers of cannon and shot for the Russian navy and army. The foundry was to diversify, producing all manner of machinery, including steam engines, and a wide range of ironware, domestic and ornamental (as early as December 1786 Gascoigne produced bas-reliefs of the empress and of the grand duke and duchess to demonstrate casting techniques).

Gascoigne's success at Petrozavodsk – work at the reconstruction of the iron foundry at nearby Konchezer was finished by 1789, although it was to suffer great fire damage within a very few years – led to a renewal of his contract for a further four years with a continuing salary of £2,500 and a half share of any savings made on the agreed prices for cannons and shot. In 1793 a further contract was negotiated for a period determined only by 'his continued loyal service'.[141] This he gave until his death and he prospered accordingly, amassing a considerable fortune by fair means and foul (he apparently 'borrowed' freely from the works' account), living in considerable style in his mansions at Petrozavodsk, St Petersburg and, latterly, at Lugansk in New Russia. As his erstwhile opponent, Boulton, himself enjoying by then an officially approved commission from the Russian government, wrote to Garbett in 1803 that Gascoigne 'has a good income, lives in more splendour, and has greater connections than he can ever have in this country'.[142] Having attended his eldest daughter's marriage to Lord Haddington before he absconded from Scotland, he saw his other two daughters safely married off in St Petersburg shortly before he died. A widower of long standing, he himself married in November 1797 at the age of sixty the beautiful teenaged Anastasia-Jessy, daughter of the ubiquitous Dr Guthrie, but soon allowed her a discreet divorce on grounds of 'a Disparity of Age and Disposition'.[143] Beginning with the modest rank of collegiate councillor and the subsequent award of the Order of St Vladimir (3rd class) from Catherine, he achieved his heights of fame and influence under Paul: a gift of 2,000 serfs at the time of the coronation, the rank of actual state councillor in October 1798 and of the Order of St Anna (2nd and then 1st class). Behind these honours lay a decade of increasing and varied activity.[144]

In 1789 a new but small iron foundry was established at Kronshtadt for the purpose of reusing the large amounts of old cannon and scrap metal accumulating in the port and of providing a direct service for the fleet. It came under Gascoigne's overall control and was managed by Josiah Roebuck and George Clark with an initial work force of 190 men dispatched from Petrozavodsk.[145] In 1801, although the foundry was not closed, much of its activity was wound down when Gascoigne established another state foundry on land on the Peterhof road which belonged to him and for which he conveniently received grants from the government. It was to be managed by Clark's son, Matthew. Later in the century this was to become the famous Putilov works and, after the October Revolution, was renamed the Kirov.[146]

In April 1798 Gascoigne became president of the newly established Board of the Olonets and Kronshtadt Works, although by then much of his time was devoted to a new complex in the south. The initial stimulus came again from Zubov in the wake of the Russo-Turkish war and reflected the need to supply the Black Sea fleet and the fortresses with cannon from a more immediate base and to exploit the vast and rich coal deposits of the region. Gascoigne was sent to carry out a detailed survey and to prospect for coal and ores. In November 1795 the Ekaterinoslavskii foundry (renamed the Luganskii in 1797) was officially established on the right bank of the River Lugan', less than ten miles from the Northern Donets. Much of the machinery came from Petrozavodsk, as did part of the workforce, including British specialists. Construction was completed in 1799 and smelting was begun, using coal from the Don basin. However, the local ore proved disappointing and it was necessary to use accumulated scrap iron from the southern ports as well as to bring in large quantities of iron from Siberia. Although small-calibre guns (up to twenty-four pound carronades) were produced, Gascoigne reported that metal quality had to be considerably improved before higher calibre cannon could be attempted.[147]

Gascoigne's involvement early in Alexander's reign with the Izhora works at Kolpino and the Aleksandrovskaia textile complex has already been touched on in connection with the career of Alexander Wilson. Within months of Gascoigne beginning work at Kolpino, his patron Admiral P. V. Chichagov was writing to Vorontsov that 'cet homme a fait dans six mois un changement si étonnant dans cette fabrique, ou plutôt dans ces débris et ruines d'une fabrique, que déjà elle est en état de fournir à l'amirauté tous les objets de première nécessité en quantité et d'une perfection comme on ne les a jamais eu'.[148] Reginald Heber, fresh from his election to a fellowship at All Souls, Oxford, visited Kolpino in 1805 accompanied by Gascoigne's new son-in-law, Colonel George Pollen, and found the works 'Extremely interesting; they are constructed in a kind of amphitheatre, round a basin which communicates with a canal, the whole lined with granite quays of great beauty ... I much admired the manner in which a constant stress of water was supplied to a saw-mill, from a fall at a few yards distance; by means of a stove the water in the pipe and cistern was brought to the wheel without freezing, and the whole machinery was very simple and ingenious.'[149] Gascoigne was already dead when the dam burst in 1807 after high spring waters. A similar accident had occurred in 1800 at Petrozavodsk after torrential rains: in his initial reconstruction of the dam, Gascoigne, it has been suggested, blocked the existing relief channels.[150]

A further area of Gascoigne's activity during Paul's reign is represented by his involvement in the new Petersburg mint. A mint was one of the first buildings Peter the Great designated for the Peter and Paul Fortress and over the years it had undergone some rebuilding and much replacement of machinery. In the last year of Catherine's reign it was decided to see if the existing machinery could again be repaired with the help of British experts. Matthew Boulton, to whom the request was addressed, countered with a design for a completely new mint and samples of what he could produce by way of medals and coins.[151] In October 1796 Vorontsov was informed that 'Her Majesty has approved of the Plan proposed by Mr Boulton for erecting a Mint, and has granted a permission for the same to be erected upon the same Plan and with all that machinery which he has represented as contributing so much towards the carrying it into execution' with the proviso that 'one or two well known to him and trusty persons, who being furnished with proper instructions, should come over here to superintend the Execution'.[152]

Additionally, while the machinery was being prepared, a group of Russians was to come to Birmingham to 'acquire a further knowledge in the money-making business'. By the time they had arrived, Paul had come to the throne and the whole mint project was abandoned and the Russian workmen were recalled.

Characteristically, the tsar had his own project for a mint which was connected with his new financial strategy of replacing the hated paper money (*assignaty*), which had been issued by Catherine, with coin. Vast piles of notes were burnt on Palace Square in December 1796 and rooms in the Assignat Bank itself on Sadovaia Street were made available for the erection of a new mint that was to produce the gold and silver coins to replace the notes. The dies were made and the first coins were minted at the beginning of 1797 (with the date 1796 and no specific value indicated), but it was only in April 1797 that plans for the new 'Bank' mint were officially approved and Gascoigne was appointed to supply the necessary new machinery, including steam engines. Although Paul's proposed financial reforms soon proved impractical, leading to a cessation in the production of the 'bank' coinage by October 1797, progress on the new mint was such that it was to provide a viable, temporary solution to the problem posed by the original mint in the Peter and Paul Fortress.[153]

The old mint could now be completely closed down and workmen and some machines were transferred to the Bank; the contract with Boulton was revived and a new group of Russians sent to Soho to learn how to use the new machinery. On 12 July 1799 a public 'Act to enable Matthew Boulton, Engineer, to export the Machinery necessary for erecting a Mint in the Dominions of His Imperial Majesty, the Emperor of all the Russias' (3 Georgii III, 1799, cap. 96) was passed in London, but the emperor to see the machinery arrive was Alexander, not Paul, for opposition from Birmingham manufacturers and then an abrupt worsening in Anglo-Russian relations had occasioned a delay of some two years. Four Boulton workmen from Soho, James Walker, James Duncan, James Harley and Speedywell arrived in 1802 to supervise the installation of the machinery in a new building within the fortress designed by Antonio Porto and were later joined by Boulton's nephew, Zacchaeus Walker. Their work was eventually finished by 1805, but most of the machines they installed were to function admirably for decades.[154]

Gascoigne's mint, as opposed to Boulton's, was completed by September 1799 and was to produce all the medals and coins minted in St Petersburg between that date and 1805. Gascoigne's involvement, however, had come to an end in January 1801 when the mint was put under the control of the Mining College, presided over by A. Aliab'ev. One of Gascoigne's steam engines from the Bank Mint was sent to the fortress to be held in reserve.[155]

Mentions of fire engines or steam engines form a red thread in any account of the major technological developments in Russia in the last decades of the eighteenth century and many are connected, directly or indirectly, with Gascoigne and his associates or employees. Although in the early 1760s the Russian mining engineer I. I. Polzunov (1728–66) invented and tested a steam engine in Siberia,[156] it was to Britain – where James Watt had begun his experiments on improving the Newcomen engine at precisely the same time as Polzunov – that the Russian government preferred to turn to order machines, recruit specialists and send its own students from the 1770s. Boulton built the first successfully working model of Watt's improved version of the Newcomen engine at Soho in 1774, the very year Russia received from Carron the Smeaton-designed fire engine, ordered on the initiative of Admiral Knowles. However, Knowles's secretary, John Robison, had already attempted to attract Watt to Russia in 1771, albeit as 'Master Founder of Iron Ordnance'. When a later attempt also failed in 1775, Erasmus Darwin remarked that he hoped 'your fire-machines will keep you here' in England.[157] They did, and it was Russian apprentices and mechanics like Lev Sabakin who were to visit Watt and Boulton frequently in the 1780s and 1790s to discover, if they could, the secrets of the steam engine and other machinery.[158] Meanwhile in Russia, the great pumping engine at Kronshtadt had been opened to great acclaim and quickly became a tourist attraction. A decade later, Gascoigne was given the task of preparing at the Aleksandrovskii works a fire engine for use in the Voitskii gold mine, where the old horse-operated pump could no longer cope with the water. In the autumn of 1789 he brought to Russia a millwright, George Sheriff, who had worked at Carron. Within a few months the machine parts were ready and taken to the mine, where the engine was assembled and began operating on 8/19 July 1791 – but only for a day before breaking down. It seems to have worked only fitfully during the further three years the mine remained open, although Sheriff was released at the end of 1792 with a testimonial as to his satisfactory work.[159] In 1797 the engine was transferred from the mine to the Assignat Bank and it was Sheriff who was sent by Gascoigne from Lugan to install it.[160] At Lugan itself, a steam engine prepared at Petrozavodsk was also soon to be installed.

Working with Sheriff at the Bank Mint in 1797–9 was another engineer, Joseph Major, whose initials in their Russian variant (O. M.) appear on the gold five-ruble coin minted there in 1800.[161] When Sheriff returned to Britain in 1799, he requested on Major's behalf an estimate from Boulton and Watt for the supply of a rotative steam engine.[162] A few years later, in April 1805, Zacchaeus Walker wrote to Boulton, who had known Major in Birmingham in the 1780s, that 'after long roving about like a wandering Arab thro' Austria, Poland &c [Major] has pitched his Tent for these 2 or 3 Years past in Siberia, in which philosophic retreat he has had leisure to contemplate uninterruptedly the profoundest depths of Mechanics, & has at last brought forth a new Steam-Engine which for simplicity & cheapness in proportion to its power is to set all that has hitherto been done or thought of at nought'.[163] Walker's heavy irony at least draws attention to a remarkable incident in the life of an undoubtedly remarkable and eccentric Englishman, raised from a mere footnote to be the subject of an article in which he is hailed as 'one of the most talented mechanics of the late eighteenth and early nineteenth centuries' but which sadly appeared in a journal obscure enough to elude many British and Russian scholars.[164] It was in Mittau (present-day Elgava) that Major first surfaced after his European 'roving' and published there in 1792 *An des Mitauische Publikum. Bei Gelengenheit der neu zu erichtenden Dampfmaschine zum Wasserwerke der Stadt* from his non-extant English original. In it he proposed the use of steam engines to provide Kurland with a constant and reliable water supply and in an appendix he listed the other machines he was capable of producing, from fire pumps to grass cutters. A few years later, he seems to have joined Gascoigne at Petroza-vodsk, whence he was dispatched to work at the Assignat Bank. He next appears in 1801, when he demonstrated before the Academy of Sciences a large galvanic battery he had built; this brought him some celebrity and not a few orders from individuals for their 'physical cabinets'.[165] But within two years the Petersburg period of his life came to an end and it was in the Urals that he was to live and work for the next thirty years until his murder in 1833 by thieves searching for the gold he had mined. In April 1804 he was invited by the factory-owner A. A. Knauf to build a small steam engine at the Iugovskii zavod, a copper-smelting works he had just acquired, and a medal was struck to celebrate 'the first fire-machine in Siberia', already func-tioning in August that same year. Major subsequently improved upon the engine, adapting it for the excessive cold, and sent a description and a model to his old friend, Academician Kraft, who published an article about it the following year.[166] It was to this engine that Walker was referring. In 1812 Major entered state service as mechanic to the Perm Mining Administration and was given a piece of land near Ekaterinburg where, aided by his son and by an assigned workforce, he was to mass-produce steam engines for government works and mines. Among the many subsequent inventions and improvements he made, one in particular deserves mention: in 1821 he sought, if without success, to interest the government in a steamboat he had invented for use on Siberian rivers to aid communication and commerce.

Some of Major's Russian predecessors had already attempted to introduce steamboats to the rivers of central Russia and Siberia; but he had a much more famous predecessor in St Petersburg in Scotsman Charles Baird (d. 1843) who, in 1815, instituted the first steamship service between the capital

and Kronshtadt with the *Elizaveta*, and soon acquired the monopoly on pass-
enger and freight traffic that brought him his immense fortune and renown.[167]
By 1815, however, Baird had already achieved his reputation as capitalist
and entrepreneur; as such he essentially lies outside the frame of this chapter,
but his standing as a 'necessary foreigner', working at times for the government on prestige projects, was recognised by the several awards he received,
beginning with that of Oberhüttenverwalter, Chief Foundry Administrator
(8th class), in 1811. He had, of course, began his career in Russia with Gascoigne, as did a younger brother James, but in 1792 had set up in partnership
with Francis Morgan, who had a few years earlier established a small private
factory, and two years later he married Morgan's eldest daughter Sophia. By
coincidence, the letter of April 1805 in which Walker spoke disparagingly
of Major's steam engine in the Urals also contains much that is positive and
informative about Baird, who by this period already possessed a great and
ever-growing industrial complex, which included his iron foundry, machine
workshops and sawmill, situated on a virtual island site on the left bank of
the Neva to the west of the Admiralty district (square C7 on the Baedeker
map of 1914):[168]

about 14 years ago [he] had acquired sufficient property & knowledge of the country
under Mr Gascoigne to venture setting up for himself as founder, forger, Steam-Engine-
Maker &c, but, has chiefly been connected with the Board of Admiralty. He also under-
takes all the Ironwork for the Mint-Department, & has done a great deal for us there
. . . He is about 40 Years of age – certainly very active & intelligent, – knows the Russian
language well, which, rest assured is a very essential point & a work of time: – is pretty
intimately acquainted with the Mechanical Professors in general, both Russian & Foreigners – also with many of the principal Nobility; & with the proper mode of applying the
Key to the private Doors of the Chief-Officers in most of the Govt Departments.[169]

Walker went on to note that Baird came 'from the north side of the Tweed
which is the best recommendation a man can bring to this City, the Caledonian Phalanx being the strongest and most numerous, and moving always in
the closest Union'. Earlier chapters have shown the strength of the Scottish
presence among, for example, merchants, doctors and naval officers, but the
number of Scots among the craftsmen and technical experts at the end of
the century was truly remarkable. Gascoigne, Baird, Armstrong (who took
over the administration of the Petrozavodsk factories in 1807), Clark,
Wilson – and, Gascoigne excepted, their sons – were dominating figures on
the industrial scene, particularly in the reign of Alexander I and, in some
cases, beyond.[170] They were also controversial figures, the extent and quality
of whose contribution to the processes of Russian modernisation and technological advance remain a matter of keen debate among economic historians
and historians of science and technology. The scales are weighted with vary-

ing considerations of the existing Russian social, organisational and economic obstacles to change, of the degree of expertise and commitment among the specialists, of personality, of 'a most profound veneration for the God Plutus'.[171] They came to Russia to seek their fortunes and most of them achieved this – and conspicuously – but the majority also devoted the greater part of their lives to the service of Russia.

7

MASTERS OF THE ARTS

⌒

I

The list of foreign architects, engravers, painters and sculptors who made a direct contribution to the development and flowering of the arts in eighteenth-century Russia is a long one. Italians, French and Germans, in perhaps that order of priority, figure prominently down the decades from Peter's reign to Catherine's: Trezzini, Schlüter, Leblond, Rastrelli, Vallin de la Motte, Quarenghi were outstanding architects, each leaving their distinctive mark on the new capital; Rastrelli the Elder, Caravaque, Rotari, Grooth, Tocqué, Falconet and Mme Vigée Lebrun were among the most noted of a generally less imposing list of painters and sculptors. Only the name of architect Charles Cameron, who never worked in the capital itself but at Tsarskoe Selo and Pavlovsk, would normally be included so as to acknowledge, as it were, a British presence. British scholars, indeed, would find it difficult to produce other British names, even for a catalogue of the 'also-known-to-have-worked in Russia' variety, although Tamara Talbot Rice made a valiant attempt in one of her articles to deprive the talented Danish painter Benjamin Pattersen of his birthright by calling him 'the first in a line of British topographical artists to visit Russia'.[1] Nevertheless, while conceding that Cameron remains in a class of his own, it is possible to extend the British list to more than modest length, particularly if we include, as we should, exponents of landscape gardening, one of the most esteemed arts of the eighteenth century. At least a dozen gardeners, eight painters, three architects, two engravers, a sculptor and a medallist worked in Russia at various times, but predominantly and expectedly, during Catherine's reign. The activities in Russia of these British artists, seen in the wider context of the acquisition of works of art of British origin by Catherine and members of her court, are the concern of this chapter.

In the early decades of the century, works of English provenance were encountered only rarely in the palaces of the empresses and their magnates. It was above all examples of English silverware that found their way to Russia during this period. Unlike the renowned collection of English silver which was accumulated by the tsars during the late sixteenth and seventeenth centuries principally as gifts from visiting English embassies and from the Muscovy Company, items made by leading London-based silversmiths of the early eighteenth century, including Nicholas Clausen, Edward Vincent and especially Paul de Lamerie were acquired by purchase and not on any regular basis.[2] It was only with the establishment of the Hermitage as the home of the imperial collections early in Catherine' reign and as a result of the increased intercourse in all fields between Russia and Great Britain that English art in all its range and variety began to arrive in Russia. If the empress' own predilection for England was marked, it was undoubtedly sustained by the efforts of Lord Cathcart, British ambassador in Russia in 1768–72. Cathcart was almost as much a cultural as a diplomatic representative, a role well appreciated by British craftsmen and manufacturers

Robert Chambers, a London mason who had perfected the art of staining marble, produced a piece bearing the Cathcart coat-of-arms and asked his lordship to take it with him to Russia and attempt to interest the Russian court in his work.[3] Matthew Boulton, partner in the great manufactory at Soho, Birmingham, seeking to extend the markets for his new ormolu ware throughout Europe, addressed Cathcart as ready 'to promote every usefull and laudable Art and every branch of the Commerce of your Country':[4] the ambassador indeed managed to persuade the empress to buy a consignment of vases in 1772, although he failed to find a purchaser for the elaborate and expensive 'sidereal' clock mentioned in the previous chapter.[5] The famous potter Josiah Wedgwood, on hearing of the sale of Boulton's vases, suggested, however, that 'the Russians must have Etruscan and Grecian Vases about the 19th Century, I fear they will not be ripe for them much sooner, unless our good friend Sir William Hamilton should go Ambassador thither and prepare a hot bed to bring these Northern plants to maturity before their *natural* time'.[6] But he had obviously forgotten that Lady Cathcart was Sir William's sister; and she had already had the opportunity of introducing the empress to her brother's *Collection of Etruscan, Greek, and Roman Antiquities* (4 vols., 1766–7). On 16 January 1769 she wrote to Sir William:

I believe I told you we were repairing & new furnishing these Objects are pretty near accomplished & you will be pleased to hear that our Dining Room is painted from y^r Etruscan Collection. My Lord presided over it himself & the German Artist that Executed it, in Figures as large as the life, has succeeded surprisingly well, you can't think how much my L^d had this at heart. I was much afraid it w^d not succeed, but it really has. The Russian nobility here reported it Charming to the Empress, who will I flatter myself see it herself in the Course of the Winter in the Mean while she has the Book. We are unluckily possessed as yet but of one Vol.[7]

Wedgwood himself had reason to be grateful to the Cathcarts, for it was

20 The Wedgwood 'Frog' service, 1774 (Josiah Wedgwood and Sons Ltd).
a. Plate, painted with view of ruin and cascade.

precisely during Cathcart's embassy and with the encouragement of 'our good Patroness', as he called Lady Cathcart,[8] that he began his trade with Russia, initiated by the so-called 'Husk Service', reaching a notable peak with the 'Green Frog' service; but continuing to the end of Catherine's reign, when he was supplying quantities of Jasper ware. Working with a number of British merchant houses, initially Porter and Jackson and later Capper and Co.,

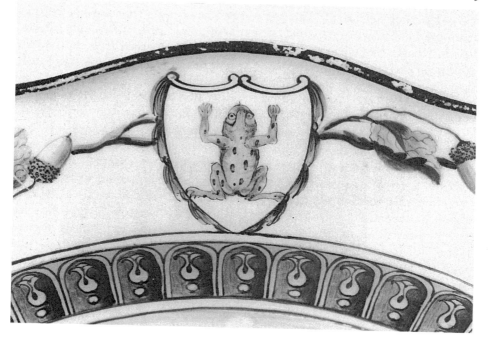

b. Frog emblem, detail from oval dish.

Wedgwood exported a considerable quantity of his 'cream ware' which became fashionable among the Russian gentry. William Coxe, passing into Russia from Poland in 1778, was surprised to find at the posthouse 'English strong beer and no less pleased to see our supper served in dishes of Wedgewood's ware'; a day later, entertained by a gentleman in Smolensk, he noted that 'the table was neatly set out, the dinner excellent, and served up in English cream-coloured ware'.[9]

The commissioning of the 'Green Frog' service through the Russian consul in London in 1773 was a prestige order, one which brought Wedgwood and his partner Bentley little financial profit but enormously enhanced their reputation both in England and in Europe. The order was for a table and dessert service for fifty people, which took the eventual form of 952 pieces of cream ware, hand-decorated in mulberry enamel, which bore 1,244 views of British country houses, castles, abbeys, monasteries, bridges, pavilions, ruins and picturesque landscapes. Catherine had particularly requested a plentiful representation of Gothic architecture and among the 200 or so British castles that were portrayed was Longford Castle in Wiltshire. It was Longford that provided the basic design for the palace that was to house the 'Frog' and was built by Iurii Fel'ten between 1774 and 1777 on the Petersburg–Tsarskoe Selo road. The palace was called Kekerekeksinskii, deriving from the Finnish word meaning 'frog marsh', and Catherine usually referred to it as 'La Grenouillère': hence the emblem of the green frog that was to appear on each piece of the service. The service was used at dinner for Joseph II in June 1780, when the palace and the nearby church, finished that year in the 'Moorish' style (perceived as a variant of 'Gothick') were renamed the 'Chesmenskii' in honour of the great Russian naval victory over the Turks a decade earlier. The service continued to be used on a number of state and more informal occasions throughout Catherine's reign, although pieces were soon broken and indeed stolen in not inconsiderable quantities as early as October 1777.[10] It was at an informal party at the palace in 1779, almost five years after the delivery of the 'Frog' to its appointed home, that the then British ambassador, Sir James Harris, was shown the service and 'this led to a conversation on English gardening, in which the Empress is a great adept'.[11] The service indeed provided, and provides, an excellent starting point for any discussion of Catherine's intense interest in landscape gardens and in the buildings that adorned them.

II

In 1772 Catherine eloquently described in a letter to Voltaire her conversion to the English style of gardening:

J'aime à la folie présentement les jardins à l'anglaise, les lignes courbes, les pentes douces, les étangs en forme de lacs, les archipels en terre ferme, et j'ai un profond mépris pour les lignes droites, les allées jumelles. Je hais les fontaines qui donnent la torture à l'eau pour lui faire prendre un cours contraire à sa nature: les statues sont reléguées dans les galeries, les vestibules, etc.; en un mot, l'anglomanie domine ma plantomanie.[12]

This was no mere flirtation but a truly deep passion she had nurtured as grand duchess and one that she could express openly as soon as she became empress in her own right. In her memoirs Catherine mentions that 'it was at this time [1755] that I took a fancy to form a garden at Oranienbaum ... I began then to plant and plant, and as this was my first whim in the constructive line, my plans assumed very grand proportions.'[13] It was to be at Oranienbaum, the former Menshikov estate on the Gulf of Finland where she had lived with the Grand Duke Peter after their marriage, that Catherine as empress was able to encourage the first hesitant signs of the new landscape garden. From 1762 Antonio Rinaldi was engaged not only in the building of the modest one-storeyed Chinese Palace and the delightful Toboggan Pavilion (*Katal'naia gorka*) on part of the estate known thereafter as 'Sobstvennaia dacha' (Catherine's first but rarely used summer residence), but also in designing both the regular and 'new' gardens. Also dating from 1762 were

Catherine's first instructions concerning the gardens of Tsarskoe Selo, when she stopped the clipping of the tops of hedges and bushes.[14]

Catherine sought increasingly to inform herself of achievements and developments in English landscape gardening and architecture. In 1766 the Russian ambassador in London conveyed to the Duke of Newcastle Catherine's wish for a plan of 'Votre magnifique Jardin' at Claremont; the Duke whose garden had been developed by William Kent, following on earlier work by Charles Bridgeman, duly obliged.[15] Three years later, Catherine decided to send one of the imperial gardeners Andrei Ekleben with an assistant trained in architecture (name not established) and two gardening apprentices, Petr Andreev and Trofim Kondrat'ev, 'to observe the art of gardening in the English manner, to take plans and to improve their knowledge by practical experience'.[16] Ekleben, whose expertise was essentially in horticulture rather than landscaping, soon returned, but Andreev and Kondrat'ev remained until 1771, although, according to Thomas Cloase (the head gardener of Hampton Court with whom they worked), they achieved very little.[17] In the interim, Catherine had in May 1770 issued orders for an English park to be laid out at Tsarskoe Selo to the west of the Great Pond. Over the next few months her architect Vasilii Neelov, who had worked at Tsarskoe Selo since the 1740s, prepared plans for changes to paths and ponds and ground elevations that were all to achieve the required effect of naturalness, but Catherine soon decided that he should also spend some time in England 'in order to visit all the notable gardens, and, having seen them, to lay out similar ones here'.[18] Neelov spent six months in England, visiting houses and estates in London and as far west certainly as Oxford, before returning to spend the last decade of his life at Tsarskoe Selo.

During the 1770s Neelov was responsible for a number of bridges and buildings in the grounds of Tsarskoe Selo, some of which are attributable to English models or designs. In 1773–4 he built the so-called Palladian Bridge in Siberian marble, which was an accomplished imitation of Roger Morris's bridge of 1737 at Wilton, which he may well have seen for himself but also could have copied from the fifth volume of *Vitruvius Britannicus* (1771), which, it has been suggested, he brought back with him from England. (It was, incidentally, in the same volume that Fel'ten would have found the plans of Longford Castle.) On the other hand, Neelov may well have been inspired by other English imitations of the Wilton bridge: indeed, a contemporary source asserts categorically that it was 'copied from that in Stowe gardens'.[19] Neelov was also prominent in catering for Catherine's taste for chinoiserie: if his Large Caprice, a Chinese summerhouse on a wide arch spanning the road leading to the Great Palace, was inspired by a print in a Dutch work, it was in William and John Halfpenny's *Rural Architecture in the Chinese Taste* (1750) that he found his design for his Cross Bridge, begun in 1776 and utilising four arches, two from each bank which met in the middle to support a Chinese pavilion.[20] Neelov was prominently involved in work on the Chinese Village, which was completed by Cameron. The wooden model of the village (constructed by Rinaldi in the early 1770s) contained a variant on the famous pagoda at Kew, although a pagoda was never to be built at Tsarskoe Selo. In 1772 money was sent to the Russian ambassador in London to pay for 'a model of the Chinese building', most probably the pagoda, and somewhat earlier Catherine had requested a copy of a recently published work on Kew.[21] The latter may well have been *Plans, Elevations, Sections, and Perspective Views of the Gardens and Buildings at Kew in Surry* (1763), containing of course a plan of the pagoda, by Sir William Chambers, whose earlier influential treatise, *Designs of Chinese Buildings, Furniture, Dresses, Machines, and Utensils. To which is annexed, a Description of their temples, houses, gardens, etc.* (1757) was already known, at least in part, to the empress.

A section from the appendix to Chambers' book, entitled 'Of the Art of Laying out Gardens among the Chinese', was published in Russian translation in St Petersburg in 1771. A handwritten version of that translation is found among Catherine's papers and is connected with one of the empress' most significant and at the same time least known initiatives to further the cause of English gardening in Russia. She acquired within months of its publication in 1771 a copy of François de Paule Latapie's very faithful French translation of Thomas Whately's influential *Observations on Modern Gardening* (1770) and she set about editing it for a Russian version. Entitling her text 'Principes pour former le jardin dans le goût anglois', she proceeded to blend parts of Latapie's extensive introduction with Whately's work, particularly the Frenchman's inclusion of Chambers' essay and other materials to further his own support for the idea of 'le jardin anglo-chinois'. Although Catherine devoted a great deal of time to the project over the years 1771–3 – precisely the period when she confessed to Voltaire that 'l'anglomanie domine ma plantomanie' – a Russian Whately was never published.[22]

One of the undoubted attractions for Catherine of Latapie's edition was the 'Description détaillée des jardins de Stowe, accompagnée du plan', the translator's own addition to the already considerable space allotted to one of the most majestic and influential of English gardens in Whately's basic text. For Catherine, Stowe proved a true inspiration and source for emulation in her own Tsarskoe Selo. It has indeed been suggested that Neelov also brought back from his visit to England the 1769 one-volume edition of Benton Seeley's *Stowe* with its numerous illustrations of buildings which were soon to find their close parallel and imitation in Catherine's garden, as it was developed by Neelov, Cameron and the best known of her 'English gardeners', John Bush.[23] Catherine was, incidentally, soon to have no less than forty-eight depictions of Stowe on the 'Green Frog' service. And in a consignment of over seventy sets of prints, representing not only British but also foreign subjects, that Catherine received from London in the summer of 1776, there were sixteen further views of Stowe.[24] Catherine assiduously collected engravings and plate books and she well understood their uses – not only for potters like Wedgwood but also for gardeners and architects. In this connection, the following instruction for Cameron, dating from around 1782, has obvious relevance: 'Show the English architect the painting which hangs behind the door in my study at Tsarskoe Selo for him to prepare the elevation and plan of a summer-house on the large island in the middle of the Grand Pond.'[25] It was on the walls of the Admiralty, one of the Gothic structures designed by Neelov for the grounds of Tsarskoe Selo, that an English visitor observed 'the English Prints of Houses and Views of different places in England'.[26]

Catherine's proposed edition of Whateley/Latapie was clearly intended to spread the vogue for the 'English garden' among her courtiers. Its dedication reads: 'To the owners of estates bordering the sea and lying along the Peterhof road this book is dedicated by one who has seen their natural attractions and capabilities, so that they should be further improved according to the principles herein prescribed.'[27] Many of her courtiers, however, were travelling on their version of the Grand Tour and were bringing back reports of the gardens and estates they had seen throughout Great Britain; some, such as Vladimir Orlov, Prince Aleksandr Kurakin and Princess Ekaterina Dashkova, were subsequently to spend much time and money on improving their estates after the English model.[28] A British comment in 1780 nicely brings together the new passion for the English garden and Latapie's Whately, which apparently exerted its influence despite the non-appearance of the empress' 'textbook':

Till of late Years the taste of Gardening among the Great was confined to fruits but the Nobles who have been in England are so much enraptured with the English pleasure gardens that they are cried up here much more beautiful than perhaps they have appeared to your or my Eye. Mr Whateley's Observations on modern Gardening translated into French perhaps has not a little contributed to this opinion. This has set them all Gardening mad. Any of the Nobility will give £100 per Ann for an English Gardener. I have been applied to for more than one but we few who are already here are not desirous of seeing any more arrive lest one scabby sheep spoil the whole flock.[29]

The empress, who never had the opportunity to see for herself the gardens and parks of Great Britain but had the authority and finances, inevitably led the way in the recruitment of British gardeners.

The first British gardener to be recruited was Charles Sparrow, a Scot, like so many of his successors, who arrived in 1769 after Catherine had instructed her ambassador in London to pay the £350 he demanded because he insisted on bringing his brother John with him![30] It was almost certainly Sparrow who was the subject of the following assessment, penned by a certain Frederick Roberts of Chiswick: 'At the request of Count Czernichew [Ivan Chernyshev, the Russian ambassador] I procured a Man qualified in an extraordinary Manner for Gardening, in all its branches; he also understood Botany, Agriculture, the designing, surveying & laying-out of Pleasure-Grounds, in the present English Taste, with rural Architecture &c.'[31] The Sparrows were set to work at Gatchina, the estate some fifteen miles south-east of Tsarskoe Selo which Catherine had presented to her lover Grigorii Orlov soon after she came to the throne. Unlike Tsarskoe Selo and Peterhof, Gatchina had no formal garden and offered a unique opportunity to impose the new style from the beginning. A Scots doctor who came to St Petersburg at the same time as the Sparrows later wrote of the 'beautiful garden, planned by one, and executed by another Englishman, of the name of Sparrow, and surely among all the fine things of this delightful summer residence, the noble plantations are the most conspicuous, and draw most attention'.[32] After the sudden death of his brother, Charles Sparrow continued to work on the pleasure grounds and park of Gatchina for more than a decade. Catherine herself took a very active interest in their development, noting in 1772 that Orlov, recognising her 'mérite jardinier', had given over the estate to her for the summer to 'y faire des incartades à ma façon'.[33] After Orlov's death in 1783, Gatchina passed into the possession of the Grand Duke Paul and Sparrow seems to have stayed in his employ for some years. In 1786, for instance, the Grand Duchess Maria Fedorovna, returning to Pavlovsk, wrote: 'J'arrive de Gatchina dans ce moment et j'ai examiné avec la plus scrupuleuse attention la manière de planter des arbres de Sparo et je vous avoue que j'ai été bien étonnée de voir la différence des soins qu'il y donne et le peu que Wisler [her German gardener at Pavlovsk] y apporte.'[34] At some stage Sparrow seemed to have gone to work for Potemkin, but no details of his last years are available. He was apparently still in the Russian capital at the end of the century: the death of his wife Mary is recorded in the register of the English Church on 5 March 1799.[35] Paul was to employ the services of a British gardener at Gatchina in the 1790s. James Hackett, whose biography is completely unknown, was engaged on new and extensive garden works. In 1798, for instance, he was supervising the excavation and landscaping of the Oval Pond near Brenna's new Forest Orangery. He was also responsible for the planning of the north-west part of the estate, known as Silvia, where features of a regular park were introduced in imitation of Chantilly and at the express wish of the Grand Duchess Maria Fedorovna.[36]

Catherine's wish to enlist further British expertise is clearly reflected in the flurry of letters between St Petersburg and the Russian ambassador in

London over the period 1770–1. Among British gardeners prepared to go to Russia was Thomas Cloase from Hampton Court, mentioned earlier in connection with the supervision of the two young Russian apprentices. In his support, no less a figure than 'Capability' Brown himself wrote on 20 October 1770 to say that 'he thought him a Person very fit for the Place he [Cloase] wishes to undertake, being a perfect Master of the Kitchen Garden, Hotwalls, Stoves, and Greenhouses. If he should meet with his Excellencys approbation, Mr Brown will be happy to give him any assistance in Plans, or other things, that may be of use to her Imperial Majesty or him.'[37] In the event Cloase did not go and there was no follow-up to what might have been a momentous direct involvement of Brown in the planning of the imperial estates. The man who did arrive in Russia at virtually the same time as the returning Neelov was to be called by Catherine 'mon jardinier anglois' but it was in German that he conversed with her, for he was by origin from Hanover.

Johann Busch (c. 1730–95), or John Bush in its anglicised form, seems to have settled in London in 1744 or somewhat later. In 1756 he rented land in Mare Street in Hackney and established what soon became a flourishing nursery garden, building up an impressive list of clients and receiving seeds and exotic plants from international correspondents.[38] Retaining the tenancy of his land, Bush sold his business to Conrad Loddiges and departed for Russia with his large family but without the trees and plants that he had unsuccessfully attempted to take with him as part of his contract. Nevertheless, according to his contract, which he signed on 19 January 1771, he was to receive 1,500 rubles a year, a generous salary compared with that of his peers.[39] The original intention was for Bush 'to keep the gardens near Moscow in the village of Kolomenskoe and not in St Petersburg',[40] but in the event it was to Oranienbaum that he went, but only for a few months, before he was installed at Tsarskoe Selo in the comfortable quarters adjoining the Orangery by the Old Garden that was to be the family home until their return to England in 1789.[41] Bush's main task was to develop the English garden begun by Neelov and gradually over the next few years it was Bush who assumed the major responsibility for the landscaping, while Neelov, as we have seen, was to make a major contribution to the garden's architectural embellishment. In 1773–4 Bush also laid out 'some pleasure ground' at nearby Pulkovo (the site of the future observatory and one of the few hills in the environs of St Petersburg).[42] His work there gave obvious satisfaction and the court journal records that in May 1774 Catherine and her suite 'walked in the English garden and after inspecting everything, they sat on the grass on a knoll and ate a cold repast'.[43] But it was Tsarskoe Selo that was to be his principal arena.

In 1781 Baroness Dimsdale, who was frequently in the company of the

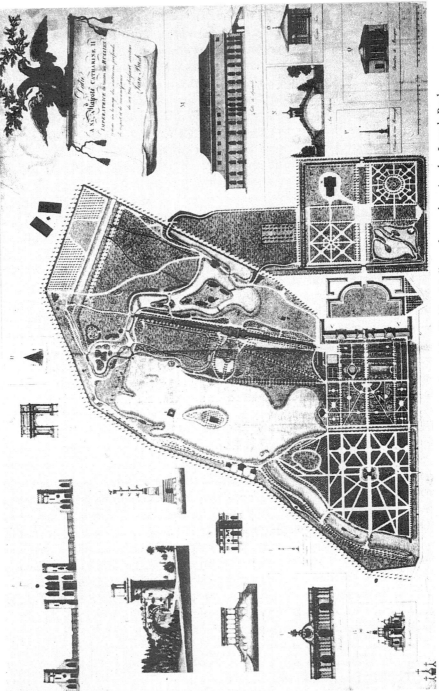

21 Plan of Park, Tsarskoe Selo. Engraving (1789) by Tobias Muller, after a drawing by Joseph Bush.

Bushs, particularly after she discovered that her social standing was not endangered by such an association, noted that 'the Gardens are laid out in the English taste and are very prettily diversified with Lawns, Gravel Walks and Wood, a very fine large piece of Water is near the centre with an island which has a building on it'.[44] The reference to the gravel paths is interesting and another British gardener asserts at about the same period that the Russians 'had no idea of Gravel walks till those of England were so much extolled & Bush & Sparrow came to this Country & set the example by introducing them; the beauty firmness & superior lustre of gravel being visible to every eye has made the great one [i.e. the empress] gravel mad'.[45] At all events, Catherine was delighted by the reactions of Baroness Dimsdale and others to her garden and in 1782 wrote to Baron Grimm that 'ce jardin, entre nous soit dit, devient une chose comme il n'y en a pas, au dire des Anglais, des voyageurs de tous pays et des notres qui ont voyagé'.[46] On his return to England in 1789, Bush had his son Joseph produce a plan of the gardens of Tsarskoe Selo, framed by illustrations of many of the buildings and monuments, which he dedicated to the empress 'comme un homage des sentimens profonds de respect et de reconnaissance'. The plan recalls an earlier plan, produced in about 1769 and probably drawn by Neelov, but well illustrates the principal changes that Bush introduced, in the contours of the Great Pond, at the west end of which Neelov erected his Palladian bridge over an outlet to a new series of interconnecting ponds, and in the disposition of copses and open meadows. The beauty of the English garden in the last decades of the eighteenth century is well caught in the watercolours of such Russian artists as Semen Shchedrin, Mikhail Ivanov and Vasilii Petrov.[47]

From about 1775 Bush's authority was extended to all aspects of horticulture, including supervision of the greenhouses and hothouses. He himself designed extensive new hothouses, where he grew all manner of exotic fruits and plants. On one occasion, as he accompanied her through the hothouses, Catherine told him to keep an eye on her courtiers, who were not averse to helping themselves to choice fruits.[48] Bush proved a devoted servant of the empress in other ways: in July 1780, during the visit of Joseph II of Austria, travelling as Count Falkenstein and known for his liking for staying in inns rather than palaces, Bush was asked to fit out as an inn one of the buildings in the park and to act as the innkeeper.[49] Catherine in her turn seems to have been genuinely fond of her gardener, although in 1788 misunderstanding about Bush's responsibility for the condition of some orange bushes may well have contributed to his decision to retire to England the following year.[50]

Bush left behind many members of his family: his eldest son Jacob had died in 1774, his second son John in 1784, and his first wife Ann in 1785, while two daughters, Catherine and Mary, were married in 1784 to Charles Cameron and Francis Forrester (a prominent merchant) respectively.[51] More importantly, in terms of garden history, he left behind another son, Joseph (1760–1838).

It was Bush's eldest son Jacob who was originally employed as one of his assistants but it was to be Joseph who ultimately became his father's successor. Joseph seems to have been assigned initially to tend the hothouses, but when he was joined in the task by the young John McLaren, who arrived at the end of 1780 and was hired by John Bush, this brought the comment from a friend that 'he suits young Bush as he can have opportunity of Pleasuring by leaving Jack in care of the stoves which he could not so well trust to a Russian'.[52] In the autumn of 1783 Joseph Bush was sent to England, but was back by July the following year, apparently 'not executing his father's Intentions which was to see every Garden worth notice and bring a large Collection of Trees & Plants which he did not'.[53] However, when his father left at the beginning of 1786 for a year in England following the death of his wife, Joseph Bush was put in charge of the gardens at Tsarskoe Selo and apparently was equal to the task. Certainly, when his father retired three years later, Joseph was confirmed as head gardener and served until 1810, when he was dismissed for refusing to work within the reduced estimates proposed by the imperial committee responsible for Tsarskoe Selo.[54] In the interim he had a particularly prominent role in laying out the park surrounding the Aleksandrovskii Palace built by Quarenghi and, on a smaller scale, he prepared the 'Little Coloured Garden' (*Tsvetnoi sadik*), designed by Cameron on the eastern side of the 'Cameron' gallery and surrounded by high iron railings.[55] In 1810 Bush was given the task of planning the landscape garden around the palace designed by Rossi on Elagin Island, which remains his finest independent creation.[56] Nothing is known about his later commissions or when he retired. He married twice and had many children, the last being called Joseph Loudon to honour the visit to Russia in 1812 of the famed Scottish horticulturist.[57]

It was in 1812 that an English gardener, whom Loudon hailed as the Capability Brown of Russia and another British visitor as its Repton, died in his native Ormskirk in Lancashire.[58] Rivalling Bush in contemporary eminence, William Gould (1735–1812) had originally worked for Richard Wilbraham-Bootle at Lathom House in Lancashire before departing for Russia in 1776. Gould is our first example of a British gardener working not for Catherine directly but for one of her courtiers, albeit Orlov's successor as favourite, the all-powerful Prince Potemkin. It was for the planning and realisation of the Taurida Garden adjoining the Taurida Palace in St Petersburg itself that Gould earned his reputation as a skilled and resourceful gardener. Potemkin's great palace was built in a severe classical style between 1782 and 1790 by Ivan Starov. Starov worked from the beginning in close cooperation with Gould, whose transformation of the flat and uninteresting land into an excellent example of English landscaping was in train over the same period. The garden façade of the palace with its great colonnade and central rotunda, which enclosed the standing statue of Catherine as legislatress executed by Fedot Shubin, was conceived in its relationship with the garden. The Russian poet Derzhavin wrote of the enchanting effect achieved by the view of the garden through the colonnade; he described 'the laurels, myrtles and other trees from moderate climes, not only growing but some burdened down with flowers, others with fruit. Beneath their peaceful shade stretches the green grass like velvet; there, flowers show colourfully, here, sanded paths wind, hills rise up, valleys fall away, cuttings open groves, ponds sparkle.'[59] John Parkinson, the Oxford don accompanying Edward Wilbraham-Bootle, son of Gould's former employer, on a visit to Russia in 1792–4, was very impressed with both palace and garden and in February 1794 recorded in his journal that 'the work at present going on is an Ah Ah and iron railing to encompass the whole garden'.[60] One of Gould's nineteenth-century successors was particularly struck by his 'great judgement in forming the ponds, out of which he got sufficient materials to make the agreeable variety of swells and declivities',[61] and something of the garden's charm can be appreciated from the contemporary watercolours of Benjamin Pattersen.

Potemkin employed Gould's expertise not only in St Petersburg but also in the south of Russia, where he had received lands as a reward for his distinguished service in the Russo-Turkish war and subsequently as Catherine's favourite. In June 1780 James Meader, another British gardener whose activities have still to be discussed, wrote that 'Gould is gone to Astracan & the Ukraine to inspect into the Estate of Prince Potemkin his master he promised me to collect every thing curious in the plant & animal way'.[62] It was, however, after the annexation of the Crimea and Potemkin's appointment as Viceroy of southern Russia that Gould was again dispatched to the south. He was certainly in the Crimea for a few months in the autumn and winter of 1784–5 and two years later he was to be responsible for preparing the 'instant gardens' at stopping points during Catherine's great progress to see her 'New Russia'. In 1787 Gould was himself given a gift of land in the Crimea; he was also called upon to 'lay out parks, plant chestnut and other trees at Kacha and in the Baidar valley', lands which Potemkin had appropriated for himself. In the following year Potemkin instructed him to landscape areas between Bogoiavlensk and Nikolaev.[63]

Back in St Petersburg, Gould was to bring to perfection the Taurida Palace's gardens – both the park and the 'winter garden' – for the last great event arranged by Potemkin: on 14/25 April 1791 the palace witnessed the magnificent entertainment attended by 3,000 guests given for Catherine to celebrate the fall of the fortress of Izmail.[64] After Potemkin's death later that year, the palace passed into the possession of the empress, and Gould became

22 The Gardener's House, Taurida Palace grounds, St Petersburg. Designed in 1793–4
by Fedor Volkov.

officially an 'imperial gardener'. In 1793 the empress instructed the architect
Fedor Volkov to build in the grounds for Gould a small Palladian villa,
known today as 'the gardener's house'. During the reign of Paul, Gould, who
was deeply offended by the emperor's unabated hatred for Potemkin that
led him to turn the palace into a stables for the horseguards and to neglect
the gardens, retired to England. In 1802 he was back again in the Russian
capital to help in the restoration of the grounds, returning finally in 1806
to Ormskirk, where he died on 6 January 1812.[65] Gould had been a prominent and colourful figure in the British community in St Petersburg, a character with a fund of frequently scurrilous anecdotes, a man whose 'true English
honesty, excellent heart, and hospitality, claim the esteem of all ranks'.[66]

In seeking to describe the careers in Russia of Sparrow, Bush and Gould
it has been necessary, in the absence of letters and documents written by the
gardeners themselves, to resort to the comments of their contemporaries.
With James Meader the situation, happily, is somewhat different. There has
survived a letter-book, covering the period 31 May 1779 to 9 May 1787
and representing the first eight years of a period of thirteen years in imperial
service.[67] It is, indeed, this letter-book that has already supplied invaluable
insights into the movements and activities of his friends Sparrow, Bush and
Gould and it is a unique source for following Meader's own vital role in
laying out one of the major gardens in the English style near the Russian

capital. It also provides a highly idiosyncratic and amusing commentary on many aspects of the contemporary scene and on many personalities in the English community.

Meader, a Scot, had worked first for the Earl of Chesterfield, then for the Duke of Northumberland at Syon House in Isleworth. It is as 'late Gardener to his Grace the Duke of Northumberland' that Meader describes himself on the title-page of the book for which he is remembered, if at all, in a British context. *The Planter's Guide: or, Pleasure Gardener's Companion*, appearing in London a few months before his departure for Russia, was essentially a manual on how to produce plantations of trees where 'the whole would be covered with verdure down to the very front, in an easy theatrical manner, and in summer scarce a stem visible'.[68] Although Meader was to suggest that he had been approached a few years earlier to go to Russia, it was in 1779 that he signed a contract to serve 'wherever Her Imperial Majesty may please to employ me as a Gardener in general and more particularly in those branches of Gardening which consist in planning, designing and laying out of Pleasure Gardens Parks &c. and to take upon me the directive part of planting Trees &c. forming pieces of Water &c. also furnishing Designs for Stoves, forcing Frames, ornamental part of the hortuary Art'.[69] He arrived with his family in Tsarskoe Selo on 23 May and after meeting the empress and renewing his acquaintance with Bush, he was sent a few weeks later to Peterhof, which was to be his home throughout his stay in Russia.

Catherine evinced little affection for Peterhof, Peter's beloved estate on the Gulf of Finland,[70] but hoped to create, in contrast to the baroque palace and elaborate formal gardens and intricate waterworks of the lower grounds, something more in harmony with her own preferences in garden design and architecture in the upper park. 'The spot allotted to me', wrote Meader, 'is a park though a great part thereof is full of fine Trees. Here are fine pieces of Water which want but little help to make them elegant, with a vale where I propose to form a magnificent Cascade, the water being above & in these affairs I am under no restraint either to extent of land or water; the bounds are only limited by the Gulf of Finland.' (f. 4v.) He was to create there what became known as the English Park; on a site selected by Meader on the west bank of the main lake or Bol'shoi prud, Giacomo Quarenghi, 'a very ingenious Italian architect' (f. 30v.), was to build the English Palace, his first commission after his arrival in January 1780. Over the next few years and aided by a workforce of some 300 men, Meader introduced gravel paths (to both upper and lower parks), 'finished a piece of Water admired by everybody, built a bridge of my own designing which is much noticed' (f. 30v.), added further bridges, including 'a most remarkable Bridge with petrified Moss & roots; numbers of People come to see it; also four curious Bridges of an original construction (I detest copying)' (f. 41v.) Catherine herself was among

23 a-c. Views of English Park, Peterhof. Watercolours by James Meader, 1780s.

those who came to see: she made several visits in the early years, walking the grounds and resting in the modestly named but sumptuously appointed Birch Cottage (*Berezovyi domik*) Quarenghi built her in the summer of 1780.[71] The cottage is depicted on one of four watercolours which Meader himself painted in 1782.[72] They catch something of the early charm of the park with its bridges over winding streams, waterfall, temples, ruins and maturing trees. None, however, shows a grotto; and it was to build a grotto to outdo all other grottoes that became Meader's obsession.

In truth, there was one grotto in particular that he had in his sights – the grotto built in the 1760s by Joseph Lane for the Hon. Charles Hamilton at Painshill. Painshill was well known to the empress; she had no less than six views of the pleasure grounds in the consignment of engravings she purchased in 1773 and four on the 'Green Frog' service that arrived the following year. By coincidence it was in 1775 that Princess Ekaterina Dashkova published a description of a tour she had made in England five years earlier; it included a visit to Painshill, where amidst other delights 'we found to our amazement a large cave, done from top to bottom in different crystals, attached to the walls and vaults like icicles ... At the far end the cave forms a very large grotto, also done in a natural way with crystal spar. The sun, penetrating through specially contrived cracks, was so blinding that our eyes could scarce bear it. All the walls are covered or rather, are composed of precious crystals and fossils, such as all types of coral, amethyst, topaz and amber which had been assembled so astutely that nature itself would have been deceived.'[73] In 1784 he at last managed to get a specimen of the Derbyshire spar that would meet the approval of the empress and thereupon ordered two barrels of the same. 'As I have orders to build a Grotto with our petrified Stones I want the Spar long & thin to represent Icicles. These stuck on the sides & roof of the grotto will have a most beautiful effect, much superior to Pains Hill Grot.' (f. 52v.) It is not known whether he ever received sufficient supplies to complete the project; in December 1784 he was still waiting and there are no further references to the grotto in his letters or in any other source. His overall success, however, in transforming the site into pleasure grounds of variety and beauty is attested by several visitors. In the opinion of the British ambassador's sister, visiting the park in 1783, 'le Jardin mériteroit même en Angleterre d'être classé *Jolie*', while Andrew Swinton, the author of a travel account published in 1792, found it 'a very beautiful spot; and when the natural flatness of the ground is considered, it is amazing what art and taste have been exerted in finishing it. – Here are winding rivulets, cascades dashing over moss-clad rocks, antique bridges, temples, ruins, and cottages amazing.'[74] Most telling of all was the high esteem in which Meader's skill was held by Quarenghi.[75]

Quarenghi was to build, or at least, to plan and begin, three imperial residences or 'pavilions', as he was wont to call them: the great English Palace itself for Catherine, a residence for the Grand Duke Paul, and a further little palace for Paul's sons, Alexander and Constantine. The position of the three palaces in relation to the general lay-out of the park can be seen on the planometric plan drawn up by Quarenghi himself.[76] There seems little doubt that the actual sites were chosen by Meader: he says that himself of the English Palace; and Quarenghi in a letter of 18 July 1783 specifically mentions his intention to 'commencer la batisse pour le Palais de Monsegn. le Grand Duc dans l'endroit choisi par le Jardinier'.[77] The third palace was begun only in 1786 and never went beyond the first floor. Work on all three palaces was suspended in 1787 with the outbreak of war against Turkey and funds were not available. Building was resumed only in 1791 on the English Palace, which, however, was never occupied as an imperial residence by either Catherine or Paul. In 1799 Paul gave orders for the other two palaces to be dismantled. It is said in Russian sources that after work on the English park had also come to a halt, Catherine decreed in 1789 that 'Meader be released in accordance with his wishes and that his account be settled with him and he be allowed all that belonged to him', and that precisely in that year he returned to England.[78] Meader, however, returned only in the summer of 1792, when his name appeared among the list of those preparing to leave the country.[79] It has been suggested that Gould's help was enlisted

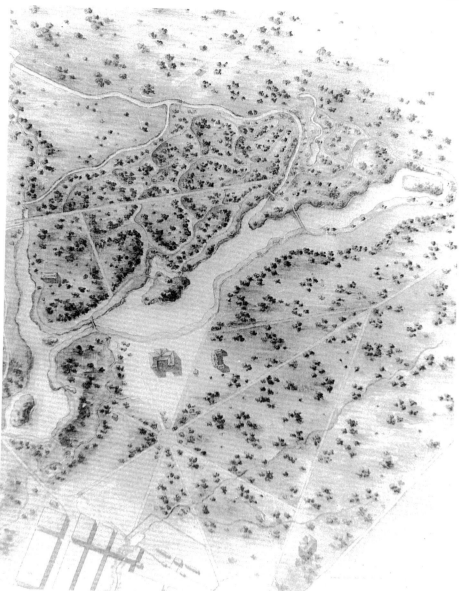

24 Plan of English Park, Peterhof. Drawing by Giacomo Quarenghi, 1780s.

in 1791 and it is possible that Meader, who had suffered from chronic gout and rheumatism throughout his stay in Russia, was by that time virtually incapacitated, but continued to live in the large wooden house he had built for his family in 1780 near the entrance to the English garden.[80]

The harmonious cooperation between British gardener and Italian architect found admirable resolution in the Palladianism of the English Palace set
in a landscape garden worthy of 'Capability' Brown. Sadly, it was never
really enjoyed by the monarch for whom the whole was created, nor by her
successors. Even more regrettably, it became an area for shelling by both the
German and Soviet forces during World War II and both park and palace
were utterly destroyed. Despite plans for restoration, apparently approved
in 1975, nothing has been done.

Meader's letter-book contains much that is relevant to gardening matters
and much that throws new light on his activities outside Peterhof. In the
summer of 1783, for instance, Meader received a commission to design a
landscape garden at a village he calls 'Velia' in the Ukraine, some 300 miles
from St Petersburg and south of Pskov:

Velia where I went to design & Plan a Grand Garden is a small Village but finely situated
by 2 fine Lakes which are separated from the 3ᵈ by a piece of low land which is proposed
to be cut through for a communication. the spot where the Gardens are to be is very fine
laid & planted by nature so that it only wants a little polishing & planting to complete
it. on the Top of an imminence where are the Ruins of fortifications the house is proposed
to be built which commands a most extensive view of the Lakes & Country adjacent.
(ff. 48–48v.)

Unfortunately, no further information is available to identify the estate or
when Meader's plans for its 'capabilities' were ever realised.

Part of Meader's contract was the 'furnishing Designs for Stoves, forcing
Frames', and one of his first tasks was to build a whole series of hothouses
near to his house and begin to cultivate the melons, oranges, apricots,
peaches and pineapples, such as he had seen Bush raising with success at
Tsarskoe Selo. He was soon to enter into a business partnership with Bush,
dealing initially in seeds and plants and working through a nurseryman by
the name of Subert in Hackney. His correspondent seems to have been
another of the gardeners working for the Duke of Northumberland and
Meader sent seeds for the Duke and was soon receiving requests for more.
Meader also saw a profit to be made in dealing in engravings and prints,
'new good Prints which are finely Engraved sell here at an Enormous Price'
(f. 4). Interesting in this connection and specifically relevant to Catherine's
own collectomania is his mentioning a number of drawings which were sent
to him by a Mr Spyers and bought by the empress for 1,000 rubles, 'more
than they are worth tho' Mr Spyers valued them at more'. (f. 44) This was
the John Spyers who had joined 'Capability' Brown in 1764 as a surveyor
and draughtsman and produced many watercolours of views of estates.[81]

Meader was generally scathing about Russian gardening practices and
practitioners, including the two apprentices assigned to him: 'one of them

has been 20 years and the other 10 years in Peterhoff gardens. They are both as ignorant of Gardening as though they had not been 6 months, nor do they seem desirous to know more.' (f. 27v.) But he was also anxious to discourage too great an influx of underqualified British gardeners. Soon after his arrival, he wrote of a gardener who 'is just arrived upon an adventure he was engaged this week with one of the Princes but I believe will do no good as he can neither survey or draw plans which is very essential for a foreign Gardener to know in this Country for the Germans here excell the English'. (f. 6v.) John McLaren seems to have pleased Bush, but Meader told his correspondent, who apparently was responsible for sending another Scot by the name of Duncan Menzies at the end of 1781 that 'I know the Young Man you sent to Bush he is no Conjuror at Gardening for he cut off all the Young Wood from the Fig Trees of Dr Johnson's Syon Hill' (f. 31v.).

Catherine's demand for British gardeners was insatiable, matched only, it seems, by the desire of British gardeners to enter her service. Meader mentions that the Duke of Devonshire's gardener Knowlton failed to negotiate terms (f. 28), but others did. The Russian consul in London, Alexander Baxter, said that there had been no fewer than 150 applicants when the empress' wish to engage three or four gardeners was made known in 1782. In the event, four-year contracts were signed by John Munro and Francis Reid, of whom Baxter wrote 'Munro & Reid ne sont formés au dessein, mais ils peuvent tracer un plan après avoir examiné le terrain qui doit être travaillé dans le gout anglais'.[82] Almost from the time Catherine purchased the Kantemir estate of Chernaia Griaz' near Kolomenskoe south of Moscow and renamed it Tsaritsyno in May 1775, the search for a suitable British gardener began in earnest.[83] It was only with the employment of Munro and Reid that the search ended. The building of the great palace at Tsaritsyno had been entrusted to the ill-fated Vasilii Bazhenov, who worked for ten years on the weird and wonderful fusion of Moscow Baroque, fashionable European Gothic, and masonic symbols that Catherine was to reject on her cruelly brief visit in 1785. For some reason it was only Reid, the less well-paid of the duo, who eventually appeared at Tsaritsyno in the spring of 1784. Where they had worked in St Petersburg in the interim is unknown, as is the reason for not sending Munro, of whom there is no more information. Bazhenov was not at all pleased with Reid's arrival, considering that the landscape 'in the last nine years had been adorned with such attractive copses and different picturesque views that it would be difficult to find its equal even in England and in only a few places does it need a little improvement in keeping with the positioning of nature itself'.[84] Reid, however, was intent on making great changes and cutting down trees and pointedly avoided meetings with Bazhenov. In August 1784 'Her Imperial Majesty was pleased to order 5000 rubles in the first instance to be released from the imperial office for the realisation of the plan for a garden in the English taste at Tsaritsyno, prepared by the gardener Reid and approved by Her Majesty.'[85] Work began in March 1785 and continued until 1790, thus straddling the dismissal of Bazhenov in 1785 and his replacement by Matvei Kazakov. The travel diaries of the Oxford don John Parkinson contain a description of a rare visit by an Englishman to Tsaritsyno in November 1793. Parkinson is totally but interestingly dismissive of the buildings of this 'imperial bauble', but appreciative of the setting:

> The Country about it is well wooded and the ground lies exactly as the Gardener would wish. In the particular situation of Zaritzina, a deep valley very bold on one side and formed by gentle slopes on the other but well wooded on both, winds along, watered formerly by a small stream, which they have now by damming it converted, as at Blenheim, into a broad lake or river.[86]

Reid continued to live with his family at Tsaritsyno until his death in 1798, but his expertise as a gardener was recognised by other commissions in the 1790s, most notably at Count Sheremetev's Ostankino. Until very recently, Reid's role in creating the Tsaritsyno park was deliberately overlooked: indeed, the most authoritative monograph on Tsaritsyno makes no mention of Reid and hails Bazhenov as the guiding spirit of both palace and park.[87]

Meader mentions two other British gardeners working in Moscow in 1784, one of whom he names as Harrison (f. 55v.). They were not, as far as is known, in imperial employ, but were representative of a growing number of gardeners working away from the capital. Henry Mowat, who was head gardener at Thoresby Hall in Nottinghamshire, was summoned to Russia in 1778 by the Duchess of Kingston to take charge of her newly acquired estate near Narva, overlooking the Baltic. Around 1781 he seems to have left the duchess' service, moved to the capital and been appointed 'Gardener of Her Imperial Majesty'.[88] The capital was the ultimate hoped-for destination of John Aiton, nephew of William Aiton, the king's gardener at Kew. Aiton, who had trained under his uncle at Kew and had also worked at Syon House, was recruited by Jeremy Bentham to work with his brother Samuel on Potemkin's estate at Krichev in Belorussia and proved to be a very able man, 'a compleat master of his business'.[89] In November 1787, following the dissolution of the Krichev enterprise, Aiton found employment with a neighbour of Potemkin's, designing hothouses and drawing up a plan for 'a kind of pleasure ground'.[90] The Benthams sought employment for him and his family in St Petersburg, commending him to the British ambassador and Russian acquaintances.[91] Nothing, however, is known of the further activities of either Mowat or Aiton, but in the 1790s there appeared other gardeners whose careers can be followed, at least in somewhat blurred outline. The fame of the Dukes of Northumberland's gardeners, both at Syon House and at their northern seat, Alnwick Castle, induced Catherine to recruit three more. All three were related by marriage and it is the Call family history which provides clues and more than a few red herrings about their early activities. Martin Miller Call is said to have left Alnwick for Russia in 1792, accompanied by the two Manners brothers, Charles (d. 1824), who had married Call's sister Lucy earlier that year, and Robert (1771–1831). Precisely where they worked initially is difficult to establish, although a whole series of imperial estates are named, including Tsarskoe Selo, Peterhof, the Taurida Palace, even Schlüsselburg.[92] While it is known that Charles Manners' eldest daughter Catherine was born in the Russian capital in 1796, documentary evidence about his and the others' appointments is available only from Alexander I's reign. Charles Manners (usually transcribed as Menas) seems to have followed Gould at the Taurida Garden, before replacing Joseph Bush at Tsarskoe Selo in 1810 and working on the park surrounding Quarenghi's Alexander Palace. He left there in 1814, possibly to work at Peterhof.[93] His brother Robert went to Moscow and in June 1796 signed a contract to work for Count Sheremetev at Ostankino. He was to stay there for more than thirty years and he was the 'scotch gardener' noted by Loudon in 1814.[94] Martin Call is best known for his work at the Taurida Garden and he was also the author of an informative essay on the 'Introduction of the Modern Style of Laying out Grounds into Russia', published anonymously in London in 1827.[95] Call and apparently other members of the family were buried at Grafskaia Slavianka near Tsarskoe Selo. The heyday of the activities of the Manners and Call is thus beyond the strict chronological boundaries of this study, but provides evidence of the continuing authority of British gardeners in Alexander's reign. As further substantiation, a further name might be cited, that of Thomas Gray, who laid out at the end of the eighteenth century the English garden at Ropsha, an estate that had belonged successively to Peter II, Grigorii Orlov and Count Ivan Chernyshev, before passing in 1785 to the Armenian banker Ovanes Lazarian. Gray was still at work at Ropsha in 1825 when he was suddenly summoned to Taganrog by Alexander I to lay out a garden in a spot by the sea that had appealed to the Empress Elizabeth.[96]

III

To the names of Sparrow, Bush, Gould and Meader – representing perhaps the most important British landscape gardeners working in Catherine's Russia – might be added a fifth, that of Charles Cameron; to the names of Joseph Bush, Gray, the Manners and Call, whose activities were at their height after Catherine's death, should be added that of Adam Menelaws. Although recognised first and foremost as architects, their work at Pavlovsk

25 Tsarskoe Selo, Sadovaia Street, showing the homes of the Bushs and Camerons and the Orangery. Sketch (1790s) by Giacomo Quarenghi.

(Cameron) and at Tsarskoe Selo and Aleksandriia/Peterhof (Menelaws) respectively may justly be seen in the tradition of such British architect-landscape designers as Kent and Chambers.

When Cameron arrived in Russia in 1779, he seems to have given the empress a romanticised version of his biography, which she passed on in letters to Melchior Grimm. 'A présent je me suis emparée de mister Cameron, écossais de nation, jacobite de profession, grand dessinateur nourri d'antiquités, connu par un livre sur les bains anciens,' she wrote on 23 August/ 3 September, and in subsequent letters she reported that he had been brought up in the household of the Pretender in Rome and was a nephew of Jenny Campbell.[97] He claimed to be a direct descendant of Cameron of Lochiel and indeed appropriated the Lochiel coat of arms which he stamped on his books. But the truth, as the most recent researchers have demonstrated, was somewhat different. Isobel Rae, who unearthed the first reliable information about Cameron's origins and early years, indicates that he was born in London, but advances a birth year of 1743, which is contradicted, however, by the entry in the register of the English Church in St Petersburg, stating that he was sixty-six at his death on 19/31 March 1812 and was thus born in 1745 or 1746.[98] His father, Walter Cameron, was a member of the

Carpenters' Company and a speculative builder in London. It was under his father that Charles served his apprenticeship, but he was also able to benefit from the instruction of Isaac Ware (d. 1766), Master of the Carpenters' Company and author of the influential *Complete Body of Architecture* (1756). At the time of Ware's death Cameron had been preparing for him engravings for a second edition of Lord Burlington's *Fabbriche Antiche disegnate de Andrea Palladio* (1730) and he decided to use some of these engravings for a work of his own on the baths of imperial Rome. Cameron was to spend the year 1768 in Rome, making further drawings on the spot for the book that was to appear only in 1772 as *The Baths of the Romans*. It was also in Rome that he seems to have made contact with the Scottish Jacobite community and, according to the conjectures of the leading Russian Cameron scholar Dmitrii Shvidkovskii, to have met another Charles Cameron, truly of Lochiel, whose 'biography' he was later to appropriate.[99] Returning to England, Cameron exhibited several engravings of Roman baths at the Society of Arts in 1772 to coincide with the publication of his book, but neither event seems to have brought him either the reputation or the commissions he sought. It has recently been established, however, that in 1770 he embarked with his father on the reconstruction of a house at 15 Hanover Square, a project that was to last until 1775.[100] It allowed Cameron to demonstrate his ability for interior decoration in the neo-classical style after the example of Robert Adam and to provide a foretaste of his work for Catherine a decade later. This familial cooperation was soon to break down into litigation brought by an irate Cameron against his father who had sold off many of his prized drawings and possessions to avoid bankruptcy. Walter Cameron was committed to a debtors' prison, where he was still languishing when his son left for Russia. The circumstances in which Cameron received the invitation to go to Russia are not known, but it was probably secured by his book, which had further editions in 1774 and 1775. At all events his prospects in England were not bright and doubts were expressed about his integrity. Such doubts were to resurface in 1791, when he paid his first and last visit to England from Russia and was blackballed when he was proposed for honorary membership of the recently formed Architects' Club. Not only were his abilities questioned on that occasion but his actions against his father and in an 'affair of the heart' with the daughter of his mentor Ware were also condemned.[101] In Russia Cameron could slough off his past, assume a new persona and embark upon a career that promised the fame and fortune his homeland denied him.

Cameron proved to be the ideal architect for Catherine. Acquainted with Hamilton's *Collection of Antiquities* since 1769, the empress had also received a book of engravings of Roman ruins in 1772 from the sculptor Falconet that gave her the notion of having a 'Graeco-Roman house' built

26 Charles Cameron (1746–1812). Charcoal and chalk drawing (1809)
by A. O. Orlovskii.

in the grounds of Tsarskoe Selo. Charles Clérisseau in Paris was given the
task of designing the building, but instead of the relatively modest structure
Catherine envisaged, he produced plans for a huge and grandiose Roman
palace at an equally huge estimated cost which were rejected out of hand.[102]
As suggested earlier, it may well have been the perusal of Cameron's book
on the Roman baths that decided the empress some years later to try again
and to invite the otherwise unknown British architect to Russia. Within
months of Cameron's arrival he and Catherine had already decided on what
would become the Agate Pavilion and Colonnade (Cameron Gallery): 'Nous
façonnons avec lui ici un jardin en terrasse avec bains en dessous, galerie en
dessus',[103] but several years were to pass before work was actually begun.

Catherine had more immediate tasks for her new architect: the conversion of rooms within the walls of Rastrelli's great baroque palace at Tsarskoe Selo into more intimate accommodation in the new idiom of Classicism. She was so delighted by his success with the suite of eight rooms, known as the First Apartment, at the north end of the palace, including, most notably, the Green Dining Room and the Bedroom with its fifty slender columns of green and white porcelain, that she put him to work at the south end on two further suites. The Fourth Apartment comprised the official reception rooms, where Cameron's versatility in adapting styles other than the Graeco-Roman is revealed in the Arabesque Room, the Lyons Drawing Room and the Chinese Hall; the Fifth Apartment, a suite of six small rooms, was for the empress' private use and included a bedroom decorated with twenty-two Wedgwood plaques. It was from the Mirror Room of the Fifth Apartment that a door was to open at first-floor level onto the hanging garden that led to the Agate Pavilion and the Colonnade. Cameron emerged, as it were, to design an exterior as well as an interior.

Work on the new wing which overlooked the lake in the English garden was completed by 1787. Cameron was able to bring the traditional Russian love of the bath-house (Catherine already had a bath-house in the grounds) and his expert knowledge of the Roman thermae to a happy creative fusion in the bath complex beneath the Agate Pavilion. The décor was more modest than Cameron's original designs would have required and resulted from one of Catherine's occasional twinges of conscience at the costs involved in her passion for building. John Parkinson, always a rich source of anecdote, notes that the whole building 'cost 500,000 roubles: not including the Agate and Jasper, which comes from the mines of Kolgwan [Kolyvan]. When it was finished the Empress walked over it holding Cameron by the Arm and said, It is indeed very handsome "mais ça coûte".'[104] The first floor, which was the first to be completed, presented in its several rooms (Vestibule, Great Hall, Oval Room, Jasper Study and Agate Room) dazzling variations on the natural stone that Russia provided in abundance – coloured marbles, malachite, agate, jasper, lapis lazuli, porphyry. The complement to the Agate Pavilion and Cameron's most famous building (by virtue of the posthumous honour of having it designated by his name) was the Colonnade or Gallery which so enthused the empress. A long gallery with a roof supported by Ionic columns, it was open on both sides but contained a glazed central area, where the empress could sit or entertain in cold or inclement weather; it ended in a portico, from which descended two graceful staircases, merging into one at the halfway stage. In 1792, when Catherine was no longer able to negotiate the steep stairs, Cameron built at right angles to the gallery a *pente douce* (*pandus* in Russian), allowing a more gradual access to the park. From the gallery there was a magnificent view of the park and surrounding

27 The Cameron Gallery and *pente douce* from across the lake. Engraving from a watercolour by M. N. Vorob'ev.

28 The Cameron Gallery, Tsarskoe Selo, 1783–6.

countryside. 'Sitting on my gallery, I see before me Pella, although it is at least thirty five versts away, and in addition to Pella I can see for about 100 versts around,' wrote Catherine with pride and pardonable exaggeration.[105] What she could see, for it had, among other things, been designed as a notable 'eye-catcher', was her new 'model' town of Sofiia, Cameron's second great project.

Today only the cathedral of St Sophia, recently returned to the care of the Orthodox Church and at a very early stage of restoration, serves as a reminder of the town of Sofiia, which was established by Catherine in 1779 and enjoyed a mere thirty years of existence before Alexander I gave orders for it to be razed virtually to the ground in 1808. Begun in 1782 and consecrated only in 1788, the impressive but not grandiose church stood in the middle of a wide square which was surrounded by other stone buildings designed by Cameron. Once again it is a watercolour by Quarenghi that has preserved for posterity the view of the recently completed church in its original setting. It stands as yet another monument to the arrival of Palladianism in Russia, even if the design of the central cupola reflects 'a manner that is closer to Lord Burlington than to Palladio'.[106] Its interior, however, holds surprises. Parkinson might regret missing 'the Granite Columns in the

29 The cathedral of Sofiia, near Tsarskoe Selo, designed by Cameron, 1782–8.
Sketch (1790s) by Giacomo Quarenghi.

Church of Sophia', about which Catherine wrote to Grimm, increasing their
number from eight to ten in her rapture,[107] but it was the imitation of the
dome of the Hagia Sophia in distant Constantinople that earned the cathedral
its special renown as 'the first example of Byzantinism in Russian architecture'.[108] The name of the town might seem to some a compliment by Catherine to herself under her German name of Sophie, but the empress had her
sights firmly directed elsewhere. 'Order Cameron to produce a plan and
façade of the cathedral church for the new town near Tsarskoe Selo and tell
him to imitate Constantinople's Sophia' ('... podognal ego tsaregradskoi
sofiiskoi').[109] As one researcher has recently put it, it was 'at this point that
Catherine's expansionist schemes intersect with her sense of architectural
symbolism'.[110]

Virtually throughout her reign Catherine was obsessed with what became
known as her 'Greek project'. Russia's two great wars against the Turks
during her reign were in the nature of a crusade; the annexation of the
Crimea in 1783 and the development of 'New Russia' under its viceroy Potemkin firmly established Russia by the Black Sea. Just across the water was
Constantinople, designated throne of the empress' second grandson Constantine, who was nurtured by a Greek nurse and fluent in her language.
From 1768 onwards it is difficult to think of any area of Russia's political,
social and cultural life that was not at some time and to some degree touched
by the Russo-Turkish confrontation. It was inevitable that architecture and

landscape gardening should mirror the empress' preoccupations and in Cameron she found a willing and understanding ally. Not that the symbolic adaptation of garden and building to the Greek cause begins and ends with Cameron. In 1775 for the celebrations to mark the first anniversary of the Treaty of Kuchuk Kainardzhi Catherine instructed Bazhenov to lay out a map of the Black Sea on the Khodynka Field north of Moscow and to build pavilions and fortresses to mark the places of victorious battles.[111] To the south of Moscow Bazhenov was to plan to connect Tsaritsyno to the Serpukhov road by which embassies from Turkey and Persia traditionally approached the old capital. This road from the south was to join the Petersburg highway, near to which was situated the Khodynka Field and Kazakov's Petrovskii Palace. In this way there was intended to be a great road from Petersburg to Constantinople. Within Tsarskoe Selo itself Cameron helped to realise a similar journey in miniature through the victory monuments which had begun to proliferate in the English garden from the early 1770s and by way of the Great Pond (Black Sea) to the town of Sofiia.[112] The Cathedral church satisfied both the empress and the architect, for whom Hagia Sophia represented the organic development of the Roman traditions he revered.[113]

Cameron's work at Tsarkoe Selo and Sofiia was demanding but he was obliged to find the time to undertake another project of considerable importance. In 1777 the empress had given the estate of Pavlovsk to her son and his wife on the birth of her first grandson Alexander. Cameron was given the challenge of designing a new palace to replace the original two wooden houses, called Paullust and Marienthal after the grand duke and duchess, and of planning and landscaping a garden amidst the thick woodland on the steep banks of the River Slavianka. Near the palace, the foundation stone of which was laid on 25 May/5 June 1782, Cameron designed formal areas, known as the Private and Aviary Gardens, as well as the Lime Avenue, the main approach, but he also laid out other areas of the park in the English style, damming the river to form a lake, constructing a cascade, opening pleasing prospects, threading paths and walks along river banks and through groves and woodland. He built in strategic spots a number of pavilions: his Temple to Friendship (1780–2) in the Slavianka valley was possibly the first building he designed after his arrival in Russia and the Pavilion of the Three Graces (1800–1) was one of the last and the only one he completed during Paul's reign. His hand was only one of the several that were to create the park in the form it eventually achieved by the 1820s, but it was the initial and decisive one. Loudon considered it 'the best specimen of the English style, in the neighbourhood of the Russian capital, or indeed in the empire'.[114] His subsequent suggestion that the man responsible for it had been Gould,

30 View of the Palace at Pavlovsk, designed by Cameron,
from across the River Slavianka.

furnished with a design by 'Capability' Brown, does an injustice to
Cameron's memory and is not supported by the known facts, but the feeling
that the result was not unworthy of Brown is appropriate enough.

It was to the beloved model of the Palladian villa that Cameron turned in
designing a central three-storeyed building surmounted by a shallow dome
on a column-encircled drum, which was flanked by curving single-storeyed
colonnaded galleries. The courtyard aspect was changed by additions from
Cameron's successor, Vicenzo Brenna, but it has always been the view from
the park that has allowed Cameron's masterpiece to be seen at its most
poetic, perched on the hill across the Slavianka. The park itself provided an
environment of natural beauty and classical antiquity, such as found in a
Claude landscape. Cameron furnished his park with buildings which not only
demonstrated the classical orders but were frequently in the nature of elegant
settings for classical statuary: such, pre-eminently, was the Pavilion sheltering
Paolo Triscorni's marble Three Graces or the double Colonnade surrounding
the statue of Apollo. Statues were everywhere throughout the park in the
more formal areas – and in the interior of the palace as well. When Paul
and his wife were travelling in Italy in 1782 Cameron was insistent that they
should buy on the spot as many ancient statues, ornaments and bas-reliefs
as possible or at least the closest of close copies from the originals.[115]

It was in the Italian Hall, the central space in the palace, high-domed and with deep wall niches that Cameron wished to concentrate his antique statues and create a sort of museum of classical art. Statues were in the niches of the adjoining Greek Hall, rectangular in shape and with sixteen columns of green false marble. Designed to recall a classical temple, this room completed the central enfilade of the first floor. That Cameron was responsible for the general planning of these rooms and many others on this floor as well as the ground floor seems clear and is substantiated by sketches and other documents, although there is much dispute among architectural historians about precisely where Cameron ends and Brenna begins, a problem complicated by Voronikhin's considerable role after the fire of 1803 – to say nothing of the complete re-creation necessary after World War II.[116]

Cameron had worked in harmony with the empress, who by and large indulged his desire to have only the best, and the costliest, of materials, only the genuine articles. Working with and for the grand duke and his wife was altogether a different matter. Accustomed to have his way, Cameron found himself frequently at odds with the ducal couple in matters of taste as well as of expense. On a number of occasions he was reluctantly obliged to cede to the wishes of the grand duchess, who had equally strong views about what she wanted. The correspondence between Maria Fedorovna and her overseer at Pavlovsk, Kiukhel'beker, reveals many of the tensions and frustrations between all involved.[117] Cameron's responsibilities were gradually taken over by Brenna, whom Paul and Maria had met in Italy and who had worked as Cameron's assistant for a few years. Cameron ceased to supervise building at Pavlovsk after 1787, but it was only at the very end of 1796, within days of his mother's death, that Paul issued an *ukaz*, relieving Cameron of all his duties.[118] In 1799 Paul seems to have had something of a change of heart and Cameron was once more employed at Pavlovsk to build a simple, elegant bridge over the Slavianka (subsequently called the Bridge of the Centaurs from the additions by Voronikhin in 1805), a number of buildings in the park, including the Cold Bath-house (plans for which he had submitted back in the 1780s) and, most notably, the colonnade that became known as the Pavilion of the Three Graces.

It was, however, only at the beginning of Alexander I's reign that he was again given an official position. Early in 1802 Cameron was appointed chief architect to the Admiralty and given a flat in the Michael Castle in St Petersburg. His initial brief was to 'visiter tous les ports de Russie, d'examiner tous les batimens publics qui s'y trouvent, et de donner des plans d'amélioration sur tous les objets',[119] but in the event his energies were directed to nearby Kronshtadt and Oranienbaum. Although Cameron was to hold his new post for only three years (he was dismissed for reasons unknown in 1805), recent research has revealed just how active he was. He designed and built sheds for the naval galleys and a naval hospital complex at Oranienbaum, consisting of twelve buildings and able to accommodate 400 patients. This latter building, in its siting on a hill, its generous layout and general design, incorporates many of the progressive ideas championed by John Howard and embraced by Catherine herself. Of Cameron's unrealised projects of these years the most interesting is the design for what was intended to be the Russian naval cathedral, the Andreevskii church at Kronshtadt. Two variants exist: of the first it has been suggested that it is strongly reminiscent of Robert Adam's parish church (1776) at Mistley in Essex and thus provides further evidence not merely of Cameron's general devotion to Palladianism but specifically of his knowledge of Adam's work, revealed in his very first interiors for Catherine two decades earlier.[120]

Of Cameron's last years little is known. He and his wife continued to live in the Michael Castle, along with other 'state pensioners'. Cameron found the company of the naval engineer, collector and bibliophile Petr Sukhtelen particularly congenial; there are two sketches of Cameron by A. O. Orlovskii, dating from 1809, one of which is an amusing portrayal of him with the two Sukhtelen brothers and another companion.[121] After Cameron's death in March 1812 his widow sold off his considerable library and collection of paintings and prints and successfully petitioned the tsar for a pension. She intended to return to England, but died in St Petersburg on 31 December 1816/12 January 1817.[122] Walter Cameron, a relation and a Russia Company merchant, took with him to London Cameron's architectural drawings, which a few years later were acquired by the Russian ambassador in London to help in the reconstruction of the fire-ravaged palace at Tsarskoe Selo.[123]

Cameron the man remains a shadowy figure. He was proud and aloof and difficult. He seems to have taken little part in the life of the British community and to have had few friends among the Russians. He was a member of the English Club in St Petersburg, but only briefly (1781–3).[124] He undoubtedly had a capacity to create a bad impression, carrying on where he left off in England: the Russian architect Fel'ten seems to have successfully thwarted his attempt to become a member of the Academy of Arts in 1781,[125] and Dr John Rogerson described him in 1804 as 'le plus grand gueux qui existe sur terre'.[126] Although a number of British visitors record meetings with him at Tsarskoe Selo, none gives any details about his personality or way of life.[127] It is in fact striking that nowhere do we find any attempt to characterise him as a person: even the imperial gardeners who must have come into frequent contact with him seem to have ignored him (with the exception of John Bush, of course, for it was Bush's daughter Catherine whom Cameron married in 1784, and the Bushes who gave them rooms by the Orangery). The Camerons seem to have had a daughter, although her birth, unlike their wedding and deaths, is not recorded in the church register.

Mary Cameron left Russia in 1798 as the extremely young fiancée of James Grange, who in a letter written many years later speaks of her as 'Miss Cameron the Daughter of the Celebrated Architect of the Palace of Pawlosky & the Baths & Galery at Zarskoe selo'.[128] It is possible that Grange, who enjoyed the protection of Alexander I and who was back in Russia in 1803, may have influenced the tsar's benevolence towards Cameron at the beginning of his reign. At all events Mary Grange had seven children living in 1839 – and there may be (unsuspecting) descendants of Cameron still alive today.

It is Charles Cameron's achievement not only as architect but also as landscape designer and town planner that justly claims the attention of posterity. Research by Russian and British scholars over recent years has revealed the full extent of his varied activities, but if we discount the wealth of architectural drawings, the extant architectural legacy is comparatively small. It is also concentrated within a very limited geographical area and even when the cathedral at Sofiia – restored eventually, it is to be hoped, to its former glory – is included in the itinerary, all can be encompassed in a day's tour. Cameron is not the architect of the imperial capital; he is an architect solely connected with its environs and loses nothing thereby. Unlike his great contemporary Giacomo Quarenghi, whose presence is so strongly felt in central Petersburg and elsewhere but whose work suffers almost from its predictability, Cameron, working virtually in the same idiom, achieved a sense of delicacy and poetry that owes much to the appropriateness of setting, to the genius of place. The Cameron Gallery, seen side-on from the lake or from the front, directly towards its wonderful staircase, and the palace at Pavlovsk, viewed preferably from across the river to where it stands on the hilltop, remain long in the mind's eye and are among the monuments best loved by Russians and now much admired by British visitors. Cameron has been hailed as 'Russia's most famous Scot', which is probably true, while at the same time remaining 'almost unknown in his own land', which is no longer so.[129]

Adam Menelaws and William Hastie, who were among the workmen Cameron brought from Scotland to Tsarskoe Selo in 1784, do, however, belong to the category of the 'almost unknown'. Although it was more appropriate to describe the activity of the group and of individuals such as the Wilsons in the earlier chapter devoted to craftsmen and specialists, the emergence of Menelaws and Hastie as architects in their own right more than justifies their inclusion at this juncture.

Menelaws (1749–1831) was one of four master stonemasons hired, but one of the two with a particular expertise in the construction of vaulting – and designated therefore in Russian as a 'vaulting master' (master svodnogo dela).[130] His special skills were immediately employed on the vaulting in the Cold Baths, but within a year his collaboration with Cameron came to an

end and there began his long and important association with the remarkable
Russian architect, landscape designer, inventor, man of letters and government official Nikolai L'vov (1751–1803).[131]

Throughout the 1780s and 1790s up to his sudden death in 1803 L'vov
was involved in a bewildering variety of projects, in many of which Menelaws came to play a key role. It was on 15/26 May 1785 that Menelaws left
Tsarkoe Selo, bound for Torzhok, a little town near Tver' on the St Petersburg–Moscow post-road, where he was to be engaged in the initial stages of
the building of the cathedral of the monastery of Boris and Gleb. One of a
number of churches that L'vov designed in the 1780s, Boris and Gleb is of
particular interest for the features it shares with Cameron's St Sophia,
notably the arrangement of its five domes, and, overall, it points to the Palladianism that both L'vov and Cameron had imbibed during their respective
visits to Italy.[132] A decade later, in 1794–6, and possibly earlier, Menelaws
was involved with L'vov's second cathedral, the St Joseph in Mogilev in Belorussia, commissioned by Catherine II to mark her meeting in that city in
1780 with the Emperor Joseph II which had strengthened the anti-Turkish
alliance.[133] In the interim Menelaws possibly worked for L'vov on buildings
on his estate of Nikol'skoe near Torzhok and in St Petersburg. One of his
more surprising activities, however, was his assisting L'vov to prospect for
coal in the region of Valdai. L'vov had long been concerned to find alternative sources of fuel that would save Russia's trees and also obviate the need
to import British coal. In August 1786 he was able to announce that he had
found at Borovichi, some fifty miles to the north-east of Valdai, substantial
deposits of good quality coal 'not inferior to that from Newcastle'.[134] Menelaws was soon joined at Borovichi by other Scottish workmen seconded from
Tsarskoe Selo and he was responsible for organising the digging of the coal
and its dispatch by barge to the capital.

Menelaws himself had ample opportunities during these years to get to St
Petersburg. His association with L'vov brought him into contact with some
of the most enlightened and cultured people in the capital, pre-eminently
members of the so-called L'vov–Derzhavin circle, which included in addition
to his mentor, the outstanding poet of the age Gavrila Derzhavin, the poet
Vasilii Kapnist, the painter V. L. Borovikovskii, who, incidentally, had
painted the murals and icons for the St Joseph Cathedral, and A. N. Olenin,
the future president of the Academy of Arts.[135] On 15 February 1792 Menelaws married Elizabeth Cave (d. 1841) and the witnesses to the marriage
included L'vov and Olenin as well as three of the most prominent members
of the British community in St Petersburg – John Rogerson, Catherine's body-
physician, Robert Hynam, the imperial watchmaker, and Charles Gascoigne,
head of important state cannon foundries.[136] It was about this time that Boro-

vikovskii painted the delightful portrait miniatures of Menelaws and his wife
that are now in the Russian Museum in St Petersburg.[137]

The reign of Paul brought disgrace to many favoured by Catherine, but
for L'vov's patron, Count A. A. Bezborodko, soon to be made chancellor,
it was a time of high honours. L'vov, partly in consequence, was not devoid
of recognition and commissions; and on account of this, the sun shone, if
considerably more weakly, on his good and faithful ally Adam Menelaws.
L'vov was soon dispatched to Moscow to design modifications to parts of the
Kremlin palace in time for Paul's coronation in April 1797 and immediately
summoned Menelaws from his work on the Mogilev cathedral. The following year Menelaws found himself back at L'vov's estate of Nikol'skoe,
employed on yet another seemingly utopian scheme. In August 1797 the
emperor had given approval to the establishment of a 'school of compressed-
earth construction' (uchilishche zemlianogo bitnogo stroeniia), at which
L'vov wished to instruct peasants in the building of huts and farm buildings
out of 'blocks' made in large moulds from earth mixed with a lime solution
which set as hard as concrete and had all the virtues of being accessible,
cheap and fireproof. L'vov had already conducted experiments in and around
Pavlovsk to the great satisfaction of the imperial family and the great and
still existing monument to this form of building was to be the Priory or
'Priorat', built in a matter of months in the summer of 1798 at Gatchina for
never-to-be-held meetings of the Knights of the Maltese Order of St John,
of which Paul was Grand Master. L'vov, not content with the school on his
estate, soon opened a second one on land he had acquired near the Simonov
Monastery outside Moscow, a spot made famous a few years earlier as the
setting for Nikolai Karamzin's sentimental tale of blighted love and suicide
'Poor Liza' (Bednaia Liza, 1792). Menelaws was put in charge of operations
at Tiufeli, constructing various buildings from the new material and
instructing young peasants in the art.[138] In addition, during these years,
Menelaws was again involved in prospecting for further deposits of coal,
L'vov's efforts in this area having received strong imperial support. It was
largely in connection with L'vov's mining concerns, his need for further
experienced workers and for machines, such as steam engines, that Menelaws
was sent at the beginning of 1800 on his first and only return visit to Britain,
but to England and not to the land of his birth. Apart from London, he is
known to have visited Boulton's famous works at Soho outside
Birmingham.[139] He had no success with recruiting workmen, as this was
against English law, but he fared better with machines. Among other commissions which he was able to fulfil was obtaining 'le plan de la cuisine telle
qu'on a ici dans la maison des enfants trouvés, suivant l'ordre qu'il a eu de
Sa Majesté l'Impératrice'.[140] On his return Menelaws resumed his duties at

Tiufeli, combining them with further prospecting in the Moscow region for deposits of peat, another of L'vov's favoured alternative sources of fuel.

L'vov's death in December 1803 to all intents and purposes also sounded the knell of many of the activities of his 'team' (*komanda*) of assistants, of which Menelaws was the most prominent and longest-serving member. Menelaws's first attempt soon afterwards to retire with promotion and retention of his salary met with no success, but in 1806, following the closure of the Tiufeli school, he was promoted to Collegiate Assessor and allowed to retire.[141] He was then fifty-seven years old, three or four years younger than Cameron, who had been retired the previous year. But to leave Menelaws at this juncture would essentially be to ignore what makes him worthy of special attention rather than of passing mention. Ahead lay no less than twenty-five years of private commissions and conspicuous official employment.

Although in one or two documents from the end of the eighteenth century, Menelaws is referred to as an 'architect' (the Russian ambassador in London called him, for instance, 'un architecte attaché à notre cour'),[142] A. K. Andreev in his article of 1977 argues that such a description of Menelaws at this stage of his career is misleading.[143] Menelaws, referred to as 'l'homme de M-r Lwow' in another letter at this time,[144] was pre-eminently L'vov's lieutenant and right-hand man, a skilled master mason, an able instructor in building techniques and a successful prospector. The late burgeoning of Menelaws' talents as designer and architect may well, however, have its origins already in the late 1790s in a commission from Count Kirill Razumovskii.

Menelaws' involvement with the Razumovskiis has usually been dated from around 1806, subsequent to his retirement, but D. O. Shvidkovskii argues that it was Menelaws, rather than Cameron, Quarenghi or L'vov, who was responsible for 'building a palace which has been championed as one of the most accomplished products of Russian Classicism' and that he was involved at Baturin, the principal seat of Razumovskii in the Ukraine, from before his visit to England in 1800.[145] If Menelaws designed this massive but long since ruined three-storeyed building, it was a remarkable achievement and was to be followed by no less imposing work for the Razumovskiis on other estates in the Ukraine such as Iagotino and Teplovka and on houses and estates in and around Moscow. Menelaws seems also to have embarked on the designing of the surrounding gardens and parks of these buildings. The degree of Menelaws' authorship is a matter of great debate, encouraged by a paucity of documentation. It seems inconceivable, given the short period of time (1799–1814) and other factors involved, that Menelaws would have achieved so much and moreover been unrecognised as the responsible architect. Menelaws did accompany Count Aleksei Kirillovich

Razumovskii on his tour of his Ukrainian estates in 1806, during which he was commissioned to undertake substantial rebuilding of the house at Iagotino and to lay out a park in the English style.[146] His involvement at Gorenki, the Razumovskii estate some twenty miles east of Moscow, is better attested and would indeed be sufficient to win him a notable place in the Russian architectural pantheon. This was a palace of enormous dimensions with attached side conservatories, resembling a sweeping colonnade and overlooking the lake. It was one of the estates visited by Loudon, who considered the palace 'highly elegant; and the attached conservatories and stoves, and decorated lawn, form a splendid and delightful scene, unequalled in Russia'.[147] Although he says the palace was 'built by an English artisan', he does not name Menelaws here or elsewhere.

Aleksei Razumovskii and Olenin, Menelaws' influential friend of long-standing, who both stressed his 'practical knowledge in the area of building' rather than naming specific notable achievements as an architect, wrote the recommendations that secured his return to government service in 1814 as a permanent member of the Building Committee responsible to the Ministry of Internal Affairs in St Petersburg.[148] It was to Tsarskoe Selo that he was to return to initiate the remarkable last phase of his long career, although his increasing expertise as a landscape designer was to be enlisted by Carlo Rossi in the planning of the gardens of the Anichkov and Mikhailovskii Palaces in St Petersburg in 1818 and 1826 respectively. His immediate task was the creation of the Aleksandrovskii Park on the territory of the former imperial hunting forest known as the Menagerie (*Zverinets*). This park was to stand in much the same relationship to Quarenghi's great, but nowadays still sadly inaccessible Aleksandrovskii Palace as the Ekaterininskii Park was to the Ekaterininskii Palace.

Menelaws was to be fully responsible for the overall planning of the park and its various buildings, for drawing up estimates and approving expenditure. He set about creating his own workforce, no doubt inspired by L'vov's example. Indeed, the person who proved most vital to the successful realisation of his projects was Ivan Alekseevich Ivanov (1779–1848), who as a young twenty-year-old had been brought from the Academy of Arts into L'vov's *komanda* in 1799 as a draughtsman and who had worked closely with Menelaws at Tiufeli. In the interim Ivanov had taught at the Academy of Arts (of which he was later to become an Academician) and gained wide experience both as painter and architectural designer. The nature of their close and harmonious collaboration over more than a decade is alluded to by Dr A. B. Granville, an English visitor to the park in 1827 and our most informative contemporary source on Menelaws. Describing one of Menelaws' last and most impressive structures, the Egyptian Gates, Granville refers to the projected bas-reliefs, 'composed from compilations taken from

31 The Chapel, Aleksandrovskii Park, Tsarskoe Selo, 1825–8.
Designed by Adam Menelaws (1756–1831).

the great French work on Egypt, designed by Menelas himself, and drawn
by Ivanoff for the use of the artist, who is to cast them in iron'.[149] The extent
to which Ivanov contributed other than a skilled pen or brush to the planning
of the Aleksandrovskii Park and its buildings remains an open question.

Menelaws is generally credited in part or in full with at least twelve struc-

32 The Egyptian Gates at Tsarskoe Selo, 1827–30. Designed by Adam Menelaws.

tures in the grounds of Tsarskoe Selo (mainly in Aleksandrovskii Park, but one or two in the Ekaterininskii). In Ekaterininskii Park he was responsible for the iron Cadet Gates (1821) (so named for allowing cadets from the institute across the road access to the park) and for the iron railing surrounding V. P. Stasov's 'Comrades-in-Arms' Gate (celebrating 1812), which was moved to a new site in 1821. Two further ironwork gates were later built by Menelaws in the Aleksandrovskii Park, the Babolovskii and the already mentioned Egyptian Gates. During Alexander I's reign he built the Farm (1818–22), the Llama House (1820–2) (to house, of course, the llamas sent as a present to the emperor), the White Tower (1821–4) (at nearly 38 metres the highest building in the park), and began the Arsenal (1818–34) on the foundations of Rastrelli's mid-eighteenth-century baroque pavilion Mon Bijou. All of these buildings are in the fashionable Gothic style of the age, although early examples of the style were created in the Ekaterininskii Park in the 1770s by Catherine's architects Il'ia Neelov and Iurii Fel'ten. Crenellated towers, romantic ruins were the common currency of the day and particularly appealed to Alexander I's brother Nicholas, who succeeded him in 1825. It was in the Arsenal, modelled on a British castle, that Nicholas, a great admirer of chivalry and all its trappings, was to hold a great masquerade in the form of a medieval tournament in 1842.[150] Working for Nicholas, Menelaws completed the quaintly named Pensioners' Stables (1827–9), another Gothic structure designed for Nicholas' retired horses with an adjacent cemetery, and also the Chapel (1825–8), described by Granville as 'a Gothic chapel in ruins, situated in the midst of a wood at the south-western extremity of the Park, erected by Menelas, in which is deposited a crucifix of white marble, seven feet high, the work of Danneker, together with an Egyptian sarcophagus, sent as a present by Count Tolstoy, from Alexandria. The effect is imposing.'[151] In the Hermitage collection there is, incidentally, a rare watercolour by Menelaws of his chapel, glimpsed above the tree line.[152] In strong and unique contrast to Menelaw's otherwise dominating Gothic are, finally, the Egyptian Gates (1827–32) with their two 40-foot piers clad in cast-iron bas-reliefs that Granville saw in their early stages of construction.

While still grand duke, Nicholas had visited England in 1817 and conceived a genuine admiration for much that he saw, not least in the area of architecture. Soon after his accession, he invited Menelaws to work at his beloved Peterhof and create for his consort a typical English cottage on land that had originally been an estate of Peter I's favourite, Prince Menshikov and was to become known as 'Aleksandriia'. Menelaws took Granville to see 'an exceedingly pretty and picturesque cottage, built by himself, in which the Gothic style predominates'. Granville provides what is probably the most detailed description of the 'Cottage' (*Kottedzh*) available in English and while emphasising its Gothic features, draws attention to Menelaws' predilection for ironwork: 'Externally, the four sides of the cottage are greatly improved in appearance by the introduction of a bowered balcony, supported by rich and tasteful fretwork, made of cast-iron at the foundry of Alexandrovsky, under the direction of Mr Clark, forming in front of the building a semicircular porch of five Gothic arches'.[153] Within a few years Menelaws had supervised the laying out of a park on an attractive undulating and wooded site, bordered by the Gulf of Finland, and adding in his well-tried Gothic style the Farm, the Guardhouse and the Ruined Bridge as well as building, to the design of the German architect K.-F. Schinkel, the large Gothic Chapel.[154]

On 31 August 1831 the cholera epidemic that gripped many parts of central Russia claimed the life of Adam Menelaws. He had worked no fewer than forty-seven years in Russia, forty of them in government service. He came to Russia as an experienced master stonemason, whose particular skill in the difficult art of building vaults and arches was immediately appreciated by L'vov. For nearly twenty years L'vov was his mentor and teacher, widening his social and intellectual horizons as well as imparting some of his own immense versatility. It was after L'vov's death that Menelaws became his own man and began to exercise his own creative talents and undoubted building skills, firstly under the patronage of the Razumovskiis and then, increasingly confidently and expansively, under the Emperors Alexander and Nicholas. Nicholas was perhaps his most appreciative patron, who provided him with the opportunity at a very advanced stage of life to create his most characteristic and complete monument. The variety and number of his buildings at Tsarskoe Selo notwithstanding, it was at Aleksandriia that Menelaws created a whole series of gothicised structures, among which the Cottage is justly the best known, and set them in a park, expressing, as one writer puts it, 'the poetic ideals of the age'.[155]

Menelaws' younger compatriot William Hastie (1755–1832) worked for six years as a stonemason at Tsarskoe Selo, although in 1786 he was sent for a short period to join Menelaws, who was prospecting for coal near Valdai.[156] Unlike Menelaws, however, Hastie came directly under Cameron's influence and it seems probable that he developed his skills as a draughtsman while working in Cameron's design team. At all events, Hastie was taken into Catherine's private service in 1792 and two years later she was explaining to Baron Grimm, who seems already to have heard of him, that 'Ce Hastie, architecte, dont vous me parlez, je l'ai pris à mon service; c'est un sujet très recommandable: il a fait des choses charmantes.'[157] Catherine's enthusiasm was based on his submission in August 1794 of designs for a country mansion which were an addition to the album of fifty-seven architectural drawings submitted earlier by 'architectural candidate Hastie'. Hastie had thus passed his probationary period to the empress' satisfaction and was now taken fully into her private service. The drawings that pleased Catherine were plans and elevations of a neo-Palladian house which, according to Militsa Korshunova, 'drew heavily on the plans of Lord Scarsdale's country house at Kedleston'; the album itself contained drawings of villas, pavilions and other structures, most of them classical in design but a few in the Gothic style.[158] As far as is known, no actual building ever resulted from these designs, but this was no impediment, it seems, to Hastie's appointment within a year to a position of some eminence in southern Russia.

In January 1795 Hastie married Margaret Bryce, the daughter of one of his fellow stonemasons,[159] and in July of the same year he left the capital to become chief architect to the governor of Ekaterinoslav and Taurida regions, Catherine's last favourite Count Platon Zubov. Thus, a decade after Cameron's supposed visit to the Crimea, his protégé Hastie found himself at work on the restoration of the Khan's palace at Bakhchisarai.[160] In 1798 Hastie prepared another album which, in addition to measured drawings of the palace and of other Crimean monuments, contained panoramic views of such towns as Kaffa and Kozlov.[161] No details are available about any other work that Hastie did in the area, where he was to remain four years in all until June 1799.

Still without a known building to his name, Hastie began a new phase in his career following Alexander I's accession to the throne. He was soon involved in the reconstruction of the ironworks at Kolpino near St Petersburg, where the director from 1803 was Charles Gascoigne and his main assistant was Alexander Wilson, son of James Wilson, one of the smiths with whom Hastie had sailed from Scotland in 1784. It was probably from Gascoigne and his associates that Hastie learnt of the latest techniques in cast-iron bridge-building developed in England and Germany in the 1790s. In the event, his appointment in 1804 to the Office of Waterways gave him the opportunity to design a number of bridges in St Petersburg that brought him wide recognition. On 14 November 1806 the Politseiskii ('Police') Bridge, 27 metres long and 21 metres wide and constructed of fourteen bolted cast-iron arches, was officially opened. It replaced the earlier wooden bridge and was the first bridge on Nevskii Prospekt at the point where it crossed the Moika. It set the standard design for a whole series of bridges over the Moika and other canals, constructed not only by Hastie but also by other builders during the first quarter of the nineteenth century. Over the period 1806–10 Hastie built five out of the ten bridges he designed: the Politseiskii (renamed the Narodnyi), the Novo-Moskovskii (1808) on the Zabalkanskii Prospekt, crossing the relief canal, the Krasnyi ('Red') (1814) on Gorokhovaia Street and the Potseluev ('Bridge of Kisses') (1816) on Glinka Street, both crossing the Moika; finally, the Aleksandrovskii (1814) across the Vvedenskii Canal, where it leaves the Fontanka. By 1842 the Politseiskii Bridge had undergone the first of several reconstructions and today only the Red Bridge with its four corner granite pillars surmounted by golden orbs remains virtually intact as a reminder of the basic Hastie design.[162]

While continuing to work in St Petersburg, Hastie became chief architect at Tsarskoe Selo from 1808. In that year Alexander I raised Tsarskoe Selo to the status of a regional town and ordered nearby Sofiia to be dismantled;

thus, by a cruel irony, Cameron's unique essay in town planning was obliterated to allow an opportunity in the same field to one of his former workmen. Hastie produced a plan of the new town, but did not oversee the town's construction, which was delayed by the war of 1812–14. Although some changes were subsequently introduced, the essential features of Hastie's plan are still preserved in the central layout of the modern town of Pushkin. One of the few houses Hastie built there – a two-storeyed wooden house in 1820 – still stands and is the house in which Anna Akhmatova spent many of her early years.[163]

Hastie's renown as a builder of bridges was rivalled and indeed eclipsed by his sudden reputation as a planner of towns.[164] His appointment at Tsarskoe Selo had been a consequence of his activities as a member of the Building Committee of the Ministry of Internal Affairs, to which he had been appointed in 1806, along with Menelaws and A. Mel'nikov.[165] In 1809 he and the Italian architect Luigi Rusca produced an album of standardised façades for private two- and three-storeyed houses in towns throughout Russia; this album, together with others published in subsequent years by Stasov and Rusca and extending to all manner of civic and private buildings, were widely distributed and were to be strictly followed: indeed, they became appendices to the Full Collection of Laws of the Russian Empire. The designs which Hastie and Rusca produced provided for various types of buildings, dependent on their location on a street and on the financial means of the owners. The designs were part of a grand overall strategy for imposing classical conformity and regularity on Russian towns and in essence were a fulfilment of the vision Peter I had had for his new capital and which Catherine II had begun to impose throughout the empire. House design was but part of Hastie's overall responsibilities and involvement. At the behest of the Building Committee he produced in 1811 a series of twenty-six plans for standardised town areas or quarters (*kvartaly*) and squares, which were engraved and published in 450 sets the following year. Here were all possible variations on three-, four-, five- and six-sided, indeed circular, town blocks and imposing city squares.[166]

Full layouts of towns were the peak of his planning and regulating activities. In 1810 this particular area of responsibility passed to the Ministry of Police, to which Hastie was assigned in 1811. It had been decreed that all provincial governors seeking to redevelop towns or rebuild after fire could only do so in accordance with architectural plans originating or finalised in St Petersburg. This was to give Hastie enormous authority and responsibility and for over twenty years, nearly up to his death in 1832, he was the empire's master planner. Following the great fire that devastated Moscow in 1812, Hastie produced a plan for the city's reconstruction which won the approval of the tsar but was ultimately rejected as inordinately expensive, impractical and insensitive. It paid scant attention to the history and topography of the ancient capital and proposed vast open squares, raking prospects and wide boulevards on a scale achieved only in the Soviet period.[167] Hastie's imprint was to be more lasting, for better and worse, on many other Russian towns, from Belorussia and the Baltic to Siberia (Omsk and Tomsk), from Onega in the north to Kiev and Ekaterinoslav in the south. Only occasionally did Hastie visit the towns, whose future face depended on his pen: he went to Vilna and its governor was delighted with the resulting recommendations; he intended to go to Siberia but never did, but had the good sense to suggest that his plans for Tomsk and Omsk in the late 1820s be modified in accordance with local conditions. He had learnt from his failure to visit Saratov after its fire in 1811 and his preparation of plans ignoring the local topography to such a degree that local protests brought their rejection. Hastie was the standard-bearer of uniformity and its frequent companion, monotony. Throughout his career he remained true to his original concept of the town planned on classical principles, such as he had encountered in Cameron's Sofiia. Nonetheless, his influence over Russian town-planning, extending beyond his death, was enormous and far-reaching.

IV

As we have seen, British gardeners and architects made a very positive contribution to the Russian cultural scene; British painters, whom Catherine began to attract into her service from the late 1770s, made considerably less impact. Few had established any sort of reputation in England before they left with hopes of finding fame and fortune in Russia; consequently British sources carry little or no information about their lives and careers and are usually ignorant about their activities in Russia. It is in letters, memoirs and travel literature of the period that scattered references are found but they are rarely adequate to provide more than a fleeting glimpse.

Perhaps the best known of the painters working for Catherine was Richard Brompton (1734–83), a pupil of Benjamin Wilson and, later, of Raphael Mengs in Italy, where he was to spend several years in the 1760s.[168] It was in Venice in 1764 that he painted for his patron, the Earl of Northampton, the conversation piece of the Duke of York and several friends that was to be exhibited at the Society of Artists in 1767 and bring him to the attention of the British public for the first time. In the 1770s he painted full-length portraits of the Prince of Wales and his brother Prince Frederick which were shown at the Royal Academy, but it was at the Society of Artists, of which he became president in 1773, that he preferred to exhibit his work. Some twenty paintings were displayed there, up to and including the year 1780. Perhaps his finest accomplishment during these years was his portrait of the

Earl of Chatham, a copy of which is now in the National Portrait Gallery. Brompton, however, seems to have caused more stir by his irascible nature, his pretensions, his inability to live within his means, and his reluctance to pay his debts. It was this last failing which brought him in 1779 to the King's Bench debtors prison, from which he was rescued by the magnanimous Catherine. Such at least is the version of events that is most often advanced to account for Brompton's departure for Russia and is given its most romantic inflation in an entry in Joseph Farington's diary for 14 February 1804:

His wife went to Russia & carried with Her a picture that He had painted of the great Lord Chatham & some other works, and exhibited them to the Empress Catherine, & represented that the artist was confined in prison for debts of £600 or £1000. The Empress ordered the debts to be paid & that He shd. come to Russia upon an establishment . . .[169]

That Brompton was in debtors prison is corroborated in a letter of 30 November 1779 from Jeremy Bentham to his brother, in which he speaks of a conversation with the husband of a woman, whose 'sister is married to a harum-scarum ingenious sort of an artist a painter, whose name is Brompton, whom Offenberg I believe used to go and see in the King's Bench – where he was in jail, and who has been taken out of jail by your people, who have sent for him over to paint, and he is patronized I understand by Sr. J. and so I suppose you see him now and again'.[170] Samuel obviously did see him and was unimpressed; writing to Jeremy on 28 November/9 December, he called Brompton 'a great scoundrel'.[171] The British ambassador Sir James Harris, however, claimed to have 'got him a good berth, six hundred a year salary, paid bonds for his extraordinary work, & leave to paint *en ville*', adding that 'he behaves well on the whole, a little lazy, & not quite so fond of truth as an honest man'.[172] The particular 'berth' Harris had secured for Brompton was greatly improved in July 1780, when he was officially appointed painter to the imperial court, following the death of the previous incumbent Stefano Torelli.[173]

Brompton's name had appeared in the empress' correspondence with Grimm already in May of that year, when she mentions that he was painting a portrait of Grand Duke Alexander.[174] This was followed by a portrait of the Grand Duke Constantine.[175] Soon Brompton was at work at what became perhaps the most widely known painting of his Russian period, a heavily allegorical portrayal of the two young grand dukes which delighted the empress: 'il a peint mes deux petits-fils, et c'est un tableau charmant: l'aîné s'amuse à couper le noeud gordien, et l'autre insolement a mis sur son épaule le drapeau de Constantin. Ce tableau dans ma galerie n'est point défiguré par les *Van Dyck*.'[176] The last remark would have struck English artistic circles as deliciously ironic, since one of Brompton's more notorious acts was his heavy-handed, insensitive restoration of Van Dyck's famous Pembroke family group at Wilton. For Catherine, however, the picture was a triumph, incorporating, undoubtedly in accordance with her wishes, the realisation of her 'Greek Project' with her little grandsons in the starring roles of a future Alexander the Great and a Constantine the Great. A miniature of the painting was made for her favourite Lanskoi and a full-size copy was dispatched to Grimm in Paris, where 'tout le monde trouve ce tableau charmant, on vient en foule le voir chez moi'. In the same letter Grimm alludes to the death of 'cet habile peintre', which occurred on 1/12 January 1783, and inquires whether Brompton had painted the empress.[177] Brompton in fact produced three portraits of Catherine. The first seems to date from 1782 and to be not from life but a variation on an earlier half-length original by Roslin. An engraving from it by Charles Ruotte was to appear in William Coxe's *Travels into Poland, Russia, Sweden, and Denmark*, published for the first time in 1784 and several times thereafter, although the indication in the 'List of the Plates' that it was a 'Head of the Empress of Russia, from an original painting in Brumpton' would do little to advance the painter's fame.[178] It was also in 1782 that Brompton completed his own half-length portrait of Catherine, now in the Hermitage collection, which earned a not undeserved contemporary assessment of it as 'highly successful'.[179] The same source refers also to a full-length portrait 'with various allegorical attributes and a view of the Russian fleet in the distance', which was almost certainly the one mentioned by Catherine as unfinished at Brompton's death and recently tentatively identified in the collection at Tsarskoe Selo.[180] Surviving full-length portraits of two members of the aristocracy, Countess A. V. Branitskaia and Prince A. B. Kurakin, testify to Brompton's success in painting *en ville* and are certainly among his best canvases. Free from the allegorical trappings and formal constraints of his portraits of the imperial family, those of Branitskaia and Kurakin are much closer to the English tradition of the portrait of the country gentleman and/or his wife in a poetic landscape setting.[181]

Brompton was in Russia for a little over three years and despite his generous appointments – but true to character – he managed to leave his widow debts of 5,000 rubles. Ann Brompton called a meeting of creditors to sort out the situation and Katherine Harris, the ambassador's sister, noted that the empress gave her a year's salary and Potemkin added 1,000 rubles.[182] Given that British sources suggest that the Bromptons had no children, it is pertinent to add that their first child was born in St Petersburg on 30 April/ 11 May 1780 and was followed by two more in 1781 and 1782. Sadly, their two daughters, Alexandra and Katherina, both died in 1782, while their son, named almost predictably Alexander Constantine, survived his father. Ann Brompton, who, according to Katharine Harris, was again pregnant when

33 Countess A. V. Branitskaia. Oil Painting (*c.* 1781) by Richard Brompton (1734–83).

34 Prince A. B. Kurakin. Oil painting (*c.* 1781) by Richard Brompton.

her husband died, married James Hill, a Russia Company merchant, in May 1783 and was soon to return to England.[183]

While Brompton left a mark of sorts in Russia, two other artists, whose visits to St Petersburg overlapped his, received barely a mention in a Russian context. A pupil of Raphael Mengs, like Brompton, was the Scot Edward Francis Cunningham (1742–95?), whose association with Italy was such that he was often called an Italian and was frequently known by the name of Francesco Calze. Born in Kelso, he left Scotland as a young boy with his parents who had been involved in the rebellion of 1745. His early training and career as a painter were in various Italian cities and in Paris. He also spent time in London and exhibited at the Royal Academy in the 1770s. His visit to Russia seems to have been as a consequence of an invitation from the notorious Duchess of Kingston to join her suite on either her first or second voyage to St Petersburg in 1777 or 1779.[184] What is known of his activities amounts to very little. It is said that he was an associate of Brompton, after whose death he worked with the Italian architect G. Trombara. Like Brompton, Cunningham also produced a painting of Catherine after Roslin, which was eventually engraved by Charles Townley and published c. 1786 in Berlin, where Cunningham had settled after leaving St Petersburg in the summer of 1783.[185] The illustrator Daniel Chodowiecki's letters from Berlin, which provide the date of Cunningham's arrival there, also offer an initially unfavourable view of his talent: 'uses crayon better than oil paint. I recently saw a family portrait which he had begun in Russia and has brought with him to finish here. The figures are full-length, the father, mother and two children are one third natural size. The drawing is not bad, the composition unremarkable, the colouring untrue and harsh, his hand heavy and rough.'[186] The identity or whereabouts of the painting to which Chodowiecki refers have never been established, but his description provides an indication of the sort of commission Cunningham received in the Russian capital.

The trio of British painters in the Russian capital in 1779 was completed by George Carter (1737–94), a product of the Royal Academy schools and exhibiting at both the Society of Artists and the Royal Academy in the 1770s.[187] He may well have travelled out from England with Brompton: such, indeed, is the impression gained from an unpublished letter written from St Petersburg on 25 October/5 November 1780 by Father Andrei Samborskii, former chaplain at the Russian embassy church in London, to his friend Baron Thomas Dimsdale, Catherine's famed inoculator.[188] It was Dimsdale who was the first to bring Brompton's work to the attention of the imperial family: in August 1778 Grand Duke Paul wrote to thank Dimsdale for 'la connoissance que vous m'avez procurée du Sieur Brompton'. That the acquaintance was through the gift of prints of, perhaps, Brompton's paintings of the Prince of Wales and his brother is supported by the following reflection that 'si les productions de l'art meritent notre estime, nous en devons bien plus encore à ceux, a qui nous en sommes redevables'.[189] The invitation to Brompton followed the next year and Dimsdale, as Samborskii makes clear, also recommended Carter. Mentioning that Brompton was prospering, Samborskii devoted most of his letter to Carter, who was already on his way back to England and was to begin portraits of Dimsdale and his son Nathaniel later that year.[190] Carter had received 5,000 rubles and a gold medal from the empress, but remained dissatisfied: 'Mr. Carter doubtless is convinced of his own merit; but every body here, even all the english with one voice pronounce him to be more enterprizing, than skilfull; and his pencill inferior by many degrees to the Majestic Subject.' Carter was active in England for a few years, arranging a pretentious private exhibition in 1785 of some thirty-five historical paintings on such subjects as 'The Siege of Gibraltar' and 'The Death of Captain Cook' before leaving for India. Carter's painting of the empress has not been identified; it may be hanging in some former imperial palace or stored amidst the vast reserve collections of the Hermitage. It is in the Hermitage's Department of Drawings that the watercolours of an even more shadowy English artist are located.

In the context of a recent survey of romantic elements in Russian architecture at the end of the eighteenth century and of emphasising the stimulus given to an 'asiatic style' by Russia's annexation of the Crimea, the Russian art historian L. N. Timofeev almost casually wrote that 'the image of the Crimea was first caught in the watercolours of the Englishman Hadfield, who accompanied Catherine on her journey in 1787' and footnoted their present whereabouts.[191] The name of Hadfield is not encountered in any account of Catherine's journey or in any work on Anglo-Russian relations, but his watercolours are there in the Hermitage. In a folder in green morocco, bearing the title 'Voyage de la Crimée fait par Sa Majesté Impériale de Toutes les Russies 1787', there are, or should be, twenty-six watercolours. At the time of my visit, fourteen could not be located, but the card index listed the titles of the complete set.[192] Although the watercolours are not remarkable for their quality, they are a most remarkable and unique pictorial record of the places Catherine visited on her journey south. The first of the series is called 'Ville de Smolensko' and bears the inscription 'Hadfield 1787'; on the last of the series is written 'Hadfield – 1787 St Petersburg'. While the majority of the watercolours are views of, for instance, Kiev and the Crimea, several importantly depict actual scenes, such as the fire that swept through Smolensk at the time of the Empress's visit, the festivities in Kiev, Catherine's departure by boat from the city, groups of Ukrainian maidens awaiting with flowers her arrival, the launching of a ship at Kherson, and the public baths at Bakhchisarai. Not a Potemkin village in sight, but there are views of

apprentices in the art of mezzotint engraving, for which in 1793 he was given the typical award of extra supplies of logs and candles.[204] Walker's work on the Hermitage paintings led in 1792, during a visit to London, to the publication of the first two folders of *A Collection of Prints, from the most celebrated pictures in the Gallery of Her Imperial Majesty Catherine the Second, Empress and Autocratix of all the Russias.* The collection contained eleven engravings prepared over the preceding eight years; in addition to the four works already mentioned, there were engravings of paintings by Reynolds, Murillo, Rembrandt, Moise Valentin, Eriksen, Batoni and Verkoyelle. Walker's eminence in Russia, however, was due principally to his engravings from portraits of members of the Russian imperial family and aristocracy. Over forty such engravings include three of Catherine (among them the famous portraits by Shibanov (1787) and Lampi (1794)), three of Paul and three of Alexander I, and such notables as Potemkin, Suvorov, Stroganov, Bezborodko, Lanskoi, Zubov, Platon and, of particular Anglo-Russian interest, Admiral Greig. The great Russian art historian, D. A. Rovinskii, suggests that Walker's engravings 'are notable for the extreme beauty and elegance of the workmanship and represent the most prized and handsome sheets in the folder of Russian portraiture'.[205]

Walker arrived in St Petersburg in 1784; he was accompanied by his wife Mary, a daughter, and a nine-year-old boy by the name of John Augustus Atkinson. The relationship of Walker and Atkinson has remained something of a mystery. Most sources suggest that Walker was Atkinson's uncle, although a contemporary Russian document refers to him as his stepson (*pasynok*), which corresponds to Walker's own overlooked description of him as 'son-in-law'.[206] Possibly, Atkinson was Mary Walker's son by an earlier marriage or the son of a deceased sister whom Walker adopted. At any event the relationship between Walker and Atkinson grew into a strong creative bond. Atkinson was soon to reveal his precocious talents as a painter, and Walker describes how Catherine requested him (when he was fifteen or sixteen, i.e. in about 1790) to include in a painting he was completing of the Easter festival in St Petersburg a 'portrait of the Grand Chamberlain [Naryshkin], sitting in his own balcony, with a large damask napkin tucked under his chin, 'pour demontrer' (as she put it) 'qu'il etoit bien eleve'.[207] It was during Paul's reign that Atkinson's career really took shape and his collaboration with Walker began. In 1800 the German playwright A. von Kotzebue describes Atkinson at work in Paul's Michael Castle painting two huge historical canvases on the subjects of Dimitrii Donskoi's victory at the Field of Kulikovo and of the baptism of Prince Vladimir, and comments that his 'pencil has a bold and striking effect, though he is far from being faultless with regard to his outlines'.[208] Early in 1801 he completed a full-length study of Count Nikolai Petrovich Sheremetev in his robes as a Knight of the Order of Malta, which still hangs at Kuskovo. None of these paintings was engraved by Walker, although he did produce engravings of three earlier works by Atkinson, dating from 1797. The first was of Paul on a white horse and the other two of Suvorov, one full-length with sword in one hand and hat in the other, the second, with his marshal's baton in his right hand. Sending copies of the engravings to Semen Vorontsov in London, Count Fedor Rostopchin wrote: 'Je vous envoie deux portraits du Cte Souworow. Celui qui est avec la bâton de commandement est frappant par le maintien. L'autre le représente mieux.'[209]

In the early months of Alexander I's reign Atkinson made a series of drawings from the Observatory of the Academy of Sciences. They were duly dedicated to the tsar and published in London as four coloured aquatints prefaced by an uncoloured vignette of Falconet's 'Bronze Horseman' under the title of *The Panorama of St Petersburg*. The first two depict the left bank of the Neva from the Marble Palace to the Winter Palace and from the Admiralty to the end of the English Line respectively, and the remaining two, the right bank, from the Academy of Arts to the Twelve Colleges and from the Old Exchange to the Peter and Paul Fortress. They provide an interesting parallel to the Makhaev drawings made fifty years earlier and show the magnificence of the Neva embankments on the eve of the city's centenary. There is no year of publication, but it was probably the year after Atkinson and the Walkers returned to England in 1802.[210] Atkinson was seemingly responsible for both the drawings and etchings and Walker's involvement is nowhere acknowledged. Walker made his own act of homage to Alexander I at this time, publishing on 1 May 1803 his engravings of both the tsar and his consort after paintings by Kügelgen. In 1803–4 there appeared a work of importance that was the result of collaboration between Walker and Atkinson and is their most enduring monument. It was a collaboration of a perhaps unexpected kind. For over a decade Atkinson had been making sketches of Russian scenes and types which he himself (and not Walker, as is sometimes erroneously asserted) etched for *A Picturesque Representation of the Manners, Customs, and Amusements of the Russians in one hundred coloured plates* (3 folio vols.). Atkinson succeeded in creating a rich mosaic of Russian life in town and country, portraying not only the traditional costumes of various classes, but also means of transport, religious ceremonies, sports and pastimes, and vivid genre scenes of, for instance, taverns and race-meetings. It was Walker who was responsible for the 'accurate explanation of each plate', as he makes clear at a later date, suggesting that reviewers had 'complimented Mr A. on the truth, freedom, and spirit of the etched prints; and were kind enough to select a few of the Author of these Scraps' best descriptions, which they recommended particularly to the public attention'.[211]

36 The Russian Bath-house. Drawn and etched by John Augustus Atkinson (1775–1831) for his and James Walker's *Picturesque Representation of the Manners, Customs, and Amusements of the Russians* (London, 1803–4).

Walker was not active as an engraver in the years following his return from St Petersburg. The last *published* joint work by Atkinson and Walker was a full-length portrait of Alexander I, dated 1 September 1814 in the wake of the emperor's triumphant visit to England, although among the copper plates (twelve in all) auctioned by Sotheby in 1822 was a 'new plate, never published', of Atkinson's portrait of the Empress Elizabeth. There were also other plates on non-Russian subjects after 1815. Atkinson frequently exhibited at the Water-Colour Society at the Royal Academy, including his huge 'Battle of Waterloo', exhibited in 1819 and based on studies he had made at the battlefield in 1815. His last known work dates from 1829 and it is assumed that he died shortly afterwards. Most authorities have also assumed that Walker had died in 1808, but in this case the assumption is quite wrong. He died, it would appear, not before 1822 and it was on 29 November of that year that Sotheby held the sale of Walker's plates and impressions. It is from the sale catalogue that we learn of the misfortune that had befallen Walker, who lost all his copper plates when the ship in which he was travelling from St Petersburg was shipwrecked off Great Yarmouth in 1802.[212] In 1821, the previous year, Walker also published, anonymously, a valuable collection of anecdotes under the title of *Paramythia; or, Mental Pastimes*, mainly relating to his years in Russia but also containing some information about his movements after 1808.[213]

Walker's reputation rests solidly on his series of formal portraits of many of the notable figures of the reign of Catherine the Great, but *Paramythia* reveals more of the man and his reaction to the world in which he lived. *Paramythia* is full of Walker's sincere admiration for Catherine; 'it was', he wrote, 'my peculiar good fortune to have passed many years of my life in the very bosom of a splendid court, almost daily honoured by the confidence and conversation of a truly great and amiable sovereign'.[214] His many anecdotes about her illustrate what he saw as her 'affability, kindness, presence of mind, and ready wit', and stand in stark contrast to the few about Paul, who on one occasion 'half laughing said, "savez vous, Mons. W., que si je voulois je pouvois vous cracher dans la figure". The reply it deserved might have packed me off to Siberia, and therefore, I pocketted the affront.'[215] The Russian anecdotes tell us much about Walker's activities, his relations with members of the English community, as well as about the less formal behaviour of a whole procession of Russian aristocrats whose public image he fixed in his engravings.

The last item in *Paramythia* concerns Catherine's inspection in the Hermitage of a painting she had commissioned from Sir Joshua Reynolds on a subject of his own choosing. 'He selected that of the infant Hercules strangling the serpent, in allusion to the infant exertions of the colossal empire of Russia. The subject was generally well chosen, and certainly not inapplicable; but I am rather disposed to think it was not entirely pleasing to her Imperial Majesty, who perhaps did not quite agree with the painter, that her empire was in its leading-strings.'[216] Walker nevertheless commented on Catherine's admiration for Reynolds both as a painter and as author of the *Discourses* to the Royal Academy which he had sent to her with the painting and which Catherine had had immediately translated into Russian; it is also interesting to note that in 1791 Walker made an engraving of the painting, which became the opening plate of his *Collection*. The commission to Reynolds had arisen as a result of Lord Carysfort's comment during his visit to the Hermitage in 1785 that the English school was not represented in Catherine's collection; Carysfort, who conveyed the order to Reynolds, also brought one from Potemkin, which resulted in 'The Continence of Scipio'.[217] Catherine, however, already possessed paintings by English artists, including a few by contemporary painters. The first paintings came to Russia not through purchase but as an unexpected gift. Richard Paton (1717–91), a successful marine painter who exhibited annually at the Society of Artists between 1762 and 1770, was inspired by the Russian naval victory over the Turks at Chesme Bay in 1770 to paint four huge canvases depicting the battle. These paintings were dispatched to Russia in the summer of 1772; the following year, Paton was informed by the Russian ambassador in London that the empress had put the paintings on public display prior to placing them in her gallery and that she had graciously awarded him £1,000 and a gold medal.[218] The paintings were originally hung in the Hermitage but transferred in 1779 to the Throne Room in the Great Palace at Peterhof, where they were seen in 1790 by a kinsman of Admiral Greig, Andrew Swinton, who commented that 'the Turkish fleet, the town and fortress of Tschesma were totally destroyed, and here they appear still burning upon the canvas!'[219] With her interest in English painting possibly stimulated by Paton's gift, the empress was to acquire in the 1770s a succession of other important canvases, beginning with portraits of George III and Queen Charlotte, painted by George Dance in 1773. In a letter of 12 February 1773 the British ambassador in Russia, Lord Cathcart, had informed the king that Catherine was seeking portraits of both the king and queen and royal princes.[220] The portrait of the Prince of Wales and his brother Henry Frederick by Benjamin West was to follow in 1778 as a personal gift from George III to the empress. All three portraits were soon installed in the Chesmenskii Palace, where they were seen and admired by Baroness Dimsdale, who does not, however, mention Dance's name and attributes West's work to Brompton:

In the Room on the second floor, were Pictures of all the crowned Heads in Europe, the Empress Grand Duke and his first Dutchess were placed at the upper end of the Room, and I was pleased to observe that our King and Queen were hung next to them, very near was a fine picture of the Prince of Wales and the Duke of York, at the Age of eleven or twelve with their hands placed on each others shoulder. This was painted by Brompton, and esteemed a very fine Picture.[221]

At much the same time Catherine – through the agency of the Russian consul in London, Alexander Baxter – was acquiring three paintings by Joseph Wright of Derby. 'The Iron Forge' was bought in London after being exhibited there in 1773 and was joined in the Hermitage collection in 1779 by a pair of landscapes, 'The Eruption of Vesuvius' and 'Firework Display at the Castle Sant'Angelo'.[222] Catherine's patronage of Wright undoubtedly helped the artist to gain more widespread recognition. Finally, it was in 1779 also that Catherine acquired a number of paintings by English artists of the seventeenth and early eighteenth centuries, such as Lely, Dobson and Kneller, as part of one of her most spectacular purchases: after receiving a favourable report on the condition of the paintings from her ambassador and the painter Giovanni Cipriani, she paid £43,000 for the famous collection formed by Sir Robert Walpole at Houghton Hall in Norfolk and offered to her by his impecunious nephew.[223]

The contacts which had been established with Reynolds prompted Catherine to seek his advice on a possible English portrait painter to come to work in Russia. Reynolds suggested the young Thomas Lawrence, who was, however, reluctant to be away from England for more than a year; Lord Carysfort proposed John Hoppner, but in the event neither painter was engaged.[224] It was to be only during Paul's reign that the next English painter made his way to Russia, but from the early 1790s another English engraver was to be found working in the Russian capital.

It is the fate of Joseph Saunders (1773–1845) to be virtually unknown in England or to be hopelessly confused with other Saunders and Sanders working in London in the last decades of the eighteenth century. It is impossible to establish with any assurance his career before his departure for Russia and how or precisely when he was recruited. Redgrave, suggesting that he, in this case John Sanders, was born in London around 1750 and became a student of Bartolozzi, states that he went to St Petersburg, but is imprecise both about dates and what he did; Thieme-Becker supplies apparently correct birth and death dates and describes him as working in the Russian capital between 1794 and 1810; Chaloner Smith and Foskett both identify only a Joseph Saunders working and exhibiting in London from 1772 into the next century.[225] It is only Rovinskii who gives a brief sketch of his career in Russia and, most importantly, lists eighty-five engravings he is known to have executed there. However, giving 1794 as the date of Saunders' arrival in Russia, Rovinskii lists an engraving for the year 1792 but nothing else before 1796.[226]

Saunders produced a number of engravings during Paul's reign, the most interesting of which was perhaps that of Guido Reni's *Roman Charity*, published in 1799. James Walker relates in one of his anecdotes how Count A. A. Bezborodko, who became chancellor under Paul, wanted him to organise the engraving of paintings in his collection and publish them as 'La Galerie de Bezborodko'.[227] The project was not completed because of the chancellor's death in 1799, but Saunders's engraving of a Reni from his collection shows that it had begun. The engraving was, however, to be one of two submitted by Saunders to the Academy of Arts and leading to his election as an Academician on 18/30 August 1800.[228] The second engraving was of Mieris' *The Morning of a Dutchwoman* and was from a painting in the Hermitage, where Saunders seems to have been allowed to work from at least 1796. Saunders was to follow Walker as imperial engraver (*c.* 1802) and his engraving of Mieris was to become part of what was essentially a continuation of Walker's *Collection of Prints* of 1792. In 1805 there was published in St Petersburg (and also on sale at Boydell's in London) the first two volumes of *La Galerie de l'Hermitage*, to which Saunders contributed forty-eight of the seventy-five engravings of paintings as well as engravings of Catherine (after Lampi) and Alexander (after Gérard). Saunders produced engravings of paintings by

Leonardo, Titian, Rubens, Raphael, Van Dyck, Rembrandt, Velasquez, Poussin and many others.[229]

Unlike Walker, Saunders left few portrait engravings – there is one of his patron A. L. Naryshkin, another of the Grand Duchess Ekaterina Pavlovna, and, best known of all, of the Italian architect Quarenghi – but he created in the first decade of Alexander's reign a distinctive niche for himself as the engraver of vignettes for literary and scholarly works. He was also employed from 1805 by the Heraldry Office in the engraving of family crests and assigned a number of apprentices to instruct in the art. It was Gavrila Derzhavin, retired in 1803 from his post as Minister of Justice and with time to devote to the publication of his literary works, who gave Saunders important encouragement. Derzhavin agreed to pay Saunders 2,000 roubles for the vignettes to the first three volumes of his collected works (*Sochineniia*, pts I–III (1808)) and tried him out initially with three vignettes for an edition of his *Anacreontic Songs* (*Anakreonticheskie pesni* (1804)).[230] The Derzhavin circle was obviously impressed by Saunders's ability. In 1806 there appeared seven of his engravings in the *Lyrical Compositions* (*Liricheskie sochineniia*) of Derzhavin's brother-in-law, V. V. Kapnist, and he contributed three vignettes to *The Inexperienced Muse* (*Neopytnaia muza*, 3 pts, 1809–12), the first collected poetry of the poetess Anna Bunina.[231]

It was in 1809 or 1810 that Saunders was appointed Professor of Engraving at the University of Vilna/Vilnius – the second of his Bunina engravings is signed 'J. S. Vilna 1810'. Rovinskii lists a mere two engravings for the more than three remaining decades of his life, which remain a virtual blank page in his biography. Many more blank pages are found in the career of an English miniature painter who, two or three years before Saunders left the Russian capital for Vilna, departed for Philadelphia after a decade in Russia.

At the beginning of August 1797 the Russian ambassador in London, Vorontsov, wrote to St Petersburg, recommending 'm-r Miles, peintre en miniature, qui a peint avec beaucoup de succès toute la famille royale d'Angleterre et qui s'est mis en tête, Dieu sait pourquoi, qu'il ferait une plus belle fortune en Russia qu'à Londres. La princesse Auguste, seconde fille du roi, protégeant beaucoup cet artiste, m'a fait prier par mademoiselle Gomm et m'a fait l'honneur de me prier elle-même de le recommander à l'Impératrice.'[232] Edward Miles (1752–1828), like Walker a native of Great Yarmouth, practised initially in that town before moving to London in 1771.[233] One of his earliest surviving works, dating from that year, is a miniature in Indian ink of the Norfolk doctor and diarist Sylas Neville (now in the Norfolk Record Office) and hailed by the sitter as 'a striking likeness'.[234] The following year Neville records seeing a Miles miniature from Reynolds' painting of Lord Carlisle and adds that 'the young man is much taken notice of by Sir Joshua & I hope he will do well'.[235] It was precisely for miniatures after Reynolds that Miles made his reputation and it may well be that Miles owed to Reynolds not only the royal patronage he enjoyed in England but also the idea of going to Russia. The Empress Maria Fedorovna was soon informing Vorontsov in October 1797 that Miles 'a peint ma fille ainée, il me peint aujourd'hui, son talent est bien agréable, il a très réussi avec le portrait de ma fille'.[236] But a year later, another correspondent wrote to the ambassador that 'le peintre Miles va son petit train. Ce n'est pas un grand talent, et nous avons icy Ritt [August-Christian Ritt, another miniaturist, trained in Paris and St Petersburg] qui vaut mieux que lui. Il parait faire plus de fortune avec la bourgeoisie qu'avec la cour et la haute noblesse.'[237] Information about Miles's remaining years in Russia is scant, although he was there until 1807, and the whereabouts of his paintings of the empress and her daughter is not known.

                                    V

Russian medallic art, to which Benjamin Scott's contribution under Elizabeth has been examined in an earlier chapter, attained a high level of excellence under Catherine. Indeed Catherine herself was anxious that the outstanding events of her reign should be commemorated in medals and she also initiated the great series of medals on subjects from ancient Russian history to complement her own historical researches in 1783–4. Nevertheless, as a collector she did not seek to acquire collections of foreign medals: when she turned down a collection formed by Lord Pembroke, Sir James Harris wrote that 'medals are not to her Imp. Maj. taste'.[238] Much more to her liking were 'pierres gravées': in 1780 she purchased the collection of the British antiquary James Byers on the recommendation of Princess Dashkova in Rome,[239] and followed this with a similar collection belonging to Lord Algernon Percy in 1785,[240] the same year that Vorontsov was requested to acquire the best pieces from the Duchess of Portland's collection.[241] But of much greater significance was her patronage in the 1780s of British masters working in London. Early in 1781 James Tassie (1735–99), the Scottish portrait medallionist and reproducer of gemstones who had moved to London in 1766, received an order from the empress for the full range of his work, complete with specially made cabinets and a detailed catalogue. A satin wood cabinet, made by Roach after a design by James Wyatt and containing 200 drawers, was sent to St Petersburg in September 1782. The collection then stood at 6,076 items and Tassie sent both paste intaglios and white enamel cameos of each. The manuscript catalogue was prepared by Rudolph Eric Raspe (the creator of the immortal Baron Munchausen); in 1791, when the total number of items supplied had reached 15,800, the revised catalogue was printed in two volumes.[242] Tassie had included casts from many of the great European collections as well as from the work of contemporary gemstone artists. Among the latter were William Brown (1748–1828) and his brother Charles (1749–95), whose work Catherine began to acquire from 1786. The Browns, who cut gemstones as both intaglios and cameos, worked almost exclusively during the last decade of Catherine's life to fulfil her orders. The 200 gems which came to the Hermitage represent about one half of their known output; in addition to themes from classical mythology, allegories, animals and historical portraits, they include a specially created Russian series with allegories on the death of Potemkin, the capture of Ochakov, Russian victories over the Turks and Swedes as well as portraits of Catherine.[243] It seems that one of the Browns, almost certainly William, visited St Petersburg, possibly to consult about the Russian series, according to one of Walker's anecdotes,[244] but there is no known corroboration from Russian sources. It is also only in English sources that the visit to Russia of an English sculptor is recorded.

The Russian episode in the long career of Thomas Banks (1735–1805), one of the most noted British sculptors of the second half of the century, occurred during a lull in his fortunes. After years of apprenticeship and study in England, he had gone to Italy, where he spent seven years (1772–9) perfecting his art and producing a number of sculptures on classical themes, including 'The Death of Germanicus' (now at Holkham Hall in Norfolk) and 'Thetis and her Nymphs' (in the Victoria and Albert). While in Rome, Banks produced the model of a statue of 'Cupid', which he carved in marble after his return to London. Short of commissions and without a buyer for his 'Cupid', he decided to take it to St Petersburg in 1781, where, according to the *European Magazine*, 'it was, by the recommendation of Lord Malmesbury and Prince Potemkin, shown to the Empress who purchased it for 4,000 roubles (about 380*l*. sterling), and ordered it to be placed in a building called the Grotto in the gardens at Czarsco-Zelo'.[245] Although available descriptions of Rastrelli's lakeside Baroque pavilion and its contents make no mention of the statue, the suggestion that it was housed there is plausible: in the 1780s the Grotto, then usually known as the Morning Room, was used to display a large collection of vases and sculpture that included Houdon's famous seated 'Voltaire' (1781).[246] Banks remained for a year in St Petersburg, preparing the model of a statue of the Empress for Potemkin, and, according to his daughter's testimony, also executing for the empress herself a bas relief on the subject of the 'Armed Neutrality'.[247] If this were in fact true – and once again there is no other evidence – it would have appealed to Catherine's sense of humour to have a British sculptor prepare a work on the subject of a treaty so antipathetic to the British. Banks returned to England to produce busts of such as Sir Joshua Reynolds, Warren Hastings, Sir

Joseph Banks and Horne Tooke, and commemorative monuments in numerous churches up and down the country, including St Paul's Cathedral and Westminster Abbey (where a tablet to his memory is to be found).[248]

In 1788 Catherine turned to England to acquire a famous collection of classical sculpture, which had been formed over many years by Lyde Browne of Wimbledon. Later that year 230 pieces arrived in Russia and were deposited mainly at Pavlovsk. The Empress agreed to pay £23,000 for the collection, but apparently Browne received only the first instalment.[249] Three years later the Hermitage received its first piece of contemporary English sculpture, a bust in marble of Charles James Fox by Joseph Nollekens.[250] Catherine's admiration for Fox (to whom, incidentally, she had sent a case of firearms in 1785) knew no bounds after his speech in Parliament opposing Pitt's plans to intervene during the 'Ochakov Crisis', and she instructed her chancellor Bezborodko to get her a bust that she could place 'sur ma colonnade entre ceux de Demonsthene et Ciceron'.[251] In fact she placed Nollekens' original in the Hermitage and had a bronze copy made for the Cameron Gallery. The event caused considerable stir in England and gave rise to a cartoon (published on 15 March 1792) depicting, under the title 'The Patriot Exalted', Demosthenes and Cicero attempting to leave their pedestals in their terror at their new companion.[252] The story has an interesting sequel, for when Fox later expressed support for Poland and sympathy for the French revolutionaries, Catherine quickly became disillusioned in her champion. An English visitor in St Petersburg in 1793 was informed that she 'would throw a veil over his bust, which she sent for, if it would not look like an imitation of the French, and that she would even sell but that it was not worth while, for that she could not get thirty roubles for it'.[253]

37a 'The Patriot Exalted'.
Two caricatures, published in London, March 1792, mocking Catherine's removal of
the bust of Charles Fox from the Cameron Gallery.

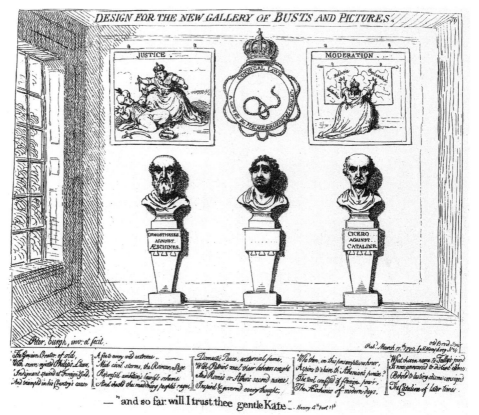

37b. 'Design for the New Gallery of Busts and Pictures'.

8

'OUT OF CURIOSITY': TOURISTS AND VISITORS

⌒

I

By the beginning of the eighteenth century the Grand Tour was well and truly established as a highly recommended, if not an altogether indispensable, part of a young gentleman's education. The classic itinerary took the tourist across the Channel to Paris and south to Italy – and Rome, 'the famousest place in the world and the first motive that induced me to become a travel-ler'.[1] The classic actors in the rite were the scion of a noble house, freshly emerged from public school or, indeed, in fewer cases, from university, and his tutor, more likely than not an Oxbridge don, a man of assumed maturity and probity, a Mentor to an English Telemachus. The pupil was supposedly keen to add a smattering of modern languages, primarily of French, to his school Latin, to refine his taste and broaden his knowledge, and to return to become an enlightened landowner, parliamentarian or leader. The travel-ling tutor, or bearleader, as he was commonly called, was to instruct and guide and to guard his pupil from the perils and snares of the world. Not unexpectedly, the reality frequently fell far short of the ideal. Many a callow youth preferred to tilt the eighteenth-century balance between utility and pleasure decidedly in favour of the latter, when it was interpreted as gam-bling, gallivanting and whoring, while the poor tutor as often found that the world he confronted was very different from the world of books he was accustomed to inhabit. Parents, moralists and critics were not slow to count the costs and enumerate the disadvantages that the tour was seen to bring. Nevertheless the tour survived in its classic form virtually until the end of the century, but not uniquely.

Dr Johnson might still assert in 1772 that Italy and the Mediterranean remained 'the grand object of travelling', but by then travellers had long followed numerous variants on routes through Europe which included many that did not lead to Italy.[2] Young milords and their bearleaders might still be found in considerable numbers in Europe, but there were thousands of other Britons of both sexes and all ages, if not all classes, travelling for a variety of reasons, including health, education, profession or diplomacy. And not only were the British on the move. The aristocracy and gentry of France, Italy and Germany and, later, of Russia were also carrying out their own versions of the Grand Tour that increasingly included England. The watering places of Europe, pre-eminently Spa, as well as the great cities of France, Germany and Austria, the Low Countries and Italy became hosts to international and largely temporary communities. Travel, however, even through the most frequented areas of Europe was fraught with dangers and discomforts. Roads were usually bad, carriages uncomfortable; inns were few and far between outside the big cities and the food and accommodation they offered were of poor standard; robbers abounded in the countryside and thieves were active in the towns; disease was rampant and medical help minimal; wars indeed were ever likely to break out and sever communications. There would therefore seem to be little to entice tourists to stray beyond the usual routes into unknown lands; there could only be worse hardships and greater dangers. Nonetheless, there were always intrepid souls whose curiosity to see the unknown or the exotic overcame their apprehension. Spain and Greece were counted among the countries off the beaten track, although towards the end of the century the numbers of visitors to both increased. The same held true of Scandinavia, Poland and Russia.

Down the century Russia attracted not only British subjects into its service as doctors, technical experts or military officers, not only merchants into the British Factory and chaplains for the British church, not only diplomats and their staff and families to represent British interests, not only governesses, ostlers, craftsmen and performers, but also tourists and visitors, staying for a few weeks or a few months. Not all who fall into this category were Grand Tourists in any strict sense, young men and their bearleaders or adult travellers, doing the sights, before moving on to the next destination on their itinerary; some travelled to Russia to stay with friends or relatives, to become acquainted with the practices of the business community, to pursue a specific investigation or commission, or even to learn the language (rare, but there are interesting examples). Nevertheless, given the nature of the British community in St Petersburg (and to a much lesser degree, in Moscow) and the particular networks of acquaintances available to the visitors, it is not surprising that such differences are hardly noticeable in the extant letters, diaries and notebooks that convey their first impressions and reactions to Russia (or a small and untypical part of it). Greater differences are not unexpectedly to be found between the contemporary published accounts and the materials that remained unpublished or were only published at a much later date. While the unpublished texts have generally an appealing freshness and an unguarded frankness, it was the published accounts that informed the contemporary public and prepared, as it were, the future travellers. At the same time the published works performing this function include writings by more permanent British residents and these will quite properly be given their place in the context of the more specific focus on the patterns of British 'tourism' and the fates and fortunes of individual tourists and visitors.[3]

Peter the Great created St Petersburg and St Petersburg created tourism in Russia. British accounts of pre-Petrine Muscovy, such as those gathered in Hakluyt or later collections, are in the nature of voyages of discovery, of the exploration of a 'rude and barbarous kingdom', from which the advantages might be commercial or diplomatic but hardly cultural. The phenomenon that was Peter the Great, who descended on England at the beginning of 1698, was to change British perceptions of Russia radically, if not overnight. St Petersburg, founded in 1703, became a focus of British interest, particularly when it became first the capital, then the commercial centre of the Russian empire. Its position on the Gulf of Finland and its considerable British community, which included a permanent diplomatic representative and members of the British Factory, made it seem both more accessible and less daunting than Moscow. Stories of the city's rapid growth and beauty began to reach Britain but it was only in 1722, when Anglo-Russian diplomatic relations were already formally suspended, that there was published in London the first enthusiastic and detailed account of Peter's city, together with a plan. Friedrich Weber, the Hanoverian Resident in the Russian capital between 1714 and 1719, describes how, 'when I first arrived there, I was surprized to find instead of a regular City, as I expected, a Heap of Villages linked together, like some Plantation in the West Indies. However at present Petersburg may with Reason be looked upon as a Wonder of the World, considering its magnificent Palaces, sixty odd thousand Houses, and the short time that was employed in the building of it.'[4] He later cites the words of Prince Aleksandr Menshikov that 'Petersburg should become another Venice, to see which Foreigners would travel thither purely out of Curiosity'.[5] A decade after the publication of Weber's book and a year after the resumption of diplomatic relations, there sailed for St Petersburg a contender for the title of the first English tourist.

In May 1733, when George, Baron Forbes (1685–1765) was sent as British envoy extraordinary to begin negotiations for a commercial treaty with Russia, Sir Francis Dashwood (1708–81) took the opportunity to accompany him on board 'the Lowstoft Man of war, of twenty Guns, Commanded by Captain Cotterell'.[6] Dashwood was then a young man of twenty-five with considerable experience of European travel. He had been in France in 1726 and, more recently and ambitiously, he had spent two years on the Continent, visiting Italy but also Constantinople, Vienna and Warsaw. While he was later to assume the title of Baron Le Despencer and become Chancellor of the Exchequer, he was to achieve notoriety by founding in 1751 the Brotherhood of the Friars of St Francis of Wycombe, otherwise known as the Hell-Fire Club. He had indeed been a member of an earlier London hell-fire club in the 1720s and his scandalous exploits on the Continent had long been the talk of the town.[7] Horace Walpole was later to suggest that Dashwood remained true to form in St Petersburg, where, as we have seen, the British Monastery had been scandalously active only a few years before.[8] However, the journal Dashwood has left of his three-week sojourn in St Petersburg in June 1733 is replete with sober observations on the architecture and early history of the city, the state of the army and navy, the Orthodox church, crimes and punishments, and on the personalities at the court. He is obviously intrigued by what he is witnessing and anxious to record both facts and impressions at an interesting stage in the city's history, when its fortunes were beginning to revive after years of neglect under Catherine I and Peter II. As the century wore on, what he sees and describes, whether it be the view of the city along the Neva, the contents of the Kunstkammer, the layout of the Peter and Paul Fortress, or the attractions of nearby estates such as 'Oranyboom, the Country Seat of Prince Mempsicoff', would become the common currency of the tourist account, but Dashwood was essentially first-footing. He is an informed and informative tourist, confessing that 'I am well contented with my journey, and think it very much, worth any curious man's while, going to See, and to Stay there three weeks or a month, but after curiosity is Satisfied, I think one could amuse oneself better, in more Southern Climates.'[9] This is, on the one hand, a fulfilling of Menshikov's prediction; on the other, it is the verdict of a seasoned traveller, anticipating what many tourists would feel about their visit to St Petersburg.

The impression left by Dashwood's diary is a mixed one of immediacy but also of a certain amount of careful fact-finding, witnessed not least in his lists of regiments. While not destined for publication, his notebook was almost certainly circulated among his friends for their edification and instruction. In this respect it is not essentially different from the memoranda and reports prepared around this time and subsequently by British diplomats. Baron Forbes also kept a diary and prepared an 'Account of Russia, the extent, population, produce, revenues, forces, government and court manners, &c' (since lost), which he presented to Queen Caroline on his return to England early in 1734.[10] Earlier, during Peter I's reign, Charles Whitworth (1675–1725), the British ambassador, had compiled a similar report, which was posthumously published as *An Account of Russia as it was in the Year 1710* at the Strawberry Hill Press in 1758.[11] Likewise, John Deane, who had served in the Russian navy between 1712 and 1722 and who had returned to Russia as British consul-general in 1725 but was soon expelled, produced a much more specific 'History of the Russian Fleet during the Reign of Peter the Great', and dedicated to George I.[12] Dashwood's circle also had its strong royal connections in the shape of Frederick, Prince of Wales, in whose household he had obtained a post in 1731, together with Charles Calvert, fifth Lord Baltimore (1699–1751), who was appointed a gentleman of the bedchamber. It was Baltimore who soon emulated Dashwood by making a cruise to St Petersburg on his yacht *Augusta*.

Baltimore's visit was in response to an invitation from the Russian court to attend the marriage of Anna Leopol'dovna and Prince Anton-Ulrich of Brunswick-Bevern-Lüneburg. The *St Petersburg News* duly recorded on 12 June 1739 his arrival, on 26 June his presentation at court, and on 17 July his departure:

with the completion of the festivities here and having seen in the imperial capital everything worthy of note, especially the Library of the Academy and the Kunstkammer, Milord Baltimore yesterday with particular pleasure returned to England, accompanied by Count Algarotti and the two mathematicians, namely, Messrs King and Desaguliers.[13]

As far as is known, Baltimore himself kept no record of the voyage, but it was to have its chronicler in one of his companions, the young Italian poet and scholar Count Francesco Algarotti (1712–64), who had arrived in London from France in 1736. Algarotti soon became a friend of the Russian resident, Prince Antiokh Kantemir, also a poet and scholar. Kantemir's Anglophilia was rivalled only by his love of all things Italian, both of which brought him into close contact with the circle of the Prince of Wales, with whom, incidentally he had had a private audience soon after his arrival in London in 1732.[14] It was undoubtedly Kantemir who helped to stimulate new interest in Russia during his six years as resident and it was he who possibly suggested to the Russian court the invitation for Baltimore.

Algarotti's account of his visit to Petersburg with Baltimore appeared for the first time only in 1759 in Italian, and a decade later in English. It was cast in the increasingly popular form of letters, the first eight of which, constituting the Russian part of their travels, were addressed to John Hervey, Lord Hervey of Ickworth (1696–1743), another long-standing member of the Prince of Wales's circle who rose to be Lord Privy Seal. Algarotti presents a view of the capital that echoes in many respects Dashwood's, particularly the poor state of repair evident everywhere, and gives amusing expression to its greater attractiveness from afar,

we no longer found it so superb as it seemed to us from a distance; whether it be that the gloominess of the forest had ceased to embellish the perspective, or that travellers resemble sportsmen and lovers, I will not pretend to determine.[15]

However, as the full title of the English edition makes clear, there was a marked emphasis once again on 'the state of the trade, marine, revenues, and forces of the Russian Empire', the factual information characteristic of the diplomatic accounts already mentioned, but generally conveyed in a more engaging style.

On the return journey, Baltimore sailed as far as Danzig, where they left the yacht in order to travel by road to Rheinsberg to see the Crown Prince of Prussia, the future Frederick the Great. The point of mentioning this stage of their tour is that they obviously spoke at length with Frederick about Russia and it is in one of Frederick's letters to Voltaire that he gives a rapid character sketch of Baltimore ('un homme tres-sensé, qui possède beaucoup de connaissances') and cites what are in fact his only known comments on his visit to St Petersburg:

Il appelle un Russien un animal mécanique; il dit que Petersbourg est l'oeil de la Russie, avec lequel elle regarde les pays policés; que si on lui éborgnait cet oeil, elle ne manquerait pas de retomber dans la barbarie dont elle est à peine sortie.[16]

If the image seems to some extent familiar, it is because a variant has gained wide currency: it is the window on Europe, incorporated by Pushkin in his *Bronze Horseman*, where he notes 'Algarotti said somewhere: "Petersbourg est la fenêtre par laquelle la Russie regarde en Europe."'' He was referring to the opening lines of Algarotti's fourth letter to Hervey, dated 30 June 1739, which in the French version of 1769 read in fact 'Je vais enfin vous parler de cette nouvelle ville, de cette grande fenêtre, ouverte récemment dans le Nord, par où la Russie regarde en Europe.'[17] Algarotti's words lack the sense of superiority that pervades Baltimore's view of both Russia and the Russians, but taken together, their remarks reflect the sort of discussions their visit to Russia stimulated.

In the years following the Baltimore/Algarotti visit, there are glimpses of other British tourists making the journey to St Petersburg, such as Richard Meggot, 'whose curiosity brought him to see this country' in 1740, in the words of Edward Finch, the British minister in St Petersburg. The letter was addressed to Lord Harrington, the principal Secretary of State, whose younger son William Stanhope (1719–43) also spent a few months with Finch during the summer of 1740.[18] The curiosity about Russia continued to be strongest in government circles and it was to be the sons of Sir Clement Cottrell, the master of ceremonies to George III, and of John, Lord Carteret, soon to become Earl Granville and Secretary of State, who set out on 14 July 1740 on what was very much a variant of a Grand Tour. Charles Cottrell (1720–79) and his friend Robert Carteret, styled Lord Carteret (1721–76), were indeed accompanied by a seasoned bearleader in Johann Caspar Wetstein, who had been tutor to Lord Dysart in Italy in 1728 and who was, incidentally, to become librarian to the Prince of Wales. They were to be away some fifteen months and their movements and activities may to some extent be followed from twelve letters Cottrell wrote to members of his family between 20 July 1740 (from Elsinore) and 22 September 1741 (from Holland). Their family connections and letters of introduction ensured a warm reception in the Russian capital, where they arrived on 30 July. The English minister introduced them to the empress' favourite, Ernst Bühren (Biron), the Duke of Courland, and also to Count Burchard von Münnich. A day later they kissed the empress' hand and continued their social whirl. It seems that later they made an excursion to see the Ladoga canal and were also at Peterhof, but the three letters that Cottrell wrote from St Petersburg convey little other than court and society gossip. The travellers intended to leave St Petersburg early in November but in the event set out only at the beginning of January 1741, when snow and hard frosts made the journey by sledge possible. But it was a delay that allowed them to witness the funeral procession of the late Empress Anna on 12/23 December and add the macabre detail that 'she had lain in state a month but not having been rightly embalmed was almost fallen to pieces before her burial'.[19] Their route from St Petersburg took them via Narva to Königsberg, Danzig, Dresden, Vienna, Pressburg (where they witnessed Maria Teresa's arrival to be crowned Queen of Hungary), Munich, Basel and back through Holland. The most informative letter as regards Cottrell's reaction to Russia was the one he wrote to his brother Robert from Basel in August 1741. He gives his only impression of the Russian capital, but it is a striking one:

The Dutch may brag that Amsterdam is built out of the water, but I insist that Petersburg is built in spite of all the four elements, Earth, air, water, and fire; the Earth is all a bog, the air commonly foggy, the Water sometimes fills half the Houses, and the fire burns down half the Town at a time, the Houses being for the most part built of wood.[20]

Most remarkable in the letter are, however, his characterisation of Anna ('that incomparable Princess') and her court and his account of the fall of Bühren, the regent, in November 1740.[21]

The visits of Dashwood, Baltimore and Cottrell during the reign of Anna established the tradition of British visits prompted primarily, if not in all cases uniquely, by curiosity. Regrettably, they are not matched by similar sources for the ensuing reign of Elizabeth, although references are to be found, for instance, to visits by Bruce Brudenell, Lord Bruce of Tottenham, as part of a wide-ranging tour of Holland, Germany and Scandinavia in 1754 and by Richard Woodward and Richard Combe in 1756.[22] An unexpected variant on the purely tourist visit was, however, to be provided by William Willes (1732–1815), son of the Bishop of Bath and Wells. A year after leaving Wadham, Oxford, he arrived in St Petersburg in May 1751 with letters from John, Earl of Granville (John Carteret's father) for Baron Wolff, the British minister resident, and the Rev. Daniel Dumaresq, the Factory's chaplain, in

which it was said that 'the intention of his journey is to learn the Russian
language perfectly, he being imployed in public business here, to the carrying
on of wch the R. language is necessary'.[23] Dumaresq, who had refrained from
learning the language because of 'too great a Confusion in a Person of my
Age, who has a Smattering of several other languages', was nevertheless
spurred to try and at the end of June wrote that 'it is now about a Month,
since I began to learn Russ with Mr Willes'.[24] Willes stayed some eight
months in all before setting out on a return journey that took him home via
Königsberg, Danzig, Berlin, Dresden and Hanover. He was later to remark
that 'in my Expedition I had an Opportunity of seeing the Russian, Saxon, &
Prussian courts, but ye former for Grandeur & Magnificence has (I think)
by far ye Preeminence'.[25] He then went to Oxford 'for two terms' and was
soon dreaming of a tour to Portugal. He was, however, to join the Post
Office's Deciphering Branch (answerable to the Secretaries of State), where
his elder brother Edward was already working and of which his father had
indeed been chief decipherer for many years before he became Bishop of Bath
and Wells in 1734.[26] It would seem that the 'public business' to which the
Earl of Granville referred was very much of a secret nature. In 1764 Willes
retired and, like his father before him, devoted himself to church matters as
rector of a Wiltshire parish and as Archdeacon of Wells. We can only surmise
that he was able to use his knowledge of Russian during his work as a
decipherer. At all events his retirement coincided with the return from St
Petersburg of a young man who certainly did employ his Russian to good
effect in service most secret.

John Maddison (1742–1808) was sent at the end of 1762 'by the King's
express commands to St Petersburg to learn the Russian language, as he
already understood the German. He arrived there in the midst of that winter,
and accomplished the task so as to return hither in the spring of 1764.'[27]
There is no information about his studies or sojourn in Russia, but on his
return he joined the Post Office, of which his uncle, Anthony Todd, was
the foreign secretary. Maddison worked in the Secret Office where foreign
correspondence was intercepted and copied. It was said of him in 1772 that:

he has constantly attended the dispatch and arrival of mails at the General Post Office,
to copy the Russian letters, there being no person ever before that time for it; nor is there
yet, except his brother, to whom he taught the language. In the course of these eight
years he has made out three of the Russian Minister's cyphers; two in their language,
and one in French.[28]

Maddison succeeded his uncle as foreign secretary in 1787, but when this
post was abolished in 1793, he continued as the head of the Secret Office,
while 'disappearing' from the list of acknowledged officials. Maddison, a shy
and retiring bachelor, was an assiduous collector of coins – and books. In

1809, some three months after his death, there began a twenty-two-day sale of over 5,000 of his books which were described in *Bibliotheca Maddisoniana: A Catalogue of the Extensive and Valuable Library of the Late John Maddison*. It included some 130 titles in Russian, mainly published during his years in St Petersburg. Their fate is unknown and, regrettably, there are no copies of most of them in British libraries.[29]

None of the visitors to Russia during the reigns of Anna and Elizabeth published accounts of their travels. Although information about Russia circulated among certain circles, the curiosity of the wider public at this period was possibly whetted – but far from satisfied – by a very few works emanating not from tourists but from other categories of British residents in Russia. In the interval between the visits to St Petersburg of Dashwood and Baltimore a certain Mrs Elizabeth Justice had sailed out from London and away from her husband, convicted of stealing books in Cambridge, to spend three years as a governess to a British merchant's family and had returned home. In 1739, the year Baltimore sailed with Algarotti for Russia, her *Voyage to Russia* appeared in an edition of 600 copies. For the first time an English author provided the reading public with an often naive and strongly prejudiced but always entertaining account of Russian customs and habits, covering dress, food, pastimes, weather, religion, festivals, funerals and marriages, interspersed with comments on the city and on the court, seen from somewhat lower down the social scale than usual. A second edition was published in 1746, augmented by four further letters, in which Mrs Justice was even freer with her criticisms. She suggests, for instance, that 'the Ladies are, or can be, just what you please. For, only say, what Complexion you like, and they will instantly put it on; being well versed in Painting'; she evinces particular disdain for Russians in service: 'as for their Servants, they are the most ignorant Creatures living, and have every thing which attends Ignorance, that is, Ingratitude, Dirt and Sauciness; and are, in my Opinion, far inferior to a well-taught Bear'.[30]

Mrs Justice's employer, Hill Evans,[31] was a member of the British Factory, as were the authors of two accounts published during Elizabeth's reign. James Spilman's dry and brief *Journey through Russia into Persia* (1742) and Jonas Hanway's much more extensive and wide-ranging *Historical Account of the British Trade over the Caspian: with the Author's Journal of Travels from England through Russia into Persia; and back through Russia, Germany and Holland* (1753) are both devoted to questions of British exploitation of the Persian silk market. The wider significance of Hanway's, if not Spilman's, work lies in the description of towns along the trade route and in the information he supplies about Russian history and society, including some interesting remarks about St Petersburg itself. However, when he disarmingly admits, prior to embarking on his 'short account of the city and court', that 'nothing is more common than to be ignorant of that which we have had a good opportunity of learning, but particularly in the instance of an accurate inquiry into things relating to a place which a man considers as his home',[32] there seems little reason to disbelieve him. Not until the reign of Catherine II, however, were there other examples against which to test the generalisation.

II

Catherine's reign was a watershed in many aspects of Anglo-Russian relations, not least in the availability of publications about Russia for the British reader, produced in response to a marked increase of interest in that seemingly not so distant and not so barbarous country.[33] That the interest was not only in contemporary Russia is seen in the popularity of at least two of three works appearing in the 1760s and 1770s that are concerned with earlier reigns and complement the accounts of Mrs Justice and Hanway. It is pertinent to note that all three authors were still alive and had been back in Britain for decades before seeking to publish. Samuel Johnson once remarked of Hanway that he had 'won some reputation by travelling abroad, but lost it all by travelling at home', but for John Bell he had nothing but praise.[34] Bell, whose years in Russia covered 1714 to 1746, and his fellow Scot, John Cook, who worked in Russia from 1735 until 1751, were medical practitioners whose careers have been described earlier (chapter 4). The accounts they published of their extensive travels with embassies and armies in the south and east of Russia belong more obviously to the genre of exploration than of tourism, but within a decade or two tourists would begin to diversify their itineraries. Possibly, the travels of Bell and Cook, together with translations, such as Krasheninnikov's *History of Kamtschatka* (by James Grieve, 1764) or Georgi's *Russia* (by William Tooke, 1780), helped to stimulate the sense of adventure. But for most, St Petersburg was exotic enough. A series of endlessly gossipy and anecdotal but nonetheless valuable letters from the British resident's wife in the Russian capital during Anna's reign, appeared only in 1775 and anonymously as *Letters from a Lady, who resided some years in Russia, to her Friend in England*. The reviewers were quick to establish her identity, which was at the time of publication Jane Vigor (1700–83), widow of a Russian merchant. She had, however, gone out to Russia in 1728 as the wife of Thomas Ward, the British consul-general, and on his death in 1731, she married within months Claudius Rondeau, the British resident (for whom Bell, incidentally, worked as secretary and whom Elizabeth Justice described in reverential terms 'from below'). Again widowed in 1739, Mrs Rondeau returned to England with Vigor, whom she married in 1740.[35]

The unknown editor of the letters of Mrs Ward/Rondeau/Vigor added a number of footnotes, sometimes giving information about the subsequent fate of some of the Russian notables mentioned in the text. Reference was made on one occasion to *Cursory Remarks Made in a Tour through some of the Northern Parts of Europe, particularly Copenhagen, Stockholm and Petersburgh* by Nathaniel Wraxall (1751–1831), which had been published earlier that same year of 1775. Indeed, a second, 'corrected' edition also appeared in 1775 with the title already changed to the less diffident *A Tour through some of the Northern Parts* ... A third edition followed in 1776 (as well as a Dublin pirate edition) and a fourth and final 'corrected and augmented' edition as late as 1807 with a new title, *A Tour round the Baltic, thro' the Northern Countries of Europe, particularly Denmark, Sweden, Finland, Russia, & Prussia*, giving it an importance and comprehensiveness it scarcely deserves. Wraxall's *Tour*, however, was undoubtedly popular and it has a particular place as the first *published* account of a visit to Russia of a British Grand Tourist travelling, pen in hand. The twenty-three-year-old Wraxall already had behind him two years' service in India with the East India Company and a tour of Portugal when he set out on his voyage to the north in April 1774. In the first of his 'letters' he writes the apologia for his travelogue.

It must likewise be confessed, that the survey of nations and view of foreign and dissimilar modes of acting and thinking to our own, is not only formed to enlarge the human mind, and correct its early prejudices, but is calculated to charm and delight in a supreme degree, as it has for its basis two passions most powerfully conducing to pleasure, I mean novelty and admiration.[36]

He goes on to suggest that one must be prepared, however, to go further afield nowadays in search of the novel and 'the unpolished gems [that] only glitter in the eye of clear and perspicuous observation':

Such are the kingdoms which I am about to visit, covered during many months with snow, and wrapt in all the horrors of a polar winter: unpolished in their manners, and still retaining the vestiges of Gothic ignorance, they present not many charms to tempt the traveller. The Roman arms never penetrated into these inhospitable climes, nor is the Antiquarian allured to pass their snows by the venerable remains of amphitheatres, temples, and naumachiae. Yet even in these remote and inclement kingdoms, are the seeds of knowledge scattered; and if the mind receives no pleasure from the reflection of their past greatness or refinement, yet may it be enlarged and improved from the consideration of their comparative power and importance in the scale of Europe. I purpose, as you know, to visit the three northern capitals, and to spend some small time in each, though probably more in St Petersburg than in either of the other two, as I regard it by far the greatest object of true curiosity. (pp. 4–5)

Wraxall eventually arrived in the Russian capital at the beginning of July and was to stay just a month. His impressions are contained in a mere two letters (out of a total of eighteen), although there is some relevant Russian material in the subsequent three letters, assigned to Narva, Riga and Mittau. He is honest enough to say at his departure that 'of the genius, manners, and real character of the Muscovites, I neither pretend nor can possibly know any thing from the short stay I have made' (p. 264). He further regrets that he has not been outside the capital to Moscow – and beyond, indeed, he dreams of returning and travelling via Kazan to Astrakhan and on to Constantinople. For all the inevitable superficiality of much that he writes – and the generally unsystematic way in which he presents his impressions – there emerges a genuine admiration for St Petersburg, 'where every month adds to the beauty and magnificence of this new-born metropolis' (p. 266). There are other aspects of the work and several passages which a contemporary English reviewer found illuminating and perceptive.

The *Critical Review* first highlights Wraxall's 'astonishment at beholding a city, which had risen, as by enchantment, within the memory of men still alive'[37] and returns at intervals to his comments on the vast scale of the architecture, on the spaces to be filled in the city ('this city is yet only an immense outline, which will require future empresses, and almost future ages, to complete', Wraxall writes (p. 231)), and his response to the river Neva:

Along its banks is beyond all doubt the finest walk in the world. It is not a quay, as vessels never come up to this part, but a parade, running a mile in length; the buildings on which are hardly to be exceeded in elegance. (p. 244)

Wraxall's account of his visit to Peterhof for the celebrations in connection with the anniversary of the empress' accession is quoted at length. This includes one of the first British eye-witness descriptions of Catherine, in which Wraxall turns from admiring her famous equestrian portrait by Eriksen to see the empress entering the great hall of the palace:

I felt a pleasure corrected with awe as I gazed upon this extraordinary woman, whose vigor and policy, without any right of blood, has seated and maintains her in the throne of the Czars. Though she is now become rather corpulent, there is a dignity tempered with graciousness in her deportment and manner, which strikingly impresses. (p. 201)

The reviewer was most taken, and rightly, with the pages Wraxall devotes to Peter I. To write extensively about Peter was virtually to become *de rigueur* for any publishing tourist, but Wraxall was among the first to reflect not merely the habitual eulogy of the hero of the enlightenment but also the doubts and misgivings associated in Catherine's time above all with such as Prince Shcherbatov and somewhat later with the Slavophiles. He presents the arguments of those he terms 'the impartial and discerning few, who can divest themselves of prejudice, and view objects free from the blaze which usually dazzles and deludes the multitude' within inverted commas over some six pages (pp. 217–23), but the reviewer is inclined to see them as Wraxall's own. The eleventh letter is a remarkable document and is wholly devoted to the Petrine theme, for in the second half Wraxall provided the first description of the Bronze Horseman and his conversations with the sculptor Falconet (pp. 224–30). This anticipates by two years the Rev. William Tooke's compilation, *Pieces by Mons. Falconet and Mons. Diderot on Sculpture in General, and Particularly on the Celebrated Statue of Peter the Great Now Finishing at St. Petersburg* (London, 1777). On balance the *Critical Review* is justified in 'recommending the work to the perusal of such readers as are desirous of information relative to the northern parts of Europe. The traveller has everywhere described his route with clearness and energy, and his Remarks, though entitled Cursory, are extremely judicious.'[38] A century later, a Russian historian certainly thought so, arguing that Wraxall's account had been unjustly overlooked and that there were many passages (including, incidentally, most of those cited by the *Critical Review*) that merited serious attention.[39]

Within weeks of the book's appearance Dr Johnson had perused it and advised Mrs Thrale that 'Wraxel is too fond of words, but you may read him'.[40] A few years later, Wraxall, characterised as 'a very agreeable ingenious man', was to be found in the learned doctor's company, together with George Macartney, the former ambassador to Russia and author of *An Account of Russia, MDCCLXVII*, produced for private circulation in 1768.[41] Although the talk on this occasion was not, as far as is known, about Russia, Johnson often spoke with Boswell in these years of 'our scheme of going up the Baltick' and Boswell was to regret that he himself had not insisted:

Besides the other objects of curiosity and observation, to have seen my illustrious friend received, as he probably would have been ... by the Empress of Russia, whose extraordinary abilities, information, and magnanimity, astonish the world, would have afforded a noble subject for contemplation and record.[42]

If the venerable Johnson was not to be received by Catherine, there was an increasing stream of milords and gentlemen who were. Horace Walpole, who had no love for the empress, noted sardonically that 'we have had two or three simpletons return from Russia, charmed with the murderess, and believing her innocent, because she spoke to them in the drawing-room'.[43] Among them, as Walpole probably knew, was none other than Frederick Calvert, sixth Lord Baltimore (1731–71), who was visiting St Petersburg not only exactly thirty years after his father but also precisely in the year when the English translation of Algarotti's description of that voyage was published.

The sixth Lord Baltimore had spent a lot of time abroad, particularly in Italy, where the celebrated Winckelmann was to dismiss him as 'one of those worn-out beings, a hipped Englishman, who had lost all moral and physical taste'.[44] It was from Italy that he journeyed to Constantinople on a tour that was to give rise to his first and best-known work, *A Tour to the East, in the Years 1763 and 1764* (London, 1767). This is a curious ragbag of a book, which, in Walpole's opinion, 'no more deserved to be published than his bills on the road for post-horses'.[45] Part of it, the fourth section entitled 'A Journey by Land from Constantinople, through Romelia, Wallachia, Bulgaria, Moldavia, Poland, and Germany, to England in the Year 1764', was, however, to appear in Russian translation in 1776, long after Baltimore himself had been to Russia. He had slipped away from England after his surprising acquittal on a charge of rape, considering it prudent to visit distant lands where his title might still command some respect and deference. On 3/14 July 1769 the British ambassador Lord Cathcart reported that 'Ld Baltimore arrived here last week from Sweden, I had the honour to present him to the Empress who was pleased to receive his Ld extremely graciously'.[46] There was no whiff of scandal here and Baltimore's visit would have disappeared without a trace, if he had not decided to celebrate it himself.

In the September 1769 issue of the *London Magazine* there appeared a letter to the editor from someone signing himself 'Musaphilus' and including a poem in Latin, 'which is written by a noble lord of this country, now on a tour through the north, and was lately presented to the empress of Russia at Petersburg, and received most gracefully'. There were in fact two poems: the first, entitled 'Reliquenda sunt palatia' and dated 26 July 1769, is devoted to a description of Peterhof and its fountains and the empress' reception of foreign envoys and guests, and its sequel, untitled and dated 7 August 1769, to a description of the palace of Tsarskoe Selo and a hair-raising run over the 'flying mountains' in the grounds.[47] The following year these poems and others appeared in a wierd and wonderful volume, so rare that it is found in very few of the great libraries of the world and so unrevealingly titled that it has escaped the attention of all bibliographers of travel literature to which in many respects it belongs. *Gaudia Poetica. Latina, Anglica, et Gallica Lingua Composita A° 1769* was printed for the author in the summer of 1770 in Augsburg: Baltimore had presumably gone to Germany from Russia and was later to travel to Naples, where he died the following year. The quarto volume is magnificently produced and has many inset engravings of high quality (several of Russian scenes), as well as decorative head and tail pieces of a mainly allegorical nature. A dedication in Latin hexameters to the Swedish botanist Linnaeus, whom Baltimore had visited on his recent tour, is followed by a prologue justifying the use of Latin (and Greek) in preference to modern tongues and then follow four 'Carmina', entitled 'Carmen itinerarium', 'Upsala', 'Palatia', 'Sarscocello' and 'Venatio', and the correspondence between Linnaeus and Baltimore. Baltimore also provided English and French prose versions of the poems.[48] *Gaudia Poetica*, the pretentious production of an eccentric English aristocrat, is a mere curiosity, adding little but another title to the literature of the Northern Tour and in no way ousting Wraxall's account from the niche assigned to it earlier. It is interesting, however, that Baltimore's descriptions of the imperial palaces and of the Eriksen equestrian portrait in particular are a direct anticipation of Wraxall's. At least Baltimore did not attempt to versify his impressions of the Russian bath-house, which Wraxall termed 'a sight rather excitive of disgust than desire, and to which only curiosity could ever have led me'.[49]

Curiosity had a lot to answer for, and the British tourists dutifully trooped off to bath-houses to observe, to linger – and to commit to paper their outrage and disgust.[50] The British naval captains John Jervis, later Earl of St Vincent (1735–1823) and Samuel Barrington (1729–1800), also to become an admiral, were in St Petersburg at the same time as Wraxall, and Jervis records in his diary that they witnessed 'such a monstrous Scene of beastly Women and indecent men mix'd together naked as our first parents without the least appearance of Shame, as to shock our feelings'.[51] Naval matters, however, expectedly loom large in Jervis's record of their month's stay in Russia: they were particularly attentive at Kronshtadt, managed with great difficulty to get into the Admiralty in St Petersburg, where they met Lambe Yeames, the venerable shipbuilder, and went on board a yacht, designed by Sir Charles Knowles. They did the usual round of palaces, buildings and estates, and were almost exclusively in the company of the British ambassador and of members of the British Factory, whom they found hospitable and admirable. Like so many unpublished diaries of this period, Jervis' remains valuable for its occasional detail of people and meetings and events (i.e. the Te Deum on the Peace with Turkey in the Kazan Cathedral on 14 August; the visit to William Gomm's house at Krasnoe Selo; John Bush's work at Pulkovo) rather than for its penetrating observations or profound meditations on the Russian character, autocracy and the church. The latter were to be the province of the publishing traveller, of whom Wraxall was the first but, soon, far from the only representative. However, there are two travellers from an increasing number heading northwards in these years who merit some attention for what they wrote, or in one case, failed to write.

John Henniker (1752–1821), later 2nd Lord Henniker, recently down from Cambridge and also in his twenty-third year, had much in common with Wraxall, not least in fashioning a travel journal from letters. 'A

Northern Tour in the Years 1775 and 1776 through Copenhagen and Petersburgh to the River Swir joining the Lakes of Onega and Ladoga in a Series
of Letters' was enlivened with his own coloured sketches mainly of village
scenes and modes of transport, and was, it seems, originally intended for
publication. Henniker, however, soon gave up the idea and the album stayed
within the family until it was sold, along with most of the library at
Thornham Hall, before World War II: it has recently come to Cambridge.[52]
The work is notable for the use for the first time, as far as is known, of the
description 'northern tour' and for the extension of the usual itinerary into
new regions. Henniker seems originally to have planned merely a voyage to
Copenhagen, but once there decided to proceed to St Petersburg. Ill-health
was to prevent him from going on to Moscow in July 1775 to see the 'triumph' arranged for Field Marshal Rumiantsev following the end of the
Russo-Turkish war and he had to be content with witnessing, and describing
vividly, the celebrations in the capital.[53] He 'did' the obligatory sights of
Petersburg and environs, but it is an excursion that he made in the company
of Timothy Raikes, a prominent member of the British Factory, that is of
particular interest. Henniker and Raikes travelled by boat up the Neva to
Lake Ladoga and then left Ladoga by the River Svir'. He inspected mills
belonging to another British merchant, William Glen, and then a factory
established by Raikes himself on the Uslianka river, a tributary of the Svir'.[54]
Henniker's interest in this area is possibly explained by the fact that his
grandfather, John Henniker of Rochester (1691–1749), had been a Russia
merchant and was considered perhaps the most significant importer of masts
for the Royal Navy in the early decades of the century.[55]

Two years after Wraxall and a year after Henniker, but for a similarly
short summer period, Patrick Brydone (1736–1818) made his way to St
Petersburg as the most distant point on a round trip from Berlin via Warsaw.
About seventy sides of a small notebook are covered with his unsystematic
and generally disapproving impressions of Russia in August 1776,[56] but
more, much more, might have been expected from his pen. For Brydone was
already the author of A Tour through Sicily and Malta (1773), a runaway
bestseller that went into numerous editions and French and German translations by the end of the century.[57] He had seen service in the Seven Years'
War and indeed it seems that he wore his uniform on occasion in St Petersburg. A graduate of St Andrew's University, he had already won his spurs
as a travelling tutor in the late 1760s to William Beckford of Somerly in
Suffolk, to whom he addressed the letters that describe his tour of Sicily, and
he was to continue to perform that function not only in Sicily but also later
on the Continent for the sons of Lord North. In his fortieth year when he
arrived in St Petersburg – and a Fellow of the Royal Society for his writings
on electricity – he had been hailed in the Monthly Review as 'the gentleman,

the scholar, and the man of science: a rational observer, a philosophical enquirer, and a polite and pleasing companion'.[58] He obviously considered Russia unworthy of his gifts and found little to commend outside the British community, whose congenial company he enjoyed. He acknowledged Peter's immense contribution but reflected that 'since the so much boasted civiliz-ation of this nation I have never heard an instance of any Native whose name has been distinguished in the world for any fine art or science'. Indeed, 'barbarism' is never far beneath the surface and the Orthodox Church is an 'absurdity', while he evinces on more than one occasion sympathy for the plight of the serfs. He is most complimentary about the gardens of the Naryshkins and at Tsarskoe Selo in the new 'English' taste, while finding the statuary of Peterhof 'hideous' and disliking the architecture of the Winter Palace.

All that one might have expected from Brydone's pen is, however, to be found in the work of another lowland Scot, William Richardson's disarm-ingly entitled *Anecdotes of the Russian Empire* (1784), albeit purveyed in the fashionable epistolary form. By the time *Anecdotes* appeared, Richardson (1743–1814) had been professor of humanity at the University of Glasgow for over a decade, but when the letters were originally written, he was tutor to the sons of the British ambassador Charles, Lord Cathcart. He was only a travelling tutor in the sense that he sailed out to Russia in 1768 with the Cathcart family and returned with them in 1772, but his four years were essentially sedentary with almost no visits outside the capital other than to Kronshtadt and imperial estates. Nevertheless, in his writings about the 'Rus-sian condition', he achieved an intellectual depth and perspicacity that seem to give the lie to his limited geographical horizons and his modest stated aim of 'conveying such information as might be useful or amusing to his Readers'.[59]

The fifty-six letters that comprise the volume are in no sense homogeneous. In his 'Advertisement' Richardson points out that his work was 'A publi-cation in which a very close method is not proposed' and that several letters are included simply because 'they were written during the time he remained in Russia' (p. viii). Letters with translations of German poetry, letters with his own poetic effusions, a tediously long letter on the abdication of the king of Sardinia in 1730, and even letters supplied by other correspondents do not obscure the very real significance of what Richardson writes about Russia. There are a number of letters on events in the Russian capital that are precisely located in time, rich in detail, and retain the immediacy of the eye-witness account. 'I am just returned from witnessing the ceremony of the Empress's laying the foundation-stone of a church dedicated to St. Isaac', he begins his letter of 19 August 1768 (p. 15); 'I was lately present at a meeting of the deputies summoned by the Empress from all the nations of her empire, and who have been assembled to assist her Majesty in forming a system of legislation' (p. 28) is the introduction to his unique description of a working session of the Legislative Commission. He is present at the service of thanksgiving for the empress' recovery from the smallpox inoculation administered by Dr Dimsdale; he describes the funeral of a Princess Kurakina; he sees a prize-giving in the Academy of Sciences and a performance of a Russian tragedy by the young ladies of the Smol'nyi Institute. He is in Russia in dramatic times – he describes, for example, the outbreak and progress of the war with Turkey in a number of letters; and he communicates news about the plague in Moscow and the murder of Archbishop Ambrosii.

The importance of *Anecdotes*, however, lies not, or not primarily, in these letters but in others which are in the form of essays or meditations on subjects of perennial interest. Such is the sequence of letters, beginning with Letter XXVIII, entitled 'The Slavery of the Russian Peasants', and continuing to Letter XXXIV, 'National Character of the Russians', and later letters, particularly Letter XLV, 'Concerning the Progress of the Feudal System in Russia'. Richardson exhibits an awareness of Russian history and of the interplay of economic, social, religious and cultural factors that was rare in foreign commentators. His analysis is frequently bleak, but he seems to believe that Catherine (of whom, incidentally, he provides one of the more insightful pen portraits (pp. 19–20, 23–6)) is generally and sincerely committed to improving the lot of her subjects. He has no doubts, however, about the perniciousness of the existing system and in particular of serfdom's corrosive effects on character. With respect to the peasants, he poses the following questions: 'Exposed to corporal punishment, and put on the footing of irrational animals, how can they possess that spirit and elevation of sentiment which distinguish the natives of a free state? treated with so much inhumanity, how can they be humane? I am confident that most of the defects which appear in their national character, are in consequence of the despotism of the Russian government' (p. 197). Richardson may be the first, but certainly not the last, to modify a classical line to emphasise his own inspiration and allegiances: 'O fortunatos nimium, sua si bona norint, Britannos!' (p. 200). The intonations and implications of much that he writes from a British standpoint, nevertheless, anticipate by a few years what a Russian, Aleksandr Radishchev, was to write, and suffer for.

A contemporary reviewer might opine that 'whether owing to the important light in which a stranger is frequently apt to regard the affairs of a foreign country, or to the desire of furnishing a volume, we cannot help being of opinion that he [Richardson] has extended these Letters far beyond the bounds to which they were entitled, either from their novelty, or the nature of the information they contain',[60] but for modern commentators, *Anecdotes* 'is a cogent and thorough account of Russia, presented with an unusual degree of sophistication', 'a skeletal framework for a really synthetic interpretation of a whole society, taking into consideration, although in varying proportion, economic, intellectual, religious, and political influences'.[61] As a result, *Anecdotes* has stood the test of time and merited its re-issue in 1968, although in its own day it did not go into a second edition or even attain the dubious reward of a Dublin pirate edition and was not quoted or referred to as an authoritative source. That distinction was awarded to the work of another tutor, this time very much a travelling one.

III

The year 1784 was something of an *annus mirabilis* for the appearance not only of Richardson's *Anecdotes* but also of the little-known *Observations on the Present State of Denmark, Russia and Switzerland* by Thomas Randolph, which was published anonymously and also referred back to the 1770s, and, most significantly, of the Reverend William Coxe's *Travels into Poland, Russia, Sweden, and Denmark*. When the *Critical Review* said of Randolph that 'we think that the author, without any detriment to information, might have withheld these Letters from the public; for they contain little of any consequence, that is not generally known', it had the authority of Coxe's volumes, published earlier that year, very much in mind.[62]

Coxe (1747–1828) simply overwhelmed both reviewers and public. Of all the accounts of travels in Catherine's Russia, Coxe's was the best known, most quoted, most frequently republished and certainly the longest. The first two volumes of the first edition appeared in 1784 and were followed by two further editions in 1785 and 1787, before the first edition was itself completed in 1790 by a third supplementary volume. Two further rearranged and expanded versions in five volumes were published in 1792 and 1802. Finally in 1803 there appeared a sumptuous three-volume set in an edition of fifty copies for private distribution and representing his envoi to Russia. Coxe became more or less the Russian Baedeker of the eighteenth century, and not only for the British – translations in German, French, Dutch, Swedish and Italian followed; people would take his bulky volumes with them on their own journeys; travellers would test their own impressions against his and check the accuracy of his observations; aristocratic mothers, indeed, would follow from afar their sons' progress by reference to the work and its maps.[63] It even made an impact of sorts on the Empress Catherine. In May 1785 she was urged by her correspondent J. G. Zimmermann to acquire the German translation which was the first to appear: 'Elle [i.e. Catherine] a trouvé un historien qui dans un style nerveux, simple et rempli de gout parle d'Elle et de Son règne comme on le doit.' Catherine did not disagree, adding that 'Mr. Coxe, dont vous me parlès, a été deux fois en Russie; il vient de

38 Rev. William Coxe (1747–1828). Watercolour by unknown English artist.
(National Portrait Gallery, London.)

nous quitter tout récemment, il m'a donné son ouvrage que j'ai feuilleté; il
m'a paru dire les choses telles qu'il les a appris, cependant il se trompe
quelques fois, mais c'est de bonne foi'.[64]

Catherine was referring to the second visit Coxe made to the Russian
capital (and to a second audience she had graciously granted him) between
November 1784 and April 1785, when once again he had assumed the
mantle of travelling tutor, on this occasion to a young man just down from
Cambridge, Samuel Whitbread II (1764–1815), son of the founder of the
famous brewery. The materials gathered during this trip gave rise to the third
volume of the first edition that appeared in 1790, but the tomes through
which the Empress deigned to leaf were the fruit of his first trip as tutor to
George, Lord Herbert (1759–1827), son of the Earl of Pembroke. Herbert,
Coxe and a Captain John Floyd (1748–1818), who was appointed to look

after the young milord's physical well-being during their travels but with whom Coxe did not always see eye-to-eye, entered Russia from Poland in August 1778 and proceeded via Smolensk and Moscow to St Petersburg, where they were to remain until February of the following year. The travellers had spent nearly three years on the Continent before heading for Poland and Russia and were then to go to Sweden and Denmark and down to Italy. It was there that Coxe left his charge and returned to his Cambridge college, where he was soon at work on the first of his three works on Russia.

Already in 1780 there appeared the substantial and important *Account of the Russian Discoveries between Asia and America*, which was devoted to subjects of considerable interest both for Russia and its European competitors: exploration and trade, the discovery and exploitation of new resources and new markets, particularly in the eastern parts of Russia, in China and along the west coast of America. Coxe had been greatly assisted in his researches by the historian G. F. Müller, whom he had met in Moscow, and he also acknowledges his indebtedness to fundamental works published by other Russia-based German scholars such as Georgi, Gmelin and Pallas. Professor Peter Pallas, indeed, in a letter to the British naturalist Thomas Pennant speaks of Coxe, 'a very ingenious & inquisitive Man, who is about extracting part of my Itineraries which I make no doubt he will send to England to be printed'.[65] By the beginning of 1781 Coxe had published a slimmer but no less interesting *Account of the Prisons and Hospitals in Russia, Sweden, and Denmark*. This work was dedicated to the famed philanthropist and prison reformer John Howard, from conversations with whom Coxe said his attention had been turned to prison conditions and who was himself at that time on his way to Russia. Coxe supplies detailed descriptions of prisons and hospitals in Moscow, Tver', Vyshnii Volochek, St Petersburg and Kronshtadt and records his thanks to his informants, including the British ambassador Sir James Harris 'for the readiness with which he assisted and promoted my researches'.[66] Harris for his part was to write of the 'many very tiresome moments his interrogatory disposition exposed me to'.[67] The empress was also on the receiving end of Coxe's enquiries and he is fulsome in his praise for her readiness to grant him an audience and to supply written answers to some specific queries. Further praise and the text of Catherine's answers were to be included in *Travels*, which appeared early enough in 1784 for him to take her a presentation set, as we have seen.

In presenting his work to Catherine, Coxe obviously considered that his picture of her Russia was basically a positive one and hardly likely to give offence, even to an empress notoriously quick to ridicule what foreigners might write of her country. By comparison with Richardson's broadsides, Coxe's criticisms are comparatively moderate. He is not slow to condemn serfdom, point out malpractices and highlight inadequacies in the laws, but he tries everywhere to be objective, to understand what might appear at first strange and unattractive, to praise when he feels it is merited. His analysis is underpinned by a basic optimism, by a belief that enlightenment is spreading, if excruciatingly slowly, but he is well aware that the masses will long remain virtually untouched. At various times and in differing contexts we read: 'their progress towards civilization is very inconsiderable, and many instances of the grossest barbarism fell under our observation' (of life in villages near St Petersburg); 'it is impossible even for a monarch, however inclined to protect merit, or for a few of the nobility who follow such an illustrious example, to diffuse a love for the works of art among a people who must first imbibe a degree of taste, which can only be acquired by experience' (on the Academy of Arts); 'the civilization of a numerous and widely dispersed people is not the work of a moment, and can only be effected by a gradual and almost insensible progress' (on the ineffectiveness of Petrine reforms); 'if it be allowed that many evils have been reformed and many improvements introduced, it cannot at the same time be supposed that the national manners should be suddenly changed or that the most absolute sovereign can venture to shake those fundamental customs which have been sanctioned by ages' (on Catherine's reform programme); and, as a final verdict, 'it may be perceived, that, though proceeding towards civilization, they are still far removed from that state; that a general improvement cannot take place while the greater part continue in complete vassalage; nor can any effectual change be introduced in the national manners, until the people enjoy full security in their persons and property'.[68] It may have been the greater delay in progress than ever Coxe imagined that made *Travels* 'a strictly forbidden' book in Nicholas I's reign, according to the testimony of the journalist Nikolai Grech.[69]

When he is not seeking to lucubrate, Coxe reveals himself to be an attentive observer, conveying accurately and often entertainingly what he and his companions encountered on the road, at posthouses, in villages and towns. There is much here that is new to published British accounts, and, surprising though it may seem, Coxe is the first to provide a detailed description of the old capital Moscow, where they spent two weeks and received generous hospitality from Count Aleksei Orlov in particular. Coxe is always anxious, however, to expand the travel diary into the travel guide and plunders the best authorities available in French and German for historical, geographical and literary information. The tutor who passes on information to his pupil transforms himself into the Cambridge don, reading a course of lectures to the British public on the history of Russia, particularly its rulers, on the development of Anglo-Russian trade, on the Russian literary scene and the rise of the theatre, and on the freezing of mercury. The public was obviously very prepared to be instructed; shortly after his death *Blackwood's Magazine* could hail him as 'the accomplished and famed traveller of Cambridge. He is a most favourable specimen of English travellers, and does honour to the great University of which he was a distinguished ornament.'[70]

A close study of the various redactions of Coxe's travels would reveal the immense amount of amplification, rearrangement and rewriting that took place over some twenty years. In 1780 Sir James Harris had confided to Lord Herbert that Coxe 'with all his admirable qualities, distinguished so little between what is to be said and what is to be secret, that I fear he will promiscuously publish all he knows'.[71] In the event Coxe was the soul of discretion, and he withheld information and the identity of several of his sources until death or the historical moment allowed him to disclose them. His prefaces to the fifth and sixth editions are particularly revealing in this respect. Among the informants whose assistance he could, however, freely acknowledge from the very first edition were Wraxall and Captain Floyd. Floyd had thought long and hard about publishing his own account, but by May 1781 had 'given up all thoughts of appearing before the publick in the shape of *Letters from a Traveller to his Friends in England* & I send Coxe my Journal'.[72] Coxe, however, makes no mention of another Englishman, who not only supplied him with materials gathered during his own travels in Russia but also read at least part of the proofs of the first edition.[73]

Reginald Pole Carew (1753–1835), a graduate of University College, Oxford, who had succeeded to the Antony estate in Cornwall in 1772, left on extensive European travels at virtually the same time as Herbert and his tutors, but arrived in the Russian capital only in November 1780, some eighteen months after their departure. He took rooms in the house where Samuel Bentham, who had been informed by his brother of Pole Carew's imminent arrival, was then living. The two soon became fast friends and Samuel described him as 'a man certainly of great abilities a vast stock of knowledge from all opportunities I have had of judging, of a most excellent heart'.[74] Pole Carew remained in St Petersburg until July of the following year before heading for Moscow and then south to Kherson. He was back in England by the spring of 1782 and soon entered upon a long parliamentary career, strongly supporting, incidentally, Pitt during the Ochakov crisis.

Jeremy Bentham had advised his brother that Pole Carew was 'very assiduous in informing himself of everything',[75] and his archive provides ample evidence to demonstrate his systematic inquiry into many aspects of contemporary Russia. It is possible that Pole Carew would have published his own account of 'the present state of Russia', but abandoned such an undertaking on learning of Coxe's plans. There is a succession of documents, varying in length and in degree of completion, that cover such subjects as 'Manners & Customs of the Russians', 'Population in Russia', 'Interiour [sic] Government', 'Manufactures', 'Agriculture', 'Revenues, Taxes, etc', 'Bank', 'Mines',

'Learning' and 'Of the Church'. In some cases Pole Carew never progressed beyond a heading, such as 'Arts in Russia'. What he did write on most subjects, however, is informative and in an English context, frequently original.

His remarks on 'learning' are particularly worthy of note, concerned as they are almost exclusively with the conditions of the parish clergy.[76] He argues that

it were to be wished perhaps for the Advantage of Learning in Russia that the Lot of the Lower Clergy were ameliorated. It is necessary that there should be a Body of Men in every State whose particular Profession & whose Interest it be to preserve what is thought worth preserving & to cultivate what may be profitable to ye Publick to see cultivated.

However, the Russian clergy

are vilified to ye last Degree & his annual Portion is so small that the Poorest Peasant lives better than he can; he must even labour like the Peasant to better his Situation, & must be beholding to ye Peasant for what the latter can or will spare to assist him, & he is too happy when the former will suffer him to Eat & Drink under his Roof, which the greater Part do to Excess.

In other parts of Europe it is the clergy who 'promote the Cause of Learning'. If Peter I had carried out his school programme and encouraged literature and learning to greater effect in all towns and parishes, the 'Parish Priests would have been so many Professors who with a small augmentation of their Salaries, from the Revenues once belonging to yr Clergy, would have worked more change in fifty years, than will be produced in the Present Situation of things in Fifty Ages'. It seems likely that his informant on such questions was Andrei Samborskii (1732–1815), the remarkable Anglophile Ukrainian who had recently returned to Russia after many years as chaplain to the Russian Mission in London.[77] Samborskii was also a noted agronomist, a passionate devotee of English practical agricultural methods. It was Samborskii whom Pole Carew specifically identifies and quotes in his detailed examination of the state of agriculture in Russia.[78]

Pole Carew was indeed well served by knowledgeable informants, both English and Russian. His wish to visit southern Russia and the Crimea was undoubtedly encouraged by friends who had recently been there, Samuel Bentham and William Eton, a merchant experienced in trade on the Black Sea, but above all by Prince Potemkin. Pole Carew was frequently in the company of the Prince, visiting estates and factories belonging to him in and around St Petersburg. When he went to Moscow, Potemkin supplied him with a list of things to see, including yet another of his own estates. Among Pole Carew's papers there is a remarkable document which begins with a description of 'an ordinary Dinner' he attended at Potemkin's, where he was regaled with 'exquisite & rare Dishes' and fine wines, and follows with a characterisation of 'This Extraordinary Man & voluptuous Favourite, [who] is possessed with very great abilities & very little Application; endowed with a Prodigious Memory, which has been enriched with a pretty copious Reading in his earlier years when he is said to have been destined for the Church, & his Knowledge of & Taste for the Greek Language to have been gained at that Time, a most quick & rapid Conception of whatever is presented to him, great & solid Views in Politicks, some perhaps Romantick Ideas relative to the Extension of the Empire . . .'[79] Writing to Potemkin from Kherson in October 1781, Pole Carew would seem himself to have been affected by, or to affect, similar romanticism, giving vent both to his love of things Greek and to his Turcophobia. He also described with enthusiasm a trip he had paid to the Crimea, which could not but benefit, he opined, from the protection of 'une Souveraine aussi sage, aussi benevole qu'Elle est magnanime'.[80]

On his return to England and entry into parliament, Pole Carew drew up a memorandum, dated 16 April 1782, that attempted to survey and analyse Russian foreign policy and strategies in the wake of the Declaration of Armed Neutrality of 1780 and against the background of Russian aspirations in the Black Sea. It was perused by the new Secretary of State for Foreign Affairs, Charles James Fox – and it was again disinterred in 1791, when it was read by Charles Grenville, Secretary of State at the time of the Ochakov crisis.[81] In the interim another British MP, Sir John Sinclair (1754–1835), had paid a rapid visit to the north during the seven-month parliamentary recess between June 1786 and January 1787, taking with him numerous letters of recommendation, including one from Semen Vorontsov, the Russian ambassador in London, for his brother, the head of the Commerce College, which introduces him as 'd'une naissance très distinguée, membre du parlement, mais encore plus distingué par son caractère et son savoir; il y a peu de personnes qui jouissent d'une estime aussi universelle que lui'.[82] Back in London, Sinclair also immediately produced a report destined to guide and influence political thinking on Russia, but unlike Pole Carew, he had his account privately printed for distribution among ministers and colleagues under the title *General Observations Regarding the Present State of the Russian Empire* (1787).[83]

General Observations provides a virtual counterpoint to Pole Carew's memorandum and other writings, and includes 'sections' entitled 'Of the Character and Manners of the Russians', 'Of the Government of Russia', 'Of Its Late Acquisitions, the Crimea and the Kuban', 'Of Its Accession to the Armed Neutrality', etc., as well as concise pen portraits of influential ministers and dignitaries at Catherine's court, the most extensive of which is devoted to Potemkin. Sinclair's view of him is more negative than Pole Carew's, emphasising that 'on the whole, with great abilities, he is a worthless and dangerous character, and will stand at nothing to procure any object he may have in view'.[84] The last section, 'Of the Conduct to be Observed by Britain towards Russia', reveals the particular context in which Sinclair's work was sited. In the year Sinclair left for Russia the Anglo-Russian commercial treaty of 1766 was due to expire, but Prime Minister William Pitt had rejected Russia's new proposals for its renewal. Virtually coinciding with Sinclair's return to London was the signing of a first commercial treaty between France and Russia on 11/22 January 1787, and in April, when that treaty was ratified, Pitt allowed the Anglo-Russian agreement to lapse. It is likely that Sinclair's arguments proved influential in that unfortunate decision. While not opposed in principle to a new agreement, Sinclair suggested that 'our best chance of obtaining an advantageous treaty of commerce with Russia, is to prove that we can make ourselves independent of it, either by raising at home the articles we draw from it, or procuring them from other countries'.[85]

The energetic Sinclair, who had spent a month in St Petersburg, chose to travel home via Moscow and down through the Ukraine as far as Kiev before turning into Poland. He did not get down to New Russia, as Pole Carew had done. It was from here that an English traveller came whose route had crossed with Sinclair's in Moscow in September 1786. Sir Richard Worsley (1751–1805), a Fellow of the Royal Society and the Society of Antiquaries, had set out from Rome in February 1785 on unusually extensive travels through the Levant that took him first to Athens. He saw much of Greece before proceeding to Constantinople, via Rhodes and Cairo. As he went, he collected statues, bas-reliefs and gems for the great collection that was to be displayed at his home on the Isle of Wight and registered in the sumptuous publication known as the *Museum Worsleyanum* (1794–1803). He was accompanied throughout his journey by Willey Reveley, his draughtsman, who prepared for him drawings of antiquities and views. It was in Constantinople on 4 May 1786 that Worsley met Elizabeth, Lady Craven (1750–1828), who had recently arrived after travels through Russia and who, according to her own account, 'obtained for him a permission to go in the frigate, that brought me hither, to the Crimea'.[86] Worsley, now without Reveley, duly arrived in Sevastopol at the beginning of June and was immediately placed in quarantine for a fortnight before beginning his Crimean tour, which he records with his customary succinctness. On 8 July Worsley left the Crimea 'and set off for Kioff, Moscow & St Petersburg by the Way of Cherson & the Ukraine', a journey that was to take until 17 October.[87] It was punctuated with quite lengthy stays in Kiev, where he was constantly in the company of Edinburgh University graduate Prince Pavel Dashkov, at Krichev, Prince Potemkin's estate in Belorussia, where Samuel Bentham had recently been joined by his brother Jeremy (travelling virtually the same route

39 Sir John Sinclair (1754–1835). Oil painting by Thomas Lawrence.

as Worsley), and in Moscow. He was in fact in Moscow for three weeks and his diary is interesting mainly for the descriptions of the personalities, Russian and British, whose hospitality he enjoyed, rather than for new information on the city. Indeed, such was the authority of Coxe's description that Worsley writes: 'Mr Coxe having published a very accurate account of the city of Moskow, to which I think little alteration can be made, I have here transcribed it' (f. 197). The two months Worsley spent in St Petersburg are covered in a mere five sides of his diary (out of a total of 155 devoted to the Russian part of his travels). A few laconic remarks on the various buildings in the city apart, Worsley is mainly content to write 'D^{itto}' to indicate the passage of days. He does, however, record his presentation to Catherine on 22 October and adds, two days later, that she and Potemkin 'staid two hours to see my drawings' (f. 205). The empress herself mentioned the visit to Baron Grimm and the French ambassador Ségur also noted the interest aroused by Worsley's (or rather Reveley's) Egyptian drawings.[88]

IV

Lady Craven's itinerary had been the reverse of Worsley's. She was also the opposite to Worsley in being a publishing traveller. While his diary was very obviously kept as an *aide-mémoire*, her letters to the Margrave of Anspach were equally obviously written with an eye to their future publication. Her introduction might carry the usual disclaimer that she was publishing 'merely to oblige many of my friends; who, knowing that I had taken a long and extraordinary journey, have desired me to give some account of it', but from an early age she had indulged her literary bent with a flood of poetry and dramas.[89] When she did publish, *Gentleman's Magazine* was ungentlemanly enough to suggest that she 'never wrote a line' of the letters that comprised her *Journey through the Crimea to Constantinople* (1789).[90] She was to incorporate much of the material in the memoirs she published two years before her death and spelt out in full the names she had earlier suppressed or designated merely by initials. Not that by nature the beautiful Lady Craven was ever discreet or free from the attentions of the then 'tabloid press': long parted from her husband, after being caught *in flagrante* with the French ambassador to the Court of St James's, she embarked on her travels with Henry Vernon, a grand nephew of Admiral Vernon, while writing letters to her 'brother', the Margrave, whom she was to marry in 1791. It was undoubtedly her reputation rather than her literary gifts (although she writes with some style and panache) that ensured the quite astonishing popularity of her *Journey*. The London edition was reprinted within months and there also appeared in 1789 a Dublin pirate edition and a German and at least two French translations. A Dutch translation appeared in the following year and there were further French editions by the end of the century, when another English edition appeared, this time in Vienna.[91] What is even more extraordinary was the appearance of a Russian translation (via the French) in 1795.

Lady Craven's book is misleadingly entitled, perhaps deliberately so. The period covered by the sixty-eight letters is from 15 June 1785 to 30 August 1786, as she travels from Paris to the south of France, then on to Italy, Austria, Poland, before arriving in St Petersburg at the beginning of February 1786. After little more than two weeks in the Russian capital, from where her letters are full of the social chit-chat more often found in unpublished letters and journals, she travelled to Moscow and then south to the Ukraine and New Russia. Two letters are date-lined St Petersburg and two, Moscow

40 Lady Elizabeth Craven (1750–1828) and the Margrave of Anspach. Engraving (1789) for the *Town and Country Magazine*.

(Letters XXXII–XXXV). Of these letters, the first refers to the journey from Warsaw to St Petersburg and the third and fourth contain not a single reference to Moscow. Lady Craven had in fact become totally obsessed with the Crimea. It is evident from one of her letters from St Petersburg that she had originally intended to do the northern tour, to turn into Scandinavia, but instead 'I shall now prepare every thing to visit the Crimea or rather the Tauride; I have been told it is a very beautiful country; and I confess I am not sorry this *enfant perdu* gives me a good excuse for turning my steps towards Constantinople' (p. 177). Letter XXXV becomes a treatise on the history of the Crimea, adapted from some conveniently acquired account, and 'Notwithstanding all that has been said to deter me from continuing my tour, I shall certainly go on, and if I am not poisoned by the waters in Tartary, or drowned in my passage by the Black Sea to Constantinople, I shall, I hope, afford you some amusement in the geographical descriptions I shall give you' (pp. 202–3). Her next letter is dated 12 March 1786 from Kherson, and she was to remain in the south, principally in the Crimea, for a month before crossing to Constantinople and proceeding to her ultimate destination, Vienna, via Greece and Romania.

The title of her book promises far more than it delivers, but it would seem that the emphasis on the Crimea was one of the reasons for its popularity.

In fact, only some forty pages (or approximately one tenth of the book) describe a journey through the Crimea and they are not distinguished by any profundity or fine detail. She is, however, enthusiastic about what she sees, admires the natural beauty and advantages of the peninsula, and passes on some observations about the appearance and customs of the local inhabitants. She writes:

Though I have not been absolutely all over this peninsula, I think I am perfectly acquainted with it, and though it is a new acquaintance to me, I sincerely wish it to be peopled by the industrious, who may restore to it that commerce and opulence, which the natural productions of it demand from the hand of man. Can any rational being, dear Sir, see nature, without the least assistance from art, in all her grace and beauty, stretching out her liberal hand to industry, and not wish to do her justice? Yes, I confess, I wish to see a colony of honest English families here; establishing manufactures, such as England produces, and returning the produce of this country to ours . . . (pp. 248–9)

This was undoubtedly written in ignorance of one of Potemkin's more hare-brained schemes, dating precisely from this period, to create a colony of deported British convicts in the region.[92]

Craven was also penning her letter at a time when 'the only account of the Krimea ever given to the [British] publick' was being published in *Gentleman's Magazine*.[93] Succinct and far more informative than Craven's rhapsodies, it was said to be the work of a British Captain P*, who had just returned from the region, and it was edited for publication by the Rev. William Tooke, the British chaplain in St Petersburg. Tooke, who himself got no nearer to the Crimea that Azov, remarked with some justice that it was 'now so much the subject of conversation'.[94] An indication of that interest was the reprinting of the essay on the Crimea in the *Annual Register* in 1787,[95] the year Catherine made her famous progress through her new territories and stayed at the palace of Bakhchisaray, which Craven had seen being prepared for her. Craven's *Journey* nevertheless remained the only description of a visit to the Crimea by a British traveller published in book form in the eighteenth century. By the time it appeared, the Crimea was no longer open to the tourist, for in August 1787 the Porte had declared war on Russia. One Englishman did plan, however, to get to the Crimea at this period. He got as far as Kherson in October 1789, but it was in Kherson that he was to die in January the following year.

John Howard (1726?–90) was of course no ordinary traveller. As he sternly and characteristically wrote in the introduction to his famous *State of Prisons* (1777): 'The journies were not undertaken for the traveller's amusement; and the collections are not published for general entertainment, but for the perusal of those who have it in their power to give redress to the sufferers.'[96] It was in the third edition (1784) of that work that he was able to include impressions from a first visit he paid to Russia in the last months of 1781. It will be remembered that William Coxe had dedicated his *Account of the Prisons and Hospitals in Russia, Sweden, and Denmark* (1781) to Howard, who was responsible, he said, for directing his attention to prison conditions. Inevitably, what Coxe saw and described anticipates Howard's own notes and indeed on one occasion Howard refers his readers to Coxe for further details.[97] Nevertheless, Howard was very much his own man, and a man quite different from the Cambridge don. Howard spurned the court and let it be known that his 'Object is not to see Great People', the empress included.[98] Not without pride Howard wrote to a friend that 'I have unremittedly pursued the object of my journey and have lookt into no palaces or seen any Curiosities – so my letters can afford little entertainmᵗ to my friends . . .'.[99] During that first visit he stayed in St Petersburg for three weeks before travelling on to Moscow and then back to England via Poland. He visited hospitals and prisons and institutions such as the Smol'nyi Institute for Young Noblewomen. His descriptions of Russian prisons are generally far less harrowing than many he provided of conditions in Great Britain and Europe and he was delighted to find no incidence of gaol-fever in Russia.

In the second half of the 1780s Howard's attention was directed to problems of plague-control and conditions in lazarettos. He once more set off on extensive travels throughout Europe, which involved his own confinement for forty-two days in a lazaretto. In July 1789 he embarked upon what was to be his last journey, taking him eventually to Russia. At the beginning of September he was in St Petersburg, having earlier inspected the various prisons and hospitals in Riga. He toured most of the institutions he had seen on his first visit, noting improvement and deterioration. He was particularly saddened to discover that the prison at Kronshtadt which the recently deceased Admiral Greig had promoted had never been built and that the marine hospital was squalid and inadequate. In Moscow he wrote that 'the Hospitals are in a sad state: upwards of 70 thousand sailors and recruits died in them last year. I labour to convey the torch of Philanthropy into these distant regions, as in God's hand no Instrument is weak, and in whose presence no flesh must glory.'[100] That torch he was to carry south, for his plans to travel through Poland and then Hungary were changed by the possibility of taking a ship under a neutral flag from the Crimea to Constantinople. He was also persuaded by news of 'the sickly state of the Russian army on the confines of Turkey, where I hope to do some good; and I shall first, with them fairly try the powders of Dr. James'.[101]

The depressing and often harrowing scenes of disease, filth and death he encountered in the south – at Kremenchug, Kherson, Bogoiavlenskoe and Nikolaev – were recorded in his letters to friends and in his journal, whence extracts were incorporated by the editors in the posthumous second edition

41 John Howard (1726–90). Oil painting by Mather Brown.
(National Portrait Gallery, London.)

(1791) of his *Account of the Principal Lazarettos in Europe* (first published in 1789). Conditions bore no comparison with those under the direct gaze of 'the benevolent Empress': 'the abuses of office are glaring, and I want not the courage to tell them so'.[102] These words occur in a remarkable letter, in which he also relates how, having been robbed of his trunk and hat-box while travelling to Kherson, he tracked down the 'banditti', caused them to be apprehended, and eventually recovered his belongings intact. He also speaks of his intention to visit the naval hospital at Sevastopol in the Crimea and 'to take possession of some poor Turk's deserted house' for two months or so.[103] Unlike Pole Carew, Worsley and Craven, Howard saw the unhappy consequences of the Russian annexation.

In December 1789, while treating a young noblewoman, Howard contracted the fever that was to end his life. Indignant during his lifetime at the intention in England to erect a statue to him, he specifically sought to avoid all pomp at his death and demanded 'qu'on l'inhumât cinq jours après sa mort dans un champ inculte, distant de cinq vestes environ de Cherson'.[104] Although his wishes were carried out to the letter as to the place and manner of his burial, it was a vain hope that he would not be immortalised by monuments both in his native land (in London at St Paul's Cathedral) and in Russia. His burial mound in Dofinovka (the estate of his French friend Dauphigné) was soon surmounted by a stone pyramid, and in Alexander I's reign an impressive cenotaph was erected before the new prison building in Kherson. His grave in turn became a place of pilgrimage and a number of later British travellers have left detailed accounts of their visits and their emotions.[105]

If British interest in the Crimea was one possible reason for the success of Craven's book, the fact that its author was a woman was another. That the lady in question had a somewhat colourful reputation only added to the interest. Hearing that Lady Craven was in the Russian capital, Horace Walpole made a connection and comparison that would not have escaped others: 'I have lately received a letter from the Lady at Petersburg . . . Petersburgh I think a very congenial asylum; the Sovereign has already fostered the Ducal Countess of Bristol – for in the family of Hervey double dignities couple with facility. Formerly our outlaws used to concentrate at Boulogne; they are now spread over the face of the earth.'[106] Walpole was here referring also to another lady whose exploits in England and St Petersburg easily eclipsed Elizabeth Craven's and who had left Russia for the last time just two years previously. She was universally known as the Duchess of Kingston, a title to which she probably had least claim and reflected only in Walpole's allusion to 'ducal'. Born Elizabeth Chudleigh in 1720, she married secretly in 1744 Augustus Hervey, but was to contract a bigamous marriage in 1769 with the Duke of Kingston (d. 1773). For this she was brought to trial in 1776, found guilty and only escaped branding on the hand by the fact that the fortuitous death of her legal husband's brother had given her the right to the title of Countess of Bristol and exemption as a noblewoman from the penalty. Immediately after her trial and on the very day that the heirs of the Duke of Kingston procured an order of *non exeat regno* against her, she slipped away to Calais, where she was to elaborate plans to visit Russia and exert her charms on the great Catherine.[107]

The duchess decided that she must arrive with due style in the Russian capital. During a clandestine visit to London in March 1777 she ordered a sumptuously appointed yacht, complete with dining-room and drawing-room, large kitchen and, apparently, a picture gallery, and she sent to Thoresby Hall for furniture, ornaments and china to fit it out in the grand manner. In due course she set sail under a French flag with a French crew, but spiritually comforted by her English chaplain, the Rev. John Forster, who, as mentioned in an earlier chapter, had visited Russia in 1745 as chaplain to the Earl of Hyndford. It was Forster who took it upon himself to send a letter to *Gentleman's Magazine*, describing the duchess' reception in St Petersburg.[108] After receiving the duchess at Tsarskoe Selo Catherine subsequently bestowed on her 'the highest mark of distinction, by placing her on her right' – at the theatre. 'The Empress had the goodness to express to the Duchess the pleasure she had in seeing her, adding, that she hoped to have the happiness to see her again in Russia. Indeed so many honours were never paid in this court to any person whatsoever.' The duchess responded by arranging for 'a magnificent entertainment' on her yacht. 'As soon as dinner was served, a band of music, composed of fifes, drums, clarinettes, and French-horns, played some English marches, and other pieces suitable to the occasion. After dinner there were some concertos on the organ, which is placed in the antichamber.' The Rev. William Tooke, however, expressed the generally negative attitude of the British community, when he commented: 'the duchess, instead of exhibiting that dignity of behaviour and elegance of manners which might have been expected from a person of such exalted rank, seemed at times by ostentatious displays of her wealth, to rival the entertainments of the palace; and at others, behaved with such servility and meanness, as to excite universal contempt'.[109] Universal curiosity rather than contempt was, however, dominant during the duchess' first visit. The *St Petersburg News* carried reports of her trial earlier in the year, but the Petersburg *beau monde* was fascinated rather than scandalised, particularly as the empress seemed well disposed towards her English guest. Catherine wrote to Baron Grimm shortly after the duchess' arrival that 'ce n'est pas l'esprit qui lui manque', and added amusingly that 'elle me trouve fort aimable, mais comme elle est un peu sourde et que je ne puis élever la voix fort haut, elle n'en profitera guère'.[110]

The duchess' visit in the summer of 1777 was designed to be impressive and short. The grand exit was, however, thwarted by the great storm and flood which hit Petersburg at the end of September. The duchess' yacht, which had quickly become a tourist's sight, was severely damaged. Although the repairs were carried out swiftly and at the empress' expense, the duchess decided to return overland, given that it was already November. Her chaplain, who had managed to be left behind, later informed Jeremy Bentham that 'the difficulties She met with upon ye Road are not to be expressed. Her Coach alone weigh'd three Tons, and was oblig'd frequently to be dug out, when twenty Horses could not move it. But Vanity and Obstinacy are the most shining parts of her Character.'[111]

In the summer of 1779 she was back, sailing into Petersburg with an escort of Russian warships kindly arranged by her admirer, Count Ivan Chernyshev, former ambassador to London and now vice president of the Admiralty College. She soon acquired a house in the capital, described by her English head gardener from Thoresby to his friends in distant Nottinghamshire as 'fitted up . . . in the most Elegant manner possible Crimson Damask hanging, Do. Window Curtains, Most splendid five Musical Lustres! Grand Organ, plate, paintings! and other ornaments displayed to the greatest advantage'.[112] She was nonetheless far from satisfied with a town house, however lavishly appointed, and aspired also to a country estate in emulation of the Russian aristocracy. An estate overlooking the Baltic near Narva was duly purchased in 1781 and renamed 'Chudleigh' or 'Chudleiskie myzy'. Once more the Thoresby estate was ransacked: furniture, plants, trees, farming implements, cows and dogs were brought (and, by mistake, the silver from the local parish church) and a young Lincolnshire farmer by the name of Richard Maws was hired to be her steward. Unfortunately, the duchess' hopes for the estate were never fully realised. There was much to do and much was indeed done, but it never became quite the place of elegance she intended and instead came to be associated by her contemporaries more with the vodka distillery that she had been ill-advised to set up in the grounds. The remains of this distillery apparently survived until the October Revolution and, together with eight cannons, bearing her cypher, and the huge anchor from her yacht, were posterity's only reminder of the duchess' life there.[113]

The duchess was perpetually on the move. She was back in Calais from July 1781 until the summer of the following year. By July of 1783 she was writing to the empress 'to be allowed to go to Carlsbad to take the waters without delay'. Catherine for her part was becoming increasingly impatient with the duchess, to whom she referred slightingly as 'Kingstonsha' ('the Kingston woman') and dismissed with the words 'let her go where she pleases'.[114] The duchess returned to Russia for the fourth and last time in 1784 and left finally at the beginning of 1785. She was to die in Paris in 1788, after drawing up a will two years earlier in which she asked to be buried in St Petersburg, should she die in Russia, 'so that her remains should stay in the place to which in her lifetime her heart was constantly attached'.[115]

An English visitor to the Russian capital might write in August 1784 that 'the Dutchess of Kingston is sunk into neglect, nobody thinks of her',[116] but memories of her were to remain strong for decades. Immediately following her death there was a spate of generally scurrilous 'authentic' biographies and accounts. One even appeared in Russian translation in Moscow in 1793. References in it to her life in Russia were highly inaccurate, but much was made of the fact that 'Milady became a supplier of vodka' ('postavshchitsa vodki') on her estate.[117] British travellers frequently evoked her name and adventures when they passed near that estate on their way to or from St Petersburg.[118] Elizabeth Craven, travelling the route in February 1786, was not among them, but some five years earlier, another itinerant English lady,

42 Elizabeth Chudleigh, Duchess of Kingston (1720–88).
Engraving by unknown artist.

Baroness Dimsdale, indeed spoke and breakfasted at a posthouse with the
duchess, who was on the way to France, and was invited to proceed to Chudleigh, where she and her husband 'lay very comfortably in her Ladyship's
Bed, every part of the Bedstead was Iron, and the Furniture white Dimity'.[119]
Baroness Elizabeth Dimsdale, third wife of Catherine's famed English
inoculator, was on her way to St Petersburg, where her husband was to treat
the Grand Dukes Alexander and Constantine. She belongs to the comparatively rare breed of British women travellers in eighteenth-century Russia,
among whom Lady Craven could claim to be the only one seeking publication of what she had written, while others were content to keep their jour-

nals to themselves and their close circle.[120] Baroness Dimsdale has now joined the ranks of published, rather than publishing, ladies with the appearance of the journal she wrote over 200 years ago. The extant copy of the journal is not in the Baroness' hand and incorporates material that she gathered to augment the original day-to-day impressions. A note by a niece of the baroness (dated July 1853) suggests that the original was destroyed 'as it was feared it might in those days get into print in some way or other'.[121] The charm and novelty of the baroness' diary lie on the one hand in her personality and circumstances and, on the other, in the privileged view she had of life at Tsarskoe Selo in particular.

Despite the ring of her title, Baroness Dimsdale was a most unlikely candidate as a chronicler of European travel, the very antithesis of a Lady Craven. The baron was already sixty-eight when he and the forty-eight-year-old spinster-daughter of his cousin William Dimsdale of Bishops Stortford married early in 1781. Within months Elizabeth found herself whisked from the obscurity of English provincial life and pitched into a new and often bewildering world that was to involve visiting a succession of foreign lands with their strange customs, conventions, and food and bring audiences with a king, various dukes and duchesses and, finally, with the Empress of Russia. There is a somewhat malicious anecdote in James Walker's *Paramythia* about the last of those occasions, when the baroness, 'more to be admired for the warmth of her honest feelings, than her knowledge of the graces, etiquette, and forms of a court', 'instead of half kneeling to kiss the hand held out with so much grace, flew towards her like a tiger, and almost smothered the poor empress with hugging and kissing'.[122] The incident is possibly apochryphal; certainly, the baroness's account of her meetings with the empress is somewhat different, but there are several occasions in the journal where she reveals herself as not knowing precisely what to do or what was 'agreeable to my Quality' (p. 66). The view of the *ingénue*, and a middle-aged one at that, rather than of a sophisticate is a distinctive attraction of the baroness' journal.

Although her journal as a whole is of interest and enlivened by fresh and unexpected comments, it is the Russian section, where the diary form is abandoned for a series of jottings and impressions covering many disparate subjects and with few indications of date, that contains valuable and in certain respects unique information. Inevitably the baroness visits and describes the main tourist attactions in the Russian capital, but there is a strong sense of recording what particularly strikes her and of omitting 'many more things too tedious to mention' (p. 42), as she comments during her tour of the Kunstkammer. Many of her entries reflect her 'housewifely' concerns with the costs of meat and of cloth, and of hiring and running houses, with the preparation of food and recipes. The Dimsdales arrived in St Petersburg on

8 August 1781 and remained there for three weeks before moving on 27 August to Tsarskoe Selo, where they were to live until 25 September in 'exceeding good Apartments' (p. 51) in the great palace by Rastrelli. The baroness was with reason flattered by the empress' invitation to accompany her husband while he carried out the inoculation of the grand dukes, 'for I was informed she is supposed to live in retirement there, and has no public Courts' (p. 49). She thus had a rare opportunity to observe the private life lived by Catherine and her family. Of especial interest are the pages devoted to the young grand dukes, in whose upbringing and education Catherine, rather than their parents, took the leading role. The baroness became very friendly with the nurses of the young boys, two English sisters, Mrs Gessler and Mrs Nicholls.[123] Pauline Gessler, the wife of Alexander's German valet, told the baroness that the empress had instructed that the grand dukes should be called simply by their first names, 'as she said Pride would come fast enough without encouraging it' (p. 52). On a later occasion she gave the baroness one of Alexander's suits which the empress had designed herself and which is still preserved in the family collection. Catherine herself much impressed the baroness who describes her reviewing her guards, at informal and formal gatherings and dinners, walking in the garden, wearing her white bonnet and accompanied by a greyhound, just as she is depicted on the famous painting by Borovikovskii or in the closing scenes of Pushkin's *The Captain's Daughter*.

Her journal inevitably abounds in the names of the people she met from the Russian aristocracy and from the British community. Her visit to St Petersburg also coincided with the visits of John Howard, who was much in their company, and of Sir Gilbert Elliot (1751–1814), the future 1st Earl of Minto. Elliot had married Anna Maria Amyand in 1777 and later that same year his wife's younger sister Harriet, then only sixteen, married Sir James Harris and left with him for St Petersburg. Harriet Harris's health had deteriorated in Russia and Elliot had arrived to escort her and her two children home to England, as noted by Baroness Dimsdale (p. 40). In one of his entertaining letters to his wife Elliot describes their leave-taking of the empress, who was, incidentally, godmother to young Catherine Harris (b. 1780), and how they were invited into her barge for a cruise on the Great Pond at Tsarskoe Selo. 'Her whole behaviour on the occasion of Harriet's *congé* was infinitely gracious; and as a humble retainer in her suite, I had the advantage of receiving a share of that civility which was addressed to her.'[124]

Lady Harris kept a journal of her voyage to St Petersburg as a young bride, but it contains little of interest.[125] Much more substantial are the diaries of an earlier ambassador's wife, who by a strange coincidence, exactly ten years before Lady Harris, had given birth in St Petersburg to a daughter who was also to be called Catherine and for whom the empress had also been god-mother. Jane, Lady Cathcart, née Hamilton and sister of Sir William, British ambassador to the Court of Naples, was, however, then in her forty-fourth year and already the mother of six children. She was also soon to die tragically in the Russian capital on 2/13 November 1771. She was a woman of uncommon virtue and modesty, endlessly devoted to her large family and self-effacing to a fault. She once wrote to a friend that people at the Russian court 'have grown used to me, find me harmless, and having got over the disappointment of an Ambassadress of no personal figure, they at last let me alone and seem to see me with all symptoms of good humour'.[126] She kept journals throughout her married life (and earlier). Twenty-four little volumes, written mainly in French, are extant in the family archive; the last four relate to the period in Russia. The bereaved Lord Cathcart, returning to England with his large family in August following his wife's death, read on board ship 'ye journal from ye day she left London to the last days of her health' and stressed for his children the ethical principles and precepts that they contain.[127] The journals in fact are largely an intimate record of religious and moral meditations, punctuated by entries that contain information about events and personalities in the Russian capital. Volume 22 is an exception in that not only is it written in English but is devoted, as its title indicates, to 'Memoranda of Russia with Voyage to St Peter also of Residence there'. These memoranda are neither extensive nor systematic, but there are revealing references to, for example, the controversy raised by Chappe d'Auteroche's critique of Russia. Lady Cathcart, who was exceptional among British ladies (and not only ladies) in her assiduous study of the Russian language, was also a patient observer of the Russian scene. 'Two years stay in this Country', she wrote in July 1770, 'having in a great degree taken off the Ideal from novelty, I now am seeking to seize those [?] wch a constant repetition of the same things may give thereby exactly to catch the true character of those we are living among.'[128] Her remarks on the common people, their qualities, their singing and music-making, and the abuses of serfdom are a modest parallel to the sweeping generalisations of the Cathcart family tutor, William Richardson, author of the *Anecdotes of the Russian Empire*. Lady Cathcart also wrote one of the more detailed personal pen-portraits of the empress in which contemporary British sources abound and which are scarcely known to or used by historians.[129]

Perhaps the most important journals of any of the British ladies who left written evidence of the time they spent in Russia during Catherine's reign come from Katherine Gertrude Harris, the elder sister of Sir James. She accompanied her brother and sister-in-law to St Petersburg and her first two journals cover the outward journey, replicating Harriet's journal. Katherine Harris, however, continued to keep journals throughout her stay, which

43 Jane Hamilton, Lady Cathcart (1726–71). Engraving by Francesco Bartolozzi,
1770s, from original marble medallion by Anne-Marie Collot.

lasted until 18 October 1779. She was to return to St Petersburg again at
the beginning of 1783 and return home with her brother when he finally left
Russia at the end of August. There are seven journals in all, of which three,
dealing with life in Russia rather than outward and return journeys, contain
much of value for the chronicler of the life of the British community and of
diplomatic and social life in general. The glimpses she provides of her brother
show him spending time on the tennis court with his secretary Richard
Oakes, fishing on the Neva with his sister, and giving a splendid ball at his
house on the Moika for the king's birthday, 'but kept according to the old
stile [4 June 1778] for the sake of the Weather':

We danced on the Platform as you land, it was cover'd with an Awning & near 60 feet
long wide enough for two setts, there were near 80, much dancing and cards in four
rooms in the House. at ten there was supper in 3 rooms & covers for 72 persons, besides

PARTICULARS

A D D R E S T   T O

LADY CATHCART'S FRIENDS.

―――――――――――

"Foolifh Eyes! muft you be fwimming in Tears
"becaufe of thofe Things? is not the Day of our Death as
"natural as that of our Birth? Yes. But this is Na-
"ture too.

"I mix thofe very few tears with yours, dear kind
"fellow Creatures; we fhall meet again; I truft in Hap-
"pinefs through the merits of a crucified Saviour.

"Weep not long, but ever remember me with the
"Balm of Friendfhip. „

*Letter from Lady CATHCART to her Husband
during her laft pregnancy dated St. Petersburg April $\frac{11}{22}$ but not
delivered in her life time, and received after her Death
November $\frac{2}{13}$ 1771.*

44 *Particulars Addrest to Lady Cathcart's Friends* by Charles, 9th Lord Cathcart
(1721–76), St Petersburg (?), 1771.

side boards, every body seem'd easy & pleased after supper they sung God save the
King & then we return'd to dancing till two a fine calm morning.[130]

The journals are rich in information about theatrical activity in St Petersburg and in Moscow. Miss Harris was a most assiduous attender of plays
and *bals masqués* in the homes of the Petersburg nobility, in institutions such

as the Smol'nyi Institute, and in the theatres. Much that she writes about performances and actors is not matched in any other known source.[131] This is especially true about her visit to Moscow in the autumn of 1778, when she met for the first time the impresario Michael Maddox. Here, for example, is her description of a visit to see a performance (unrecorded in Russian sources) of Aleksandr Sumarokov's famous tragedy *Dimitrii Samozvanets* on 7/18 October 1778 at Prince P. V. Urusov's theatre in the Vorontsov house on Znamenka:

Went to the Russian Play the False Demetrius. That Part said to be well written. The Actor performed it perfectly well, and had much change of countenance and good action, tho in this last he failed at the death when he gave a box in the Ear to a friend who was rather tardy in his assistance. The dresses fine, but those of the men not exactly according to the old Russian coustome, those of the Women quite so, & with the Virgins fillet round their foreheads. Between the acts they play'd solemn music analogous to the performance. After it was over, they gave one of Bachs Concertos an old acquaintance of mine. Then follow'd a Farce. We went from the Theatre to the Masquerade which was in the same House, paid a rouble for admittance. A tolerable appearance of company, many pretty Women. Round polonaise without end. I danced a few dances a quadrille and came away at half past Eleven. I was introduced to Prince Ourouzoff the proprietor of the Theatre.[132]

Where other visitors are generally content to note simply that they went 'to a Russ play', Miss Harris develops a lively vignette. This tendency is everywhere apparent in her notebooks. She rarely attempts to generalise at any length, but she is a truly interested and intelligent observer of Russian life, while noting somewhat wryly that 'living in Russia [is] like living in the time of ones Great grandfather to all other civilised European Nations'.[133]

V

Katherine Harris and the Harrises travelled out to St Petersburg with William Morton Pitt (1754–1836). In May 1778 he decided to make a trip to Moscow, and in a letter to Sir James Harris he declared himself not only 'perfectly surprized to find the Country so agreable' on the way there but also the people 'extremely tractable and civil, and I saw nothing that put me in mind of ye prudent counsels of some of my Friends.'[134] However, he was soon to have an unpleasant brush with minor Russian officialdom, giving him an unsought opportunity to experience conditions in Russian prisons that would have struck a chord with the likes of Coxe and Howard. After a fracas at a crossing over the Moscow River, when Pitt, armed with pistols, intervened to save his footman who was himself aiding peasants being beaten by police, he and his companions were marched off to the local prison, disarmed by a trick and then 'hurried to the Dungeon':

you can easily conceive how agreable a small room without much air can be with eight Russian Thieves, Deserters, & three of our Companions were chained, we were not, the door was locked with a Padlock, and so we continued six hours, I shall keep till I see you an account of ye Heat, the Smell, the Lice, the filth, and the conversation, and the amusements of this place.[135]

Pitt survived to complete his journey back to St Petersburg, setting out again in August 1778 to spend many months in Scandinavia, where he was to meet Coxe and Lord Herbert at a later stage.[136] Miss Harris, on her return from her Moscow trip, had met Coxe and Herbert in the company of Francis Hale (c. 1758–1827), who, like Pitt, was soon to enter parliament and who had been traversing Europe for a number of years.[137]

British visitors and travellers to Russia were being mentioned with increasing frequency in both unpublished journals and correspondence and, indeed, in the few published accounts. Lady Craven, for instance, notes that in St Petersburg in February 1786 she enjoyed the company and conversation of Alleyne Fitzherbert, Harris' successor as ambassador, and of George Ellis (1753–1813).[138] Like Worsley, Ellis was FSA and FRS and, in addition, a satirical poet of note and a future founder of the *Anti-Jacobin*. His visit to Russia is generally unknown, although confirmation that he had been there for virtually a year is found in a letter from the empress to Grimm, describing how she had shown him, Fitzherbert and Lord Carysfort her collection of gemstones and *pierres gravées*.[139] Ellis' sojourn in Russia lends credence to the attribution to him of a *Memoir of a Map of the Countries Comprehended between the Black Sea and the Caspian; with an Account of the Caucasian Nations, and Vocabularies of their Languages* (1788). The memoir represents an attempt to classify the inhabitants of the Caucasus according to information communicated to the author by Professor Pallas and incorporated material from the researches of Güldenstadt and Müller. In addition, it provides specimens of the various languages (Ossetian, Caucasian, Georgian, Abkhasian), drawn from the universal comparative dictionary, compiled by Pallas with the encouragement and involvement of the empress.

John Joshua Proby, Lord Carysfort (1751–1828) seems to have lingered in Russia even longer than Ellis. The young George Norman, who visited the Russian capital in August 1784, relates that he had declined Carysfort's invitation to join his party departing for Moscow; 'there are parties continually going to Moscow, Astracan, Warsaw & Constantinople, to which a Man might join himself, but I should prefer travelling in the more civilised parts of Europe'.[140] The following year Carysfort visited the Hermitage and, as was indicated in chapter 7, suggested to the empress that she might improve her under-represented English school by ordering a picture from his friend Sir Joshua Reynolds. In 1787 Jeremy Bentham found it surprising that Carysfort was not in Catherine's party for her imperial progress to the Crimea.[141]

He had, however, by then left Russia, but not without regret, if the following anecdote is to be believed: 'Lord Carysfort was in love with the late Dutchess of Sierra Capriola [wife of the Neapolitan ambassador] and caused himself to be put into the papers so often as on the point of going that the Dutchess told him at last that he would be taken for a diligence.'[142]

The coincidental arrival in St Petersburg in the autumn of 1789 of two pairs of English travellers who in fact had much in common prompted another British tourist to remark that 'Russia begins now to make a part of the grand tour, and not the least curious or useful part of it'[143] and brought forth an enthusiastic appraisal from the ever solicitous Dr Matthew Guthrie. Guthrie writes of a

Count Bentick a most aimiable young sailor who does honor to the British Navy as does his Companion Cap[t] Hawkins, nay we have had a third Post Captain of the same stamp (all three at same time) Mr. Markam son of the Archbishop of York and certainly the true British Character was never better supported in a foreign Country nor could we easyly I should think have picked out a better triumvirate or the British Navy must be rich in fine fellows indeed. I must own to you that I was affraid our men of fashion in the fleet carried there with them a share of that *fopish ton* which disgusted me so much when last in Britain, and were probably too much of the fine Gentleman to assimilate with the bold spirit of the British Tar, but I find myself most agreeably mistaken by the sample here lately, as they possess all that energy and manlyness of Character which has ever given and ever will give (whilst it lasts) a decided superiority to the British Fleets.[144]

The three naval captains in question were Count William Bentinck (1764–1813), later to achieve the rank of Rear-Admiral, who was travelling with James Hawkins (1762–1849), later Admiral Sir James Hawkins-Whitshed and future brother-in-law of Bentinck, whilst Captain John Markham (1761–1827), later Admiral of the Blue, had come to St Petersburg with John, Earl Wycombe (1765–1809), later 2nd Marquis of Landsdowne, a seasoned traveller who had been in Croatia and Slovakia a few years earlier.[145] Markham and Wycombe had come from Sweden and were soon to go on to Moscow before heading towards Warsaw. Bentinck's and Hawkins' experience of Russia was limited to a month in St Petersburg, to which they had come overland from Reval, after cruising in the North Sea and visiting Bentinck's illustrious grandmother, Charlotte Sophie, Countess Bentinck, then in her seventy-fifth year, at Embsbüttel. It was the Countess Bentinck's close friendship with Catherine the Great's mother that ensured Bentinck and Hawkins a cordial reception at the Russian court. Both men kept journals of their visit to the Russian capital but to judge by the evidence of the available extracts from Hawkins' diary,[146] they did or saw nothing that distinguishes them from other British visitors of the period. There was, however, considerable attention paid to naval matters and in this respect their visit strongly recalls that of Barrington and Jervis some fifteen years earlier.

Hawkins records how on one occasion they went onto the roof of Rinaldi's unfinished St Isaac's Church on Senate Square:

The church looks immediately into Narishkin's windows, and because the girls [Lev Naryshkin's daughters] happened to be looking at us when we were on the ridge, Bentinck took it into his head to walk along it from one end to the other for no one reason that could possibly be given, for he did not better his view in the least by it, and the way was much worse than that we had come up. If he had slipped his foot in the least nothing could have prevented his fall to the ground, which from the ridge of the roof is as near as I can guess near two hundred feet. When I attributed to vanity his having performed this exploit, he was quite angry.[147]

Such exploits give substance to the reputation for eccentricity and wildness that attached itself to many Englishmen, and in particular, to the young bear-cubs, unrestrained by their hapless tutors.

Lady Craven had an opinion about most things and the young British on the Grand Tour did not escape her attention. After praising the community of British merchants in the Russian capital, she declared that 'a little Latin and Greek in the schools of Westminster and Eton, and a great deal of vulgar rioting, make our young men a strange mixture of pedantism and vice, which can only produce impudence and folly. Thus tutored, at sixteen they are turned upon the hands of some unhappy man, who is to present them at foreign courts, with no other improvement or alteration in the boys heads, than that of their hair being powdered and tied behind.'[148] A British merchant is pitted favourably against a titled but callow tourist in one of James Walker's *Paramythia*. The youth, having visited the menagerie, inquires how an elephant could possibly withstand the rigours of a Russian winter and is told that 'each elephant eats a pood, or about forty pounds weight of nutmegs every day, to warm its system. The traveller stared, calculated the expense to a fraction, noted the information he had received in his common-place book, and in his next letter to his honoured papa and mamma, delighted them with the results of his judicious statistic enquiries.'[149]

The extremely young milords do not seem to have got to Russia, or at least those who arrived with their tutors had already spent some years travelling elsewhere on the Continent and by the time they descended on St Petersburg they were relatively seasoned travellers. The accompanied Lord Herbert at nineteen and Whitbread at twenty were not much younger than many tourists arriving in pairs or alone, such as Wraxall or Henniker. The same holds true of the next young tourists travelling under the supervision of tutors in the early 1790s. The very end of 1792 saw a veritable confluence of young

milords coming by various routes from Europe and Scandinavia. First to
arrive was Charles William Henry Montagu Scott, Lord Dalkeith (1772–
1807), eldest son of the Duke of Buccleuch, who had come via Scandinavia
with his companion and tutor William Garthshore (1764–1806), an Oxford
don. The relationship between Dalkeith and Garthshore was as warm as that
between Herbert and Coxe and in both cases led to preferments for the
tutors: Garthshore became successively private secretary to Lord Melville,
MP and finally a Lord of the Admiralty.[150] They were soon joined by Charles
Beauclerk (b. 1774), son of Topham and Lady Diana Beauclerk and nephew
of the Duke of Marlborough, who had been travelling with Charles James
Fox's nephew, Lord Holland. Holland had fallen ill in Berlin and Beauclerk
had decided to pay a rapid visit to St Petersburg before returning to rejoin his
friend and proceed to Italy.[151] Soon after Beauclerk's departure, two young
aristocrats, recently down from Oxford, took in Russia as part of a vast
sweep of Europe (minus revolutionary France). Lord Granville Leveson-
Gower (1772–1846), later 1st Earl Granville, and John Parker, 2nd Baron
Borringdon (1772–1840), later 1st Earl of Morley, had travelled through
Holland to Berlin; they left St Petersburg at the end of November to visit
Moscow before returning via Warsaw to Vienna and Prague and were back
in England by mid-March 1793.[152] Still very much in Russia at that period
were Edward Wilbraham-Bootle (1771–1853), later 1st Lord Skelmersdale,
who was travelling with his tutor John Parkinson (1754–1840), an Oxford
don like Garthshore and recently defeated in an election for the presidency
of Magdalen College. They arrived in St Petersburg on 4 November 1792
after some weeks in Scandinavia and were accompanied by Sir William
Watkins Wynn (1772–1840). Lord Leveson-Gower informed his sister that
'there is arrived here Booth and Sir W. Wynn; they both look in high beauty
and as like each other as two peas'.[153] Wynn was to leave for Moscow at
the beginnning of February 1793 and was to be joined there by Bootle and
Parkinson some days later. He seems to have then left Russia sometime in
March, while the other two were to embark on further extraordinary and
extensive travels through the Russian empire.

   All these young men were aged between eighteen and twenty-one; they
had much in common in education, wealth and family; they were all strong
Pittites, who were soon to enter parliament (with the exception of Borringdon, already in the Lords, and Beauclerk). Their well-being in St Petersburg
was looked after by the current ambassador, Charles Whitworth (1752–
1825), later Baron Whitworth, who earned their fulsome gratitude by his
hospitality, kindness and demeanour. He was aided and abetted by his secretary of legation, the Hon. Arthur Paget (1771–1840), son of the Earl of
Uxbridge, later Marquis of Anglesea, a future ambassador to Vienna and
Constantinople, who, by a cruel irony, was to elope many years later with

Borringdon's wife. A weakness for the fair sex or a reputation as a wom-
aniser was worn as a badge of honour. Certainly in Russia, British ambassadors frequently provided a shining example: Sir George Macartney had had
his 'intrigue galante' with Mlle Khitrovo, one of the empress' ladies-in-
waiting;[154] and Whitworth's liaison with the current favourite's married
sister, Ol'ga Zherebtsova, was common knowledge and led Hugh Elliot to
quip that 'he has proved himself an able Plenipo, as much by the exertion
of his physical as of his mental powers'.[155] Leveson-Gower was noted also
as a handsome lady-killer. He was to return to St Petersburg in 1804 as
British ambassador and have an affair with Princess Evdokiia Golitsyna, the
'Princess Nocturne'.[156] Dalkeith portrayed Wynn as 'imagining himself to be
an object much admired by the Fair Sex'[157] and much space was generally
devoted in journals and letters to amours and affairs in society, to the physical attributes of various ladies, young and old. There was a frankness of
language to match the habitual subject matter of conversation – and even
the clergymen-tutors were not spared. Herbert used the most colourful language in his letters to Coxe, writing for instance that 'the Narishkin girls are
married ere this & f-k-g about Petersburg like rabbits'.[158] Parkinson records
a passage of conversation at a dinner, 'where Paget asked me first who were
the best w– in Petersburg, and soon afterwards whether I was in orders'.[159]
On one occasion at least, incidentally, 'Bootle and Sir Watkin went to the –
and I [Parkinson] came home' (p. 80). The young men frequently made a
point of being outrageous. Parkinson with disapproval notes Wynn's conduct
at a ball in Moscow: 'sir Watkin's speech: To see it [a dance] in perfection
you ought to see it danced sans culotte – I only dance to make myself sweat.
He turned his back on Mad^e Potemkin; and afterwards fell asleep between
her and the Governor' (p. 102). The tutor was more content on another
occasion, when 'the young men amused themselves with wrestling, taking up
a candle out of water with the mouth, and with other such gambols. It might
put one in mind of the amusements in an English country gentleman's house'
(p. 72).

  None of these young men had much time for writing, although they dutifully sent back the necessary bland letters to reassure anxious parents. A
representative of the breed who did appear in print within a few years, but
not by his own devising, was Lionel Colmore (1765–1807), who preceded
Dalkeith and the other milords to Russia by a few months. He was in the
Russian capital from mid-October 1790 until at least the end of April 1791,
when his departure was announced in the *St Petersburg News*.[160] Only after
his death, however, were his letters published by the friend to whom they
were addressed as the anonymous *Letters from the Continent; Describing
the Manners and Customs of Germany, Poland, Russia and Switzerland ...*
(1812). Colmore, like Garthshore, had been at Christ Church, Oxford; he

was a staunch Pittite and a tub-thumping patriot, who was also in the words
of his friend, the editor of his letters, 'an elegant classical scholar, and an
accomplished gentleman',[161] thereby in no wise different from the Baltimores
and many others we have seen on their travels. He was, however, appraised
through the eyes of the thirteen-year-old Elizabeth Wynne as 'a young
Englishman [he was then twenty-seven] who travels who is charming, wise
and without frivolity, an excellent boy'.[162] Colmore is the recorder of society
tittle-tattle, prone to name-dropping, and frequently scathing and dismissive
in his characterisations of all and sundry, but particularly and expectedly,
of the high and mighty. Indeed, what Colmore writes about Russian society
is consistently damning, patronising, and frequently unfair, but it is all delivered with great verve and style and penned to an intimate friend who shares
his tastes and his humour.[163]

The young Leveson-Gower had been urged, in vain, by his mother to 'keep
a Journal, which will be a great Amusement to us, as well as to yourself',[164]
but many other travellers filled their notebooks and kept copies of their letters, recording all they had seen and done in what was for most people still
a remote area of the world. Two coevals of Colmore, but of more sober
disposition and differing political persuasion, who did provide detailed
accounts of their visits were James Brogden and Charles Hatchett (1765–
1847). They were not strictly or simply Grand Tourists, for both were combining pleasure with a certain amount of business: Brogden's father was a
prominent member of the Russia Company, which James himself would join
on his return, and Hatchett's father was the great coachmaker of Long Acre
in London and recently by appointment to the Russian court. They thus came
to the Russian capital to meet old acquaintances or with ample letters to
make new ones. Brogden found not only a welcome among the British merchants but also a friend from Eton days in the British acting chargé-d'affaires
Charles Fraser. As was shown in chapter 2, he became a privileged insider
within the British community, moving into a room in the courtyard of the
Cayley home on the English Embankment.

Both Brogden (in the series of letters he sent originally to his father and
sister and then copied into a book as a permanent record) and Hatchett (in
a set of small notebooks) provide a rich picture of life in the Russian capital,
predominantly and expectedly in its British-oriented aspects. But both also
travelled to Moscow and much of what they write about the old capital and
about villages on the way proves equally valuable. Brogden, incidentally,
travelled not by the post road but skirted Ladoga before turning south-west
and travelling to Moscow via Tikhvin, Iaroslavl' and Kostroma, a long and
arduous journey enlivened by the stay in Iaroslavl' to visit the Zatrapeznyis'
linen manufactory. At the Zatrapeznyi home they were 'ushered into a very
handsome suite of Apartments furnished entirely in the English manner –

English furniture, Clocks, Barometer by Dolland & even a Library of the best English and french authors'. Later the young Zatrapeznyi brothers 'treated us with an excellent English breakfast, who read the English newspapers & talked about Hasting's trial & Mrs Seddons'.[165] What more could a good Briton desire, but Brogden had persuaded his father to let him extend his tour beyond St Petersburg and return by the overland route by his 'sincere desire to obtain solid improvement & fit myself to be a useful member of Society . . . nothing can do this more than travelling'. It is a moot point, but Brogden continues: 'I have often heard this repeated but was never so much convinced of its truth as at this moment, from the numberless false ideas I had entertained of a place which I had so often heard described as Petersburg & which nothing but having been actually upon the spot cd have corrected.'[166] Hatchett, an amateur chemist, future FRS and honorary member of foreign, including Russian, societies, would probably have agreed. His diaries show his serious interest in all aspects of Russian life, but particularly the scientific and industrial. Brogden and Hatchett remained in Russia for longer periods than the average traveller and tourist. Brogden was there from mid-October 1787 and left St Petersburg on his return journey in the middle of the following June; Hatchett, travelling overland on both outward and return journeys, was in Russia between October 1790 and mid-May 1791, by which time Brogden was back in St Petersburg on a return visit.[167] Both therefore overlapped with Colmore, whom Hatchett indeed mentions.[168]

It is John Parkinson, the already oft-quoted tutor of Wilbraham-Bootle who may be seen as the real chronicler of the Grand Tour in its Russian or northern variant. Parkinson had gone up to Oxford at the age of sixteen in 1770 and remained virtually until the end of the century, receiving his DD in 1797. In 1785 he was presented to the living at Brocklesby in Lincolnshire, which he retained until his death in 1840, the year in which three companions from his days in Russia, Borringdon, Paget and Wynn, also died. Parkinson was a seasoned bear-leader and one who kept meticulously detailed journals of his travels. There exist diaries of British and Continental tours over some fifteen years, beginning with a Swiss tour in 1780, including tours of the United Provinces and then of Italy, and finishing with the Northern tour, the name he gave to his travels through Scandinavia, Russia and Poland in 1792–4. None saw the light of day during his lifetime and he never had any pretensions to rival Coxe or similar travel writers. Six manuscript volumes cover the northern tour and of these four are devoted to Russia. The edition that eventually appeared in 1971 represents a streamlined version of the original, losing the detailed listings of paintings and buildings and much else that was of great interest to Parkinson, FSA but retaining the elements which make it an entertaining and revealing account

both of Russian high society and Grand Touring. At the same time it should
be said that Parkinson was a knowledgeable and discriminating observer of
art and architecture. He obviously came to St Petersburg with an excitement
well caught in his first impressions of the city recorded on 4 November
1792:

I cannnot describe the impressions which were made this morning on my mind by the
first sight of this magnificent town, which in grandeur very far exceeds every other that
I have seen. But I am particularly struck in all the private as well as public edifices with
such an uncommon display of Grecian Architecture, which might lead us to fancy
ourselves under the general atmosphere of Athens, instead of so northern a latitude.
(pp. 20–1)

A week later, he acutely observes that 'in walking through this fine Town
one cannot help forseeing that if ever it comes to be neglected it must neces-
sarily become very forlorn and ragged, from the stucco dropping off, which
will expose the shabby brickwork behind' (p. 25). During his stay in the
Russian capital, Parkinson much enjoyed the company of the Italian architect
Giacomo Quarenghi, who was responsible for many of the new buildings he
visited.

Parkinson spared himself the problem of public image and private personality such as beset Coxe. The rich vein of outrageous gossip and scurrilous
anecdote that runs through the diaries would have been mined by him only
over port in the Combination Room or in the society of well-tried friends.
He was writing essentially for himself (although some of the information
found its way in the letters he also sent from Russia to a variety of
correspondents);[169] he had no axes to grind and made no attempt to provide
a finished picture or interpretation of Russia. Nevertheless, his gift for precise
reportage allowed him to create an absorbing mosaic of facts, anecdotes and
impressions of the contemporary scene. He was a most diligent diarist, noting
what he saw and did each day and recording snippets of conversation and
information as and when they became available. He had no wish or need to
project himself and his views, rather the contrary, although his distaste for
aspects of Russian high society life and his compassion for the peasants in
'the degrading circumstances of their servile condition' (p. 71) are apparent.
Parkinson absorbed the information purveyed by others, but there is an
occasional glimpse of his sensitivity about his own position: he notes with
some irritation Bootle's lack of consideration (pp. 93–4), and when Admiral
Mordvinov made a distinction in his attitude towards the young English
milord Bootle and his companion, Parkinson confesses that 'this is what
begins to give me a perfect surfeit of my situation' (p. 198).

Parkinson's work is first and foremost a travel diary, but it is also a political notebook. There is essentially no historical dimension in the accumulated

material devoted to current affairs and personalities. Catherine the Great, her favourites (particularly the late Potemkin and Zubov), the Grand Duke Paul, the aristocrats who thronged the court or were temporarily or permanently scattered throughout the country on their estates, in Moscow, or in provincial towns – these are the constant subjects of pen-pictures and all manner of anecdotes and gossip. In Petersburg and Moscow and in other places on their route, Parkinson was showered with tales about Catherine's love-life and the intrigues and scandals of the court, all of which he carefully records with an indication of source. The names of Russians and of British residents in St Petersburg with whom the English visitors came into contact read like an abbreviated *Who's Who* of the contemporary scene. Their particular informants in the capital's British community were the late Potemkin's gardener William Gould and Robert Hynam, the imperial watchmaker; in Moscow they were frequently in the company of Maddox, Dickinson and Dr William Halliday; while in Bakhchisarai in the Crimea, they were greeted by Major Thomas Cobley, Admiral Mordvinov's brother-in-law.

The timing of Parkinson's visit adds to his diary's general importance. The last years of Catherine's reign are not particularly well reflected in British contemporary sources and only in Parkinson are the effects of the French Revolution on the climate of Russian intellectual and social life at that time perceptibly and consciously registered. Parkinson was in St Petersburg when news arrived of the execution of Louis XVI and his diary carries several entries concerning Russian reactions. On 13 February 1793, for example, he notes that 'the Empress in her orders for going into mourning expresses herself to the Russians in such manner as this "For the death of the King of France who has been cruelly murdered by his rebellious subjects" ' and three days later he records that the events in France 'make the subject of every conversation' (p. 87). Soon he is giving details of the oath of allegiance to the Russian throne demanded of all Frenchmen resident in the capital and mentions the abuse showered on the French by 'the common people' (p. 91). Rumours of alleged assassination plots against the empress (p. 58) were another of the reasons or excuses for the increasingly repressive measures marking the last years of her reign. Parkinson registers moves against the Moscow freemasons, including the imprisonment of the famous publisher Nikolai Novikov (p. 39). And the last entry in his St Petersburg diary recalls the fate of Aleksandr Radishchev, whose denunciation of conditions he alleged to have witnessed on the very post road to Moscow along which they were about to journey had brought him exile to that distant Siberia to which they were also momentously to travel (p. 95).

The extraordinary itinerary which Parkinson and Bootle covered in the Russian part of their 'Northern Tour' highlights the unique significance of the diaries. It seems that the travellers originally intended to travel across

Russia to China, but were dissuaded from this plan by Princess Dashkova. Instead, they decided on a round trip that would take them to Siberia as far as Tobol'sk and then south to the Caspian and the edge of the Caucasus before crossing to the Crimea and returning through the Ukraine to Moscow and St Petersburg. They spent the whole of the spring, summer and autumn of 1793 on the journey and it seems it was Bootle rather than Parkinson who was the more intrepid traveller. In February 1793 Parkinson confessed that a recent 'thaw begins to make us hesitate about our tour; which I would relinquish for my own part without the slightest regret; especially since I have discovered that Dresden and Vienna are to be sacrificed for it' (p. 92). In the event, they did go on to Dresden and Vienna in the spring of 1794, but the travelling through Siberia was often as hazardous as Parkinson feared. Britons of course had penetrated into Siberia earlier in the century for various official reasons and Parkinson and Bootle had the opportunity to talk in St Petersburg with the Siberian ironmaster Hill as well as Samuel Bentham, whose own journal of extensive travels through the area a decade earlier is extant.[170] Parkinson's diary, however, is the first tourist's account of Siberia. They crossed into Siberia on 9 April 1793 and arrived a week later in Tobol'sk, where they were to remain until 16 May. At this point there is a gap in the diary, which resumes with their arrival a month later at Sarepta on the lower reaches of the Volga. It may be assumed therefore that they penetrated no further into Siberia but retraced their steps to Tiumen' before heading south-west. The Siberian journey is thus essentially the account of a month's stay in the town of Tobol'sk, but these lively pages contain unique impressions and information about personalities and social life. Although they did not meet Radishchev, who two years previously had spent a few months in Tobol'sk before moving to Ilimsk, his ultimate place of exile, they met many people who knew him. These included both officials, such as the governor, Aliab'ev, and the vice-governor, Selifontov, and exiles among whom the most colourful were Pankratii Sumarokov, nephew of the dramatist who had been banished for forging bank-notes, and Naum Choglo-kov, whose parents are often mentioned in Catherine's memoirs. Choglokov himself was very much of an *enfant terrible* both before his exile and in Tobol'sk: he provided Parkinson with an endless supply of scandalous stories and outspoken comments, in addition to a detailed biography. Parkinson tells us much about the social life in Tobol'sk, particularly about the local theatre, where he was impressed by performances by a most motley company: '15 soldiers, 6 actrices, 6 writers, an old man who had acted formerly on the German stage at Petersburgh, 14 dancing girls and the man who had personated Prince Volkonski compose the greatest part of the troop. The old German was sent here for poignarding his wife' (p. 140).

On their return journey from Siberia to Moscow Parkinson and Bootle made often prolonged stays in Sarepta, Astrakhan, Georgievsk, Bakhchisarai and Kiev. Although some of the sights and people Parkinson describes in the south of Russia are found in accounts by such as Lady Craven, Worsley and Pole Carew, the pages he devotes to Sarepta, the great Herrhut settlement on the Volga, are unparalleled. They stayed there for a week, renewing their acquaintance with the naturalist and traveller Professor Peter Pallas and his wife, to whom frequent reference is made during their first sojourn in the capital. They were able to witness at first hand life in the society of Moravian Brothers which so charmed Parkinson that he wrote: 'I never saw a place equal for the goodness of the people and for all the comforts of life' (p. 151).[171]

VI

The year Parkinson and his charge arrived for the first time in St Petersburg there appeared in London one of the few published accounts by a British tourist of contemporary Russia. The book was conventionally entitled *Travels into Norway, Denmark, and Russia, in the Years 1788, 1789, 1790, and 1791* and bore the name of an author, 'A. Swinton, Esq.', who to this day remains very much a shadowy figure. Swinton was in Russia from the end of 1788 until 1790 and it was his meetings with Hawkins, Bentinck, Markham and Wycombe in 1789 that had prompted his already quoted remark that 'Russia begins to make a part of the grand tour'. That his own account was not discussed at that juncture is to be explained, on the one hand, by certain features which make it distinct from all other published travelogues on Russia in the eighteenth century and, on the other, by its relevance to a controversy about travel writing best treated as a coda to this survey of visitors and residents in Catherine's Russia.

Virtually all that is known about Swinton is derived from his book. Neither of the Swinton genealogies finds a place for Andrew Swinton, although one mentions him in a footnote.[172] As Swinton makes clear, however, in his preface, Admiral Samuel Greig was 'his honourable and near relation' (p. x), and it seems likely that Swinton was one of the Inverkeithing Swintons, also related to the Roxburghs.[173] Swinton arrived in Riga just a few days after the admiral's death and the book contains a great deal about his funeral, his career and his family, whom Swinton visited in Kronshtadt. Naval affairs inevitably occupy much space because of the current campaign against the Swedes and also because of Swinton's genuine interest, evinced by a paper on Russian marine hospitals which he prepared during his stay (pp. 484–7).

A reviewer in the *Scots Magazine* suggested that 'overlooking the occasional flippancy of the writer, this volume contains a variety of amusing information; and he is always interesting, when he condescends to be serious',[174] but the manner is inseparable from the matter and is part and parcel of the book's attractiveness (or for some, its lack of appeal). Swinton is in the mould of Sterne's Sentimental Traveller, not prone to excessive tears or melancholy, however, but of a happy, optimistic disposition, seeking communion with peoples and their cultures. 'Wherever I travel, my first enquiries relate to the customs, manners, and amusements of the people, by which alone their real characters are to be estimated' (p. 126). He tries to avoid prejudice or hasty generalisations and 'I will not therefore give way to first impressions: have patience with me until I have resided for some time in Russia, and I promise a faithful portrait of the children of Peter, for whose sake I am disposed to think the best of them' (p. 128). And generally he succeeds, even against the odds, to think and write the best of them. He is sympathetic to their language, their songs and their dances, their courtship and wedding rites, their superstitions and traditions, and their dress, and is mild and understanding in his criticisms. The dominant notes are the idyllic and the pastoral, even within an urban setting. There is much, however, that is truly informative and perceptive on all manner of subjects.

Swinton skilfully manipulates the epistolary form and imaginary interlocutor to give his prose the flow and intonations of conversation, now chatty, now lyrical, now descriptive, now narrational. His periods are relatively short; the clauses balanced; the effects controlled. 'The first day of the year is a great day at Court: every star, garter, and ribbon, is waiting upon her Imperial Majesty. The cannons, drums, and trumpets are all at work: these are the drawing-room furniture of an Imperial Palace' (p. 217); 'The dress of the women is the reverse of the men, both in fashion and colour. Every part of it being as short and tight as decency will allow, and as gaudy as their copics [copecks] will admit' (p. 227). At times he resorts to the favoured orthographic devices of the sentimental writer, particularly the exclamation mark, to highlight the emotion of the moment: 'I walked the streets in a melancholy mood: – I viewed before me the residence of its late Governor [Admiral Greig], now no more! Tears filled my eyes as I entered – the Admiral's youngest son was in the parlour. I placed him upon my knee, and pressed him to my bosom!' (p. 213). He has an eye for the picturesque: 'We now see nothing but villages, half buried in snow. The roads are only distinguishable by the tracks of sledges, and red painted verst-poles' (p. 196); 'Figure to yourself the peasants travelling in their sledges, loaded with cheese, butter, and poultry, where lately a ship of the line had been tossed in a hurricane! We are jogging on to Cronstadt by the light of the snow' (pp. 212–13); 'when they have rowed the boat against the stream, beating time to their songs with the oars, they allow her to drive with the current, fixing their oars in a horizonal position from the boat's sides; and the rowers collect in a circle. It is at this period they exert their vocal powers, and make such exquisite harmony, as to draw the inhabitants to the galleries of their houses upon the river's banks, and the foot passengers to the water's edge, to listen to the music; and many follow the boat, to enjoy their native tunes' (p. 352).

Swinton's manner was unlikely to elicit universal approval. Swinton would, however, have scarce expected the swingeing attack on his 'matter' that soon came from the aptly named *Critical Review*.

Before we dismiss this volume, we have only to observe, that where the author has adhered to the narrative of travellers, his account of the northern nations, though imperfect, and void of novelty, may be considered in general as faithful; but every addition of his own is suspicious, if not in reality ill-founded; and when he indulges himself in politics, it is rather in vague speculations than judicious reflections.[175]

This is the concluding paragraph to a long notice that had begun with an exposé of the wiles and stratagems of armchair travellers, to whose ranks the reviewer believed Swinton unquestionably belonged. 'We have read a circumstantial narrative of the travels of persons, who, during the time of their supposed peregrinations, were scarcely ever out of their closets; and have seen works of this kind published in the name of authors who had no other existence than in the title-page of the book.'[176] What the reviewer has to say about the 'manufacture' of spurious accounts for financial gain would of course have been more telling if he had picked an appropriate target. Russia did attract its full quota of armchair travellers – and this may be seen, on the one hand, as an indication of public interest in the Northern Tour, and, on the other, as evidence of its ignorance of the geography, history and culture of the places described – but Swinton was not one of them. The *Critical Review* was to reveal only two years later how gullible it was itself to skilful manufacture, when it welcomed the English translation of P. N. Chantreau's *Voyage philosophique, politique et littéraire fait en Russie pendant les années 1788 et 1789*.[177] Chantreau's armchair compilation has, however, continued to fool many people, including some who might have known better. Harry Nerhood's bibliography of travel accounts of Russia (1968) includes with approving comment not only Chantreau but also a trio of British authors from the last quarter of the eighteenth century over whom hang similar question marks.[178]

Of John Richard's superficial, imprecise and totally uninformative *Tour from London to Petersburgh* (1778) Jeremy Bentham wrote, 'no such person I dare swear – a catch-penny performance – an imposture' and, indeed, nothing has ever been established about the author.[179] Somewhat earlier, both the *Monthly Review* and the *Annual Register* had voiced their suspicions about Joseph Marshall's *Travels through Holland, Flanders, Germany, Denmark, Sweden, Lapland, Russia, the Ukraine and Poland in the years 1768, 1769, and 1770* (1772) and there were other sceptical voices raised before the century closed, including Parkinson's who suggested that

'Mr Marshall has published travels through various parts of Europe without having once crossed the Channel'.[180] This was a mystification on a grand scale, of quite a different order from Richard's. Three volumes, replete with details of dates, itineraries, meetings, seemed a convincing demonstration of an observant and meticulous traveller through parts of Europe then little known to British reader. *Letters from Scandinavia on the Past and Present State of the Northern Nations of Europe* appeared anonymously in 1796; it contained quite a lot of information about St Petersburg, lifted from Coxe but overwhelmingly from Swinton. The work was subsequently attributed to William Thomson (1746–1817), one of the more prolific and skilful writers of the time. He finds an entry in the *DNB*, where he is not in fact given as the author of *Letters from Scandinavia* but of Swinton's *Travels*.[181] Poor Swinton, once suspected of plagiarism, was now said not to have existed![182]

VII

During her lifetime Catherine II had been described in letters and journals by many of the visiting British who were presented to her at court. With her death there came a veritable flood of biographies and assessments of her reign, largely based on roundly hostile French originals.[183] The most extensive, the most popular and overall the most sympathetic treatment of Catherine was the three-volumed *Life of Catharine II. Empress of Russia*, which appeared in 1798 and went into its fifth edition by 1800. It was essentially a reworking of a French work by Jean Castéra, revised and augmented in subsequent editions to such an extent that by the fifth edition the Rev. William Tooke could consider himself the 'author'. Tooke, who had returned to England in 1792 after retiring from the Petersburg chaplaincy, dominated British writing on Russia in the last years of the century, adding a vast *View of the Russian Empire during the Reign of Catharine the Second, and to the Close of the Present Century* in 1799. The only new published work by a traveller was the promisingly entitled *Journey from Bengal to England, through the Northern Part of India, Kashmire, Afghanistan, and Persia, and into Russia, by the Caspian Sea* (1798) by George Forster, a member of the civil service of the East India Company. Although the route through Russia was initially along not too familiar ground, Astrakhan to Tsaritsyn, the time of the journey was 1784, the content was superficial, and the Russian section was limited to a mere thirty pages in the second volume. There were, however, British travellers in Russia during Paul's short reign, one in particular achieving a fame virtually rivalling that of Coxe.

Although Anglo-Russian relations were initially good and reached a high in 1799 with an extension of the commercial agreement and the forming of a coalition against France, they rapidly deteriorated in the latter part of the year. The following year, as Paul's admiration for Napoleon grew, he moved to renew the League of Armed Neutrality, put an embargo on British shipping, and broke off diplomatic relations. It was precisely in the second half of 1800 that there arrived the last of the publishing or published travellers to visit Russia during Paul's reign but the first to appear in print. Within months of his visit, William Hunter, a member of the Inner Temple and prolific publicist, produced his *Short View of the Political Situation of the Northern Powers* (1801), in which he described the expulsion of the British ambassador two weeks before his arrival and the embargo against British ships. A mere twenty-five pages of his small book are devoted to Russia and are dominated by his negative portrayal of 'crazy Paul', as the Emperor was now dubbed by the British.[184] This negative reaction to Paul is, however, very apparent even in the letters of a British traveller at the very beginning of Paul's reign.

John Tweddell (1769–99), Fellow of Trinity College, Cambridge and member of the Middle Temple, began in 1795 his travels to acquire 'a knowledge of the manners, policy, and characters of the principal courts and most interesting countries of Europe, which were not yet inaccessible to an Englishman, through the overwhelming dominion of republican France' with a view to entering eventually the diplomatic service.[185] After extensive travels over a period of nearly four years Tweddell was, however, to die of fever in Athens. Russia seems not to have figured in Tweddell's itinerary until late in 1796 when he received an invitation from the Countess Potocka to stay at her estate at Tulczyn in the Ukraine. He arrived there at the beginning of January 1797 to find Field Marshal Suvorov quartered with his officers in a wing of the palace. He was to spend some three months in Tulczyn, writing in February that 'At present we are reduced to about 16 persons, and our society is somewhat select and pleasant. Among these is the Marshal Suvarrow, the hero of Ismäel. He is a most extraordinary character. He dines every morning about nine o'clock. He sleeps almost naked. He affects a perfect indifference to heat and cold – and quits his chamber, which approaches to suffocation, in order to review his troops, in a thin linen jacket, while the thermometer of Réamur is at 10 degrees below freezing . . .' (pp. 135–6). Tweddell was thus at Tulczyn when Suvorov received his dismissal by Paul and was ordered into internal exile. He writes of the unrest among the officers caused by Paul's military reforms, of which he himself seems to approve in principle, and senses that 'there will be some great event soon in the russian empire. I dare not say more – but I fear it' (p. 137). He travels to Moscow for Paul's coronation and provides a remarkable and extended assessment of the emperor, highlighting the contradictions in his character and actions and ending with damning words:

In short, Paul is a poor thing; he does not want sense, but he has not capacity to embrace a comprehensive system of measures. He is a little man standing on tip-toe – he libels dignity when he struts; and reminds me of a poultry yard, when he traverses the palace in the midst of dames of honor. He has the air of endeavouring to reign with double pomp, in order to make up for the time he has lost. (p. 145)

Tweddell went on to St Petersburg, which impressed him, and to Stockholm, before retracing his steps and travelling down to the Crimea, which enchanted him.

The southern coast, along which I travelled during a fortnight, with the high mountains above my head, and the sea at my feet, amongst groves of laurel, and fig-trees, and olives, and almost all the productions of Anatolia, still in high verdure, offered some points of view more romantic and more picturesque than the most romantic and most picturesque part of Switzerland. (pp. 201–2)

He stayed for some two months in the Crimea, spending some time with the Pallases. He made many sketches, copied down inscriptions on tombs and monuments and all the time kept a detailed diary, which disappeared after his death, leaving only a number of letters to various correspondents and gathered together by his brother as the record of his travels.

'Of former English travellers Tweddell seems to have made the greatest impression; an impression augmented, no doubt, by his melancholy and romantic death.'[186] So wrote Reginald Heber (1783–1826), Fellow of All Souls, Oxford and future Bishop of Calcutta, who was himself on a tour of Russia in 1805–6. Heber's journal, unlike Tweddell's, survived and was used with his permission by another Cambridge man who had travelled earlier to Paul's Russia and wrote its most vehement denunciation.

There are obvious points of comparison between William Coxe and Edward Daniel Clarke (1769–1821), although they belonged to different generations and the Russia they knew and their reaction to it were in many ways poles apart. Both went to Russia at the age of thirty-one, virtually at the beginning of careers in which they were to achieve eminence as prolific authors and scholars; both were Cambridge graduates and Fellows – Clarke became senior tutor at Jesus and the university's first professor of mineralogy (from 1808); both were ordained – Clarke, the son of a clergyman who was also an author and traveller, in 1806, two years after receiving his LLD; both willingly fulfilled the functions of tutors and companions to affluent young men embarking upon the Grand Tour – Clarke had a decade's experience behind him before he accompanied John Marten Cripps (1780–1853) on a journey that was to take them via the northern capitals to St Petersburg in January 1800. Clarke and Cripps travelled to Moscow and then to the Crimea and Odessa, before crossing over to Constantinople, but it was typical of Clarke to write from Tula that 'we intend to leave the common track to the Crimea; because I hate wearing other people's shoes, and it has been made by Lady Craven and others'.[187] Having hired 'the servant who accompanied poor Tweddell upon the same expedition', they proceeded via Voronezh, Cherkask, Taganrog, and skirted the Caucasus.

Unlike Coxe, however, Clarke from the very beginning did not feel constrained to hide what he thought about Russia and was unashamedly partisan and unrelentingly vitriolic in his denunciation of Russian men, manners and methods, beginning with the emperor himself. In another of his letters, sent with the diplomatic courier, he had delighted in 'laying aside the order of Mum!' and wrote that 'it is impossible to say what will be the end of things here; or whether the Emperor is more of a madman, a fool, a knave, or a tyrant. If I were to relate the ravings, the follies, the villanies, the cruelties, of that detestable beast I shall never reach the end of my letter. Certainly things cannot long go on as they do now.'[188] It is interesting that when he came to publish the account of their journey (and he uses 'we' to emphasise throughout the shared views of him and his companion), he says absolutely nothing about St Petersburg (which impressed him with its beauty, as his letters reveal) and launched into an attack on Paul, giving numerous examples of 'the Sovereign's absurdities and tyranny, which seemed to originate in absolute insanity'.[189] Not surprisingly, the profile that Clarke himself drew of the emperor as a vignette to Chapter I is hardly flattering (p. 1).

It is difficult for Clarke to find much to commend. Rastrelli's great palace at Tsarskoe Selo strikes him as 'a compound of what an architect ought to avoid, rather than to imitate' (p. 19). He finds the rooms in hotels like squalid kennels 'in which an Englishman would blush to keep his dogs' (p. 56). He argues that 'in whatsoever country we seek for original genius, we must go to Russia for the talent of imitation. This is the acme of Russian intellect; the principle of all Russian attainments' (pp. 86–7). He is prepared to make the occasional concession – Moscow intrigues him and 'after London and Constantinople, Moscow is doubtless the most remarkable city in Europe' (p. 94), but Russians generally get short shrift. The following passage is a supreme example of a Clarke broadside:

The picture of Russian manners varies little with reference to the Prince or the peasant. The first nobleman in the empire, when dismissed by his Sovereign from attendance upon his person, or withdrawing to his estate in consequence of dissipation and debt, betakes himself to a mode of life little superior to that of brutes. You will then find him, throughout the day, with his neck bare, his beard lengthened, his body wrapped in a sheep's skin, eating raw turnips, and drinking *quass*; sleeping on half of the day, and growling at his wife and family the other. The same feelings, the same wants, wishes, and gratifications, then characterize the nobleman and the peasant; and the same system of tyranny, extending from the throne downwards, through all the bearings and ramifications of society, even to the cottage of the lowest boor, has entirely extinguished every spark of liberality in the breasts of a people composed entirely of slaves. They are all, high and low, rich and poor, alike servile to superiors; haughty and cruel to their dependants; ignorant, superstitious, cunning, brutal, dirty, mean. (p. 46)

We are back to Russia depicted in the sixteenth and seventeenth centuries by Giles Fletcher and Samuel Collins, and, lest the connection be lost, Clarke elsewhere spells it out in clear, directing his readers to the accounts in Hakluyt and commenting that 'by the accounts they sent home, it appears the situation of Englishmen in Russia was precisely what we experienced two hundred and thirty years afterwards, under the tyranny of the Emperor Paul; the same disgusting race around them; the same dread of being communicative in their letters; the same desire to quit a scene of barbarity' (p. 134). He quotes passages on the manners of the Russians from the poems of George Turbervile, who visited Russia a few years before Fletcher, for 'they prove that Russia, when they were written, appeared as it does at this day' (p. 136). Russians, in short, are what they always were, and 'neither ... the drivellings of Voltaire, nor all the hired deceptions of French philosophers and *savans*' can disguise the fact (pp. ii–iii).

With Clarke, the last of the early influential Cambridge 'image-makers' of Russia, we seem to have come full circle. Clarke's account of his visit to Russia appeared in print for the first time only in 1810 under the title 'Russia, Tahtary and Turkey', representing the first part of what was to become the three-part *Travels in Various Countries of Europe, Asia and Africa*. By the time it had gone into a fourth edition by 1816 it had spanned the years of Anglo-Russian rapprochement, the defeat of Napoleon, the visit of Alexander I to England – years that had left Clarke unrepentant about his account of Russian society. As Britain moved into another period of Russophobia during the reign of Nicholas I, intensified by the suppression of the Polish revolt in 1830 and fears of Russian expansionism, Clarke's strictures on the Russians seemed to gain added weight and new editions of his work appeared in 1839 and 1848.

It was James Walker, the imperial engraver with eighteen years' experience of Russia, who wrote in *Paramythia* that 'Many travellers are much to be censured for the unqualified blame they bestow on the countries they have passed through, forgetting the bounties and hospitalities they have received. Nothing is so easy as to find fault ... It would be well if travellers were to recollect that there are pick-pockets, thieves, extortionate inn-keepers, dirt, and even a sprinkling of naughty women, at home as well as abroad.[190] Leitch Ritchie, travelling to Russia much later, in 1835, reported with obvious sympathy a Russian acquaintance's charge that 'you English should travel in Russia for the avowed purpose of making yourself acquainted with the manners and character of the people, yet without comprehending a single word of their language. You come here with the greatest prejudices against us as a nation. You see everything different from what you have been accustomed to at home, except the manners of some dozen families whom you visit. You make no inquiries, no reflections, no allowances . . .'[191] Such statements could be multiplied without difficulty down the decades – and are as likely as not to come from writers who are about to propose their own work as embodying all the virtues. The benefits or otherwise of travel remain a matter of debate. Fools returned as bigger fools and wise men often learnt from what they saw and heard. How the individual experience of Russia related to public understanding is more problematical. That the British public became increasingly aware of Russia down the century is obvious, but awareness is not understanding. Negative stereotypes remained strong and, as Clarke demonstrates, are given a new validity with every downturn in political relations. Nevertheless, intercourse between the two countries greatly increased and during Catherine's reign there was a contant flow of people between Russia and England, travelling for all manner of reasons, including, as this chapter has shown, tourism and curiosity. Published information about Russia grew, varying inevitably in quality and reliability, and while much was ephemeral and passed without any impact, there were works, notably by Coxe and, to a lesser extent, by Wraxall and later by Tooke, that sought to enlighten and helped to form opinion. The evidence of the unpublished letters and journals shows a spirit of enquiry and curiosity among the majority of visitors. However, the travellers not unnaturally tended to be happier with what was nearer to their experience in their native land, be it architecture, food, dress, conduct in society, to say nothing of laws and institutions. Petersburg at least proved the magnet and did not generally disappoint by the magnificence of its setting and prevailing character of its buildings. It, and its founder the great Peter (or at least, enlightened Europe's perception of him), remained the window by which the West not only entered but also could attempt to understand.

EPILOGUE

Johnson Newman, who has not been previously named in these pages, was a devoted servant of Russia during a career spanning some fifty years, beginning in 1755 in the reign of Elizabeth and ending early in the reign of Alexander I.[1] Initially an 'informator in the English language' at the Naval Cadet Corps, he moved to the College of Foreign Affairs as a translator, but in the 1770s he was to be found at the Russian embassy in London. He subsequently served in Lisbon, before returning to England in 1785 to take up the newly created post of Russian consul at Hull. He is an interesting figure not least because of his largely unsung efforts to be useful 'tant à la Russie qu'à ma Patrie' by the translation of literary and historical works. His own command of languages, specifically English, French and Russian, led him to recognise that ignorance of foreign languages formed a huge barrier between nations and that British ignorance of Russian was a particularly depressing example. He wrote in 1789:

Depuis l'année 1755 que je suis entré en Russie au Service, j'ai souvent été témoin oculaire par Terre et par Mer de quantité d'Anglois qui sont entrés au Service de la Russie dans tous les Departments et qui faute de sauvoir et la Langue et l'Histoire de Russie, n'ont pu communiquer leurs Idées, ni par consequent lui être util sans Interprète, avec toute leur Fidelité, Zèle, Courage et Sciences reconnus.[2]

Newman was essentially correct in highlighting the problem and indeed, he took steps to alleviate it. He composed what he described as a 'Grammaire russienne pour un Gentilhomme Anglois', but sadly, his work was never published and the manuscript was lost.

Had it been published, it would have been a unique event. During the whole of the eighteenth century no Russian grammar and no Russian–English or English–Russian dictionaries were published in Britain. At the end of the preceding century, in 1696, Ludolf's *Grammatica Russica* had appeared in Oxford, representing a highpoint in early English knowledge of Russian. During the eighteenth and nineteenth centuries, however, the British, in the view of an eminent Russian scholar of Anglo-Russian relations, 'were the least receptive of all Europeans to the Russian tongue' and no work appeared equal in significance to Ludolf's.[3] In contrast, Russian interest in English during the same period grew apace and there were a number of English grammars, model conversation guides and dictionaries published in St Petersburg and composed by Russians, almost all of whom had spent some time in Britain. Among them was Prokhor Zhdanov who in 1772 published a grammar and a 'Vocabulary English–Russian', arranged according to subjects and themes; it was, however, his *New Dictionary English and Russian* (1784), containing some 30,000 words in alphabetical order, that proved invaluable for Russians and British alike. Other English–Russian dictionaries were produced in St Petersburg at the beginning of the nineteenth century and in 1808–11 there appeared the first two volumes of Ivan Shishukov's unfinished Russian–English dictionary. It was 'the Want of ... any kind of Lexicon where the Russian words stand first' of which the British chaplain Daniel Dumaresq had complained in 1751.[4] Russian–French and Russian–German dictionaries had to fill the gap in the interim: a set of French–Russian and Russian–French dictionaries with the ownership inscription of Charles Gascoigne is preserved in the Library of the School of Slavonic Studies in London.

Dumaresq also complained of the lack of a 'tolerable Grammar' and again it was a French intermediary that proved the gateway to Russian for many British in the second half of the eighteenth century. In 1757 Mikhail Lomonosov's *Rossiiskaia grammatika*, the first Russian grammar to be printed in Russian, appeared in St Petersburg. It was translated into German in 1764 and, more importantly, formed the basis of Jean-Baptiste Charpentier's *Elemens de la langue russe*, published in St Petersburg in 1768, with further editions in 1791 and 1795. It was, for instance, a copy of Charpentier that Samuel Bentham sent to his brother Jeremy in triumph in January 1784 – 'a Russian grammar I sent you' – and the copy, bearing Jeremy's ownership inscription, is now in the University Library, Cambridge.[5] More interestingly, Lady Cathcart, wife of the British ambassador in St Petersburg, began in 1769 her love affair with the Russian language, noting in her diary for 29 January: 'J'ai commencé le 18 avec Mons Charpentier l'étude de la langue Russe. Cela me diverti c'est mon jouet.'[6] A final fascinating reference dates from the very beginning of the nineteenth century and thus just over a decade after Newman's abortive attempt to publish his grammar, which was also modelled on Lomonosov's original. The Rev. Alexander John Scott, who had been appointed chaplain, interpreter and translator of languages to the British naval expedition setting out for Copenhagen in 1801, began to learn Danish and also Russian, using Charpentier. The copy, which Scott used and was kept in the family, bore the following inscription: 'This book kindly lent by Dr Rogers, late of St Petersburg, to John Sewell, 32 Cornhill, for the express purpose of accommodating the Rev. Scott, going in the present armament to the North. Sewell procured it from Dr R., with intent to have it translated into English, and printed, in which work Mr Scott can probably assist. – 32 Cornhill, 4th March, 1801.'[7] Sadly, all efforts on the British side to advance the cause of Russian came down to *A Commercial Dictionary in the English and Russian Languages*, produced at the end of 1800 by a naturalised British subject from Riga, Adam Kroll, who was awarded twenty guineas by the Russia Company probably assuming it would be useful to its members. The work promised more than it delivered, offering merely a sixty-page list of English words with their Russian equivalents in would-be phonetic transcriptions to obviate 'the laborious and difficult task of learning the Russian characters, which would appear so formidable to his [i.e. a British merchant's] imagination that he would be deterred from making the attempt'.[8]

There were many who down the century made the attempt to acquire Russian and not always out of necessity. The degree of necessity was a moot point. In one of the model conversations Zhdanov devised for his 1772 work, his Russian is delighted to learn that his English interlocutor, just arrived in Russia, is attempting to learn Russian and he asserts that ''tis a Language of great use in this country: & without it one labours under great many inconveniences here. All the Russ Merchants speak mostly Russ; and in short, everything transacted here is in Russ. Consequently all foreigners are under a necessity to learn the Russ language.'[9] Zacchaeus Walker, in the approving characterisation of Charles Baird which he sent to Matthew Boulton in 1805, made virtually the same argument, stressing that 'he knows the Russian language well, which, rest assured is a very essential point & a work of time'.[10] On the other hand, there was a number of factors virtually conspiring to persuade the British in Russia that it was not worth devoting the time to acquire the language. The first of course was that French and German were much more useful in everyday life, certainly in the Russian capital: French for those operating at court or governmental levels, German among the merchants and artisans. Even in such 'British' institutions as the notorious 'British Monastery' during Peter's reign and the more sedate English Club during Catherine's it was German that was the first language. The comments of James Brogden, visiting Russia for the first time in 1787–8, are valid for much of the century. He visited one of the great fashionable balls held in the English Inn and found that 'French is the universal language', but in an earlier letter he had written:

I shall endeavour to do what I can in learning Russ, but must own I almost despair when I find even Mr Cayleys Sons, who were born in the Country, by no means master of it. All the Russians who are above the condition of Peasants speak either German or French, & the intercourse with the com people is so small that very little advantage is to be derived from it [learning Russian].[11]

It would appear that very few British had to learn Russian to survive; whether they should have learnt it, and whether, as Newman implied, Russia would thereby have more obviously benefitted, is a different matter. There were literally thousands of British subjects in Russia down the century and undoubtedly hundreds came to speak the language with varying degrees of accuracy and fluency. Some, but distinctly the minority, found themselves in purely Russian-speaking environments, in the interior, away from the capitals; the occupations of others made the acquisition of the language very necessary. By and large, the British could get by without Russian, and most did, including most naval officers, it would seem, and many members of the merchant family dynasties, some of which were in their third generation by the end of the eighteenth century.

Questions of language and degrees of integration and contact with Russian society remained predictably unresolved until the British colony itself was swept away in 1917. Herbert Swann, father of Donald Swann and a descendant of Catherine's watchmaker Robert Hynam, wrote of the life of the British in St Petersburg in the early years of this century and how 'like my father and brothers I was christened in the English church in St Petersburg ... and like them I retained the unmistakable traits of an expatriate Englishman despite all the environmental pressures of my surroundings, the influence of affectionate Russian nannies, and the more pervasive authority of German tutors'.[12] However, as he later writes:

The small colony of Britishers in St Petersburg, probably not more than four to five hundred strong, could be divided into two groups – those who had integrated into Russian or Baltic German society, and those who held themselves aloof, mixing almost entirely with others of their own nationality.[13]

His family belonged to the first group: his mother was Danish–German, his father, a clerk, later manager, but fluent in four languages; Herbert and his brothers went to a German school and spoke English as their third language. They were outside the fashionable, embassy-led British group and contented themselves with the occasional Stilton from the English Shop and a Christmas pudding from 'home' and their father collected 'Cries of London' pictures and said grace in English before lapsing into other, more comfortable languages. The lifestyle of the upper echelons of the colony, of those who 'knew little or no Russian or German', may be glimpsed in the voluminous writings of the ambassador's own daughter, Meriel Buchanan.[14] The complementary accounts of Swann and Buchanan, and those of other insiders and outsiders alike from the turn of the century, recall in many respects – inevitably and expectedly – the life of the British colony in Catherine II's reign with its rituals and prejudices and divisions. The colony, however, like Russia itself and Anglo-Russian relations, had also changed and evolved.

Lives and careers rarely fit neatly into decades or reigns or even centuries. Many of the people who have appeared in the various chapters of this book lived and worked in Russia into the first decades of the nineteenth century and their descendants frequently remained until 1917 and some are still there. It is the reign of Alexander I, however, that is more often than not seen as the highpoint of British influence in Russia and, in terms of Russian awareness of English culture and literature and the fashionableness of all things English, that may be so. On the other hand, the evidence as regards the situation of the British community in St Petersburg seems contradictory. It certainly grew in size during Alexander's reign (as did the British presence elsewhere in Russia – in Moscow, Archangel and Odessa, for example). The opening of the reconstructed English Church in 1815 would seem to emphasise the permanence of the British presence in the heart of the Russian capital, as did the adoption of the name 'English Embankment' for the road on which it stood, but British ownership of the adjacent houses, which supplied the main reason for the name, was gradually and inexorably reduced. The Russian aristocracy and others took over the houses, just as they took over the English Club. British membership of that venerable institution gradually diminished until in 1842 the fourteen British members of the club resigned in protest at the blackballing of a fellow-countryman in the annual election.[15] The English Shop continued to be the place at which to be seen to shop and British imported goods were in high demand, not least among the dandies of the Onegin stamp:

> Whatever, for the lavish whim,
> London the trinketer deals in
> and o'er the Baltic waves to us
> ships in exchange for timber and for tallow.[16]

It was, nevertheless, among members of the British Factory that the feeling grew that the best days had passed: despite the upswing in relations between the two countries after 1812 and the signing of a fourth commercial treaty in the following year, the repressive measures against the British in 1800 and again at the time of Tilsit were not easily forgotten. Britain was no longer seen as the most favoured nation and Russia was certainly no longer viewed as the most faithful ally.

The British undoubtedly continued to organise themselves conspicuously and to make their contribution in many areas of Russian life. The story of the British in the nineteenth century, when it comes to be written, will hold many fascinating pages, but it will lack the vitality and vibrancy, the sense of excitement and optimism that mark the first century of their presence in the new Russian capital of St Petersburg.

NOTES

ABBREVIATIONS

AGM	*Arkhiv grafov Mordvinovykh*
AKV	*Arkhiv kniazia Vorontsova*
AVPR	Arkhiv vneshnei politiki Rossii, Moscow
BL	British Library
DNB	*Dictionary of National Biography*
GL	Guildhall Library, London
GLRO	Greater London Record Office
IRLI	Institut russkoi literatury (Pushkinskii Dom), St Petersburg
MIRF	*Materialy dlia istorii russkogo flota*
M-L	Moscow-Leningrad
NL of Wales	National Library of Wales, Aberystwyth
OMS	*Obshchii morskoi spisok*
OSP	*Oxford Slavonic Papers*
POARAN	Peterburgskoe otdelenie Arkhiva Rossiiskoi Akademii nauk
PRO	Public Record Office, London
PRONI	Public Record Office of North Ireland, Belfast
RBS	*Russkii biograficheskii slovar'*
RGADA	Rossiiskii gosudarstvennyi arkhiv drevnikh aktov, Moscow
RNL	Russian National Library, St Petersburg
SEER	*Slavonic and East European Review*
SGECRN	*Study Group on Eighteenth-Century Russia Newsletter*
SIRIO	*Sbornik Imperatorskogo Russkogo istoricheskogo obshchestva*
spb	St Petersburg
SRO	Scottish Record Office, Edinburgh
TSGAVMF	Tsentral'nyi gosudarstvennyi arkhiv voenno-morskogo flota, St Petersburg

INTRODUCTION

1 See A. G. Cross, *The Russian Theme in English Literature: From the Sixteenth Century to 1980* (Oxford, 1985).
2 *View of the Importance of the Trade between Great Britain and Russia* (London, 1789), p. 45.
3 *AKV*, XVII (Moscow, 1880), 118.
4 *Ibid.*, VIII (1876), 341. Count F. V. Rostopchin, whose words are quoted, visited England in 1780 and again in 1820, when his enthusiasm was considerably diminished by finding an England affected by 'la contagion du siècle' (*ibid.*, 389).

5 *Arkhiv kniazia F. A. Kurakina*, VI (Saratov, 1896), 332. (Letter from Prince Aleksandr Kurakin to Count Nikita Panin.)

6 See Geraldine Marie Phipps, *Britons in Seventeenth-Century Russia: A Study in the Origins of Modernization*, PhD thesis, University of Pennsylvania, 1971 (available through University Microfilms), ch. VI, 'Britons in the Russian Army'.

7 An excellent start has been made by M. S. Anderson, 'British Officers in the Russian Army in the Eighteenth and Early Nineteenth Centuries', *Journal of the Society for Army Historical Research*, XXXVIII (1960), 168–73.

8 *Russkii arkhiv*, no. 1 (1879), 100.

1 THE COLONY BY THE BANKS OF THE NEVA

1 William Coxe, *Travels into Poland, Russia, Sweden, and Denmark*, II, 5th edn (London, 1802), p. 104.

2 Said to be the words of one of Peter I's jesters and quoted by Christopher Marsden, *Palmyra of the North* (London, 1942), p. 51.

3 See P. N. Stolpianskii, *Kak voznik, osnovalsia i ros Sanktpiterburkh* (Petrograd, 1918), pp. 217–21; his *Staryi Peterburg: Dvorets truda* (Petrograd, 1923), pp. 17–21. I am also extremely grateful to Mme Larisa Broitman of St Petersburg who kindly put at my disposal her unpublished typescript about the English Embankment.

4 A. G. Cross (ed.), *An English Lady at the Court of Catherine the Great: The Journal of Baroness Elizabeth Dimsdale, 1781* (Cambridge, 1989), p. 41.

5 In a letter from Carron Company of Falkirk to the engineer John Smeaton in 1773, as quoted by R. H. Campbell, *Carron Company* (Edinburgh and London, 1961), p. 74.

6 British Factory in Russia Register 1706–1815, MS 11, 192B, f. 72, GL.

7 *The Picture of Petersburg* (London, 1801), p. 88; John Parkinson, *A Tour of Russia, Siberia and the Crimea 1791–1794*, ed. W. Collier (London, 1971), p. 93. Parkinson in fact writes 15,000, which I take as a slip of the pen; the figure of 1,800 at the end of the century is given in J. Meerman, *Russland* (Haarlem, 1804), pp. 175–6.

8 *Leningrad: Entsiklopedicheskii spravochnik* (M-L, 1957), p. 33; W. H. Parker, *An Historical Geography of Russia* (London, 1968), p. 204.

9 Robert Lyall, *The Character of the Russians and a Detailed History of Moscow* (London, 1823), p. 532.

10 E. D. Clarke, *Travels in Various Countries of Europe, Asia and Africa*, I (London, 1810), p. 90.

11 POARAN, Razriad IV, *op. 1, d. 999, f. 20* (Letterbook of James Meader).

12 Anthony Cross (ed.), *Engraved in the Memory: James Walker, Engraver to the Empress Catherine the Great, and His Russian Anecdotes* (Oxford and Providence, 1993), p. 46.

13 *Biografiia A. N. Radishcheva napisannaia ego synov'iami*, ed. D. S. Babkin (M-L, 1959), pp. 42–3.

14 *Sanktpeterburgskie vedomosti*, no. 26 (1 April 1791), p. 463. In 1787–8 there had been at least two earlier and different ones, owned by Benjamin Hawkesford on Sennaia and John Pickersgill on Nevskii Prospekt: *Sankpeterburgskie vedomosti*, no. 1 (1 January 1787), 10; no. 1 (4 January 1788), 16.

15 *Ibid.*, no. 43 (28 May 1790), 700; no. 45 (4 June 1790), 735.

16 *Ibid.*, no. 9 (30 January 1792), 144.

17 *Ibid.*, no. 11 (5 February 1790), 165; no. 48 (14 June), 791; no. 104 (27 December), 1703; no. 51 (27 June 1791), 1052.

18 *Ibid.*, no. 40 (20 May 1793), 893.

19 *The Wynne Diaries*, III (London, 1940), p. 59.

20 I. G. Georgi, *Opisanie rossiisko-imperatorskogo stolichnogo goroda Sankt-Peterburga i dostopamiatnostei v okrestnostiakh onogo* (spb, 1794), pp. 213–14.

21 M. M. Shcherbatov, *On the Corruption of Morals in Russia*, ed. and trans. A. Lentin (Cambridge, 1969), p. 222.

22 Lewis Melville, *Lady Suffolk and Her Circle* (London, 1929), p. 272; Coxe, *Travels*, II, p. 151.

23 Auchindoune, Cawdor, Nairne, Cathcart papers, Folio I, no. 42.

24 Shcherbatov, *Corruption of Morals*, p. 222.

25 M. I. Pyliaev, *Staryi Peterburg* (spb, 1887), pp. 251, 446.

26 Lincolnshire Record Office, Lincoln, Dixon 16/6/17, letter from John Parkinson of 19 January 1793.

27 Georgi, *Opisanie*, p. 214.

28 *Sanktpeterburgskie vedomosti*, no. 2 (5 February 1790), p. 22.

29 *Morning Chronicle and London Advertiser*, Thursday 31 July 1783.

30 The journey was a success. On 18 May 1791 the *Gazetteer* reported that two carriages were being built for a Prince Golitsyn.

31 *Sanktpeterburgskie vedomosti*, no. 53 (2 July 1792), 1030.

32 *Edinburgh Review*, CXXXVIII (1873), p. 433; V. O. Vitt, *Iz istorii russkogo konnozavodstva* (Moscow, 1952), pp. 25ff.

33 Cross, *English Lady*, p. 65.

34 *Sanktpeterburgskie vedomosti*, no. 14 (18 February 1793), 294; no. 69 (27 August 1792), 1340; no. 53 (2 July 1792), 1027.

35 *Ibid.*, no. 69 (27 April 1790), 1122; no. 73 (10 September 1790), 1186; no. 68 (26 August 1791), 1378–9. See A. G. Cross, 'Early Miss Emmies: English Nannies, Governesses and Companions in Pre-Emancipation Russia', *New Zealand Slavonic Journal*, no. 1 (1981), 1–20.

36 John Carr, *A Northern Summer* (London, 1805), p. 293.

37 *Sanktpeterburgskie vedomosti*, no. 90 (11 November 1793), 2058.

38 James Cracraft, 'James Brogden in Russia, 1787–1788', *SEER*, XLVII (1969), 223.

39 'From Mother Bumboatis, at the Dancing Bears in Petersburg', *The Bee, or Literary Weekly Intelligence* XII (1792), 59–63; 'Chockablock's Letter', XVI, 324–8.

40 Cross, *Engraved in the Memory*, pp. 42–4.

41 POARAN, Razriad IV, op. 1, d. 999, ff. 58v.–9.

42 *The Picture of Petersburg*, p. 574. (Addition by the translator, Rev William Tooke.)

43 *A Journey through the Crimea to Constantinople* (London, 1789), pp. 125–6.

44 Cracraft, 'James Brogden in Russia', p. 231.

45 *Letters from the Continent; Describing the Manners and Customs of Germany, Poland, Russia and Switzerland, in the Years 1790, 1791 and 1792* (London, 1812), pp. 113–14.

46 BL, Egerton MS 2697, f. 259; Cathcart Papers, Folio I, no. 48, ff. 3–3v.

47 A. B. Granville, *St. Petersburg*, II (London, 1828), p. 482.

48 SRO, Adam of Blair Adam MSS. 1454/4/438 (Journal no. 18), unfoliated; Cross, *English Lady*, p. 77; Parkinson, *Tour*, p. 89.

49 Cathcart Papers, Folio I, no. 48, f. 3v.

50 Cracraft, 'James Brogden in Russia', p. 233.

51 Cross, *Engraved in the Memory*, pp. 108–10.

52 Mrs Aubrey Le Blond, *Charlotte Sophie Countess Bentinck: Her Life and Times 1715–1800*, I (London, 1912), pp. 114–15; *The Farington Diary*, I (London, 1923), p. 105; 'K. A. G. S[everin]oi', in I. I. Dmitriev, *Polnoe sobranie stikhotvorenii* (Leningrad, 1967), p. 125.

53 *Sanktpeterburgskie vedomosti*, no. 91 (12 November 1787), 1237.

54 See Stolpianskii, *Staryi Peterburg: Dvorets truda*, pp. 24–5. Fawell was still arranging masquerades in 1789: *Sanktpeterburgskie vedomosti*, no. 8 (26 January 1789), 106.

55 Stolpianskii, *Staryi Peterburg*, pp. 23–4.

56 SRO, MSS. 1454/4/438, unfoliated.

57 Private Collection, 'Journal of Charles Hatchett's Journey to Russia, August 1790–November 1791', Notebook III, f. [4].

58 *Ibid.*, f. [13v]; *Sanktpeterburgskie vedomosti*, no. 53 (2 July 1790), 872.

59 Cathcart Papers, Folio I, no. 57, ff. 1–IV.

60 *Svodnyi katalog knig na inostrannykh iazykakh, izdannykh v Rossii v XVIII veke 1701–1800*, II (Leningrad, 1985), 45–6, no. 1372. See V. D. Rak, 'Petr Khol'sten, bibliotekar' britanskoi faktorii, i tsikl "Kratkie istoricheskie izvestiia" v tobol'skom zhurnale', *XVIII vek*, XVII (St Petersburg, 1991), 88–122.

61 *Archivo del general Miranda, Viajes* II (Caracas, 1929), pp. 395, 432, 433.

62 *Catalogue of Books Belonging to the British Factory St. Petersburg* (spb, 1821), p. 4. Further catalogues were issued in 1837 and 1882. See A. G. Cross, 'The Subscription Library of the British Factory in St Petersburg', *SGECRN*, no. 7 (1979), 41–6.

63 *Stoletie Sankt-Peterburgskogo Angliiskogo sobraniia* (spb, 1870), pp. 1–15. The members of the committee during the eighteenth century are given in the Appendix, pp. 1–18, and of the Club, pp. 43–76.

64 The portrait is reproduced facing the title page of the above work.

65 Cross, *Engraved in the Memory*, pp. 98–101.

66 Hatchett, Notebook III, f. [23].

67 Georgi, *Opisanie*, pp. 629–30.

68 Hatchett, Notebook III, f. [25].

69 Nicholas Hans, 'The Moscow School of Mathematics and Navigation (1701)', *SEER*, XXIX (1951), 535.

70 A. N. Pypin, *Russkoe masonstvo XVIII i pervaia chetvert' XIX v.* (Petrograd, 1916), pp. 89–90.

71 Robert Freke Gould, *The History of Freemasonry, its Antiquities, Symbols, Constitutions, Customs* etc., III (London, n.d.), p. 214.

72 United Grand Lodge of England, London, 'Journal of the Lodge of Perfect Union from the 13th June 1771 to the 30 May 1772', f. 29.

73 Robison gives some very interesting details of the Lodge in the introduction to his *Proofs of a Conspiracy against all the Religions and Governments of Europe*, 5th edn (Dublin, 1798), pp. 2–4.

74 'Journal of the Lodge of Perfect Union', f. 44.

75 *Ibid.*, f. 35.

76 *Ibid.*, ff. 37–8.

77 P. Pekarskii, *Dopolneniia k istorii masonstva v Rossii XVIII stoletiia* (spb, 1869), p. 52.

78 G. V. Vernadskii, *Russkoe masonstvo v tsarstvovanie Ekateriny II* (Petrograd, 1916), pp. 21 n.1, 200 n.4.

79 S. F. Platonov, 'Iz bytovoi istorii Petrovskoi epokhi. I: Bengo-Kollegiia ili Velikobrit-

anskii monastyr' v S.- Peterburge pri Petre Velikom', *Izvestiia Akademii Nauk SSSR*, nos. 7–8 (1926) (Seriia: Istoriia), 527–46.

80 *Pis'ma i bumagi imperatora Petra Velikogo*, VII, vyp. 1 (Petrograd, 1918), pp. 449–52.

81 See A. G. Cross, 'The Bung College or British Monastery in Petrine Russia', *SGECRN*, no. 12 (1984), 14–24.

82 Jonas Hanway, *An Historical Account of the British Trade over the Caspian Sea*, II (London, 1753), p. 123.

83 A unique source of information about the Order is the *Records of the Most Ancient and Puissant Order of the Beggar's Benison and Merryland, Anstruther* (Anstruther, 1892), and its *Supplement*, published the same year. Both are now available in a one-volume photomechanic reprint, with an introduction by Alan Bold, as *Gems of British Social History*, no. 6 (Edinburgh, 1982).

84 Derbyshire County Record Office, Matlock, D239M/0478 Fitzherbert. The documents are printed in A. G. Cross, 'An Unknown Episode in Scoto-Russian Relations in the Eighteenth Century: The Order of the Beggar's Benison in Russia', *Scottish Slavonic Review*, no. 3 (1984), 45–63.

85 Porter was a Scot who was elected to the Society of Antiquaries of Scotland on 2 April 1782 (*Archaeologica Scotica*, III (Edinburgh, 1831), Appendix p. 22). In the early 1770s he was in partnership with John Jackson and was involved in the import of wares manufactured by Wedgwood and Matthew Boulton.

86 *The Correspondence of Jeremy Bentham*, ed. T. L. S. Sprigge, II (London, 1968), pp. 500–1.

87 A. M. Skabichevskii, *Ocherki istorii russkoi tsenzury (1700–1863 gg.)* (spb, 1892), p. 49.

88 An example of the medal, previously in the collection of masonic insignia formed by D. Burylin, is now in the Hermitage and was photographed for Larissa Dukelskaia (ed.), *The Hermitage: English Art, Sixteenth to Nineteenth Century* (Leningrad, London, Wellingborough, 1969), plates 62–3.

89 Stählin's *Zur Geschichte des Theaters in Russland* (1769), quoted in P. N. Berkov, 'English Plays in St. Petersburg in the 1760s and 1770s', *OSP*, VIII (1958), 92.

90 *SIRIO*, XIX (1876), pp. 123–4. (The Mr Fawkener referred to was William Fawkener (1747–1811), then a volunteer in the Russian army.)

91 *Anecdotes of the Russian Empire* (London, 1784), pp. 396–8.

92 Quoted in V. N. Gerngross, 'Inostrannye antreprizy Ekaterininskogo vremeni', *Russkii bibliofil*, no. 6 (1915), p. 78.

93 *Scots Magazine*, XXXIII (March 1771), 151–2.

94 Berkov, 'English Plays', pp. 94–5.

95 *Satiricheskie zhurnaly N. I. Novikova*, ed. P. N. Berkov (M-L, 1951), p. 329.

96 *The Picture of Petersburg*, p. 456 (Addition by William Tooke).

97 'Narrative Private and Commercial by the Late Stephen Cattley of Camberwell', p. 10. (Typescript made available by Mr Eric Cattley of Kingston, Devon.). On Fisher's company, see, in addition to Berkov, A. G. Cross, 'Mr Fisher's Company of English Actors in Eighteenth-Century Petersburg', *SGECRN*, no. 4 (1976), 49–56; A. G. Cross, 'Catherine the Great "Come from Russia to Liberate Ireland" ', *Irish Slavonic Studies*, no. 10 (1989/91), 89–92; and M. P. Alekseev (ed.), *Shekspir i russkaia kul'tura* (M-L, 1965), pp. 61–4.

98 *Sanktpeterburgskie vedomosti*, no. 1 (1 January 1773), 4.

99 'Journal of the Lodge of Perfect Union', f. 69. (The theatre later passed to the Italian impresario Bertolotti.)

100 SRO, MS 1454/4/438, unfoliated.
101 The pioneering work in this field was V. N. Vsevolovskii-Gerngross, 'Nachalo tsirka v Rossii', in *O teatre*, II (Leningrad, 1927), pp. 66–106. M. Burgess, 'Fairs and Entertainers in 18th-century Russia', *SEER*, XXXVIII (1959), 95–113, is essentially an amplification of Gerngross's article. The most recent work is Iu. Dmitriev, *Tsirk v Rossii* (Moscow, 1977), pp. 24–44.
102 Preceding Gerngross's work was the article by I. G. Inozemtsev, which is particularly informative on Sanders, 'Obshchestvo ekvilibristov', *Istoricheskii vestnik*, LXXXIV (1901), 274–9.
103 See M. Willson Disher, *Greatest Show on Earth* (London, 1937), pp. 10–16.
104 *Ibid.*, pp. 29–51.
105 *Sanktpeterburgskie vedomosti*, no. 53 (2 July 1792), 1032.
106 M. P. Alekseev, 'Angliiskii iazyk v Rossii i russkii iazyk v Anglii', *Uchenye zapiski Leningradskogo gos. universiteta, Seriia filologicheskikh nauk*, vyp. 9 (1945), p. 95. *Istoriia Moskvy*, II (Moscow, 1955), p. 585, wrongly gives 1770, the year of the St Petersburg club's founding.
107 *Moskovskii kur'er*, I (1805), p. 54.
108 Hatchett, Notebook V, f. [27].
109 *Ibid.*, f. [25v.].
110 V. Veresaev, *Pushkin v zhizni*, I, 6th edn (Moscow, 1936), p. 44.
111 Parkinson, *Tour*, p. 103. See also Hatchett, Notebook V, f. [5].
112 Lincolnshire Record Office, Worsley MSS. no. 24, f. 188.
113 The basic source is Ol'ga Chaianova, *Teatr Maddoksa v Moskve 1776–1805* (Moscow, 1927). See also Malcolm Burgess, 'Fairs and Entertainers in 18th century Russia', *SEER*, XXXVIII (1959), 109–10; A. G. Cross, 'The Eighteenth-Century Russian Theatre through British Eyes', *Studies in Voltaire and the Eighteenth Century*, CCXIX (1983), 231–3; Gerald R. Seaman, 'Michael Maddox – English Impresario in Eighteenth-Century Russia', in B. Christa *et al.*, *Slavic Themes: Papers from Two Hemispheres* (Neuried, 1988), pp. 321–5.
114 PRO, Lowry Cole Papers 30/43. 12, f. 46 (Diary of Katherine Harris).
115 Coxe, *Travels*, I, p. 315.
116 William Tooke, *History of Russia, from the Foundation of the Monarchy by Rurik, to the Accession of Catharine the Second*, II (London, 1800), p. 428.
117 Hatchett, Notebook VI, f. [1].
118 *Plany i fasady teatra i maskeradnoi zaly v Moskve, postroennykh soderzhatelem publichnykh uveselenii anglichaninom Mikhailom Maddoksom* (Moscow, 1797).
119 Clarke, *Travels*, I, p. 143.
120 *Moskovskie vedomosti*, no. 2 (1795), 33, 38; no. 3, 56; no. 23, 580; no. 71, 1381.
121 *Ibid.*, no. 1, 16.
122 S. P. Zhikharev, *Zapiski sovremmenika* (M-L, 1955), p. 15; Vel. Kn. Nikolai Mikhailovich, *Moskovskii nekropol'*, I (spb, 1907), p. 74.
123 *Moskovskie vedomosti*, no. 7 (1795), 176; no. 8, 201; no. 15, 375; no. 18, 461; no. 73, 1406.
124 *Ibid.*, no. 8, 200; *Moskovskii nekropol'*, I, p. 348. For other 'English' shops, see *Moskovskie vedomosti*, no. 15 (1795), 373; no. 21, 538; (1796), no. 3, 42.
125 *Ibid.*, no. 58 (1795), 1178; *Times*, 24 November 1933.
126 See A. G. Cross, *'By the Banks of the Thames': Russians in Eighteenth-Century Britain* (Newtonville, Mass., 1980), pp. 268–9. In 1787, however, a certain James advertising English lessons in St Petersburg, described himself as a former teacher

of English in the Naval Cadet Corps: *Sanktpeterburgskie vedomosti*, no. 80 (5 October 1787), 1088.

127 *Moskovskii nekropol'*, I, p. 96; Derbyshire Record Office 239m/o613; *Biograficheskii slovar' professorov i prepodavatelei Im. Moskovskogo universiteta*, I (Moscow, 1855), pp. 90-1.

2 FACTORY MATTERS AND THE 'HONORABLE OF THE EARTH'

1 T. S. Willan, *The Early History of the Russia Company 1553-1603* (London, 1956), pp. 4-5.

2 John Milton, *A Brief History of Moscovia and of Other Less-Known Countries Lying Eastward of Russia as far as Cathay* (London, 1682), p. 69.

3 See David. S. Macmillan, 'The Russia Company of London in the Eighteenth Century: The Effective Survival of a 'Regulated' Chartered Company', *Guildhall Miscellany*, IV (1973), 222-36.

4 These records are now held in the Guildhall Library, London, and include the Court Minute Books, MS 11, 741/1-14; the Treasurers' Account Books, MS 11, 893/1-7; Miscellaneous Correspondence and Documents, MS 11,749 (3 boxes); Register of the British Church in St Petersburg, MS 11,192B.

5 David S. Macmillan, 'Problems in the Scottish Trade with Russia in the Eighteenth Century', in A. G. Cross (ed.), *Great Britain and Russia in the Eighteenth Century: Contacts and Comparisions* (Newtonville, Mass., 1979), pp. 165-7.

6 *SIRIO*, LXXVI (spb, 1891), 319, 337, 341.

7 *Ibid.*, 335.

8 F. Martens (ed.), *Sobranie traktatov i konventsii, zakliuchennykh Rossiei s inostrannymi derzhavami*, IX(X) (spb, 1892), 89.

9 Douglas K. Reading, *The Anglo-Russian Commercial Treaty of 1734* (New Haven and London, 1938), p. 301.

10 N. C. Hunt, 'The Russia Company and the Government, 1730-42', *OSP*, VII (1957), 64.

11 Herbert H. Kaplan, 'Russia's Impact on the Industrial Revolution in Great Britain during the Second Half of the Eighteenth Century: The Significance of International Commerce', *Forschungen zur Osteuropäischen Geschichte*, XXIX (Berlin, 1981), 9.

12 Arcadius Kahan, *The Plow, the Hammer and the Knout* (Chicago and London, 1985), p. 198.

13 Britain's pursuit of the Persian silk trade via Russia is a well-known episode in Anglo-Russian relations, not least for the involvement of the colourful adventurer Captain John Elton. His diary was published by a former member of the British Factory James Spilman in 1742 as *A Journey through Russia into Persia* and was included also in Jonas Hanway's vast *Historical Account of the British Trade over the Caspian Sea* (1753).

14 PRONI, Macartney Papers, D2225/1/2. For the treaty, see Martens, *Sobranie traktatov*, IX(X), pp. 242-59. For analyses of the treaty, see Knud Rahbek Schmidt, 'The Treaty of Commerce between Great Britain and Russia 1766: A Study on the Development of Count Panin's Northern System', *Scando-Slavica*, I (1954), 115-34; P. H. Clendenning, 'The Background and Negotiations for the Anglo-Russian Commercial Treaty of 1766', in Cross (ed.), *Great Britain and Russia*, pp. 145-63.

15 See also Kaplan's later article, 'Observations on the Value of Russia's Overseas Commerce with Great Britain during the Second Half of the Eighteenth Century', *Slavic*

Review, XLV *(1986), 85–94. Cf.* Arcadius Kahan, '*Eighteenth-Century Russian–British Trade: Russia's Contribution to the Industrial Revolution in Great Britain*', in Cross (ed.), *Great Britain and Russia*, pp. 185–9.

16 GL, MS 11,741/8, f. 328.

17 For the text of the treaty, see Martens, *Sobranie traktatov*, IX(X), 354–8.

18 See David S. Macmillan, 'Paul's "Retributive Measures" of 1800 against Britain: The Final Turning-Point in British Commercial Attitudes towards Russia', *Canadian–American Slavic Studies*, VII (1973), 68–77; and Macmillan's 'Russo-British Trade Relations under Alexander I', *Canadian–American Slavic Studies*, IX (1975), 437–48.

19 Kahan, *The Plow*, pp. 199–200; Jennifer Newman, ' "A very delicate Experiment": British Mercantile Strategies for Financing Trade in Russia, 1680–1780', in Ian Blanchard, Anthony Goodman and Jennifer Newman (eds.), *Industry and Finance in Early Modern History* (Stuttgart, 1992), pp. 116–41.

20 GL, MS 11,747/7, ff. 158, 163, 344–5; *SIRIO*, XIX (1876), 342–5; *Scots Magazine*, XXXV (1773), 157–8.

21 See D. B. Horn, *The British Diplomatic Service 1689–1789* (Oxford, 1961), ch. XIII: 'Diplomatists and Consuls'.

22 Quoted in *ibid.*, p. 239.

23 *Ibid.*, p. 253.

24 Letter from E. Forster, governor of the Russia Company, to Stephen Shairp, 1 December 1795, made available to me by Mrs Eleanor Rosser, a descendant of Shairp.

25 See O. J. Frederiksen, 'Virginia Tobacco in Russia under Peter the Great', *SEER*, XXI (1943), 40–56; and especially Jacob M. Price, 'The Tobacco Adventure to Russia', *Transactions of the American Philosophical Society*, NS LI, pt. 1 (1961), 3–120.

26 Information on Goodfellow is taken principally from Price, see index, p. 113, but particularly pp. 78–9, 110. See also D. B. Horn, *British Diplomatic Representatives, 1689–1789* (London, 1932), p. 110.

27 GL, MS 11,741/5, ff. 173, 289.

28 Quoted in Price, p. 78.

29 *SIRIO*, LXVIII (1889), 400, 412; Reading, *Anglo-Russian Commercial Treaty*, pp. 96–7. (Reading, incidentally, expresses his incomprehension at the 'peculiar distinction between a consul and public minister'.)

30 GL, MS 11,741/5, ff. 283, 284, 287.

31 *Ibid.*, ff. 302–3, 307–8.

32 *SIRIO*, LXVI (1889), 37–8.

33 *Ibid.*, p. 105.

34 *Ibid.*, pp. 202–3, 221–2.

35 *Ibid.*, p. 401. Jane Rondeau was the author of *Letters from a Lady, who resided some years in Russia, to her friend in England* (1775). See chapter 8.

36 *Ibid.*, p. 409. Cf. p. 455.

37 GL, MS 11,741/5, ff. 381–92.

38 *SIRIO*, LXVI, 555.

39 GL, MS 11,741/6, f. 15.

40 *SIRIO*, LXXXV (1893), 9.

41 *Ibid.*, 32, 35, 36, 43, 45, 72, 149; GL, MS 11,741/6, f. 167.

42 Macmillan, 'Russia Company', p. 228.

43 A. V. Demkin (comp.), *Russko-britanskie torgovye otnosheniia v XVIII veke* (Moscow, 1994), pp. 14–21.

44 GL, MS 11,741, ff. 262, 436; Lewis Namier and John Brooke, *The History of Parliament: The House of Commons 1754–1790*, III (Members K–Y) (London, 1985), 434–6 (Henry Shiffner).

45 *SIRIO*, CIII (1897), 144.

46 F. W. Steer, *The Shiffner Archives: A Catalogue* (Lewes, 1959), pp. xii–xiii.

47 Reading, *Anglo-Russian Commercial Treaty*, pp. 44–5. (This was the deal to which some of the Factory subsequently objected in 1732: see note 37.)

48 *Ibid.*

49 Clifford M. Foust, *Rhubarb the Wondrous Drug* (Princeton, 1992), p. 62. (In his notes, p. 262, Foust refers to the unholy row raised by Joseph Chitty, a London merchant and free of the Russia Company, who said he had bought up all the rhubarb through his factor Ernst Bardewick and that Shiffner & Wolff had used improper means to secure it. Foust is not aware of the Company minutes which reflect the affair in great detail: MS 11,741/6, ff. 40–3, 47–50, 73–9.)

50 *SIRIO*, LXVI, 530. (The particular culprit was a naturalised British merchant named Meyer, see *ibid.*, 504. The loss of the wool contract to the Prussians had been a bitter blow for the British, who were frequently known as 'the wool merchants' in Russia.)

51 GL, MS 11,741/6, f. 307.

52 *Ibid.*, ff. 309, 314.

53 *SIRIO*, CX (1901), 89–90.

54 *Ibid.*, CXLVIII (1916), 168.

55 *Ibid.*, 149–52. See also 206–7, 211–12, 216–17.

56 *Ibid.*, CIII, 183–4; GL, MS 11,741/6, ff. 414–15, 418, 427.

57 GL, MS 11, 741/6, f. 465.

58 *SIRIO*, CIII, 144; Hanway, *Historical Account of the British Trade over the Caspian Sea*, II (London, 1753), 122, 151–65.

59 GL, MS 11,741/6, ff. 447, 498.

60 GL, MS 741/7, ff. 103, 104.

61 Horn, *British Diplomatic Representatives*, p. 116.

62 SRO, Shairp of Houston, GD 30/1583/13.

63 Sir N. William Wraxall, *Historical Memoirs of My Own Time* (London, 1904), p. 110. See pp. 109–13.

64 See Carol S. Leonard, *Reform and Regicide: The Reign of Peter III of Russia* (Bloomington and Indianapolis, 1993), pp. 132–3 and references, pp. 197–8. (Leonard refers misleadingly to Wroughton as an 'agent' of the British government.)

65 SRO, GD 30/1583/17 and 18.

66 Horn, *British Diplomatic Representatives*, p. 116.

67 Earl of Ilchester and Mrs Langford-Brooke (eds. and trans.), *Correspondence of Catherine the Great When Grand Duchess, with Sir Charles Hanbury-Williams and Letters from Count Poniatowski* (London, 1928), p. 56. See also index for numerous other references to Swallow.

68 BL, Egerton MS 6,864.

69 Compare N. Wraxall, jr., *A Tour through Some of the Northern Parts of Europe, particularly Copenhagen, Stockholm, and Petersburgh*, 2nd edn (London, 1775) pp. 247ff, with N. W. Wraxall, *A Tour Round the Baltic, Thro' the Northern Countries of Europe, Particularly Denmark, Sweden, Finland, Russia, & Prussia*, 4th edn (London, 1807), pp. 278ff.

70 GL, MS 11,741/6, f. 487; MS 11,741/7, ff. 125–6, 128, 171, 178.

71 D. B. Horn, 'The Board of Trade and Consular Reports, 1696–1782', *English*

Historical Review, LIV (1939), 479; GL, MS 11,741/7, ff. 252-3, 378, 402 (brak); 305, 312, 313, 314, 326 (plague); 384 (cattle). For the brak problem up to and including 1734, see Reading, *Anglo-Russian Commercial Treaty*, pp. 201-19.

72 GL, MS 11,741/9, f. 272. Mrs Swallow died in 1807. Swallow's only son Samuel, jr. (b. 1765) received his freedom by patrimony only in November 1800 (MS 11,741/9, f. 272).

73 GL, MS 11,741/7, ff. 415, 417.

74 SRO, GD 30/1583/3 and 7; GL, MS 11, 741/6, ff. 365 (Allen), 393 (Shairp), 451, 498 (Maister).

75 SRO, GD 30/1583/4; GL, MS 11,192B, f. 23.

76 SRO, GD 30/1583/10; GL, MS 11,192B, f. 31 (W. Maister); MS 11,741/7, f. 109; SRO, GD 30/1583/18 (A. Maister).

77 GL, MS 11,741/8, ff. 8, 96. The Shairp of Shairp, Maude & Co., Russia merchants of Broad Street, London, was Alexander Shairp (d. 1789), Walter's nephew and apprenticed to him from 1757 to 1765.

78 Georgi, *Opisanie rossiisko-imperatorskogo stolichnogo goroda Sankt-Peterburga i dostopamiatnostei v okrestnostniakh onogo* (spb, 1794), p. 67; P. G. Liubomirov, *Ocherki po istorii russkoi promyshlennosti* (Moscow, 1947), p. 490; E. Amburger, *Ingermanland*, I (Cologne and Vienna, 1980), 339, 369.

79 GL, MS 11,741/8, ff. 70, 94-5.

80 *AKV*, XII (Moscow, 1877), 50; XIII (1879), 130.

81 GL, MS 11,741/8, ff. 226-7, 232.

82 GL, MS 11,741/6, f. 502.

83 Anthony Cross, 'British Freemasons in Russia during the Reign of Catherine the Great', *OSP*, NS IV (1971), pp. 54-6; *Stoletie Sankt-Peterburgskogo Angliiskogo sobraniia* (spb, 1870), pp. 4, 54.

84 Anthony Cross (ed.), *Engraved in the Memory James Walker, Engraver to the Empress Catherine the Great, and His Russian Anecdotes* (Oxford and Providence, 1993), p. 55.

85 GL, MS 11,741/8, ff. 222, 233, 240. See the comments of the Russian ambassador in London on this abuse: *AKV*, IX, 103-4.

86 *Ibid.*, ff. 296, 326; GL, MS 11,741/9, ff. 46-7, 49.

87 GL, MS 11,741/9, ff. 53-4.

88 *Ibid.*, f. 87; *Gentleman's Magazine*, LXV, pt. 2 (1795), 705.

89 GL, MS 11,741/9, ff. 91-3, 95, 98, 100. On 11 July 1789 Stephen signed 'Articles of Agreement & Partnership' with his brother Walter in London (copy made available to me by Mrs Rosser). When he became consul, his brother Alexander took over officially the running of the Petersburg end of the business.

90 Horn, *British Diplomatic Representatives*, p. 118.

91 GL, MS 11,741/9, ff. 122, 228.

92 *Ibid.*, f. 250.

93 V. N. Aleksandrenko, *Russkie diplomaticheskie agenty v Londone v XVIII v.*, II (Warsaw, 1897), 279-81.

94 *Ibid.*, p. 281. See also Rosalin Barker, *Prisoners of the Tsar: East Coast Sailors Held in Russia 1800-1801* (Beverley, 1992).

95 *Ibid.*, pp. 282-4. See also Macmillan, 'Paul's "Retributive Measures" of 1800', pp. 73-4.

96 *The Observer*, no. 469 (21 December 1800), back page; Aleksandrenko, *Russkie diplomaticheskie agenty*, II, 284, 294.

97 Derbyshire Record Office, Matlock, Fitzherbert Papers, 239M/O. 492.

98 GL, MS 11,741/9, ff. 160, 161.

99 The term is used to cover 'factories' (*fabriki*), 'manufactories' (*manufaktury*) and 'works' (*zavody*), which are all used in the eighteenth century but with far from complete consistency.

100 AVPR, Fond Snosheniia s Angliei, opis' 35/1 1720, no. 488, f. 8. (The phrase in the document is 'zavedenie zavodov'.)

101 See D. Baburin, *Ocherki po istorii Manufaktur-Kollegii* (Moscow, 1939). See also Kahan, *The Plow*, ch. III: 'Industry'.

102 A. Bychkov (ed.), *Bumagi Imperatora Petra I* (spb, 1873), pp. 125–6. See also a similar order of the same date from Peter to P. P. Shafirov: RGADA, Fond 35 Snosheniia s Angliei, op. 1, no. 329, ff. 1–2.

103 RGADA, Fond 9, Kabinet Petra I, Otdel II, Kn. 25, f. 212; E. I. Zaozerskaia, *Razvitie legkoi promyshlennosti v Moskve v pervoi chetverti XVIII v.* (Moscow, 1953), pp. 177–84.

104 D. G. Kirby, 'The Balance of the North and Baltic Trade: George Mackenzie's Relation, August 1715', SEER, LIV (1976), 449.

105 RGADA, Fond 9, Otdel II, kn. 58, f. 111.

106 V. G. Geiman, 'Manufakturnaia promyshlennost' Peterburga petrovskogo vremeni', in A. I. Andreev (ed.), *Petr Velikii: sbornik statei* (M-L, 1947), pp. 277–9.

107 *Ibid.*, p. 279.

108 P. N. Petrov, *Istoriia Sankt Peterburga* (spb, 1885), pp. 594–5. On James Gardner, see SIRIO, LXVI (1889), 408–9, 454, 521; GL, MS. 11,192B, ff. 20, 28; on Francis, his son, see: MS 11,192B, ff. 66, 69, 74, 81, 100, 181, 190, 270; *Zhurnal Komiteta ministrov*, I (spb, 1888), p. 364; Tatiana Bakounine, *Répertoire biographique des franc-maçons russes* (Paris, 1968), p. 167.

109 'Vedomost' sostoiashchim v S.-Peterburge fabrikam, manufakturam i zavodam 1794 sentiabriia 1 dnia', SIRIO, I (1867), 352–61.

110 F. Veselago (ed.), MIRF, XII (spb, 1886), 226.

111 University of Edinburgh, Black Correspondence, Gen 873/II, ff. 125–6; Gen 875/II, ff. 115–16.

112 Georgi, *Opisanie*, pp. 243–4; *Sanktpeterburgskie vedomosti*, no. 12 (8 Feb. 1790), 180.

113 SIRIO, I, 358; Birmingham Reference Libraries, Matthew Boulton papers, Russian Mint Box I, Letter of 2 April 1803 (Rev. Smirnov to M. Boulton).

114 The owner of the playing-card manufactory in 1794 was Henry Klausing. An earlier British owner of a similar factory was James Dunant (d. 1780) and the business was continued for a while by his wife. 'Kartochnyi/kartoshnyi zavod' was, incidentally, rendered as a 'potato factory' by William L. Blackwell, *The Beginnings of Russian Industrialization 1800–1860* (Princeton, 1968), p. 245.

115 *Sanktpeterburgskie vedomosti*, no. 4 (14 Jan. 1791), 56–7; Georgi, *Opisanie*, p. 230 (starch).

116 Georgi, *Opisanie*, pp. 140, 162, 228; Petrov, *Istoriia Sankt-Peterburga*, p. 595; National Library of Ireland, Dublin, Kavanagh Papers, MS 8049/13 'The Russian Cavanaughs'; BL, Add. MS 38340, ff. 215–221v.; John H. Appleby, 'Mills, Models and Magdalens – the Dingley Brothers and the Society of Arts', *Journal of the Royal Society of Arts*, CXL (1992), 271–2; E. I. Indova, 'O rossiiskikh manufakturakh vtoroi poloviny XVIII v.', in A. L. Narochnitskii (ed.), *Istoricheskaia geografiia Rossii XII – nachalo XX v.* (Moscow, 1975), p. 237.

117 Marchioness of Londonderry and H. M. Hyde (eds.), *The Russian Diaries of Martha and Catherine Wilmot* (London, 1934), p. 175.

118 [Cte de Fortia Piles], *Voyage de deux français en Allemagne, Danemarck, Suède, Russie et Pologne, fait en 1790–1792*, III (Paris, 1796), 143–5.

119 *The Political Register*, IV (1769), 243. First quoted in Appleby, 'Mills', p. 271.

120 *SIRIO*, CXLVIII (1916), 401–4.

121 William Tooke, *View of the Russian Empire during the Reign of Catharine the Second and to the Close of the Present Century*, III (London, 1799), 505.

122 M. I. Tugan-Baranovsky, *The Russian Factory in the 19th Century* (Homewood, Ill., 1970), p. 30, note 68, referring to *Polnoe sobranie zakonov*, XIV, no. 10,376 and XV, no. 11,080; NL of Wales, Wms 474, Add. MS 272c, letter of 30 August (OS) 1770.

123 'The Strange Effects of Some Effervescent Mixtures; in a letter from Dr James Mounsey, Physician, to Mr Henry Baker', *Philosophical Transactions for the Year 1757*, L, pt. 1 (1758), 19–22.

124 For contemporary references to the manufactory, see William Richardson, *Anecdotes of the Russian Empire* (London, 1784), p. 68; Georgi, *Opisanie*, pp. 706–7. For accounts, see Petrov, *Istoriia Sankt-Peterburga*, p. 596; Liubomirov, *Ocherki*, pp. 143, 255, 630; K. A. Pazhitnov, *Ocherki istorii tekstil'noi promyshlennosti dorevoliutsionnoi Rossii* (Moscow, 1958), pp. 47–9; Peter Struve, 'English Tissue-Printing in Russia: An Episode in Russian Economic History', *SEER*, XIX (1940), 303–10. Blackwell's few lines on 'Chamberlain and Cuzzins' are confused: *Beginnings*, p. 245.

125 The other guarantor was the well-known linen manufacturer A. I. Zatrapeznov, with whom Cavanaugh was closely connected. See James Cracraft, 'James Brogden in Russia, 1787–1788', *SEER*, XLVII (1969), 240 and note. See also Cavanaugh's testimony on the Anglo-Russian linen trade to a Parliamentary committee in 1774; A. V. Demkin (ed.), *Russko-britanskie torgovye otnosheniia v XVIII veke*, pp. 57–67.

126 The spelling of Chamberline's name is in accord with entries in the Church register: MS 11,192B, f. 23. For information on his daughter's purchase of the house I am grateful to Mme Broitova of St Petersburg.

127 For details on his father, see chapter 5. Cozens' baptism on 27 April/8 May 1726 is recorded in the Church register, MS 11,192B, f. 13.

128 RGADA, Fond 168, d. 101, ff. 15–15v. I am grateful to Dr R. Bartlett for this reference.

129 'Druzheskie pis'ma', *Priiatnoe i poleznoe preprovozhdenie vremeni*, IX (1796), 137–8. Cozens' wife Margaret (née Bosanquet) was buried at Krasnoe Selo on 13/24 June 1767: MS 11,192B, f. 43. See also *ibid.*, ff. 31, 32, 35, 40, 43, 47, 146 for other references to the Cozens family.

130 Brotherton Library, Leeds University, Special Collections, Leeds Russian Archive, Last Will & Testament of John Cayley (1794), f. 3.

131 Tooke, *View*, III, p. 546.

132 See note 108. The Petersburg Gardners originated in Staffordshire and were said to be distant relations of Admiral Gardner, Lord Gardner of Uttoxeter (1742–1809). See William S. Childe-Pemberton, *The Baroness de Bode 1775–1803* (London, 1900), pp. 250, 254. The Moscow Gardners were also often said to have come from Staffordshire, but they have recently been 'claimed' by the Aberdeen Gardners: see Marvin C. Ross, *Russian Porcelains* (Norman, Oklahoma, 1968), pp. 3–4.

133 The account that follows is based largely on Iu. Arbat, *Farforovyi gorodok* (Moscow, 1957) (on which Ross's *Russian Porcelains*, pp. 3–4, 37–50, also draws

heavily) and N. V. Chernyi, *Farfor Verbilok* (Moscow, 1970), pp. 1–58. Other sources are separately noted.

134 Andrei Bolotov, quoted in Arbat, p. 21.

135 I. S. Kriukova, *Russkaia skul'ptura malykh form* (Moscow, 1969), pp. 30–7.

136 For an analysis of the pieces in the Marjorie Merriweather Post Collection at Hillwood, Washington D.C., see Ross, pp. 52–105; for the Talbot Collection, see G. Bernard Hughes, 'An English Potter's Triumph in Imperial Russia', *Country Life*, CXXXIII (28 Feb. 1963), 408–10.

137 *AKV*, XXII (1881), 523.

138 See P. H. Clendenning, 'William Gomm: A Case Study of the Foreign Entrepreneur in Eighteenth Century Russia', *Journal of European Economic History*, VI (1977), 533–48. Clendenning concentrates solely on Gomm's timber concerns, but sadly, even here his use of sources is not always reliable.

139 GL, MS 11,741/6, ff. 356, 421. See also Appleby, 'Mills', p. 272, who has Gomm apprenticed to another William Gomm of London. Clendenning gives 1745 as the year of Gomm's freedom.

140 Price, 'Tobacco Adventure', p. 94.

141 Percy A. Scholes, *The Great Dr Burney*, II (London, 1948), p. 307.

142 Unless otherwise noted, the account which follows of Gomm's timber enterprises is based on: 'Ekstrakt ot kommisii mednykh deneg o angliiskom kuptse Gome s kompaniei v dannom emu lesnom promysle, po kotoromu on nyne v kazne v dolgu sostoit, so vsepoddanneishim na to kommiskim mneniem' [1764], *Senatskii arkhiv*, XII (spb, 1893), 652–8; N. Iukhantsov (ed.), *Sbornik svedenii i materialov po vedomstvu ministerstva finansov* (spb, 1866), pp. 223–8; M. A. Tseitlin, *Ocherki razvitiia lesozagotovok i lesopileniia v Rossii* (Moscow, 1968), pp. 117–21.

143 Gomm's marriage to Mrs Jeanne Marie Barraud on 13/24 October 1750 is recorded in the Church register, GL MS 11,192B, f. 22. The 'Pedigree of the Gomm Family' in Francis Culling Carr-Gomm (ed.), *Letters and Journals of Field-Marshal Sir William Maynard Gomm* (London, 1881), p. [12], refers to Marie Jeanne, daughter of Russian Councillor Poggenpohl and his wife Marie de Barraud of Normandy.

144 Ramsbottom in a 'memoire' of 28 February/11 March 1777 describes himself as 'associé en 1753 dans la Maison de Gomm et Comp', who 'residois en personne a Kola, a Meçen et ensuite a Onega': RGADA, Fond 19, Kommissiia o kommertsii, ed. khr. 286, ch. 3, ff. 240–3.

145 The British ambassador the Earl of Buckinghamshire mentions in a dispatch of 24 September/5 October 1764 the shipping of goods to Britain in Russian ships built by Gomm: Adelaide D'Arcy Collyer (ed.), *The Despatches and Correspondence of John, Second Earl of Buckinghamshire, Ambassador to the Court of Catherine II, of Russia 1762–1765*, II (London, 1902), 239.

146 K. L. Blum, *Ein Russische Staatsmann: Des Grafen Jakob Johann Sievers. Dentwürdigkeiten zur Geschichte Russlands*, I (Leipzig, 1857), 230, 294; [George Macartney], *Account of Russia in the Year MDCCLXVII* (London, 1768), p. 5; Scholes, *The Great Dr Burney*, I, 131. See also the letter of Fanny Burney of 14 August 1798 on the 'Russian funds': *The Journals and Letters of Fanny Burney*, IV (Oxford, 1973), 166.

147 *SIRIO*, CXL (1912), 535, 564–5.

148 Aleksandrenko, *Russkie diplomaticheskie agenty*, I, 276.

149 RGADA, Fond Kabinet Ee Velichestva, op. 3, ed. khr. 69, ff. 3v.–4.

150 *SIRIO*, X (1972), 192–3, 203, 206, 250–1.

151 *Ibid.*, CXLI, 319.

152 A. I. Komissarenko and I. S. Sharkova (eds.), *Vneshniaia torgovlia Rossii cherez Peterburgskii port vo vtoroi polovine XVIII–nachala XIX v.* (Moscow, 1981), pp. 17, 38, 79.

153 *Sankpeterburgskie vedomosti*, no. 1 (2 Jan 1775), p. [3].

154 BL, Add. MS 32, 192, f. 100.

155 PRONI, Macartney Papers, D572/7/63.

156 Kaplan, 'Russia's Impact', p. 9. Gomm was also anxious that Russia should have young Russians skilled in European banking and book-keeping methods: see A. G. Cross, *'By the Banks of the Thames': Russians in Eighteenth-Century Britain* (Newtonville, Mass., 1980), p. 207.

157 Iukhantsov, *Sbornik svedenii*, p. 227.

158 *Diaries and Correspondence of James Harris, First Earl of Malmesbury*, I (London, 1844), 411. See also Horn, *British Diplomatic Representatives*, p. 167; S. T. Bindoff *et al.*, *British Diplomatic Representatives 1789–1852* (London, 1934), p. 177.

159 The family pedigree already cited (note 143) is inaccurate in several respects. Gomm's elder daughter Jane Gomm (1753–1822), who became governess to George III's daughters, is buried alongside her father, as is his other daughter Sophia, Countess de Brühl (b. 1761) and his niece Sophia Louisa (1788–1917).

160 *Letters and Journals of Field-Marshal Sir William Maynard Gomm*, p. 23.

161 *Gentleman's Magazine*, LXI, pt. 2 (1791), 1064.

162 GL, MS 11,741/7, f. 154.

163 Cracraft, 'James Brogden in Russia', p. 232, *Dnevnik A.V. Khrapovitskogo 1782–93* (spb, 1874), p. 376; John Parkinson, *A Tour of Russia, Siberia and the Crimea 1792–1794* (London, 1971), p. 228. Potemkin loved his food as much as Sutherland. The Rev. William Coxe told (but only published in the fifth edition) the story of Potemkin so liking the roast beef he was served at Sutherland's that he took the rest home with him: *Travels into Poland, Russia, Sweden, and Denmark*, II (London, 1802), 373. Sutherland was also the subject of a wonderful anecdote of misunderstanding in the memoirs of the French ambassador (*Mémoires ou souvenirs et anecdotes par M. le Comte de Ségur*, II (Paris, 1826), 249–53) and earned a place in the pantheon of the fabulously rich of Catherine's reign (E. P. Karnovich, *Zamechatel'nye bogatstva chastnykh lits v Rossii* (spb, 1874), pp. 361–3).

164 *Dnevnik Khrapovitskogo*, p. 203.

165 N. N. Firsov, *Pravitel'stvo i obshchestvo v ikh otnosheniiakh k vneshnei torgovle Rossii v tsarstvovanie Imperatritsy Ekateriny II* (Kazan, 1902), 108–9.

166 *Sochineniia Derzhavina*, VI (spb, 1871), 4.

167 *Ibid.*, p. 627.

168 *Ibid.*, V, 755, 771, 843.

169 *Ibid.*, VI, p. 648. Khrapovitskii reports that a court doctor, Blok, had said Sutherland had been ill for the previous two years: *Dnevnik Khrapovitskogo*, p. 376.

170 *Sochineniia Derzhavina*, VI, 648.

171 AKV, XII (1877), 338.

172 Bedfordshire County Office, Bedford, Whitbread Papers, MS. 5699, 4474–81. Substantial extracts were published in A. G. Cross, 'The Sutherland Affair and its Aftermath', SEER, L (1972), 257–75.

173 Quoted in Roger Fulford, *Samuel Whitbread 1764–1815: A Study in Opposition* (London, 1967), pp. 20–1.

174 Whitbread Papers, MS 4479, letter of 16/28 October 1800; GL, MS 11,192B, f. 109 (marriage of Sarah Sutherland to Browne).

175 GL, MS 11,741/8, f. 347. Richard Rigail (b. 1761) was a son of the merchant Jacob

Rigail and his wife Mary-Anne, widow of Baron Sutherland's brother John (d. 1757).

176 Whitbread Papers, MS 5699, letter of 6/17 April 1792.

177 *Ibid.*, MS 4479.

178 A. H. Sutherland was very prominent in the Russia Company, being an assistant for over fifteen years and elected a consul between 1799 and 1801. He was not only a respected merchant, but a very rich one. He accumulated an immense collection of prints and engravings, which his widow extended and left to the Bodleian Library: *Catalogue of the Sutherland Collection*, 2 vols. (London, 1837–8).

179 See James Whishaw, *A History of the Whishaw Family* (London, 1935).

180 Whitbread Papers, MS 4480.

181 See note 130.

182 NL of Wales, Wms 474, Add. MS 272c.

183 It is from the Church register (GL, MS 11,192B) that much of the evidence for the family connections is taken; it would seem unnecessary to cite here the many folio numbers involved.

184 Francisco de Miranda was often in the company of Moberly and Anderson in 1787: *Archivo del general Miranda, Viajes*, II (Caracas, 1929), 428, 430, 432.

185 On Wilhelm and Elizabeth Poggenpohl, see AKV, IX, 59, 68, 106, 107; XXII, 3, 40, 142; Aleksandrenko, *Russkie diplomaticheskie agenty*, II, 396; C. A. E. Moberly, *Dolce Domum: George Moberly, His Family and Friends* (London, 1911), p. 20. There is a wonderful and long description by Fanny Burney of her meeting in 1772 with Poggenpohl, her first 'Russian' and who spoke excellent English: Annie Raine Ellis (ed.), *The Early Diary of Frances Burney 1768–1778* (London, 1913), pp. 151–60.

186 Cracraft, 'James Brogden in Russia', p. 222; GL, MS 11,741/8, f. 258.

187 Cracraft, 'James Brogden in Russia', pp. 227–8.

188 GL, MS 11,741/8, ff. 166, 281, 295. On George Cayley, see chapter 4.

189 Cracraft, 'James Brogden in Russia', p. 235.

190 GL, MS 11,741/6, ff. 365, 498; MS 11,192B, f. 63.

191 There are references to Saffree and Raikes in the correspondence between William Raikes in London and Robert Duesbery in St Petersburg: Brynmor Jones Library, University of Hull, Duesbery Papers, DDDU/20/8a–b.

192 Cracraft, 'James Brogden in Russia', p. 230; Brotherton Library, Leeds, Gunning Papers, VII, Egerton 2702, ff. 10–11.

193 Liubomirov, *Ocherki*, p. 491.

194 *The Russian Journals of Martha and Catherine Wilmot*, p. 175. See also pp. 29, 168–9.

195 Parkinson, *Tour*, p. 41; *Archivo del general Miranda*, II 387, 408, 434–5, M. P. Alekseev (ed.), *Shekspir i russkaia kul'tura* (M-L, 1965), pp. 61–2; Kent Archives Office, Maidstone, Norman MSS U310c3, no. 3, f. 2v.

196 J. Henry Harris (ed.), *Robert Raikes: The Man and His World* (Bristol, 1899), pp. 240–85.

197 Frederick Boase, *Modern English Biography*, I (London, 1901), 577; IV, 623–4; *Akademiia nauk SSSR: Personal'nyi sostav*, I (Moscow, 1974), 374.

198 Moberly, *Dolce Domum*, p. 18.

199 V. I. Maikov, *Izbrannye sochineniia* (M-L, 1966), p. 105.

200 Paul Dukes (ed.), *Catherine the Great's Instruction (Nakaz) to the Legislative Commission* (Newtonville, Mass., 1977), p. 84.

201 Whitbread Papers, MS 4478; SRO, Shairp of Huston, GD 30/1583/14 and 17.

202 Hanway, *Historical Account*, II, 123.
203 Glasgow University Library, MS Murray 503, f. 12.

3 'IN ANGLORUM TEMPLO': THE ENGLISH CHURCH AND ITS CHAPLAINS

1 A. B. Granville, *St Petersburgh*, II (London, 1828), 202–3.
2 *The Picture of Petersburg* (London, 1801), pp. 107–10.
3 *The Character of the Russians, and a Detailed History of Moscow* (London, 1823), p. 375.
4 *The Travels of Olearius in Seventeenth-Century Russia*, trans. S. H. Baron (Stamford, 1967), p. 282.
5 See John H. Appleby, 'Some of Arthur Dee's Associations before Visiting Russia Clarified, Including Two Letters from Sir Theodore Mayerne', *Ambix*, XXVI (March 1979), 8.
6 *Ibid.*
7 United Society for the Propagation of the Gospel, London, Correspondence A.1/85.
8 *Ibid.*, A.1/138.
9 BL, Add. MSS 37, 354, f. 279v.
10 United Society for the Propagation of the Gospel, Correspondence A.5/12. See other letters at A.5/13, 69, 171.
11 C. F. Pascoe, *Two Hundred Years of S.P.G. An Historical Account of the Society for the Propagation of the Gospel in Foreign Parts 1701–1900*, II (London, 1901), 850.
12 J. and J. A. Venn, *Alumni Cantabrigienses*, pt. 1, IV (Cambridge, 1927), 217.
13 GL, British Factory in Russia Register 1706–1815, MS 11,192B, first pages unfoliated.
14 *Ibid.*, f. 4.
15 Venn, pt. 1, I (1922), 380.
16 GL, MS 11, 192B, f. 6.
17 Bodleian Library, Oxford, Robinson Papers, A. 286, f. 75.
18 Quoted in Russian version of Latin original in P. N. Berkov, 'Tomas Konsett, kapellan angliiskoi faktorii v Rossii', in *Problemy mezhdunarodnykh literaturnykh sviazei*, ed. B.G. Reizov (Leningrad, 1962), p. 4.
19 Kh. Grasgoff (H. Grasshoff), 'Iz istorii sviazei Berlinskogo obshchestva nauk s Rossiei v 20-kh godakh XVIII v.', *XVIII vek*, VII (M-L, 1966), 60.
20 PRO, SP 91/9, ff. 396–7, 407–10.
21 See Berkov, 'Tomas Konsett', pp. 10–13.
22 *The Present State and Regulations of the Church of Russia* (London, 1729), p. i.
23 *For God and Peter the Great: The Works of Thomas Consett, 1723–1729*, ed. J. Cracraft (New York, 1982). Cracraft's introduction (pp. 9–37) is the most thorough discussion available of Consett's life and works.
24 *The Picture of Petersburg*, p. 108.
25 Grasshoff, p. 65.
26 GL, Court Minute Books of the Russia Company, MS 11,741/6, f. 106.
27 *Ibid.*
28 *Ibid.*, f.111.
29 Venn, pt.1, III (1924), 75.
30 John Cook, *Voyages and Travels through the Russian Empire, Tartary, and Part of the Kingdom of Persia*, I (Edinburgh, 1770), 447.

31 GL, Russia Company, MS 11,741/6, ff. 256–7.

32 Cf. *Picture of Petersburg*, pp. 108–9 and British Factory Register MS II, 192B, ff. 19, 70 .

33 *Gentleman's Magazine*, XLVIII (1777), III; *The Correspondence of Jeremy Bentham*, ed. T. L. S. Sprigge, II (London, 1968), 98–115; *The Diary of Sylas Neville 1767–1788* (London, 1950), pp. 31–2.

34 GL, Russia Company MS 11,741/6, f. 370.

35 Joseph Foster, *Alumni Oxonienses 1715–1886*, I (London, 1887), 393.

36 BL, Add. MSS 32, 420, f. 81.

37 GL, Russia Company MS 11, 741/7, f. 29.

38 BL, Add. MSS 32, 419, ff. 327–27v.

39 *Istoriia Akademii Nauk SSSR*, I (M-L, 1958), 408.

40 BL, Add. MSS 32, 419, ff. 14, 279; 32, 420, f. 159. [The translation referred to was *Sinave et Trouvore, tragédie*. Traduit du russe par le prince Alexandre Dolgorouky (spb, 1751)].

41 POARAN, Fond 21, Miller, Gerard Fridrikh, op. 3, ed. khr. 73, ff. 2v., 6v.

42 B. L. Modzalevskii, *Spisok chlenov Imp. Akademii Nauk* (spb, 1908), p. 128.

43 POARAN, Fond 21, op. 3, ed. khr. 73, ff. 8, 10.

44 M. F. Shabaeva (ed.), *Ocherki istorii shkoly i pedagogicheskoi mysli narodov SSSR* (Moscow, 1973), pp. 119–22; J. L. Black, *G.-F. Müller and the Imperial Russian Academy* (Kingston and Montreal, 1986), pp. 166–8.

45 POARAN, Fond 21, op. 3, ed. khr. 73, f. 48v., 51; A. G. Cross, 'Russian Students in Eighteenth-Century Oxford (1766–75)', *Journal of European Studies*, V (1975), 91–110.

46 *The Correspondence of King George the Third*, I (London, 1927), 194. See N. Hans, 'Dumaresq, Brown and Some Early Educational Projects of Catherine II', *SEER*, XL (1961), 229–35; M. P. Alekseev, *Iz istorii angliiskoi literatury* (M-L, 1960), pp. 237–9.

47 POARAN, Fond 21, op. 3, ed. khr. 73, f. 93.

48 *Ibid.*, ff. 82–82v., 87–8, 91; D. Kobeko, *Tsesarevich Pavel Petrovich (1754–1776)*, 3rd edn (spb, 1889), pp. 28–9.

49 Russia Company MS 11,741/7, ff. 230–1.

50 POARAN Fond 21, op. 3, ed. khr. 73, ff. 101–101v.

51 Peterburgskoe otdelenie Instituta istorii RAN, Fond 36, Vorontsovy, op. 2, ed. khr. 425, ff. 1–2. [The portrait was painted in 1798 by Thomas Le Hardy and subsequently engraved by William Nutter.]

52 *Ibid.*, f. 3. Since these pages on Dumaresq were written there has appeared a typically thorough study by John H. Appleby, 'Daniel Dumaresq, D.D., F.R.S. (1712–1805) as a Promoter of Anglo-Russian Science and Culture', *Notes and Records of the Royal Society of London*, XLIV (1990), 25–50.

53 PRO, Kew, SP 91/107, ff. 162–3.

54 Information in a letter from I. A. Lapis of the then Office for the Preservation of the Monuments of Leningrad; Berkov, 'Tomas Konsett', p. 10.

55 GL, Russia Company MS 11,741/6, f. 424.

56 BL, Add. MSS. 32,19, f. 28v.

57 GL, Russia Company MS 11, 741/6, ff. 439, 457.

58 *Ibid.*, f. 454.

59 BL, Add. MSS. 32,419, f. 279.

60 GL, Russia Company MS 11,741/6, f. 496.

61 GL, Russia Company MS 11,741/7, f. 87.

62 *Ibid.*, ff. 87, 88.

63 BL, Add. MSS 32,420, f. 159v.

64 *Gentleman's Magazine*, LXVI, pt. 1 (1796), 373; British Factory Register MS 11,192B, f. 25.

65 *Picture of Petersburg*, p. 109.

66 Venn, pt. 1, III, 20; DNB, XI (London, 1909), 141–2.

67 *Some Account of the Public Life, and a Selection from the Unpublished Writings of the Earl of Macartney*, II (London, 1807), 62–93.

68 *Account of Russia, MDCCLXVII*, (London, 1768), pp. 183–230.

69 *The Rites and Ceremonies of the Greek Church, in Russia* (London, 1772), pp. xi–xiii, xviii.

70 GL, Russia Company MS 11,741/7, f. 282.

71 British Factory Register MS 11,192B, f. 49; Lewis Melville, *The Life of William Makepeace Thackeray* (London, n.d.), pp. 2–3.

72 *Correspondance de Falconet avec Catherine II 1767–1778* (Paris, 1921), pp. 129–30; H. H. Robbins, *Our First Ambassador to China: An Account of the Life of George, Earl of Macartney*, I (London, 1908), 82.

73 Robbins, I, 84.

74 *Ibid.*, pp. 82–4.

75 *The Early Diary of Frances Burney 1768–1778*, ed. A. R. Ellis, I (London, 1913), 151.

76 *The Rites and Ceremonies of the Greek Church, in Russia*, p. 43, note.

77 *The Early Diary*, I, 119, 134–5, 151–60.

78 P. A. Scholes, *The Great Doctor Burney*, I (London, 1948), 307; *The Journals and Letters of Fanny Burney*, IV (Oxford, 1973), 166.

79 *Mémoires de la Princesse Dashkoff* (Paris, 1966), p. 275.

80 *The Life of Reginald Heber, D.D. Lord Bishop of Calcutta*, I (London, 1830), 177.

81 RNL, Fond 871, Ia. Ia. Shtelin, N. 201 (five letters from King, 1775–81); N. 202 (three draft letters from Stählin, 1775).

82 Letter of 5 October 1778, *ibid.*, N. 201, f. 6v. It is relevant to note that Catherine had recently ordered a set of medals bearing the likeness of Russian rulers to be struck. Some 102 plates of King's work appeared shortly after his death with the title of *Nummi Familiarum et Imperatorum Romanorum*.

83 W. Tooke, *The Life of Catharine II*, III, 5th edn (Dublin, 1800), 66–7, note. King travelled to Russia in 1781 with Baron Dimsdale, who was to inoculate the Grand Dukes Alexander and Constantine.

84 GL, Russia Company MS 11,741/7, f. 303.

85 United Grand Lodge of England, London, Journal of the Lodge of Perfect Union at St Petersburg, f. 28.

86 Dr William's Library, London, MS Modern 4, 24. 47 (1).

87 *Russia, or a Compleat Historical Account of All the Nations which Compose That Empire*, 4 vols. (London, 1780–3).

88 J. Nichols, *Literary Anecdotes of the Eighteenth Century*, IX (London, 1815), 170.

89 T. Thomson, *History of the Royal Society* (London, 1812), p. lix.

90 J. S. G. Simmons, 'Samuel Johnson "on the Banks of the Wolga" ', XI (1964), 29–30.

91 *Correspondence of Jeremy Bentham*, III (1971), 309.

92 *Gentleman's Magazine*, LV, pt. 2 (1785), 519–22, 761, 933–5; LVI, pt. 1 (1786), 455–60; LVI, pt. 2, 547–52, 643–8, 846–51, 921–4, 1013–15; LVII, pt. 1 (1787), 390–5.

93 *Life of Catharine II*, III, 88–9.

94 *Protokoly zasedanii konferentsii Akademii Nauk s 1725 po 1803 god*, IV (spb, 1911), 306–7.

95 Nichols, IX, 171–3.

96 See D. Griffiths, 'Castéra-Tooke: The First Western Biographer(s) of Catherine II', *SGECRN*, no. 10 (1982), 50–62.

97 *History of Russia*, I (London, 1800), x.

98 See in more detail A. G. Cross, 'The Reverend William Tooke's Contribution to English Knowledge of Russia at the End of the Eighteenth Century', *Canadian Slavic Studies*, III (1969), 113–15.

99 'The Voyage of Gregory Shelekoff', in *Varieties of Literature from Foreign Library Journals and Original Mss now First Published*, II (London, 1795), 1–42; 'Observations on Spontaneous Inflammations', in *The Pocket Magazine*, III (London, 1795), 88–97.

100 'Of the Russian Annals, Four Dissertations', in *Selections from the Most Celebrated Foreign Literary Journals and Other Periodical Publications*, II (London, 1798), 293–438.

101 *Secret Memoirs of the Court of Petersburg*, 2 vols. (London, 1800).

102 Venn, pt. 2, V (1953), p. 91; British Factory Register, MS 11,192B, f. 132.

103 *Picture of Petersburg*, p. 110.

104 British Factory Register MS 11,192B, ff. 116, 192.

105 K. A. Papmehl, 'Letters by L. K. Pitt, British Chaplain in St. Petersburg, on the Person and Policies of the Emperor Paul', *Canadian–American Slavic Studies*, VII (1973), 85–105.

106 *A Sermon preached in the Chapel of the British Factory in St Petersburg, on Sunday 10th/22nd Dec. 1805, on the occasion of the late glorious victory obtained over the combined fleets of France and Spain and on the lamented death of Lord Viscount Nelson* (spb, 1805).

107 Foster, *Alumni Oxonienses*, III, 1121.

108 AKV, XXX (Moscow, 1881), 224.

109 A. N. Pypin, *Religioznoe dvizhenie pri Aleksandre I* (Petrograd, 1916), pp. 27–8.

110 N. F. Von-Kruze, 'Imperatritsa Elisaveta Alekseevna', *Russkaia starina*, VII (1873), pp. 212–27. Includes the texts of correspondence between the empress and Mrs Pitt.

111 GL, Russia Company MS 11,741/9, f. 188.

112 *Ibid.*, f. 194.

113 *Ibid.*, f. 200.

114 *Ibid.*, ff. 200–1.

115 *Ibid.*, f. 200.

116 *Ibid.*, ff. 232–5.

117 *Ibid.*, ff. 237, 239.

118 British Factory Register MS 11,192B, f. 165.

119 GL, Russia Company MS 11,741/9, ff. 262, 263.

120 *Ibid.*, f. 340. The Court acknowledged that one of its unspoken objections to Pitt had now been met: 'Mr Pitt now in priests orders and consequently capable of holding the Chaplaincy' (*ibid.*, f. 342).

121 *Ibid.*, ff. 350–1, 354.

122 GL, Russia Company MS 11,741/10, f. 171.

123 *Ibid.*, f. 172.

124 *Ibid.*, ff. 195, 197.

125 GL, Russia Company MS 11,749/1, document 9.

126 GL, Russia Company MS 11,741/8, f. 129.

127 *Ibid.*, f. 135.

128 *Ibid.*, f. 360.

129 GL, Russia Company MS 11,741/10, ff. 173, 195, 229.

130 'A Surgeon in the British Navy', *A Voyage to St. Petersburg in 1814* (London, 1822), p. 32.

131 *Ibid.*, p. 33.

132 J. C. Grot, *Bemerkungen über die Religionsfreiheit der Ausländer im Russischen Reich*, I (Leipzig, 1797), 454–60.

133 Russia Company MS 11,741/7, f. 94.

134 *Ibid.*, ff. 161, 174.

135 B. A. Rozadeev, R. A. Somina and L. S. Kleshcheva, *Kronshtadt: arkhitekturnyi ocherk* (Leningrad, 1977), pp. 73–4.

136 Abel Burja, *Observations d'un voyageur sur la Russie, la Finlande, la Livonie, la Curlande et la Prusse* (Berlin, 1785), p. 87. Cf. *Novyi i polnyi geograficheskii slovar'* I (Moscow, 1788), 332.

137 GL, Russia Company MS 11,741/7, f. 308.

138 *Ibid.*, ff. 379–80.

139 GL, Russia Company MS 11,741/8, f. 100. See also J. M. Bullock, 'How a Monymusk Dominie Founded a Family', *Huntly Express* (31 May 1907). I am grateful to Mr A. G. Bagnall of Eastbourne, New Zealand, a descendant of Gordon, for sending me a copy of this item.

140 GL, Russia Company MS 11,741/8, ff. 113, 342; Venn, pt. 2, II, 591.

141 *Ibid.*, ff. 355, 372, 375; MS 11,741/9, f. 208; MS 11,741/10, f. 3.

142 See the detailed letter of Martha Wilmot, dated 9/21 March 1805, in *The Russian Journals of Martha and Catherine Wilmot,* ed. Marchioness of Londonderry and H. M. Hyde (London, 1934), p. 136. Cf. GL, Russia Company, MS 11,741/10, ff. 21–2, 294; MS 11,741/11, ff. 39, 52.

143 GL, Russia Company, MS 11,741/8, ff. 234–5, 240.

4 'DOCTORS ARE SCARCE AND GENERALLY SCOTCH'

1 John Richard, *A Tour from London to Petersburgh, From thence to Moscow, and Return to London by Way of Courland, Poland, Germany and Holland,* 2nd edn (London, 1780), p. 35.

2 Richard Hakluyt, *The Principal Navigations, Voyages, Traffiques and Discoveries of the English Nation,* I (London, 1907), 421.

3 See generally: George Lefevre, 'Sketch of the Origin and Present State of Medicine, and of Medical Institutions, in Russia', *British and Foreign Medical Review,* I (1836), 597–606; Frank G. Clemow, 'English Physicians at the Court of Moscow in the XVIth XVIIth centuries', *Anglo-Russian Literary Society Proceedings,* no. 21 (April–June 1898), 35–47; W. J. Bishop, 'English Physicians in Russia in the Sixteenth and Seventeenth Centuries', *Proceedings of the Royal Society of Medicine,* XXXIII (1929), 144–53. See also A. G. Cross, *Cambridge – Some Russia Connections* (Cambridge, 1987), pp. 5–6.

4 J. Hamel, *England and Russia* (London 1854; reprint 1968), p. 177. (Hamel suggests the verb is an English version of *pozhalovannyi*.)

5 John H. Appleby, 'Doctor Christopher Reitinger and a Seal of Tsar Boris Godunov', *OSP,* NS XII (1979), 34. It is fitting to mention at this juncture the massive contri-

bution made by Appleby to the study of the activities of British doctors in Russia over three centuries. His doctoral thesis, 'British Doctors in Russia, 1657–1807: Their Contribution to Anglo-Russian Medical and Natural History', was completed under my supervision at the University of East Anglia, Norwich, in 1979. The numerous articles spawned by that thesis as well as by subsequent research are duly noted in the appropriate places.

6 Hamel, *England and Russia*, pp. 235, 422 (Latin version).
7 See generally: Geraldine M. Phipps, 'Britons in Russia: 1613–82', *Societas*, VII (1977), 19–45, especially 36–8.
8 John H. Appleby, 'Dr Arthur Dee: Merchant and Litigant', *SEER*, LVII (1979), 32–55; 'Some of Arthur Dee's Associations before Visiting Russia Clarified, Including Two Letters from Sir Theodore Mayerne', *Ambix*, XXVI (1979), 1–15.
9 Leo Loewenson, 'The Works of Robert Boyle and "The Present State of Russia" by Samuel Collins (1671)', *SEER*, XXXIII (1955), 470–85.
10 For an able exposition of the structures and changes in the Russian medical services in the eighteenth century, see John T. Alexander, *Bubonic Plague in Early Modern Russia: Public Health and Urban Disaster* (Baltimore and London, 1980), pp. 36–50.
11 *Gentleman's Magazine*, LXVI, pt. 1 (1796), 521–2.
12 Robert Paul (ed.), 'Letters and Documents relating to Robert Erskine, Physician to Peter the Great, Czar of Russia 1677–1720', *Miscellany of the Scottish History Society*, II (Edinburgh, 1904), 399.
13 BL, Whitworth Papers, Add. MSS 37,354, f. 278v.
14 Paul (ed.), 'Letters and Documents', p. 400.
15 Alexander Gordon, *The History of Peter the Great, Emperor of Russia*, II (Aberdeen, 1755), 171.
16 John H. Appleby, 'Robert Erskine: Scottish Pioneer of Russian Natural History', *Archives of Natural History*, X (1982), 377–98.
17 Paul (ed.), 'Letters and Documents', pp. 413–14 (original Latin text and English translation).
18 *Ibid.*, pp. 383–7, 414–24.
19 Henrietta Taylor (ed.), *The Seven Sons of the Provost* (London, 1949), p. 91.
20 Paul (ed.), 'Letters and Documents', pp. 425–6 (in English translation by W. R. Morfill).
21 Appleby, 'Erskine', pp. 390–3. See also: S. P. Luppov, *Kniga v Rossii v pervoi chetverti XVIII veka* (Leningrad, 1973), pp. 238–40; John H. Appleby and Andrew Cunningham, 'Robert Erskine and Archibald Pitcairne: Two Scottish Physicians' Outstanding Libraries', *Bibliotheck*, XI (1982), 3–16.
22 Lefevre, 'Sketch', p. 604.
23 Iakov Chistovich, *Istoriia pervykh meditsinskikh shkol v Rossii* (SPB, 1883), appendix X, pp. lxvi–ccclxvi.
24 Information in letter from Mr D. L. L. Howells, 20 January 1977; GL, MS 11,192B, first unfoliated sheet.
25 Paul (ed.), 'Letters and Documents', p. 403.
26 [F.C. Weber], *The Present State of Russia*, II (London, 1722; reprint 1968), 3–36.
27 Renate Burgess, 'Thomas Garvine: Ayrshire Surgeon Active in Russia', *Medical History*, XIX (1975), 91–4.
28 John Bell, *Travels from St Petersburgh in Russia, to Various Ports of Asia*, I (new edn, Edinburgh, 1788), vii.
29 *Ibid.*, p. vi.

30 J. L. Stevenson (ed.), *A Journey from St Petersburg to Pekin 1719–22 by John Bell of Antermony* (Edinburgh, 1965), p. 1. Stevenson's Introduction, pp. 1–27, provides the fullest account of Bell's career.

31 Bell, *Travels*, I, 11.

32 *Ibid.*, II, 467.

33 Bell's dispatches are printed in SIRIO, LXXX (spb, 1892), 539–40, 544–6.

34 SRO, GD 30/1583/6 (letter of 10 August 1752 from Walter Shairp in St Petersburg).

35 I intend to publish this manuscript (National Library of Scotland, MS 109, ff. 10–29) as an appendix to my 'Petrus Britannicus: The British Perception of Peter the Great' (in preparation).

36 GL, MS 11,192B, f. 11.

37 John Cook, *Voyages and Travels through the Russian Empire, Tartary, and Part of the Kingdom of Persia*, I (Edinburgh, 1770), 86, 102.

38 *Ibid.*, pp. 81–2.

39 Chistovich, pp. clxxxi–ii.

40 SRO, Abercairny muniments, GD 24/856, sec. I, f. 107.

41 *Ibid.*, GD 30/1583/6; GL, MS 11,192B, f. 21.

42 SIRIO, LXVI (1889), 352.

43 Chistovich, p. clix; Cook, I, 461–2.

44 BL, Add. MSS 32,419, f. 278v.

45 Cook, *Voyages and Travels*, I, 359, 361–3, 411–13.

46 *Sochineniia Pushkina. Perepiska*, edited by V. I. Saitov, III (spb, 1911), 259.

47 Cook, *Voyages and Travels*, I, 3–4.

48 *Ibid.*, pp. 253–8; *Critical Review*, XXX (1770), 428–9.

49 Cook, *Voyages and Travels*, I, 83.

50 *Ibid.*, p. 428; GL, MS 11,192B, f. 17.

51 Cook, *Voyages and Travels*, I, 84–5; II, 433, 543–4.

52 Information in letter from the Keeper of the Muniments, University of St Andrews.

53 *Nomine eorum qui gradum medicinae doctoris in Academia Jacobi Sexti Scotorum regis, quae Edinburgi est, adepta sunt* (Edinburgh, 1846), p. 2.

54 Chistovich, p. clii.

55 *Historical Sketch and Laws of the Royal College of Physicians of Edinburgh* (Edinburgh, 1925), p. 3.

56 William Munk, *The Roll of the Royal College of Physicians of London*, II (London, 1878), 297.

57 James Tamesz Grieve became heir to the Tames fortune on the death of his mother and returned himself at a later date to Moscow. But, as Count Semen Vorontsov wrote to his brother, 'Grèves, l'héritier de Thames, n'a pas voulu s'établir chez nous, mais est venu mourir en Angleterre' (AKV, IX, 104). He died on 9 May 1787, aged 43, and is also buried in Bath Abbey.

58 *Critical Review* (Feb. 1764), p. 81. *Sbornik Otdeleniia russkogo iazyka i slovesnosti Imperatorskogo Akademii nauk*, XIII (spb, 1875), 352.

59 *History of Kamtschatka and the Kurilski Islands, with the Countries Adjacent*, 2nd edn (Glocester, 1764), Advertisement, 2nd unnumbered sheet.

60 AVPR, Moscow, Snosheniia Rossii s Angliei, Opis' No. 35/1, d. 829.

61 SRO, GD 24/1/846, f. 2.

62 Graham G. C. Thomas, 'Some Correspondence of Dr James Mounsey, Physician to the Empress Elizabeth of Russia', *Scottish Slavonic Review*, no.4 (Spring 1985), 13.

63 John B. Wilson, 'Three Scots in the Service of the Czars', *The Practitioner*, CCX

(1973), 574. See also R. W. Innes Smith, 'Dr James Mounsey of Rammerscales', *Edinburgh Medical Journal* (May 1926), p. 278.

64 Thomas, 'Some Correspondence of Mounsey', pp. 12–13.

65 *Calendar of Home State Papers of the Reign of George III 1770–1772* (London, 1881), pp. 491–2.

66 Cook, *Voyages and Travels*, I, 32–5.

67 Chistovich, p. ccxxxiii.

68 SRO, GD 24/1/846, ff. 1–IV.

69 *Ibid.*, f. 2.

70 Chistovich, pp. 320–6, lxi–lxvi; Alexander, *Bubonic Plague*, pp. 41, 51, 53, 58, 282.

71 Royal Society Archives, Certificates, I, f. 416.

72 On Baker, see G. L'E. Turner, 'Henry Baker, FRS., Founder of the Bakerian Lecture', *Notes and Records of the Royal Society of London*, XXIX (1974), 53–79.

73 John H. Appleby, ' "Rhubarb" Mounsey and the Surinam Toad: A Scottish Physician–Naturalist in Russia', *Archives of Natural History*, XI (1982), 137–52.

74 *Historical Sketch*, p. 22. Robert Dossie, *Memoirs of Agriculture and Other Oeconomical Arts*, III (London, 1782), 208–22.

75 'Extract of a Letter from Dr John Hope, Professor of Medicine and Botany in the University of Edinburgh, to Dr Pringle', *Philosophical Transactions*, LV (1765), 290–3.

76 Royal Society of Arts, S. A. General Meeting, Minutes, 11 Jan. 1770. See, in addition to Appleby and Turner, Clifford M. Foust, 'The Society of Arts and Rhubarb', *RSA Journal* (March 1988), 275–8; (April), 350–3; (May), 434–7. See also Foust's magnificent monograph, *Rhubarb: The Wondrous Drug* (Princeton, 1992).

77 *Nomina eorum qui gradum medicinae doctoris*, p. 3; Chistovich, p. cxxiv; *Historical sketch*, p. 3.

78 POARAN, Fond 21, Miller G.F., op. 3, ed. khr. 73, f. 10v.

79 Thomas Dimsdale, *Tracts on Inoculation* (London, 1781), p. 44.

80 See A. G. Cross, *'By the Banks of the Thames': Russians in Eighteenth-Century Britain* (Newtonville, Mass., 1980), pp. 117–18.

81 RGADA, Moscow, Fond 10, Kabinet ee velichestva, op. 3, ed. khr. 605 (Catherine to P. I. Saltykov 27 October 1768). For a recent appraisal of Catherine's attitude to medicine that includes some discussion of the contribution of three British doctors, see J. T. Alexander, 'Medicine at the Court of Catherine the Great of Russia', in Vivian Nutton (ed.), *Medicine at the Courts of Europe, 1500–1837* (London and New York, 1990), pp. 182–208.

82 R. P. Bartlett, 'Russia in the Eighteenth-Century European Adoption of Inoculation for Smallpox', in R. P. Bartlett, A. G. Cross and K. Rasmussen (eds.), *Russia and the World of the Eighteenth Century* (Columbus, Ohio, 1988), pp. 193–213.

83 The most detailed accounts of Dimsdale's career and visits to Russia are W. J. Bishop, 'Thomas Dimsdale, MD., FRS, and the Inoculation of Catherine the Great of Russia', *Annals of Medical History*, NS IV (1932), 321–38; Philip H. Clendinning, 'Dr Thomas Dimsdale and Smallpox Inoculation in Russia', *Journal of the History of Medicine and Allied Sciences*, XXVII (1973), 109–25.

84 Thomas, 'Some Correspondence of Mounsey', p. 17.

85 RGADA, Fond 10, op. 3, ed. khr. 605.

86 William Richardson, *Anecdotes of the Russian Empire* (London, 1784), p. 36.

87 SIRIO, XII (spb, 1873), 405–6. Information about the inoculation and Dimsdale's rewards was soon published in the British press. See *Scots Magazine*, XXX (1768), 656; XXXI (1769), 43, 101.

88 Auchindoune, Cawdor, Nairne, Cathcart Papers, Journal of Jane Hamilton, Lady Cathcart, xx, f. 14.

89 Even the poets joined in: Vasilii Maikov, for example, wrote a sonnet on Catherine's recovery and a poetic 'inscription' to a portrait of Dimsdale (*Sochineniia i perevody Vasiliia Ivanovicha Maikova* (spb, 1867), pp. 55, 494, 501, 534).

90 A. Lentin, 'Shcherbatov, Inoculation and Dr Dimsdale', SGECRN, no. 17 (1989), 8–11.

91 Simon Houfe, 'Portraits from St Petersburg', *Country Life*, CLXXXIII, no. 46 (16 November 1989), 78–81.

92 RGADA, Fond 5, ed. khr. 160, ff. 2–3 (letter of 25 June 1771).

93 *Ibid.*, f. 1.

94 A. G. Cross (ed.), *An English Lady at the Court of Catherine the Great: The Journal of Baroness Elizabeth Dimsdale, 1781* (Cambridge, 1989), p. 63.

95 RGADA, Fond 5, ed. khr. 160, ff. 8–8v.

96 Institute of Russian Literature (Pushkin House), St Petersburg, Fond 620, Arkhiv A. A. Samborskogo, ed. khr. 173, ff. 1–3. See also RGADA, Fond 5, ed. khr. 160, f. 9 (letter of 17 October 1787).

97 For example, *Azbuchnyi ukazatel' imen russkikh deiatelei dlia russkogo biograficheskogo slovaria*, I (reprint Vaduz, 1963), 129; A. Francis Steuart, *Scottish Influences in Russian History* (Glasgow, 1913), p. 121.

98 GL, MS 11,192B, f. 31.

99 Thomas, 'Some Correspondence of Mounsey', pp. 14–15.

100 *Sankpeterburgskie vedomosti*, no. 19 (7 March 1790), 323.

101 RGADA, Fond 10, op. 2, ed. khr. 283; Spb. Otd. Instituta Istorii RAN, Fond 36, op. 1, d. 1247, f. 6v., 8v.

102 *Pavlovsk: ocherk istorii i opisanie 1777–1877* (Spb. 1877), pp. 68–70.

103 RGADA, Fond 10, op. 3, d. 1774, ff. 2–2v. (letter to Count Aleksandr Vorontsov). Three years later a young Scots doctor by the name of Keir, who became Vorontsov's personal physician, started to carry out vaccinations on Vorontsov's peasants (AKV, XXX, 222). Two rivals for the honour of introducing vaccination are Dr Otto Gunn (1764–1832) in Riga also in 1800 (K. T. Vasil'ev, F. F. Grigorash, *Ocherki istorii meditsiny i zdravookhraneniia Latvii* (Moscow, 1964), pp. 32–41) and Dr E. O. Mukhin in October 1801 (V. V. Kuprianov, *Iz istorii meditsinskoi sluzhby na russkom flote* (Moscow, 1963), p. 74). I am indebted for these last two references to Dr Roger Bartlett.

104 *Scots Magazine*, XXXIII (1771), 659.

105 Alexander, *Bubonic Plague*, pp. 238–9, 241, 245.

106 Thomas, 'Some Correspondence of Mounsey', p. 16.

107 AKV, XVII, 11–12; XXII, 517.

108 Chistovich, p. cxxxii; Fechner, *Chronik der evangelischen Gemeinden in Moskau*, II (Moscow, 1876), 38, 49, 55, 552, 554; *Life of Reginald Heber*, I (London, 1830), 206; *The Russian Journals of Martha and Catherine Wilmot 1803–1808* (London, 1934), pp. 29, 41, 44; John Parkinson, *A Tour of Russia, Siberia and the Crimea, 1792–1792* (London, 1971), p. 105.

109 GL, MS 11,192B, f. 245; RGADA, Fond 1261, op. 3, d. 1774, ff. 5–5v.

110 See W. L. Johnstone, 'Dr John Rogerson of Dumcrief, Physician to the Empress of Russia', in *The Bard and the Belted Knight* (Edinburgh, 1867), pp. 173–81; W. A. J. Prevost, 'Dumcrief and Its Owners', *Transactions of the Dumfrieshire and Galloway Natural History and Antiquarian Society*, XLV (1968), 200–10; A. G. Cross, 'John Rogerson: Physician to Catherine the Great', *Canadian Slavic Studies*, IV (1970),

594–601; Wilson, 'Three Scots'; A. El'nitskii, 'Rodzherson', *RBS*, XVI (reprint New York, 1962), 290–5.

111 *Nomina eorum qui gradum . . .*, pp. 8, 18.

112 Chistovich, p. cclxxxiv; Thomas, 'Some Correspondence of Mounsey', p. 17; BL, Add. MS 6826, ff. 175–175v. (Cathcart to Sir Andrew Mitchell, 28 February OS 1769).

113 Thomas, 'Some Correspondence of Mounsey', pp. 15, 17.

114 Edward Daniel Clarke, *Travels in Various Countries of Europe, Asia and Africa*, I (London, 1810), 88.

115 Kyril Fitzlyon (tr. and ed.), *Memoirs of Princess Dashkov* (London, 1958), pp. 139, 194.

116 *Vosemnadtsatyi vek*, I (Moscow, 1904), 24; *Un diplomate français à la cour de Catherine II 1775–1780. Journal intime du Chevalier de Corberon, chargé d'affaires de France en Russie*, II (Paris, 1901), 137; Cathcart Papers, Journal of Jane Hamilton, Lady Cathcart, XXI, f. 13v.

117 Cf. Dmitrii Kobeko, *Tsesarevich Pavel Petrovich (1754–1776)*, 3rd edn (spb, 1887), pp. 123–4, 308; *Dnevnik A.V. Krapovitskogo 1782–1793* (spb, 1874), pp. 174, 376; *AKV*, XXX (1881), 75.

118 *Dnevnik Khrapovitskogo*, p. 105.

119 *SIRIO*, XIII (1878), 253 (letter of 30 Sept. OS 1782).

120 *Archivo del general Miranda, Viajes*, II (Caracas, 1929), 256; S. P. Zhikharev, *Zapiski sovremennika* (M-L, 1955), p. 340.

121 National Library of Scotland, MSS 3942, ff. 137–41, 277–8.

122 *Protokoly zasedanii Konferentsii Imperatorskoi Akademii nauk s 1725 po 1803 god*, III (spb, 1900), 276; *Transactions of the Royal Society of Edinburgh*, I (Edinburgh, 1788), 93; Royal Society Archives, Certificates, IV, f.19; *Historical Sketch*, p. 22.

123 *Dnevnik Khrapovitskogo*, p. 51.

124 *AKV*, XVIII, 149 (V. P. Kochubei to S. R. Vorontsov, 29 July OS 1798).

125 Steuart, *Scottish Influences*, pp. 121–2; F. Golovkin, *Dvor i tsarstvovanie Pavla I* (Moscow, 1912), p. 210.

126 *RBS*, XVI, 291.

127 *AKV*, XXX, 96.

128 *Ibid.*, pp. 79, 99.

129 Thomas, 'Some Correspondence of Mounsey', p. 18; Cathcart Papers, Folio I, no. 47, f. 2. Guthrie's uncle was William Guthrie (1708–70), geographer and historian. On the Guthrie family, see C. E. Guthrie Wright (ed.), *Gideon Guthrie – A Monograph Written 1712 to 1730* (London and Edinburgh, 1900).

130 BL, Add. MS 8099, f. 166 (letter of Guthrie to Sir Joseph Banks of 14 January OS 1802); *Materialy dlia istorii russkogo flota*, XII (spb, 1888), 65; Derbyshire Record Office, Matlock, MS 239 m, Fitzherbert, 0555 (letter of 24 September OS 1800).

131 'Observations on the Plague, Quarantine &c.', *Medical and Philosophical Commentaries*, VIII (1781), 355–6.

132 *Azbuchnyi ukazatel'*, II, 642; Chistovich, p. cliii.

133 GL, MS 11,192 B, ff. 68 (death of first husband), 69 (marriage to Guthrie), 71, 81, 82, 112 (births of children).

134 Golovkin, *Dvor*, p. 195.

135 Chistovich, pp. clili–iv.

136 John Carr, *A Northern Summer; or, Travels round the Baltic through Denmark, Sweden, Russia, Prussia, and Part of Germany, in the Year 1804* (London, 1805), pp. 327–9; [Lionel Colmore], *Letters from the Continent, Describing the Manners*

and Customs of Germany, Poland, Russia, and Switzerland, in the Years 1790, 1791, and 1792 (London, 1812), p. 148.

137   *Archivo del general Miranda, Viajes* II, 448 and *passim*.

138   N. Findeizen, *Ocherki po istorii muzyki v Rossii*, vyp. 6 (M-L, 1929), 327; Heinz Mohrmann, *Studien über russisch-deutsche Begegnungen in der Wirtschaftswissenschaft (1750–1825)* (Berlin, 1959), p. 114.

139   *Transactions of the Royal Society of Edinburgh*, I (1788), 93; Thomas Thomson, *History of the Royal Society* (London, 1812), appendix IV, p. lviii; *Archaelogica Scotica: or Transactions of the Society of Antiquaries of Scotland*, III (Edinburgh, 1831), appendix, 22.

140   Jessie M. Sweet, 'Matthew Guthrie (1743–1807): An Eighteenth-Century Gemmologist', *Annals of Science*, XX (1964), 245–302 (pp. 289–95 bibliography); John H. Appleby, 'St Petersburg to Edinburgh: Matthew Guthrie's Introduction of Medicinal Plants in the Context of Scottish–Russian Natural History Exchange', *Archives of Natural History*, XIV (1987), 45–58.

141   *The Bee*, I (1790), vii–xii. See A. G. Cross, 'Arcticus and *The Bee* (1790–4): An Episode in Anglo-Russian Cultural Relations', *OSP*, NS II (1969), 62–76.

142   'The Oration of Plato, Archbishop of Mosco, on crowning Alexander the First, 15th of Sept. 1801', *London Chronicle*, XCI, no. 66880 (1802), 49.

143   BL, Add. MS 14390. See K.A. Papmehl, 'Matthew Guthrie: The Forgotten Student of 18th Century Russia', *Canadian Slavonic Papers*, XI (1969), 172–81.

144   *Sochineniia Derzhavina*, VII (spb, 1872), 65. B. Modzalevskii, 'Biblioteka A. S. Pushkina', *Pushkin i ego sovremenniki*, IX–X (spb, 1910), 243–4. (It is interesting that Pushkin also possessed three volumes of the *English Review* (1783–5) with Guthrie's ex-libris: *ibid.*, p. 368). See also the influence of Guthrie's book on the Wilmot sisters: The Marchioness of Londonderry and H. M. Hyde (eds.), *The Russian Journals of Martha and Catherine Wilmot* (London, 1934), pp. 238, 336.

145   TSGAVMF, St Petersburg, Fond 8, op. 1, ed. khr. 60, ff. 132–6.

146   Chistovich, pp. ccxiv–v.

147   GL, MS. 11,192B, ff. 144, 148, 155, 161, 170, 178, 187, 200, 208, 219, 230, 253; *Peterburgskii nekropol'*, IV (spb, 1913), 78. A photograph of the monument, wrongly captioned, appears in *Istoricheskaia panorama Peterburga*, vyp. 2 (Moscow, 1914), no. 39.

148   *Scots Magazine*, XXXII (Dec. 1770), 661.

149   See the letters from Robert Rutherford to Greig in 1772–4: TSGAVMF, Fond 8, op. 1, delo 58. In 1770 Rogers was aboard the *Sv. Pavel* under Captain James Preston: *An Authentic Account of the Russian Expedition against the Turks by Sea and Land* (London, 1772), p. 114.

150   Parkinson, *Tour*, p. 36 (the editor confuses Rogers with Rogerson, *ibid.*, p. 276).

151   Aleksandr Nikitin, *Kratkii obzor sostoianiia meditsiny v Rossii v tsarstvovanie Imperatritsy Ekateriny II* (spb, 1855), p. 59; *Russkii biograficheskii slovar'*, XVI, 334.

152   GL, MS 11,196, f.845; MS. 11,192B, f. 255.

153   *Ibid.*, MS 11,192B, f. 218; *Religious Monitor*, IV (1806), 119.

154   *The Laws of the Royal Physical Society* (Edinburgh, 1819), p. 47; W. I. Addison, *A Roll of the Graduates of the University of Glasgow, from 31 December, 1727, to 31st December, 1897* (Glasgow, 1898), p. 240.

155 TSGAVMF, Fond 8, op. 1, d. 57, f. 59. See also letter of Samuel Charters to Greig, *ibid.*, d. 54, f.31.

156 *Transactions of the Royal Society of Edinburgh*, I, 94; Thomson, *History of the Royal Society*, appendix IV, p. lxiii.

157 *Medical Commentaries*, IX (1784), 286–302; 'An Account of the Method of Making a Wine, called by the Tartars koumiss; with observations on its use in medicine', *Transactions of the Royal Society of Edinburgh*, I, 178–90. For more on Grieve's publications etc., see John H. Appleby, 'John Grieve's Correspondence with Joseph Black and Some Contemporaneous Russo-Scottish Medical Intercommunication', *Medical History*, XXIX (1985), 401–13.

158 *AKV*, XXX, 99. See also 84, 91, 110.

159 *Ibid.*, XXII, 99 (letter of L. H. Nicolay to A. R. Vorontsov).

160 Chistovich, p. clii.

161 GL, MS 11,192B, ff. 170, 180, 187, 221, 203, 254.

162 See Cross, *By the Banks of the Thames*, pp. 128–45.

163 *Gentleman's Magazine*, LVI, pt. 1 (1786), 130–1. See Cross, *By the Banks of the Thames*, pp. 140–1.

164 Chistovich, p. ccciii.

165 *Laws of the Society instituted at Edinburgh MDCCLXXXII, for the Investigation of Natural History* (Edinburgh, 1803), p. 28; 'Obligation Book of the Edinburgh Medical Society' (Edinburgh University Library MS), unfoliated (16 December 1786).

166 Chistovich, p. clxxiv; Parkinson, *Tour*, pp. 101, 106, 211, 220.

167 *London Chronicle*, no. 4178 (9–12 August 1783), 146.

168 *Correspondence of Jeremy Bentham*, IV (London, 1981), 9.

169 IRLI, Fond 620, ed. khr. 157, no. 3, f. 4.

170 Chistovich, p. cvi.

171 *Correspondence of Jeremy Bentham*, III (1971), 320, 465, 616.

172 Christovich, pp. cvi–ii; Stephen Watrous (ed.), *John Ledyard's Journey through Russia and Siberia* (Madison, 1966), pp. 23–4; John D. Comrie, *History of Scottish Medicine*, I, 2nd edn (London, 1932), 333.

173 Venn, pt. 2, III, 492; John Venn, *Biographical History of Gonville and Caius College 1349–1897*, II (Cambridge, 1898), 86; Chistovich, p. cxxxv.

174 Robert Lyall, *Travels in Russia, the Krimea, the Caucasus, and Georgia*, I (London, 1825), 68–70; Edward Morton, *Travels in Russia, and a Residence at St. Petersburg and Odessa in the Years 1827–1829* (London, 1830), p. 109 (quoting Lyall).

175 *Correspondence of Jeremy Bentham*, IV, 10. See also III, 496, 497–501, 503–5, 528–9, 548–9.

176 POARAN, Fond 36, op. 1, d. 1248, ff. 58–9. Mrs Debraw, whom the good doctor seems to have married bigamously at Riga (*Correspondence to Jeremy Bentham*, III, 548), also suggested that her husband had established 'the great Hospital at Creechoff'.

177 There is a considerable literature on Wylie, as well as numerous references to him in memoir and travel literature. See in particular Ia. Chistovich, *Pamiatnik doktoru meditsiny i khirurgii, deistvitel'nomu tainomu sovetniku, baronetu Iakovu Vasil'evichu Villie* (spb, 1860) and V. S. Sakharov, 'Iakov Vasil'evich Villie', *Russkaia starina*, XVI (1876), 712–18.

178 Lyall, *Travels*, II, 466.

179 *AKV*, XXX, 110. (Johann Bek was a body-physician.)

5 'SUR LE PIED ANGLAIS': SHIPBUILDERS AND OFFICERS IN
THE RUSSIAN NAVY

1 *AKV*, IX (Moscow, 1876), 198.

2 The introduction appeared in a contemporary English translation as 'The Story of the Ship's-Boat, which gave his Majesty the Thought of building Ships of War', in Thomas Consett, *The Present State and Regulations of the Church of Russia*, II (London, 1729), 209.

3 *Ibid.*, p. 215.

4 See in particular Ian Grey, 'Peter the Great in England', *History Today*, VI (1956), 225–34; Bernard Pool, 'Peter the Great on the Thames', *Mariner's Mirror*, LIX (1973), 9–12; W. F. Ryan, 'Peter the Great's Yacht, Admiral Lord Carmarthen and the Russian Tobacco Monopoly', *Mariner's Mirror*, LXIX (1983), 65–88.

5 Compare John Perry, *The State of Russia under the Present Czar* (London, 1716), p. 164, with L. N. Maikov (ed.), *Rasskazy Nartova o Petre Velikom* (spb, 1891), p. 10.

6 The document is reproduced in Ryan, 'Peter the Great's Yacht', p. 85.

7 See D. Bonner Smith, 'The Authorship of the *Russian Fleet under Peter the Great*', *Mariner's Mirror*, XX (1934), 373–6. Smith supplies the full text of the additional material.

8 *OMS*, I (spb, 1885), 132–3.

9 D. B. Horn, *British Diplomatic Representatives*, Camden Third Series, XLVI (London 1932), p. 112. Deane's 'Account of Affairs in Russia' in 1725 is in PRO, SP XCI, 9, ff. 107ff. After years as British Consul in Flanders and Ostend both before and after his last abortive attempt to visit Russia, Deane retired in 1738 to the village of Wilford near Nottingham. His gravestone gives details of his career and shows that he died on 8 August 1761, one day after his wife.

10 [John Barrow], *A Memoir of the Life of Peter the Great* (London, 1832), p. 96.

11 *OMS*, I, 326; Ryan, 'Peter the Great's Yacht', p. 76.

12 Deane, *Letter from Moscow to the Marquess of Carmarthen* (London, 1699), in Ryan, pp. 86–7. On Deane, see *OMS*, I, 131; Perry, *State of Russia*, pp. 165, 169.

13 Perry, *State of Russia*, p. 186; Charles Whitworth, *Account of Russia as it was in the Year 1710* (Strawberry Hill, 1758), p. 112. (Whitworth's book has recently been reissued, together with a Russian translation (by N. G. Bespiatykh) and an excellent commentary and notes (by Iu. N. Bespiatykh): *Rossiia v nachale XVIII veka. Sochinenie Ch. Uitvorta* (M-L, 1988).

14 *OMS*, I, 179 (Cozens), 271–2 (Nye).

15 Whitworth, *Account*, p. 130.

16 *Ibid.*, pp. 128–48. Iu. Bespiatykh, in his commentary on Whitworth's work, supplies further information about these and other British specialists: *Rossiia v nachale XVIII veka*, pp. 195–201.

17 BL Add. MS 37,354, f. 279.

18 *OMS*, I, 38.

19 Ryan, 'Peter the Great's Yacht', p. 87.

20 Perry, *State of Russia*, pp. 54–5. The best account of Perry's career and his book is by Peter Putnam, *Seven Britons in Imperial Russia 1698–1812* (Princeton, 1952), pp. 3–20.

21 Simpson was the other British officer serving with the Azov fleet. He was detained for a short time by the Turks in Constantinople before returning to Russia via England and serving with the Baltic Fleet until 1715. See *OMS*, I, 338–9 and *History of*

the Russian Fleet During the Reign of Peter the Great (London, 1899), pp. 27–8, 30. On the fate of Peter's southern fleet, see R. C. Anderson, *Naval Wars in the Levant 1559–1853* (Liverpool, 1952), p. 242.

22 Whitworth, *Account*, p. 149; *Rossiia v nachale* XVIII *veka*, pp. 196, 200–1; OMS, I, 116–7.

23 *History of the Russian Fleet*, p. 11.

24 OMS, I, 92–3 (Hadley), 123 (Davenport), 31–8 (Ramsey).

25 M. S. Anderson, 'Great Britain and the Growth of the Russian Navy in the Eighteenth Century', *Mariner's Mirror*, XLII (1956), 134.

26 *History of the Russian Fleet*, p. 101.

27 *Dnevnik kamer-iunkera F.V. Berkhol'tsa*, IV (Moscow, 1903), p. 52.

28 DNB, XII (London, 1887), 424; GL, MS 11,192B, ff. 11, 13, 28.

29 *History of the Russian Fleet*, pp. 10, 17, 20, 100, 124.

30 OMS, I, 63–4; T. M. Matveeva, *Ubranstvo russkikh korablei* (Leningrad, 1979), pp. 45, 47–8.

31 Fred T. Jane, *The Imperial Russian Navy: Its Past, Present, and Future* (London, 1899), pp. 714–24; R. C. Anderson, 'British and American Officers in the Russian Navy', *Mariner's Mirror*, XXXIII (1947), 17–27.

32 Deane gives a list of eighty-two officers, Russian and foreign, as mentioned in his *History* (although he overlooks some he in fact named): of these, twenty-three are British, nineteen are Russian, and the rest mainly Scandinavian and Dutch: *History of the Russian Fleet*, pp. 128–30.

33 *Ibid.*, pp. 96–9, together with the editor, Admiral Cyprian Bridge's invaluable commentary in footnotes.

34 Jane, *The Imperial Russian Navy*, pp. 725, 727.

35 R. C. Anderson, *Naval Wars in the Baltic 1522–1850* (London, 1969), pp. 206–7.

36 *History of the Russian Fleet*, pp. 87–8.

37 F. Veselago, *Kratkaia istoriia russkogo flota*, I (spb, 1893), 39.

38 *History of the Russian Fleet*, pp. 90–1.

39 *Truth is but Truth, as it is Timed!* (London, 1719), p. 7.

40 Perry, *State of Russia*, pp. 19–21; *History of the Russian Fleet*, pp. 73, 89; SIRIO, LXVI (spb, 1889), 49–50.

41 OMS, I, 280–2.

42 *Ibid.*, 144.

43 *History of the Russian Fleet*, pp. 41, 44–5, 71; OMS, I, 83–4.

44 OMS, I, 436.

45 *History of the Russian Fleet*, pp. 72, 89; OMS, I, 219–20.

46 *History of the Russian Fleet*, pp. 85–6.

47 *Ibid.*, pp. 54–5. See also pp. 52, 58, 61.

48 OMS, I, 293–4; Alexander Gordon, *History of Peter the Great, Emperor of Russia*, II (Aberdeen, 1755), 171 (death and burial of Paddon). George Paddon's son George also joined the Russian navy and served until his death in 1749 (OMS, I, 295–6).

49 OMS, I, 110–12 (Gordon), 332–3 (Saunders).

50 Quoted in W. M. Parker, 'A Scots Admiral of the Russian Navy', *Journal of the Royal United Service Institution*, XCII (1947), 270. Parker's article (pp. 268–73) uses Gordon's letterbook and other materials which are in the Register House, Edinburgh, Abercainy Muniments GD 24/854–6.

51 *History of the Russian Fleet*, p. 92.

52 OMS, I, 142–4.

53 Quoted in Parker, 'A Scots Admiral', p. 273.

54 *Ibid.*

55 *OMS*, I, 213–15; *SIRIO*, LXI (1888), 224–6. (Whitworth's dispatch of 17/28 June 1712 is a valuable description of Lane's early work at Kronshlot.)

56 Bonner Smith, 'The Authorship of *The Russian Fleet under Peter the Great*', p. 374.

57 The account of Lane's work at Kronshtadt is based on *History of the Russian Fleet*, pp. 66, 75, 90, 123; B. A. Rozadeev, R. A. Somina and L. S. Kleshcheva, *Kronshtadt: arkhitekturnyi ocherk* (Leningrad, 1977), pp. 6–30; A. A. Razdolgin, Iu. A. Skorikov, *Kronshtadtskaia krepost'* (Leningrad, 1988), pp. 20–57.

58 *History of the Russian Fleet*, pp. 25, 92–3; *OMS*, I, 214.

59 *History of the Russian Fleet*, pp. 59, 90, 122, 123.

60 Quoted in Jeremy Black, *European Warfare 1660–1815* (London, 1994), p. 116.

61 Bonner Smith, 'The Authorship of *The Russian Fleet under Peter the Great*', p. 374.

62 *History of the Russian Fleet*, p. 93; *SIRIO*, LXVI (1889), 59.

63 See the chapter 'On British Ships and in British Yards' in A. G. Cross, *'By the Banks of the Thames': Russians in Eighteenth-Century Britain* (Newtonville, Mass., 1980), pp. 146–73.

64 Narcissus Luttrell, *A Brief Historical Relation of State Affairs from September 1678 to April 1714*, IV (Oxford, 1857), 207.

65 See generally F. Veselago, *Ocherk istorii morskogo kadetskogo korpusa* (spb, 1852).

66 Perry, *State of Russia*, p. 212.

67 Nicholas Hans, 'The Moscow School of Mathematics and Navigation (1701)', *SEER*, XXIX (1951), 534.

68 Perry, *State of Russia*, pp. 211–12.

69 Veselago, *Ocherk istorii*, p. 22; Hans, 'Moscow School', p. 535. On Bruce, see Valentin Boss, 'Russia's First Newtonian: Newton and J. D. Bruce', *Archives internationales d'histoire des sciences*, nos. 60–1 (1962), 233–64. Farquharson, it will be remembered from chapter 1, later became a member of the notorious 'British Monastery' in St Petersburg.

70 Perry, *State of Russia*, p. 280.

71 See, in addition to sources already cited, A. Sokolov, 'Andrei Danilovich Farvarson', *Morskoi sbornik*, no 15 (Dec 1856), 172–8; *OMS*, I, 392–3; Nicholas Hans, 'Henry Farquharson, Pioneer of Russian Education, 1698–1739', *Aberdeen University Review*, XXXVIII (1959), 26–9; Valentin Boss, *Newton & Russia: The Early Influence, 1698–1796* (Cambridge, Mass., 1972), pp. 78–89.

72 L. V., 'Farvarson, Andrei Danilovich', *RBS*, XXI (Reprint: New York, 1962), 22–3.

73 John Cook, *Voyages and Travels through the Russian Empire, Tartary, and Part of the Kingdom of Persia*, I (Edinburgh, 1770), 94.

74 *History of the Russian Fleet*, p. 126.

75 *SIRIO*, LXVI, 10.

76 *Ibid.*, 550–1.

77 Veselago, *Kratkaia istoriia*, I, 96.

78 Anderson, 'Great Britain and the Growth of the Russian Navy', p. 137.

79 *OMS*, II, 72.

80 A. S. Berg, *Otkrytie Kamchatki i ekspeditsii Beringa* (M-L, 1946), pp. 119–24, 170–82; Leonard Stejneger, *Georg Wilhelm Steller, the Pioneer of Alaskan Natural History* (Cambridge, Mass., 1936), pp. 189–92; George V. Lantzeff and Richard A. Pierce, *Eastward to Empire: Exploration and Conquest on the Russian Open Frontier, to 1750* (Montreal and London, 1973), pp. 215–17.

81 Erik Amburger, *Beiträge zur Geschichte der deutsch-russischen kulturellen Bezie-*

hungen (Geissen, 1961), p. 211. Walton's wife's name was Dorothea Clark and his son's, William Patrick.

82 *OMS*, I, 172–4.

83 *Ibid.*, 231–4.

84 V. N. Aleksandrenko (ed.), *Reliatsii kn. A.D. Kantemira iz Londona (1732–1733 g.)*, I (Moscow, 1892), 124.

85 Anderson, 'Great Britain and the Growth', p. 134.

86 *OMS*, II, 419; *RBS*, XX, 271.

87 *OMS*, II, 418–9; *RBS*, XX, 271; *SIRIO*, LXXXV, 61; GL, MS 11, 192B, ff. 19, 34, 92.

88 *OMS*, II, 500–1. On the *Trekh Ierarkhov* (Yeames's second ship of this name), see Matveeva, *Ubranstvo russkikh korablei*, pp. 53–4.

89 *Archivo del general Miranda*, II (Caracas, 1929), 396–7.

90 *Correspondence of Jeremy Bentham*, II (London, 1968), 209; GL, MS 11,192B, ff. 42, 62, 74, 102. See also the anecdote in James Walker's *Paramythia: Engraved in the Memory James Walker: Engraver to the Empress Catherine the Great, and His Russian Anecdotes* (Oxford and Providence, 1993), p. 133.

91 For a detailed examination of this episode, see R. J. Morda Evans, 'Recruitment of British Personnel for the Russian Service 1734–1738', *Mariner's Mirror*, XLVII (1961), 126–37.

92 *SIRIO*, LXXVI, 442. See also L. N. Maikov, *Materialy dlia biografii kn. A.D. Kantemira* (spb, 1903), pp. 31, 319.

93 *SIRIO*, LXXX, 158.

94 *OMS*, II, 296. O'Brien's son and nephew also joined the Russian navy at the end of Anna's reign.

95 *SIRIO*, LXXX, 99.

96 *OMS*, II, 110 (Griffiths); *SIRIO*, LXXX, 279 (Master and Talbot).

97 Succinct accounts of the war are to be found in Anderson, *Naval Wars in the Levant*, pp. 270–6 and Veselago, *Kratkaia istoriia*, pp. 86–90.

98 Cook, *Voyages and Travels*, I, pp. 208–9.

99 *Ibid.*, pp. 209–16.

100 *OMS*, II, 173–4, 498.

101 *Ibid.*, pp. 6–7, 245–7.

102 Veselago, *Ocherk istorii morskogo kadetskogo korpusa*, pp. 103–7; Edward Hughes, 'The Early Journal of Thomas Wright of Durham', *Annals of Science*, VII (1951), 17; A. G. Cross, *By the Banks of the Thames*, pp. 96–7.

103 Veselago, *Ocherk istorii*, p. 126.

104 *SIRIO*, X (1876), 28.

105 See A. G. Cross, *By the Banks of the Thames*, pp. 156–73.

106 *OMS*, III, 511–12; DNB, XV, 288–91.

107 Dmitrii Bantysh-Kamenskii, *Slovar' dostopamiatnykh liudei russkoi zemli*, I (Moscow, 1836), 157–63. See also on Greig: 'Memoir of Sir Samuel Greig', *Dublin University Magazine*, XLIV (1854), 156–67; A. G. Cross, 'Samuel Greig, Catherine the Great's Scottish Admiral', *Mariner's Mirror*, LX (1964), 251–65; Margaret M. Page, 'Admiral Samuil Karlovich Greig: A Scot in the Service of Catherine the Great', *Scottish Slavonic Papers*, no. 15 (1990), 7–18.

108 *OMS*, III, 421 (Gordon); IV, 87 (Cleland); 682 (Roxburgh). All are in Anderson's list. On Roxburgh, see also William Stephens, *History of Inverkeithing and Rosyth* (Aberdeen, 1921), pp. 487–8, 522 and *SIRIO*, XIX, 99.

109 TSGAVMF, Fond 8, opis' 2, ed. khr. 44, ff. 1–2 (letter of 10/21 May 1768 to unknown (probably A. S. Musin-Pushkin, Russian ambassador in London).

110 *SIRIO*, I (1868), 30.
111 See M. S. Anderson, 'Great Britain and the Russian Fleet, 1769–70', *SEER*, XXXI (1952), 148–63; William C. Chapman, 'Prelude to Chesme', *Mariner's Mirror*, LII (1966), 61–76.
112 'Sobstvennoruchnyi zhurnal kapitana-komandora S. K. Greiga v chesmenskii pokhod', *Morskoi sbornik*, II (spb, 1849), 645–60, 715–30, 785–827. See also Anderson, *Naval Wars in the Levant*, pp. 285–91, and E. V. Tarle, *Chesmenskii boi i pervaia russkaia ekspeditsiia v Arkhipelag* (ML, 1945).
113 *Middlesex Journal* (1–4 September 1770); *General Evening Post* (25–7 September 1770); *Scots Magazine*, XXXII (1770), 504–5.
114 *SIRIO*, XIX, 107; TSGAVMF, Fond 8, opis' 1, delo 57, ff. 77–77v. See also Christopher Lloyd and R. C. Anderson (eds.), *A Memoir of James Trevenen* (London, 1959), p. 159; John Parkinson, *A Tour of Russia, Siberia and the Crimea 1792–4* (London, 1971), p. 79.
115 *An Authentic Narrative of the Russian Expedition against the Turks by Land and Sea* (London, 1772), pp. 26–7. Newberry returned to Kronshtadt with a transport in 1771 and became o/c the Admiralty College's yacht. He took part in the Don expedition in 1773, but later that year retired from Russian service (see *OMS*, IV, 477–8).
116 *Scots Magazine*, XXXIV (1772), 79–82. Cf. *Critical Review*, XXXIII, 138–42.
117 *An Authentic Narrative*, p. 74.
118 *Ibid.*, p. 30.
119 John Charnock, *Biographia Navalis*, VI (London, 1798), 358; DNB, VI, 730.
120 *SIRIO*, I, 57.
121 *AGM*, II (spb, 1901), 48–9.
122 *Scots Magazine*, XXXIII (1771), 153, 549.
123 Samuel (1758–89) was to re-enter Russian service in 1783 with his younger brother Robert (1769–1822) and both served in the war against Sweden, during which Samuel was killed. Samuel's son, Alexander Francis, born at Kronshtadt in 1788, later served in the Royal Navy. On 30 March 1836 he petitioned the Emperor Nicholas I for 'honors and rewards' apparently due to his grandfather (*AGM*, VII (1903), 192–4).
124 *Scots Magazine*, XXXIII (1771), 549. Cf. Anderson, *Naval Wars in the Levant*, p. 294.
125 *SIRIO*, XIX, 88.
126 *Scots Magazine*, XXXI (1769), 599. See also pp. 161, 210, 493, 550, 658.
127 *An Authentic Narrative*, pp. 117, 123, 138–9.
128 See *OMS*, III, 67 (Arnold), 187–8 (Body); *SIRIO*, XIX, 78–80; Anderson, 'Great Britain and the Russian Fleet', p. 156.
129 *An Authentic Narrative*, pp. 114–20; *OMS*, IV, 613–14.
130 The main secondary sources on Knowles are: 'Biographical Memoir of the Late Sir Charles Knowles', *Naval Chronicle*, I (1799), 89–124; II, 265–82; Al. Sk. [Aleksandr Sokolov], 'Admiral Noul's', *Morskoi sbornik*, II (1849), 509–27; Philip H. Clendenning, 'Admiral Sir Charles Knowles and Russia, 1771–1774', *Mariner's Mirror*, LXI (1975), 39–49.
131 National Maritime Museum, Greenwich, 'Copy Notebook containing correspondence between Admiral Sir Charles Knowles and Catherine the Great regarding the former's review of the Russian Navy, 1771–1774', [f. 1].
132 *Scots Magazine*, XXXII (1770), 675; XXXIII (1771), 155, 264. Knowles was accompanied to Russia by his daughter Anna (1752–1839), who was appointed a

maid of honour to the Empress in 1772 (P. F. Karabanov, 'Freiliny russkogo dvora v XVIII i XIX stoletiiakh', *Russkaia starina*, IV (1871), 385), and by his secretary John Robison (1739–1805), who became a professor at Noble Naval Cadet Corps at Kronshtadt in 1772 (on him, see A. G. Cross, *By the Banks of the Thames*, pp. 129–30).

133 F. Veselago (ed.), MIRF, XI (spb, 1886), 720, 743; 'Biographical Memoir', II, 270, 271; DNB, XXXI (1892), 295.

134 'Reskript Ekateriny II P.A. Rumiantsevu s rekomendatsiei admirala Pollisa [*sic*]', in N. M. Korobkov (ed.), *Fel'dmarshal Rumiantsev: sbornik dokumentov i materialov* (Moscow, 1947), p. 208.

135 *Ibid.*, pp. 197–200. Knowles is not even mentioned in connection with the creation of the Danube flotilla in Iu. R. Klokman, *Fel'dmarshal Rumiantsev v period russko-turetskoi voiny 1768–1774 gg.* (Moscow, 1951), pp. 118–19. Clendenning's account ('Admiral Sir Charles Knowles and Russia', pp. 33–4) makes little sense, since he persists in speaking of the Don Flotilla and turns the Danube (Dunai) into the Duna River!

136 Veselago, MIRF, XII (1888), 65. Catherine also sent Major-General E. Kashkin to accompany Knowles' party: SIRIO, XIII (1874), 215–16. Catherine's instructions to Knowles are found at *ibid.*, 216–18.

137 SIRIO, XIX, 318 (letter from Robert Gunning, British minister in St Petersburg, to Earl of Suffolk, 28 July/8 August 1772).

138 *Ibid.*, XIII, 219–20, 250–4; XXVII (1880), 34.

139 'Copy Letterbook', [ff. 50–21].

140 *Ibid.*, [ff. IV.–2].

141 *Scots Magazine*, XXXV (1773), 661.

142 *Ibid.*, XXXVII (1775), 279.

143 *Memoir of James Trevenen*, p. 159.

144 RNL, Fond 73, Arkhiv Bil'basova, V. A. i Kraevskogo, A. A., No. 215 'Sud'ba printsessy Tarakanovoi', f. 9v. See Mikhail Longinov, 'Zametka o kniazhne Tarakanovoi. Po povodu kartiny g. Flavitskogo', *Russkii arkhiv*, no. 1 (1865), 89–94.

145 *Scots Magazine*, XXXIX (1777), 562.

146 Thomas Thomson, *History of the Royal Society* (London, 1812), Appendix IV, p. viii; *Novi Acta Academiae Scientiarum Imperialis Petropolitanae*, I (4th series) (spb, 1787), 20–1.

147 RNL, Fond 216, Letter of Bezborodko to Greig, 25 July/5 August 1781, f. 1. (I was allowed to examine this archive, for long inaccessible to scholars and still uncatalogued, through the kindness of the Keeper of the Manuscript Department, Mme B. Gradova.).

148 *Memoir of Sir Samuel Greig*, p. 161.

149 Veselago, MIRF, XII, 211–12.

150 P. P. Zabarinskii, *Pervye 'ognevye' mashiny v Kronshtadtskom portu* (M-L, 1936), pp. 47–50, 75–7, 124–30.

151 SIRIO, XXIII, 246.

152 AKV, XIX, 339.

153 William Tooke, *The Life of Catharine* II, Empress of Russia, I, 5th edn (Dublin, 1800), 197.

154 John Hill Burton, *The Scot Abroad*, II (Edinburgh, 1864), 221–2.

155 Razdolgin, Skorikov, *Kronshtadtskaia krepost'*, pp. 68–9.

156 Rozadeev *et al.*, *Kronshtadt*, pp. 36–46. The principal architect was initially the little-known M. N. Vetoshnikov.

157 J. B. Brown, *Memoirs of the Public and Private Life of John Howard* (London, 1818), p. 613.

158 *Archivo del general Miranda*, II (Caracas, 1929), 402–6.

159 R. H. Campbell, *The Carron Company* (Edinburgh and London, 1961), p. 151.

160 *Diaries and Correspondence of James Harris, First Earl of Malmesbury*, I (London, 1844), 306–7.

161 RNL, Fond 216, Draft of letter to unknown lady in Britain.

162 *Diaries and Correspondence of James Harris*, I, 327–8.

163 *The Correspondence of Jeremy Bentham*, II (London, 1968), 469.

164 *A Memoir of James Trevenen*, p. 160.

165 AKV, XIX, 502–6.

166 See Tira Sokolovskaia, 'O masonstve v prezhnem russkom flote', *More*, no. 8 (1907), 216–52; A. G. Cross, 'British Freemasons in Russia during the Reign of Catherine the Great', OSP, NS IV (1971), 58–9. All the British officers are in OMS with the exception of Nasse. On him, see his letter to Bezborodko from a St Petersburg debtors prison, 28 July/8 August 1794 (RGADA, Fond 10, opis' i, ed. khr. 651, ff. 168–70).

167 See *Memoirs of Paul Jones, Late Rear-Admiral in the Russian Service*, 2 vols. (London, 1843); Lincoln Lorenz, *The Admiral and the Empress: John Paul Jones and Catherine the Great* (New York, 1954).

168 *A Memoir of James Trevenen*, p. 124.

169 National Library of Scotland, Edinburgh, No. 8389, letter of 1/12 March 1777.

170 *Scots Magazine*, L (1788), 348. Cf. RGADA, Fond 1261, opis' 3, ed. khr. 1790, ff. 46–7.

171 *Scots Magazine*, L, 459.

172 Jane, *Imperial Russian Navy*, pp. 630–4.

173 Cf. *ibid.*, p. 637; Parkinson, *Tour*, p. 79; Tatiana Bakounine, *Répertoire biographique des francs-maçons russes* (Paris, 1967), p. 188.

174 Comte de Ségur, *Memoirs ou souvenirs et anecdotes*, III (Paris, 1826), 350–1.

175 See the description in Andrew Swinton, *Travels into Norway, Denmark and Russia, in the Years 1788, 1789, 1790, and 1791* (London, 1792), pp. 152–9. See also Viktor Antonov, 'Admiral Greig's Tomb', SGECRN, no. 12 (1984), 25–34.

176 *An Grabe Greghs* (spb, 1788); *Slovo na smert' V.D. Greikha* (spb, 1788). Quotations are translated from A. N. Pypin, *Russkoe masonstvo XVIII i pervaia chetvert' XIX v.* (Petrograd, 1916), pp. 162–6. See also N. Struiskii, 'Elegiia v pamiat' S.K. Greiga', *Moskovskie vedomosti*, no. 100 (13 December 1788), 899; 'Stikhi na smert' Greiga', *Novye ezhemesiachnye sochineniia*, XXIX (1788), 85; XXX, 63.

177 *A Memoir of James Trevenen*, pp. 160–1.

178 See A. Aslanberov, *Admiral Aleksei Samuilovich Greig* (spb, 1873); Iu. S. Kriuchkov, *Aleksei Samuilovich Greig* (Moscow, 1984).

179 See Stephens, *History of Inverkeithing and Rosyth*, pp. 488–97; OMS, III, 433–41; Elizabeth Chambers Patterson, *Mary Somerville and the Cultivation of Science, 1815–1840* (Boston, 1983), pp. 1–5.

180 AKV, XII (1877), 62; XIII, 156.

181 *Ibid.*, XXVIII (1883), 89–90.

182 *Diaries and Correspondence of James Harris*, II, 36, letter from Harris to Lord Grantham, 17/28 February 1783.

183 *London Chronicle*, LIV, no. 4189 (4–6 September 1783), 240; no. 4190 (6–9 September), 248.

184 *Russkii arkhiv*, bk 1 (1879), 100–1.

185 *AKV*, XXVIII, 74.

186 *AGM*, III (1902), 337–8.

187 *Russkii arkhiv*, bk 1 (1879), 100.

188 *Archivo del general Miranda*, II, 229.

189 *OMS*, III, 510–11.

190 E.g. Captain Crown (St Petersburg Branch of Institute of History, Fond 36, opis' 1, d. 1248, ff. 80–80v.; Vincent Barrer (RGADA, Fond 10, op. 1, ed. khr. 650, ff. 42–42v.).

191 *OMS*, IV, 356 (Mettam), *AGM*, I, 302–6, 515–16; *OMS*, V, 186–7 (Teesdale).

192 Jones's journal of the Liman campaign is in *Memoirs of Paul Jones*, II, 4–117.

193 TSGAVMF, Fond 8, op. 1, d. 58, f. 99, letter of Harris to Greig, 25 April/6 May 1780.

194 *Correspondence of Jeremy Bentham*, IV (1981), 2.

195 *Ibid.*, pp. 1–9. On Bentham, see Ian R. Christie, 'Samuel Bentham and the Russian Dnieper Flotilla, 1787–1788', *SEER*, L (1972), 173–97 and his *The Benthams in Russia* (Oxford and Providence, 1993).

196 William Eton, *A Survey of the Turkish Empire* (London, 1798), pp. 78–9; SIRIO, LIV, 182 (here called Foot); *Correspondence of Jeremy Bentham*, IV, 12.

197 Edward Daniel Clarke, *Travels in Various Countries of Europe Asia and Africa*, II (4th edn, London, 1816), 365. See *OMS*, IV, 612–13; *Archivo del general Miranda*, II, 216, 222; *The Life of Richard Heber, D.D.*, I (London, 1830), 277, 326.

198 Anderson, 'British and American Officers', p. 19; *Naval Battles in the Levant*, pp. 376, 431–4.

199 *AGM*, I, 212; *OMS*, III, 160–3 (Bailey), IV, 351–4 (Messer).

200 M. S. Anderson, 'Russia in the Mediterranean, 1788–1791: A Little-Known Chapter in the History of Naval Warfare and Privateering', *Mariner's Mirror*, XLV (1959), 25–35. On Gibbs, see SIRIO, XCII, 55; *AGM*, I, 490; on Smith, *OMS*, V, 98; *AGM*, I, 554–5.

201 Anderson, 'Russia in the Mediterranean', p. 30, note 2. A manuscript copy is in the Dartmouth Papers, D(W) 1778/V/953 in the Staffordshire Record Office and another copy, belonging to E. H. Hooker, was advertised in *Bernard Quaritch's Catalogue 1006: Travel* (1980), p. 60, item 263. The journal is most readily available in C. Redding (ed.), *History of Shipwrecks and Disasters at Sea*, III (London, 1835), 185–205.

202 See M. S. Anderson, *Britain's Discovery of Russia 1553–1815* (London, 1958), pp. 143–85.

203 Anderson, *Naval Wars in the Baltic*, p. 293.

204 *The Bee*, XIV (1793), 280–2 (Greig); XV, 13–19 (Trevenen), 60–4 (Elphinstone), 316–19 (Marshall).

205 Swinton, *Travels*, p. 365, *OMS*, III, 338 (Hay), 448 (Green).

206 Tooke, *Life of Catharine II*, III, 193.

207 *OMS*, IV, 328; *AGM*, III, 337; *AKV*, IX, 181 (and not Greig, as the editor suggests); XIII, 160; Mrs Aubrey Le Blond, *Charlotte Sophie Countess Bentinck, Her Life and Times, 1715–1800*, I (London, 1912), 110–11.

208 *A Memoir of James Trevenen*, p. 218.

209 Dennison married Ruth Farquharson (date unknown) and Trevenen, Elizabeth Farquharson on 8/19 February 1789. John Farquharson was a relation of Peter's Aberdonian Professor of Navigation.

210 *OMS*, III, 477–8.

211 *Ibid.*, IV, 359 (Miller); V, 396–7 (Aiken). Vorontsov and his sister Princess Dashkova were successful in securing Aiken an increased pension: *AKV*, XII, 341; XVIII, 48.

John Parkinson learnt much of the events of the war from Aiken in St Petersburg in 1792: Parkinson, *Tour*, pp. 60, 79, 226.

212 Tooke, *Life of Catharine II*, III, 193–4; *Memoir of Trevenen*, p. xiv. (The obituary was written by a long-standing friend of Trevenen, David Samwell, a naval surgeon.).

213 *AKV*, XIII, 154. Cf. *ibid.*, 156, 161.

214 See the anecdote in James Walker's *Paramythia*: A. G. Cross (ed.), *Engraved in the Memory: James Walker, Engraver to the Empress Catherine the Great, and His Russian Anecdotes* (Oxford and Providence, 1993), pp. 78–9. There was, incidentally, another Samuel Elphinston, an 'engineer', who also joined in 1783 and died in 1790 (*OMS*, V, 402).

215 *Memoir of James Trevenen*, pp. 191–3; *OMS*, III, 124 (Barrer); IV, 288–9 (Lally), 485–7 (Ogilvie).

216 *Pamiatnye zapiski A.V. Khrapovitskogo stats-sekretaria Imperatritsy Ekateriny Vtoroi* (Moscow, 1990), p. 209.

217 *Memoir of James Trevenen*, pp. 198–208. Cf. Trevenen's long letter of justification to his patron Vorontsov, 30 October/10 November 1789 (*AKV*, XIX, 507–15).

218 *RBS*, IX (Knappe-Kiukhel'beker), 450–1.

219 *Memoir of James Trevenen*, p. 173.

220 RNL, Fond 609, Popov V.S., No. 151, ff. 1–2; *The Russian Journals of Martha and Catherine Wilmot* (London, 1934), pp. 317–18.

221 GL, MS 11,192B, f. 155; *Memoir of James Trevenen*, p. x.

222 *Memoir of James Trevenen*, p. 93.

223 *Ibid.*, p. 113.

224 *Correspondence of Jeremy Bentham*, III, 28. Cf. Veselago, *MIRF*, XIII, 45.

225 Martin Sauer, *An Account of a Geographical and Astronomical Expedition to the Northern Parts of Russia, for Ascertaining the Degrees of Latitude and Longtitude of the River Kovima; of the Whole Coast of Tsutski, to East Cape; and of the Islands in the Eastern Ocean, Stretching to the American Coast* (London, 1802), p. viii. Pallas in a letter to Sir Joseph Banks of 2/13 June 1785 says that he proposed Billings to the empress (BL, Add. MSS 8096, f. 148v).

226 V. A. Divin, *Russkie moreplavateli na Tikhom okeane v XVIII veke* (Moscow, 1971), p. 258. In his petition Edwards speaks of his skill as an instrument-maker in St Petersburg. He is not to be confused with the Joseph Edwards who joined the navy as a midshipman in 1783 and later served in Paul Jones's squadron (*OMS*, V, 396).

227 [John Sinclair], *General Observations Regarding the Present State of the Russian Empire* (London, 1787), p. 17; 'Notice of Billings's Discoveries in the Northern Archipelago', *The Bee*, XI (1792), 224; 'News from Captain Billings', *ibid.*, XVI (1793), 9–17, 45–9.

228 *Memoir of James Trevenen*, p. 114.

229 See generally *OMS*, III, 175–6; A. I. Alekseev, 'Joseph Billings', *Geographical Journal*, CXXXII (1966), 233–8. A third member of Cook's third voyage, the American John Ledyard (1751–89), was also in Siberia at the same time as Billings and having met up with him, got as far as Irkutsk before he was expelled by Catherine. See Stephen D. Watrous (ed.), *John Ledyard's Journey through Russia and Siberia 1787–1788: The Journal and Selected Letters* (Madison, 1966).

230 Clarke, *Travels*, II, pp. 201, 208. See also Clarke's anecdote about how Pallas contrived to get the empress to favour Billings: I, 20.

231 *OMS*, III, 341–3; GL, MS 11,194/1, f. 301.

232 See Eunice H. Turner, 'The Russian Squadron with Admiral Duncan's North Sea Fleet, 1795–1800', *Mariner's Mirror*, XLIX (1963), 212–22; A. G. Cross, *By the Banks of the Thames*, pp. 165–7.

233 Rosalin Barker, *Prisoners of the Tsar: East Coast Sailors Held in Russia 1800–1801* (Beverley, 1992), p. 28. See Roderick E. McGrew, *Paul of Russia 1754–1801* (Oxford, 1992), pp. 308–16.

234 For information on officers not cited earlier, see *OMS*, III, 191–2 (Boyle), 349–51 (Hamilton); IV, 21–4 (Chandler), 485–7 (Ogilvy); V, 398–9 (Elliot).

235 Repeating an experiment of 1805: see 'The Diaries of James Hall', in L. King-Hall (ed.), *Sea Saga: Being the Naval Diaries of Four Generations of the King-Hall Family* (London, 1935), pp. 17–27.

236 A Surgeon in the British Navy, *A Voyage to St. Petersburg in 1814, with Remarks on the Imperial Russian Navy* (London, 1822), p. 3.

237 *Ibid.*, pp. 18–19.

238 Veselago, *Kratkaia istoriia*, II, 449. See *OMS*, II, 207–9 (Borthwick); IV, 388–9 (Monk). See also the very sympathetic note on Borthwick by P. Belavenets, *RBS*, III (Betankur-Biakster), 284–5.

239 Quoted in Barker, *Prisoners of the Tsar*, p. 18.

240 *SIRIO*, XIX, 313.

241 'Memorandum by Sir George Collier', *Correspondence of King George the Third*, II (London, 1927), 348–9. Cf. Robert R. Rea, 'John Blankett and the Russian Navy in 1774', *Mariner's Mirror*, XLI (1955), 247–9. Admiral Sir George Collier had been captain of the ship bringing the British ambassador Lord Cathcart back from Russia in 1772. His memorandum is undated, but judged by M. S. Anderson as not earlier than 1775 (*Britain's Discovery of Russia*, p. 132, n. 1). Lieutenant (later Rear-Admiral) Blankett had visited Russia in 1774. His views are expounded in a letter to Earl of Shelburne, dated 25 December 1777, sixteen days after Knowles' death. According to a letter from Jeremy Bentham to Samuel, dated 21 November 1778, Blankett was with Knowles when he died and gained possession of many of Knowles's papers (*Correspondence of Jeremy Bentham*, II, 193 and note).

6 'NECESSARY FOREIGNERS': SPECIALISTS AND CRAFTSMEN IN RUSSIAN SERVICE

1 Maia Jansson and Nikolai Rogozhin (eds.), *England and the North: The Russian Embassy of 1613–1614* (Philadelphia, 1994), p. 181 (translation of Paul Bushkovitch).

2 Vladimir Chekhmarev, 'Angliiskie mastera na sluzhbe u Mikhaila Fedorovicha', *Arkhitektura i stroitel'stvo Moskvy*, no. 9 (1990), 19–21. (An English variant appeared under the title 'British Craftsmen in the Service of the Tsar', *Britain–USSR*, no. 87 (1990), 3–7.) See also A. A. Lappo-Danilevskii, 'Inozemtsy v Rossii v tsartsvovanie Mikhaila Fedorovicha', *Zhurnal Ministerstva narodnogo prosveshcheniia* (September 1885), 84–99; Geraldine M. Phipps, 'Britons in Russia: 1613–82', *Societas*, VII (1977), 19–45.

3 Chekhmarev, 'Angliiskie mastera', pp. 20–1. See also on Halloway, Valentin L. Chenakal, *Watchmakers and Clockmakers in Russia 1400 to 1850* (London, 1972), p. 25; D. S. Likhachev, *Poeziia sadov: k semantike sadovo-parkovykh stilei* (Leningrad, 1982), pp. 110–12.

4 See Joseph T. Fuhrmann, *Tsar Alexis, His Reign and His Russia* (Gulf Breeze, Florida, 1981), particularly chs. 15–17.

5 See Joseph Robertson (ed.), *Passages from the Diary of General Patrick Gordon of Auchleuchries* (Aberdeen, 1859; reprint London, 1968).

6 Dmitry G. Fedosov, 'The First Russian Bruces', in Grant G. Simpson (ed.), *The Scottish Soldier Abroad 1247–1967* (Edinburgh, 1992), pp. 55–66. Bruce is a figure of major importance, known in particular for his invention of the first Russian secular calendar ('Briusov kalendar'') and for his great library, the catalogue of which was recently published: E. A. Savel'eva (comp.), *Biblioteka Ia. V. Briusa* (Leningrad, 1989).

7 RGADA, Fond 196, Sobraniia Mazurina, opis' 3, delo 195, ff. 1–3.

8 Valentin L. Chenakal, 'The Astronomical Instruments of John Rowley in Eighteenth-Century Russia', *Journal for the History of Astronomy*, III (1972), 119–35.

9 Valentin L. Chenakal, 'John Bradlee and His Sundials', *Journal for the History of Astronomy*, IV (1973), 159–67.

10 A. S. Britkin, S. S. Vidonov, *Vydaiushchiisia mashinostroitel' XVIII veka A. K. Nartov* (Moscow, 1950), pp. 51–64; F. N. Zagorskii, *Andrei Konstantinovich Nartov* (Leningrad, 1969), pp. 20, 24; M. Iu. Matveev, *Tokarnia Petra I* (Leningrad, 1979), M. E. Gize, *Nartov v Peterburge* (Leningrad, 1988), pp. 7–24. On Nartov in England, see A. G. Cross, *'By the Banks of the Thames': Russians in Eighteenth-Century Britain* (Newtonville, Mass., 1981), pp. 186–7.

11 Gize, *Nartov v Peterburge*, p. 19.

12 GL MS 11,192B, f. 22.

13 S. P. Luppov, *Istoriia stroitel'stva Peterburga v pervoi chetverti XVIII veka* (M-L, 1957), p. 124. According to P. N. Stolpianskii, the Fontanka was originally known as 'Nameless Erik' ('Bezymiannyi Erik'): *Peterburg: Kak voznik, osnovalsia i ros Sanktpiterburkh* (Petrograd, 1918), p. 282.

14 RGADA, Fond 9, Kabinet Petra I, otdelenie I, kn., 57, f. 44.

15 Luppov, *Istoriia stroitel'stva Peterburga*, p. 120; Aubry de LaMotraye, *Voyage en anglois et en françois en diverses provinces et places de la Prusse Ducale et Royale, de la Russie, de la Pologne* (The Hague, London and Dublin, 1732), p. 230; G. N. Komelova, *Vidy Peterburga i ego okrestnostei serediny XVIII veka: Graviury po risunkam M. Makhaeva* (Leningrad, 1968), pp. 43, 48.

16 Komelova, *Vidy Peterburga*, pp. 6–7. M. I. Sukhomlinov, *Materialy dlia istorii Akademii nauk*, VIII (spb, 1895), 164.

17 On Thomas Truscott, see Iu. Kh. Kopelevich, *Osnovanie Peterburgskoi Akademii nauk* (Leningrad, 1977), pp. 139, 157, note 16. Amburger gives his profession as 'wine-waiter' ('Weinschenk'): Erik Amburger, *Beiträge zur Geschichte der deutsch-russishcen kulturellen Beziehungen* (Geissen, 1961), p. 197. Truscott's wife was named Elizabeth (d. 1751) (GL, MS 11,192B, f. 23). Different birth years for John Truscott are given in *Istoriia Akademii nauk SSSR*, I (M-L, 1958), 456 (gives 1719 and spells his name Troscott/Trescott); *Akademiia nauk SSSR: personal'nyi sostav*, I (Moscow, 1974), 14 (gives 1721 and name as Truscott, but Johann instead of John). Truscott and his wife Juliana Gertrude were members of the English congregation. The baptisms of their sons, John Frederic and Charles Gustavus, are registered in December 1755 and March 1760 respectively (MS 11,192B, ff. 27, 33).

18 V. F. Gnucheva, *Geograficheskii departament Akademii nauk XVIII veka* (M-L, 1946), p. 47.

19 *Ibid.*, p. 243, no. 53 and p. 276, no. 43.

20 *Ibid.*, p. 88, note 3.

21 *Ibid.*, pp. 85–6, 199–201 (text of memorandum).

22 Sukhomlinov, *Materialy*, IX (1897), 198.

23 *Ibid.*, 292–3. On Truscott, see also Amburger, *Beiträge*, p. 197.

24 Chenakal, *Watchmakers*, p. 53; R. T. Gunther, *Early Science in Oxford*, I (Oxford, 1923), 184.

25 R. J. Morda Evans, 'Recruitment of British Personnel for the Russian Service 1734–1738', *Mariner's Mirror*, XLVII (1961), 136–7. Kantemir was also instructed to purchase mathematical instruments in 1737: *ibid.*, 132.

26 Sukhomlinov, *Materialy*, VIII, 645–6, 652–4. See also *ibid.*, X (1900), 337–8.

27 *Ibid.*, IX, 1–2; Britkin and Vidonov, *Nartov*, p. 146.

28 V. L. Chenakal, 'Astronomicheskie instrumenty Dzhona Berda v Rossii XVIII v.', *Istoriko-astronomicheskie issledovaniia*, vyp. VI (Moscow, 1960), 74–5. On Scott's death in 1751 his heirs apparently decided to sell his house by lottery (the first in Russia), selling sixty-four tickets at five rubles each and the draw was made in the English Inn: P. N. Petrov, *Istoriia Sankt-Peterburga* (spb, 1885), p. 535.

29 V. L. Chenakal *et al. Letopis' zhizni i tvorchestva M.V. Lomonosova* (M-L, 1961), pp. 120, 123, 124, 125, 143, 146, 149, 150, 151, 161.

30 A. Sivers, 'Medal'er Ben'iamin Skott', *Izvestiia GAIMK*, V (1927), 163.

31 Leonard Forrer, *Biographical Dictionary of Medallists*, V (London, 1912), 445.

32 GL, MS 11,192B, f. 34. See also ff. 20, 23, 25, 26, 27, 29, 31. Only the burial of the first son, Benjamin, (as opposed to the baptisms of the others) is recorded in March 1748 (f. 20), suggesting that the Scotts had indeed arrived in 1747.

33 K. V. Malinovskii (ed.), *Zapiski Iakoba Shtelina ob iziashchnykh iskusstvakh v Rossii*, I (Moscow, 1990), 317. (Incidentally, Stählin says quite categorically that the Scotts are father and son.)

34 E. S. Shchukina, *Medal'ernoe iskusstvo v Rossii XVIII veka* (Leningrad, 1962), p. 38. See also pp. 59, 64, 66.

35 *Obshchii morskoi spisok*, I (spb, 1885), 52; GL, MS 11,192B, f. 1.

36 GL, MS 11,192B, ff. 10, 25. See also ff. 11, 12, 13, 14.

37 *Ibid.*, f. 62. (His wife was Anna Elizabeth Schlotzer, *ibid.*, f. 33); SIRIO, XL (1887), 60 (name and patronym given there as Osip *Ivanovich*). See also Erik Amburger, *Ingermanland*, I (Cologne and Vienna, 1980), 211–2.

38 A. E. Fersman, N. I. Vlodavets, *Gosudarstvennaia Petergofskaia granil'naia fabrika v ee proshlom, nastoiashchem i budushchem* (Petrograd, 1922), pp. 2–7; Sukhomlinov, *Materialy*, IX (1899); M. G. Voronov, G. D. Khodasevich, *Arkhitekturnyi ansambl' Kamerona v Pushkine* (Leningrad, 1982), pp. 45–8. Bottom's widow received an annual pension of 300 rubles from the empress on 12/23 July 1779: *200-letie Kabineta Ego Imperatorskogo Velichestva 1704–1904* (spb, 1911), p. 377.

39 Fersman and Vlodavets, *Gosudarstvennaia Petergofskaia*, p. 7.

40 Chenakal, *Watchmakers*, p. 14; *Sanktpeterburgskie vedomosti*, no. 68 (26 August 1791), 1378–9. There are many entries about the various Bottoms in the church register. See also Grand Duke Nikolai Mikhailovich, *Petersburgskii nekropol'*, I (spb, 1912), 277.

41 GL, MS 11,192B, f. 32.

42 Iakob Shtelin, *Muzyka i balet v Rossii XVIII veka* (Leningrad, 1935), pp. 104–5.

43 Basil Cozens-Hardy (ed.), *The Diary of Sylas Neville 1767–1788* (London, 1950), p. 52.

44 A version of the misfortunes of Winrowe and his organ remains in the possession of the descendants of Tucker and was made available to me through the good offices of Mr Robert Dimsdale.

45 Nicholas Goodison, *Ormolu: The Work of Matthew Boulton* (London, 1974), pp. 96–100, 119–23.

46 *Ibid.*, p. 123.

47 See *The Times* (26 March 1987), p. 16a; (8 April), p. 5a.

48 L. A. Dukel'skaia, *Iskusstvo Anglii XVI–XIX vekov: Ocherk-putevoditel'* (Leningrad, 1983), pp. 29–32. For excellent illustrations of three of Cox's clocks (not including the 'Peacock'), see Dukel'skaia (comp.), *The Hermitage: English Art Sixteenth to Nineteenth Century* (Leningrad, London and Wellingborough, 1979), nos. 205, 207–9. For a detailed description of Kulibin's repairs and the working of the 'Peacock' clock, see V. N. Pipunyrov, N. M. Raskin, *Ivan Petrovich Kulibin 1735–1818* (Leningrad, 1986), pp. 126–9.

49 S. R. Mikulinsky *et al.* (eds.), *USSR Academy of Sciences: Scientific Relations with Great Britain* (Moscow, 1977), pp. 194–6. In 1764 Arnold made a miniature watch for George III, so small that it could fit into a ring. Catherine wanted Arnold to make one for her, offering him 1,000 gold rubles, but he declined: Pipunyrov, Raskin, *Kulibin*, p. 193 note.

50 See V. L. Chenakal, 'Zerkal'nye teleskopy Vil'iama Gershelia v Rossii', *Istoriko-astronomicheskie issledovaniia*, IV (1958), 253–340; 'Dzhems Short i russkaia astronomiia XVIII v.', *ibid.*, V (1959), 3–82; 'Astronomicheskie instrumenty Dzhona Berda v Rossii XVIII v.', *ibid.*, 53–119.

51 See Cross, *By the Banks of the Thames*, pp. 187–9.

52 *Protokoly zasedanii konferentsii Imperatorskoi Akademii nauk*, III (spb, 1900), 567.

53 PRO, SP 91/88, ff. 283–4; 289–90 (contract). Francis's father John, who was one of the witnesses to the agreement, was also an instrument-maker, to whom one of the workmen accompanying Francis, Daniel McMillan, had been apprenticed. McMillan soon set up on his own in St Petersburg.

54 P. N. Petrov (ed.), *Sbornik materialov dlia istorii Imperatorskoi S.-Peterburgskoi Akademii khudozhestv za sto let ee sushchestvovaniia*, I (spb, 1864), 208–9.

55 *Ibid.*, p. 283.

56 G. Gorodkov, *Admiralteiskie izhorskie zavody. Kratkii istoricheskii ocherk ikh vozniknoveniia, razvitiia i deiatel'nosti. (S 1710 – 1902 gg.)* (spb, 1903), pp. 24–5.

57 AVPR, Moscow, Fond Londonskaia missiia, opis' 36/1, delo 450, f. 2.

58 Gorodkov, *Admiralteiskie izhorskie zavody*. p. 33.

59 *MIRF*, XVI (1902), 64–5.

60 *Protokoly zasedanii*, III, 152–5.

61 *Ibid.*, pp. 189, 192–3; Chenakal, 'Astronomical Instruments of John Rowley', pp. 131–2. (Pipunyrov and Raskin do not mention the orrery.)

62 *Protokoly zasedanii*, III, 699, 733.

63 Pipunyrov, Raskin, *Kulibin*, pp. 82–3.

64 I. G. Georgi, *Opisanie rossiisko-imperatorskogo stolichnogo goroda Sanktpeterburga i dostopamiatnostei v okrestnostiakh onogo* (spb, 1794), p. 572.

65 Chenakal, *Watchmakers*, p. 43.

66 Herbert Swann, *Home on the Neva: A Life of a British Family in Tsarist St Petersburg – and after the Revolution* (London, 1968), pp. 46–7.

67 Birmingham Reference Library, Matthew Boulton Papers, Letter Book G, f. 666; Letter Book H, ff. 523–4.

68 GLRO, Peachey Papers, F/PEY/142.

69 Chenakal, *Watchmakers*, p. 25; F. J. Britten, *Watchmakers and Clockmakers of the World*, 7th edn (London, 1969), p. 410; Swann, *Home on the Neva*, photograph facing p. 97.

70 *Protokoly zasedanii*, III, 542, 693.

71 GLRO, Peachey Papers, F/PEY/ 148–9.

72 See A. G. Cross, 'Early Contacts of the Society with Russia', in D. G. C. Allan and John L. Abbott (eds.), *The Virtuoso Tribe of Arts & Sciences: Studies in the Eighteenth-Century Work and Membership of the London Society of Arts* (Athens, Georgia, and London, 1992), p. 269.

73 GLRO, Peachey Papers, F/PEY/169 (letter of 12/24 August 1813).

74 *Ibid.*, F/PEY/150.

75 *Ibid.*, F/PEY/152, 154.

76 *Ibid.*, F/PEY/147, 153. (Swann, who quotes these letters, confuses the chronology and the tsars and also suggests the standards project was abandoned: *Home on the Neva*, pp. 54–5.)

77 E. I. Kamentseva, 'Rol' Peterburga v snabzhenii gorodov Rossii merami dliny (pervaia chetvert' XIX v.), in V. I. Shunkov (ed.), *Goroda feodal'noi Rossii* (Moscow, 1966), pp. 538–9.

78 *Ibid.*, pp. 542–6.

79 GLRO, Peachey Papers, F/PEY/156 (letter of 7/19 October 1812).

80 Pushkin House, St Petersburg, Fond 620, Arkhiv A. A. Samborskogo, ed. khr. 100, f. 2v.; *200-letie Kabineta E.I. Velichestva*, p. 373.

81 The Hynams were prolific breeders and if the children survived their early years, they lived on to ripe old age. See GL, MS 11,192B and 11,194/1, *passim*, and *Peterburgskii nekropol'*, I, 524, in addition to Swann, *Home on the Neva*.

82 Chenakal, *Watchmakers*, p. 27.

83 GLRO, Peachey Papers, F/PEY/174.

84 Information in a letter dated 25 November 1974 from the late Professor N. A. Erofeev of Moscow, based on archival materials which were inaccessible to me. Another Englishman, Edward Bull, was also arrested on Senate Square and expelled. As to Hynam's 'innocence', one can only speculate – and also wonder whether his unexplained second expulsion, coming a few months after the death of Pushkin, was in any way connected with the demonstrations following that event.

85 Letter from the Carron Company to John Smeaton, quoted in R. A. Campbell, *Carron Company* (Edinburgh and London, 1961), p. 74; *Public Advertiser*, no. 15373 (4 September 1783), p. 2; no. 15391 (25 September 1783), p. 2.

86 Roger P. Bartlett, *Human Capital: The Settlement of Foreigners in Russia 1762–1804* (Cambridge, 1979).

87 Adelaide D'Arcy Collyer (ed.), *The Despatches and Correspondence of John, Second Earl of Buckinghamshire, Ambassador to the Court of Catherine II of Russia 1762–1765*, II (London, 1902), 122–3.

88 *Russkii arkhiv*, bk. 1 (1879), 97. See also *ibid.*, 98–100; AKV, IX, 46, 406–7; XI, 177–8; XIII, 101–2.

89 Bartlett, *Human Capital*, pp. 128–9.

90 *Correspondence of Jeremy Bentham*, III (London, 1971), 271.

91 *Ibid.*, pp. 270–1, 268.

92 Ian R. Christie, *The Benthams in Russia 1780–1791* (London and Providence, 1993), chs. 6–9.

93 *Lloyds Evening Post and British Chronicle*, IV (9–12 March 1764), 243, quoted in full in Bartlett, *Human Capital*, pp. 248–9.

94 AVPR, Fond Londonskaia missiia, delo 398, ff. 32v. There are several letters in this file concerning Catherine's desire for British families to settle her newly acquired lands, as well as one containing the terms demanded by one Marmaduke Stalkartt, a Deptford shipwright, to build a new dockyard in the Crimea.

95 Quoted in Tamara Talbot Rice, 'Charles Cameron, Architect to the Imperial Russian

Court', in *Charles Cameron c. 1740–1812* (Edinburgh, 1967), pp. 21–2; E. A. Jones, 'The Enticement of Scottish Artificers to Russia and Denmark in 1784 and 1786', *Scottish Historical Review*, XVIII, no. 3 (1920–1), 233–4.

96 See the examples quoted in Eric Robinson, 'The Transference of British Technology to Russia, 1760–1820: A Preliminary Enquiry', in Barrie M. Ratcliffe (ed.), *Great Britain and Her World 1750–1914* (Manchester, 1975), pp. 8–10.

97 RGADA, Fond 10, Op. 1, ed. khr. 648, ff. 192–8.

98 National Maritime Museum, Greenwich, MS 84/075, [ff. 6–6v.].

99 SRO, Carron Papers, GD 58/1/12, f. 71, quoted in R. P. Bartlett, 'Scottish Cannon Founders and the Russian Navy, 1768–85', *OSP*, NS X (1977).

100 National Maritime Museum, MS 84/075, [f. 34].

101 Gosudarstvennyi arkhiv Voronezhskoi oblasti, Voronezh, Fond 181, op. 1, d. 37, ff. 11–12.

102 BL, Add. MSS 37, 354, Whitworth Papers, f. 279v.

103 PRO, SP 91/88, ff. 283, 287 (contract).

104 Document in RGADA, quoted in Bartlett, 'Scottish Cannon Founders', p. 69.

105 O. I. Vasil'evskaia, 'Angliiskii prokhodimets Poul' i russkie pushechnye mastera na Aleksandrovskom zavode', *Na rubezhe*, no. 4 (1949), pp. 95ff.

106 V. Rodzevich, *Istoricheskoe opisanie S.-Peterburgskogo Arsenala za 200 let ego sushchestvovaniia 1712–1912 gg.* (spb, 1914), pp. 138–41.

107 *Ibid.*, pp. 142–33. The recognisable British names include Stewart, Henry Taylor, Davie, Ward and Clark, of whom Stewart and Davie were smiths who had worked with the Wilsons for Charles Cameron.

108 P. P. Zabarinskii, *Pervye 'ognevye' mashiny v Kronshtadtskom portu (K istorii vvedeniia parovykh dvigatelei v Rossii)* (M-L, 1936), pp. 47–130. See also Robinson, 'Transference of British Technology', pp. 9–10.

109 For a detailed examination of this episode, see A. G. Cross, 'Charles Cameron's Scottish Workmen', *Scottish Slavonic Review*, no. 10 (1988), 51–74.

110 SRO, Seafield Papers, GD 248/518/6, quoted in full in Rice, *Charles Cameron c.1740–1812*, pp. 19–21.

111 See A. G. Cross, 'British Freemasons in Russia during the Reign of Catherine the Great', *OSP*, NS IV (1971), 60–2.

112 *SIRIO*, XXVII (1880), 355–6.

113 RGADA, Fond 14, d. 52 (III), f. 284.

114 N. K. Shil'der, *Imperator Nikolai Pervyi: ego zhizn' i tsarstvovanie*, I (spb, 1903), pp. 3–4. See also the delightful cameo in W. A. L. Seaman and J. R. Sewell (eds.), *The Russian Journal of Lady Londonderry 1836–37* (London, 1973), p. 54. George Lyon (b. 1764) married Helen Auld in 1786 and was witness at his sister Margaret's wedding in March 1797: GL, MS 1194B, ff. 89, 156.

115 GL, MS 11,192B, ff. 126 (marriage), 131, 140, 148, 158, 172, 189, 220, 228, 229.

116 RGADA, Fond 14, d. 52 (III), f. 269.

117 C. F. Adams (ed.), *Memoirs of John Quincy Adams*, II (Philadelphia, 1874), 111–14 (reproduced in my Russia under *European Eyes, 1517–1825* (London, 1971), pp. 289–93); A. B. Granville, *St Petersburg. A Journal of Travels to and from That Capital*, II (London, 1828), 319–28.

118 G. Gorodkov, *Admiralteiskie zavody* (spb, 1903), pp. 75–7 (with portrait); Iu. B. Iversen, *Medali v chest' russkikh gosudarstvennykh deiatelei i chastnykh lits* (spb, 1877), pp. 91–2 (gold medal struck to honour fifty years in government service); Erik Amburger, *Ingermanland*, I (Cologne and Vienna, 1980), 336–8, 374; II, 776.

119 V. I. Saitov (ed.), *Perepiska Pushkina: Perepiska*, III (spb, 1911), 258–9. See M. P.

Alekseev, *Russko-angliiskie literaturnye sviazi (XVIII vek – pervaia polovina XIX veka) (Literaturnoe nasledstvo,* XCI) (Moscow, 1962), p. 174.

120 *AKV,* XIX (Moscow, 1881), 339. The three letters are on pp. 339-45.

121 Rostislav Gladkikh, 'Tainoe stanovitsia iavnym', in V. N. Verkhogliadov (ed.), *Kraeved Karelii* (Petrozavodsk, 1990), pp. 68-87. Gladkikh speculates, implausibly, about masonic links between Greig and Gascoigne.

122 Edward Daniel Clarke, *Travels in Various Countries of Europe, Asia and Africa,* I (London, 1810), 256. See also *The Life of Reginald Heber, D.D. Lord Bishop of Calcutta* I (London, 1830), p. 105; R. H. Campbell, *Carron Company* (Edinburgh and London, 1961), p. 151; A. H. Cross, 'Great Britain and the Growth of the Russian Navy', *Mariner's Mirror,* XLIII (1957), 75-6; John M. Norris, 'The Struggle for Carron: Samuel Garbett and Charles Gascoigne', *Scottish Historical Review,* XXXVII (1958), 136-45.

123 The letters are split between two St Petersburg archives: the Central Naval Archive (TSGAVMF) and the Russian National (Public) Library (RNL). The Greig archive in the latter repository was for many years unsorted and I am deeply grateful to the Head of the Manuscript Department, Mme Bronislava Gradova, for allowing me access to the papers. The letters have no folio numbers and reference is made by date only.

124 TSGAVMF, Fond 8, Greig, op. 2, ed. khr. 8, f. 20.

125 RNL, Fond 216, Greig, Letter of 21 December 1786 (OS). (For Bowie in 1774, see Bartlett, 'Scottish Cannon-Founders', p. 87, citing Ia. A. Balagurov, *Olonetskie gornye zavody v doreformennyi period* (Petrozavodsk, 1958), p. 44.).

126 *Ibid.,* letter of 2 December 1786.

127 TSGAVMF, Fond 8, op. 1, ed. khr. 50, ff. 40-40v.

128 *Ibid.,* ff. 18-18v., 91. The introduction of the cupola furnace brought admiration and a detailed description from the Swedish engineer J. E. Norberg, visiting Petrozavodsk in 1792 (J. G. James, 'Russian Iron Bridges to 1850', pre-print of paper delivered to the Newcomen Society in 1982, p. 28, note 17 (not included in printed version)).

129 See Norris, 'Struggle for Carron', p. 143; Robinson, 'Transference', p. 9.

130 RNL, Fond 216, Letter of 7/18 December 1786.

131 On 30 July/10 August 1787 Catherine told Potemkin that Greig would be ordered to establish how many cannon Gascoigne could supply and how many it would be necessary to order from Britain for the Black Sea fleet; on 31 August/11 September of the following year she told him of the arrival of Carron guns (SIRIO, XXVII (1880), 420, 519).

132 TSGAVMF, Fond 8, op. 1, ed. khr. 50, f. 112.

133 *Ibid.,* f. 6.

134 *Ibid.,* ff. 23, 112; RNL, Fond 216, Letter of 11 April 1788. (No further information is available about Ingram or his specialism.)

135 See A. G. Cross, 'Cameron's Scottish Workmen', p. 60. There was a teacher by 1800 in the factory school, possibly named Falkener (Folkern), see Ivan German, *Opisanie petrozavodskogo i konchezerskogo zavodov, i proizvodimogo pri onykh lit'ia pushek i snariadov* (spb, 1803), p. 138. I owe the suggestion of the masonic lodge to Dr Bartlett, following his conversation with scholars in Petrozavodsk.

136 Balagurov, *Olonetskie zavody,* p. 90; German, *Opisanie,* pp. 133-40.

137 RGADA, Fond 10, op. 1, ed. khr. 648, ff. 373-373v.

138 TSGAVMF, Fond 8, op. 1, ed. khr. 50, f. 116.

139 *Ibid.,* f. 130.

140 RNL, Fond 216, Letter of 11/22 April 1788.

141 K. I. Arsen'ev, '*Opisanie* Olonetskikh zavodov, s samogo ikh osnovaniia, do poslednego vremeni, s kratkim obozreniem Olonetskoi gubernii', *Trudy mineralogicheskogo obshchestva*, I (spb, 1830), 316–17; *RBS*, vol. Gaag-Gerbel' (Moscow, 1914; reprint 1962), 258–9.

142 Quoted in Campbell, *Carron Company*, p. 153. See the comments on the Gascoigne lifestyle at Petrozavodsk in a letter of 1803 from Mary Kynnersley, Baroness de Bode, whose son Harry was employed in the factory design office: William S. Childe-Pemberton, *The Baroness de Bode 1775–1803* (London, 1900), pp. 269–70.

143 GL, MS 11,192B, ff. 160 (Gascoigne's wedding), 192 (Elizabeth to George Pollen, 1803), 217 (Mary to Edward Row, 1805). Court gossip had it that Anastasia-Jessy soon became the mistress of the Procurator-General P. V. Lopukhin (1744–1827) and thus gained some influence (F. Golovkine, *La Cour et le règne de Paul I* (Paris, 1905), pp. 183–6), but Guthrie provided a disarming and detailed defence of his daughter's honour in a letter of 24 September (OS) 1800 to the former ambassador Fitzherbert (Derbyshire Record Office, Matlock, MS 239m, Fitzherbert, 0555).

144 The best survey of Gascoigne's career is Roger P. Bartlett, 'Charles Gascoigne in Russia: A Case Study in the Diffusion of British Technology, 1786–1806', in A. G. Cross (ed.), *Russia and the West in the Eighteenth Century* (Newtonville, Mass., 1983), pp. 354–67.

145 German, *Opisanie*, p. 139.

146 M. Mitel'man, B. Glebov, A. Ul'ianskii, *Istoriia Putilovskogo zavoda (1801–1917)* (Moscow, 1961), pp. 11–12; James, 'Russian Iron Bridges', pre-print, p. 29, note 26. See also P. N. Stolpianskii, *Petergofskaia pershpektiva* (spb, 1923).

147 Nosov, 'Istoricheskii ocherk Luganskogo liteinogo zavoda', *Gornyi zhurnal*, IV, bk 10 (1855), 78–93; F. F. Veselago (ed.), *Materialy dlia istorii russkogo flota*, XV (1895), 496–500; E. I. Druzhinina, *Severnoe Prichernomor'e v 1775–1800 gg.* (Moscow, 1959), pp. 241–4; Druzhinina, *Iuzhnaia Ukraina v 1800–1825 gg.* (Moscow, 1970), pp. 287–92,

148 AKV, XIX, 110.

149 *Life of Reginald Heber*, I, 125–6.

150 Balagurov, *Olonetskie gornye zavody*, pp. 34–5.

151 Birmingham Reference Library, Matthew Boulton Papers, Russian Mint Box II, letter of Boulton to Baxter, 15 August 1796.

152 *Ibid.*, Russian Mint Box I, translation of letter from Count A. N. Samoilov to Vorontsov, 10/21 October 1796, supplied to Boulton by the Russian Embassy in London.

153 I. G. Spasskii, *Peterburgskii monetnyi dvor ot vozniknoveniia do nachala XIX veka* (Leningrad, 1949), pp. 53–9; V. T. Koretskii, 'Bankovskii monetnyi dvor', in D. B. Shelov (ed.), *Pamiatniki russkogo denezhnogo obrashcheniia XVIII–XX vv.* (Moscow, 1980), pp. 70–84; Bartlett, 'Charles Gascoigne', pp. 360–1.

154 For the activities of the Russian workmen in England, see A. G. Cross, *By the Banks of the Thames*, pp. 198–206. Duncan, one of the English workers, is recorded as still servicing the machines in 1827: A. B. Granville, *St Petersburgh*, II, 98. See also Eric Robinson, 'Birmingham Capitalists and Russian Workers', *History Today*, VI, no. 10 (1956), 673–9. A steam-engine was, however, replaced in 1820 by a more powerful model, designed by Matthew Clark, another of Gascoigne's former associates: M. Klark, 'O parovykh mashinakh voobshche s prisovokupleniem chertezha parovoi mashiny, siloiu protivu 60 loshadei, ustroennoi pri S-Peterburgskom monetnom dvore', *Gornyi magazin*, bk. 10 (1826).

155 Spasskii, *Peterburgskii monetnyi*, p. 58.

156 See I. Ia. Konfederatov, *Ivan Ivanovich Polzunov* (M-L, 1951), 295ff.

157 E. Robinson, D. McKie, *Partners in Science: James Watt and James Black* (London, 1970), pp. 24, 412; Robinson, 'Transference', p. 27; Zabarinskii, *Pervye 'ognevye' mashiny*, pp. 150–2.

158 Zabarinskii, *Pervye 'ognevye' mashiny*, pp. 131–46; A. G. Cross, *By the Banks of the Thames*, pp. 194–8, 204.

159 Balagurov, *Olonetskie gornye zavody*, pp. 60–2. On 1/12 September 1792 Sheriff married Sarah Roper, the daughter of another of Gascoigne's workmen; GL, MS 11,192B, f. 133.

160 RNL, Fond 542, Oleniny, No. 373, ff. 1, 29. Balagurov, p. 62, for the transfer, but there is some question whether there was another steam engine installed. Zavadovskii in a letter of 12/23 August 1799 to Vorontsov, writes of 'the steam engine built by English masters to designs by Gascoigne', and on 12/23 September, mentions Sheriff as a 'man of great skill in the construction of steam engines which he has completed at the Bank mint': AKV, XII (1877), 234, 237.

161 Koretskii, 'Bankovskii monetnyi dvor', p. 77.

162 Robinson, 'Transference', p. 15.

163 Russian Mint Box II, letter of 4 April 1805. See also Jennifer Tann (ed.), *The Selected Papers of Boulton & Watt*, I (London, 1981), 362.

164 V. L. Chenakal, 'Iosif Medzher – talantlivyi mekhanik kontsa XVIII – pervoi treti XIX v.', *Iz istorii estestvoznaniia i tekhniki Pribaltiki*, V (Riga, 1976), 37–51.

165 *Ibid.*, pp. 38–41. See 'O gal'vanievykh opytakh', *Pribavlenie k Sankt-Peterburgskim vedomostiam*, no. 41 (23 May 1803), 16–17.

166 'Kraft o Medzherovoi parovoi makhine', *Tekhnologicheskii zhurnal*, II (spb, 1805), 75–84. See Chenakal, pp. 42–44.

167 V. S. Virginsky, 'The Birth of Steam Navigation in Russia and Robert Fulton', *Technology and Culture*, IX (1968), 562–9.

168 On Baird, see RBS, vol. Aleksinskii-Bestuzhev (spb, 1900; New York, 1964), 728; Bartlett, *Human Capital*, pp. 178–9; Robinson, 'Transference', pp. 12–14; James, 'Iron Bridges', pre-print, pp. 4, 28–9; William L. Blackwell, *The Beginnings of Russian Industrialization 1800–1860* (Princeton, 1968), pp. 251–3. By 1800 Baird had installed small steam engines in his Petersburg works: see MIRF, XVI (spb, 1902), 485–6.

169 Tann, *Selected Papers*, I, p. 360.

170 For a general survey, with excellent photographs, of the activities of Gascoigne, Baird and others, see: John R. Bowles, 'From the Banks of the Neva to the Shores of Lake Baikal: Some Enterprising Scots in Russia', in *The Caledonian Phalanx: Scots in Russia* (Edinburgh, 1987), pp. 65–75.

171 As perceived by Walker in Charles Baird: Russian Mint Box I, letter of 5 October 1805.

7 MASTERS OF THE ARTS

1 Tamara Talbot Rice, 'The Conflux of Influences in Eighteenth-Century Russian Art and Architecture: A Journey from the Spiritual to the Realistic', in J. G. Garrard (ed.), *The Eighteenth Century in Russia* (Oxford, 1973), p. 398.

2 See Larissa Dukelskaya (ed.), *The Hermitage: English Art Sixteenth to Nineteenth Century* (Leningrad and London, 1979).

3 Auchindoune, Cawdor House, Nairne, Cathcart Papers, Folio H, no. 16.

4 Birmingham Reference Libraries, Matthew Boulton Papers, Letter Book E, f. 236.

5 Nicholas Goodison, *Ormolu: The Work of Matthew Boulton* (London, 1974), pp. 96–100.

6 Ann Finer and George Savage (eds.), *The Selected Letters of Josiah Wedgwood* (London, 1965), p. 120.

7 Cathcart Papers, Folio I, no. 43, ff. 1v.–2.

8 Finer and Savage, *Selected Letters of Josiah Wedgwood*, p. 106.

9 William Coxe, *Travels in Poland, Russia, Sweden, and Denmark*, I, 5th ed. (London, 1802), 253–4, 264.

10 See Finer and Savage, *Selected Letters of Josiah Wedgwood*, pp. 144ff.; G. C. Williamson, *The Imperial Russian Dinner Service* (London, 1909); L. N. Voronikhina, *Serviz s zelenoi liagushkoi* (Leningrad, 1962); C. A. Johnson, 'Wedgwood and Bentley's "Frog" Service for Catherine the Great', in A. G. Cross (ed.), *Great Britain and Russia in the Eighteenth Century: Contacts and Comparisons* (Newtonville, Mass., 1979), pp. 123–33; Peter Hayden, 'British Seats on Imperial Russian Tables', *Garden History*, XIII (1985), 17–23; L. N. Voronikhina, 'O peizazhakh 'serviza s zelenoi liagushkoi' ', *Muzei*, no. 9 (1988), 166–74. 'The Genius of Wedgwood' exhibition at the Victoria and Albert Museum in the summer of 1995 has re-awakened British interest in the Service.

11 *Diaries and Correspondence of James Harris, First Earl of Malmesbury*, I (London, 1844), 231.

12 *Voltaire's Correspondence*, ed. T. Besterman, LXXXII (Geneva, 1963), 130. See A. G. Cross, 'Catherine the Great and the English Garden', in John O. Norman (ed.), *New Perspectives on Russian and Soviet Artistic Culture* (London, 1994), pp. 17–24.

13 *Memoirs of the Empress Catherine II, Written by Herself* (London, 1859), p. 228.

14 G. P. Balog *et al.*, *Muzei i parki Pushkina* (Leningrad, 1972), p. 16.

15 BL, Add. MS 33070, ff. 425, 443v., 445.

16 AVPR, Moscow, Fond Londonskaia missiia, opis' 36/1, delo 261, f. 85.

17 *Ibid.*, opis' 36/1, delo 299, f. 4.

18 *Ibid.*, opis' 36/1, delo 296, f. 22. On Neelov in England, see A. G. Cross, *'By the Banks of the Thames': Russians in Eighteenth Century Britain* (Newtonville, Mass., 1980), pp. 219–22.

19 William Tooke, *The Life of Catharine II, Empress of Russia*, II, 5th edn (Dublin, 1800), 13. Irina Stepanenko, however, says that Neelov produced a model of 'the marble gallery' before his visit to England: 'Sadovye mastera Iogann i Iosif Bushi', *SGECRN*, no. 22 (1994), 36.

20 A. N. Petrov, *Pushkin: dvortsy i parki* (Leningrad, 1969), p. 97.

21 *Ibid.*, p. 131, n. 17; AVPR, opis' 36/1, delo 261, f. 69.

22 For a detailed study of the manuscript, see A. G. Cross, 'Catherine the Great and Whately's *Observations on Modern Gardening*', *SGECRN*, no. 18 (1990), 21–9.

23 Peter Hayden, 'The Russian Stowe: Benton Seeley's Guidebooks as a Source of Catherine the Great's Park at Tsarskoe Selo', *Garden History*, XIX (1991), 21–7.

24 RGADA, Moscow, Kabinet Ee Velichestva, Fond 10, opis' 1, delo 654, ff. 293–4.

25 *Ibid.*, delo 302, f. 10v.

26 See A. G. Cross (ed.), *An English Lady at the Court of Catherine the Great: The Journal of Baroness Elizabeth Dimsdale, 1781* (Cambridge, 1989), p. 55.

27 RGADA, Fond 10, opis' 1, delo 383, ff. 1, 2.

28 See A. G. Cross, *By the Banks of the Thames*, pp. 247–8.

29 POARAN, Razriad IV, opis' 1, delo 999, ff. 27v.–28.

30 *Russkii arkhiv*, VIII (1871), 1327, 1335.

31 AVPR, opis' 36/1, delo 283, f. 21.

32 'Arcticus' [Dr Matthew Guthrie], 'On Rearing Timber Trees in Russia', *The Bee*, IX (1792), 156. See also Cambridge University Library, Add. MS 8720, John, 2nd Lord Henniker, 'A Northern Tour in the Years 1775 and 1776 through Copenhagen and Petersburgh to the River Swir Joining the Lakes of Onega and Ladoga in a series of letters', f. 146.

33 *SIRIO*, XIII (1874), 238.

34 *Pavlovsk: Ocherk istorii i opisanie 1777–1877* (spb, 1877), p. 545.

35 GL, British Factory in Russia Register 1706–1815, MS 11,192B, f. 169.

36 V. Makarov, A. Petrov, *Gatchina* (Leningrad, 1974), pp. 45, 49, 61.

37 AVPR, opis' 36/1, delo 261, f. 56.

38 Bush's early activities have been the subject of much recent research. See Marcus Köhler, ' "Wenn wir erst einem ins Wilde angelegten Garten zu sehen gewohnt sind …" ', *Die Gartenkunst*, V, no. 1 (1993), 113–4; D. Solman and G. Douglas, *Loddiges Nursery* (London, 1994).

39 AVPR, delo 261, ff. 1–7v., 16–16v., 21–21v. According to Elizabeth Dimsdale, he was receiving 1,900 rubles in 1781, when the ruble was worth four English shillings: Cross (ed.), *An English Lady*, p. 83.

40 AVPR, opis' 36/1, delo 261, f. 4 (letter from Catherine's secretary Ivan Elagin to the Russian ambassador in London, 6/17 April 1771).

41 Baroness Dimsdale writes that 'one way to his house was through the Green House, as it joins it, therefore I always used to go that way being very pleasant walking between the Orange Trees': Cross (ed.), *An English Lady*, p. 70.

42 BL, Add. MS 31,192, Journal of Visit to St Petersburg by John Jervis, later Earl of St Vincent, ff. 88–88v.; *Gardener's Magazine*, II (July 1827), 386.

43 *Kamerfur'erskii tseremonial'nyi zhurnal 1774 goda* (spb, 1864), pp. 252–3.

44 Cross (ed.), *An English Lady*, p. 54.

45 POARAN, delo 999, ff. 26–26v.

46 *SIRIO*, XXIII (spb, 1878), 239.

47 For the plan, engraved in London by Tobias Müller, see Cross (ed.), *An English Lady*, between pp. 54–5; for the watercolours, see G. A. Printseva (comp.), *Russkaia akvarel'v sobranii gosudarstvennogo Ermitazha*, Leningrad (Moscow, 1988), plates 1–3, 13–14.

48 A. G. Cross (ed.), *Engraved in the Memory: James Walker, Engraver to the Empress Catherine the Great, and His Russian Anecdotes* (Oxford and Providence, 1993), p. 80.

49 Cross (ed.), *An English Lady*, p. 70.

50 Stepanenko, 'Sadovye mastera', p. 39.

51 GL, MS 11,192B, ff. 56, 78, 81, 86.

52 POARAN, delo 999, f. 28.

53 *Ibid.*, f. 58v.

54 Il'ia Iakovkin, *Istoriia Sela Tsarskogo*, III (spb, 1831), 498–502.

55 M. G. Voronov and G. D. Khodasevich, *Arkhitekturnyi ansambl' Kamerona v Pushkine* (Leningrad, 1982), pp. 96–8.

56 [Martin Call], 'History of the First Introduction of the Modern Style of Laying out Grounds into Russia', *Gardener's Magazine*, II (1827), 387.

57 GL, MS 11,192B, ff. 136 (first marriage), 243 (second marriage), 268 (last child).

58 J. C. Loudon, *An Encyclopaedia of Gardening*, new edn (London, 1834), p. 265;

Robert Ker Porter, *Travelling Sketches in Russia and Sweden during the years 1805, 1806, 1807, 1808*, I (London, 1809), 58.

59 Quoted in A. A. Kiuchariants, *Ivan Starov* (Leningrad, 1982), p. 43.

60 John Parkinson, *A Tour of Russia, Siberia and the Crimea 1792–1794*, ed. W. Collier (London, 1971), p. 226. See also *ibid.*, pp. 37–8.

61 *Gardener's Magazine*, II, 388.

62 POARAN, delo 999, f. 11.

63 'Ordera kniazia Potemkina pravitelia Tavricheskoi oblasti 1778oi god', *Izvestiia Tavricheskoi uchenoi arkhivnoi kommissii*, no. 6 (1888), 21; *ibid.*, no.11 (1891), 89; *Morskoi sbornik*, XLVI (1860), 502; E. I. Druzhinina, *Severnoe Prichernomor'e v 1775–1800 gg.* (Moscow, 1959), pp. 121, 135.

64 Several descriptions of this event appeared in English at the beginning of the nineteenth century. See, for example, *Secret Memoirs of the Court of Petersburg*, II (Dublin, 1801), 95–9.

65 *European Magazine*, LXI (January 1812), 58. Gould left all his possessions to his natural daughter Elizabeth (by Jane Worthington of Ormskirk). See his will, Lancashire Record Office, Preston, WOW (William Gould, 1812).

66 Porter, *Travelling Sketches*, I, 58.

67 The letter book was presented to the Soviet authorities in 1942 by H. M. Cox, who had previously published extracts from it in his 'An English Gardener at the Russian Court, 1779–87', *New Flora and Silva*, II (1939), 103–12. Details of the whereabouts of the letter book are given in note 29 of this chapter and in the discussion which follows, reference is made in the text to the letter book by folio number.

68 *The Planter's Guide: or, Pleasure Gardener's Companion* (London, 1779), pages unnumbered.

69 AVPR, Fond Snosheniia Rossii s Angliei, opis' 35/6, delo 296, ff. 23–4.

70 In 1772 Catherine wrote to her friend Mme de Bielke: 'J'ai quitté aujourd'hui mon cher, mon charmant Tsarskoe-Sélo pour m'en aller au détestable, au haïssable Péterhof, que je ne puis souffrir' (SIRIO, XII, 259).

71 V. I. Piliavskii, *Dzhakomo Kvarengi: arkhitektor, khudozhnik* (Leningrad, 1981), pp. 140–1.

72 I have examined the originals in the Department of Prints in the Hermitage. Black and white reproductions are found in E. N. Glezer, *Arkhitekturnyi ansambl' angliiskogo parka* (Leningrad, 1979) and in my 'Russian Gardens, British Gardens', *Garden History*, XIX (1991), 17–18.

73 'Puteshestvie odnoi rossiiskoi znatnoi gospozhi, po nekotorym aglinskim provintsiiam', *Opyt trudov Vol'nogo rossiiskogo sobraniia pri Imperatorskom Moskovskom universitete*, I (1775), 111–12.

74 PRO, Kew, Lowry Cole Papers, 30/43, 19, f. 43v.; Andrew Swinton, *Travels into Norway, Denmark and Russia in 1788, 1789, 1790, 1791* (London, 1792), p. 414. See also *Archivo del general Miranda, Viajes* II (Caracas, 1929), 410.

75 *Edifices construits à Saint-Pétersbourg d'après les plans du Chevalier de Quarenghi et sous sa direction* (spb, 1810), p. 11.

76 Giacomo Quarenghi, *Architetto a Pietroburgo: Lettere e altri scritti*, ed. Vanni Zanella (Venice, 1987), plate 124.

77 *Ibid.*, p. 48.

78 Glezer, *Arkhitekturnyi ansambl'*, p. 23.

79 *Sanktpeterburgskie vedomosti*, no. 53 (2 July 1792), 1036.

80 Glezer, *Arkhitekturnyi ansambl'*, p. 20 (Meader's house); p. 23 (Gould's involvement).

81 Dorothy Stroud, *Capability Brown* (London, 1975), p. 206; David Jacques, *Georgian Gardens: The Reign of Nature* (London, 1983), pp. 81, 112 (reproduction of watercolour of Fisherwick in Staffordshire).

82 AVPR, opis' 35/6, delo 695, ff. 1-4.

83 *Ibid*, opis' 35/6, delo 591, ff. 1-1v.; delo 593, ff. 1-1v.

84 RGADA, Fond 14, opis' 1, ed.kh. 51, ff. 440-440v.

85 *Ibid*., Fond 1239, opis' 3, chast' 118, ed. kh. 64991, f. 140v.

86 Parkinson, *Tour*, pp. 211-12.

87 K. I. Mineeva, *Tsaritsyno: dvortsovo-parkovyi ansambl'* (Moscow, 1988), pp. 59ff. The record has been put aright by B. B. Mikhailov, 'Sadovnik Frensis Rid v Tsaritsyne i Ostankine', *Arkhitektura SSSR*, no. 4 (July-August 1990), 104-9.

88 Nottingham University Library, Manvers Collection, M. 4147; *Correspondence of Jeremy Bentham*, II (London, 1968), 207.

89 *Correspondence of Jeremy Bentham*, III (1971), 574-5. Cf. p. 469.

90 *Ibid*., p. 592.

91 *Ibid*., pp. 564, 574. See Ian R. Christie, *The Benthams in Russia, 1780-1791* (London and Providence, 1993), pp. 141, 192, 195, 204.

92 Charles S. Romanes, *The Calls of Norfolk and Suffolk* (London, 1920), pp. 63-7.

93 Iakovkin, *Istoriia Sela Tsarskogo*, III, 498, 515; Petrov, *Pushkin: dvortsy i parki*, pp. 107, 132, n. 49.

94 Loudon, *Encyclopaedia*, pp. 249, 252; Mikhailov, 'Sadovnik Frensis Rid', pp. 106, 108.

95 Loudon, who makes much use of Call's article, mentions his meeting with him in 1813: Loudon, *Encyclopaedia*, p. 249. Call is also mentioned several times in William Howison, 'An Account of Several of the Most Important Culinary Vegetables of the Interior of the Russian Empire', *Memoirs of the Caledonian Horticultural Society*, III (1819), 77-109.

96 Iu. M. Gogolitsyn, T. M. Gogolitsyna, *Pamiatniki arkhitektury Leningradskoi oblasti* (Leningrad, 1987), p. 181; N. K. Shil'der, *Aleksandr pervyi: ego zhizn' i tsarstvovanie*, IV (SPB, 1898), 358.

97 SIRIO, XXIII, 157-8, 179.

98 Isobel Rae, *Charles Cameron, Architect to the Court of Russia* (London, 1971), p. 18. The error persists, despite my chapter 'The British in Russia: A Preliminary Survey', in J. G. Garrard (ed.), *The Eighteenth Century in Russia* (Oxford, 1973), pp. 249-50, where I refer to the church register held in the Guildhall, MS 11,192B, f. 261.

99 D. O. Shvidkovskii, 'Cameron Discoveries', *Architectural Review*, CLXXII, no. 1030 (1982), 46.

100 John Martin Robinson, 'A Dazzling Adventurer. Charles Cameron: The Lost Early Years', *Apollo* (January 1992), 31-5.

101 Letter of S. P. Cockerell to Henry Holland, dated 20 November 1791, quoted by Rae, p. 69. For evidence that Cameron actually visited London, see the letter of Count A. A. Bezborodko to Count S. R. Vorontsov of 5/16 August 1791: AKV, XIII (Moscow, 1879), 205.

102 See V. N. Taleporovskii, *Charl'z Kameron* (Moscow, 1939), p. 10.

103 SIRIO, XXIII, 158.

104 Parkinson, *Tour*, p. 83.

105 Quoted in D. O. Shvidkovskii, 'Ideal'nyi gorod russkogo klassitsizma', in V. G. Kisun'ko (ed.), *Denis Didro i kul'tura ego vremeni* (Moscow, 1986), pp. 180-1. This article (pp. 163-214) represents the fullest exposition of Shvidkovskii's brilliant

thesis on the significance of Sofiia both as 'ideal' town and as an integral part of the parks of Tsarskoe Selo.

106 Anthony Cutler, 'Recovering St. Sophia: Cameron, Catherine II, and the Idea of Constantinople in Late Eighteenth-Century Russia', in Henry A. Millon and Susan Scott Munshower (eds.), *An Architectural Progress in the Renaissance and Baroque Sojourns in and out of Italy, Papers in Art History from the Pennsylvania State University*, VII (Philadelphia, 1992), 891. Cutler's interesting article, based on research he did many years ago, was written in ignorance of the work of Shvidkovskii and other scholars.

107 Parkinson, *Tour*, p. 84; *SIRIO*, XXIII, 612.

108 D. O. Shvidkovskii, 'Prosvetitel'skaia kontseptsiia sredy v russkikh dvortsovo-parkovykh ansambliakh vtoroi poloviny XVIII veka', *Vek Prosveshcheniia: Rossiia i Frantsiia, Vipperskie chteniia*, XX (Moscow, 1989), 196.

109 RGADA, Fond 10, opis' 1, no. 302, f. 11.

110 Cutler, 'Recovering St. Sophia', p. 890.

111 Mineeva, *Tsaritsyno*, pp. 24–30. There is a reproduction of an engraving of the Khodynka Field on pp. 26–7.

112 See D. O. Shvidkovskii, 'Tsarskosel'skii park', in his *Gorod russkogo Prosveshcheniia* (Moscow, 1991), pp. 28–32.

113 Cutler, 'Recovering St. Sophia', p. 893.

114 Loudon, *Encyclopaedia*, p. 247.

115 T. Sapozhnikova, 'Kameron v Pavlovske', *Sredi kollektsionerov*, no. 5 (1923), 30–1.

116 I have consulted, in addition to the works by Sapozhnikova, Shvidkovskii and Taleporovskii, A. Kuchumov, *Pavlovsk* (Leningrad, 1972); his *Pavlovsk, Palace & Park* (Leningrad, 1975); A. I. Zelenova, *Dvorets v Pavlovske* (Leningrad, 1986), G. K. Koz'mian, *Charlz Kameron* (Leningrad, 1987); V. K. Shuiskii, *Vinchentso Brenna* (Leningrad, 1986).

117 See *Pavlovsk: Ocherk istorii i opisanie 1777–1877*, pp. 517–52.

118 'To release the architect Cameron as not needed (*po nenadobnosti*)', quoted in Koz'min, p. 128.

119 AKV, XVIII (1880), 286.

120 Shvidkovskii, 'Cameron Discoveries', pp. 48–51; his 'Poslednii period tvorchestva arkhitektora Ch. Kamerona v dokumentakh Admiralteistva', *Pamiatniki kul'tury, Ezhegodnik 1984* (Leningrad, 1986), pp. 523–30.

121 T. Diadkovskaia, 'Neizvestnye portrety Charl'za Kamerona', *Arkhitektura SSSR*, vyp. 2 (1939), 78–9.

122 GL, MS 11,192B, f. 8.

123 Walter Cameron's name, along with that of the ailing Mrs Cameron, appears in the list of departures in *Sanktpeterburgskie vedomosti*, no. 62 (4 August 1816), 615.

124 *Stoletie Sankt-Peterburgskoi Angliiskogo sobraniia* (spb, 1870), Appendix, p. 61.

125 Taleporovskii, *Charl'z Kameron*, p. 25; P. N. Petrov (ed.), *Sbornik materialov dlia istorii Imperatorskoi S.-Peterburgskoi Akademii khudozhestv*, I (spb, 1864), 240.

126 AKV, XXX, 212.

127 Apart from the references in the diaries of Baroness Dimsdale and Parkinson, there are mentions of meetings with Cameron in Sir Richard Worsley's diary (1786) (Lincolnshire Record Office, Lincoln, Yarborough Collection, Worsely MSS 24, f. 203) and in the journals of Captain James Hawkins (1789) (Mrs Aubrey Le Blond, *Charlotte Sophie Countess Bentinck*, I (London, 1912), 121).

128 See A. G. Cross, 'An Anglo-Russian Medley: Semen Vorontsov's Other Son, Charles

Cameron's Daughter, Grand Duke Alexander Pavlovich's English Playmate, and Not Forgetting His English Nurse', *SEER*, LXX (1992), 717–18.

129 *The Observer* 'Colour Section', 6 August 1972, 66. On the perils of calling Cameron 'a Scot', see the correspondence in *The Scotsman*, 2, 9, 18 and 24 March 1992.

130 On Menelaws, see A. K. Andreev, 'Adam Menelas', *Problemy sinteza iskusstv i arkhitektury*, vyp. 7 (1977), 39; A. G. Cross, 'In Cameron's Shadow: Adam Menelaws, Stonemason Turned Architect', *Scottish Slavonic Review*, no. 17 (1991), 7–19; and Dmitrij Shvidkovsky, 'Architect to Three Emperors: Adam Menelas in Russia', *Apollo* (January 1992), 36–41.

131 On L'vov's life and career, see M. V. Budylina *et al.*, *Arkhitektor N. A. L'vov* (Moscow, 1961); N. I. Nikulina, *Nikolai L'vov* (Leningrad, 1971) and A. Glumov, *N. A. L'vov* (Moscow, 1980).

132 The comparison was made by Budylina, *L'vov*, p. 126, and expanded by Cutler, 'Recovering St Sophia', p. 891 and Shvidkovskii, 'Ideal'nyi gorod', p. 195.

133 Nikulina suggests that Menelaws worked first at Mogilev (*L'vov*, pp. 30–1), but Andreev cites documentary evidence for Torzhok ('Menelas', pp. 40, 42). However, it seems likely that he worked at Mogilev before 1792; he certainly visited the town in September 1789; *Correspondence of Jeremy Bentham*, IV (1981), 90, where he is referred to as 'Monilaw'.

134 Glumov, *L'vov*, pp. 76–7.

135 T. V. Alekseeva, *Vladimir Lukich Borovikovskii i russkaia kul'tura na rubezhe 18–19 vekov* (Moscow, 1975), ch. 2.

136 GL, MS 11,192B, f. 128.

137 Reproduced in Alekseeva, pp. 70, 376.

138 Nikulina, pp. 103–15; Andreev, pp. 44–8.

139 Birmingham Reference Libraries, Matthew Boulton Papers, Russian Mint Box II, Letter of Iakov Smirnov to Matthew Boulton.

140 *AKV*, XXII (1881), 529.

141 Andreev, p. 49, citing imperial edict of 18 August 1806.

142 *AKV*, XXII, 529.

143 Andreev, pp. 48–9.

144 *AKV*, XXX (1883), 119.

145 Shvidkovskii, 'Architect to Three Emperors', p. 37.

146 Andreev, pp. 50–2, quoting Count Razumovskii's doctor, Otto Gun's *Poverkhnostnye zamechaniia po doroge ot Moskvy v Malorossiiu k oseni 1806 g.* (Moscow, 1806).

147 Loudon, *Encyclopaedia*, p. 250 (with drawing). Menelaws's plan of Gorenki is reproduced in M. Iljin, 'Russian Parks of the Eighteenth Century', *Architectural Review*, CXXXV (1976), 109.

148 Andreev, p. 53.

149 A. B. Granville, *St Petersburgh. A Journal of Travels to and from that Capital*, II (London, 1828), 495.

150 A. Benua and N. Lansere, 'Dvortsovoe stroitel'stvo Imperatora Nikolaia I', *Starye gody* (July–September 1913), p. 184.

151 Granville, *St Petersburgh*, II, 495–6.

152 Dukelskaya, *The Hermitage: English Art*, plate 161.

153 Granville, *St Petersburgh*, II, 507–8.

154 V. M. Tenikhina, *Petrodvorets: Kottedzh* (Leningrad, 1986). See also A. G. Raskin, *Petrodvorets: dvortsy-muzei, parki, fontany* (Leningrad, 1988), pp. 162–78.

155 Tenikhina, *Petrodvorets*, p. [3].

156 Glumov, *L'vov*, pp. 76–8.

157 *SIRIO*, XXIII, 611–2.

158 Miliza Korshunova, 'William Hastie in Russia', *Architectural History*, XVII (1974), 15.

159 GL, MS 11,192B, f. 146.

160 For Cameron's supposed visit, see Rae, *Cameron*, pp. 62–5.

161 V. Gerngross, 'Khanskii dvorets v Bakhchisarae', *Starye gody* (April 1912), pp. 20–1, 27.

162 See Korshunova, p. 17; I. Blek, A. Rotach, 'Chugunnye arochnye mosty v Leningrade', *Arkhitekturnoe nasledstvo*, VII (1955), 143–56; J. G. James, 'Russian Iron Bridges to 1850', *The Newcomen Society Transactions*, LIV (1982–3), 88–90, 99; M. S. Bunin, *Mosty Leningrada* (Leningrad, 1986), pp. 68–70, 178–80.

163 Korshunova, pp. 17–18. There is a photograph of the house as fig. 16b.

164 The major work in English on this aspect of Hastie's career is A. J. Schmidt, 'William Hastie, Scottish Planner of Russian Cities', *Proceedings of the American Philosophical Society*, CXIV (1970), 226–43. See also Dmitri Shvidkovsky, 'Classical Edinburgh and Russian Town-Planning of the Late 18th and Early 19th Centuries: The Role of William Hastie (1755–1832)', *Scottish Architects Abroad: Architectural Heritage*, II (Edinburgh 1991), 69–78.

165 T. F. Savarenskaia, D. O. Shvidkovskii, F. A. Petrov, *Istoriia gradostroitel'nogo iskusstva: pozdnii feodalizm i kapitalizm* (Moscow, 1989), p. 164.

166 Many of the designs are reproduced in the works cited in notes 164–5.

167 Schmidt, pp. 232–7; I. Gol'denburg, *Staraia Moskva* (Moscow, 1947), 57–60.

168 The principal English sources are Edward Edwards, *Anecdotes of Painters Who Have Resided or Been Born in England* (London, 1808), pp. 174–6; Samuel Redgrave, *A Dictionary of Artists of the English School*, 2nd edn (London, 1878), p. 56; William T. Whiteley, *Artists and Their Friends in England, 1700–1799*, II (London and Boston, 1928), 255–61.

169 *The Farington Diary*, I (London, 1922), 191.

170 *Correspondence of Jeremy Bentham*, II, 512. (Offenbach was the Duke of Courland's ambassador in Britain.)

171 *Ibid.*, II, 512, n. 13.

172 *Pembroke Papers*, ed. Lord Herbert (London, 1950), p. 111.

173 *Zapiski Iakova Shtelina ob iziashchnykh iskusstvakh v Rossii*, ed. K. V. Malinovskii, I (Moscow, 1990), 110.

174 *SIRIO*, XXIII, 176.

175 See E. P. Renne, 'Kartiny Bromptona v Ermitazhe', *Zapadnoevropeiskoe iskusstvo XVIII veka: publikatsii i issledovaniia* (Leningrad, 1987), p. 59.

176 *SIRIO*, XXIII, 262.

177 *Ibid.*, XLIV (1885), 322. See also *ibid.*, XXXIII. For date of death, see GL, MS 11,192B, f. 75.

178 Coxe, *Travels*, II, 5th edn (1802), [iv], 129; D. A. Rovinskii, *Podrobnyi slovar' russkikh gravirovannykh portretov*, I (spb, 1886), 673, no. 109.

179 *Zapiski Iakova Shtelina*, I, 92.

180 *Ibid.*; *SIRIO*, XXIII, 274; Renne, 'Kartiny Bromptona', pp. 59–60.

181 See G. B. Andreeva, 'K voprosu o russko-angliiskikh khudozhestvennykh sviaziakh vtoroi poloviny XVIII veka: tvorchestvo Richarda Bromptona', *Tezisy dokladov ... muzeia izobrazitel'nykh iskusstv imeni A. S. Pushkina* (Moscow, 1986), pp. 47–8.

182 Notice in *Sanktpeterburgskie vedomosti*, no. 8 (1783), quoted in A. P. Miuller, *Byt*

inostrannykh khudozhnikov v Rossii (Leningrad, 1927), p. 83; PRO, Lowry Cole Papers, 30/43, 19, ff. 7v.–8.

183 GL, MS 11,192B, ff. 67, 70, 71, 74, 76.

184 Edwards, *Anecdotes*, p. 42; *Bryan's Biographical Dictionary of Painters and Engravers*, I, rev. edn (London, 1904), 361–2; Ellis Waterhouse, *Dictionary of British 18th Century Painters in Oils and Crayons* (London, 1981), p. 96. For the Duchess of Kingston, see chapter 8 of the present work.

185 Rovinskii, I, 672–3, no. 106.

186 *Briefe Daniel Chodowiecki's an Anton Graff* (Berlin and Leipzig, 1921), quoted in P. Ettinger, 'Inostrannye khudozhniki v Rossii: E. F. Kanningkhem', *Sredi kollektsionerov*, no. 10 (1922), 25.

187 Waterhouse, *Dictionary*, p. 72.

188 Barkway House, Barkway, Dimsdale Collection, A/39.

189 *Ibid.*, C/2.

190 The two portraits, signed and dated, are at Barkway House.

191 L. N. Timofeev, 'Romanticheskie tendentsii v arkhitekture vtoroi poloviny XVIII v. – pervoi poloviny XIX v.', *Problemy sinteza iskusstv i arkhitektury*, vyp. 4 (Leningrad, 1974), 76.

192 State Hermitage, St Petersburg, Department of Drawings, inventory numbers 3815–39. The watercolours bear the cypher of Paul I. I wish to express my thanks to Militsa Korshunova for showing me the folder.

193 It is reproduced in Jeremy Black, *The British Abroad: The Grand Tour in the Eighteenth Century* (Stroud and New York, 1993), p. 208.

194 G. C. Williamson, *Richard Cosway, His Life and Pupils* (London, 1897), p. 11. A George Hadfield was admitted to the Royal Academy schools on 28 September 1781 as an eighteen-year-old and was awarded a gold medal in 1784: Sidney Hutchinson, 'The Royal Academy Schools', *Walpole Society*, XXXIII (1962), 146.

195 See, for instance, Galina Andreeva, 'Ital'ianskie vstrechi: Russkie i britanskie zhivopistsy v Rime vo vtoroi polovine XVIII veka', *SGECRN*, no. 19 (1991), 9–12.

196 Williamson, *Richard Cosway*, pp. 12, 16.

197 In a letter of 10 October 1994, Stephen Lloyd, Assistant Keeper at the Scottish National Portrait Gallery and the leading authority on the Cosways, confirmed that very little is known of George Hadfield, but thought that my 'attribution may well be plausible'.

198 Hearn has no entry in DNB, but the barest details are found in SIRIO, LX (1887), 155.

199 *Sanktpeterburgskie vedomosti*, no. 98 (1790), 1600.

200 GL, MS 11,192B, ff. 137, 144, 208.

201 The fullest study of Walker's career is in A. G. Cross's introduction to *Engraved in the Memory*, pp. 1–25.

202 See A. G. Cross, *By the Banks of the Thames*, pp. 211–17, 305–6 (bibliography).

203 For a full chronological listing of Walker's engravings throughout his career, see Cross (ed.), *Engraved in the Memory*, pp. 187–92.

204 Petrov, *Sbornik materialov*, I, 145, 315, 333, 334.

205 D. A. Rovinskii, *Podrobnyi slovar' russkikh graverov XVI–XIX vv.*, I (spb, 1895), pp. 129–45. See also N. G. Saprykina, 'Gravirovannye listy Dzheimsa Uokera v sobranii nauchnoi biblioteki imeni A.M. Gor'kogo MGU', in E. S. Karpova (ed.), *Iz kollektsii redkikh knig i rukopisei nauchnoi biblioteki Moskovskogo universiteta* (Moscow, 1981), pp. 81–9.

206 V. Staniukovich, 'Neizvestnaia rabota Dzh. Atkinsona v Rossii', *Zapiski istoriko-*

bytovogo otdela GRM, I (1928), 328; Cross (ed.), *Engraved in the Memory*, p. 105.

207 Cross (ed.), *Engraved in the Memory*, p. 106.

208 *The Most Remarkable Year in the Life of Augustus von Kotzebue*, III (London, 1802), 24–5.

209 *AKV*, VIII (1876), 225.

210 There was possibly a second edition in 1805–7: J. R. Abbey, *Travel in Acquatint and Lithography 1770–1860*, I (Folkestone and London, 1972), 195–6. Rovinskii believes that Walker was responsible for engraving the vignette: Rovinskii, *Podrobnyi slovar' graverov*, I, 142–3.

211 Cross (ed.), *Engraved in the Memory*, p. 29. (A selection of these descriptions is included at pp. 153–86.)

212 *A Catalogue of the Valuable Stock of Copper Plates, with Impressions, the Property of Mr Horace Rodd ... to Which Are Added, Mezzotint Plates, by Mr. Walker, Engraver to the Emperor Alexander, Together with the Remaining Impressions of the Copper Plates Which Were Lost ...(London, 1822).*

213 The text of this rare work is reprinted in Cross (ed.), *Engraved in the Memory*, pp. 27–152.

214 *Ibid.*, p. 28.

215 *Ibid.*, pp. 50, 41.

216 *Ibid.*, p. 146.

217 On Reynolds and Catherine, see 'Kartiny Reinol'dsa', *Starye gody* (July 1913), pp. 40–3; J. S. G. Simmons, 'Samuel Johnson "On the Banks of the Neva": A Note on a Picture by Reynolds in the Hermitage', in *Johnson, Boswell and Their Circle* (Oxford, 1965), pp. 208–14; Frederick W. Hilles, 'Sir Joshua and the Empress Catherine', in *Eighteenth-Century Studies in Honor of Donald F. Hyde* (New York, 1970), pp. 267–77.

218 The correspondence was published as an appendix to *Skazanie o morskom srazhenii, proiskhodivshem mezhdu rossiianami i turkami pri brege Natolii iiunia 24 25 i 26 1770 goda* (spb, 1770), pp. 17–26. Paton's gold medal is now in the British Museum. Around its rim is the following inscription: 'A Token of Approbation, from the Empress, to R. Paton of London, of his Gift of Four Pictures of her Naval Victory off the coast of Natolia, Anno 1770'. See A. G. Cross, 'Richard Paton and the Battle of Chesme', *SGECRN*, no. 14 (1986), 31–7.

219 Swinton, *Travels*, p. 408.

220 *Correspondence of George III*, ed. Sir John Fortescue, II (London, 1927), 452–3; L. A. Dukel'skaia, E. P. Renne, *Angliiskaia zhivopis' XVI–XIX veka (Gos. Ermitazh sobranie zapadnoevropeiskoi zhivopisi: katalog, t. XIII)* (Leningrad, 1990), pp. 42–4.

221 *An English Lady*, p. 82; Dukel'skaia, Renne, *Angliiskaia zhivopis'*, pp. 169–70.

222 Dukel'skaia, Renne, *Angliiskaia zhivopis'*, pp. 178–81.

223 AVPR, opis' 35/6, delo 287, ff. 19–20v; delo 296, ff. 4v., 7–12.

224 A. Krol', 'Neopublikovannoe pis'mo Dzhoshua Reinol'dsa iz arkhiva Vorontsovykh', *Soobshcheniia Gos. Ermitazha*, XVIII (1960), 42–4.

225 Redgrave, *Dictionary of Artists*, p. 377; U. Thieme, F. Becker, *Allgemeines Lexicon der Bildenden Kunstler*, XXIX (Leipzig, 1923), 493; John Chaloner Smith, *British Mezzotint Portraits*, IV, pt. I (London, 1882), 1046–9; Daphne Foskett, *A Dictionary of British Miniature Painters*, I (London, 1972), 493.

226 Rovinskii, *Podrobnyi slovar'*, II, 867–78.

227 Cross (ed.), *Engraved in the Memory*, pp. 116–18.

228 Petrov, *Sbornik materialov*, I, 414.

229 Rovinskii, *Podrobnyi slovar'*, II, 874–8.
230 See the letter from Derzhavin to V. V. Kapnist, dated 21 March (OS) 1804, in *Sochineniia Derzhavina*, VI, 2nd acad. edn (spb, 1876), 163.
231 Details in Rovinskii, nos. 15–17, 24–30, 32–4.
232 *AKV*, XXII, 501.
233 Graves, *The Royal Academy of Arts*, V (London, 1906), 242; Foskett, *Dictionary*, I, 406–7.
234 *The Diary of Sylas Neville 1767–1788* (London, 1950), p. 96. (The miniature is reproduced facing the title page.)
235 *Ibid.*, p. 181.
236 *AKV*, XXVII (1883), 340.
237 *Ibid.*, XXII, 77.
238 *The Pembroke Papers*, p. 22.
239 *The Memoirs of Princess Dashkov*, trans. Kyril Fitzlyon (London, 1958), p. 22.
240 *SIRIO*, XXIII (1878), 328–9, 384, 387, 413.
241 *AKV*, XIII (1870), 102.
242 John M. Gray, *James and William Tassie* (Edinburgh, 1894), pp. 16–31; Iu. O. Kogan, 'Kabinet slepkov Dzheimsa Tassi v Ermitazhe', *Trudy Gos. Ermitazha*, XIV (1973), 82–96; Duncan Thomson, 'Two Medallionists in Georgian London', *Country Life* (27 January 1972), 214–19; Janet M. Hartley, 'Crown Jewels and Cameos: Notes from the Irish Archives', *SGECRN*, no. 22 (1994), 21–4.
243 Iu. Etkind, 'Russian Themes in the Work of the English Gem Cutters William and Charles Brown', *Burlington Magazine* (August 1965), 421–4; Iu. O. Kogan, *Reznye kamni Uil'iama i Charl'za Braunov: katalog vystavki* (Leningrad, 1976), pp. 5–18.
244 Cross (ed.), *Engraved in the Memory*, pp. 134–5.
245 *European Magazine*, XVIII (1790), 24.
246 Petrov, *Gorod Pushkin: dvortsy i parki*, p. 105.
247 *Builder*, XXI (1 Jan 1863), 4.
248 DNB, I, 1053–4; C. F. Bell (ed.), *Annals of Thomas Banks* (Cambridge, 1938), pp. 49–52; Rupert Gunnis, *Dictionary of British Sculptors 1660–1851*, new edn (London, n.d.), pp. 37–40.
249 James Dallaway, *Anecdotes of the Arts in England* (London, 1800), p. 389 and note; Xenia Gorbunova, 'Classical Sculpture from the Lyde Browne Collection', *Apollo*, C (Dec. 1974), 460–7.
250 Dukelskaya, *The Hermitage: English Art*, plate 135.
251 The Earl of Ilchester, *The Home of the Hollands 1605–1820* (London, 1937), pp. 117–18.
252 See A. G. Cross, *Anglo-Russian Relations in the Eighteenth Century: Exhibition Catalogue* (Norwich, 1977), p. 12, item 29.
253 Parkinson, *Tour*, p. 78.

8 'OUT OF CURIOSITY': TOURISTS AND VISITORS

1 Metcalfe Robinson to his father in 1705. Quoted in Jeremy Black, *The British Abroad: The Grand Tour in the Eighteenth Century* (London, 1992), p. 48.
2 Boswell, *Life of Johnson*, edited by R. W. Chapman (Oxford, 1970), p. 742. On the Grand Tour, in addition to Black, see Christopher Hibbert, *The Grand Tour* (London, 1969) and R. S. Lambert (ed.), *Grand Tour: A Journey in the Tracks of the Aristocracy* (London, 1935).

3 See A. G. Cross, 'British Residents and Visitors in Russia during the Reign of Catherine the Great: Tapped and Untapped Sources from British Archives', in Janet Hartley (ed.), *The Study of Russian History from British Archival Sources* (London, 1986), pp. 89–106.

4 [F. C. Weber], *The Present State of Russia*, I (London, 1723), 4. (For a valuable investigation into foreign accounts of Petrine Petersburg, see Iu. N. Bespiatykh, *Petersburg Petra I v inostrannykh opisaniiakh* (Leningrad, 1991). See my review of this work, *SGECRN*, no. 20 (1992), 66–8.)

5 *Ibid.*, 190.

6 Betty Kemp, 'Sir Francis Dashwood's Diary of His Visit to St Petersburg in 1733', *SEER*, XXXVIII (1959), 197.

7 Generally on Dashwood, see Ronald Fuller, *Hell-Fire Francis* (London, 1939).

8 Kemp, 'Dashwood', 194, note 5.

9 *Ibid.*, 206. Cf. a similar statement on p. 213.

10 Extracts are published in HMC, *Second Report* (London, 1871), pp. 215–6. See Kemp, 'Dashwood', 196, note 15.

11 This has recently been published in English and Russian translation with an excellent commentary by Iu. N. Bespiatykh, *Rossiia v nachale XVIII veka. Sochinenie Ch. Uitvorta* (M-L, 1988).

12 Published as volume XV of the Publications of the Navy Record Society, edited by Cyprian A. G. Bridge (London, 1899), but unattributed. See further on Deane in chapter 5 of this volume.

13 *Sankpeterburgskie vedomosti* (12 June 1739), p. 4; (26 June), p. 6; (17 July), p. 7. (I am grateful to Ms S. Ia. Somova of St Peterburg for these references.) Erasmus King had apparently given lectures on 'experimental philosophy', while Thomas Desaguliers (1725–90), a future FRS, had been sent 'to learn the practice of navigation' by his father, a prominent scientist and chaplain to the Prince of Wales: *Letters from Count Algarotti to Lord Hervey and the Marquis Scipio Maffei*, I (London, 1769), 3. See also John H. Appleby, 'Erasmus King: Eighteenth-Century Experimental Philosopher', *Annals of Science*, XLVII (1990), 376–7.

14 Igor Vinogradoff, 'Russian Missions to London, 1711–1789: Further Extracts from the Cottrell Papers', *OSP*, NS XV (1982), 53. See also A. G. Cross, 'The Lords Baltimore in Russia', *Journal of European Studies*, XVIII (1988), 77–91.

15 *Letters from Count Algarotti*, I, 75.

16 *Oeuvres de Frédéric le Grand*, XXXI (Berlin, 1850), pp. 326–7.

17 *Lettres du Comte Algarotti sur la Russie* (London, 1769), p. 64.

18 Black, *The British Abroad*, p. 74; *Sbornik Imperatorskogo Russkogo istoricheskogo obshchestva*, LXXXV (spb, 1893), 93–4, 104, 190; LXXXVI, 515.

19 Vinogradov, 'Russian Missions', p. 71. (The twelve letters are on pp. 68–79.)

20 *Ibid.*, p. 76.

21 *Ibid.*, pp. 76–8.

22 *Arkhiv kniazia Kurakina*, VI (Saratov, 1896), 236; HMC, *Rawdon Hastings* MS, III (London, 1934), 105; Black, *The British Abroad*, p. 73.

23 BL, Add. MS 32,419, f. 306.

24 *Ibid.*, f. 327v. See also *ibid.*, f. 334.

25 Wiltshire County Record Office, Trowbridge, MS 161/24/1 (letter to his brother Francis, 7 October 1752). On Willes's career, see Robert Gardiner, *The Registers of Wadham College, Oxford*, II (London, 1895), 79.

26 Kenneth Ellis, *The Post Office in the Eighteenth Century* (London, 1958), pp. 127–31. On Willes's father, see William Gibson 'An Eighteenth-Century Paradox: The

Career of the Decipherer-Bishop, Edward Willes', *British Journal for Eighteenth-Century Studies*, XII (1989), 69–76.

27 *Calendar of Home State Papers of the Reign of George III 1770–1772* (London, 1881), p. 553.

28 *Ibid.*

29 See A. G. Cross, 'John Maddison – Breaker of Russian Ciphers and Collector of Russian Books', *SGECRN*, no. 15 (1987), 25–30.

30 *A Voyage to Russia, Describing the Laws, Manners and Customs of the Great Empire as Governed at this Present by that Excellent Princess the Czarina ...* (London, 1746), pp. 56–7. On Mrs Justice's husband, see P. Gaskell, 'Henry Justice: A Cambridge Book Thief', *Transactions of the Cambridge Bibliographical Society*, I (1952), 348–57. A Russian translation of Mrs Justice's book has appeared in *Neva*, no. 5 (1988), 197–207.

31 Mrs Justice gives her employer as Mr Evans, whom I identify as the prominent English merchant Hill Evans, who married Mrs Mary Ramsey on 1 September 1725 and died on 2 May 1740 (GL, MS 11,192B, ff. 11, 17).

32 *Historical Account of the British Trade over the Caspian Sea*, I, 2nd edn, London, 1754, 372.

33 See A. G. Cross, 'British Awareness of Russian Culture (1698–1801)', *Canadian Slavic Studies*, XIII (1979), 212–35.

34 Boswell, *Life of Johnson*, pp. 440, 393.

35 See Leo Loewenson, 'Lady Rondeau's Letters from Russia (1728–1739)', *SEER*, XXXV(1956–7), 399–408. This important article with its information about the eleven additional letters published posthumously in 1784 is apparently unknown to Russian scholars. See, for instance, E. Anisimov's commentary and notes to a new Russian translation of the 1775 edition (by Nadezhda Bespiatykh) in *Bezvremen'e i vremenshchiki: vospominaniia ob 'epokhe dvortsovykh perevorotov' (1720-e – 1760-e gody)* (Leningrad, 1991). (Rondeau, incidentally, was not knighted, so his wife was just plain Mrs. The confusion probably arises from 'the Lady' in the original title.)

36 N. Wraxall, *A Tour through Some of the Northern Parts of Europe*, 2nd edn (London, 1775), p. 2. (Subsequent references in the text are by page number to this edition.)

37 *Critical Review*, LX (1775), 106.

38 *Ibid.*, p. 111.

39 E.M.L., 'Angliiskii turist v Peterburge v 1774 godu', *Istoricheskii vestnik*, VI (1881), 822–37.

40 Letter of 22 May 1775, *The Letters of Samuel Johnson with Mrs Thrale's Genuine Letters to Him*, ed. R. W. Chapman, II (Oxford, 1952), 395.

41 Boswell, *Life of Johnson*, p. 1052.

42 *Ibid.*, p. 824. See also p. 570.

43 *Horace Walpole's Correspondence*, ed. W. S. Lewis, XXIII (London, 1967), 195.

44 Quoted in John G. Morris, *The Lords Baltimore* (Philadelphia, 1874), pp. 58–9.

45 *Ibid.*, p. 54. See also *Gentleman's Magazine*, XXXVII (1767), 458.

46 Auchidoune, Cawdor, Cathcart Papers, MSS A/73.

47 *London Magazine*, XXXVIII (1769), 484–5.

48 See in more detail A. G. Cross, 'The Lords Baltimore in Russia', pp. 84–9.

49 Wraxall, *Tour*, p. 249.

50 See A. G. Cross, 'The Russian Banya in the Descriptions of Foreign Travellers and in the Depictions of Foreign and Russian Artists', *OSP*, NS XXIV (1991), 34–59.

51 BL, Add. MS 31192, f. 98.

52 University Library, Cambridge, 'A Northern Tour', Add. MS 8720. (For Henniker's intention to publish, see the letter of William Raikes (a cousin of Timothy Raikes) to Robert Duesbery in St Petersburg, 14 June 1777 (Brynmor Jones Library, University of Hull, MS DDDU/20/86, f. [7].)

53 'A Northern Tour', ff. 93-7. (The passage has been published in A. G. Cross, 'The Eighteenth-Century Russian Theatre under British Eyes', *Studies on Voltaire and the Eighteenth Century*, CCXIX (1983), 228-9.)

54 'A Northern Tour', ff. 173-213.

55 J. H. Major, Baron Henniker, *Some Account of the Families of Major and Henniker* (London, 1803), p. 3.

56 SRO, Adam of Blair Adam, MS 4/438, Journal No. 18. (The journal is unfoliated and references in the text are not footnoted.)

57 Paul Fussell, jr., 'Patrick Brydone: The Eighteenth-Century Traveler as Representative Man', *New York Public Library Bulletin* (June 1962), pp. 349-63. (Fussell was unaware of the extensive Adam of Blair Adam materials and thus of Brydone's visit to Russia.)

58 *Monthly Review*, XLIX (1973), 22.

59 *Anecdotes of the Russian Empire in a Series of Letters Written, a Few Years Ago, from St. Petersburg* (London, 1784), p. vii. (Further references are by page in the text.)

60 *Critical Review*, LVII (1784), 194. (The reviewer quotes in full the letter on the plight of the peasantry as 'sufficient to excite the commiseration of every person of humanity' (p. 18).)

61 H. J. Pitcher, 'A Scottish View of Catherine's Russia: William Richardson's *Anecdotes of the Russian Empire* (1784)', *Forum for Modern Language Studies*, III (1967), 247; Peter Putnam (ed.), *Seven Britons in Imperial Russia 1698-1812* (Princeton, 1952), pp. 133-4.

62 *Critical Review*, LVII (1784), 200. (Randolph's authorship was established in G. E. von Haller, *Bibliothek der Schweizer-Geschichte*, I (Bern, 1785), 288-9.)

63 Cf. *Archivo del general Miranda*, II (Caracas, 1929), 372, 376; Elizabeth, Lady Craven, *A Journey through the Crimea to Constantinople* (Dublin, 1789), p. 158; [Lionel Colmore], *Letters from the Continent* (London, 1812), p. 94; John Parkinson, *A Tour of Russia, Siberia and the Crimea 1792-1794* (London, 1971), p. 96; *Private Correspondence of Lord Granville Leveson-Gower*, I (London, 1916), 58.

64 *Der Briefwechsel zwischen der Kaiserin Katharina II von Russland und Joh. Georg Zimmermann*, ed. Eduard Bodemann (Hannover and Leipzig, 1906), pp. 13-15.

65 Carol Urness (ed.), *A Naturalist in Russia: Letters from Peter Simon Pallas to Thomas Pennant* (Minneapolis, 1967), p. 47.

66 *Account of the Prisons and Hospitals in Russia, Sweden, and Denmark. With Occasional Remarks on the Different Modes of Punishment in Those Countries* (London, 1781), p. 24.

67 Lord Herbert (ed.), *Henry, Elizabeth and George (1734-80): Letters and Diaries of Henry, Tenth Earl of Pembroke and His Circle* (London, 1939), pp. 306-7.

68 *Travels into Poland, Russia, Sweden, and Denmark*, II, 5th edn (London, 1802), 72; III, 193, 135, 131, 158.

69 N. I. Grech, *Zapiski o moei zhizni* (M-L, 1930), pp. 224-5.

70 Quoted in S. A. Allibone, *A Critical Dictionary of English Literature and British and American Authors*, I (Philadelphia, 1897), 389. The best essay on Coxe's *Travels* remains Putnam's, *Seven Britons*, pp. 237-49.

71 Herbert, *Henry, Elizabeth and George*, p. 382.

72 Lord Herbert (ed.), *The Pembroke Papers (1780–1794)* (London, 1950), p. 122.

73 Antony House, Torpoint, Cornwall, Carew-Pole MSS, CC/J/12–13.

74 I. R. Christie (ed.), *The Correspondence of Jeremy Bentham*, III (London, 1971), 6.

75 *Ibid.*, II (1968), 496.

76 Carew-Pole MSS, CO/R/3/113.

77 For Samborskii, see A. G. Cross, *'By the Banks of the Thames': Russians in Eighteenth-Century Britain* (Newtonville, Mass., 1980), pp. 39–44, 60–73.

78 Carew-Pole MSS, CO/R/3/102.

79 *Ibid.*, CO/R/3/95.

80 *Ibid.*, CO/R/3/175.

81 *Ibid.*, CO/R/5/1-4. See Fred Zartz, 'The 'Pole-Carew Memorandum' in the Context of British Policy towards Russia in the 1780s', *SGECRN*, no. 10 (1982), 12–17.

82 *AKV*, IX (1876), 49.

83 See A. G. Cross, ' "Zamechaniia" Sera Dzhona Sinklera o Rossii', *XVIII vek*, X (1975), 160–8. (A slightly expanded English version has been published in A. G. Cross, *Anglo-Russica: Aspects of Cultural Relations between Great Britain and Russia in the Eighteenth and Early Nineteenth Centuries* (Oxford and Providence, 1993), pp. 51–61.)

84 *General Observations Regarding the Present State of the Russian Empire* (n.p., n.d.), p. 32. (My copy of this rare work belonged to Pole Carew, who has made a marginal correction to a passage on p. 32 in which he is named by Sinclair.)

85 *Ibid.*, p. 44.

86 Craven, *Journey*, p. 282.

87 Lincolnshire Archives Office, Lincoln, Yarborough Collection, Worsley MS, no. 24, f. 172. (Further references are in the text by folio number.)

88 *SIRIO*, XXIII (1878), 433; Comte de Ségur, *Mémoires, ou souvenirs et anecdotes*, I, 2nd edn (Paris, 1826), 424.

89 Craven, *Journey*, p. 4. (Further references are in the text by page number.) The best outline of Lady Craven's life is provided by A. M. Broadley and Lewis Melville's introduction to their edition of her memoirs: *The Beautiful Lady Craven*, I (London, 1914), xiii–cxxxvi.

90 *Gentleman's Magazine*, LIX (1789), 287–8.

91 In 1814 there appeared a 'second edition, including a variety of letters not before published', with a changed title: *Letters from the Right Honourable Lady Craven to His Serene Highness the Margrave of Anspach, during Her Travels through France, Germany, & Russia in 1785 and 1786.*

92 See Roger P. Bartlett, *Human Capital: The Settlement of Foreigners in Russia 1762–1804* (Cambridge, 1979), p. 128.

93 *Gentleman's Magazine*, LVI, pt. 2 (1786), 648. The full account is on pp. 644–8, 847–51.

94 *Ibid.*, 552.

95 *Annual Register for the Year 1786* (1787), 'Miscellaneous Essays', pp. 129–34.

96 John Howard, *State of the Prisons in England and Wales, with Preliminary Observations, and an Account of Some Foreign Prisons* (Warrington, 1777), p. 6.

97 See A. G. Cross, 'The Philanthropist, the Travelling Tutor and the Empress: British Visitors and Catherine II's Plans for Penal and Medical Reform', in R. P. Bartlett, A. G. Cross and Karen Rasmussen (eds.), *Russia and the World of the Eighteenth Century* (Columbus, Ohio, 1988), pp. 214–28.

 98 A. G. Cross (ed.), *An English Lady at the Court of Catherine the Great: The Journal of Baroness Elizabeth Dimsdale, 1781* (Cambridge, 1989), p. 49.

 99 Letter of 7 September 1781 from Moscow, quoted in J. B. Brown, *Memoirs of the Public and Private Life of John Howard, the Philanthropist* (London, 1818), p. 368.

100 Letter of 22 September 1789, *ibid.*, p. 615.

101 Letter of 2 October 1789 to Samuel Whitbread I, in J. Field (ed.), *Correspondence of John Howard, the Philanthropist, not before published* (London, 1855), p. 171.

102 Letter of 14 November 1789 to Whitbread, in Field, *Correspondence*, p. 175. See *An Account of the Principal Lazarettos in Europe*, 2nd edn (London, 1791), Appendix, pp. 17–21.

103 Field, *Correspondence*, p. 176.

104 Bedfordshire Record Office, Bedford, Whitbread Papers, No. 2366.

105 E. D. Clarke, *Travels in Various Countries of Europe, Asia and Africa*, I (London, 1810), 603–11; Robert Lyall, *Travels in Russia, the Krimea, the Caucasus, and Georgia*, I (London, 1825), 206–10; Ebenezer Henderson, *Biblical Researches and Travels in Russia, Including a Tour of the Crimea and the Passage of the Caucasus* (London, 1826), pp. 283–5; Amelia Heber, *The Life of Richard Heber D.D., Bishop of Calcutta*, I (London, 1830), 277. For a recent Russian account of Howard and his career, see E. E. Pisarenko, 'Bastiliia, Peterburg, Novorossiia v sud'be Dzhona Govarda', *Novaia i noveishaia istoriia*, no. 5 (1989), 161–73.

106 Letter of 16 March 1786 to Sir Horace Mann, *Horace Walpole's Correspondence*, XXV (1971), 632.

107 There is a vast literature on the Duchess of Kingston, ranging from the informative to the highly fanciful. For general, book-length accounts, see Charles E. Pearce, *The Amazing Duchess. Being the Romantic History of Elizabeth Chudleigh*, 2 vols. (London, 1911) and Elizabeth Mavor, *The Virgin Mistress. A Study in Survival. The Life of the Duchess of Kingston* (London, 1964). For her sojourn in Russia, see A. G. Cross, 'The Duchess of Kingston in Russia', *History Today*, XXVII (1977), 390–5; A. E. Fel'kerzam, 'Gertsoginia Kingston i ee prebyvanie v Rossii', *Starye gody* (June 1913), pp. 3–35; E. P. Karnovich, 'Gertsoginia Kingston', in his *Zamechatel'nye i zagadochnye lichnosti XVIII i XIX stoletii* (spb, 1881; reprint, L., 1990), pp. 156–90.

108 *Gentleman's Magazine*, XLVIII (1778), 111–12.

109 William Tooke, *Life of Catharine II, Empress of Russia*, II, 5th edn (Dublin, 1800), 269–70.

110 *SIRIO*, XXIII (1878), 63.

111 *Correspondence of Jeremy Bentham*, II, 207.

112 Letter from Richard Mowat to Charles Standley, April 1781, University of Nottingham Library Manuscript Department, Manvers Papers 4147.

113 Fel'kerzam, 'Gertsoginia Kingston', p. 34.

114 *SIRIO*, XXVII (1880), 273–4.

115 Fel'kerzam, 'Gertsoginia Kingston', p. 26.

116 Letter from George Norman to Eleonora Norman, 10 August 1784, Kent Archives Office, Maidstone, Norman MS U310 c3, f. 2v.

117 *Dostopamiatnaia zhizn' i osobennye prikliucheniia Gertsogini Kingston* (Moscow, 1793), p. 229.

118 For example, Letter of 10 September 1784, Norman MS U310 c3, ff. 1–1v.; Worsley MS 24, f. 208; A. B. Granville, *St Petersburgh*, I (London, 1828), 409.

119 Cross (ed.), *An English Lady*, p. 38.

120 I am conscious that I have excluded here, and in the earlier discussion of British

travellers in the Crimea, the name of Maria Guthrie, née de Romaud-Survesnes (d. 1800), who was in the Crimea for health reasons in 1795–6 and stayed and travelled through the peninsula with P. S. Pallas and his wife. Mrs Guthrie's letters were translated from the French and published with numerous additions by her husband Matthew Guthrie as *A Tour, Performed in the Years 1795–6, through the Taurida, or Crimea . . . Described in a Series of Letters to Her Husband* (London, 1802).

121 Cross (ed.), *An English Lady*, p. 17.

122 A. G. Cross (ed.), *Engraved in the Memory: James Walker, Engraver to the Empress Catherine the Great, and His Russian Anecdotes* (Oxford and Providence, 1993), p. 107.

123 See A. G. Cross, 'An Anglo-Russian Medley: Semen Vorontsov's Other Son, Charles Cameron's Daughter, Grand Duke Alexander Pavlovich's English Playmate, and Not Forgetting His English Nanny', *SEER*, LXX (1992), 719–21.

124 The Countess of Minto (ed.), *Life and Letters of Sir Gilbert Elliot, First Earl Minto, from 1751 to 1806*, I (London, 1874), 65.

125 Public Record Office, Kew, Lowry Cole Papers, 30/43, 35.

126 Letter of 8/19 February 1768 to Mrs Walkinshaw, quoted in E. Maxtone Graham, *The Beautiful Mrs. Graham and the Cathcart Circle* (London, 1927), p. 13.

127 *Ibid.*, p. 29. Cathcart published *Particulars Addrest to Lady Cathcart's Friends* (spb, 1771), describing her last illness and death (*ibid.*, pp. 24–8).

128 Auchindoune, Cawdor, Cathcart MSS, Journal of Lady Cathcart, XXIV, f. 15.

129 Graham, *The Beautiful Mrs Graham*, pp. 10–13.

130 Lowry Cole Papers 30/43, 11, ff. 40, 41, 42v.–43.

131 See Cross, 'Eighteenth-Century Russian Theatre through British Eyes', pp. 229–31.

132 Lowry Cole Papers 30/43, 12, ff. 44v.–45.

133 *Ibid.*, 30/43, 11, f. 94.

134 Letter of 20/31 May 1778, Hampshire Record Office, Winchester, Malmesbury Collection, 9M73/163.

135 Letter of 11 June (OS?) 1778, *ibid.*

136 On Pitt, see *Arkhiv kniazia Kurakina*, X (Saratov, 1902), 338–9, 445–6; *Russkii arkhiv*, i (1879), 101.

137 Herbert, *Henry, Elizabeth and George, passim*; BL Ad. MS 35515, ff. 47, 72, 94, 110–11, 136; Lewis Namier and John Brooke, *The House of Commons, III Members K–Y* (London, 1985), 302.

138 Craven, *Journey*, p. 171.

139 *SIRIO*, XXIII, 328.

140 Norman MS U310 c 3, f. 2v.–3.

141 *Correspondence of Jeremy Bentham*, III, 525.

142 Parkinson, *Tour*, p. 63.

143 A. Swinton, *Travels into Norway, Denmark, and Russia, in the Years 1788, 1789, 1790, and 1791* (London, 1792), p. 341.

144 *Archivo del general Miranda*, V, 428–9.

145 On Bentinck and Hawkins, see Mrs Aubrey Le Blond, *Charlotte Sophie Countess Bentinck: Her Life and Times, 1715–1800*, I (London, 1912), 102–24; II, 265–9 (biography of Hawkins). Bentinck was to die on a visit to St Petersburg on 9 February 1813: GL, MS 11,192B, f. 266. On Wycombe, see *Archivo del general Miranda*, V, 429; Black, *The British Abroad*, pp. 66, 69–70. On Markham, see *A Naval Career during the Old War: A Narrative of the Life of Admiral John Markham* (London, 1883).

146 The present whereabouts of Bentinck's and Hawkins' journals is not known.

147 Le Blond, *Countess Bentinck*, I, 120–1.

148 Craven, *Journey*, p. 170.

149 Cross (ed.), *Engraved in the Memory*, p. 73.

150 SRO, Edinburgh, Buccleugh Muniments GD 224/655/5. On Garthshore's sorry fate, see *Farington Diary*, II (London, 1923), 164–5 and note. On Dalkeith, see the letter by S. R. Vorontsov to his brother, 2/13 July 1792, *AKV*, IX, 248.

151 *AKV*, XVIII (1880), 51; RGADA, Fond 10 (Vorontsovy), op. 1, ed. khr. 650, ff. 345–6 (Letters of recommendation by S. R. Vorontsov to A. A. Bezborodko on behalf of Holland and Beauclerk).

152 See *Private Correspondence of Lord Granville Leveson-Gower*, I, 54–9.

153 *Ibid.*, p. 56.

154 See Michael Roberts, *Macartney in Russia* (London, 1974), pp. 73–4.

155 Lord Ilchester, *The Home of the Hollands 1605–1820* (London, 1937), p. 161.

156 Marchioness of Londonderry and W. H. Hyde (eds.), *The Russian Diaries of Martha and Catherine Wilmot 1803–1808* (London, 1934), pp. 173–4.

157 *Private Correspondence of Lord Granville Leveson-Gower*, I, 56.

158 Herbert, *Pembroke Papers*, p. 276.

159 Parkinson, *Tour*, p. 86. (Subsequent references are in the text by page number.)

160 *Sanktpeterburgskie vedomosti*, no. 34 (29 April 1791), 637.

161 *Letters from the Continent: Describing the Manners and Customs of Germany, Poland, Russia, and Switzerland, in the Years 1790, 1791, and 1792* (London, 1812), p. iii. Colmore's authorship was established by Gavin de Beer, 'An Anonymous Identified: Lionel Colmore (1765–1807)', *Notes and Queries* (August 1967), pp. 303–4.

162 Anne Fremantle (ed.), *The Wynne Diaries*, I (Oxford, 1935), 151.

163 See A. G. Cross, 'British Sources for Catherine's Russia: I. Lionel Colmore's Letters from St Petersburg, 1790–1', *SGECRN*, 17 (1989), 17–34.

164 *Private Correspondence of Lord Granville Leveson-Gower*, I, 58.

165 James Cracraft, 'James Brogden in Russia, 1787–1788', *SEER*, XLVII (1969), 240.

166 *Ibid.*, 237.

167 *Sanktpeterburgskie vedomosti* (29 July 1791), 1232.

168 Private Collection, Manuscript Journals of Charles Hatchett, III, [f.23] (entry for 15 November 1790). In addition to the manuscript diaries the same collection holds twenty letters from Russia from Hatchett to his father. There are also letters to Hatchett from Russian correspondents in the Library of the University College of Wales, Swansea.

169 Lincolnshire Archives Office, Dixon 16/6/14–31.

170 See Walther Kirchner, 'Samuel Bentham and Siberia', *SEER*, XXXVI (1958), 471–80.

171 On Sarepta, and its increasing attraction for visitors, see Bartlett, *Human Capital*, pp. 104–5. Further on Parkinson's tour, see A. G. Cross, 'An Oxford Don in Catherine the Great's Russia', *Journal of European Studies*, I (1971), 166–74.

172 *The Swintons of That Ilk and Their Cadets* (Edinburgh, 1883), p. 61; A. C. and J. L. C. Swinton (comps.), *Concerning Swinton Family Records and Portraits at Kimmerghane* (Edinburgh, 1908).

173 William Stephen, *History of Inverkeithing and Rosyth* (Aberdeen, 1921), p. 38.

174 *Scots Magazine*, LIV (September 1792), 544.

175 *Critical Review*, NS V (1792), 299.

176 *Ibid.*, p. 294.

177 *Ibid.*, NS X (1794), 297.

178 Harry W. Nerhood, *To Russia and Return: An Annotated Bibliography of Travelers'*

English-Language Accounts of Russia from the Ninth Century to the Present (Columbus, 1968), items 98, 102, 120, 125. For an interesting investigation into the general question (including reference to Chantreau), see Percy G. Adams, *Travelers and Travel Liars 1660–1800* (Berkeley and Los Angeles, 1962).

179 *Correspondence of Jeremy Bentham*, II, 124.

180 Parkinson, *Tour*, p. 11; *Monthly Review*, XLVII (1772), 252; *Annual Register for 1772* (1773), p. 241. See also William Edgerton, *Russia in the Eighteenth Century: An Exhibition of Rare Books in the Lilly Library* (Bloomington, 1984), pp. 8–9; J. Lough, 'Joseph Marshall's Travels', *Factotum*, no. 21 (1985), 12–13.

181 DNB, LVI (1898), 275. See also Robert Chambers, *A Biographical Dictionary of Eminent Scotsmen*, IV (Glasgow, Edinburgh and London, 1855), 378 and its revised edition by Thomas Thomson, III (London, 1875), 458.

182 Incidentally, notice of Swinton's impending departure from the Russian capital was published in *Sankpeterburgskie vedomosti*, no. 69 (27 August 1791), 1128. Also p. 1348. No such evidence has been found for the other 'travellers'. For a general discussion of the problem, see A. G. Cross, 'The Armchair Traveller "in" Catherine II's Russia', forthcoming in a volume of essays in memory of M. P. Alekseev to be published in St Petersburg in 1996.

183 See A. G. Cross, 'Catherine the Great: Views from the Distaff Side', in Roger Bartlett and Janet M. Hartley (eds.), *Russia in the Age of the Enlightenment* (London, 1990), pp. 208–9.

184 William Hunter, *A Short View of the Political Situation of the Northern Powers: Founded on Observations Made during a Tour through Russia, Sweden, and Denmark, in the Last Seven Months of the Year 1800. With Conjectures on the Probable Issue of the Approaching Contest* (London, 1801), pp. 23–54, 80–2.

185 Robert Tweddell (ed.), *Remains of John Tweddell*, 2nd edn (London, 1816), p. 9. (Further references are in the text by page number.)

186 *Life of Reginald Heber*, I, 195.

187 William Otter (ed.), *The Life and Remains of the Rev. Edward Daniel Clarke* (London, 1824), p. 407.

188 *Ibid.*, p. 394.

189 E. D. Clarke, *Travels in Various Countries of Europe, Asia and Africa*, I, 4th edn (London, 1816), 4. The examples fill pp. 4–11. (Further references are in the text by page number.)

190 Cross (ed.), *Engraved in the Memory*, pp. 127–8.

191 Leitch Ritchie, *A Journey to St. Petersburg and Moscow through Courland and Livonia* (London, 1836), p. 156.

EPILOGUE

1 See A. G. Cross, 'Johnson Newman, a Little-known Englishman in Russian Service in the Second Half of the Eighteenth Century', SGECRN, no. 21 (1993), 36–47.

2 AVPR, Fond Snosheniia Rossii s Angliei, delo 772, f. 2v.

3 M. P. Alekseev, 'Angliiskii iazyk v Rossii i russkii iazyk v Anglii', *Uchenye zapiski Leningradskogo gos. universiteta*, seriia filologicheskikh nauk, vyp. 9 (1944), 78.

4 BL, Add. MS 32, 419, f. 327v.

5 *Correspondence of Jeremy Bentham*, III (London, 1971), 242.

6 Auchindoune, Cawdor, Cathcart MSS, Journal of Lady Cathcart, XX, f. 22. Cf. ff. 26v.–27.

7 *Recollections of the Life of the Rev. A. J. Scott, D.D., Lord Nelson's Chaplain* (London, 1842), p. 64. Dr Jonathan Rogers is discussed in chapter 4 of this volume.

8 Adam Kroll, *A Commercial Dictionary, in the English and Russian Languages: with a Full Explanation of the Russia Trade, &c. &c.* (London, 1800), p. iii; GL, MS 11,741/9, f. 275.

9 Prokhor Zhdanov, *Angliska grammatika* (spb, 1772), p. 204.

10 Jennifer Tann (ed.), *The Selected Papers of Boulton & Watt*, I (London, 1981), 360.

11 James Cracraft, 'James Brogden in Russia, 1787-1788', *SEER*, XLVII (1969), 233, 232.

12 Herbert Swann, *Home on the Neva: A Life of a British Family in Tsarist St Petersburg – and after the Revolution* (London, 1968), p. 26.

13 *Ibid.*, pp. 29–30.

14 Cf. *Petrograd: The City of Trouble, 1914–1918* (London, 1918); *Recollections of Imperial Russia* (London, 1923); *The Dissolution of an Empire* (London, 1932).

15 *Stoletie Angliiskogo sobraniia* (spb, 1870), p. 7.

16 *Eugene Onegin. A Novel in Verse by Aleksandr Pushkin*, translated from the Russian, with a Commentary, by Vladimir Nabokov, I (London, 1964), 106.

INDEX